The Singer's Repertoire

by

Berton Coffin

College of Music, University of Colorado

The Scarecrow Press

New Brunswick, N. J.   1956

To my wife

Mildred Wantland Coffin

Whose faith, encouragement and assistance
have meant so much in this effort.

FOREWORD

The Singer's Repertoire is an effort to aid all singers
and teachers of singing in their repertoire problems. The
singer at no stage in his career is free from this problem.
In the beginning he has to select the suitable songs for his
vocal powers and development. As he becomes a successful
amateur singer he secures various engagements which are
always presenting new song needs. Should he become a pro-
fessional singer the needs will be multiplied many times
with a changing repertoire required season after season.
Should be become a teacher of singing or a vocal coach he
will have hundreds of potential singers, each one with differ-
ent needs. Therefore, no matter with what phase of vocal
work one is concerned the repertoire problem is always
present and one's storehouse is always changing, always be-
ing added to.

The Singer's Repertoire has profited in its growth and development by the advice, counsel and criticism of many ex-
perienced singers and many noted teachers of singing. From
these discussions, four repertoire aids appear to be paramount:

1. Aids for program building (for this problem the
Guide lists recital songs in the various languages; songs for
opening and closing recitals; and lists songs by song classification).

2. Aids for training repertoire (this problem has been
approached by indexing technical characteriestics of songs).

3. Aids for specific or seasonal occasions (see Christ-
mas, Easter, Wedding, Patriotic lists).

4. Aids in sacred repertoire (hundreds of songs have
been studied and those appropriate are listed).

The above aids are based on contemporarily performed
songs and arias as programmed in countless recitals, in re-
cordings, and in the media of radio and television. This mass
of material has been interpolated into appropriate listings.
The compiler has not assumed the position of the musical
analyist except for the Sacred listings and in augmenting the
smaller lists. Questions have not been asked as to why cer-
tain songs are sung or not sung; if the song has been found
in the above mentioned sources, it is listed, otherwise it is

not included in this volume. This book is based on the pre-selection of songs sung by noteworthy or accepted singers, and is not a compendium of all vocal repertoire which would surely approximate 100,000 song titles. It is merely a distribution of some 7500 songs into 752 lists for the nine voice classifications (coloratura soprano, lyric soprano, dramatic soprano, mezzo soprano, contralto, lyric tenor, dramatic tenor, baritone and bass) rather than an annotated bibliography of songs. For each voice classification there are 71 - 92 lists whereby the characteristics of various songs are shown. It is well known to all teachers that a matching of song traits to the strengths and limitations of any singing personality will assure the individual's best success. This is a very difficult thing to do and it is hoped will be made easier by the multiple listings of this work.

Due to the large number of programs examined, all voices should be represented in proportion to their natural distribution. The largest segments will be the lyric soprano and baritone, because there are more of those voices; the smallest segments will be the coloratura soprano, dramatic tenor and bass since these voices occur less frequently. The compiler has made no attempt to reclassify voices, only listing songs according to the voice classification as stated on the programs. The voice classifications have been accepted as having the following general connotations:

The Coloratura Soprano is the lightest of the soprano voices. It has brilliance of color, great agility and a range of d^1 to f^3.

The Lyric Soprano has more weight and color contrast than the coloratura soprano. This voice has agility and a range of $b - d^3$.

The Dramatic Soprano has weight, nobility, and great color contrast with less effectiveness in agility. It has a range of $a - c^3$ (includes Lyrico Spinto).

The Mezzo Soprano is the medium female voice. It is a sonorous and heavy voice with a tendency toward the darker vocal colors and has a range of $a - b \text{ flat}^2$.

The Contralto is the lowest female voice, large in extensity, and dark in color. It has a range of $g - a \text{ flat}^2$.

The Lyric Tenor is the lightest and brightest of the male voices. It possesses agility and a range of $c - c^2$.

The Dramatic Tenor is the heavy tenor voice, large in climaxes, and more sombre in color. It is not as agile as the lyric tenor but instead has a heavier production effective in parlando singing. The range is approximately the same as the lyric tenor (in many cases dramatic tenors have previously sung as baritones).

The Baritone voice is the medium male voice. Its high range has a tenor quality, this is sometimes called tenor-baritone. It has fine color contrast from bright to the sombre with a range of A flat - a flat[1].

The Bass voice includes bass-baritone, basso cantante and basso profondo. The bass voice has the largest extensity of all voices, the darkest color and greatest weight. It has wide color range from darkest hues to the medium bright, and a range of $G - g^1$, $F - f^1$, or E flat - e flat[1].

Spellings, capitalizations, and diacritical markings have been verified in source books and publishers' catalogues as far as possible, although it is reasonable to assume that some errors have resulted from the varied sources used. Linguistic experts have assisted in this clarification and questionable titles have been deleted. Some errors have resulted in the continual card sorting of over one million card sorts on the International Business Machines. It is to be expected that some errors will have eluded the writer and the reader's indulgence is requested.

Such a work as this could not have been possible without the assistance of a large number of people, including Dr. Eugene Wilson, Director of Libraries of the University of Colorado; the International Business Machines Services of the University of Colorado; and the staff of the Newberry Library in Chicago. Valuable assistance was also given by the music publishing houses who made a large amount of music available for analysis for the Sacred listings, contemporary American listings, and supplementary listings. Without a grant by the Research Committee of the University of Colorado this study would not have been accomplished.

A work of this kind can never be complete in contemporary song, since new songs are continually appearing and others are falling into disuse. However, the classic, romantic and impressionistic repertoire is now relatively stable. These 7500 songs comprise the living repertoire of today.

Boulder, Colorado
November 10, 1955

PUBLISHER CODE

† - Published by more than one company

ABC - ABC Music Corp.
AHC - Asherberg, Hopwood
and Crew
AMP - Associated Music
Publishers
ARR - Arrow Music Press
ASC - Arthur P. Schmidt
ASH - Ashdown
AUG - Augener
AXE - Axelrod

BAF - Bayley and
Ferguson
BAR - Barenreiter
BER - Berlin
BES - Bessel
BIR - Birchard
BLO - C. A. Blodgett
BMI - Broadcast Music, Inc.
BOH - Boosey and Hawkes
BOO - Boosey
BON - Bongiovani
BOS - Boston
BOT - Bote and Bock
BRA - Brandus and Cie
BRE - Bregeman
BRH - Breitkof and Haertel
BRM - Barton and Mead
BRO - Broude
BVC - Bregman, Vocco and
Conn

CAR - Cardilli
CFI - Carl Fischer
CHA - Chappell
CHE - Chester
CHM - Champagne
CHO - Choudens

CMC - Composers Music
Corp.
CMP - Composers Press
CNN - Conn
CRA - Cramer
CRF - Crawford
CRZ - Cranz
CSC - Cos Cob
CST - Costallet
CUR - Curwen

DBH - Desylvia, Brown and
Henderson
DES - DeSantis
DIT - Ditson
DRE - Dreiklang
DUR - Durand

ECS - E. C. Schirmer
ELK - Elkin
ELV - Elkan-Vogel
ENO - Enoch
ESC - Eschig

FAM - Famous
FEI - Feist
FLA - Flammer
FOE - Foetisch
FOX - Fox
FRA - Frank
FRL - Forlivesi
FRS - Forster
FST - Forsyth
FTZ - FitzSimmons

GAL - Galaxy
GAM - Gamble Hinged (GAH)
GER - Gershwin

GLO - Glocken Verlag
GOL - Goldsea
GOT - Goodwin and Tabb
GRA - H. W. Gray
GSC - G. Schirmer

HAC - Hachette
HAM - Hamelle
HAN - Hansen
HAR - Harms
HEU - Heugel
HHE - Hinds, Haydn and
      Eldredge
HNR - Heinrichofen
HNZ - Hunzinger
HOM - Homeyer
HRM - Harmonia (HMP)
HSC - Hans Schneider

INT - International

JCH - John Church
JFI - J. Fischer
JOB - Jobert
JUR - Jurgenson
JWI - J. Williams

KAL - Kalmus
KIS - Kistner
KSS - Kustner and Siegel

LAC - Lacour
LED - Leduc
LEE - Leeds
LEM - Lemoine

MAR - Marks
MAT - Mathot
MCG - MacGimsey
MCR - McLaughlin, Reilly
MER - Mercury
MET - Methuen
MLR - Miller
MLS - Mills
MOR - Morris, E. H.
MOV - Movietone
MUP - Music Press

Nag - Nagel Verlag
NEM - New Music
NOR - Norsky Verlag
NOV - Novello

OCT - Octava Music Co.
OXF - Oxford

PAR - Paragon
PEE - Peer
PET - Peters
PON - William Pond
PRE - Presser
PRM - Paramount
PRO - Prowse
PTR - Paterson

RBR - Riker, Brown and
      Wellington
REM - Remick
RIC - Ricordi
ROB - Robbins
ROG - Winthrop Rogers
ROM - Roma
ROU - Rouart, Lerolle
ROW - Row

SAL - Salabert
SC - Schott
SCH - Schlesinger
SEN - Senart
SHA - Shapiro
SHU - Schuberth
SIM - Simroch
SIR - Sirene
SON - Sonzogno
SOU - Southern Music Co.
STB - Stainer Bell
SUM - Summy

TRA - Transcontinental

UME - Union Musical
      Española
UNI - Universal

VIC - Victoria
VLP - Valley Press

WEI - Weinberger
WHI - White Smith
WIL - Williamson
WIT - Witmark
WLL - Willis
WOO - Wood
WOR - Words and Music
WTR - Weintraub

DIRECTIONS FOR USE

All songs are listed alphabetically by composer with the song listings alphabetized under each composer. The lists are to be read in the following manner: first, the composer's name is given, then the title, then the opera, operetta, cantata, oratorio, if it is an aria. In cases where a solo instrument accompanies the voice and piano that instrument has been indicated.

Next are shown the keys HML. The last letter of the key is important: should it be L - the low range is shown; if the last is M, the medium range is shown; and if it is H - the high. BF-EF indicates a range of B flat to E flat (CS -FS would indicate C sharp to F sharp). The three letters at the extreme right of page are a code for the publisher (code at front of book, i.e. GSC indicates G. Schirmer; SC indicates Schott). Where a dagger (†) appears the song is published by more than one firm.

The Miscellaneous listings are total lists including songs other than those found in the American, British, French, German and Italian listings. However, if there is a void in any of these lists (American, British, French, German, Italian), those songs will be included in the Miscellaneous list. Latin songs always appear in the Miscellaneous lists as do the Portuguese, Hungarian, Hebrew, etc.

This book does not include popular music as such but does have a separate listing of the lighter numbers which are so frequently needed. These songs are found under the heading - Songs of Popular Appeal.

The Handel songs are found in the British, German and Italian lists; Wagner in the German and French; and Mozart in the Italian, German and French. American compositions are found in the American lists regardless of whether French, German or Italian texts are used. Likewise English composers are in the English lists.

The classical Italian arias are listed under song rather than opera because the works are no longer staged and they are thought of as song literature.

13

A book on vocal repertoire can never be absolutely complete since new songs are continually appearing and others after their time are falling into disuse. However, the classic, romantic and impressionistic repertories are now quite stable. I believe that the literature included in The Singer's Repertoire is the most complete record of living song that has been prepared to date.

Repertoire for the Coloratura Soprano Voice

15

Repertoire for the Lyric Soprano Voice

16

Repertoire for the Dramatic Soprano Voice

Repertoire for the Mezzo Soprano Voice

Repertoire for the Contralto Voice

Repertoire for the Lyric Tenor Voice

Repertoire for the Dramatic Tenor Voice

Repertoire for the Baritone Voice

Repertoire for the Bass Voice

American Recital Songs

Coloratura Soprano

Alberti	Oriental serenade	H	CS-A	CFI
Bacon	Is there such a thing as day?	M	DS-FS	AMP
Barber	Monks and raisons	M	DF-E	GSC
-----	Nuovoletta	H	BS-BS	GSC
-----	Secrets of old	LH	EF-G	GSC
-----	Sleep now	MH	EF-AF	GSC
-----	The daisies	M	C-F	GSC
Beach	Fairy lullaby			ASC
Boyd	Adoration	H	C-A	GAL
Granscombe	At the postern gate	MH	DF-AF	ASC
Burleigh	By the pool at the third roses	H		RIC
Buzzi-Peccia	Little birdies			
-----	Under the greenwood tree	LMH	EF-A	DIT
Cadman	I hear a thrush at eve			MOR
-----	Joy	MH	E-A	GSC
-----	Welcome, sweet wind	H	E-B	GSC
Carpenter	Serenade	LH	CS-A	GSC
Chanler	Wind			GSC
Charles	A wish	LH	E-GS	GSC
-----	And so, goodbye	LH	EF-AF	GSC
-----	Let my song fill your heart	LH	EF-AF	GSC
-----	The white swan	HL	C-F	GSC
Clough-Leighter	My lover he comes on the skee	HM	D-F	BOS
Cottenet	Red, red rose	H	D-BF	CFI
Cowles	Desire	H	F-A	GSC
Creston	Bird of the wilderness	MH	FS-A	GSC
Crist	By a silent seashore	H	CS-GS	GSC
-----	Into a ship dreaming	LMH	EF-GS	CFI
-----	O come hither	HM	B-GS	CFI
-----	White hours like snow	HL	CS-BF	CFI
Curran	Bird songs	MH	EF-AF	GSC
Davis	Nancy Hanks	H	D-G	GAL
Dougherty	Primavera	H	C-BF	GSC
Duke	A piper	H	CS-B	GSC

(Duke)	Bells in the rain	H	E-GS	CFI
-----	Little elegy	H	FS-A	GSC
Edmunds	Fare you well	MH	F-AF	ROW
-----	Milk maids	M	DF-F	MER
Ganz	The angels are stooping	MH	GF-A	GSC
Gaynor	May magic			
-----	Pierrot	H	E-B	BOS
Giannini	Tell me, o blue, blue sky	H		RIC
Gilberte	Two roses	LMH	CS-G	CFI
Grant-Schaeffer	The cuckoo clock	H	EF-BF	SUM
Griffes	Elves	H	F-AF	GSC
-----	In a myrtle shade	H	FS-A	GSC
-----	The rose of the night	H	CS-A	GSC
-----	Thy dark eyes to mine	H	EF-AF	GSC
-----	To-night			
-----	Upon their grave	M	C-G	GSC
-----	Waikiki	H	DS-GS	GSC
Hageman	At the well	LH	EF-AF	GSC
-----	Me company along	LH	F-BF	CFI
-----	Music I heard with you	MH	E-A	GAL
Harmati	Spring night			
Harris	Winter	H	F-A	GAL
Horsman	The bird of the wilderness	LMH	DF-BF	GSC
-----	Thus wisdom sings	H	EF-A	GSC
Josten	Cupid's counsel	H	EF-AF	GSC
Kramer	Swans	HL		RIC
La Forge	Bird song	H		RIC
-----	Come unto these yellow sands	H	FS-B	GSC
-----	Cupid captive	H		GAL
-----	Pastorale			
-----	The sand			
Lubin	The piper	H	C-A	GSC
Mana-Zucca	Fluttering birds	H	EF-BF	GSC
-----	Sleep, my darling			CNG
-----	There's joy in my heart			CNG
Miller	The blue bell			
-----	The bumblebee			
Naginski	Look down, fair moon			
Nevin	Good night, good night beloved	LH	E-FS	BOS
Nordoff	Fair Annette's song			AMP
-----	Serenade	H	CS-FS	AMP
-----	There shall be more joy	M	CS-FS	AMP
Parker	The lark now leaves her watery nest	LH		JCH
Popper	Gavotte	H	D-B	GSC

Proctor	I light the blessed candles	H	DF-A	GSC
Rorem	Alleluia			
-----	The silver swan	H	F-C	PEE
		HL		GSC
Rybner	Pierrot	MH	FS-BF	GSC
Sacco	Rapunzel	H	D-A	CFI
Saminsky	Queen Estherka's laugh			JCH
Spross	Will o' the wisp	H	EF-A	GSC
Thomson	Preciosilla			
Treharne	A widow bird sat mourning	H	FS-AF	BOS
Vanderpool	Values			WIT
Vene	Age and youth	H	E-A	RIC
-----	The rats	H	E-A	RIC
Ware	By the fountain			FLA
-----	This day is mine	MH	EF-AF	BOS
Warren	Down in the glen	H	F-A	GSC
-----	My lady Lo-Fu			DIT
-----	Snow towards evening	LH	EF-AF	GSC
-----	Who calls?	LH	E-A	CFI
Watts	Joy	HL	D-F	GSC
-----	Stresa	H	EF-BF	DIT
-----	The little shepherd's song	H	G-BF	RIC
-----	The poet sings	MH	EF-AF	DIT
Woodman	Love's in my heart	LH	F-BF	GSC

British Recital Songs

Coloratura Soprano

Anon	Willow song from Otello			GSC
Arne, M.	The lass with the delicate air	MH	D-G	†
Arne, T.	Where the bee sucks	HM		†
Aylward	Deep in my heart	LMH		CHA
Bainton	The nightingale near the house			CUR
Bantock	A feast of lanterns	HM	D-F	GAL
Bax	I heard a piper piping	LH	D-G	CFI
-----	O green grow the rushes	MH	EF-BF	OXF
-----	Shieling song	H	CS-A	CHE
Bayly	I'd be a butterfly			
Benedict	The carnival of Venice	H	D-EF	GSC
-----	The gypsy and the bird	H	D-E	GSC
-----	The wren Flute	H	F-C	PRE
Benjamin	The piper			BOO
Besley	Listening	H	E-AF	CUR
Bishop	Echo song Flute	H	D-C	GSC
-----	Love has eyes	M		†

27

(Bishop)	Should he upbraid	H		†
Bliss	Three jolly gentlemen	H		†
Brahe	Piper from over the hill			
Brewer	The fairy pipers	HML		BOH
Bridge	Adoration	H		ROG
Brown	Shepherd thy demeanor vary!			BOO
Clarke	Shy one	HL	BF–G	BOH
Coleridge-Taylor	Willow song	MH		CRA
Edmunds	I know my love	HL	BF–EF	ROW
-----	The faucon	M	D–F	MER
Forsyth	Dew fairy			
-----	The stranger Organ	H	A–B	GRA
German	Charming Chloe	HML		NOV
Gibbs	To one who passed whistling through the night	H	F–G	CUR
Goossens	The fan song			
Head	A piper	HL		BOO
Holst	A little music	H		AUG
Horn	Cherry ripe	M	D–G	†
Ireland	Bed in summer			CUR
Lehmann	Snake charmer			BOO
Mallinson	My heart, the bird of the wilderness	H	DF–AF	CRA
Quilter	Love's philosophy	LMH	D–A	BOO
-----	To daisies			BOO
Ronald	Down in the forest	HML	C–D	ENO
Sharp	My mother did so before me			MEU
Stanford	Sea wrack	H	EF–A	STB
Taylor	O can ye sew			
Walton	Sunset			
Warlock	Pretty ring time	H	D–G	CFI
-----	The passionate shepherd	HM		ELK

French Recital Songs

Coloratura Soprano

Anon	Dites, que faut-il faire?			
Bachelet	Chère nuit	H	DF–BF	GSC
Bizet	Douce mer			GSC
-----	Le matin			GSC
-----	Vielle chanson	H	EF–A	GSC
Boieldieu	Essayons's il se peut de parler			LEM

Busser	La meilleure pensée			DUR
Chaminade	L' été	MH	E-A	†
Charpentier	Les chevaux de bois	H	E-A	HEU
-----	Les yeux de Berthe			HEU
-----	Serenade à Watteau			
Chausson	Sérénade			
Dalcroze	Le coeur de ma mie	HML		†
-----	L' oiseau bleu			CFI
Debussy	Apparition			DUR
-----	Beau soir	LH	C-FS	†
-----	Chevaux de bois	H	C-G	†
-----	Clair de lune	M	CS-FS	JOB
-----	De fleurs	H	C-AF	†
-----	Fantoches	H	D-A	JOB
-----	Green	H	C-AF	†
-----	Harmonie du soir			DUR
-----	Il pleur dans mon coeur	LH	CS-GS	†
-----	L'ombre des arbres			DIT
-----	La mer est plus belle	HL		†
-----	Le faune			DUR
-----	Mandoline	HM	BF-F	†
-----	Noël des enfants qui n'ont plus de maisons			DUR
-----	Nuits d'etoiles	LH	E-A	MAR
-----	Pierrot			DUR
-----	Romance	HM	C-E	†
-----	Rondeau			
-----	Rondel chinois			DUR
-----	Voici que le printemps	LH	CS-G	BOS
Délibes	Coppelia waltz	H	BF-BF	GSC
-----	Jours passés			GSC
-----	Les filles de Cadix	HM	A-A	†
-----	Passepied	LH	DS-CS	GSC
Duparc	Chanson triste	MH	FS-AF	†
-----	Extase	LMH	FS-A	†
-----	L'invitation au voyage	HM	E-F	†
-----	Soupir	HL	CS-F	BOS
Dupont	Chanson des noisettes			HEU
-----	Mandoline			DUR
Fauré	Apres un Rêve	HM	C-F	†
-----	Clair de lune	MH	C-G	†
-----	La fée aux chansons	LH	F-F	†
-----	La lune blanche	HL		†
-----	Les roses D'Ispahan	HM	D-FS	DIT
-----	Nell	LH	FS-AF	†
-----	Notre amour	H	DS-B	†
-----	Rencontre	H	EF-AF	†
-----	Sylvie	HL	E-F	†
-----	Vocalise	H		LED

29

Fourdrain	Le papillon			RIC
Gounod	Au printemps	LMH	DF-AF	GSC
Grovlez	Guitares et mandolines			DUR
Hahn	Le printemps			
-----	Le rossignol des lilas			
Honegger	Le Delphinium			
Hue	Il a neigé des fleurs	H	EF-AF	
-----	Le passant	H	D-G	†
Jacobson	Song of Marie Antoinette	MH	DS-GS	CFI
Koechlin	L'air	M	F-FS	ROU
-----	La lune	M	C-F	ROU
-----	Le thé	HM	C-E	BOS
Lalo	La chanson d'Alouette	H	EF-B	GSC
Letorey	La fontaine de Caramouet			HAM
Liszt	Comment, disaient-ils	H	C-AF	†
-----	Oh! quand je dors	H	E-A	†
Messiaen	Le sourire	H		DUR
-----	Pourquoi	H		DUR
Milhaud	A une fontaine			
-----	Chansons de Ronsard	H		BOH
-----	Tais-toi, Babillarde	H	G-C	BOH
Moret	Le nélumbo	H	E-DF	HEU
Paladilhe	Le roitelet	MH	DS-GS	GSC
Pierné	Le moulin	ML	C-E	BOS
Poldowski	Dansons la gigue	M	EF-G	MAR
-----	Nocturne	H	DS-GS	CHE
Poulenc	Air champêtre			ROU
-----	Air vif	H	C-AF	ROU
-----	C. (J'ai traversé les ponts de c.)			ROU
-----	Fêtes galantes			SAL
Quilitsky	La rose et le rossignol			
Ravel	D'Anne jouant de l'espinette	H	CS-GS	GSC
-----	Ronde			
Roussel	Coeur en péril			DUR
-----	Sarabande			
Saint-Saëns	Aimons-nous			DUR
-----	Au cimetière			
-----	Le bonheur est une chose légère	H	C-A	CHO
	Violin and piano			
-----	The nightingale and the rose	H	C-D	GSC
Sauguet	Amour			
Severac	Chanson pour le petit cheval			ROU
Szulc	Mandoline	H	D-B	ROU
Vidal	Ariette	LH	F-A	GSC

Vuillermoz	Jardin d'amours			SAL
Weckerlin	Je connais un berger			
	discret	M	EF-EF	BOS

German Recital Songs

Coloratura Soprano

Beethoven	Lied aus der Ferne			
-----	Mit einem gemalten Band			RIC
Brahms	Auf dem Schiffe	LH	GS-A	†
-----	Botschaft	HL	D-F	†
-----	Das Maedchen spricht	H	E-FS	†
-----	Eine gute, gute Nacht			†
-----	Es liebt sich so lieblich			
	im Lenze	LH	D-GS	†
-----	Feldeinsamkeit	HL	C-EF	†
-----	Geheimnis			†
-----	Lerchengesang	LH	FS-GS	†
-----	Maedchenlied	HL		†
-----	Nachtigall	MHL	BF-FS	†
-----	Regenlied	HL	CS-F	†
-----	Vergebliches staendchen	LMH	E-FS	†
-----	Vorueber			†
-----	Wiegenlied			
-----	Wie Melodien zieht es	HL	A-E	†
-----	Wir wandelten	LH	EF-GF	†
Haydn	My mother bids me bind			
	my hair	M	E-E	†
Jensen	Murmuring zephyr	LH	E-AF	GSC
Liszt	Kling leise, mein Lied	HL		†
Loesch	Auf der Kirmes			
Loewe	Canzonetta	MH	B-A	DIT
-----	Niemand hat's gesehen	LM	DS-FS	†
Marx	Marienlied	MH	EF-AF	AMP
-----	Nocturne	H	EF-AF	AMP
-----	Selige Nacht	M	DF-GF	AMP
-----	Und gestern hat er mir			
	Rosen gebracht	H	E-A	AMP
Mendelssohn	Fruehlingslied	H	DS-GS	†
-----	Im Gruenen	H	E-BF	AUG
-----	Neue Liebe	H	CS-A	†
-----	O for the wings of a dove	MLH	D-G	†
-----	O Jugend	H	E-A	†
-----	On wings of song			†
Mozart	Warnung	HM	C-D	

31

(Mozart)	Wiegenlied	MH	G-G	†
Oboussier	Weine du nicht			
	Oboe and harpsichord			
Proch	Theme and variations	H	C-DF	†
	Flute			
Schubert	An die Laute	LH	D-F	†
-----	An die Nachtigall	H	C-G	†
-----	Auf dem Wasser zu singen	MH	EF-GF	†
-----	Ave Maria	LMH	F-F	†
-----	Das Lied im Gruenen			PET
-----	Das Rosenband			PET
-----	Der Hirt auf dem	H	BF-B	†
	Felsen			
	Clarinet or violoncello			
-----	Der Juengling an der	LH	E-A	†
	Quelle			
-----	Der Knabe			PET
-----	Der Musensohn	LH	FS-G	†
-----	Der Schmetterling	LH	E-F	†
-----	Die Forelle	MLH	EF-GF	†
-----	Die Rose	M	G-FS	PET
-----	Die Spinnerin			†
-----	Geheimes	HL	BF-EF	†
-----	Gott im Fruehling			PET
-----	Gretchen am	H	F-A	†
	Spinnrade			
-----	Klaerchens Lied			
-----	Liebesbotschaft	H	E-G	†
-----	Nachtviolen			PET
-----	Rastlose Liebe	M	B-F	†
-----	Ungeduld	HML		†
-----	Wiegenlied (Op. 98)			†
-----	Wohin?	HL	B-E	†
Schumann	Auftraege	HL	C-E	†
-----	Der Nussbaum	LMH	D-FS	†
-----	Die Meerfee			
-----	Er ist's	HL	BF-EF	†
-----	Geisternaehe			
-----	Intermezzo	HL	C-D	GSC
-----	Marienwuermchen	HL	D-D	†
-----	Mondnacht	M	E-FS	†
-----	O wie lieblich ist das			
	Maedchen			
-----	Schneegloeckchen	HL		†
-----	Volksliedchen	HL		†
Strauss	All' mein' Gedanken	H	CS-GS	
-----	Barcarolle	H	DF-BF	†
-----	Fruehlingsgedraenge			
-----	Kornblumen	LH	DF-AF	†

32

(Straus)	Liebeshymnus			†
-----	Mohnblumen			
-----	Schlagende Herzen			†
-----	Schlechtes Wetter			†
-----	Staendchen	HM	A-FS	†
Taubert	Der Vogel im Wald			
Trunk	In meiner Heimat			
Wolf	Ach, im Maien	HL	C-E	†
-----	Bedeckt mich mit Blumen	HL	B-D	†
-----	Das grosse Karussell			
-----	Der Knabe und das Immlein	L	CS-A	†
-----	Fruehling uebers Jahr			PET
-----	Gleich und Gleich			†
-----	Ich hab' in Penna	LH		†
-----	Zum neuen Jahr			PET

Italian Recital Songs

Coloratura Soprano

Arditi	Il bacio	H	CS-B	†
-----	Parla	H	CS-CS	GSC
Bononcini	Deh, più a me non v'ascondete	LH	EF-F	†
-----	Per la gloria	HL	C-EF	†
-----	Più non ti voglio credere	H	D-AF	PET
-----	Si che fedele			DUR
Brogi	Le lucciole			
Buzzeleni	Si che morte			
Caccini	Amarilli, mia bella	ML	C-D	†
-----	Deh, dove son fuggite	M		CUR
-----	Tu ch'hai le penne, amore			
Castelnuovo-Tedesco	Orpheus	H		CHE
Cavalli	Donzelle fuggite	HL	C-EF	†
-----	In amor			DUR
Cesti	Intorno all'idol mio	MH	D-F	†
Cimara	Inutile precauzione Flute			
-----	Scherzo			
-----	Stornellata marinara	HM		RIC
-----	Stornello			BON
Cimarosa	Bel nume che adoro			RIC
D'Astorga	Vo' cercando in queste valli	H	D-G	STB
Defesch	Tu fai la superbetta			GSC

33

De Luca	Non posso disperar	HL	C-E	GSC
Donaudy	Perduto ho la speranza			
Donizetti	La zingara	H	DS-A	GSC
Gagliano	Dormi amore	HL	CS-E	DIT
Gasparini	Caro laccio, dolce nodo	M	EF-EF	GSC
-----	Lasciar d'amarti			
Gluck	O del mio dolce ardor	LH	D-FS	GSC
-----	Ritorna l'eta dell'oro (Il Trionfo di Clelia)			
Handel	Alma mia (Floridante)	HM	CS-E	†
-----	Care selve (Atalanta)	MH	FS-A	†
-----	Lusinghe più care (Alessandro)	H	D-G	†
-----	Mi restano le lagrime (Alcina)			BOO
-----	Parolette vezzi e squardi			
-----	Qual farfalletta (Partenope)	H	E-A	†
Haydn	Al tuo seno fortunato (Orfeo ed Euridice)			
Jommelli	Chi vuol comprar la bella	H	B-G	GSC
Legrenzi	Che fiero costume	HML	C-D	†
Malipiero	L'eco	H	E-G	CHE
Marchesi	La folletta	M		RIC
Mayr	La biondina in gondoleta			
Mozart	Ridente la calma			BOS
Paisiello	Chi vuol la zingarella	L	C-F	GSC
Paradies	Quel ruscelletto	L	BF-F	CFI
Pergolesi	Dite ch'ogni momento			BOS
-----	Nina	HL	CS-D	DIT
-----	Se tu m'ami	LMH	C-G	GSC
Pizzetti	I pastori			FRL
Porpora	Non più fra sassi			PET
Respighi	Scherzo			BON
-----	Son come farfalletta			BON
Ricci	Domi, domi del bambino			
Rode	Al dolce canto			
Rosa	Star vicino	HL	D-E	†
Rossini	La danza	MH	E-A	†
Santoliguido	Riflessi			FOR
Scarlatti, A.	Cara e dolce rimembranza			
-----	Già il sole dal Gange	LH	EF-F	GSC
-----	Rugiadose odorose	HL	D-E	DIT

(Scarlatti, A.)	Sento nel core	M	E-F	†
Sibella	La Girometta	HML	D-E	GSC
-----	O bimba bimbetta	LMH	D-G	GSC
Tirindelli	Primavera			
Tocchi	In riva al fiume			
-----	Serenata			
Tosti	'A vucchella	LH	F-G	RIC
Venzano	Grand waltz			

Russian Recital Songs

Coloratura Soprano

Alabieff	The nightingale Flute	H	EF-C	†
Arensky	The little fish's song	H	D-A	†
-----	Valse	H	DF-GF	GSC
Glazounoff	The nereid	H	FS-A	GSC
Gretchaninoff	Il s' est tu, le charmant rossignol	H	EF-G	†
-----	The snowdrop	HM	BF-F	DIT
Prokofieff	The gray eyed king			
Rachmaninoff	Before my window	HM	C-G	†
-----	Daisies			†
-----	Here beauty dwells	H	D-B	CFI
-----	Into my open window	HL	B-FS	BOS
-----	I wait for thee			
-----	Lilacs	LH	EF-G	†
-----	Oh cease thy singing, maiden fair	H	E-A	CFI
-----	Sorrow in spring	H	D-BF	DIT
-----	The alder tree			
-----	The songs of Grusia	H	E-A	GSC
-----	Vocalise	LH	CS-A	GSC
Rimsky-Korsakov	The nightingale and the rose	H	FS-FS	DIT
Rubinstein	The piper			
Stravinsky	Pastorale			GSC
-----	Russian maiden's song			
Tcherepnin	Quiet night			DIT
Vassilenko	Longing	H	E-A	DIT

Scandinavian Recital Songs

Coloratura Soprano

Bodenhoff	Bølge mod kyst			
Grieg	In the boat	LM	D-ES	†
-----	Pretty Margaret			
-----	Solvejg's cradle song	M	CS-FS	GSC
-----	Solvejg's song	MH	E-A	†
-----	The first meeting			PET
Kjerulf	Synnove's song	M	C-F	GSC
Sibelius	A dragon fly			
-----	From the north	H	DS-G	GSC
Weyse	Den store, stille natt			
-----	Teklas sang			
Winding	Den evige sne			

Spanish Recital Songs

Coloratura Soprano

Alvarez	La partida	HL	DS-E	GSC
Granados	Andalusia			
-----	El majo discreto	H		INT
-----	El tra la la y el punteado			INT
-----	Manañica era			
Lara	Granada			SOU
Lecuona	Lament			
Longas	Lavanderas			
-----	Mi jota			SEN
Nin	Montañesa			AMP
Obradors	Al amor			INT
-----	Coplas de curro dulce			
-----	La mi sola laureola			
Turina	Cantares			UME
-----	Cantilena	M	C-EF	UME
Valverde	Clavelitos	MH	E-F	GSC

Miscellaneous Recital Songs

Coloratura Soprano

Bach- Gounod	Ave Maria			
Bizet	Agnus dei	HLM	C-AF	
Cherubini	Ave Maria	H	E-A	GSC †

36

Chopin	My delight	HL		
-----	The birdling			JCH
Dvořák	The lark			
Mozart	Alleluia	LMH	F-C	

Songs and Arias for Opening Recitals

Coloratura Soprano

Anon	Dites, que faut-il faire?			
Bach, J. S.	Jauchzet Gott in allen Landen (Cantata 51)			BRO
Beethoven	Ich liebe dich	HL	BF-DF	†
Bononcini	Deh, più a me non v'ascondete	LH	EF-F	†
Brahms	Nachtigall	MHL	BF-FS	†
Caccini	Amarilli, mia bella	ML	C-D	†
Cavalli	Donzelle fuggite	HL	C-EF	†
Cimara	Stornellata marinara	HM		RIC
Gluck	O del mio dolce ardor (Paride ed Elena)	LH	D-FS	GSC
-----	Ritorna l'eta dell' oro (Il Trionfo di Clelia)			
Gretry	La fauvette avec ses petits (Zémire et Azor) Flute			LEM
Handel	Care selve (Atalanta)	MH	FS-A	†
-----	Let the bright seraphim (Samson) Trumpet	H	E-A	†
-----	O sleep why dost thou leave me (Semele)	H	DS-GS	†
-----	Sweet bird (L'Allegro) Flute			NOV
Haydn	Al tuo seno fortunato (Orfeo ed Euridice)			
-----	With verdure clad (The Creation)	H	E-BF	GSC
Jommelli	Chi vuol comprar la bella	H	B-G	GSC
Mendelssohn	Fruehlingslied	H	DS-GS	†
Mozart	A questo seno, deh vieni			BOO
-----	Alleluja	LMH	F-C	†
-----	Batti, batti, o bel Masetto (Don Giovanni)	H	C-BF	†
				BOO

(Mozart)	Bella mia fiamma, addio			BOO
-----	Mia speranza adorata			
-----	Ridente la calma			BOS
Paisiello	Chi vuol la zingarella	L	C-F	GSC
Pergolesi	A lui donnai			
	(Il Flaminio)			
-----	Se tu m'ami	LMH	C-G	GSC
-----	Stizzoso, mio stizzoso	H	C-AF	†
	(La Serva Padrona)			
Porpora	Non più fra sassi			PET
Rosa	Star vicino	HL	D-E	†
Scarlatti, A.	Cara e dolce			
	rimembranza			
-----	Già il sole dal Gange	LH	EF-F	GSC
-----	Sento nel core	M	E-F	†
Schubert	Gott im Fruehling			PET
-----	Liebesbotschaft	H	E-G	†

American Songs for Closing Recitals

Coloratura Soprano

Branscombe	At the postern gate	MH	DF-AF	ASC
Cadman	Joy	MH	E-A	GSC
Carpenter	Serenade	LH	CS-A	GSC
Charles	And so, goodbye	LH	EF-AF	GSC
-----	Let my song fill your heart	LH	EF-AF	GSC
Clough-Leighter	My lover he comes on the skee	HM	D-F	BOS
Creston	Bird of the wilderness	MH	FS-A	GSC
Dougherty	Primavera	H	C-BF	GSC
Giannini	Sing to my heart a song	H	D-B	ELV
Hageman	At the well	LH	EF-AF	GSC
-----	Me company along	LH	F-BF	CFI
Horsman	The bird of the wilderness	LMH	DF-BF	GSC
La Forge	Cupid captive	H		GAL
Mana Zucca	There's joy in my heart!			CNG
Poldini	Dance of the dolls			CHM
Rorem	Alleluia			
Sacco	Rapunzel	MH	FS-BF	GSC
Saminsky	Queen Estherka's laugh	H	D-A	CFI
Ware	This day is mine	MH	EF-AF	BOS
Warren	Fulfilment	H	D-BF	GAL
-----	Who calls?	LH	E-A	CFI

Watts	Joy	HL	D-F	GSC
-----	Stresa	H	EF-BF	DIT

(See also Folk Songs)

Miscellaneous Songs for Closing Recitals

Coloratura Soprano

Alabieff	The nightingale Flute	H	EF-C	†
Besley	Listening	H	E-AF	CUR
Bliss	Three jolly gentlemen	H		†
Debussy	Chevaux de bois	H	C-G	†
Falla	Polo	HL		AMP
Head	A piper	HL		BOO
Hughes	The leprehaun			
Lara	Granada			
Obradors	Coplas de curro dulce			
Poulenc	Air vif	H	C-AF	ROU
Quilter	Love's philosophy	LMH	D-A	BOO
Ronald	Love, I have won you	HML	EF-EF	ENO
Schubert	Die Forelle	MLH	EF-GF	†
Schumann	Er ist's	HL	BF-EF	†
Strauss, J.	Blue Danube waltz			GSC
Strauss, R.	Staendchen	HM	A-FS	†

Atmospheric Songs and Arias

Coloratura Soprano

Barber	Secrets of old	LH	EF-G	GSC
-----	Sleep now	MH	EF-AF	GSC
Bizet	Douce mer			GSC
Crist	Into a ship dreaming	LMH	EF-GS	CFI
Davis	Nancy Hanks	H	D-G	GAL
Debussy	Nuits d'etoiles	LH	E-A	MAR
Delibes	Pourquoi dans les grands bois (Lakmé)	H	FS-AF	BRO
Duke	Bells in the rain	H	E-GS	CFI
-----	Little elegy	H	FS-A	GSC
Duparc	Soupir	HL	CS-F	BOS
Dvořák	The lark			
Forsyth	The stranger (Organ)	H	A-B	GRA
Ganz	The angels are stooping	MH	GF-A	GSC

39

Gounod	Sérénade	LMH	D-A	GSC
Handel	O sleep why dost thou leave me (Semele)	H	DS-GS	†
Kjerulf	Synnove's song	M	C-F	GSC
Kramer	Swans	HL		RIC
Marx	Marienlied	MH	EF-AF	AMP
Naginski	Look down, fair moon			
Niles	I wonder as I wander	HL	BF-D	GSC
Proctor	I light the blessed candles	H	DF-A	GSC
Rachmaninoff	Lilacs	LH	EF-G	†
Ravel	D'Anne jouant de l'espinette	H	CS-GS	GSC
Reger	The Virgin's slumber song	MMH	G-G	†
Schubert	An die Nachtigall	H	C-G	†
-----	Nachtviolen			PET
Schumann	Der Nussbaum	LMH	D-FS	†

Dramatic Songs and Arias

Coloratura Soprano

Alvarez	La partida	HL	DS-E	GSC
Bainton	The nightingale near the house			CUR
Besley	Listening	H	E-AF	CUR
Burleigh	By the pool at the third roses	H		RIC
Debussy	Chevaux de bois	H	C-G	†
-----	De fleurs	H	C-AF	†
-----	Noël des enfants qui n'ont plus de maisons			DUR
Dougherty	Primavera	H	C-BF	GSC
Geehl	For you alone			SHU
Giannini	Sing to my heart a song	H	D-B	ELV
Grieg	In the boat	LM	D-ES	†
Griffes	The rose of the night	H	CS-A	GSC
-----	Thy dark eyes to mine	H	EF-AF	GSC
-----	Waikiki	H	DS-GS	GSC
Hageman	Christ went up into the hills	LH	EF-AF	CFI
-----	Music I heard with you	MH	E-A	GAL
Handel	Let the bright seraphim (Samson) Trumpet	H	E-A	†
Horsman	The bird of the wilderness	LMH	DF-BF	GSC
Malotte	Among the living	LMH	E-G	GSC
Marx	Selige Nacht	M	DF-GF	AMP
Meyerbeer	Roberto, o tu che odoro	H	C-C	DEI

(Meyerbeer)	(Robert le Diable)			
Mozart	Der Hoelle Rache (Die Zauberfloete)	H	F-F	GSC
-----	Martern aller Arten (Abduction from Seraglio)	H	B-D	†
Poldowski	Dansons la gigue	M	EF-G	MAR
Rachmaninoff	Sorrow in spring	H	D-BF	DIT
Ronald	Down in the forest	HML	C-D	ENO
Severac	Chanson pour le petit cheval			ROU
Vene	Age and youth	H	E-A	RIC
Ware	This day is mine	MH	EF-AF	BOS
Warren	Fulfilment	H	D-BF	GAL

Humorous Songs

Coloratura Soprano

Bach, J. S.	Patron, das macht der Wind (Phoebus and Pan)	M	C-G	GSC
Bax	Oh dear what can the matter be?	M	D-EF	CHE
Bliss	Three jolly gentlemen	H		†
Boieldieu	Essayons s'il se peut de parler			LEM
Brahms	Vergebliches Staendchen	LHM	E-FS	†
Clarke	Shy one	HL	BF-G	BOH
Dalcroze	Le coeur de ma mie	HML		†
Debussy	Voici que le printemps	LH	CS-G	BOS
Duke	A piper	H	CS-B	GSC
Josten	Cupid's counsel	H	EF-AF	GSC
Lehmann	The cuckoo	HH	D-B	BOH
Mopper	The lemon-colored dodo	H	F-BF	BOS
Mozart	Durch Zaertlichkeit (Abduction from Seraglio)			†
-----	Warnung	HM	C-D	
Nordoff	Serenade	H	CS-FS	AMP
-----	There shall be more joy	M	CS-FS	AMP
Paisiello	Chi vuol la zingarella	L	C-F	GSC
Pergolesi	Stizzoso, mio stizzoso (La Serva Padrona)	H	C-AF	†
Pinkham	A partridge in a pear tree	H	D-BF	ROW
Powell	The deaf woman's courtship	M		JFI
Spross	Will o' the wisp			JCH
Strauss, J.	Adele's laughing song	H	D-B	GSC

(Strauss, J.)	(Die Fledermaus)			
Vene	The rats	H	E-A	RIC
Wolf	Jack in the box			
-----	Der Knabe und das Immlein	L	CS-A	†
-----	Ich hab' in Penna	LH		†

Folk Songs (Arr.)

Coloratura Soprano

Bacon	Careless love			
Bax	Oh dear what can the matter be?	M	D-EF	CHE
Britten	O can ye sew cushions?			BOH
-----	The Sally gardens			BOH
Falla	Asturiana	HL		AMP
-----	El pano moruno	HL		AMP
-----	Nana	HL		AMP
-----	Polo	HL		AMP
-----	Seguidilla murciana	HL		AMP
Ferrari	Le jardin d'amour	LM	EF-F	GSC
Hopekirk	Coming through the rye			DIT
-----	Flow gently, sweet Afton			DIT
Hughes	I know my love			BOO
-----	The leprehaun			
Kennedy-Fraser	Isle' of my heart			BOO
-----	Land of heart's desire			BOO
Liebling	Mother dear	H	D-E	GSC
McFeeters	Gentle Mary	H	EF-AF	GSC
Niles	Go 'way from my window	MH	C-G	GSC
-----	I wonder as I wander	HL	BF-D	GSC
-----	If I had a ribbon bow			GSC
Page	The meeting of the waters			DIT
Peel	The early morning			CHA
Powell	The deaf woman's courtship	M		JFI
Siegmeister	He's gone away			
Vaughan Williams	Rolling in the dew			OXF
Weckerlin	Maman, dites-moi	M	E-FS	BOS
-----	Menuet de Martino			
-----	Mon petit coeur soupire			

42

American Songs Employing Agility

Coloratura Soprano

Beach	Fairy lullaby			ASC
Buzzi-Peccia	Under the greenwood tree	LMH	EF-A	DIT
Charles	Let my song fill your heart	LH	EF-AF	GSC
Clough- Leighter	My lover he comes on on the skee	HM	D-F	BOS
Crist	O come hither	HM	B-GS	CFI
Curran	Ho! Mr. Piper	LH	D-G	GSC
Gaynor	Pierrot	H	E-B	BOS
La Forge	Come unto these yellow sands	H	FS-B	GSC
Lubin	The piper	H	C-A	GSC
Manning	Shoes	M	EF-F	GSC
Menotti	Lucy's arietta (The Telephone)			GSC
Nordoff	There shall be more joy	M	CS-FS	AMP
Parker	The lark now leaves her watery nest	LH	D-BF	JCH
Treharne	A widow bird sat mourning	H	FS-AF	BOS

British Songs and Arias
Employing Agility

Coloratura Soprano

Arne, M.	The lass with the delicate air	MH	D-G	†
Arne, T.	Where the bee sucks	HM		†
Bainton	The nightingale near the house			CUR
Bax	Shieling song	H	CS-A	CHE
Benedict	The carnival of Venice	H	D-EF	GSC
-----	The gypsy and the bird Flute	H	D-E	GSC
-----	The wren Flute	H	F-C	PRE
Besley	Listening	H	E-AF	CUR
Bishop	Echo song Flute	H	D-C	GSC
-----	Lo! here the gentle lark Flute	H		†
-----	Love has eyes	M		†

(Bishop)	Pretty mocking bird Flute	H		†
-----	Should he upbraid	H		†
Bliss	Three jolly gentlemen	H		†
Carey	A pastoral			GSC
German	Charming Chloe	HML		NOV
Gibbs	To one who passed whistling through the night	H	F-G	CUR
Handel	Hallelujah (Esther)	H	E-B	CFI
-----	Let the bright seraphim (Samson) Trumpet	H	E-A	†
-----	Oh, had I Jubal's lyre (Joshua)	H	E-FS	GSC
-----	Rejoice Greatly (The Messiah)	H	E-A	†
-----	What's sweeter than a new blown rose? (Joseph)	H	EF-AF	†
Horn	Cherry ripe	M	D-G	†
Quilter	Love's philosophy	LMH	D-A	BOO
Scott	Blackbird's song			ELK

French Songs and Arias
Employing Agility

Coloratura Soprano

Adam	Ah vous dirais-je maman (Le Toreador) Flute			GSC
Auber	Quel bonheur (Fra Diavolo)			BOO
Bizet	Ouvre ton coeur	MH	DS-GS	†
-----	Vielle chanson	H	EF-A	GSC
Boieldieu	Essayons s'il se peut de parler			LEM
Campra	Charmant papillon (Les Fêtes Venitiennes)	MH	D-G	GSC
Chaminade	L'été	MH	E-A	†
Dalcroze	L'oiseau bleu			CFI
David	Charmant oiseau (La Perle du Bresil)	M	D-E	†
Debussy	Fêtes galantes	LH	CS-A	†
Delibes	Bell song (Lakmé)	MH	E-DS	†
-----	Chant de l'almée	H	D-E	GSC
-----	Les filles de Cadix	HM	A-A	†
-----	Passepied	LH	DS-CS	GSC

44

Dupont	Chanson des noisettes			HEU
Falla	Polo	HL		AMP
Ferrari	Le jardin d'amour	LM	EF-F	GSC
Gounod	Je veux vivre	H	F-C	†
	(Roméo et Juliette)			
-----	Mon coeur ne peut			GSC
	changer! (Mireille)			
-----	O légère hirondelle	H	FS-D	CFI
	(Mireille)			
-----	Sérénade	LMH	D-A	GSC
Grétry	Je ne le dis qu'à vous			LEM
	(La Fausse Magie)			
-----	La fauvette avec ses			LEM
	petits			
	(Zémire et Azor) Flute			
-----	Plus de dépit			LEM
	(Les Deux Avares)			
Isouard	Non, je ne veux pas			LEM
	chanter			
	(Le Billet de Loterie)			
Massé	Air du rossignol			
	(Les Noces de Jeannette) Flute			
-----	Sa couleur est blonde			JCH
	et vermeille (Galathée)			
Massenet	Gavotte			†
	(Manon)			
Meyerbeer	La, la, la air cheri			BRA
	(L'Etoile du Nord) Two flutes			
-----	Shadow song	H	DF-D	†
	(Dinorah)			
Milhaud	Tais-toi,	H	G-C	BOH
	Babillarde			
Offenbach	Les oiseaux dans la	H	EF-EF	†
	charmille			
	(Tales of Hoffman)			
Poulenc	Air vif	H	C-AF	ROU
Ravel	Air du feu			DUR
	(L'Enfant et les Sortilèges)			
Saint-Saëns	The nightingale and the	H	C-D	GSC
	rose			
Thomas	Je connais un pauvre	H	C-B	†
	enfant (Mignon)			
-----	Je suis Titania	H	C-EF	GSC
	(Mignon)			
Vidal	Ariette	LH	F-A	GSC

Coloratura Soprano

Bach, J. S.	Jauchzet Gott in allen Landen (Cantata 51)			BRO
Beethoven	Mit einem gemalten Band			RIC
-----	O waer'ich schon mit dir vereint (Fidelio)			†
Brahms	Botschaft	HL	D-F	†
-----	Das Maedchen spricht	H	E-FS	†
Eckert	Swiss echo song	H	A-B	GSC
Haydn	My mother bids me bind my hair	M	E-E	†
-----	On mighty pens uplifted soars (The Creation)	H	E-A	†
Loewe	Niemand hat's gesehen	LM	DS-FS	†
Marx	Und gestern hat er mir Rosen gebracht	H	E-A	AMP
Mozart	Ach, ich liebte (Abduction from Seraglio)			†
-----	Der Hoelle Rache (Die Zauberfloete)	H	F-F	†
-----	Durch Zaertlichkeit (Abduction from Seraglio)			†
-----	Martern aller Arten (Abduction from Seraglio)	H	B-D	†
Proch	Theme and variations Flute	H	C-DF	†
Schubert	Auf dem Wasser zu singen	MH	EF-GF	†
-----	Der Hirt auf dem Felsen (Clarinet or violoncello	H	BF-B	GSC
-----	Liebesbotschaft	H	E-G	†
-----	Ungeduld	HML		†
Schumann	Auftraege	HL	C-E	†
Strauss, J.	Adele's laughing song (Die Fledermaus)	H	D-B	GSC
-----	Blue Danube Waltz			GSC
-----	Czardas (Die Fledermaus)			BOO
-----	Tales from the Vienna forest	H	EF-C	GSC
-----	Voci di primavera	LMH	EF-C	GSC
Strauss, R.	Staendchen	HM	A-FS	†
Weber	Truebe Augen (Der Freischuetz)			GSC

Italian Songs and Arias
Employing Agility

Coloratura Soprano

Arditi	Il bacio	H	CS-B	†
-----	Parla	H	CS-CS	GSC
Bellini	Ah! non credea mirarti			GSC
	(La Sonnambula)			
-----	Son vergin vezzosa	H	E-B	GSC
	(I Puritani)			
Bononcini	Deh, più a me non v'ascondete	LH	EF-F	†
-----	Per la gloria	HL	C-EF	†
Cimarosa	Perdonate signor mio			RIC
	(Il Matrimonio Segreto)			
Defesch	Tu fai la superbetta			GSC
Donizetti	Chacun le sait	H	C-A	RIC
	(La Fille du Régiment)			
-----	Mad scene	H	FS-C	†
	(Lucia di Lammermoor) Flute			
-----	O luce di quest' anima	H	C-E	GSC
	(Linda di Chamounix)			
-----	Prendi, prendi per mei sei libero			BRO
	(L'Elisir d'Amore)			
-----	Quel guardo			BRO
	(Don Pasquale)			
Handel	Lusinghe più care	H	D-G	†
	(Alessandro)			
-----	Qual farfalletta	H	E-A	†
	(Partenope)			
Jommelli	Chi vuol comprar la bella	H	B-G	GSC
Mozart	Batti, batti, o bel Masetto (Don Giovanni)	H	C-BF	†
-----	Ma che vi fece, o stelle			PET
-----	Mia speranza adorata			
-----	Misera, dove son			BOO
Paradies	Quel ruscelletto	L	BF-F	CFI
Porpora	Non più fra sassi			PET
Rossini	La danza	MH	E-A	†
-----	La pastorella delle Alpi	H	E-C	CFI
Scarlatti, A.	Già il sole dal Gange	LH	EF-F	GSC
-----	Rugiadose odorose	HL	D-E	DIT
	(Il Pirro e Demetrio)			
Sibella	O bimba bimbetta	LMH	D-G	GSC
Veracini	Pastorale	MH	C-G	BOO
	(Rosalinda)			

47

Verdi	Ah fors' è lui	H	C-DF	†
	(La Traviata)			
-----	Merce, dilette amiche	MH	A-CS	GSC
	(I Vespri Siciliani)			
-----	Saper vorreste	H	D-B	GSC
	(Un Ballo in Maschera)			
-----	Tacea la notte placida	H	D-DF	†
	(Il Trovatore)			
-----	Volta la Terrea	H	D-BF	GSC
	(Un Ballo in Maschera)			

Miscellaneous Songs and Arias
Employing Agility

Coloratura Soprano

Alabieff	The nightingale	H	EF-C	†
	Flute			
Alvarez	La partida	HL	DS-E	GSC
Chopin	My delight	HL		
Falla	Nana	HL		AMP
-----	Seguidilla murciana	HL		AMP
Glazounoff	La primavera d'or	H	D-BF	GSC
Granados	El majo discreto	H		INT
Mozart	Alleluja	LMH	F-C	†
-----	Et incarnatus est			PET
	(C Minor Mass)			
Rimsky Korsakov	Hymn to the sun	H	FS-B	GSC
	(Le Coq d'Or)			
Rossini	Inflammatus			GSC
	(Stabat Mater)			
Stravinsky	Pastorale			GSC
Thrane	Norwegian echo song	H	D-B	GSC
Turina	Cantares			UME
-----	Cantilena	M	C-EF	UME

American Songs Employing
Crescendo and Diminuendo

Coloratura Soprano

Bacon	Is there such a thing as	M	DS-FS	AMP
	day?			
Barber	Secrets of old	LH	EF-G	GSC
-----	Sleep now	MH	EF-AF	GSC
-----	The daisies	M	C-F	GSC

48

Beach	Fairy lullaby			ASC
Carpenter	When I bring to you coloured toys	LM		GSC
Duke	Bells in the rain	H	E-GS	CFI
Lubin	The piper	H	C-A	GSC
Niles	I wonder as I wander	HL	BF-D	GSC
Nordoff	Fair Annette's song			AMP
-----	Serenade	H	CS-FS	AMP
Ware	By the fountain			FLA
Watts	Wings of night	LH	CS-G	GSC

British Songs and Arias Employing Crescendo and Diminuendo

Coloratura Soprano

Bantock	A dream of spring	H		CHE
Clarke	Shy one	HL	BF-G	BOH
Gibbs	To one who passed whistling through the night	H	F-G	CUR
Handel	As when the dove (Acis and Galatea)	H	D-G	†
-----	O sleep why dost thou leave me (Semele)	H	DS-GS	†
-----	Sweet bird (L' Allegro) Flute			NOV
-----	What's sweeter than a new blown rose? (Joseph)	H	EF-AF	†
Horn	Cherry ripe	M	D-G	†
Ireland	Bed in summer			CUR
Quilter	Dream valley	H	EF-GF	ROG
-----	To daisies			BOO

French Songs and Arias Employing Crescendo and Diminuendo

Coloratura Soprano

Auber	Quel bonheur (Fra Diavolo)			BOO
Bachelet	Chère nuit	H	DF-BF	GSC
Bizet	Vielle chanson	H	EF-A	GSC
Dalcroze	Le coeur de ma mie	HML		†
-----	L'oiseau bleu			CFI
David	Charmant oiseau (La Perle du Brésil)	M	D-E	†
Debussy	Green	H	C-AF	†

49

(Debussy)	Voici que le printemps	LH	CS-G	BOS
Duparc	Chanson triste	MH	FS-AF	†
-----	L'invitation au voyage	HM	E-F	†
Fauré	Clair de lune	MH	C-G	†
-----	Les roses d'Ispahan	HM	D-FS	†
-----	Nell	LH	FS-AF	†
-----	Sylvie	HL	E-F	†
Gounod	Le jour se lève (Mireille)			CHO
Grétry	Je crains de lui (Richard Coeur-de-Lion)			LEM
-----	Plus de dépit (Les Deux Avares)			LEM
Hahn	Le rossignol des lilas			
Herold	Air de Nicette (Le Pré aux Clercs)			BRA
Lalo	La chanson d'Alouette	H	EF-B	GSC
Liszt	Comment, disaient-ils?	H	C-AF	GSC
Massé	Air du rossignol (Les Noces de Jeannette) Flute			
Massenet	Gavotte (Manon)			†
-----	Je suis encore toute étourdie (Manon)			HEU
Meyerbeer	Nobles seigneurs, salut! (Les Huguenots)	LH	C-C	†
Saint-Saëns	Le bonheur est une chose légère Violin and piano	H	C-A	CHO

German Songs and Arias Employing Crescendo and Diminuendo

Coloratura Soprano

Beethoven	Mit einem gemalten Band			RIC
-----	O waer' ich schon mit dir vereint (Fidelio)			†
Brahms	Geheimnis			†
-----	Wie Melodien zieht es	HL	A-E	†
Haydn	On mighty pens uplifted soars (The Creation)	H	E-A	†
Liszt	Kling' leise, mein Lied	HL		†
Mendelssohn	O for the wings of a dove	MLH	D-G	†
Mozart	Durch Zaertlichkeit (Abduction from Seraglio)			†
Schubert	An die Laute	LH	D-F	†

50

(Schubert)	Auf dem Wasser zu singen	MH	EF-GF	†
-----	Das Lied im Gruenen			PET
-----	Das Rosenband			PET
-----	Der Knabe			PET
-----	Der Musensohn	LH	FS-G	†
-----	Der Schmetterling	LH	E-F	†
-----	Geheimes	HL	BF-EF	†
-----	Gott im Fruehling			PET
-----	Gretchen am Spinnrade	H	F-A	†
-----	Hark! hark! the lark	LMH	F-G	†
-----	Liebesbotschaft	H	E-G	GSC
-----	Wiegenlied (op. 98)			†
Schumann	Der Nussbaum	LMH	D-FS	†
-----	Die Meerfee			
-----	Intermezzo	HL	C-D	†
-----	Lieder der Braut	H	D-A	†
-----	Marienwuermchen	HL	D-D	†
-----	Schneegloeckchen	HL		†
-----	Volksliedchen	HL		†
Strauss	All' mein' Gedanken	H	CS-GS	
-----	Barcarolle	H	DF-BF	†
-----	Schlagende Herzen			†
Wolf	Der Knabe und das Immlein	L	CS-A	†
-----	Fruehling uebers Jahr			†
-----	Gleich und gleich			†

Italian Songs and Arias Employing
Crescendo and Diminuendo

Coloratura Soprano

Bononcini	Per la gloria	HL	C-EF	†
-----	Si che fedele			DUR
Cavalli	In amor (Eritrea)			DUR
Cesti	Intorno all'idol mio (Orontea)	MH	D-F	†
De Luca	Non posso disperar	HL	C-E	GSC
Donizetti	Chacun le sait (La Fille du Régiment)	H	C-A	RIC
Handel	Mi restano le lagrime (Alcina)			BOO
Mozart	L'amero, saro costante (Il Re Pastore) Violin or flute	H	D-B	GSC
Pergolesi	Se tu m'ami	LMH	C-G	GSC
Scarlatti, A.	Sento nel core	M	E-F	†

Miscellaneous Songs Employing
Crescendo and Diminuendo

Coloratura Soprano

Arensky	The little fish's song	H	D-A	†
Dvořák	Songs my mother taugh me			†
Gretchaninoff	The snowdrop	HM	BF-F	DIT
Grieg	In the boat	LM	D-ES	†
-----	Solvejg's song			
Lilljebjorn	When I was seventeen			RIC
Rachmaninoff	Daisies			†
-----	Lilacs			
-----	Oh cease thy singing, maiden fair	H	E-A	CFI
-----	The songs of Grusia	H	E-A	GSC
-----	Vocalise	LH	CS-A	GSC
Stravinsky	Pastorale			GSC
Turina	Cantilena	M	C-EF	UME

American Songs Employing Piano Singing

Coloratura Soprano

Barber	Sleep now	MH	EF-AF	GSC
Burleigh	By the pool at the third roses	H		RIC
Crist	White hours like snow	HL	CS-BF	CFI
Davis	Nancy Hanks	H	D-G	GAL
Duke	Bells in the rain	H	E-GS	CFI
-----	Little elegy	H	FS-A	GSC
Ganz	The angels are stooping	MH	GF-A	GSC
Giannini	Tell me, o blue, blue sky	H		RIC
Griffes	In a myrtle shade	H	FS-A	GSC
-----	Thy dark eyes to mine	H	EF-AF	GSC
Kramer	Swans	HL		RIC
Manning	Shoes	M	EF-F	GSC
Niles	I wonder as I wander	HL	BF-D	GSC
Nordoff	Serenade	H	CS-FS	AMP
Watts	Stressa	H	EF-BF	DIT
-----	The little shepherd's song	H	G-BF	RIC

British Songs Employing Piano Singing

Coloratura Soprano

Arne, M.	The lass with the delicate air	MH	D-G	†

Bainton	The nightingale near the house			CUR
Bax	I heard a piper piping	LH	D-G	CFI
-----	Shieling song	H	CS-A	CHE
Brewer	The fairy pipers	HML		BOH
Clarke	Shy one	HL	BF-G	BOH
Gibbs	To one who passed whistling through the night	H	F-G	CUR
Head	A piper	HL		BOO
Ronald	Down in the forest	HML	C-D	ENO
Warlock	Pretty ring time	H	D-G	CFI

French Songs and Arias Employing
Piano Singing

Coloratura Soprano

Bizet	Douce mer			GSC
Dalcroze	Le coeur de ma mie	HML		†
Debussy	Clair de lune	M	CS-FS	JOB
-----	Fantoches	H	D-A	JOB
-----	Green	H	C-AF	†
-----	Harmonie du soir			DUR
-----	Il pleure dans mon coeur	LH	CS-GS	†
-----	L'ombre des arbres			†
-----	La mer est plus belle	HL		†
-----	Mandoline	HM	BF-F	†
-----	Nuits d'etoiles	LH	E-A	MAR
-----	Voici que le printemps	LH	CS-G	BOS
Delibes	Sous le ciel tout étoile (Lakmé)			HEU
Duparc	Extase	LMH	FS-A	†
-----	Soupir	HL	CS-F	BOS
Dupont	Mandoline			DUR
Fauré	Après un rêve	HM	C-F	†
-----	Clair de lune	MH	C-G	†
-----	La lune blanche	HL		†
-----	Notre amour	H	DS-B	†
-----	Sylvie	HL	E-F	†
Gounod	Sérénade	LMH	D-A	GSC
Grétry	Je ne fais semblant de rien (L'Ami de la Maison)			LEM
-----	Rose chérie (Zémire et Azor)			LEM
Hahn	Le rossignol des lilas			
Koechlin	L'air	M	F-FS	ROU
-----	La lune	M	C-F	ROU
-----	Le thé	HM	C-E	BOS

Liszt	Comment, disaient-ils?	H	C-AF	†
-----	Oh! quand je dors	H	E-A	†
Moret	Le nélumbo	H	E-DF	HEU
Poulenc	Air champêtre			ROU
-----	C. (J'ai traversé les ponts de C.)			ROU
Rabey	Tes yeux Violin and piano	H	EF-G	DUR
Ravel	D'Anne jouant de l'espinette	H	CS-GS	GSC
Saint-Saëns	Le bonheur est une chose H légère Violin and piano		C-A	CHO
Weckerlin	Je connais un berger discret	M	EF-EF	BOS
-----	Maman, dites-moi	M	E-FS	BOS

German Songs Employing
Piano Singing

Coloratura Soprano

Beethoven	Ich liebe dich	HL	BF-DF	†
Brahms	Auf dem Schiffe	LH	GS-A	†
-----	Botschaft	HL	D-F	†
-----	Das Maedchen spricht	H	E-FS	†
-----	Eine gute, gute Nacht			†
-----	Geheimnis			†
-----	Lerchengesang	LH	FS-GS	†
-----	Vergebliches Staendchen	LHM	E-FS	†
Jensen	Murmuring zephyr	LH	E-AF	GSC
Liszt	Kling' leise, mein Lied	HL		†
Marx	Marienlied	MH	EF-AF	AMP
-----	Selige Nacht	M	DF-GF	AMP
Schubert	An die Laute	LH	D-F	†
-----	Auf dem Wasser zu singen	MH	EF-GF	†
-----	Ave Maria	LMH	F-F	†
-----	Das Rosenband			PET
-----	Der Schmetterling	LH	E-F	†
-----	Du bist die Ruh	LMH	EF-AF	†
-----	Geheimes	HL	BF-EF	†
-----	Gott im Fruehling			PET
-----	Liebesbotschaft	H	E-G	GSC
-----	Nachtviolen			PET
-----	Wiegenlied (op. 98)			†
-----	Wohin?	HL	B-E	†
Schumann	Auftraege	HL	C-E	†
-----	Der Nussbaum	LMH	D-FS	†

54

(Schumann)	Die Meerfee			
-----	Marienwuermchen	HL	D-D	†
-----	Mondnacht	M	E-FS	†
-----	Volksliedchen	HL		†
Strauss, R.	All' mein' Gedanken	H	CS-GS	
-----	Barcarolle	H	DF-BF	†
Trunk	In meiner Heimat			
Wolf	Ach, im Maien	HL	C-E	†
-----	Fruehling uebers Jahr			†
-----	Gleich und gleich			†
-----	Schlafendes Jesuskind	HL	AS-F	†

Italian Songs and Arias Employing
Piano Singing

Coloratura Soprano

Bononcini	Deh, più a me non v'ascondete	LH	EF-F	†
d'Astorga	Vo' cercando in queste valli	H	D-G	STB
Donizetti	Mad scene (Lucia di Lammermoor) Flute	H	FS-C	
Gagliano	Dormi, amore (La Flora)	HL	CS-E	DIT
Gluck	O del mio dolce ardor (Paride ed Elena)	LH	D-FS	GSC
Handel	Care selve (Atalanta)	MH	FS-A	†
Jommelli	Chi vuol comprar la bella	H	B-G	GSC
Mozart	A questo seno, deh vieni			BOO
-----	Deh vieni non tardar (Le Nozze di Figaro)	H	A-A	†
-----	Non so più cosa son (Le Nozze di Figaro)	H	EF-G	†
	Un moto di gioja (Le Nozze di Figaro)			
Pizzetti	I pastori			FRL
Verdi	Addio del passato (La Traviata)			†
-----	Sul fil d'un soffio etesio (Falstaff)	H	DS-A	RIC

Miscellaneous Songs Employing
Piano Singing

Coloratura Soprano

Arensky	Valse	H	DF-GF	GSC
Dvořák	Songs my mother taught me			
Gretchaninoff	Hushed the song of the nightingale			DIT
Grieg	In the boat	LM	D-ES	†
-----	Solvejg's song	MH	E-A	†
Lie	Soft-footed snow	HM		DIT
Rachmaninoff	Before my window	HM	C-G	†
-----	Here beauty dwells	H	D-B	CFI

American Songs Employing
Rapid Enunciation

Coloratura Soprano

Bacon	Four songs	H	DF-G	MUP
Beach	The year's at the spring			ASC
Clough-Leighter	My lover he comes on the skee	HM	D-F	BOS
Curran	Ho! Mr. piper	LH	D-G	GSC
Griffes	Elves	H	F-AF	GSC
Hageman	At the well	LH	EF-AF	GSC
Hageman	Miranda	HL		GAL
Josten	Cupid's counsel	H	EF-AF	GSC
Manning	Shoes	M	EF-F	GSC
Spross	Will o' the wisp			JCH

British Songs Employing
Rapid Enunciation

Coloratura Soprano

Bantock	A feast of lanterns	HM	D-F	GAL
Bartlet	Whither runneth my sweetheart?			BOO
Bax	Oh dear, what can the matter be?	M	D-EF	CHE
Bishop	Love has eyes	M		†

(Bishop)	Pretty mocking bird	H		†
	Flute			
Brewer	The fairy pipers	HML		BOH
German	Charming Choe	HML		NOV
Head	A piper	HL		BOO
Holst	A little music	H		AUG
Hughes	Hey diddle diddle			CRA
Morley	It was a lover and his			DIT
	lass			

French Songs and Arias Employing
Rapid Enunciation

Coloratura Soprano

Auber	L' eclat de rire			DUR
	(Manon Lescaut)			
Dalcroze	L'oiseau bleu			CFI
Debussy	Chevaux de bois	H	C-G	†
-----	Fantoches	H	D-A	JOB
-----	Fêtes galantes	LH	CS-A	†
-----	Green	H	C-AF	†
-----	Mandoline	HM	BF-F	†
-----	Voici que le printemps	LH	CS-G	BOS
Delibes	Les filles de Cadox	HM	A-A	†
Dupont	Chanson des noisettes			HEU
Fauré	Notre amour	H	DS-B	†
-----	Sylvie	HL	E-F	†
Ferrari	Le Jardin d'amour	LM	EF-F	GSC
Hue	A des oiseaux	H	E-G	†
Koechlin	La lune	M	C-F	ROU
Milhaud	Tais-toi, Babillarde	H	G-C	BOH
Poldowski	Dansons la gigue	M	EF-G	MAR
Severac	Chanson pour le petit			ROU
	cheval			
Vuillermoz	Jardin d' amours			SAL
Weckerlin	Maman, dites-moi	M	E-FS	BOS

German Songs and Arias Employing
Rapid Enunciation

Coloratura Soprano

Bach, J. S.	Patron, das macht der	M	C-G	GSC
	Wind			
	(Phoebus and Pan)			
Brahms	Das Maedchen spricht	H	E-FS	†

(Brahms)	Vergebliches Staendchen	LHM	E-FS	†
Mendelssohn	Im Gruenen	H	E-BF	AUG
-----	Neue Liebe	H	CS-A	†
Mozart	Warnung	HM	C-D	
-----	Welche Wonne, welche Lust (Abduction from Seraglio)			†
Schubert	Das Lied im Gruenen			PET
-----	Der Musensohn	LH	FS-G	†
-----	Der Schmetterling	LH	E-F	†
-----	Die Forelle	MLH	EF-GF	†
-----	Ungeduld	HML		†
-----	Wohin?	HL	B-E	†
Schumann	Auftraege	HL	C-E	†
-----	Volksliedchen	HL		†
Strauss	Staendchen	HM	A-FS	†
Wolf	Ich hab' in Penna	LH		†

Italian Songs and Arias Employing Rapid Enunciation

Coloratura Soprano

Bononcini	Si che fedele			DUR
Cavalli	Donzelle fuggite	HL	C-EF	†
Cimarosa	Perdonate signor mio (Il Matrimonio Segreto)			RIC
De Luca	Non posso disperar	HL	C-E	GSC
Durante	Danza, danza fanciulla gentile			†
Legrenzi	Che fiero costume	HML	C-D	†
Mozart	Non so più cosa son (Le Nozze di Figaro)	H	EF-G	†
Paisiello	Chi vuol la zingarella	L	C-F	GSC
Pergolesi	A Serpina penserete (La Serva Padrona)			
------	Stizzoso, mio stizzoso (La Serva Padrona)	H	C-AF	†
Rossini	La danza	MH	E-A	†
Tosti	'A vucchella	LH	F-G	RIC

Miscellaneous Songs Employing Rapid Enunciation

Coloratura Soprano

Falla	Seguidilla Murciana	HL		AMP

58

Grieg	In the boat	LM	D-ES	†
-----	My Johann			
-----	With a water lilly			†

American Songs Employing
Sustained Singing

Coloratura Soprano

Bacon	Is there such a thing as day?	M	DS-FS	AMP
Barber	Sleep now	MH	EF-AF	GSC
Burleigh	By the pool at the third roses	H		RIC
-----	Were you there?	HML		RIC
Charles	And so, goodbye	LH	EF-AF	GSC
Crist	White hours like snow	HL	CS-BF	CFI
Ganz	The angels are stooping	MH	GF-A	GSC
Giannini	Tell me, o blue, blue sky	H		RIC
Griffes	In a myrtle shade	H	FS-A	GSC
-----	The rose of the night	H	CS-A	GSC
-----	Thy dark eyes to mine	H	EF-AF	GSC
Hageman	Music I heard with you	MH	E-A	GAL
Horsman	The bird of the wilderness	LMH	DF-BF	GSC
Kramer	Swans	HL		RIC
Sacco	Rapunzel	MH	FS-BF	GSC
Watts	Stresa	H	EF-BF	DIT
-----	The poet sings	MH	EF-AF	DIT

British Songs and Arias Employing
Sustained Singing

Coloratura Soprano

Bax	I heard a piper piping	LH	D-G	CFI
Britten	The Sally gardens			BOH
Handel	How beautiful are the feet of them (The Messiah)	H		†
-----	I know that my Redeemer liveth (The Messiah)	MH	E-GS	†
-----	O sleep why dost thou leave me (Semele)	H	DS-GS	†
-----	Sweet bird (L' Allegro) Flute			NOV
Purcell	Cease, o my sad soul			
-----	Had I but love			DUN
Quilter	To daisies			BOO

Ronald	Down in the forest	HML	C-D	ENO
-----	Prelude			ENO
-----	O lovely night	HML		BOO

French Songs and Arias Employing Sustained Singing

Coloratura Soprano

Bachelet	Chère nuit	H	DF-BF	GSC
Bizet	Comme autrefois dans la nuit sombre (Les Pêcheurs des Perles)			CHO
-----	Douce mer			GSC
-----	O dieu Brahma (Les Pêcheurs des Perles)	H	B-D	GSC
Debussy	Beau soir	LH	C-FS	†
-----	Clair de lune	M	CS-FS	JOB
-----	De fleurs	H	C-AF	†
-----	Harmonie du soir			DUR
-----	Il pleure dans mon coeur	LH	CS-GS	†
-----	L'ombre des arbres			†
-----	Nuits d'etoiles	LH	E-A	MAR
-----	Romance	HM	C-E	†
Délibes	Jours passés			GSC
-----	Sous le ciel tout étoile (Lakmé)			HEU
Duparc	Chanson triste	MH	FS-AF	†
-----	Extase	LMH	FS-A	†
-----	L'invitation au voyage	HM	E-F	†
-----	Soupir	HL	CS-F	BOS
Fauré	Après un rêve	HM	C-F	†
-----	La lune blanche	HL		†
-----	Les Roses d'Ispahan	HM	D-FS	†
-----	Rencontre	H	EF-AF	†
-----	Vocalise	H		LED
Gounod	Le jour se lève (Mireille)			CHO
Grétry	Rose chérie (Zémire et Azor)			LEM
Hahn	Le rossignol des lilas			
Koechlin	L'air	M	F-FS	ROU
Liszt	Oh! quand je dors	H	E-A	†
Massenet	Je suis encore tout étourdie (Manon)			HEU
Meyerbeer	Nobles Seigneurs, salut! (Les Huguenots)	LH	C-C	†

60

(Meyerbeer)	Roberto, o tu che odoro (Robert le Diable)	H	C-C	DEI
Moret	Le nélumbo	H	E-DF	HEU
Poulenc	C. (J'ai traversé les ponts de C.)			ROU
Rabey	Tes yeux Violin and piano	H	EF-G	DUR
Ravel	D'Anne jouant de l'espinette	H	CS-GS	GSC
Saint-Saëns	Aimons-nous			DUR

German Songs and Arias Employing
Sustained singing

Coloratura Soprano

Beethoven	Ich liebe dich	HL	BF-DF	†
Brahms	Feldeinsamkeit	HL	C-EF	†
-----	Lerchengesang	LH	FS-GS	†
-----	Nachtigall	MHL	BF-FS	†
-----	Wie Melodien zieht es	HL	A-E	†
-----	Wir wandelten	LH	EF-GF	†
Haydn	With verdure clad (The Creation)	H	E-BF	†
Loewe	Canzonetta	MH	B-A	DIT
Marx	Marienlied	MH	EF-AF	AMP
-----	Nocturne	H	EF-AF	AMP
-----	Selige Nacht	M	DF-GF	AMP
Mendelssohn	Fruehlingslied	H	DS-GS	†
-----	O for the wings of a dove	MLH	D-G	†
-----	On wings of song			†
Mozart	Ach, ich fuehl's (Die Zauberfloete)	H	CS-BF	†
-----	Wiegenlied	MH	G-G	†
Schubert	An die Nachtigall	H	C-G	†
-----	Ave Maria	LMH	F-F	†
-----	Der Juengling an der Quelle	LH	E-A	†
-----	Du bist die Ruh	LMH	EF-AF	†
-----	Gretchen am Spinnrade	H	F-A	†
-----	Nachtviolen			PET
-----	Wiegenlied (op. 98)			†
Schumann	Der Nussbaum	LMH	D-FS	†
-----	Intermezzo	HL	C-D	GSC
-----	Lieder der Braut	H	D-A	†
-----	Mondnacht	M	E-FS	†
Strauss	Kornblumen	LH	DF-AF	†
-----	Liebeshymnus			†

Trunk	In meiner Heimat			
Wolf	Ach, im Maien	HL	C-E	†
-----	Bedeckt mich mit Blumen	HL	B-D	†
-----	Schlafendes Jesuskind	HL	AS-F	†

Italian Songs and Arias Employing
Sustained Singing

Coloratura Soprano

Braga	Angel's serenade	LH	D-G	†
	Violin			
Caccini	Amarilli, mia bella	ML	C-D	†
Cesti	Intorno all'idol mio	MH	D-F	†
	(Orontea)			
Cimara	Stornellata marinara	HM		RIC
Cimarosa	Bel nume che adoro			RIC
Donizetti	Regnava nel silenzio	H	CS-D	GSC
	(Lucia di Lammermoor)			
Gagliano	Dormi amore	HL	CS-E	DIT
	(La Flora)			
Gluck	O del mio dolce ardor	LH	D-FS	GSC
	(Paride ed Elena)			
Handel	Care selve	MH	FS-A	†
	(Atalanta)			
-----	Mi restano le lagrime			BOO
	(Alcina)			
Mozart	Bella mia fiamma, addio			BOO
-----	Deh vieni non tardar	H	A-A	†
	(Le Nozze di Figaro)			
-----	L'amero, saro costante	H	D-B	GSC
	(Il Re Pastore)			
	Violin or flute			
-----	Ridente la calma			BOS
Pergolesi	Dite ch'ogni momento			BOS
-----	Nina	HL	CS-D	DIT
Pizzetti	I pastori			FRL
Puccini	Musetta's waltz	H	EF-BF	RIC
	(La Boheme)			
Rosa	Star vicino	HL	D-E	†
Rossini	Una voce poco fa	HM	GS-E	GSC
	(Il Barbiere di Siviglia)			
Verdi	Addio del passato			†
	(La Traviata)			
-----	Caro nome	H	DS-DS	†
	(Rigoletto)			

Miscellaneous Songs Employing
Sustained Singing

Coloratura Soprano

Arensky	The little fish's song	H	D-A	†
-----	Valse	H	DF-GF	GSC
Bach-Gounod	Ave Maria			†
Cherubini	Ave Maria	H	E-A	GSC
Dvořák	The lark			
Gretchaninoff	The snowdrop	HM	BF-F	DIT
Grieg	I love Thee	HML	E-F	†
-----	Solvejg's song	MH	E-A	†
Kjerulf	Synnove's song	M	C-F	GSC
Lilljebjorn	When I was seventeen			RIC
Rachmaninoff	Before my window	HM	C-G	†
-----	Daisies			†
-----	Here beauty dwells	H	D-B	CFI
-----	Into my open window	HL	B-FS	BOS
-----	Oh cease thy singing, maiden fair	H	E-A	CFI
-----	Vocalise	LH	CS-A	GSC
Sibelius	From the north	H	DS-G	GSC

American Songs Employing
Spirited Singing

Coloratura Soprano

Brown	Love is where you find it (The Kissing Bandit)			
Buzzi-Peccia	Under the greenwood tree	LMH	EF-A	DIT
Carpenter	Serenade	LH	CS-A	GSC
Charles	Let my song fill your heart	LH	EF-AF	GSC
Clough-Leighter	My lover he comes on the skee	HM	D-F	BOS
Crist	O come hither	HM	B-GS	CFI
Curran	Ho! Mr. Piper	LH	D-G	GSC
Giannini	Sing to my heart a song	H	D-B	ELV
Griffes	Elves	H	F-AF	GSC
Hageman	At the well	LH	EF-AF	GSC
-----	Me company along	LH	F-BF	CFI
Josten	Cupid's counsel	H	EF-AF	GSC
Nordoff	There shall be more joy	M	CS-FS	AMP
Robyn	A heart that's free	MH	EF-AF	FEI
Saar	The little gray dove	MH	D-BF	GSC

Sacco	Rapunzel	MH	FS-BF	GSC
Spross	Will o' the wisp			JCH
Vene	The rats	H	E-A	RIC

British Songs and Arias Employing
Spirited Singing

Coloratura Soprano

Bantock	A feast of lanterns	HM	D-F	GAL
Bax	Oh dear what can the matter be?	M	D-EF	CHE
-----	Shieling song	H	CS-A	CHE
Besley	Listening	H	E-AF	CUR
Bishop	Lo! here the gentle lark Flute	H		†
-----	Love has eyes	M		†
-----	Should he upbraid	H		†
Bliss	Three jolly gentlemen	H		†
Brewer	The fairy pipers	HML		BOH
Carey	A pastoral			GSC
German	Charming Chloe	HML		NOV
Handel	Hallelujah (Esther)	H	E-B	CFI
-----	Rejoice greatly (The Messiah)	H	E-A	†
Head	A piper	HL		BOO
Lehmann	The cuckoo	HH	D-B	BOH
Quilter	Love's philosophy	LMH	D-A	BOO
Ronald	Love, I have won you	HML	EF-EF	ENO
Warlock	Pretty ring time	H	D-G	CFI

French Songs and Arias Employing
Spirited Singing

Coloratura Soprano

Auber	L' eclat de rire (Manon Lescaut)			DUR
Bizet	Ouvre ton coeur	MH	DS-GS	†
Chaminade	L'été	MH	E-A	†
Charpentier	Les chevaux de bois	H	E-A	HEU
Debussy	Chevaux de bois	H	C-G	†
-----	Fantoches	H	D-A	JOB
-----	Fêtes galantes	LH	CS-A	†
-----	La mer est plus belle	HL		†
-----	Le faune			DUR

(Debussy)	Mandoline	HM	BF-F	†
-----	Noël des enfants qui n'ont plus de maisons			DUR
Dupont	Mandoline			DUR
Fauré	Notre amour	H	DS-B	†
Gounod	Au printemps	LMH	DF-AF	GSC
-----	Je veux vivre (Roméo et Juliette)	H	F-C	†
-----	O légère hirondelle (Mireille)	H	FS-D	CFI
Grétry	Je ne fais semblant de rein (L' Ami de la Maison)			LEM
-----	La fauvette avec ses petits (Zémire et Azor) Flute			LEM
Hahn	Le printemps			
Isouard	Non, je ne veux pas chanter (Le Billet de Loterie)			LEM
Koechlin	La lune	M	C-F	ROU
-----	Le thé	HM	C-E	BOS
Massé	Sa couleur est blonde et vermeille (Galathée)			JCH
Meyerbeer	Shadow song (Dinorah)	H	DF-D	†
Milhaud	Tais-toi, Babillarde	H	G-C	BOH
Pierné	La moulin	ML	C-E	BOS
Poldowski	Dansons la gigue	M	EF-G	MAR
Poulenc	Air champêtre			ROU
-----	Air vif	H	C-AF	ROU
Ravel	Air du feu (L'Enfant et les Sortilèges)			DUR
Severac	Chanson pour le petit cheval			ROU
Thomas	Je connais un pauvre enfant (Mignon)	H	C-B	†
Vidal	Ariette	LH	F-A	GSC
Vuillermoz	Jardin d'amours			SAL

German Songs and Arias Employing
Spirited Singing

Coloratura Soprano

Bach, J. S.	Jauchzet Gott in allen Landen (Cantata 51)			BRO
-----	Patron, das macht der Wind (Phoebus and Pan)	M	C-G	GSC
Brahms	Auf dem Schiffe	LH	GS-A	†

65

(Brahms)	Botschaft	HL	D-F	†
-----	Das Maedchen spricht	H	E-FS	†
-----	Es liebt sich so lieblich im Lenze	LH	D-GS	†
-----	Vergebliches Staendchen	LHM	E-FS	†
Eckert	Swiss echo song	H	A-B	GSC
Haydn	O how pleasing to the senses (The Seasons)	H		†
Jensen	Murmuring zephyr	LH	E-AF	GSC
Loewe	Niemand hat's gesehen	LM	DS-FS	†
Marx	Und gestern hat er mir Rosen gebracht	H	E-A	AMP
Mendelssohn	Fruehlingslied	H	DS-GS	†
-----	Im Gruenen	H	E-BF	AUG
-----	Neue Liebe	H	CS-A	†
-----	O Jugend	H	E-A	†
Mozart	Ach, ich liebte (Abduction from Seraglio)			†
-----	Martern aller Arten (Abduction from Seraglio)	H	B-D	†
Schubert	Die Forelle	MLH	EF-GF	†
-----	Rastlose Liebe	M	B-F	†
-----	Wohin?	HL	B-E	DIT
Schumann	Auftraege	HL	C-E	†
-----	Er ist's	HL	BF-EF	†
-----	Geisternaehe			
Strauss, J.	Adele's laughing song (Die Fledermaus)	H	D-B	GSC
-----	Tales from the Vienna forest	H	EF-C	GSC
-----	Voci di primavera	LMH	EF-C	GSC
Strauss, R.	Schlechtes Wetter			†
-----	Staendchen	HM	A-FS	†
Wolf	Ach, im Maien	HL	C-E	†
-----	Ich hab' in Penna	LH		†
-----	Zum neuen Jahr			PET

Italian Songs and Arias Employing Spirited Singing

Coloratura Soprano

Arditi	Il bacio	H	CS-B	
-----	Parla	H	CS-CS	GSC
Bellini	Ah! non credea mirarti (La Sonnambula)			GSC
-----	Son vergin vezzosa (I Puritani)	H	E-B	GSC

Cavalli	Donzelle fuggite	HL	C-EF	†
Cimarosa	Perdonate signor mio			RIC
	(Il Matrimonio Segreto)			
D'Astorga	Vo' cercando in queste	H	D-G	STB
	valli			
Donizetti	Prendi, prendi per mei			BRO
	sei libero			
	(L' Elisir d'Amore)			
-----	Regnava nel silenzio	H	CS-D	GSC
	(Lucia di Lammermoor)			
Handel	Lusinghe più care	H	D-G	†
	(Alessandro)			
-----	Qual farfalletta	H	E-A	†
	(Partenope)			
Legrenzi	Che fiero costume	HML	C-D	
Mozart	A questo seno, deh vieni			BOO
-----	Non so più cosa son	H	EF-G	
	(Le Nozze di Figaro)			
-----	Un moto di gioja			
	(Le Nozze di Figaro)			
Paisiello	Chi vuol la zingarella	L	C-F	GSC
Pergolesi	Stizzoso, mio stizzoso	H	C-AF	†
	(La Serva Padrona)			
Porpora	Non più fra sassi			PET
Respighi	Scherzo			BON
Rossini	La pastorella delle Alpi	H	E-C	CFI
-----	Una voce poco fa	HM	GS-E	GSC
	(Il Barbiere di Siviglia)			
Scarlatti, A.	Già il sole dal Gange	LH	EF-F	GSC
Veracini	Pastorale	MH	C-G	BOO
	(Rosalinda)			
Verdi	Merce, dilette amiche	MH	A-CS	GSC
	(I Vespri Siciliani)			

Miscellaneous Songs Employing Spirited Singing

Coloratura Soprano

Alabieff	The nightingale	H	EF-C	†
	Flute			
Dvořák	The lark			
-----	Tune thy fiddle gypsy			SIM
Falla	El paño moruno	HL		AMP
-----	Seguidilla murciana	HL		AMP
Glazounoff	La primavera d'or	H	D-BF	GSC
Granados	El majo discreto	H		INT
Grieg	My Johann	H		†

Rachmaninoff	Sorrow in spring	H	D-BF	DIT
Thrane	Norwegian echo song	H	D-B	GSC
Turina	Cantares			UME
Turina	Madrigal	H	D-BF	UME

Songs and Arias Employing Staccato

Coloratura Soprano

Arne, M.	The lass with the delicate air	MH	D-B	
Arne, T.	Where the bee sucks	HM		†
Delibes	Bell song (Lakmé)	MH	E-DS	†
-----	Les filles de Cadix	HM	A-A	†
-----	Passepied	LH	DS-CS	GSC
Dupont	Chanson des noisettes			HEU
Gaynor	Pierrot	H	E-B	BOS
Grieg	Solvejg's song	MH	E-A	†
Handel	Oh, had I Jubal's lyre (Joshua)	H	E-FS	†
Haydn	My mother bids me bind my hair	M	E-E	†
La Forge	Come unto these yellow sands	H	FS-B	GSC
Liadoff	The musical snuff box	H	CS-D	GSC
Mozart	Der Hoelle Rache (Die Zauberfloete)	H	F-F	†
Offenbach	Les oiseaux dans la charmille (Tales of Hoffman)	H	EF-EF	†
Saminsky	Queen Estherka's laugh	H	D-A	CFI
Scarlatti, A.	Rugiadose odorose (Il Pirro e Demetrio)	HL	D-E	DIT
Schubert	Der Juengling an der Quelle	LH	E-A	†
Sibella	La Girometta	HML	D-E	GSC
-----	O bimba bimbetta	LMH	D-G	GSC
Strauss	Zerbinetta's aria (Ariadne auf Naxos)			BOO
Thomas	Je suis Titania (Mignon)	H	C-EF	†
Verdi	Tacea la notte placida (Il Trovatore)	H	D-DF	†
Watts	The little shepherd's song	H	G-BF	RIC
Weckerlin	Maman, dites-moi	M	E-FS	BOS

American and British Songs
of Popular Appeal

Coloratura Soprano

Arne, M.	The lass with the delicate air	MH	D-G	†
Benedict	The carnival of Venice	H	D-EF	GSC
-----	The gypsy and the bird Flute	H	D-E	GSC
-----	The wren Flute	H	F-C	PRE
Besley	The second minuet	HL		BOO
Bishop	Echo song Flute	H	D-C	GSC
-----	Lo! here the gentle lark Flute	H		†
- ----	Love has eyes	M		†
-----	Pretty mocking bird Flute	H		†
Buzzi-Peccia	Little birdies			
-----	Under the greenwood tree	LMH	EF-A	DIT
Cadman	Joy	MH	E-A	GSC
Carey	A pastoral			GSC
Charles	And so, goodbye	LH	EF-AF	GSC
-----	Let my song fill your heart	LH	EF-AF	GSC
Clarke	Shy one	HL	BF-G	BOH
Curran	Dawn	LMH	E-BF	GSC
-----	Ho! Mr. Piper	LH	D-G	GSC
D'Hardelot	Because	MH	E-G	CHA
Dostal	I am in love			
Friml	L'amour, toujours, l'amour			HAR
Gaynor	May magic			
German	Who'll buy my lavender	HML		BOO
Giannini	Sing to my heart a song	H	D-B	ELV
Grothe	I am dreaming about one only			
Kaufman	In your eyes I find all my fortune			
Lehmann	The cuckoo	HH	D-B	BOH
Manning	Shoes	M	EF-F	GSC
Melichar	I was never in love as much as today			WEI
-----	This is the finest day in my life			
Mopper	The lemon-colored dodo	H	F-BF	BOS
Poldini	Dance of the dolls			CHM
Rasbach	Promise	LH	AF-BF	GSC

69

Robyn	A heart that's free	MH	EF-AF	FEI
Ronald	Down in the forest	HML	C-D	ENO
-----	O lovely night	HML		BOO
Rybner	Pierrot	HL		GSC
Saar	The little gray dove	MH	D-BF	GSC
Scott	Blackbird's song			ELK
Silesu	Love, here is my heart	M		FEI
Spross	Will o' the wisp			JCH
Ware	By the fountain			FLA
-----	This day is mine	MH	EF-AF	BOS
Warren	Fulfilment	H	D-BF	GAL
-----	If you feel like singing			WAR
-----	My lady Lo-Fu			DIT
Wolf	Jack in the box			
Woodman	A birthday	LH	F-BF	GSC
-----	Love's in my heart	LH	F-BF	GSC

(See also Humorous Songs, Negro Spirituals,
Folk Songs, Operetta Songs and Opera Arias.)

Miscellaneous Songs of
Popular Appeal

Coloratura Soprano

Acqua	Chanson provencale	H	D-BF	GSC
-----	Villanelle	H	EF-D	GSC
Adam	Variations on a nursery theme			GSC
Alabieff	The nightingale Flute	H	EF-C	†
Alvarez	La partida	HL	DS-E	GSC
Arditi	Il bacio	H	CS-B	†
-----	Parla	H	CS-CS	GSC
Bach-Gounod	Ave Maria			†
Bizet	Agnus Dei	HLM	C-AF	†
-----	Ouvre ton coeur	MH	DS-GS	†
Braga	Angel's serenade Violin	LH	D-G	†
Buzzi-Peccia	El morenito	LMH	F-G	GSC
Cavalli	Donzelle fuggite	HL	C-EF	†
D'Albert	Zur Drossel sprach der Fink			
Dalcroze	Le coeur de ma mie	HML		†
Délibes	Chant de l' almée	H	D-E	GSC
-----	Coppelia waltz	H	BF-BF	GSC
-----	Les filles de Cadix	HM	A-A	†
-----	Passepied	LH	DS-CS	GSC

Denza	Funiculi, funicula			†
Eckert	Swiss echo song	H	A-B	GSC
Freire	Ay, ay, ay	LH		RIC
Glazounoff	La primavera d'or	H	D-BF	GSC
Gounod	Au printemps	LMH	DF-AF	GSC
-----	Sérénade	LMH	D-A	GSC
Grieg	Solvejg's song	MH	E-A	†
Hue	A des oiseaux	H	E-G	†
Lara	Granada			SOU
Lecuona	Andalucia			MAR
Liadoff	The musical snuff box	H	CS-D	GSC
Lilljebjorn	When I was seventeen			RIC
Mendelssohn	On wings of song			†
Moret	Le nélumbo	H	E-DF	HEU
Mozart	Alleluja	LMH	F-C	†
Pestalozza	Ciribiribin			DIT
Proch	Theme and variations Flute	H	C-DF	†
Rabey	Tes yeux Violin and piano	H	EF-G	DUR
Rimsky-Korsakov	The nightingale and the rose	H	FS-FS	DIT
Rossini	La danza	MH	E-A	†
-----	La pastorella delle Alpi	H	E-C	CFI
Saint-Saëns	La libellule	H	C-D	DUR
Schubert	Ave Maria	LMH	F-F	†
-----	Hark! hark! the lark	LMH	F-G	†
Sibella	La Girometta	HML	D-E	GSC
Sieczynski	Vienna, city of my dreams			HAR
Strauss, J.	Blue Danube waltz			GSC
-----	Kaiser waltz			
-----	Tales from the Vienna forest	H	EF-C	GSC
-----	Voci di Primavera	LMH	EF-C	GSC
-----	Wein, Weib und Gesang			
-----	Wiener Blut			
Thrane	Norwegian echo song	H	D-B	GSC
Tosti	'A vucchella	LH	F-G	RIC
Veracini	Pastorale (Rosalinda)	MH	C-G	BOO
Weber	Invitation to the dance	H	EF-EF	GSC
Yradier	La paloma	HL	BF-EF	GSC

(See also Humorous Songs, Negro Spirituals,
Folk Songs, Operetta Songs and Opera Arias.)

Arias From French Operas

Coloratura Soprano

Adam	Ah vous dirais-je maman (Le Toreador) Flute			GSC
Auber	L'eclat de rire (Manon Lescaut)			DUR
-----	Quel bonheur (Fra Diavolo)			BOO
Bizet	Comme autrefois dans la nuit sombre (Les Pêcheurs des Perles)			CHO
-----	O dieu Brahma (Les Pêcheurs des Perles)	H	B-D	GSC
Campra	Charmant papillon (Les Fêtes Vénitiennes)	MH	D-G	GSC
David	Charmant oiseau (La Perle du Brésil)	M	D-E	†
Delibes	Bell song (Lakmé)	MH	E-DS	†
-----	Pourquoi dans les grands bois (Lakmé)	H	FS-AF	BRO
-----	Sous le ciel tout étoile (Lakmé)			HEU
-----	Tu m'as donné le plus doux rêve (Lakmé)			BRO
Gounod	Je veux vivre (Roméo et Juliette)	H	F-C	†
-----	Le jour se lève (Mireille)			CHO
-----	Mon coeur ne peut changer! (Mireille)			GSC
-----	O légère hirondelle (Mireille)	H	FS-D	CFI
Grétry	Je crains de lui (Richard Coeur-de-Lion)			LEM
-----	Je ne fais semblant de rein (L'Ami de la Maison)			LEM
-----	Je ne le dis qu'à vous (La Fausse Magie)			LEM
-----	La fauvette avec ses petits (Zémire et Azor) Flute			LEM
-----	Plus de dépit (Les Deux Avares)			LEM
-----	Rose chérie (Zémire et Azor)			LEM
Lecocq	Le punch scintille (Girofle)			

Massé	Air du rossignol (Les Noces de Jeannette) Flute			
-----	Cours mon aiguille dans le laine (Les Noces de Jeanette)			
-----	Sa couleur est blonde et vermeille (Galathée)			JCH
Massenet	Gavotte (Manon)			†
-----	Je suis encore tout etourdie (Manon)			HEU
-----	Sévillana (Don Cesar da Bazan)			HEU
Meyerbeer	La, la, la air cheri (L'Etoile du Nord) Two flutes			BRA
-----	Nobles Seigneurs, salut! (Les Huguenots)	LH	C-C	†
-----	Roberto, o tu che adoro (Robert le Diable)	H	C-C	DEI
-----	Shadow song (Dinorah)	H	DF-D	†
Offenbach	Les oiseaux dans la charmille (Tales of Hoffman)	H	EF-EF	†
Ravel	Air du feu (L'Enfant et les Sortilèges)			DUR
Thomas	Je connais un pauvre enfant (Mignon)	H	C-B	†
-----	Je suis Titania (Mignon)	H	C-EF	†

Arias from German Operas

Coloratura Soprano

Beethoven	O waer' ich schon mit dir vereint (Fidelio)			†
Mozart	Ach, ich fuehl's (Die Zauberfloete)	H	CS-BF	†
-----	Ach, ich liebte (Abduction from Seraglio)			†
-----	Der Hoelle Rache (Die Zauberfloete)	H	F-F	†
-----	Durch Zaertlichkeit (Abduction from Seraglio)			†
-----	Martern aller Arten (Abduction from Seraglio)	H	B-D	†

(Mozart)	Welche Wonne, welche Lust (Abduction from Seraglio)			†
Strauss, R.	Zerbinetta's aria (Ariadne auf Naxos)			BOO
Weber	Truebe Augen (Der Freischuetz)			GSC

Arias From Italian Operas

Coloratura Soprano

Bellini	Ah! non credea mirarti (La Sonnambula)			GSC
-----	Qui la voce (I Puritani)	H	EF-DF	GSC
-----	Son vergin vezzosa (I Puritani)	H	E-B	GSC
Donizetti	Chacun le sait (La Fille du Régiment)	H	C-A	RIC
-----	Il faut partir (La Fille du Régiment)	H	E-C	GSC
-----	Mad scene (Lucia di Lammermoor) Flute	H	FS-C	†
-----	O luce di quest' anima (Linda di Chamounix)	H	C-E	GSC
-----	Prendi, prendi per mei sei libero (L' Elisir d'Amore)			BRO
-----	Quel guardo (Don Pasquale)			BRO
-----	Regnava nel silenzio (Lucia di Lammermoor)	H	CS-D	GSC
-----	Salut à la France (La Fille du Régiment)			NOV
Flotow	Qui sola, vergin rosa (Martha)			BRO
Gagliano	Dormi amore (La Flora)	HL	CS-E	DIT
Giordano	Brilla sulla mia fronte (Il Re)			SON
Mascagni	Flammen perdonami (Lodoletta)			SON
Mozart	Batti, batti, o bel Masetto (Don Giovanni)	H	C-BF	†
-----	Deh vieni non tardar (Le Nozze di Figaro)	H	A-A	†

74

(Mozart)	L'amero, saro costante (Il Re Pastore) Violin or flute	H	D-B	GSC
-----	Non so più cosa son (Le Nozze di Figaro)	H	EF-G	†
-----	Un moto di gioja (Le Nozze di Figaro)			
Pergolesi	A lui donnai (Il Flaminio)			
-----	Stizzoso, mio stizzoso (La Serva Padrona)	H	C-AF	†
Ponchielli	La madre mia (Lina)			
Puccini	Musetta's waltz (La Boheme)	H	EF-BF	RIC
Rossini	Sombre forêt (Guillaume Tell)			
-----	Una voce poco fa (Il Barbiere di Siviglia)	HM	GS-E	GSC
Verdi	Addio del passato (La Traviata)			†
-----	Ah fors'è lui (La Traviata)	H	C-DF	†
-----	Caro nome (Rigoletto)	H	DS-DS	†
-----	Merce, dilette amiche (I Vespri Siciliani)	MH	A-CS	GSC
-----	Saper vorreste (Un Ballo in Maschera)	H	D-B	GSC
-----	Sul fil d'un soffio etesio (Falstaff)	H	DS-A	RIC
-----	Tacea la notte placida (Il Trovatore)	H	D-DF	†
-----	Volta la terrea (Un Ballo in Maschera)	H	D-BF	GSC
Zandonai	Paolo datemi pace (Francesca da Rimini)			RIC

Miscellaneous Opera Arias

Coloratura Soprano

Gershwin	Summertime (Porgy and Bess)	
Granados	Descúbrase el pensamiento (Goyescas)	GSC
Menotti	Lucy's arietta (The Telephone)	

Rimsky-Korsakov	Hymn to the sun (Le Coq d'Or)	H	FS-B	GSC
-----	Martha's air (The Tsar's Bride)			
-----	Song of India (Sadko)	LH	D-G	GSC

Arias From Oratorios and Latin Works

Coloratura Soprano

Beethoven	O praise him (Mount of Olives)			
Gaul	These are they (The Holy City)	H	E-GS	GSC
Handel	Hallelujah (Esther)	H	E-B	CFI
-----	How beautiful are the feet of them (The Messiah)	H		†
-----	I know that my Redeemer liveth (The Messiah)	MH	E-GS	†
-----	Let the bright seraphim (Samson) Trumpet	H	E-A	†
-----	Oh, had I Jubal's lyre (Joshua)	H	E-FS	†
-----	O sleep, why dost thou leave me? (Semele)	H	DS-GS	†
-----	Rejoice greatly (The Messiah)	H	E-A	†
-----	Sweet bird (L'Allegro) Flute			NOV
-----	What's sweeter than a new blown rose? (Joseph)	H	EF-AF	†
Haydn	O how pleasing to the senses (The Seasons)	H		†
-----	On mighty pens uplifted soars (The Creation)	H	E-A	†
-----	With verdure clad (The Creation)	H	E-BF	GSC
Mozart	Et incarnatus est (C Minor Mass)			PET
Rossini	Inflammatus (Stabat Mater)			GSC

Cantata Arias

Coloratura Soprano

Bach, J. S.	Hoert doch! der sanften Floeten (Cantata 206) 3 Flutes and continuo			
-----	Patron, das macht der Wind (Phoebus and Pan)	M	C-G	GSC
-----	Sheep may safely graze (Cantata 208) 2 Flutes and continuo	LM	EF-GF	GAL

Operetta, Musical Comedy or Show Songs

Coloratura Soprano

Brown	Love is where you find it (The Kissing Bandit)			
Coward	I'll follow my secret heart (Conversation Piece)	M	A-FS	CHA
-----	I'll see you again (Bitter Sweet)	M	C-F	HAR
Friml	Donkey Serenade (The Firefly)			WIT
Herbert	Kiss me again (Mlle. Modiste)	LHM	CS-A	WIT
-----	Romany life (The Fortune Teller)			WIT
Herold	Air de Nicette (Le Pré aux Clercs)			BRA
Kern	All the things you are (Very Warm for May)	M	BF-F	HAR
-----	I dream too much (I Dream Too Much)			CHA
-----	I'm the echo (I Dream too Much)			CHA
Milloecker	Komm, mia bella (Gasparone)	M		SC
Romberg	One kiss (New Moon)			HAR
-----	Romance (The Desert Song)	H	D-BF	HAR
Strauss, J.	Adele's laughing song (Die Fledermaus)	H	D-B	GSC

77

(Strauss, J.)	Czardas (Die Fledermaus)			BOO
-----	One thousand and one nights (Indigo)			
-----	Southern roses (Spitzentuch der Koenigin)			

Song Cycles (Or groups of songs)

Coloratura Soprano

Alberti	Four sketches from the Far East	HM	C-F	GSC
Berger	Villanescas	H	CS-B	GSC
Debussy	Fêtes galantes	LH	CS-A	†
-----	Proses lyriques	HL		JOB
Schumann	Lieder der Braut	H	D-A	†
Stravinsky	Three bird songs			
-----	Three Japanese lyrics for Voice, piano, string quartes, 2 flutes, and 2 clarinets			RUM

Solo Cantatas

Coloratura Soprano

Bach, J. S.	Jauchzet Gott in allen Landen (Cantata 51)	BRO
Scarlatti, A.	Solitude ameni apriche Collinette	

(See Solo Cantatas of Pergolesi, Handel and Scarlatti,
Kirchenkantaten of Buxtehude and Symphoniae Sacrae
of Schuetz.)

Concert Arias

Coloratura Soprano

Mozart	A questo seno, deh vieni	BOO
-----	Bella mia fiamma, addio	BOO
-----	Ma che vi fece, o stelle	PET
-----	Mia speranza adorata	
-----	Misera, dove son	BOO
-----	Non temer amato bene	BOO

Christmas Songs

Coloratura Soprano

Benjamin	Before dawn			CUR
Black	In the sky a wondrous star	H	DF-AF	GRA
Dickinson	The shepherds' story	H		GRA
Dougherty	The first Christmas	H	D-A	GSC
Forsyth	The Child Jesus Organ	H	EF-B	GRA
Hageman	Christmas eve	HML	BF-EF	GAL
Handel	How beautiful are the feet of them (The Messiah)	H		†
-----	Rejoice greatly (The Messiah)	H	E-A	†
Harris	The holy infant	H	G-AF	GAL
Head	The little road to Bethlehem	MH	EF-AF	BOO
Kaull	Unto you is born a Savior	MH	D-AF	BOS
Martin	The Holy Child	HML	G-G	ENO
McKinney	The Holy Mother sings	MH	AF-AF	JFI
Ohlson	The vigils of Mary	H		GSC
Pinkham	A partridge in a pear tree	H	D-BF	ROW
Reger	The Virgin's slumber song	MMH	G-G	†
Sadero	Fa la nana, bambin			RIC
Schubert	Ave Maria	LMH	F-F	†
Trunk	Mary	HM		AMP
Warren	Christmas candle	HML	D-E	GSC
Wolf	Schlafendes Jesuskind	HL	AS-F	

Easter Songs

Coloratura Soprano

Barnes	Easter	HM	D-EF	GSC
Curran	Crucifixion			
Dennee	Easter song	HM	B-F	ASC
Granier	Hosanna	HH	F-BF	DIT
Hageman	Christ went up into the hills	LH	EF-AF	CFI
Handel	I know that my Redeemer liveth (The Messiah)	MH	E-GS	†
Huhn	Christ is risen	HM	C-E	ASC

Lekberg	A ballad of trees and the Master	H	E-A	GAL
Ohlson	The vigils of Mary	H		GSC
Rossini	Inflammatus (Stabat Mater)			GSC
Schubert	Ave Maria	LMH	F-F	†
Scott	Angels roll the rock away	MH	E-G	HUN
Ward Stephens	Christ triumphant	MH	F-AF	CHA

Patriotic Songs

Coloratura Soprano

Alberti	A nation's prayer	H		ELV
Cadman	Glory	H	EF-G	GAL
Dungan	Eternal life	HL		PRE
Howe	To the unknown soldier	H	D-G	GSC
Ward Stephens	Phantom legions	MHH	EF-BF	CHA

Sacred Songs

Coloratura Soprano

Bach, J. S.	Sheep may safely graze (Cantata 208) 2 Flutes and continuo	LM	EF-GF	GAL
Brown	The twenty-third Psalm	LH	E-G	GRA
Campbell-Tipton	I will give thanks unto the Lord	LMH	DF-AF	GSC
Candlyn	Light at evening time	H	FS-GS	GRA
Charles	Love is of God	H	D-G	GSC
Clokey	God is in everything	LH	D-G	JFI
Gaul	These are they (The Holy City)	H	E-GS	GSC
Handel	How beautiful are the feet of them (The Messiah)	H		†
-----	I know that my Redeemer liveth (The Messiah)	MH	E-GS	†
-----	Let the bright seraphim (Samson) Trumpet	H	E-A	†
-----	Praise the Lord (Esther)	H	E-G	

Haydn	With verdure clad (The Creation)	H	E-BF	†
Mendelssohn	O for the wings of a dove	MLH	D-G	†
Scott	Come ye blessed	LMH	EF-AF	GSC
Timmings	In the evening it will be light Chimes	H		GRA

Wedding Songs

Coloratura Soprano

Beethoven	Ich liebe dich	HL	BF-DF	†
Clough-Leighter	Possession	MH	DF-AF	GSC
De Koven	Oh promise me (Robin Hood)	HML	C-D	†
D'Hardelot	Because	MH	E-G	CHA
Diggle	A wedding prayer	HM	EF-F	GSC
Geehl	For you alone			SHU
Grieg	I love thee	HML	E-F	†
Ronald	Love I have won you	HML	EF-EF	ENO
Schubert	Du bist die Ruh	LMH	EF-AF	†
Sowerby	O perfect love	MH	EF-AF	GRA
Willan	O perfect love	HM	E-FS	GRA

Songs and Arias with Added Accompanying Instrument

Coloratura Soprano

Adam	Ah vous dirais-je maman (Le Toreador) Flute			GSC
Alabieff	The nightingale Flute	H	EF-C	†
Bach, J. S.	Hoert doch! der sanften Floeten (Cantata 206) 3 Flutes and continuo			
Benedict	The gypsy and the bird Flute	H	D-E	GSC
Bishop	Echo song Flute	H	D-C	GSC
-----	Lo! here the gentle lark Flute	H		†
-----	Pretty mocking bird Flute	H		†

81

Braga	Angel's serenade	LH	D-B	†
	Violin			
Gretry	La fauvette avec ses			LEM
	petits (Zemire et Azor)			
	Flute			
Handel	Let the bright seraphim	H	E-A	†
	(Samson) Trumpet			
-----	Sweet bird			NOV
	(L'Allegro) Flute			
Massé	Air du rossignol			
	(Les Noces de Jeannette)			
	Flute			
Meyerbeer	La, la, la air cheri			BRA
	(L'Etoile du Nord)			
	Two flutes			
Mozart	L'amero, saro costante	H	D-B	GSC
	(Il Re Pastore)			
	Violin or flute			
Proch	Theme and variations	H	C-DF	†
	Flute			
Rabey	Tes yeux	H	EF-G	DUR
	Violin and piano			
Saint-Saëns	Le bonheur est une chose	H	C-A	CHO
	légère			
	Violin and piano			
Schubert	Der Hirt auf dem Felsen	H	BF-B	†
	Clarinet or violoncello			
Timmings	In the evening it will be	H		GRA
	light			
	Chimes			

American Recital Songs

Lyric Soprano

Alberti	Oriental serenade	H	CS-A	CFI
-----	The gypsy			
-----	Trees	H	C-A	CFI
-----	White swan of Samarkand			
Bacon	As if the sea should part			
-----	Is there such a thing as	M	DS-FS	AMP
	day?			
-----	The Colorado tree			
-----	The dove			
-----	The little stone			
-----	The red rose	M		BOO
-----	Where the bee sucks			
Barber	A nun takes the veil	MH	G-G	GSC

(Barber)	I hear an army	LH	D-AF	GSC
-----	Knoxville, summer of 1915	H		GSC
-----	Monks and raisons	M	DF-E	GSC
-----	Nocturne	HM	CS-FS	GSC
-----	Nuovoletta	H	BS-BS	GSC
-----	Rain has fallen	HM	D-E	GSC
-----	Sleep now	MH	EF-AF	GSC
-----	Sure on this shining night	MH	D-G	GSC
-----	The daisies	M	C-F	GSC
Barnett	Nightingale lane	H	BS-GS	GSC
Bauer	Orientale			
Beach	Ah, love but a day			ASC
-----	Fairy lullaby			ASC
-----	I send my heart up to thee	MH		ASC
-----	June	MH		ASC
-----	The year's at the spring	MH	AF-AF	ASC
Bernstein	I just found out today			
-----	Rabbit at top speed			GSC
Bloch	Psalm 114 (Snatched away by Jahveh)	H	A-A	GSC
-----	Psalm 137 (By the waters of Babel)	H	F-AS	GSC
-----	The shelter	MH	CS-GS	GSC
-----	The vagabond	M	E-E	GSC
Bone and Fenton	Deborah	LM	CS-FS	CFI
-----	Tryst	MH	FS-G	CFI
-----	Wind in the tree tops			
Bowles	Cabin	ML	CS-CS	GSC
-----	Heavenly grass	ML	B-E	GSC
-----	In the woods			AMP
-----	Letter to Freddy	M	EF-EF	GSC
-----	On a quiet conscience	M	C-F	MUP
-----	Once a lady was here	ML	C-EF	GSC
Boyd	Adoration	H	C-A	GAL
Braine	Dawn awakes	HML	A-D	ASC
Branscombe	At the postern gate	MH	DF-AF	ASC
-----	I send my heart up to thee			
Browning	The night is but a mirror			
Burleigh	By the pool at the third roses	H		RIC
-----	The sailor's wife	HM		RIC
Buzzi-Peccia	Under the greenwood tree	LMH	EF-A	DIT
Cadman	I hear a thrush at eve			MOR
-----	Joy	MH	E-A	GSC

Campbell- Tipton	A spirit flower	LHM	B-G	GSC
Carpenter	I am like a remnant of a cloud of autumn	L	BF-F	GSC
-----	If	M	D-E	GSC
-----	Light, my light	M	C-G	GSC
-----	Serenade	LH	CS-A	GSC
-----	Silhouettes	M	C-G	GSC
-----	The sleep that flits on baby's eyes	M	B-FS	GSC
-----	When I bring to you colour'd toys	LM	CS-FS	GSC
Castelnuovo- Tedesco	Heavily arise			
-----	O mistress mine			CHE
-----	Roundel	H		CHE
-----	The horn			CHE
Chadwick	Allah	LH	CS-GS	ASC
Chanler	Grandma			GSC
-----	Sleep			GSC
-----	The lamb	M	C-D	AMP
-----	Wind			GSC
Charles	And so, goodbye	LH	EF-AF	GSC
-----	Dawn	M	BF-F	BOS
-----	Let my song fill your heart	LH	EF-AF	GSC
-----	Night	MH	F-AF	GSC
-----	Remembrance			
-----	Sweet song of long ago	HML	A-D	GSC
-----	When I have sung my songs	HM	BF-EF	GSC
Chasins	Dreams			JFI
Clough- Leighter	My lover he comes on the skee	HM	D-F	BOS
Cottenet	Red, red rose	H	D-BF	CFI
Cowell	St. Agnes morning	M	C-G	MER
Cowles	Desire	H	F-A	GSC
-----	The fragrance of a song	HM	E-F	GSC
-----	The grasshopper			
Creston	Bird of the wilderness	MH	FS-A	GSC
Crist	By a silent seashore	H	CS-GS	GSC
-----	C'est mon ami	LH	CS-G	CFI
-----	Evening	H	C-G	GSC
-----	Into a ship dreaming	LMH	EF-GS	CFI
-----	Knock on the door	H	EF-AF	GSC
-----	Love's offering			
-----	O come hither	HM	B-GS	CFI
-----	The dark King's daughter			JCH

Curran	The two magicians	LH	DS-FS	GSC
Davis	Nancy Hanks	H	D-G	GAL
Deis	Come down to Kew			
Dello Joio	Mill doors	M	D-E	CFI
Diamond	David weeps for Absolom	M	D-A	MUP
-----	Even though the world keeps changing	H	CS-A	CFI
-----	To Lucasta, on going to the wars			
Dittenhaver	Hurdy-gurdy playing in the street	H	DF-AF	GAL
-----	Lady of the amber wheat	H		GAL
-----	Passage	M	C-F	GAL
Dougherty	Beauty is not caused	M		AMP
-----	If love were what the rose is			
-----	Love in the dictionary	M	C-G	GSC
-----	Loveliest of trees	HM	C-E	BOH
-----	Madonna of the evening flowers	M		BOO
-----	Music			
-----	Pianissimo	M	C-G	GSC
-----	Pied beauty			
-----	Portrait	HM	BF-G	GSC
-----	Primavera	H	C-BF	GSC
-----	Song for autumn			
-----	The K'e	M	D-F	GSC
-----	The song of the Jasmin			
-----	Weathers			
Duke	A piper	H	CS-B	GSC
-----	Bells in the rain	H	E-GS	CFI
-----	Capri			
-----	Central Park at dusk	M		BOO
-----	Evening			
-----	Hesperus	H	CS-GS	GSC
-----	I can't be talkin' of love	H	CS-G	GSC
-----	Just spring			
-----	Little elegy	H	FS-A	GSC
-----	My soul is an enchanted boat			
-----	Spray	H	CS-A	BOH
-----	The bird			GSC
-----	The puritan's ballad			
-----	To Karen, singing	M	CS-G	ELV
-----	XXth century	M		VLP
-----	Velvet shoes	H	D-A	ROW
-----	Viennese waltz	H	C-GF	ROW
-----	Voices	H	FS-A	BOH
Dukelsky	Adolescence	MH		CFI

85

Edmunds	Billy boy	ML	BF-EF	ROW
-----	Fare you well	MH	F-AF	ROW
Edwards	Little shepherd's song			MLS
-----	The fisher's widow	ML	G-EF	GSC
Elwell	In the mountains	M	DF-F	BMI
-----	The road not taken	M	B-FS	GSC
-----	The sound of the trees	M		AMP
Engel	Sea shell	M	EF-EF	GSC
Fairchild	A memory			BOS
Fisher	Sigh no more ladies			
Flood	The hermit thrush			
-----	The windows of Sainte Chapelle	H		RIC
-----	White bud			
Gaines	My heart hath a mind			
Ganz	A memory	HM	B-D	GSC
-----	The angels are stooping	MH	GF-A	GSC
Gaynor	May magic			
Giannini	Be still my heart			ELV
-----	Far above the purple hills	LH	CS-A	RIC
-----	Heart cry	H		RIC
-----	Tell me, o blue, blue sky	H		RIC
Gilberte	Two roses	LMH	CS-G	CFI
Golde	Love was with me yesterday	LMH	E-A	CFI
-----	Who knows?	HM	BF-F	GSC
Grant	Looking across	H	D-G	AMP
Grant-Schaeffer	The cuckoo clock	H	EF-BF	SUM
Griffes	By a lonely forest pathway	HML	A-EF	GSC
-----	Elves	H	F-AF	GSC
-----	Evening song	H	DS-GS	GSC
-----	In a myrtle shade	H	FS-A	GSC
-----	Symphony in yellow	M	D-GF	GSC
-----	The dreamy lake	H	BS-GS	GSC
-----	The lament of Ian the proud	MH	DS-AS	GSC
-----	The rose of the night	H	CS-A	GSC
-----	Thy dark eyes to mine	H	EF-AF	GSC
-----	Time was, when I in anguish lay	H	E-GS	GSC
-----	Waikiki	H	DS-GS	GSC
Hadley	Evening song	HM	BF-EF	GSC
-----	My shadow			ASC
Hageman	At the well	LH	EF-AF	GSC
-----	Do no go, my love	HL	B-EF	GSC
-----	Is it you?			
-----	Miranda	HL		GAL

(Hageman)	Music I heard with you	MH	E-A	GAL
-----	The donkey			BOO
-----	The night has a thousand eyes	M	C-FS	BOO
Harrington	Alas, that spring should vanish	LH	DF-AF	CFI
Harris	Someone came knocking at my door	M		GAL
Haubiel	I love you	M	B-FS	GSC
-----	To you			CMP
Hindemith	Echo	H	D-FS	AMP
-----	On hearing the last rose of summer	M	D-FS	AMP
-----	The whistling thief	M	E-F	AMP
-----	The wildflower's song	MH	E-G	AMP
Homer	House that Jack built			JCH
Hopkinson	Beneath a weeping willow's shade	H	D-G	†
-----	My days have been so wondrous free	LH	EF-G	
-----	My love is gone to sea	HL	D-E	†
-----	O'er the hills	LH	C-G	†
Horsman	In the yellow dusk	MH	FS-A	GSC
-----	The bird of the wilderness	LMH	DF-BF	GSC
-----	The dream	H	F-G	GSC
-----	Thus wisdom sings	H	EF-A	GSC
Howe	When I died in Berners Street	H	C-G	GSC
Huerter	Pirate dreams	HML		DIT
Ives	Ann Street			
-----	At sea			
-----	Mists			
-----	Two little flowers			
Josten	Cupid's counsel	H	EF-AF	GSC
Kagen	A June day	H	FS-BF	WTR
-----	All day I hear	H	F-FS	WTR
-----	I'm nobody	H	D-G	WTR
-----	Let it be forgotten	M	F-F	WTR
-----	Maybe	H	D-G	WTR
-----	War is kind			
Kernochan	We two together	H	EF-AF	GAL
Kingsford	Wallpaper for a little girl's room	M	BF-F	GSC
Klein	Illusion	M		AMP
-----	Night mist	M		AMP
Klemm	Sounds			DIT
Kramer	Clouds	H		JFI
-----	Pleading	LH	D-GF	JFI
-----	Swans	HL		RIC

(Kramer)	The crystal gazer			DIT
La Forge	Chant de joie libre			
-----	Come unto these yellow sands	H	FS-B	GSC
-----	Cupid captive	H		GAL
-----	Gypsy melodies			
-----	Hills	HL		RIC
-----	Pastorale			
Levitzki	Ah, thou beloved one	H	EF-AF	GSC
Lubin	The piper	H	C-A	GSC
MacDowell	A maid sings light	H	F-G	ASC
-----	As the gloaming shadows creep			
-----	Idyl			
-----	Long ago	HL		ASC
-----	The blue bell			GSC
-----	The sea	HL	D-D	BRH
-----	The swan bent low	LH		ELK
Malotte	A day is born			
-----	Hebrew prayer			
Mana-Zucca	Speak to me			
-----	Spring is whispering			CNG
-----	There's joy in my heart			CNG
Manning	In the Luxembourg gardens	HML	BF-D	GSC
-----	The street fair			
-----	White clouds			DIT
McArthur	Night	H	F-AF	GSC
-----	Spring came	HL	D-F	GSC
McDonald	He is gone	H	DF-BF	ELV
Metcalf	At nightfall	HML	C-DF	ASC
Moore	Sigh no more, ladies			BOO
Mopper	Amelia			
-----	Gray velvet			
-----	Men	M	D-FS	BOS
Naginski	Look down, fair moon			
-----	The pasture	M	BF-EF	GSC
-----	Under the harvest moon	M	D-E	GSC
Nordoff	Fair Annette's song			AMP
-----	Madrigals			
-----	Music I heard with you	H	DS-FS	AMP
-----	Praise			
-----	Serenade	H	CS-FS	AMP
-----	Song	H	DF-A	AMP
-----	Tell me, Thyrsis	H	E-G	AMP
-----	There shall be more joy	M	CS-FS	AMP
-----	This is the shape of the leaf	M	B-E	SC
-----	Willow River	H	D-G	AMP

Parker	A gypsy maiden, I			
-----	The lark now leaves her watery nest	LH	D-BF	JCH
Proctor	I heard a bird			
-----	I light the blessed candles	H	DF-A	GSC
Protheroe	Ah, love but a day	LMH	F-AF	GAM
-----	Sing again			
Rasbach	Mountains	LH	DF-AF	GSC
Robinson	The chudder weaver	H	C-G	GSC
Rogers	The last song	MLH	E-AF	GSC
-----	Time for making songs	HM	CS-F	DIT
Rorem	Alleluia			
-----	The silver swan	H	F-C	PEE
Rummel	Ecstasy	LMH	GF-AF	GSC
Russell	Fulfillment	LH	EF-GF	BOS
-----	Harbor night	M	D-F	CFI
Rybner	Pierrot	HL		GSC
Sacco	Let it be forgotten	LH	F-AF	CFI
-----	Little man	LH	D-F	BOS
-----	Mexican serenade	HL	D-EF	BOS
-----	Rapunzel	MH	FS-BF	GSC
-----	The ragpicker	MH	C-AF	GSC
-----	Where the lilac blows	LH	D-G	BOS
Saminsky	Queen Esterka's laugh	H	D-A	CFI
Sargent	Three a. m.	M	DF-E	GSC
-----	Twentieth century	H	EF-GS	LEE
Schneider	Flower rain			SUM
Schuman	Holiday song	M	C-F	GSC
-----	Orpheus with his lute	M	C-FS	GSC
Shepherd	Triptych String quartet	H		GSC
Silberta	Lullaby for Judith			
-----	You shall have your red rose			
-----	Wild geese			
Spencer	For whom the bell tolls	MH	F-AF	BOS
Spross	Ishtar			
-----	Will o' the wisp			JCH
Still	The breath of a rose			
Swanson	Joy	M	BF-EF	LEE
-----	Night song			
-----	The negro speaks of rivers	M		LEE
-----	The valley	L	BF-DF	LEE
Taylor	A song for lovers	MH	D-F	JFI
-----	The rivals	H	E-G	JFI
Thompson	Velvet shoes	M	C-E	ECS
Thomson	Dirge	M	D-F	GSC
-----	Preciosilla	H	EF-A	GSC
-----	The tiger			

Tyson	Like barley bending	HL	C-EF	GSC
Vene	Age and youth	H	E-A	RIC
Wagenaar	From a very little sphinx			
Walther	Sometimes	MH	EF-AF	GSC
Ware	This day is mine	MH	EF-AF	BOS
Warner	Hurdy gurdy	M	D-F	CFI
Warren	Down in the glen	H	F-A	GSC
-----	Heather	LH	FS-G	GSC
-----	I saw a little tailor			
-----	Silent noon	HL		DIT
-----	Snow towards evening	LH	EF-AF	GSC
-----	Wander shoes	LH	F-G	FLA
-----	We two	LH	E-A	GSC
-----	White horses of the sea	LH	F-G	GSC
Watts	Hushing song			
-----	Joy	HL	D-F	GSC
-----	Like music on the waters	H		GSC
-----	Pierrot	HM		DIT
-----	Stresa	H	EF-BF	DIT
-----	The little shepherd's song	H	G-BF	RIC
-----	The poet sings	MH	EF-AF	DIT
-----	Transformation	ML	AS-DS	GSC
-----	Wings of night	LH	CS-G	GSC
-----	With the tide	H	DF-A	GSC
Weaver	A book of verses	H	D-AF	GAL
Wolf	Weather forecast	H	EF-GS	GSC
Woodman	Love's in my heart	LH	F-BF	GSC
Worth	Madrigale			
-----	Midsummer	LM	E-A	GSC
Young	The tea-kettle song			

British Recital Songs

Lyric Soprano

Aiken	Sonnet XVIII			
Anon	Have you seen but a white lily grow?	H	E-F	GSC
Arne, M.	The lass with the delicate air	MH	D-G	†
Arne, T.	Blow, blow, thou winter wind	M	C-F	†
-----	In infancy			NOV
-----	Oh come my dearest			
-----	Polly Willis	H	D-G	†
-----	Under the greenwood tree			
-----	Water parted from the sea			GSC
-----	When daisies pied			AUG

(Arne, T.)	Where the bee sucks	HM		†
Bainton	The nightingale near the house			CUR
Bantock	A dream of spring	H	E-G	CHE
-----	A feast of lanterns	HM	D-F	GAL
-----	Silent strings	MH	F-G	BOO
-----	The celestial weaver			
Bartlet	Whither runneth my sweetheart			BOO
Bax	Cradle song			CHA
-----	I heard a piper piping	LH	D-G	CFI
-----	O, green grow the rushes	MH	EF-BF	OXF
-----	Shieling song	H	CS-A	CHE
-----	The white peace			CHE
Bayly	I'd be a butterfly			
Benjamin	The piper			BOO
-----	The wasp			CUR
Berners	Lullaby	M	C-G	CHE
-----	The green eyed monster	M	C-G	CHE
Besley	Listening	H	E-AF	CUR
Bishop	Bid me discourse	H	B-A	†
-----	Love has eyes	M		†
-----	Should he upbraid	H		†
Bliss	Simples			
-----	Three jolly gentlemen	H		†
Boyce	Tell me lovely shepherd			AUG
Brewer	The fairy pipers	HML		BOH
Bridge	Adoration	H		ROG
-----	All things that we clasp	HL		BOS
-----	O that it were so	LMH	D-G	CHA
Britten	As it is plenty			
-----	Les illuminations	H		BOH
-----	Let the florid music praise			
-----	Marine			
-----	Nocturne			BOH
-----	Now the leaves are falling fast			
-----	Oh, to vex me			BOO
-----	Royaute			
Brook	At Michael's Gate	H	C-AF	CUR
Brown	Shepherd thy demeanor vary!			BOO
Campion	Author of light			
-----	Beauty if thou so much desire			
-----	Fain would I wed			
-----	When to her lute Corinna sings			STB
Clarke	Shy one	HL	BF-G	BOH
Coates	The green hills o' Somerset			

Coleridge-Taylor	She rested by the broken brook	HL		DIT
-----	Willow song	MH		CRA
Delius	Cradle song			AUG
-----	In a seraglio garden			
-----	Irmelin rose			BOO
-----	Love's philosophy			†
-----	The nightingale has a lyre of gold			†
-----	The princess			
Dowland	Awake, sweet love	M	E-F	STB
-----	Come again, sweet love	M	D-E	STB
-----	Come away			BOO
-----	Flow, my tears	M	D-E	STB
-----	Shall I sue?			STB
Dunhill	To the Queen of Heaven	M	C-G	GSC
Edmunds	I know my love	HL	BF-EF	ROW
-----	The faucon	M	D-F	MER
Fellows	Willow song			
Forsyth	The stranger Organ	H	A-B	GRA
German	Charming Chloe	HML		NOV
Gibbs	Five eyes	HL	D-D	BOS
-----	Silver		CS-FS	ROG
-----	To one who passed whistling through the night	H	F-G	CUR
-----	Why do I love?			BOO
Green	My lips shall speak the praise	M	E-F	OXF
Handel	Loves' a dear deceitful jewel	LH	F-F	RBR
-----	Pack clouds away			PAT
Harty	Lane o' the thrushes			BOO
-----	The fiddler of Dooney			BOO
Head	A blackbird singing	MH		BOO
-----	A piper	HL		BOO
-----	The dreaming lake	HL.		BOO
Henschel	Morning-hymn	MH	DS-GS	†
Holbrooke	The clown's song			
Holst	A little music	H		AUG
Hook	Softly waft, ye southern breezes			GSC
Horn	Cherry ripe	M	D-G	†
-----	I've been roaming	L	B-E	DIT
Ireland	Bed in summer			CUR
Jacob	Laughing song	H	D-G	OXF

Johnson	As I walked forth one summer day			DIT
Lehmann	Alas that spring should vanish			GSC
-----	Magdalen at Michael's gate			CHA
-----	Snake charmer			BOO
Linley	O, bid your faithful Ariel fly			BOO
Mallinson	My heart, the bird of the wilderness	H	DF-AF	CRA
Matthews	Night song at Amalfi	H		RLV
Milford	Love on my heart	H	FS-FS	NOV
Morley	It was a lover and his lass	HM		DIT
-----	Love winged my hopes			
Parry	Armida's garden			NOV
-----	The maiden			NOV
-----	Whether I live			NOV
Peel	Lov'liest of trees			
Purcell	Cease, o my sad soul			POT
-----	Come unto these yellow sands			AUG
-----	Here the deities approve			
-----	If music be the food of love	M	D-G	BOO
-----	Man is for woman made			
-----	Not all my torments			NOV
-----	Since from my dear			
-----	Song of Bonvica			NOV
-----	Strike the viol			BAF
-----	The Blessed Virgin's expostulation	H		SC
-----	The fatal hour comes on			
-----	We sing to him			
Quilter	A land of silence			BOO
-----	Blow, blow, thou winter wind	HL	C-E	BOO
-----	Come away, come away death			BOO
-----	Dream valley	H	EF-GF	ROG
-----	Go, lovely rose	LHM	F-GF	CHA
-----	How should I your true love know?			BOO
-----	It was a lover and his lass	HL	CS-E	BOO
-----	Love's philosophy	LMH	D-A	BOO
-----	Take, o take those lips away			BOO
-----	To daisies			BOO
Ronald	Down in the forest	HML	C-D	ENO
-----	Drift down, drift down			BOO

93

(Ronald)	Love, I have won you	HML	EF-EF	ENO
Rosseter	What then is love but mourning			STB
-----	When Laura smiles	LM	D-E	STB
Scott	Don't come in, sir, please!	HL		GAL
-----	Lullaby	MML	BF-DF	GAL
-----	The unforeseen	HML		GAL
Sharp	My mother did so before me			MEU
Shaw	Song of the Palanquin bearers	LH	E-F	CUR
Stanford	I'll rock you to rest	HML		BOH
-----	Sea wrack	H	EF-A	STB
Stephenson	Love is a sickness	HML	C-D	BOO
-----	Ships that pass in the night	HML	DF-DF	BOO
Taylor	O can ye sew			
-----	The wind mill	M		OXF
Thiman	The silver swan	MH	EF-G	NOV
Vaughan Williams	How can the tree but wither?			OXF
-----	In dreams			
-----	Orpheus with his lute			PRO
-----	Silent noon			GSC
-----	The water mill	L	C-D	OXF
Warlock	Pretty ring time	H	D-G	CFI
-----	Rantum, tantum	H	DF-G	CHE
-----	The distracted maid	H	DF-G	CHE

French Recital Songs

Lyric Soprano

Acqua	Chanson provençale	H	D-BF	GSC
Attaignant	Puisque, voulez-vous que je vous laisse			
Aubert	La lettre			DUR
-----	Vieille chanson espagnole			DUR
Auric	Printemps			DUR
Bachelet	Chère nuit	H	DF-BF	GSC
Bemberg	Chant hindou	HML	A-EF	†
-----	Il neige	H	FS-G	GRU
Berlioz	L'absence	H	CS-FS	GSC
-----	La mort d'Ophélie			CST
-----	Le spectre de la rose			CST
-----	L'isle inconnue			CST

94

(Berlioz)	Villanelle	H	E-FS	†
Bizet	Adieu de l'hôtesse arabe	H	BF-G	†
-----	Agnus Dei	HLM	C-AF	†
-----	Après l'hiver			†
-----	Chanson d'avril	H	BF-G	†
-----	Douce mer			GSC
-----	Ouvre ton coeur	MH	DS-GS	†
-----	Pastorale	H	C-FS	GSC
-----	Vielle chanson	H	EF-A	GSC
Boulanger	Cantique	M	F-F	HAM
Britten	Antique			
Bruneau	Le passepied			
-----	Le sabot de frene			CHO
-----	Les cloches de Nantes			
-----	Les pieds nus			
Busser	Notre Père qui êtes aux cieux			
Campra	Hébé	H		ROU
Chabrier	Les cigales	HML		†
-----	L'Île heureuse	M	B-F	†
-----	Villanelle des petits canards	HML	B-E	†
Chaminade	Berceuse	LH	D-G	†
-----	L'été	MH	E-A	†
-----	The silver ring	HM	BF-F	GSC
-----	Tu me dirais	LH	BF-AF	DIT
Chausson	Chanson perpétuelle (String quartet)	H	CS-GS	ROU
-----	Dans la forêt	HL		INT
-----	La fleur des eaux			
-----	L'amour d'Antan	HL		INT
-----	Le colibri (Violin or cello)	M	F-GF	BOS
-----	Le temps des lilas	MH	D-GS	†
-----	Les papillons	M	C-F	GSC
-----	Nocturne	HL		INT
-----	Sérénade			
Couperin	Brunete			
Dalayrac	D'un époux chéri			DUR
-----	Jeune fillette	HL	GS-E	DIT
Dalcroze	Le coeur de ma mie	HML		†
-----	Le petit oiseau			
-----	L'oiseau bleu			CFI
Debussy	Apparition			DUR
-----	Beau soir	LH	C-FS	†
-----	C'est l'extase	LH	CS-A	†
-----	Chevaux de bois	H	C-G	†
-----	Clair de lune	M	CS-FS	JOB
-----	Colloque sentimental			DUR

(Debussy)	Crois mon conseil, chère Climène			DUR
-----	De fleurs	H	C-AF	†
-----	De grève	HL		†
-----	De soir	HL		†
-----	En sourdine	M	C-FS	†
-----	Fantoches	H	D-A	JOB
-----	Green	H	C-AF	†
-----	Harmonie du soir			DUR
-----	Il pleure dans mon coeur	LH	CS-GS	†
-----	L'echelonnement des haïes			HAM
-----	L'ombre des arbres			†
-----	La demoiselle Élue			DUR
-----	La flûte de Pan		B-B	†
-----	La lettre de Geneviève			DUR
-----	La mer est plus belle	HL		†
-----	La vierge Erigone			DUR
-----	Le balcon			JOB
-----	Le faune			DUR
-----	Le jet d'eau			DUR
-----	Le tombeau des naïades			JOB
-----	Le angélus			HAM
-----	Les cloches	LH	E-GS	†
-----	Les ingénus			DUR
-----	Mandoline	HM	BF-F	†
-----	Noël des enfants qui n'ont plus de maisons			DUR
-----	Nuits d'etoiles	LH	E-A	MAR
-----	Pantomime			DUR
-----	Paysages belges			JOB
-----	Pierrot			DUR
-----	Placet futile			DUR
-----	Recueillement			DUR
-----	Romance	HM	C-E	†
-----	Voici que le printemps	LH	CS-G	BOS
Delibes	Eglogue			
-----	Les filles de Cadix	HM	A-A	†
-----	Myrto	M	A-FS	GSC
-----	Passepied	LH	DS-CS	GSC
-----	Que l'heure est donc brève			
Duparc	Chanson triste	MH	FS-AF	†
-----	Extase	LMH	FS-A	†
-----	L'invitation au voyage	HM	E-F	†
-----	Phidylé	MH	EF-AF	BOS
-----	Soupir	HL	CS-F	BOS
Dupont	Chanson des noisettes			HEU
-----	Mandoline			DUR
-----	Adieu	MH	F-F	†

(Fauré)	Après un rêve	HM	C-F	†
-----	Au bord de l'eau	HL	C-F	†
-----	Aurore	H	D-G	†
-----	Chanson du pêcheur	H	E-A	HAM
-----	Clair de lune	MH	C-G	†
-----	Dans les ruines d'une abbaye	M	E-FS	†
------	Dolly			HAM
-----	En sourdine	HL	C-EF	†
-----	Hymne	MH	D-G	HAM
-----	Ici-bas!	H	FS-G	†
-----	La fée aux chansons	LH	F-F	†
-----	La lune blanche	HL		†
-----	La rose	H	F-A	MAR
-----	Le parfum impérissable	LH	GF-GF	
-----	Le secret	LH	F-G	†
-----	Les roses d'Ispahan	HM	D-FS	†
-----	Lydia	MH	G-G	†
-----	Mandoline	HL	F-E	†
-----	Nell	LH	FS-AF	†
-----	Notre amour	H	DS-B	†
-----	Rencontre	H	EF-AF	†
-----	Spleen	H	E-FS	MAR
-----	Sylvie	HL	E-F	†
-----	Vocalise	H		LED
Ferrari	Je saute, je danse			
-----	La peureuse			
-----	Le miroir	M	E-F	GSC
-----	Le roi a fait battre tambour			
-----	Les belles manieres			
Février	Le printemps			HEU
Fontenailles	Obstination	MH	EF-GF	DUR
Fourdrain	Carnaval	M	C-F	RIC
-----	Celle que je préfère	H		RIC
-----	Chanson norvégienne	H	E-G	RIC
-----	Chevauchée cosaque	H	D-G	RIC
-----	L'oasis			
-----	Le papillon			RIC
Franck	Lied	LH	FS-FS	†
-----	Nocturne	HL		†
Gaubert	Ah, fuyez à présent			
Georges	Hymne au soleil	LH	E-A	HOM
-----	La pluie	HL		INT
Godard	Florian's song	LMH	D-FS	GSC
Gounod	Adore and be still	HL		GSC
-----	Au printemps	LMH	DF-AF	GSC
-----	Au rossignol	LMH	D-G	CHO
-----	Où voulez-vous aller?	H	D-A	GSC

97

(Gounod)	Sérénade	LMH	D-A	GSC
-----	Vénise	HL		INT
Gretry	Comme un eclair			
Grovlez	Guitares et mandolines			DUR
Hahn	À Chloris	H	DS-FS	HEU
-----	En sourdine			HEU
-----	Infidélité	M		HEU
-----	L'air			HEU
-----	L'enamourée			HEU
-----	L'heure exquise	M	DF-F	†
-----	Cimetière de campagne			HEU
-----	Fêtes galantes			
-----	Le printemps			
-----	Le rossignol des lilas			
-----	Mai			HEU
-----	Offrande	M	D-D	†
-----	Paysage	MH	EF-G	HEU
-----	Quand je fus pris au pavillon	M		HEU
-----	Rêverie			HEU
-----	Si mes vers avaient des ailes	HLM	B-FS	†
-----	The rain song			
Hindemith	La belle dame sans merci	MH		SC
Honegger	Amour			
-----	Le grand étang			
-----	Les cloches			SEN
-----	Poème de Verlaine			SAL
-----	Poème de William Aguet			SAL
-----	Psalm 130 (Mimaamaquim)			SAL
-----	Psalm 138 (I will give Thee thanks with my whole heart)			SAL
Hue	A des oiseaux	H	E-G	†
-----	Il a neigé des fleurs	H	EF-AF	
-----	L'âne blanc	H	EF-G	HEU
-----	Les clochettes des muguets	HL	E-GF	INT
-----	Soir païen Flutes			ROU
-----	Vocalise-étude			
Jaubert	La chanson de Tessa			
Koechlin	L'air	M	F-FS	ROU
-----	L'hiver	H	E-G	†
-----	La lune	M	C-F	ROU
-----	La pêche			ROU
-----	Le matin	H		ROU
-----	Le thé	HM	C-E	BOS
-----	Si tu le veux	LH	FS-A	MAR
Lalo	La chanson d'Alouette	H	EF-B	GSC
Laparra	C'est une calme			

(Laparra)	Le bonheur			
-----	Le tambour			
-----	Lettre à une espagnole			ENO
Leguerney	Au sommeil			ROU
-----	Genièvres hérissés	H	D-G	ROU
Leroux	Le nil	LH	E-A	†
	Cello or violin			
Letorey	La fontaine de Caramouet			HAM
Liszt	Comment, disaient-ils?	H	C-AF	†
-----	Enfant, si j'étais roi			SC
-----	Oh! quand je dors	H	E-A	†
-----	S'il est un charmant gazon	HL		†
Lully	Au clair de la lune	H	E-D	CFI
Manning	Vielle chanson de chasse			
Martini	Plaisir d'amour	M	BF-EF	GSC
Massenet	Crépuscule	M	D-E	GSC
-----	Elégie	LM	C-GF	GSC
-----	Entchantement	HL		HEU
-----	Ouvre tes yeux bleus	MH	C-G	†
-----	Première danse	H	E-G	GSC
-----	Sérénade du passant!			HEU
Mehul	N'avoir jamais qu'une pensée			
Moret	La lettre			
-----	Le nélumbo	H	E-DF	HEU
Mozart	Dans un bois	H	EF-AF	
-----	Oiseaux, si tous les ans	H	C-G	KAL
Paladilhe	Le roitelet	MH	DS-GS	GSC
-----	Psyché	HM	BF-F	GSC
Paulin	Que deviennent les roses			
Pierné	An album for my little friends			
-----	Ils étaient trois petits chats blancs			MAR
-----	Le moulin	ML	C-E	BOS
Poldowski	Cortège	M	D-FS	CHE
-----	Effet de neige	M	EF-F	CHE
-----	L'heure exquise	LMH	DF-AF	CHE
Poulenc	A sa guitare	M	D-FS	DUR
-----	Air champêtre			ROU
-----	Air grave			ROU
-----	Air romantique			SAL
-----	Air vif	H	C-AF	ROU
-----	Allons plus vite			ROU
-----	Au delà	H	D-G	DUR
-----	Berceuse			ROU
-----	Bleuet	H	FS-GF	DUR
-----	C (J'ai traversé les ponts de C)			ROU

(Poulenc)	Chanson de la fille frivole			ESC
-----	Chanson d'Orkenise			AMP
-----	Cimetière			ROU
-----	Fêtes galantes			SAL
-----	Figure de force			DUR
-----	Fleurs	M	DF-F	ROU
-----	Hôtel			AMP
-----	Il vole			SAL
-----	La petite servante			ROU
-----	Le disparu			ROU
-----	Les chemins de l'amour	M		AMP
-----	Les gars qui vont à la fête	H	C-GF	AMP
-----	Priez pour paix	ML		ROU
-----	Reine des mouettes	M	FF-F	SAL
-----	Sanglots			AMP
-----	Une herbe pauvre	H	E-G	DUR
-----	Violon			ROU
Rabey	Tes yeux (Violin and piano)	H	EF-G	DUR
Rameau	La musette			BOS
-----	Le grillon			DUR
Ravel	Asie	M	BF-G	DUR
-----	D'Anne jouant de l'espinette	H	CS-GS	GSC
-----	D'Anne qui me jecta	HM	CS-FS	GSC
-----	Kaddisch	H	C-G	DUR
-----	La flûte enchantée	M	DS-FS	DUR
-----	Le paon	M	C-F	DUR
-----	Manteau de fleurs	H		INT
-----	Nicolette	L	B-FS	ELK
-----	Ronde			
-----	Sur l'herbe	MH	C-G	DUR
-----	Tout gai!	MH	EF-F	
-----	Trois beaux oiseaux du paradis			DUR
-----	Vocalise en forme de habanera	MH	BF-G	MAR
Rhené-Baton	Berceuse			DUR
Roussel	Jazz dans la nuit	H	C-A	DUR
-----	Le jardin mouillé	M	C-FS	ROU
-----	Response d'une épouse sage			DUR
Saint-Saëns	A swan's song (Harp or piano and cello)	H	D-G	GSC
-----	Aimons-nous			DUR
-----	Guitares et mandolines			DUR
-----	La cloche	LH	DF-AF	†

(Saint Saëns)	La libellule	H	C-D	DUR
-----	Le bonheur est une chose légère (Violin and piano)	H	C-A	CHO
-----	Mai	H	G-FS	DUR
-----	Pourquoi rester seulette	H	D-A	GSC
-----	Une flûte invisible			
Satie	Daphénéo			ROU
-----	Le chapelier			ROU
Severac	Ba, be, bi, bo, bu			ROU
-----	Chanson de Blaisine			
-----	Chanson pour le petit cheval			ROU
-----	Offrande			ROU
-----	Ma poupée chérie			ROU
-----	Ne dérangez pas le monde			ROU
-----	Zon, zon, zon			ROU
Staub	L'heure silencieuse	H	EF-G	DUR
Szulc	Claire du lune	H	E-G	AXE
-----	Hantise d'amour	H	D-BF	GSC
-----	Mandoline	H	D-B	ROU
Vidal	Ariette	LH	F-A	GSC

German Recital Songs

Lyric Soprano

Bach, C.P.E.	Das Gebet			SIM
-----	Passionslied			SIM
-----	The last judgement			
Bach, J. S.	Bist du bei mir	HML	A-EF	†
-----	Come visit ye glowing	H		
-----	Comfort sweet, Lord Jesus comes			OXF
-----	Dir, dir Jehovah			†
-----	Father what I proffer			
-----	Ich halte treulich still			
-----	Komm suesser Tod	MH	C-G	†
-----	Liebster Herr Jesu			BRH
-----	O Jesulein suess			
Beethoven	An die Hoffnung	H	B-A	†
-----	Andenken			†
-----	A song of penitence			
-----	Bitten			†
-----	Busslied			
-----	Das Geheimnis			
-----	Freudvoll und leidvoll	M	DS-E	†
-----	Ich liebe dich	HL	BF-DF	GSC

101

(Beethoven)	Mailied			RIC
-----	Mit einem gemalten Band			RIC
-----	Neue Liebe, neues Leben			†
Berg	Die Nachtigall			AMP
Blech	Heimkehr vom Feste			UNI
Brahms	An ein Veilchen	H	DS-GS	†
-----	An eine Aeolsharfe	H	EF-AF	†
-----	Auf dem Schiffe	LH	GS-A	†
-----	Auf dem See	HL	D-F	†
-----	Bei dir sind meine Gedanken	MH	E-FS	†
-----	Blinde Kuh			†
-----	Botschaft	HL	D-F	†
-----	Daemm'rung senkte sich von oben	LH	BF-G	†
-----	Das Maedchen spricht	H	E-FS	†
-----	Dein blaues Auge	MH	BF-G	†
-----	Der Jaeger	HL		†
-----	Der Tod, das ist die kuehle Nacht	L	AF-F	†
-----	Dort in den Weiden	LH	A-A	†
-----	Ein Wanderer	LH	E-AF	†
-----	Eine gute, gute Nacht			†
-----	Erinnerung	H	E-G	†
-----	Es liebt sich so lieblich im Lenze	LH	D-GS	†
-----	Es traeumte mir			RIC
-----	Feldeinsamkeit	HL	C-EF	†
-----	Fruehlingstrost	LH	E-A	†
-----	Geheimnis			†
-----	Immer leiser wird mein Schlummer	LH	DF-A	†
-----	In Waldeseinsamkeit	H	ES-G	†
-----	Juchhe!			†
-----	Lerchengesang	LH	FS-GS	†
-----	Maedchenlied	HL		†
-----	Meerfahrt			†
-----	Mein wundes Herz verlangt			
-----	Meine Lieder	HL	D-DS	†
-----	Nachtigall	MHL	BF-FS	†
-----	O liebliche Wangen	MLH	E-G	†
-----	O wuesst' ich doch den Weg zurueck	H	E-FS	†
-----	Regenlied	HL	CS-F	†
-----	Rote Abendwolken zieh'n	H	EF-AF	†
-----	Ruhe Suessliebchen	HL	BS-E	†
-----	Salamander			†
-----	Salome			†
-----	Sandmaennchen	LH	F-G	†

102

(Brahms)	Schoen war, das ich dir weihte			†
-----	Schwesterlein			†
-----	Sonntag	H	D-G	†
-----	Staendchen	HL	BF-E	†
-----	Unbewegte laue Luft			PET
Brahms	Vergebliches Staendchen			†
-----	Vorueber			†
-----	Waehrend des Regens			†
-----	Wiegenlied			
-----	Wie Melodien zieht es	HL	A-E	†
-----	Wir wandelten	LH	EF-GF	†
Cornelius	Hirschlein ging im Wald			
-----	Im Lenz			
-----	Komm, wir wandeln	H	FS-GS	SC
-----	Moechte im Walde mit dir gehen			
-----	Morgenwind			
Franck, J.W.	Auf, auf, zu Gottes Lob			SIM
Franz	Ach, wenn, ich doch ein Immchen war			
-----	Ein Stuendlein wohl vor Tag			†
-----	Er ist gekommen	HL	EF-F	†
-----	Es hat die Rose sich beklagt	LH	DF-F	†
-----	For music	ML	C-D	†
-----	Gute Nacht	HL		†
-----	Im Herbst	HM	A-F	†
-----	Liebchen ist da!	HL		GSC
-----	Mutter, o sing mich zur Ruh	HL	E-G	†
-----	Sonnenuntergang	HL	CS-FS	DIT
-----	Stille Sicherheit	M	E-F	†
-----	Vergessen	HL		DIT
-----	Voeglein wohin?	HL		GSC
Handel	Dank sei dir, Herr	M	CS-E	†
-----	Das zitternde Glaenzen der spielenden Wellen			
Haydn	Das Leben ist ein Traum			GSC
-----	Der erste Kuss			
-----	My mother bids me bind my hair	M	E-E	†
-----	O tuneful voice			
-----	Pastorella			
-----	She never told her love	HL	B-D	DIT
-----	Sympathy			
-----	The mermaid's song	M	C-F	PRE
Hiller	Sei du mit mir			
Hindemith	Geburt Marias			AMP

(Hindemith)	Pietà from Marienleben			AMP
-----	The moon	M	DS-EF	AMP
Humperdinck	Die Lerche			
Jensen	Am Ufer des Flusses des Manzanares	H	D-FS	GSC
-----	An der Linden			
-----	Fruehlingsnacht	L	D-E	GSC
-----	Murmuring zephyr	LH	E-AF	GSC
-----	Waldesgespraech			
Kienzl	Maria auf dem Berge			
Liszt	In Liebeslust			
-----	Kling'leise, mein Lied	HL		†
Loewe	Canzonetta	MH	B-A	DIT
-----	Der Edelfalk			SC
-----	Der Zahn			SC
-----	Des Glockenthuermers Tochterlein	H	CS-A	SC
-----	Die wandelnde Glocke			SC
-----	Niemand hat's gesehen	LM	DS-FS	†
Mahler	Das Irdische Leben	HL	A-F	INT
-----	Ich atmet' einen linden Duft	HL		INT
-----	Ich ging mit Lust	HL		INT
-----	Liebst du um Schoenheit	HL		INT
-----	Rheinlegendchen	M	B-FS	†
-----	Wer hat dies Liedlein erdacht?	HL	BF-E	INT
Marx	Der bescheidene Schaefer			UNI
-----	Hat dich die Liebe beruehrt	MH	EF-BF	AMP
-----	Marienlied	MH	EF-AF	AMP
-----	Nocturne	H	EF-AF	AMP
-----	Regenlied	LH	E-G	UNI
-----	Selige Nacht	M	DF-GF	AMP
-----	Und gestern hat er mir Rosen gebracht	H	E-A	AMP
-----	Valse de Chopin	M	CS-GS	AMP
-----	Venetianisches Wiegenlied			AMP
-----	Waldseligkeit	H	D-A	UNI
-----	Wie einst			UNI
Mendelssohn	And'res Maienlied			AUG
-----	Bei der Wiege	M	DF-EF	†
-----	Das erste Veilchen	M	F-F	†
-----	Der Mond	HL		†
-----	Die Liebende schreibt	HL		†
-----	Fruehlingslied	H	DS-GS	†
-----	Gruss	M	DS-FS	†
-----	Im Gruenen	H	E-BF	AUG
-----	Minnelied	H	E-G	AUG

(Mendelssohn)	Nachtlied			
-----	Neue Liebe	H	CS-A	†
-----	O Jugend	H	E-A	†
-----	On wings of song			†
-----	Suleika	H	E-GS	†
Mittler	Over the mountains	H		DIT
-----	Soft through my heart	M		AMP
Mozart	Abendempfindung	M	E-F	
-----	An Chloe	LH	EF-AF	
-----	Das Lied der Trennung			
-----	Das Traumbild			
-----	Das Veilchen	LMH	F-G	†
-----	Der Zauberer	H	F-G	
-----	Die kleine Spinnerin			
-----	Die Verschweigung			
-----	Sehnsucht nach dem Fruehling			
-----	Trennungslied			
-----	Warnung	HM	C-D	
-----	Wiegenlied	MH	G-G	†
Reger	Des Kindes Gebet	H	F-G	BOT
-----	Friede	H	EF-G	UNI
-----	Mit Rosen bestreut			UNI
-----	Waldeinsamkeit	HML	A-D	BOS
Schoeck	Das bescheidene Wuenschlein			
-----	Die drei Zigeuner			
-----	In der Fremde			
-----	Nachtlied			
-----	Sommerabend			
Schrecker	Wiegenlied der Els			
Schubert	Am Grabe Anselmos	HL	B-EF	†
-----	An den Mond	HL	F-GF	†
-----	An die Laute	LH	D-F	†
-----	An die Nachtigall	H	C-G	†
-----	An die Sonne			†
-----	An eine Quelle			PET
-----	An mein Klavier			PET
-----	Auf dem Strom Horn or violoncello			PET
-----	Auf dem Wasser zu singen	MH	EF-GF	†
-----	Aufloesung	LH	D-A	DIT
-----	Ave Maria	LMH	F-F	†
-----	Ballade			
-----	Danksagung an den Bach	HL	E-F	†
-----	Das Lied im Gruenen			PET
-----	Das Maedchen			PET
-----	Das Wandern	HLM	E-E	†

105

(Schubert)	Das Wirtshaus	HL	C-D	†
-----	Dass sie hier gewesen!			PET
-----	Delphine			PET
-----	Der Blumen Schmerz			PET
-----	Der Einsame	LH	D-G	†
-----	Der Hirt auf dem Felsen	H	BF-B	
	Clarinet or violoncello			
-----	Der Juengling an der	LH	E-A	†
	Quelle			
-----	Der Juengling und der	M	DF-FF	†
	Tod			
-----	Der Knabe			PET
-----	Der Leiermann	ML	C-D	†
-----	Der Morgenkuss			PET
-----	Der Musensohn	LH	FS-G	†
-----	Der Neugierige	HL	CS-EF	†
-----	Der Schmetterling	LH	E-F	†
-----	Der Wachtelschlag	H	DS-FS	PET
-----	Der Wegweiser	L	D-EF	†
-----	Des Fischers Liebesglueck	LH	F-A	†
-----	Des Maedchens	LH	C-E	GSC
-----	Didone's aria			
-----	Die Forelle	MLH	EF-GF	†
-----	Die Gebuesche			PET
-----	Die junge Nonne	LH	C-GF	†
-----	Die Maenner sind mechant			PET
-----	Die Post	HML	BF-EF	†
-----	Die Rose	M	G-FS	PET
-----	Die Taubenpost	HL	D-EF	†
-----	Die Voegel	LH	E-GS	†
-----	Dithyrambe	L	A-D	†
-----	Du bist die Ruh	LMH	EF-AF	†
-----	Ellens zweiter Gesang			PET
-----	Erlafsee	H	E-G	†
-----	Erntelied			PET
-----	Erstarrung	HL	D-F	†
-----	Florio			PET
-----	Freude der Kinderjahre	LH	C-G	†
-----	Fruehlingsglaube	M	EF-F	†
-----	Fruehlingssehnsucht	HL	B-E	†
-----	Fruehlingstraum	HL	C-D	†
-----	Ganymed	LH	EF-G	†
-----	Geheimes	HL	BF-EF	†
-----	Gott im Fruehling			PET
-----	Gretchen am Spinnrade	H	F-A	†
-----	Haenflings Liebeswerbung			PET
-----	Halt!	HL	E-F	†
-----	Heidenroeslein			
-----	Ihr Bild	HL	C-C	†

(Schubert)	Im Abendrot	HL	C-D	†
-----	Im Fruehling	LH	D-FS	†
-----	Klaerchens Lied			
-----	La pastorella			SC
-----	Lachen und Weinen	HL	C-EF	†
-----	Letzte Hoffnung	HL		†
-----	Liebesbotschaft	H	E-G	†
-----	Lied der Mignon	HL		†
-----	Lob der Thraenen	LM	F-F	†
-----	Meeresstille	HL	B-D	†
-----	Mein!	HL		†
-----	Mignon	HL		†
-----	Nachtstueck	LH	D-G	†
-----	Nachtviolen			PET
-----	Naehe des Geliebten	HL	D-EF	†
-----	Nur wer die Sehnsucht kennt	LH		†
-----	Rastlose Liebe	M	B-F	†
-----	Seligkeit			
-----	Sprache der Liebe			PET
-----	Staendchen			
-----	Suleika I	LH	DS-G	†
-----	Suleika II	LH	F-BF	†
-----	Ueber allen Zauber Liebe			
-----	Ungeduld	HML		GSC
-----	Verklaerung			PET
-----	Versunken			PET
-----	Viola			
-----	Vor meiner Wiege	HL	C-E	†
-----	Wanderers Nachtlied 2	LH	F-F	†
-----	Wehmuth	HL	B-D	†
-----	Wiegenlied (Op. 98)			†
-----	Wohin?	HL	B-E	†
Schuetz	Eile mich, Gott, zu erretten			BAR
-----	Herr, unser Herrscher!			BAR
Schumann	Abends am Strande			
-----	Abschied vom Walde			
-----	Alte Laute	HL	DF-DF	†
-----	An den Sonnenschein	HL	A-D	†
-----	Auftraege	HL	C-E	†
-----	Dein Angesicht	HL	B-EF	†
-----	Der Himmel hat eine Traene geweint			
-----	Der Nussbaum	LMH	D-FS	†
-----	Der Sandmann	HL	AF-DF	†
-----	Die blume der Ergebung			
-----	Die Lotusblume	HLM	BF-F	†
-----	Die Meerfee			

107

(Schumann)	Du bist wie eine Blume	HM	F-EF	†
-----	Freisinn			
-----	Fruehlingslust	HL		†
-----	Fruehlingsnacht	L	CS-E	†
-----	Geisternaehe			
-----	Herzeleid			
-----	In der Fremde	HL		†
-----	Intermezzo	HL	C-D	†
-----	Lied der Suleika			
-----	Marienwuermchen	HL	D-D	†
-----	Mein schoener Stern			
-----	Meine Rose			
-----	Mondnacht	M	E-FS	†
-----	O wie lieblich ist das Maedchen			
-----	Roeselein, Roeselein			
-----	Schneegloeckchen	HL		†
-----	Singet nicht in Trauertoenen			
-----	Stille Traenen	HL		†
-----	Volksliedchen	HL		†
-----	Wer machte dich so krank?			
-----	Widmung	HL	BF-F	†
Strauss	Ach Lieb, ich muss nun scheiden	H	D-G	
-----	All' mein' Gedanken	H	CS-GS	
-----	Als mir dein Lied erklang			
-----	An die Nacht			
-----	Beim Schlafengehen			
-----	Breit ueber mein Haupt	LH	GF-AF	†
-----	Das Rosenband			†
-----	Des Dichters Abendgang			†
-----	Die Georgine	LH	B-A	†
-----	Die Nacht	HL		†
-----	Du meines Herzens Kroenelein	HL	CS-E	†
-----	Fruendliche Vision	HL	C-F	
-----	Fruehling			
-----	Fruehlingsfeier			
-----	Fruehlingsgedraenge			
-----	Fruehlingsstimme			
-----	Hat gesagt, bleibt's nicht dabei			†
-----	Heimkehr	HL	B-E	†
-----	Heimliche Aufforderung	HL	B-E	†
-----	Ich trage meine minne	M		†
-----	Ich wollt' ein Straeusslein binden			†

108

109

(Wolf)	Der Knabe und das Immlein	L	CS-A	†
-----	Die Bekehrte			PET
-----	Die heilige Marie singt			
-----	Die Sproede			†
-----	Die Zigeunerin			†
-----	Du denkst, mit einem Faedchen			†
-----	Elfenlied	HL	D-F	†
-----	Er ist's	H	D-G	†
-----	Frage und Antwort			PET
-----	Fruehling uebers Jahr			†
-----	Fuehr' mich, Kind	H	E-FS	
-----	Ganymed	HL	CS-D	†
-----	Gesang Weylas	HL	DF-F	†
-----	Gesegnet sei das Gruen	HL		†
-----	Gleich und gleich			†
-----	Heb' auf dein blondes Haupt	HL	G-DF	†
-----	Hoch beglueckt in deiner Liebe	HL	DF-F	†
-----	Ich hab' in Penna	LH		†
-----	Ihr jungen Leute			PET
-----	Im Fruehling	HL	BF-F	†
-----	In dem Schatten meiner Locken	M	C-EF	†
-----	Kennst du das Land			†
-----	Lebe wohl	HL	BF-F	†
-----	Liebe mir in Busen zuendet	M	E-F	†
-----	Lied vom Winde			†
-----	Mausfallen Spruechlein	HL	BF-E	†
-----	Morgentau	HL	D-D	†
-----	Nachtzauber	HL	B-E	†
-----	Nimmersatte Liebe	LH	CF-AF	†
-----	Nixe Binsefuss	H	E-G	†
-----	Nun bin ich dein	M	C-F	†
-----	Nun wandre, Maria	HL	EF-D	†
-----	O waer' dein Haus			†
-----	Phaenomen			PET
-----	Rat einer Alten			†
-----	Sie blasen zum Abmarsch			
-----	Storchenbotschaft			PET
-----	Tretet ein, hoher Krieger	HL	B-F	†
-----	Und willst du deinen Liebsten sterben	HL		†
-----	Verborgenheit	HL	B-E	†
-----	Verschwiegene Liebe	LH	DF-FS	†
-----	Waldmaedchen			PET

(Wolf)	Wenn du zu den Blumen gehst	HL	B-EF	†
-----	Wer sein holdes Lieb verloren			
-----	Wie glaenzt der helle Mond			†
-----	Zitronenfalter im April	HL		†
-----	Zum neuen Jahr			PET
Wolff	Wer rief dich denn?			

Italian Recital Songs

Lyric Soprano

Abbatini	Quanto è bello il mio diletto			PET
Alfano	Non nascondere il segreto del tuo cuore			
Arditi	Il bacio	H	CS-B	†
Ariosti	Vuoi, che parta (Lucio Vero)			PET
Augustini	Tu non m'intendi amor			
Bassani	Posate, dormite (La Serenata)	H	EF-F	GSC
Bellini	Dolente immagine di fille mia			RIC
Bononcini	Deh, più a me non v'ascondete	LH	EF-F	†
-----	L'esperto nocchiero (Astarte)	HL	B-E	†
-----	Per la gloria	HL	C-EF	†
-----	Più non ti voglio credere Violin	H	D-AF	PET
-----	Si che fedele			DUR
Brogi	Gotine gialle	H		HOM
-----	Le lucciole			
Buzzi-Peccia	Colombetta			RIC
Caccini	Amarilli, mia bella	ML	C-D	†
Caldara	Come raggio di sol	HL	D-F	†
-----	Sebben crudele	HML	E-DS	†
-----	Selve amiche, ombrose piante	HM	E-E	†
Campana	Veglia			
Carissimi	Piangete, ohime			RIC
Casella	Fuor de la bella gaiba			
Castelnuovo-Tedesco	Quattro scherzi per musica			RIC
Cavalli	Donzelle fuggite	HL	C-EF	†

Cesti	Ah, quanto è vero	HL	F-F	DIT
	(Il Pomo d'Oro)			
-----	Che angoscia, che affanno	HL	C-DF	DIT
	(Il Pomo d'Oro)			
-----	Lasciatemi in pace			
Cimara	Filastrocca			
-----	Fiocca la neve	H	G-G	GSC
-----	Ondina			
-----	Scherzo			
-----	Stornello			BON
-----	Trittico primaverile			
Cimarosa	Bel nume che adoro			RIC
Cottone	Ninna, nanna	H	FS-A	MCR
D'Astorga	Qual mai fatale arcano			
-----	Vo' cercando in queste valli	H	D-G	STB
De Luca	Non posso disperar	HL	C-E	GSC
De Meglio	Una tarentella			
Donaudy	Ah mai non cessate			RIC
-----	O del mio amato ben	M	EF-F	RIC
-----	Ognun ripicchia e nicchia			RIC
-----	Quand' il tuo diavol nacque			RIC
-----	Spirate pur, spirate			RIC
Donizetti	La zingara	H	DS-A	GSC
Durante	Vergin, tutta amor	LM	C-EF	†
Falconieri	Non più d'amòre	HL	C-D	DIT
-----	Nudo arciero	HL	AF-AF	DIT
-----	O bellissimi capelli	HL	B-D	†
-----	Occhietti amati	HL	B-D	DIT
-----	Vallanella			
Freschi	Parte il pie			
Gagliano	Dormi, amore	HL	CS-E	DIT
Ghedini	La tortora			
Giordani	Caro mio ben	HML	B-D	†
Gluck	Ah ritorna			PET
	(Il Trionfo di Clelia)			
-----	O del mio dolce ardor	LH	D-FS	GSC
	(Paride ed Elena)			
-----	Spiagge amate			†
	(Paride ed Elena)			
Handel	Affani del pensier			†
	(Ottone)			
-----	Amor commanda	H		†
	(Floridante)			
-----	Bel piacere			†
	(Agrippina)			
-----	Cara sposa	M	CS-D	
	(Radamisto)			
-----	Care selve (Atalanta)	MH	FS-A	†

(Handel)	Caro voi siete all alma (Serse)	H	E-A	CFI
-----	Ch' io mai vi possa (Siroe)			†
-----	Come alla tortorella (Atalanta)	M	B-E	CFI
-----	Deh lasciatemi (Tamerlano)			
-----	Generoso chi sol (Scipione)			GSC
-----	La speranza è giunto in porto (Ottone)			
-----	Lusinghe più care (Alessandro)	H	D-G	†
-----	Mio caro bene (Rodelinda)			OXF
-----	Ne men con l'ombre (Serse)	H	E-A	CFI
-----	Ombre, piante (Rodelinda)	H	FS-A	CFI
-----	Qual farfalletta (Partenope)	H	E-A	†
-----	Rendi' l sereno al ciglio (Sosarme)	LH	EF-F	†
-----	Riportai (Atalanta)			BOO
-----	Se fedele vuoi ch'io ti creda (Orlando)			
-----	Sei, mia gioja (Partenope)			CFI
-----	Sommi Dei (Radimisto)			†
-----	Spietati, io vi giurai (Rodelinda)			BOO
-----	V' adoro pupille (Julius Caesar)			BOO
-----	Vieni o figlio caro e mi consola (Ottone)			†
-----	Voi dolce aurette al cor (Tolomeo)			GSC
Hasse	Nel mirar quel sasso amato			
Haydn	Del mio core (Orfeo ed Euridice)			GSC
-----	Pensi a me			
-----	Un tetto umil			
Jommelli	Chi vuol comprar la bella	H	B-G	GSC
Legrenzi	Bella, moro per te			
-----	Che fiero costume	HML	C-D	†
Lotti	Pur dicesti, o bocca bella	LMH	E-FS	GSC
Malipiero	Ballata	H		CHE
Marcello	O Signor chi sarà			
-----	Un guardo vogli a me	M		BOS
Monteverdi	Lettera amorosa			
-----	Maledetto sia l'aspetto			PET

113

Mortari	Il mago pistagna			
Mozart	Ridente la calma			BOS
Paisiello	Chi vuol la zingarella	L	C-F	GSC
-----	Nel cor più non mi sento	HL	C-EF	†
Paradies	M'ha preso alla sua ragna	M	EF-F	GSC
-----	Quel ruscelletto	L	BF-F	CFI
Pergolesi	Confusa, smarrita			GSC
-----	Nina	HL	CS-D	DIT
-----	Se tu m'ami	LMH	C-G	GSC
Perti	Canzonetta			
Piccini	Se il ciel mi divide	M	C-F	†
	(Alessandro di Indie)			
Pizzetti	I pastori			FRL
-----	Levommi il mio pensier			RIC
-----	Ninna nanna di uliva			
-----	Quel rosignol che si soave			RIC
	piagne			
Porpora	Non più fra sassi			PET
Quagliati	Apra il suo verde seno	HL	E-CS	DIT
Recli	Bella bellina			
Respighi	Abbandono			BON
-----	Ballata			RIC
-----	Bella porta di rubini			RIC
-----	Crepusculo			
-----	E se un giorno tornasse	M		RIC
-----	Invito alla danza			BON
-----	La najade ese un giorno			
	tornasse			
-----	Nebbie			†
-----	Nevicata	HM		BON
-----	Notte			BON
-----	Pioggia			BON
-----	Quando nasceste voi			
-----	Scherzo			BON
Rocca	La vocazione di St.	M	C-F	CHA
	Francesco			
Rontani	Or ch'io non segno più	HL	CS-E	DIT
Rosa	Selve, voi che le	MH	D-G	DIT
	speranze			
Rossini	La danza	MH	E-A	†
-----	La promessa			
Sadero	Ero la vo	M		CHE
-----	I battitori di grano	M		CHE
-----	In mezo al mar	M		CHE
Santoliquido	Io mi levai			
-----	Riflessi			FOR
Sarti	Lungi dal caro bene	HL	G-D	GSC
	(Armide)			
Sartorio	Il mio cor			

114

Scarlatti, A.	All' acquisto di gloria (Tigrane)	H	C-G	GSC
-----	Col dire a me così			
-----	Già il sole dal Gange	LH	EF-F	GSC
-----	Già mai la lontananza			DUR
-----	La fortuna			BOS
-----	La tua pena			
-----	Labbra gradite			
-----	Quanto è dolce quel velen			
-----	Rugiadose odorose (Il Pirro e Demetrio)	HL	D-E	DIT
-----	Se Florindo è fedele	LM	EF-EF	GSC
-----	Speranza			
-----	Toglietemi la vita ancor			RIC
Scarlatti, D.	Consolati e spara amante	L	BF-E	GSC
-----	Qual farfalletta			
Sgambati	Separazione	LMH	FS-G	GSC
Sibella	Ballata			
-----	La Girometta	HML	D-E	GSC
-----	O bimba bimbetta	LMH	D-G	GSC
-----	O bocca dolorosa	HM	D-F	GSC
Stradella	Così, amor, mi fai languir	HL	F-G	DIT
-----	Per pietà (Il Floridoro)	HM	D-F	DIT
-----	Pietà, Signore	HM	C-F	GSC
-----	Ragion sempre addita	H	E-G	†
Strozzi	Amor dormiglione	HL	B-E	DIT
Tocchi	Ninna, nanna			
Tosti	'A vucchella	LH	F-G	RIC
-----	Mattinata			RIC
-----	Sogno			RIC
Traetta	Ombra cara, amorosa	HL	B-F	†
Vellucci	Che fai tu luna			
Viardot	Fingo per mio diletto			
Vivaldi	Da du venti (Ercole)			
-----	La pastorella sul prima albore			
-----	Un certo no so che	HL	BF-EF	†

Russian Recital Songs

Lyric Soprano

Arensky	By the river			
-----	Revery	MH	DS-FS	DIT
-----	The little fish's song	H	D-A	†
-----	Valse	H	DF-GF	GSC
Borodin	In your far country			
Cui	Poet and critic			

115

(Cui)	The statue at Czarskoe-Selo	HM	DF-EF	†
-----	Touching the flower			
-----	Twilight			
Dargomijshky	It's all the same to me			
-----	My darling girls			
-----	Parting			
-----	Song of the mermaid			
-----	When the sun is sinking low			
Glazounoff	I am not allowed to go to the river			
-----	Romance orientale			
-----	The nereid	H	FS-A	GSC
Glinka	Ah, kindly star			
-----	How sweet it is to be with you	HM		GSC
-----	The first train			
-----	The journey			
Gretchaninoff	Hushed the song of the nightingale	MH	E-G	DIT
-----	Il s'est tu, le charmant rossignol	H	EF-G	CFI
-----	My native land	L	C-EF	GSC
-----	Over the steppe	LM	C-G	GSC
-----	The skylark			DIT
-----	Wounded birch	HL	B-EF	†
Liadoff	Le lac enchante			
Mednikoff	The hills of Gruzia	H	DS-A	LAC
Medtner	Butterfly			
-----	Roses			
-----	Spanish romance			
-----	The angel			
-----	The ravens			
-----	The singer			
-----	To a dreamer			
-----	Waltz			
-----	Winter evening			
Mussorgsky	In the corner			INT
-----	Night			GSC
-----	The orphan girl			GSC
-----	Tiny star where art thou	LH	DF-F	BOS
Prokofieff	Jewish cradle song			
-----	Snowdrops			GSC
Rachmaninoff	All is so fair			
-----	At night	LH	D-A	BOS
-----	Before my window	HM	C-G	†
-----	Daisies			†
-----	Floods of spring	HL		DIT
-----	God took away from me			GSC

116

(Rachmaninoff)	Here beauty dwells	H	D-B	CFI
-----	In the silence of night	LH	D-A	GSC
-----	Into my open window	HL	B-FS	BOS
-----	Lilacs	LH	EF-G	†
-----	Melody	H	DS-A	CFI
-----	Midsummer nights	H		BOO
-----	Morning	ML	B-DS	GSC
-----	Oh cease they singing, maiden fair	H	E-A	CFI
-----	O thou billowy harvest field	HL	CS-E	GSC
-----	Sorrow in spring	H	D-BF	DIT
-----	The answer	H		BOO
-----	The coming of spring	LH	DF-AF	BOS
-----	The island	LH	DF-F	†
-----	The soldier's bride			†
-----	The songs of Grusia	H	E-A	GSC
-----	Vocalise	LH	CS-A	GSC
-----	Why wert thou given me			
Rimsky-Korsakov	Hebrew love song	HM		GSC
-----	It is not the wind blowing			
-----	The nightingale and the rose	H	FS-FS	DIT
-----	Zuleika's song			
Rubinstein	Es blinkt der Thau	LH	EF-GF	GSC
-----	Neue Liebe			
-----	Romance			
-----	The lark	LH	EF-G	DIT
-----	The rose			GSC
Scriabin	Soft the rose			
Stravinsky	La rosée sainte			
-----	Pastorale			GSC
-----	Song of the dew			JUR
-----	Spring			
-----	The cloister (La novice)			DIT
-----	Tilibom			
Tchaikovsky	A child's song			
-----	All for you			
-----	At the ball	MH		GSC
-----	At the open window			GSC
-----	Complaint of the bride			
-----	Cradle song	LH	D-G	†
-----	Disappointment			
-----	He loved me so dear	HL		GSC
-----	If I had known			
-----	In this hour of the night	H		GSC
-----	It was early in spring			
-----	Lament			

117

(Tchaikovsky)	Les Larmes			BES
-----	Serenade			DIT
-----	Song of the gypsy girl			
-----	So soon forgotten			
-----	Why	HL		†
Zimbalist	The folk songs of little Russia			

Scandinavian Recital Songs

Lyric Soprano

Agerby	Havren			
Alfven	Skogen sover			LUN
Alnaes	A leva			
-----	Lykken mellem to mennesker	M	B-FS	HAN
-----	Sidste reis			
Backer Gröndahl	In dreaming dance			
-----	Mot kveld			
Bellman	Butterflies at Haga			
-----	Liksom en herdinna			
-----	Undan ur vågen			
Berg	Herdegossen			
Berger	Jungfrun under lind			
Ericksson	Ljus			
-----	Min själ vak upp			
Grieg	A dream			†
-----	Among roses			
-----	By the brook			GSC
-----	En fuglevise			
-----	From Monte Pincio			PET
-----	Greeting			PET
-----	Hope			
-----	I love thee	HML	E-F	†
-----	In the boat	LM	D-EF	†
-----	It was a lovely summer evening			
-----	Kveldsang for Blakken			
-----	Little hut			
-----	Modersorg			
-----	Prinsessen	HL	B-E	†
-----	Snegl, Snegl	M	B-F	HAN
-----	Solvejg's cradle song	M	CS-FS	GSC
-----	Solvejg's song	MH	E-A	†
-----	Springtide	M		DIT
-----	The first meeting			PET

118

(Grieg)	Udvandreren	M	EF-F	HAN
Heise	Loneliness in the forest			
-----	Skovensomhed			
-----	Sol deroppe ganger under lide			
Kilpinen	Der spuk			
-----	Kuessekraut			
-----	Liebessuche			
-----	The cuckoo calls			
Kjerulf	My heart and lute	H		DIT
-----	Synnove's song	M	C-F	GSC
Lange-Mueller	Lykken er ikke gods eller guld			
Lie	Soft-footed snow	HM		DIT
Lindberg	Hur skall man bruden klaeda?			
Nielson	Aebleblomsten			HAN
-----	Havren			
Nystroem	Gubben och gumma			
-----	Kaerlekens visa			
Palmgren	Spring song			
-----	When I first saw your eyes			
-----	Where is the end of the road?			
Peterson-Berger	En visa i folkton			
-----	Till bruden			
-----	Titania			
Rangstroem	A bird flew over the forest			
-----	Avskedet			
-----	Flicken under nymånen			
-----	Pan			
-----	Rondeau			
Sibelius	Black roses	M	A-ES	AMP
-----	But my bird is long in homing			
-----	From the north	H	DS-G	GSC
-----	Illalle			
-----	Ingalill			
-----	Spring is fleeting			DIT
-----	The first kiss	M		AMP
-----	The silent town			AMP
-----	Was it a dream?			BRH
Sinding	Sylvelin	M	E-E	GSC
Sjoegren	Liten prins i vaggan			
Soederberg	Fågelns visa			
Soedermann	Längtan			
-----	Tag emot krandse			

119

Lyric Soprano

Alvarez	La partida	HL	DS-E	GSC
Berger	They all dance the samba	M	A-FS	GSC
Boero	Serenata			
-----	Serrana			
Freire	Ay, ay, ay	LH		RIC
Fuste	Háblame de amores			REI
Ginastera	Arrorro			RIC
-----	Triste			RIC
Granados	El majo discreto	H		INT
-----	El mirar de la maja			INT
-----	Gracia mía			
-----	Iban al pinar			
-----	Mañanica era			
Grever	Dame tu amor			
-----	Despedida			
Guastavino	La rose y la sauce			RIC
Guridi	Jota castellana			
-----	No quiero tus avellanas			
Lecuona	Desengano			
-----	Mi vida eres tu			MAR
Longas	Lavanderas			
-----	Sevillana			
Mignone	Bella granada			
-----	El clavelito en tus lindos cabellos			
-----	Improviso			
Nin	El amor es como un niño			ESC
-----	El vito			ESC
-----	Granadina			AMP
-----	Malagueña			AMP
-----	Minué cantado			ESC
-----	Montañesa			AMP
-----	Polo			AMP
-----	Villancico catalán			
Obradors	Coplas de curro dulce			
-----	Corazón, por qué pasáis?			
-----	Del cabello mas sutil			RIC
-----	Dos cantares populares			
-----	El vito			
-----	La mi sola laureola			
Padilla	El relicario			GOL
-----	La violetera			HAR
Rogatis	Chacarera			
-----	Gato			

(Rogatis)	Vidala			
Sandoval	Copla bailable			
-----	Copla leonesa			
-----	Copla malagueña			
-----	Eres tú			
-----	Sin tu amor	H	E-G	GSC
-----	Zamorana			
Tavares	Bahía			
-----	Benedicto pretinho			
-----	Dansa de caboclo			
Turina	Cantares			UME
-----	Desa el aura			
-----	Farruca	M	A-F	UME
-----	La giralda			
-----	Las locas por amor			UME
-----	Madrigal	H	D-BF	UME
-----	Nunca olvida			
-----	Olas gigantes			
-----	Rima	H	A-A	AMP
-----	Saeta en forma de salve a la Virgen de la esperanza			
-----	Tu pupila es azul			
Yradier	La paloma	HL	BF-EF	GSC

Miscellaneous Recital Songs

Lyric Soprano

Bach-Gounod	Ave Maria			
Bizet	Agnus Dei	HLM	C-AF	
Buchardo	Chilean dance			
Carr	Ave Maria			
Caturia	Bito manue			
Cherubini	Ave Maria	H	E-A	GSC
Chopin	Lithuanian song	ML	C-C	GSC
-----	Mazurka			
-----	My beloved	HL		GSC
-----	My delight	HL		
-----	The maiden's wish	LM	CS-E	GSC
Couperin	Adolescentalus sum ergo Organ, flute and strings			
Dvořák	God is my shepherd			AMP
-----	Hear my prayer, O Lord			AMP
-----	Lord, Thou art my refuge and shield			AMP
-----	Songs my mother taught me	HM	E-E	

121

(Dvořák)	The lark			
-----	The maiden's lament			
-----	The mower			
-----	Tune thy fiddle, gypsy			SIM
-----	Turn Thee to me			AMP
Fernandez	A velha historia			
-----	Cancáo do mar			
-----	Noite de junho			
-----	Samaritana da floresta			
Fisher	Eili, Eili	LMH	E-G	DIT
Franck	Panis angelicus	LM		
Guarnieri	Sae arue			
Janacek	Spring song			
Lecuona	Always in my heart			SOU
Loeffler	Canticum fratris solis			
Mignone	Variations for soprano on popular song luar do sertao			
Mozart	Alleluia	LMH	F-C	
Saint-Saëns	Ave Maria	HM		DIT
Saminsky	Hebrew lullaby	H	D-G	CFI
Schubert	Ave Maria	LMH	F-F	
-----	Salve Regina			
Ticciati	O salutaris hostia			
Villa-Lobos	Bachianas Brazileiras no. 5 8 Celli and bass			AMP
-----	Lundu da marquesa de Santos			
-----	Nhapope			
-----	O canto da nossa terra			
-----	The lost cat			
Weinberger	The way to Emmaus Organ			GRA

British Songs and Arias for Opening Recitals

Lyric Soprano

Anon	Have you seen but a white lily grow?	H	E-F	GSC
Arne, T.	Oh come my dearest			
-----	Water parted from the sea			GSC
Green	My lips shall speak the praise	M	E-F	OXF
Handel	Have mercy Lord (Te Deum)	HM		†
-----	Let me wander not unseen (L' Allegro)	M	D-G	†

(Handel)	Let the bright seraphim (Samson) Trumpet	H	E-A	†
-----	O sleep why dost thou leave me (Semele)	H	DS-GS	†
-----	Sweet bird (L' Allegro) Flute			NOV
-----	Trip, blithe streamlet (Serse)			
-----	With artful beguiling (Alessandro)			†
Purcell	Fairest Isle (King Arthur)			NOV
-----	Hark, the echoing air (The Fairy Queen)			BAF
-----	Here the deities approve			
-----	If music be the food of love	M	D-G	BOO
-----	Music for a while (Oedipus)	LH		SC
-----	Not all my torments			NOV
-----	We sing to him			

French Songs and Arias for Opening Recitals

Lyric Soprano

Berlioz	Villanelle	H	E-FS	†
Gretry	La fauvette avec ses petits (Zemire et Azor) Flute			LEM
Lully	Chant du Vénus (Revenez Amours) (Thésée)			LEM
Mehul	N'avoir jamais qu une pensée			
Mozart	Dans un bois	H	EF-AF	
Rameau	La musette			BOS
-----	Quand le silence (Air tendre) (Diane et Acteon)			DUR
Severac	Zon, zon, zon			ROU

German Songs and Arias for Opening Recitals

Lyric Soprano

Bach, J. S.	Bist du bei mir	HML	A-EF	†
-----	Ich halte treulich still			

123

(Bach)	Jauchzet Gott in allen Landen (Cantata 51)			BRO
-----	O Jesulein suess			
-----	Seufzer, Traenen, Kummer, Noth (Cantata 21) Oboe			†
Beethoven	Andenken			†
-----	Ich liebe dich	HL	BF-DF	†
Brahms	Ein Wanderer	LH	E-AF	†
-----	Nachtigall	MHL	BF-FS	†
Handel	Dank sei dir Herr (Added to Israel in Egypt)	M	CS-E	†
Haydn	O tuneful voice			
-----	She never told her love	HL	B-D	DIT
-----	Sympathy			
-----	The mermaid's song	M	C-F	PRE
-----	With verdure clad (The Creation)	H	E-BF	†
Mendelssohn	Fruehlingslied	H	DS-GS	†
Mozart	An Chloe	LH	EF-AF	
Schubert	Das Wandern	HLM	E-E	†
-----	Der Wachtelschlag	H	DS-FS	PET
-----	Ganymed	LH	EF-G	†
-----	Gott im Fruehling			PET
-----	Liebesbotschaft	H	E-G	GSC
-----	Verklaerung			PET
Schuetz	Eile mich, Gott, zu erretten			BAR

Italian Songs and Arias for
Opening Recitals

Lyric Soprano

Bassani	Posate, dormite (La Serenata)	H	EF-F	GSC
-----	Deh, più a me non v' ascondete	LH	EF-F	†
Bononcini				
Caccini	Amarilli, mia bella	ML	C-D	†
Caldara	Sebben crudele	HML	E-DS	†
Carissimi	Lamento della figlia de Jephte (Jepthe)			
Cavalli	Donzelle fuggite	HL	C-EF	†
Cesti	Ah, quanto è vero (Il Pomo d'Oro)	HL	F-F	DIT
-----	Che angoscia, che affanno (Il Pomo d'Oro)	HL	C-DF	DIT
D'Astorga	Qual mai fatale arcano			
Durante	Vergin, tutta amor	LM	C-EF	†

Falconieri	O bellissimi capelli	HL	B-D	†
-----	Villanella			
Freschi	Parte il pie			
Gluck	Che fiero momento			HEU
	(Orfeo ed Euridice)			
-----	O del mio dolce ardor	LH	D-FS	GSC
	(Paride ed Elena)			
-----	Spiagge amate			†
	(Paride ed Elena)			
Handel	Affani del pensier			†
	(Ottone)			
-----	Cara sposa	M	CS-D	†
	(Radamisto)			
-----	Care selve (Atalanta)	MH	FS-A	BOO
-----	Ch'io mai vi possa			†
	(Siroe)			
-----	Generoso chi sol			GSC
	(Scipione)			
-----	Ne men con l'ombre	H	E-A	CFI
	(Serse)			
-----	Rendi'l sereno al ciglio	LH	EF-F	†
	(Sosarme)			
-----	Se fedele vuoi ch'io ti			
	creda (Orlando)			
-----	Sei, mia gioja			CFI
	(Partenope)			
-----	Spietati, io vi giurai			BOO
	(Rodelinda)			
-----	V'adoro pupille			BOO
	(Julius Caesar)			
-----	Voi dolce aurette al cor			GSC
	(Tolomeo)			
Hasse	Nel mirar quel sasso amato			
Haydn	Del mio core			GSC
	(Orfeo ed Euridice)			
Jommelli	Chi vuol comprar la	H	B-G	GSC
	bella			
Lotti	Pur dicesti, o bocca	LMH	E-FS	GSC
	bella			
Marcello	O Signor chi sarà			
Mozart	A questo seno, deh vieni			BOO
-----	Ah spiegarti, oh Dio			
-----	Batti, batti, o bel Masetto	H	C-BF	GSC
	(Don Giovanni)			
-----	Bella mia fiamma addio			BOO
-----	Ch'io mi scordi di te			BOO
-----	Parto, parto	H		AMP
	(La Clemenza di Tito)			
	B flat clarinet and piano			

125

(Mozart)	Ridente la calma			BOS
-----	Vado, ma dove			
Paisiello	Chi vuol la zingarella	L	C-F	GSC
-----	Nel cor più non mi sento	HL	C-EF	†
Pergolesi	Se tu m'ami	LMH	C-G	GSC
-----	Stizzoso, mio stizzoso (La Serva Padrona)	H	C-AF	†
Porpora	Non più fra sassi			PET
Sarti	Lungi dal caro bene (Armide)	HL	G-D	GSC
Scarlatti, A.	All' acquisto di gloria (Tigrane)	H	C-G	GSC
-----	Già il sole dal Gange	LH	EF-F	GSC
-----	Già mai la lontananza			DUR
Sgambati	Separazione	LMH	FS-G	GSC
Stradella	Per pietà (Il Floridoro)	HM	D-F	DIT
-----	Pietà, Signore	HM	C-F	GSC
Traetta	Ombra cara, amorosa	HL	B-F	†
Vivaldi	Un certo no so che	HL	BF-EF	GSC

American Songs for Closing Recitals

Lyric Soprano

Bacon	The Colorado tree			
Barber	I hear an army	LH	D-AF	GSC
-----	Sure on this shining night	MH	D-G	GSC
Bernstein	La bonne cuisine	H	B-B	GSC
Branscombe	At the postern gate	MH	DF-AF	ASC
Cadman	Joy	MH	E-A	GSC
Carpenter	Light, my light	M	C-G	GSC
-----	Serenade	LH	CS-A	GSC
Charles	And so, goodbye	LH	EF-AF	GSC
-----	Let my song fill your heart	LH	EF-AF	GSC
-----	Night	MH	F-AF	GSC
-----	When I have sung my songs	HM	BF-EF	GSC
Clough-Leighter	My lover he comes on the skee	HM	D-F	BOS
Creston	Bird of the wilderness	MH	FS-A	GSC
Crist	Knock on the door	H	EF-AF	GSC
Dougherty	Beauty is not caused	M		AMP
-----	Everyone sang			
-----	Portrait	HM	BF-G	GSC
-----	Primavera	H	C-BF	GSC
-----	Song for autumn			

Duke	Evening			
-----	The puritan's ballad			
-----	XXth century	M		VLP
Giannini	Sing to my heart a song	H	D-B	ELV
Golde	Who knows?	HM	BF-F	GSC
Hageman	At the well	LH	EF-AF	GSC
-----	Is it you?			
-----	Miranda	HL		GAL
Horsman	The bird of the wilderness	LMH	DF-BF	GSC
Kahn	Spring's in the air	LH	D-A	GSC
Kernochan	We two together	H	EF-AF	GAL
La Forge	Cupid captive	H		GAL
-----	Hills	HL		RIC
-----	Song of the open	MH	EF-AF	DIT
Levitzki	Ah, thou beloved one	H	EF-AF	GSC
Malotte	A day is born			
Mana-Zucca	There's joy in my heart			CNG
McArthur	Night	H	F-AF	GSC
-----	Spring came	HL	D-F	GSC
Nordoff	Tell me, Thyrsis	H	E-G	AMP
Poldini	Dance of the dolls			CHM
Protheroe	Sing again			
Rasbach	April	LH	EF-G	GSC
Rogers	The last song	MLH	E-AF	GSC
-----	Time for making songs	HM	CS-F	DIT
Rorem	Alleluia			
Rummel	Ecstasy	LMH	GF-AF	GSC
Sacco	Rapunzel	MH	FS-BF	GSC
Saminsky	Queen Estherka's laugh	H	D-A	CFI
Sargent	Twentieth century	H	EF-GS	LEE
Schuman	Holiday song	M	C-F	GSC
Swanson	Joy	M	BF-EF	LEE
Ware	This day is mine	MH	EF-AF	BOS
Warren	Fulfilment	H	D-BF	GAL
-----	Heather	LH	FS-G	GSC
-----	We two	LH	E-A	GSC
-----	White horses of the sea	LH	F-G	GSC
Watts	Joy	HL	D-F	GSC
-----	Stresa	H	EF-BF	DIT
-----	With the tide	H	DF-A	GSC
Worth	Midsummer	LM	E-A	GSC

(See also Negro Spirituals and Folk Songs.)

127

Lyric Soprano

Aiken	Sonnet no. XVIII			
Bizet	Adieu de l'hotesse arabe	H	BF-G	†
Bliss	The buckle			CUR
-----	Three jolly gentlemen	H		†
Brahms	Juchhe!			†
Britten	Les illuminations	H		BOH
Caturia	Bito manue			
Cimara	Canto di primavera		D-G	FRL
Debussy	Chevaux de bois	H	C-G	†
-----	La Demoiselle Elue			DUR
Delius	Love's philosophy			†
Falla	Jota	LH		AMP
-----	Polo	HL		AMP
Gretchaninoff	My native land	L	C-EF	GSC
Grieg	By the brook			GSC
-----	En fuglevise			
Head	A piper	HL		BOO
Henschel	Morning-hymn	MH	DS-GS	†
Jensen	Fruehlingsnacht	L	D-E	GSC
Laparra	Le bonheur			
Lecuona	Desengano			
-----	Mi vida eres tu			MAR
Mortari	Il mago pistagna			
Mozart	Schon lacht der holde Fruehling			
Nin	El vito			ESC
-----	Polo			AMP
Obradors	Chiquitita la novia			
-----	Coplas de curro dulce			
-----	El vito			
Poulenc	Air vif	H	C-AF	ROU
Quilter	Blow, blow, thou winter wind	HL	C-E	BOO
-----	Love's philosophy	LMH	D-A	BOO
Rachmaninoff	Floods of spring	HL		DIT
Respighi	Pioggia			BON
Schubert	Aufloesung	LH	D-A	†
-----	Die Forelle	MLH	EF-GF	†
Schumann	Er ist's	HL	BF-EF	†
-----	Singet nicht in Trauertoenen			
Sibelius	Was it a dream			BRH
Strauss, J.	Blue Danube waltz			GSC
Strauss, R.	Lied der Frauen			†

128

Turina	Farruca	M	A-F	UME
-----	La giralda			
Warlock	Yarmouth Fair	HL	B-E	CFI
Wolf	Er ist's	H	D-G	†

American Atmospheric Songs

Lyric Soprano

Bacon	Four songs	H	DF-G	MUP
Barber	Rain has fallen	HM	D-E	GSC
-----	Sleep now	MH	EF-AF	GSC
Bone and Fenton	Tryst	MH	FS-G	CFI
Burleigh	Sometimes I feel like a motherless child	HML		RIC
Carpenter	When I bring to you colour'd toys	LM	CS-FS	GSC
Charles	When I have sung my songs	HM	BF-EF	GSC
Crist	Into a ship dreaming	LMH	EF-GS	CFI
Davis	Nancy Hanks	H	D-G	GAL
Dougherty	Lovliest of trees	HM	C-E	BOH
Duke	Bells in the rain	H	E-GS	CFI
-----	Central Park at dusk	M		BOO
-----	I can't be talkin' of love	H	CS-G	GSC
-----	Little elegy	H	FS-A	GSC
-----	The bird			GSC
Flood	The windows of Sainte Chapelle	H		RIC
Ganz	A memory	HM	B-D	GSC
-----	The angels are stooping	MH	GF-A	GSC
Griffes	Symphony in yellow	M	D-GF	GSC
-----	The dreamy lake	H	BS-GS	GSC
Kramer	Pleading	LH	D-GF	JFI
-----	Swans	HL		RIC
MacGimsey	Sweet little Jesus boy	ML	D-D	CFI
McArthur	Night	H	F-AF	GSC
McDonald	He is gone	H	DF-BF	ELV
Naginski	Look down, fair moon			
Niles	I wonder as I wander	HL	BF-D	GSC
Nordoff	Music I heard with you	H	DS-FS	AMP
Proctor	I light the blessed candles	H	DF-A	GSC
Sacco	The ragpicker	MH	C-AF	GSC
Tyson	Like barley bending	HL	C-EF	GSC
Warren	Wander shoes	LH	F-G	FLA
Watts	Wings of night	LH	CS-G	GSC

129

British Atmospheric Songs

Lyric Soprano

Anon	Have you seen but a white lily grow?	H	E-F	GSC
Bantock	A dream of spring	H	E-G	CHE
Bax	The white peace			CHE
Forsyth	The stranger	H	A-B	GRA
Gibbs	Silver		CS-FS	ROG
Handel	O sleep why dost thou leave me (Semele)	H	DS-GS	†
Hughes	Open the door softly	LMH	G-G	ENO
Quilter	Dream valley	H	EF-GF	ROG
Ronald	Drift down, drift down			BOO
Vaughan Williams	Silent noon			GSC

French Atmospheric Songs

Lyric Soprano

Bizet	Douce mer			GSC
Breville	Prières d'enfant	M	D-F	ROU
Chaminade	The silver ring	HM	BF-F	GSC
Chausson	Les papillons	M	C-F	GSC
Debussy	C'est l'extase	LH	CS-A	†
-----	Les cloches	LH	E-GS	†
-----	Nuits d'etoiles	LH	E-A	MAR
Duparc	Soupir	HL	CS-F	BOS
Fauré	En sourdine	HL	C-EF	†
Ferrari	Le miroir	M	E-F	GSC
Gounod	Sérénade	LMH	D-A	GSC
Hahn	A Chloris	H	DS-FS	HEU
-----	L'heure exquise	M	DF-F	†
-----	Paysage	MH	EF-G	HEU
Leguerney	Genièvres hérissés	H	D-G	ROU
-----	Je vous envoie	H	C-A	ROU
Paladilhe	Psyché	HM	BF-F	GSC
Poulenc	Fleurs	M	DF-F	ROU
Ravel	D'Anne jouant de l'espinette	H	CS-GS	GSC
-----	Le réveil de la mariée	MH	G-F	DUR
-----	Sur l'herbe	MH	C-G	DUR
Roussel	Le jardin mouillé	M	C-FS	ROU
Staub	L'heure silencieuse	H	EF-G	DUR
Szulc	Claire de lune	H	E-G	AXE

German Atmospheric Songs

Lyric Soprano

Haydn	She never told her love	HL	B-D	DIT
Hindemith	The moon	M	DS-EF	AMP
Mahler	Ich ging mit Lust	HL		INT
Marx	Marienlied	MH	EF-AF	AMP
Schubert	An die Nachtigall	H	C-G	†
-----	Nachtviolen			PET
Schumann	Dein Angesicht	HL	B-EF	†
-----	Der Nussbaum	LMH	D-FS	†
Strauss	Die Nacht	HL		†
-----	Traum durch die Daemmerung	HML	BF-EF	†
Wolf	In dem Schatten meiner Locken	M	C-EF	†
-----	Verborgenheit	HL	B-E	†

Miscellaneous Atmospheric Songs

Lyric Soprano

Alnaes	Lykken mellem to mennesker	M	B-FS	HAN
Cui	The statue at Czarskoe-Selo	HM	DF-EF	†
Dvořák	The lark			
Grieg	Snegl, Snegl	M	B-F	HAN
-----	Udvandreren	M	EF-F	HAN
Kjerulf	Synnove's song	M	C-F	GSC
Lie	Soft-footed snow	HM		DIT
Mussorgsky	Tiny star where art thou?	LH	DF-F	BOS
Rachmaninoff	Lilacs	LH	EF-G	†
-----	Morning	ML	B-DS	GSC
Sinding	Sylvelin	M	E-E	GSC

American Dramatic Songs

Lyric Soprano

Barber	I hear an army	LH	D-AF	GSC
Beach	Ah, love but a day			ASC
-----	The year's at the spring	MH	AF-AF	ASC
Bloch	Psalm 114 (Snatched away by Jahveh)	H	A-A	GSC

131

(Bloch)	Psalm 137 (By the waters of Babel)	H	F-AS	GSC
Burleigh	By the pool at the third roses	H		RIC
Campbell-Tipton	A spirit flower	LHM	B-G	GSC
Carpenter	I am like a remnant of a cloud of autumn	L	BF-F	GSC
-----	Light, my light	M	C-G	GSC
Crist	The dark king's daughter			JCH
Diamond	David weeps for Absolom	M	D-A	MUP
Dougherty	Primavera	H	C-BF	GSC
Duke	Capri			
-----	Evening			
-----	Spray	H	CS-A	BOH
Geehl	For you alone			SHU
Giannini	Far above the purple hills	LH	CS-A	RIC
-----	Sing to my heart a song	H	D-B	ELV
Griffes	Evening song	H	DS-GS	GSC
-----	The lament of Ian the proud	MH	DS-AS	GSC
-----	The rose of the night	H	CS-A	GSC
-----	Thy dark eyes to mine	H	EF-AF	GSC
-----	Time was, when I in anguish lay	H	E-GS	GSC
-----	Waikiki	H	DS-GS	GSC
Hageman	Do not go, my love	HL	B-EF	GSC
-----	Music I heard with you	MH	E-A	GAL
Horsman	The bird of the wilderness	LMH	DF-BF	GSC
Kernochan	We two together	H	EF-AF	GAL
La Forge	Song of the open	MH	EF-AF	DIT
MacDowell	The sea	HL	D-D	BRH
Nordoff	Tell me, Thyrsis	H	E-G	AMP
Protheroe	Ah, love but a day	LMH	F-AF	GAM
Rogers	The last song	MLH	E-AF	GSC
-----	Time for making songs	HM	CS-F	DIT
Schuman	Holiday song	M	C-F	GSC
Vene	Age and youth	H	E-A	RIC
Ware·	This day is mine	MH	EF-AF	BOS
Warren	Fulfilment	H	D-BF	GAL
-----	We two	LH	E-A	GSC
-----	White horses of the sea	LH	F-G	GSC
Worth	Midsummer	LM	E-A	GSC

British Dramatic Songs

Lyric Soprano

Bainton	The nightingale near the house			CUR
Besley	Listening	H	E-AF	CUR
Bridge	O that it were so	LMH	D-G	CHA
Elgar	Be not extreme, O Lord (Light of Life)			NOV
Handel	Let the bright seraphim (Samson) Trumpet	H	E-A	†
Henschel	Morning-hymn	MH	DS-GS	†
Quilter	Blow, blow, thou winter wind	HL	C-E	BOO
Ronald	Down in the forest	HML	C-D	ENO
-----	Prelude	HML	B-D	ENO

French Dramatic Songs and Arias

Lyric Soprano

Berlioz	Le spectre de la rose			CST
-----	Les nuits d'été			AUG
Bizet	Je dis que rien ne m'épouvante (Carmen)	LH	D-B	†
Chausson	Chanson perpétuelle	H	CS-GS	ROU
Debussy	Air de Lia (L'Enfant Prodigue)	H	E-A	DUR
-----	Chevaux de bois	H	C-G	†
-----	Colloque sentimental			DUR
-----	De fleurs	H	C-AF	†
-----	Noël des enfants qui n'ont plus de maisons			DUR
Duparc	Phidylé	MH	EF-AF	BOS
Fauré	Poème d'un jour			HAM
Fourdrain	Chanson norvégienne	H	E-G	RIC
Gluck	L' ai-je bien entendu? (Iphigenie en Aulide)			†
-----	Non! ce n'est point (Alceste)	H	E-G	†
Gounod	Plus grand, dans son obscurité (La Reine de Saba)	MH	CS-B	†
Hahn	Offrande	M	D-D	†
Halévy	Il va venir (La Juive)	H	D-CF	†
Honegger	Les cloches			SEN

(Honegger)	O had I wings like a dove (King David)			CHE
Massenet	Charmes des jours passés (Hérodiade)			HEU
-----	Dis-moi que je suis belle (Thaïs)	H	D-B	HEU
-----	Il est doux, il est bon (Hérodiade)	MH	EF-BF	GSC
-----	L'amour est une vertu rare (Thaïs)			HEU
Meyerbeer	Roberto, o tu che adoro (Robert le Diable)	H	C-C	DEI
Poldowski	L'heure exquise	LMH	DF-AF	CHE
Severac	Chanson pour le petit cheval			ROU

German Dramatic Songs and Arias

Lyric Soprano

Franz	Im Herbst	HM	A-F	†
Mahler	Das Irdische Leben	HL	A-F	INT
Marx	Hat dich die Liebe beruehrt	MH	EF-BF	AMP
-----	Selige Nacht	M	DF-GF	AMP
Mendelssohn	Hear ye, Israel (Elijah)	H	E-A	†
Mozart	Martern aller Arten (Abduction from Seraglio)	H	B-D	†
Schubert	Die junge Nonne	LH	C-GF	†
-----	Erstarrung	HL	D-F	†
-----	Fruehlingstraum	HL	C-D	†
-----	Ganymed	LH	EF-G	†
Strauss, R.	Kling			†
Wolf	Lebe wohl	HL	BF-F	†
-----	Liebe mir in Busen zuendet	M	E-F	†
-----	Nachtzauber	HL	B-E	†

Italian Dramatic Songs and Arias

Lyric Soprano

Boito	Morte di Margherita (L' altra notte) (Mefistofele)	H	D-B	GSC
Carissimi	Piangete, ohime			RIC

Catalani	Ebben? Ne andrò lontana (La Wally)	H	E-B	RIC
Cilea	Io son' l' umile ancella (Adriana Lecouvreur)	H		AMP
-----	Poveri fiori (Adriana Lecouvreur)			SON
Cimara	Canto di primavera		D-G	FRL
Durante	Vergin, tutta amor	LM	C-EF	†
Faccio	Sortita d'Ofelia (Amleto)			GSC
Giordano	La mamma morta (Andrea Chenier)	H	CS-B	AMP
Mascagni	Son pochi fiori (L' Amico Fritz)			GSC
Mozart	Or sai, chi l' onore (Don Giovanni)			†
Pergolesi	Confusa, smarrita			GSC
Puccini	Ancora un passo (Madama Butterfly)			RIC
-----	In quelle trine morbide (Manon Lescaut)	H	DF-BF	RIC
-----	Musetta's waltz (La Boheme)	H	EF-BF	RIC
-----	Solo perduta abbandonata (Manon Lescaut)			RIC
-----	Tu, che di gel sei cinta (Turandot)			RIC
-----	Un bel di vedremo (Madama Butterfly)	H	DF-BF	RIC
-----	Vissi d' arte (Tosca)	MH	EF-BF	RIC
Respighi	Nebbie			†
Traetta	Ombra cara, amorosa	HL	B-F	†
Verdi	Ecco l' orrido campo (Un Ballo in Maschera)	H	B-C	RIC

Miscellaneous Dramatic Songs

Lyric Soprano

Alvarez	La partida	HL	DS-E	GSC
Dvořák	Hear my prayer, O Lord			AMP
Granados	La maja dolorosa	M		INT
Gretchaninoff	Over the steppe	LM	C-G	GSC
-----	The skylark			DIT
-----	Wounded birch	HL	B-EF	†
Grieg	A dream			†
-----	In the boat	LM	D-ES	†
-----	Prinsessen	HL	B-E	†

135

Mussorgsky	The orphan girl			GSC
Rachmaninoff	Floods of spring	HL		DIT
-----	God took away from me			GSC
-----	O thou billowy harvest field	HL	CS-E	GSC
-----	Sorrow in spring	H	D-BF	DIT
-----	The soldier's bride			†
-----	To the children	MH	F-G	DIT
Sibelius	Black roses	M	A-ES	AMP
-----	Was it a dream			BRH
Stravinsky	Song of the dew			JUR
-----	The cloister (La novice)			DIT
Tchaikovsky	All for you			
-----	Complaint of the bride			
-----	None but the lonely heart	HLM	C-F	DIT
-----	Why	HL		†
Turina	Madrigal	H	D-BF	UME
-----	Rima	H	A-A	AMP

American Humorous Songs

Lyric Soprano

Bergsma	Six songs	H	E-BF	CFI
Bernstein	I hate music	H	C-A	WIT
-----	I just found out today			
-----	La bonne cuisine	H	B-B	GSC
-----	Rabbit at top speed			GSC
Carpenter	If	M	D-E	GSC
Crist	Chinese mother goose rhymes	H	C-G	CFI
Davis	Deaf old woman			GAL
Dougherty	Love in the dictionary	M	C-G	GSC
-----	Weathers			
Duke	A piper	H	CS-B	GSC
-----	I can't be talkin' of love	H	CS-G	GSC
Griselle and Young	The cuckoo clock	LH	EF-G	GSC
Gruenberg	Animals and insects	H	A-A	UNI
Hadley	My shadow			ASC
Hindemith	The whistling thief	M	E-F	AMP
Josten	Cupid's counsel	H	EF-AF	GSC
Kountz	The little French clock	LH	D-G	GAL
MacDowell	A maid sings light	H	F-G	ASC
Mopper	The lemon-colored dodo	H	F-BF	BOS
Nordoff	Serenade	H	CS-FS	AMP
-----	There shall be more joy	M	CS-FS	AMP

Powell	The deaf woman's courtship	M		JFI
Rich	American lullaby	LH	C-F	GSC
Sacco	Mexican serenade	HL	D-EF	BOS
Sandoval	Theme and 3 variations on "Long ago"	H	CS-B	GSC
Schuman	Holiday song	M	C-F	GSC
Slonimsky	Gravestones at Hancock, New Hampshire	H	D-G	AXE
Spross	Will o' the wisp			JCH
Wolf	Jack in the box			
-----	Weather forecast	H	EF-GS	GSC

British Humorous Songs

Lyric Soprano

Bax	Oh dear, what can the matter be?	M	D-EF	CHE
Bliss	The buckle			CUR
-----	Three jolly gentlemen	H		†
Britten	Oliver Cromwell			BOH
Clarke	Shy one	HL	BF-G	BOH
Gibbs	Five eyes	HL	D-D	BOS
Jacob	Laughing song	H	D-G	OXF
Lehmann	The cuckoo	HH	D-B	BOH
Novello	The little damozel	LHM	C-G	BOO

French Humorous Songs

Lyric Soprano

Chabrier	Villanelle des petits canards	HML	B-E	†
Dalcroze	Le coeur de ma mie	HML		†
Debussy	Voici que le printemps	LH	CS-G	BOS
Monsigny	Il regardait mon bouquet (Le Roi et le Fermier)	H	D-G	GSC
Pierné	Ils etaient trois petits chats blancs			MAR
Ravel	Sur l' herbe	MH	C-G	DUR
Rosenthal	Le marabout			ESC
Satie	Le chapelier			ROU

German Humorous Songs and Arias

Lyric Soprano

Bach, J. S.	Patron, das macht der Wind (Phoebus and Pan)	M	C-G	GSC
Blech	Heimkehr vom Feste			UNI
Brahms	Vergebliches Staendchen	LHM	E-FS	†
Loewe	Der Zahn			SC
-----	Des glockenthuermers Tochterlein	H	CS-A	SC
Mahler	Rheinlegendchen	M	B-FS	†
-----	Wer hat dies Liedlein erdacht?	HL	BF-E	INT
Marx	Der bescheidene Schaefer			UNI
Mozart	Durch Zaertlichkeit (Abduction from Seraglio)			†
-----	Warnung	HM	C-D	
Nicolai	Now to my aid fun wit and humor (The Merry Wives)			
Reger	Waldeinsamkeit	HML	A-D	BOS
Schubert	Die Maenner sind mechant			PET
-----	Heidenroeslein			
Strauss, J.	Adele's laughing song (Die Fledermaus)	H	D-B	GSC
-----	Ein Maedchen hat es gar nicht gut (The Gypsy Baron)			CRZ
Wolf	Abschied			†
-----	Der Knabe und das Immlein	L	CS-A	†
-----	Elfenlied	HL	D-F	†
-----	Ich hab' in Penna	LH		†
-----	Nimmersatte Liebe	LH	CF-AF	†
-----	Storchenbotschaft			†
-----	Tretet ein, hoher Krieger	HL	B-F	†

Italian Humorous Songs and Arias

Lyric Soprano

Mozart	Venite inginocchiatevi (Le Nozze di Figaro)	H	D-G	†
Paisiello	Chi vuol la zingarella	L	C-F	GSC
Pergolesi	A Serpina penserete (La Serva Padrona)	HLM	D-F	†
-----	Stizzoso, mio stizzoso (La Serva Padrona)	H	C-AF	†

Rontani	Or ch' io non segno più	HL	CS-E	DIT

American Folk Songs (Arr.)

Lyric Soprano

Bacon	Careless love			
Davis	Deaf old woman			GAL
Endicott	He stole my tender heart away			BRO
Hughes	Birds' courting song			GSC
Johnson	His name so sweet	H	D-D	CFI
Niles	Down in the valley			GSC
-----	Go 'way from my window	MH	C-G	GSC
-----	I wonder as I wander	HL	BF-D	GSC
-----	If I had a ribbon bow			GSC
-----	The blue madonna	H		GSC
Powell	The deaf woman's courtship	M		JFI
-----	The rich old woman	M		JFI
Siegmeister	He's gone away			
Sowerby	He's gone away			
Taylor	Twenty, eighteen	HM	D-E	JFI
Willan	The little red lark			BOS

British Folk Songs (Arr.)

Lyric Soprano

Bax	Oh dear, what can the matter be?	M	D-EF	CHE
Benjamin	Jan (Creole melody)	M		BOO
-----	Linstead market	M		BOO
Britten	La belle est au jardin d'amour			BOH
-----	Le roi s'en va-t-en chasse			BOH
-----	O can ye sew cushions?			BOH
-----	The ash grove			BOH
-----	The Sally gardens			BOH
Gatty	Bendemeer's stream	LMH		BOO
Grainger	The sprig of thyme	LH	E-FS	GSC
Gurney	Down by the Salley gardens			OXF
Hook	Mary of Allendale			BOO
Hopekirk	Coming through the rye			DIT
-----	Flow gently, sweet Afton			DIT
-----	Loch Lomond			DIT
Hughes	Hey diddle diddle			CRA

(Hughes)	I have a bonnet trimmed with blue			BOO
-----	I know my love			BOO
-----	I know where I'm going			BOO
-----	I will walk with my love			BOO
-----	Open the door softly	LMH	G-G	ENO
-----	The leprehaun			
-----	The little boats			BOO
-----	The next market day			BOO
Kennedy- Fraser	A fairy's love song			BOO
-----	An Eriskay love lilt			BOO
-----	Land of heart's desire			BOO
-----	Isle of my heart			BOO
Page	The meeting of the waters			DIT
Peel	The early morning			C HA
Vaughn Williams	And all in the morning	L	D-E	GAL
-----	Robin Hood and the pedlar	M	D-E	OXF
-----	Rolling in the dew			OXF
Warlock	Yarmouth Fair	HL	B-E	CFI
Welsh	The ash grove			
Wilson	Come let's be merry			BOO

Miscellaneous Folk Songs (Arr.)

Lyric Soprano

Bartok	Altal mennék én a Tiszán			BOH
-----	Aszszonyok, Aszszonyok			BOH
-----	Elindultam szép hazámbul			BOH
-----	Feketeföd			BOH
-----	Istenem, Istenem			BOH
-----	Nem meszsze van ide kis Margitta			BOH
-----	Töltek a nagy erdö útját			BOH
Brahms	Da unten in Thale			†
-----	In stiller Nacht			†
-----	Mein Maedel hat einen Rosenmund	M	F-F	†
Dvořák	Gypsy songs	LH	D-A	AMP
Falla	Asturiana	HL		AMP
-----	El paño moruno	HL		AMP
-----	Jota	LH		AMP
-----	Nana	HL		AMP
-----	Polo	HL		AMP
-----	Seguidilla murciana	HL		AMP
-----	Siete canciones	HL		AMP

140

Ferrari	Il etait un bergere			GSC
-----	Le jardin d'amour	LM	EF-F	GSC
McFeeters	Gentle Mary	H	EF-AF	GSC
Obradors	Chiquitita la novia			
Ravel	Chanson italienne			DUR
-----	Cinq mélodies populaires grecques			CUR
-----	Là-bas vers l'église	MH	GS-E	DUR
-----	Le réveil de la mariée	MH	G-F	DUR
-----	Quel galant!	M	D-F	DUR
-----	Tout gai	MH	EF-F	DUR
Sadero	Stornello pugliese	M	F-F	GSC
Serradell	La golondrina	H	C-A	GSC
Tavares	Bia-ta-ta			
Tiersot	Noël provençal			
-----	Tambourin			
Weckerlin	Aminte	M	C-D	†
-----	Chantons les amours de Jean	H	D-G	GSC
-----	L'amour s'envole	H	E-G	GSC
-----	Maman, dites-moi	M	E-FS	BOS
-----	Mignonette			

Negro Spirituals

Lyric Soprano

Boatner	Oh, what a beautiful city!	HL	D-E	GSC
-----	On mah journey	LH	EF-EF	RIC
Burleigh	De gospel train	HL		RIC
-----	Joshua fit de battle ob Jericho	LH	DS-E	RIC
-----	Little child of Mary	HL		RIC
-----	Little David play on yo harp	HL		RIC
-----	Swing low, sweet chariot	HL		RIC
-----	Weepin' Mary	HL		RIC
-----	Were you there?	HML		RIC
Dett	A man goin' roun'			
-----	I couldn't hear nobody pray			
-----	In dat great gittin' up morning			
-----	Nobody knows de trouble I've seen			
-----	Ride on Jesus	H		JFI
-----	Rise up shepherd an' foller			
-----	Sit down servant			GSC

(Dell)	Were you there?			
Johnson	City called Heaven			ROB
-----	Dere's no hidin' place down dere			
-----	Ride on, King Jesus			CFI
Kerby-Forrest	He's got the whole world in His hands	M	G-E	MLS
MacGimsey	Sweet little Jesus boy	ML	D-D	CFI
-----	Workin' workin'			
Price	My soul's been anchored in the Lord			GAM
Ryder	Let us break bread together	LH	D-G	JFI
Wolff	Gimme dat ole time religion			
Work	Wasn't that a mighty day?			

American Songs Employing Agility

Lyric Soprano

Bacon	Four songs	H	DF-G	MUP
Bernstein	La bonne cuisine	H	B-B	GSC
Buzzi-Peccia	Under the greenwood tree	LMH	EF-A	DIT
Charles	Let my song fill your heart	LH	EF-AF	GSC
Clough-Leighter	My lover he comes on the skee	HM	D-F	BOS
Crist	O come hither	HM	B-GS	CFI
Curran	Ho! Mr. Piper	LH	D-G	GSC
Hageman	Miranda	HL		GAL
Hopkinson	O'er the hills	LH	C-G	†
LaForge	Come unto these yellow sands	H	FS-B	GSC
Menotti	Lucy's arietta (The Telephone)			GSC
Nevin	One spring morning	MH	DS-F	BOS
Nordoff	There shall be more joy	M	CS-FS	AMP
Parker	The lark now leaves her watery nest	LH	D-BF	JCH
Speaks	In may time	HL	D-E	JCH

142

British songs and Arias
Employing Agility

Lyric Soprano

Arne, M.	The lass with the delicate air	MH	D-G	†
Arne, T.	Where by bee sucks	HM		†
Bax	Shieling song	H	CS-A	CHE
Besley	Listening	H	E-AF	CUR
Bishop	Lo! here the gentle lark	H		†
-----	Love has eyes	M		†
-----	Pretty mocking bird Flute	H		†
-----	Should he upbraid	H		†
Bliss	Three jolly gentlemen	H		†
Carey	A pastoral			GSC
Finzi	Let us garlands bring (Shakesperian songs)	M		BOO
German	Charming Chloe	HML		NOV
-----	Waltz song (Tom Jones)	H	B-B	CHA
Green	My lips shall speak the praise	M	E-F	OXF
Handel	From mighty Kings (Judas Maccabaeus)	H	D-A	†
-----	Hallelujah (Esther)	H	E-B	CFI
-----	Let the bright seraphim (Samson) Trumpet	H	E-A	†
-----	Oh! had I Jubal's lyre (Joshua)	H	E-FS	†
-----	Rejoice greatly (The Messiah)	H	E-A	†
-----	So shall the lute and harp awake (Judas Maccabaeus)			†
Hook	Softly waft, ye southern breezes			GSC
Linley	O, bid your faithful Ariel fly			BOO
Morley	It was a lover and his lass	HM		DIT
Purcell	Come unto these yellow sands			AUG
-----	From rosey bow'rs (Don Quixote)			AUG
-----	Hark! the echoing air (The Fairy Queen)			BAF
-----	Nymphs and shepherds (The Libertine)	HM	C-F	†
-----	Strike the viol			BAF

143

Quilter	Love's philosophy	LMH	D-A	BOO
Scott	Blackbird's song			ELK
Wilson	Come let's be merry			BOO

French Songs and Arias Employing Agility

Lyric Soprano

Bizet	Ouvre ton coeur	MH	DS-GS	†
Campra	Charmant papillon	MH	D-G	GSC
	(Les Fêtes Venitiennes)			
Chaminade	L'été	MH	E-A	†
Chausson	Les papillons	M	C-F	GSC
Dalayrac	Jeune fillette	HL	GS-E	DIT
Debussy	Fêtes galantes	LH	CS-A	†
Delibes	Les filles de Cadix	HM	A-A	†
-----	Passepied	LH	DS-CS	GSC
Dupont	Chanson des noisettes			HEU
Falla	Polo	HL		AMP
Fauré	Mandoline	HL	F-E	†
Ferrari	Le jardin d'amour	LM	EF-F	GSC
Georges	La pluie	HL		INT
Gounod	Air des bijoux (Faust)	H	B-B	†
-----	Je veux vivre	H	F-C	†
	(Roméo et Juliette)			
-----	Mon coeur ne peut changer!			GSC
	(Mireille)			
Grétry	Je ne le dis qu'à vous			LEM
	(La Fausse Magie)			
-----	La fauvette avec ses petits			LEM
	(Zémire et Azor)			
Massé	Chanson du Tigre			
	(Paul et Virginie)			
Poulenc	Air vif	H	C-AF	ROU
-----	Airs chantés	H	C-AF	ROU
Saint-Saëns	Guitares et mandolines			DUR
Thomas	Je connais un pauvre	H	C-B	†
	enfant (Mignon)			
Vidal	Ariette	LH	F-A	GSC
Weckerlin	L'amour s'envole	H	E-G	GSC

German Songs and Arias Employing Agility

Lyric Soprano

Bach, J. S.	Auch mit gedaempften,			PET

144

(Bach)	schwachen Stimmen (Cantata 36) Violin			
-----	Come visit ye glowing	H		
-----	Hoert, ihr Augen auf zu weinen (Cantata 98) Oboe			PET
-----	Hoert, ihr Voelker (Cantata 76) Violin			BRO
-----	I follow thee (St. John Passion)			†
-----	Jauchzet Gott in allen Landen (Cantata 51)			BRO
-----	Mein glaeubiges Herze (Cantata 68)	HML		†
-----	Mein Seelenschatz (Cantata 18)			BRO
-----	Wie zittern und wanken (Cantata 105)			BRO
Beethoven	Mailied			RIC
Brahms	Botschaft	HL	D-F	†
-----	Das Maedchen spricht	H	E-FS	†
-----	O liebliche Wangen	MLH	E-G	†
Eckert	Swiss echo song	H	A-B	GSC
Haydn	My mother bids me bind my hair	M	E-E	†
-----	The mermaid's song	M	C-F	PRE
Jensen	Am Ufer des Flusses des Manzanares	H	D-FS	GSC
Loewe	Des Glockenthuermers Tochterlein	H	CS-A	SC
-----	Niemand hat's gesehen	LM	DS-FS	†
Mahler	Rheinlegendchen	M	B-FS	†
-----	Wer hat dies Liedlein erdacht?	HL	BF-E	INT
Marx	Und gestern hat er mir Rosen gebracht	H	E-A	AMP
Mendelssohn	Fruehlingslied	H	DS-GS	†
Mozart	Ach, ich liebte (Abduction from Seraglio)			†
-----	Martern aller Arten (Abduction from Seraglio)	H	B-D	†
Nicolai	Now to my aid fun wit and humor (The Merry Wives)			
Schubert	Ballade			
-----	Das Wandern	HLM	E-E	†
-----	Der Hirt auf dem Felsen Clarinet or violoncello	H	BF-B	†
-----	Der Wachtelschlag	H	DS-FS	PET
-----	Mein!	HL		†
-----	Ungeduld	HML		†

145

Schumann	Auftraege	HL	C-E	†
-----	Fruehlingsnacht	L	CS-E	†
Strauss, J.	Adele's laughing song	H	D-B	GSC
	(Die Fledermaus)			
-----	Blue Danube waltz			GSC
-----	Tales from the Vienna	H	EF-C	GSC
	forest			
-----	Voci di primavera	LMH	EF-C	GSC
Weber	Truebe Augen			GSC
	(Der Freischuetz)			
Wolf	Die Zigeunerin			†

Italian Songs and Arias
Employing Agility

Lyric Soprano

Abbatini	Quanto è bello il mio diletto			PET
Arditi	Il bacio	H	CS-B	†
Ariosti	Vuoi, che parta			PET
	(Lucio Vero)			
Bellini	Ah! non credea mirarti			GSC
	(La Sonnambula)			
-----	Casta diva (Norma)	H	F-C	†
Bononcini	L'esperto (Nocchiero)	HL	B-E	†
Cimara	Canto di primavera		D-G	FRL
Donaudy	Ah mai non cessate			RIC
-----	Spirate pur, spirate			RIC
Donizetti	O luce di quest' anima	H	C-E	GSC
	(Linda di Chamounix)			
-----	Prendi, prendi per mei			BRO
	sei libero			
	(L'Elisir d'Amore)			
-----	Quel guardo (Don Pasquale)			BRO
Gluck	Ah ritorna			PET
	(Il Trionfo di Clelia)			
Handel	Amor commanda	H		†
	(Floridante)			
-----	Ch'io mai vi possa (Siroe)			†
-----	Dira che amor per me	H	F-A	CFI
	(Serse)			
-----	Lusinghe più care	H	D-G	GSC
	(Alessandro)			
-----	Mio caro bene (Rodelinda)			OXF
-----	Qual farfalletta (Partenope)	H	E-A	†
-----	Riportai gloriosa palma			BOO
	(Atalanta)			

146

(Handel)	Sei, mia gioja (Partenope)			CFI
-----	Spietati, io vi giurai (Rodelinda)			BOO
Leoncavallo	Ballatella! (I Pagliacci)	H	CS-AS	†
Lotti	Pur dicesti, o bocca bella	LMH	E-FS	GSC
Mozart	Batti, batti, o bel Masetto (Don Giovanni)	H	C-BF	†
-----	Come scoglio (Così Fan Tutte)			†
-----	Dove sono Le Nozze di Figaro	H	D-A	†
-----	Mi tradi quell' alma ingrata Don Giovanni			†
-----	Misera, dove son			BOO
Paradies	Quel ruscelletto	L	BF-F	CFI
Pergolesi	A Serpina penserete (La Serva Padrona)	HLM	D-F	†
Porpora	Non più fra sassi			PET
Puccini	Ancora un passo (Madama Butterfly)			RIC
Rossini	La danza	MH	E-A	†
-----	La pastorella delle Alpi	H	E-C	CFI
-----	Una voce poco fa (Il Barbiere di Siviglia)	HM	GS-E	GSC
Scarlatti, A.	All acquisto di gloria (Tigrane)	H	C-G	GSC
-----	Già il sole dal Gange	LH	EF-F	GSC
-----	Rugiadose odorose (Il Pirro e Demetrio)	HL	D-E	DIT
-----	Se Florindo è fedele	LM	EF-EF	GSC
Scarlatti, D.	Consolati e spara amante	L	BF-E	GSC
-----	Qual farfalletta			
Sibella	O bimba bimbetta	LMH	D-G	GSC
Stradella	Ragion sempre addita	H	E-G	†
Verdi	Ah fors' è lui (La Traviata)	H	C-DF	†
-----	Ernani involami (Ernani)	H	AF-BF	GSC
-----	Tacea la notte placida (Il Trovatore)	H	D-DF	†
-----	Volta la terrea (Un Ballo in Maschera)	H	D-BF	GSC
Vivaldi	Un certo no so che	HL	BF-EF	†

Miscellaneous Songs and Arias
Employing Agility

Lyric Soprano

Alvarez	La partida	HL	DS-E	GSC
Chopin	My delight	HL		
-----	The maiden's wish	LM	CS-E	GSC
Falla	Nana	HL		AMP
-----	Seguidilla murciana	HL		AMP
Glazounoff	La primavera d'or	H	D-BF	GSC
Granados	El majo discreto	H		INT
Grieg	Solvejg's song	MH	E-G	†
Mignone	Variations for soprano on the popular song Luar do sertao			
Mozart	Et incarnatus est (C Minor Mass)			PET
Mussorgsky	Tiny star where art thou?	LH	DF-F	BOS
Rimsky-Korsakov	Hymn to the sun (Le Coq d'Or)	H	FS-B	GSC

American Songs Employing
Crescendo and Diminuendo

Lyric Soprano

Bacon	Is there such a thing as day?	M	DS-FS	AMP
Barber	Rain has fallen	HM	D-E	GSC
-----	Sleep now	MH	EF-AF	GSC
-----	The daisies	M	C-F	GSC
Beach	Ah, love but a day			ASC
-----	Fairy lullaby			ASC
Cadman	From the land of the sky-blue water			WHI
Campbell-Tipton	A spirit flower	LHM	B-G	GSC
Carpenter	The sleep that flits on baby's eyes	M	B-FS	GSC
-----	When I bring to you colour'd toys	LM	CS-FS	GSC
Duke	Bells in the rain	H	E-GS	CFI
Elwell	In the mountains	M	DF-F	BMI
Engel	Sea shell	M	EF-EF	GSC
Fairchild	A memory			BOS

Hopkinson	Beneath a weeping willow's shade	H	D-G	†
-----	My days have been so wondrous free	LH	EF-G	†
La Forge	Hills	HL		RIC
Lubin	The piper	H	C-A	GSC
Manning	White clouds			DIT
Naginski	The pasture	M	BF-EF	GSC
-----	Under the harvest moon	M	D-E	GSC
Niles	I wonder as I wander	HL	BF-D	GSC
Nordoff	Fair Annette's Song			AMP
-----	Serenade	H	CS-FS	AMP
Rogers	At parting	LH	CS-FS	GSC
Thompson	Velvet shoes	M	C-E	ECS
Watts	Wings of night	LH	CS-G	GSC

British Songs and Arias Employing Crescendo and Diminuendo

Lyric Soprano

Balfe	I dream't I dwelt in marble halls (The Bohemian Girl)			†
Bantock	A dream of spring	H	E-G	CHE
Bax	Cradle song			CHA
Benjamin	The wasp			CUR
Bliss	Lovelocks			GOT
Clarke	Shy one	HL	BF-G	BOH
Gibbs	To one who passed whistling through the night	H	F-G	CUR
Handel	Angels ever bright and fair (Theodora)	H	E-F	†
-----	Ask if yon damask rose (Susanna)			†
-----	As when the dove (Acis and Galatea)	H	D-G	†
-----	Let me wander not unseen (L'Allegro)	M	D-G	†
-----	O sleep why dost thou leave me (Semele)	H	DS-GS	†
-----	Sweet bird Flute (L'Allegro)			NOV
-----	What's sweeter than a new-blown rose (Joseph)	H	EF-AF	†
Horn	Cherry ripe	M	D-G	†
-----	I've been roaming	L	B-E	†

149

Ireland	Bed in summer			CUR
Purcell	I attempt from Love's sickness to fly (The Indian Queen)	MH	CS-E	†
Quilter	Dream Valley	H	EF-GF	ROG
-----	To daisies			BOO
Shaw	Song of the Palanquin bearers	LH	E-F	CUR

French Songs and Arias Employing
Crescendo and Diminuendo

Lyric Soprano

Auber	Quel Bonheur (Fra Diavolo)			BOO
Auric	Printemps			DUR
Bachelet	Chère nuit	H	DF-BF	GSC
Berlioz	Villanelle	H	E-FS	†
Bizet	Après l'hiver			†
-----	Vielle chanson	H	EF-A	GSC
Chaminade	The silver ring	HM	BF-F	GSC
Charpentier	Depuis le jour (Louise)	MH	D-B	†
Dalayrac	D'un époux chéri			DUR
Dalcroze	Le coeur de ma mie	HML		†
-----	L'oiseau bleu			CFI
David	Charmant oiseau (La Perle du Brésil)	M	D-E	†
Debussy	Air de Lia (L'Enfant Prodigue)	H	E-A	DUR
-----	C'est l'extase	LH	CS-A	†
-----	Crois mon conseil, chere Climène			DUR
-----	En sourdine	M	C-FS	†
-----	Green	H	C-AF	†
-----	La flûte de Pan		B-B	†
-----	Le tombeau des naïades			JOB
-----	Les angélus			HAM
-----	Les cloches	LH	E-GS	†
-----	Les ingénus			DUR
-----	Voici que le printemps	LH	CS-G	BOS
Duparc	Chanson triste	MH	FS-AF	BOS
-----	L'invitation au voyage	HM	E-F	†
-----	Phidylé	MH	EF-AF	BOS
Fauré	Adieu	MH	F-F	†
-----	Au bord de l'eau	HL	C-F	†
-----	Clair de lune	MH	C-G	†

150

(Fauré)	Le secret	LH	F-G	†
-----	Les roses d'Ispahan	HM	D-FS	†
-----	Lydia	MH	G-G	†
-----	Nell	LH	FS-AF	†
-----	Spleen	H	E-FS	MAR
-----	Sylvie	HL	E-F	†
Gounod	Ah, si je redevenais belle (Philémon et Baucis)	H	E-A	GSC
-----	Le jour se lève (Mireille)			CHO
Grétry	Je crains de lui (Richard Coeur de Lion)			LEM
-----	Plus de dépit (Les Deux Avares)			LEM
Hahn	Le rossignol des lilas			
Herold	Air de Nicette (Le Pré aux Clercs)			BRA
Koechlin	L'hiver	H	E-G	†
Lalo	La chanson d'Alouette	H	EF-B	GSC
Liszt	Comment, disaient-ils?	H	C-AF	†
-----	S'il est un charmant gazon	HL		†
Martini	Plaisir d'amour	M	BF-EF	GSC
Massé	Air du rossignol Flute (Les Noces de Jeannette)			
Massenet	Adieu, notre petite table (Manon)			GSC
-----	Gavotte (Manon)			†
-----	Je suis encore tout étourdie (Manon)			HEU
Meyerbeer	Nobles Seigneurs, salut! (Les Huguenots)	LH	C-C	†
Paladilhe	Psyché	HM	BF-F	GSC
Rameau	Dans ces doux asiles (Castor et Pollux)			LEM
-----	La musette			BOS
-----	Le grillon			DUR
Rhené-Baton	Berceuse			DUR
Saint-Saëns	Le bonheur est une chose légère Violin and piano	H	C-A	CHO
Satie	Daphénéo			ROU

German Songs and Arias Employing
Crescendo and Diminuendo

Lyric Soprano

Beethoven	Andenken		†

151

(Beethoven)	Mit einem gemalten Band			RIC
-----	O waer' ich schon mit dir vereint (Fidelio)			†
Brahms	Auf dem See	HL	D-F	†
-----	Geheimnis			†
-----	Sandmaennchen	LH	F-G	†
-----	Sonntag	H	D-G	†
-----	Wie Melodien zieht es	HL	A-E	†
Franz	Ach, wenn ich doch ein Immchen war			
-----	Es hat die Rose sich beklagt	LH	DF-F	†
-----	Gute Nacht	HL		†
-----	Stille Sicherheit	M	E-F	†
Haydn	Der erste Kuss			
-----	On might pens uplifted soars (The Creation)	H	E-A	†
Liszt	Kling' leise, mein Lied	HL		†
Mahler	Ich atmet' einen linden Duft	HL		INT
Marx	Wie einst			UNI
Mendelssohn	Das erste Veilchen	M	F-F	†
-----	I will sing of Thy great mercies (Saint Paul)	H	E-F	†
-----	O for the wings of a dove	MLH	D-G	†
Mozart	Durch Zaertlichkeit (Abduction from Seraglio)			RIC
Reger	Des Kindes Gebet	H	F-G	BOT
-----	Mit Rosen bestreut			UNI
-----	Waldeinsamkeit	HML	A-D	BOS
Schubert	An den Mond	HL	F-GF	†
-----	An die Laute	LH	D-F	†
-----	An die Nachtigall	H	C-G	†
-----	Auf dem Wasser zu singen	MH	EF-GF	†
-----	Das Lied im Gruenen			PET
-----	Der Einsame	LH	D-G	†
-----	Der Knabe			PET
-----	Der Musensohn	LH	FS-G	†
-----	Der Schmetterling	LH	E-F	†
-----	Die Taubenpost	HL	D-EF	†
-----	Fruehlingstraum	HL	C-D	†
-----	Geheimes	HL	BF-EF	†
-----	Gott im Fruehling			PET
-----	Gretchen am Spinnrade	H	F-A	†
-----	Hark! hark! the lark	LMH	F-G	†
-----	Im Fruehling	LH	D-FS	†
-----	Lachen und Weinen	HL	C-EF	†
-----	Liebe schwaermt auf allen Wegen			PET

(Schubert)	(Claudine von Villa Bella)			
-----	Liebesbotschaft	H	E-G	†
-----	Sprache der Liebe			PET
-----	Wiegenlied (op. 98)			GSC
Schumann	Der Nussbaum	LMH	D-FS	†
-----	Der Sandmann	HL	AF-DF	†
-----	Die Meerfee			
-----	Fruehlingslust	HL		†
-----	Intermezzo	HL	C-D	†
-----	Lieder der Braut	H	D-A	†
-----	Marienwuermchen	HL	D-D	†
-----	Roeselein, Roeselein			
-----	Schneegloeckchen	HL		†
-----	Volksliedchen	HL		†
Strauss, J.	Ein Maedchen hat es gar			CRZ
	nicht gut (The Gypsy Baron)			
Strauss, R.	All' mein' Gedanken	H	CS-GS	
-----	Die Nacht	HL		†
-----	Schlagende Herzen			†
Wolf	Auch kleine Dinge	HM	D-E	†
-----	Blumengruss	HL	D-E	†
-----	Der Gaertner	HL		†
-----	Der Knabe und das	L	CS-A	†
	Immlein			
-----	Fruehling uebers Jahr			†
-----	Gleich und gleich			†
-----	In dem Schatten meiner	M	C-EF	†
	Locken			
-----	Mausfallen Spruechlein	HL	BF-E	†
-----	Morgentau	HL	D-D	†
-----	Nun wandre, Maria	HL	EF-D	†
-----	Und willst du deinen	HL		DIT
	Liebsten sterben			
-----	Verschwiegene Liebe	LH	DF-FS	†
-----	Wenn du zu den Blumen	HL	B-EF	†
	gehst			

Italian Songs and Arias Employing
Crescendo and Diminuendo

Lyric Soprano

Bononcini	Per la gloria	HL	C-EF	†
-----	Si che fedele			DUR
Caldara	Sebben crudele	HML	E-DS	†
-----	Selve amiche, ombrose	HM	E-E	†
	piante			
De Luca	Non posso disperar	HL	C-E	GSC

153

Donizetti	Chacun le sait (La Fille du Régiment)	H	C-A	RIC
Falconieri	O bellissimi capelli	HL	B-D	†
Handel	Affani del pensier (Ottone)			†
-----	Bel piacere (Agrippina)			†
-----	Caro voi siete all'alma (Serse)	H	E-A	CFI
-----	Ne men con l'ombre (Serse)	H	E-A	CFI
-----	Voi dolce aurette al cor (Tolomeo)			GSC
Monteverdi	Lasciatemi morire (Arianna)	ML	D-D	†
Mozart	L'amero saro costante (Il Re Pastore) Violin or flute	H	D-B	GSC
-----	Venite inginocchiatevi (Le Nozze di Figaro)	H	D-G	†
-----	Zeffiretti lusinghieri (Idomeneo)			†
Pergolesi	Se tu m'ami	LMH	C-G	GSC
Respighi	Bella porta di rubini			RIC
Rosa	Selve, voi che le speranze	MH	D-G	DIT
Scarlatti, A.	La fortuna			BOS
Verdi	Ave Maria (Otello)	H	EF-AF	GSC

Miscellaneous Songs Employing Crescendo and Diminuendo

Lyric Soprano

Arensky	The little fish's song	H	D-A	†
Backer-Gröndahl	In dreaming dance			
Gretchaninoff	My native land	L	C-EF	GSC
Grieg	En fuglevise			
-----	In the boat	LM	D-ES	†
-----	It was a lovely summer evening			
-----	Springtide	M		DIT
Lilljebjorn	When I was seventeen			RIC
Nin	Minué cantado			ESC
Rachmaninoff	Daisies			†
-----	Lilacs	LH	EF-G	†
-----	The island	LH	DF-F	†
Stravinsky	Pastorale			GSC

154

American Songs Employing
Piano Singing

Lyric Soprano

Burleigh	By the pool at the third roses	H		RIC
Carpenter	Silhouettes	M	C-G	GSC
Charles	When I have sung my songs	HM	BF-EF	GSC
Crist	Evening	H	C-G	GSC
Davis	Nancy Hanks	H	D-G	GAL
De Rose	I heard a forest praying	MH	EF-GF	CHA
Dittenhaver	Hurdy-gurdy playing in the street	H	DF-AF	GAL
Duke	Little elegy	H	FS-A	GSC
-----	The bird			GSC
-----	To Karen, singing	M	CS-G	ELV
Gaines	My heart hath a mind			
Ganz	A memory	HM	B-D	GSC
-----	The angels are stooping	MH	GF-A	GSC
Giannini	Tell me, o blue, blue sky	H		RIC
Griffes	In a myrtle shade	H	FS-A	GSC
-----	Symphony in yellow	M	D-GF	GSC
-----	The dreamy lake	H	BS-GS	GSC
-----	Thy dark eyes to mine	H	EF-AF	GSC
Hageman	Do not go, my love	HL	B-EF	GSC
Huerter	Pirate dreams	HML		DIT
Kingsford	Wallpaper for a little girl's room	M	BF-F	GSC
Kramer	Pleading	LH	D-GF	JFI
-----	Swans	HL		RIC
MacDowell	As the gloaming shadows creep			
-----	Long ago	HL		ASC
-----	The sea	HL	D-D	BRH
MacGimsey	Sweet little Jesus boy	ML	D-D	CFI
Manning	In the Luxembourg gardens	HML	BF-D	GSC
-----	Shoes	M	EF-F	GSC
Nevin	Little boy blue			BOS
-----	Mighty lak' a rose			JCH
Nordoff	Music I heard with you	H	DS-FS	AMP
Schuman	Orpheus with his lute	M	C-FS	GSC
Taylor	A song for lovers	MH	D-F	JFI
Watts	Stresa	H	EF-BF	DIT

British Songs Employing
Piano Singing

Lyric Soprano

Anon	Have you seen but a white lily grow?	H	E-F	GSC
Bainton	The nightingale near the house			CUR
Bax	I heard a piper piping	LH	D-G	CFI
Coleridge-Taylor	She rested by the broken brook	HL		DIT
Delius	The nightingale has a lyre of gold			†
Gibbs	Silver		CS-FS	ROG
Hook	Mary of Allendale			BOO
Hughes	Open the door softly	LMH	G-G	ENO
Ronald	Down in the forest	HML	C-D	ENO
-----	Drift, down drift down			BOO
Scott	Lullaby	MML	BF-DF	GAL
Vaughan Williams	Orpheus with his lute			PRO
-----	Silent noon			GSC

French Songs and Arias Employing
Piano Singing

Lyric Soprano

Aubert	La lettre			DUR
Bizet	Douce mer			GSC
-----	Pastorale	H	C-FS	GSC
Breville	Prieres d'enfant	M	D-F	ROU
Chausson	Dans la forêt	HL		INT
-----	Nocturne	HL		INT
Debussy	Clair de lune	M	CS-FS	JOB
-----	Harmonie du soir			DUR
-----	Il pleure dans mon coeur	LH	CS-GS	†
-----	L'ombre des arbres			†
-----	Le jet d'eau			DUR
-----	Nuits d'etoiles	LH	E-A	MAR
-----	Recueillement			DUR
Duparc	Extase	LMH	FS-A	†
-----	Soupir	HL	CS-F	BOS
Faure	Après un rêve	HM	C-F	†
-----	Dans les ruines d'une abbaye	M	E-FS	†

156

(Faure)	En sourdine	HL	C-EF	†
-----	Ici-bas!	H	FS-G	†
-----	La lune blanche	HL		†
Ferrari	Le miroir	M	E-F	GSC
Godard	Cachés dans cet asile	MH	DF-F	GSC
	(Jocelyn) Violin or cello			
Gounod	Au rossignol	LMH	D-G	CHO
-----	Sérénade	LMH	D-A	GSC
Grétry	Rose chérie			LEM
	(Zémire et Azor)			
Hahn	A Chloris	H	DS-FS	HEU
-----	Infidélité	M		HEU
-----	L'heure exquise	M	DF-F	†
-----	Offrande	M	D-D	†
-----	Paysage	MH	EF-G	HEU
Koechlin	L'air	M	F-FS	ROU
Leguerney	Je vous envoie	H	C-A	ROU
Liszt	Oh! quand je dors	H	E-A	†
Lully	Au clair de la lune	H	E-D	CFI
Massenet	Crépuscule	M	D-E	GSC
Moret	Le nélumbo	H	E-DF	HEU
Mozart	Oiseaux, si tous les ans	H	C-G	KAL
Poldowski	L'heure exquise	LMH	DF-AF	CHE
Poulenc	C. (J'ai traversé les			ROU
	ponts de C.)			
Rabey	Tes yeux	H	EF-G	DUR
	Violin and piano			
Rameau	Rossignols amoureux			†
	(Hippolyte et Aricie)			
Ravel	D'Anne jouant de	H	CS-GS	GSC
	l'espinette			
-----	D'Anne qui me jecta	HM	CS-FS	GSC
-----	La flûte enchantée	M	DS-FS	DUR
-----	Noël des jouets	M	BS-FS	MAT
-----	Sur l'herbe	MH	C-G	DUR
-----	Trois beaux oiseaux du			DUR
	paradis			
Roussel	Le jardin mouillé	M	C-FS	ROU
Saint-Saëns	Mai	H	G-FS	DUR
Severac	Ma poupée chérie			ROU
Staub	L'heure silencieuse	H	EF-G	DUR
Szulc	Claire de lune	H	E-G	AXE
Weckerlin	Aminte	M	C-D	†
-----	Je connais un berger	M	EF-EF	BOS
	discret			

German Songs and Arias Employing
Piano Singing

Lyric Soprano

Bach, J. S.	Ich nehme mein Leiden (Cantata 75) Oboe d'amore			AUG
-----	Seufzer, Traenen, Kummer, Noth (Cantata 21) Oboe			†
-----	Suesser trost, mein Jesus kommt (Cantata 151) Flute			†
Beethoven	Ich liebe dich	HL	BF-DF	†
Blech	Heimkehr vom Feste			UNI
Brahms	An ein Veilchen	H	DS-GS	†
-----	Eine gute, gute Nacht			†
-----	Es traeumte mir			†
-----	In Waldeseinsamkeit	H	ES-G	†
-----	Lerchengesang	LH	FS-GS	†
-----	Staendchen	HL	BF-E	†
Franz	Ein Stuendlein wohl vor Tag			†
Hindemith	Geburt Marias			AMP
Korngold	Mariettas song (The Dead City)	MH	F-BF	AMP
Mahler	Ich ging mit Lust	HL		INT
-----	Liebst du um Schoenheit	HL		INT
Marx	Marienlied	MH	EF-AF	AMP
-----	Selige Nacht	M	DF-GF	AMP
Mendelssohn	Bei der Wiege	M	DF-EF	GSC
-----	Gruss	M	DS-FS	†
Mozart	Welche Wonne, welche Lust (Abduction from Seraglio)			†
Schubert	Ave Maria	LMH	F-F	†
-----	Danksagung an den Bach	HL	E-F	†
-----	Du bist die Ruh	LMH	EF-AF	†
-----	Erlafsee	H	E-G	†
-----	Im Abendrot	HL	C-D	†
-----	Lob der Thraenen	LM	F-F	†
-----	Nachtviolen			PET
-----	Mondnacht	M	E-FS	†
Strauss, J.	Czardas (Die Fledermaus)			BOO
Strauss, R.	Freundliche Vision	HL	C-F	†
-----	Heimkehr	HL	B-E	†
-----	Ich trage meine minne	M		†
-----	Mein Herz ist stumm	LH	EF-AF	
-----	Meinem Kinde			†
-----	Traum durch die Daemmerung	HML	BF-EF	†

Trunk	In meiner Heimat			
Wolf	Ach, des Knaben Augen	HL		†
-----	Auf ein altes Bild	HL	E-DS	†
-----	Du denkst, mit einem Faedchen			†
-----	Frage und Antwort			PET
-----	Nachtzauber	HL	B-E	INT
-----	Verborgenheit	HL	B-E	†
-----	Wie glaenzt der helle Mond			†

Italian Songs and Arias Employing Piano Singing

Lyric Soprano

Bassani	Posate, dormite (La Serenata)	H	EF-F	GSC
Bononçini	Deh, più a me non v'ascondete	LH	EF-F	†
Cimara	Fiocca la neve	H	G-G	GSC
Faccio	Sortita d'Ofelia (Amleto)			GSC
Gagliano	Dormi, amore (La Flora)	HL	CS-E	DIT
Gluck	O del mio dolce ardor (Paride ed Elena)	LH	D-FS	GSC
Handel	Care selve (Atalanta)	MH	FS-A	†
Jommelli	Chi vuol comprar la bella	H	B-G	GSC
Mozart	Deh vieni non tardar (Le Nozze di Figaro)	H	A-A	†
Pizzetti	I pastori			FRL
Puccini	O mio babbino caro (Gianni Schicchi)			RIC
Respighi	Notte			BON
Verdi	Addio del passato (La Traviata)			†
-----	Salce, salce (Otello)	H	CS-FS	RIC
-----	Sul fil d'un soffio etesio (Falstaff)	H	DS-A	RIC

Miscellaneous Songs Employing Piano Singing

Lyric Soprano

Alnaes	Lykken mellem to mennesker	M	B-FS	HAN

Arensky	Revery	MH	DS-FS	DIT
-----	Valse	H	DF-GF	GSC
Cui	The statue at Czarskoe-Selo	HM	DF-EF	†
Dvořák	God is my shepherd			AMP
-----	Songs my mother taught me	HM	E-E	†
Gretchaninoff	Hushed the song of the nightingale	MH	E-G	DIT
Grieg	A dream			†
-----	Snegl, Snegl	M	B-F	HAN
Lie	Soft-footed snow	HM		DIT
Mednikoff	The hills of Gruzia	H	DS-A	LAC
Rachmaninoff	Before my window	HM	C-G	†
-----	Here beauty dwells	H	D-B	CFI
-----	In the silence of night	LH	D-A	GSC
-----	Into my open window	HL	B-FS	BOS
Schubert	Ave Maria	LMH	F-F	†
Sinding	Sylvelin	M	E-E	GSC
Tchaikovsky	Cradle song	LH	D-G	†

American Songs Employing
Rapid Enunciation

Lyric Soprano

Bacon	Four songs	H	DF-G	MUP
Bernstein	La bonne cuisine	H	B-B	GSC
Boatner	Oh, what a beautiful city!	HL	D-E	GSC
Burleigh	Joshua fit de battle ob Jericho	LH	DS-E	RIC
-----	Little David play on you harp	HL		RIC
Clough-Leighter	My lover he comes on the skee	HM	D-F	BOS
Curran	Ho! Mr. Piper	LH	D-G	GSC
Deis	Come down to Kew			
Griffes	Elves	H	F-AF	GSC
Hadley	My shadow			ASC
Hageman	At the well	LH	EF-AF	GSC
-----	Miranda	HL		GAL
Josten	Cupid's counsel	H	EF-AF	GSC
Kountz	The sleigh	HL	D-FS	GSC
MacDowell	A maid sings light	H	F-G	ASC
Nevin	One spring morning	MH	DS-F	BOS
Sacco	Mexican serenade	HL	D-EF	BOS
Spross	Will o' the wisp			JCH

Warner	Hurdy gurdy	M	D-F	CFI

British Songs Employing
Rapid Enunciation

Lyric Soprano

Bantock	A feast of lanterns	HM	D-F	GAL
Bartlet	Whither runneth my sweetheart			BOO
Bax	Oh dear what can the matter be?	M	D-EF	CHE
Bishop	Love has eyes	M		†
-----	Pretty mocking bird Flute	H		†
Brewer	The fairy pipers	HML		BOH
Dowland	Shall I sue?			STB
German	Charming Chloe	HML		NOV
Gibbs	Five eyes	HL	D-D	BOS
Head	A piper	HL		BOO
Holst	A little music	H		AUG
Hughes	Hey diddle diddle			CRA
Molloy	The Kerry dance	LH	C-G	GSC
Morley	It was a lover and his lass	HM		DIT
Vaughan Williams	The water mill	L	C-D	OXF

French Songs Employing
Rapid Enunciation

Lyric Soprano

Bemberg	Il neige	H	FS-G	GRU
Bizet	Chanson d'avril	H	BF-G	†
Bruneau	Le sabot de frêne			CHO
Chabrier	Les cigales	HML		†
-----	Villanelle des petits canards	HML	B-E	†
Debussy	Chevaux de bois	H	C-G	†
-----	Fantoches	H	D-A	JOB
-----	Fêtes galantes	LH	CS-A	†
-----	Mandoline	HM	BF-F	†
-----	Placet futile			DUR
Delibes	Les filles de Cadix	HM	A-A	†
Dupont	Chanson des noisettes			HEU
Fauré	Mandoline	HL	F-E	†

161

(Fauré)	Notre amour	H	DS-B	†
-----	Poeme d'un jour			HAM
Ferrari	Le jardin d'amour	LM	EF-F	GSC
Fourdrain	Carnaval	M	C-F	RIC
Hahn	Quand je fus pris au pavillon	M		HEU
Hue	A des oiseaux	H	E-G	†
Koechlin	La lune	M	C-F	ROU
Massenet	Première danse	H	E-G	GSC
Monsigny	Il regardait mon bouquet (Le Roi et le Fermier)	H	D-G	GSC
Pierné	Ils étaient trois petits chats blancs			MAR
Poldowski	Cortège	M	D-FS	CHE
Ravel	Manteau de fleurs	H		INT
-----	Nicolette	L	B-FS	ELK
-----	Tout gai	MH	EF-F	DUR
Severac	Chanson pour le petit cheval			ROU
Weckerlin	Chantons les amours de Jean	H	D-G	GSC
-----	Maman, dites-moi	M	E-FS	BOS

German Songs Employing
Rapid Enunciation

Lyric Soprano

Bach, J. S.	Patron, das macht der Wind (Phoebus and Pan)	M	C-G	GSC
Beethoven	Mailied			RIC
-----	Neue Liebe, neues Leben			†
Brahms	Blinde Kuh			†
-----	Das Maedchen spricht	H	E-FS	†
-----	Der Jaeger	HL		†
-----	Dort in den Weiden	LH	A-A	†
-----	Juchhe!			†
-----	O liebliche Wangen	MLH	E-G	†
-----	Vergebliches Staendchen	LHM	E-FS	†
Mendelssohn	Im Gruenen	H	E-BF	AUG
-----	Neue Liebe	H	CS-A	†
Mozart	Warnung	HM	C-D	
Schubert	Das Wandern	HLM	E-E	†
-----	Die Forelle	MLH	EF-GF	†
-----	Die Post	HML	BF-EF	†
-----	Erstarrung	HL	D-F	†
-----	Fruehlingssehnsucht	HL	B-E	†
-----	Mein!	HL		†

(Schubert)	Ungeduld	HML		†
-----	Wohin?	HL	B-E	†
Schumann	Auftraege	HL	C-E	†
Wolf	Elfenlied	HL	D-F	†
-----	Ich hab' in Penna	LH		INT
-----	Nixe Binsefuss	H	E-G	†
-----	Waldmaedchen			PET

Italian Songs and Arias Employing
Rapid Enunciation

Lyric Soprano

Cavalli	Donzelle fuggite	HL	C-EF	†
Donaudy	Ah mai non cessate			RIC
Falconieri	Non più d'amore	HL	C-D	DIT
-----	Nudo arciero	HL	AF-AF	DIT
Handel	Ch'io mai vi possa (Siroe)			†
-----	Dira che amor per me (Serse)	H	F-A	CFI
Legrenzi	Che fiero costume	HML	C-D	†
Malipiero	Ballata	H		CHE
Mozart	Non so più cosa son (Le Nozze di Figaro)	H	EF-G	†
-----	Voi che sapete (Le Nozze di Figaro)	M	C-F	†
Paisiello	Chi vuol la zingarella	L	C-F	GSC
Paradies	M'ha preso alla sua ragna	M	EF-F	GSC
Pergolesi	A Serpina penserete (La Serva Padrona)	HLM	D-F	†
-----	Stizzoso, mio stizzoso (La Serva Padrona)	H	C-AF	†
Rontani	Or ch'io non segno più	HL	CS-E	DIT
Rossini	La danza	MH	E-A	†
Stradella	Ragion sempre addita	H	E-G	†
Tosti	'A vucchella	LH	F-G	RIC

Miscellaneous Songs Employing
Rapid Enunciation

Lyric Soprano

Falla	Seguidilla murciana	HL		AMP
Grieg	My Johann	HL	BF-EF	GSC
-----	The way of the world			
-----	With a water lily			
Mussorgsky	The evening prayer	M	C-E	GSC

163

American Songs Employing
Sustained Singing

Lyric Soprano

Barber	A nun takes the veil	MH	G-G	GSC
-----	Sure on this shining night	MH	D-G	GSC
Bloch	The shelter	MH	CS-GS	GSC
-----	The vagabond	M	E-E	GSC
Burleigh	Sometimes I feel like a motherless child	HML		RIC
-----	Were you there?	HML		RIC
Chadwick	Allah	LH	CS-GS	ASC
Charles	And so, goodbye	LH	EF-AF	GSC
Edwards	By the bend of the river	HML	C-E	GSC
-----	Into the night	HML	C-DF	GSC
Giannini	Be still my heart			ELV
-----	Far above the purple hills	LH	CS-A	RIC
Golde	Love was with me yesterday	LMH	E-A	CFI
Griffes	By a lonely forest pathway	HML	A-EF	GSC
-----	Evening song	H	DS-GS	GSC
-----	The lament of Ian the proud	MH	DS-AS	GSC
-----	The rose of the night	H	CS-A	GSC
Hageman	Music I heard with you	MH	E-A	GAL
Hindemith	The wildflower's song	MH	E-G	AMP
Horsman	In the yellow dusk	MH	FS-A	GSC
-----	The bird of the wilderness	LMH	DB-BF	GSC
Kernochan	We two together	H	EF-AF	GAL
Lang	Irish love song	HML	A-E	ASC
Lieurance	By the waters of Minnetonka			PRE
MacDowell	The swan bent low	LH		ELK
Manning	Sketches of Paris	HL	C-E	GSC
Metcalf	At nightfall	HML	C-DF	ASC
Moore	Sigh no more, ladies			BOO
Nevin	The Rosary	HML	C-D	BOS
Rasbach	Trees	LMH	CS-GS	GSC
Rogers	The star	LH	C-AF	GSC
-----	Wind song	LM	C-G	GSC
Scott	Think on me	HML	D-EF	GAL
Watts	The poet sings	MH	EF-AF	DIT
-----	Transformation	ML	AS-DS	GSC
-----	With the tide	H	DF-A	GSC

British Songs and Arias Employing
Sustained Singing

Lyric Soprano

Arne, T.	Blow, blow thou winter wind	M	C-F	†
-----	In infancy			NOV
-----	Water parted from the sea			GSC
Bantock	Silent strings	MH	F-G	BOO
Bax	The white peace			CHE
Bridge	All things that we clasp	HL		BOS
-----	O that it were so	LMH	D-G	CHA
Britten	The Sally gardens			BOH
Campion	When to her lute Corinna sings			STB
Dowland	Flow, my tears	M	D-E	STB
Dunhill	To the Queen of Heaven	M	C-G	GSC
Grainger	The sprig of thyme	LH	E-FS	GSC
Gurney	Down by the Salley Gardens			OXF
Handel	Come unto Him (The Messiah)	MH	F-G	†
-----	Farewell, ye limpid springs and floods (Jephtha)	H	D-G	†
-----	How beautiful are the feet of them (The Messiah)	H		†
-----	I know that my Redeemer liveth (The Messiah)	MH	E-GS	†
-----	If God be with us, who can be against us (The Messiah)			†
-----	With thee th'unsheltered moor (Solomon)			NOV
Henschel	Morning-hymn	MH	DS-GS	†
Johnson	As I walked forth one summer day			DIT
Purcell	Cease, o my sad soul			POT
-----	If music be the food of love	M	D-G	BOO
-----	Music for a while (Oedipus)	LH		SC
-----	Since from my dear			
Quilter	Come away, come away death			BOO
-----	Go, lovely rose	LMH	F-GF	CHA
Ronald	O, lovely night	HML		BOO
-----	Prelude	HML	B-D	ENO

Scott	The unforeseen	HML		GAL
Stephenson	Love is a sickness	HML	C-D	BOO
Thiman	The silver swan	MH	EF-G	NOV
Thomson	The knight of Bethlehem	LM		NOV
Welsh	The ash grove			

French Songs and Arias Employing Sustained Singing

Lyric Soprano

Bemberg	Chant hindou	HML	A-EF	†
Berlioz	Autrefois un roi de Thule (La Damnation de Faust)			CST
-----	Le spectre de la rose			CST
-----	Les nuits d'été			AUG
Bizet	Adieu de l'hôtesse arabe	H	BF-G	†
-----	Comme autrefois dans la nuit sombre (Les Pêcheurs des Perles)			CHO
-----	Je dis que rien ne m'épouvante (Carmen)	LH	D-B	†
-----	O dieu Brahma (Les Pêcheurs des Perles)	H	B-D	GSC
Boulanger	Cantique	M	F-F	HAM
Caplet	Les prières			DUR
Chausson	Chanson perpétuelle	H	CS-GS	ROU
-----	L'amour d'Antan	HL		INT
-----	Le colibri	M	F-GF	BOS
-----	Le temps des lilas	MH	D-GS	†
Debussy	Beau soir	LH	C-FS	†
-----	Colloque sentimental			DUR
-----	De fleurs	H	C-AF	†
-----	Romance	HM	C-E	†
Fauré	Aurore	H	D-G	MAR
-----	Le jardin clos	M	C-E	DUR
-----	Le parfum impérissable	LH	GF-GF	
-----	Rencontre	H	EF-AF	†
-----	Vocalise	H		LED
Franck	Nocturne	HL		†
Georges	Hymne au soleil	LH	E-A	HOM
Gluck	Adieu, conservez dans votre âme (Iphigénie en Aulide)			†
-----	Grands dieux (Alceste)	H	E-BF	GSC
-----	Jamais dans ces beaux lieux (Armide)			PET
-----	Non! ce n'est point (Alceste)	H	E-G	†

166

Godard	Florian's song	LMH	D-FS	GSC
Gounod	Plus grand, dans son obscurité (La Reine de Saba)	MH	CS-B	†
Halévy	Il va venir (La Juive)	H	D-CF	†
Honegger	O had I wings like a dove (King David)			CHE
Leguerney	Au sommeil			ROU
Leroux	Le nil Cello or Violin	LH	E-A	†
Lully	Fermez-vous pour jamais (Amadis)			LEM
-----	Plus j'observe ces lieux (Armide)			LEM
Massenet	Charmes des jours passés (Hérodiade)			HEU
-----	Élégie	LM	C-GF	GSC
-----	Il est doux, il est bon (Hérodiade)	MH	EF-BF	GSC
-----	L'amour est une vertu rare (Thaïs)			HEU
Messager	La maison grise (Fortuno)			CHO
Meyerbeer	O beau pays (Les Huguenots)	H	CS-D	GSC
-----	Roberto, o tu che adoro (Robert le Diable)	H	C-C	DEI
Monsigny	Adieu, chère Louise (Le Deserteur)			JOB
Mozart	Dans un bois	H	EF-AF	
Offenbach	Elle a fui, la tourterelle (Tales of Hoffman)	H	D-A	GSC
Poulenc	A sa guitare	M	D-FS	DUR
-----	Air grave			ROU
-----	Bleuet	H	FS-GF	DUR
-----	Fleurs	M	DF-F	ROU
-----	Violon			ROU
Rameau	Tristes apprêts (Castor et Pollux)			CHE
Ravel	Chanson italienne			DUR
-----	Kaddisch	H	C-G	DUR
-----	Là-bas vers l'église	MH	GS-E	DUR
-----	Le paon	M	C-F	DUR
-----	Vocalise en forme de habanera	MH	BF-G	MAR
Roussel	Response d'une épouse sage			DUR
Saint-Saëns	A swan's song Harp or piano and cello	H	D-G	GSC
------	Aimons-nous			DUR

(Saint-Saëns)	La cloche	LH	DF-AF	†

German Songs and Arias Employing
Sustained Singing

Lyric Soprano

Bach, C.P.E.	Das Gebet			SIM
-----	Passionslied			SIM
Bach, J. S.	Bist du bei mir	HML	A-EF	†
-----	Bleed and break (St. Matthew Passion)			
-----	Die Armen will der Herr umarmen (Cantata 186) Violin			PET
-----	Die Seele ruht in Jesu Haenden (Cantata 127) 2 Flutes and oboe			AUG
-----	Father what I proffer			
-----	Ruhet hie matte Toene (Cantata 210) Oboe d'amore and violin			AUG
Beethoven	Das Geheimnis			
Brahms	An eine Aeolsharfe	H	EF-AF	†
-----	Daemm'rung senkte sich von oben	LH	BF-G	†
-----	Dein blaues Auge	MH	BF-G	†
-----	Der Tod, das ist die kuehle Nacht	L	AF-F	†
-----	Erinnerung	H	E-G	†
-----	Feldeinsamkeit	HL	C-EF	†
-----	Immer leiser wird mein Schlummer	LH	DF-A	†
-----	Nachtigall	MHL	BF-FS	†
-----	O wuesst' ich doch den Weg zurueck	H	E-FS	†
-----	Ruhe Suessliebchen	HL	BS-E	CFI ●
-----	Schoen war, das ich dir weihte			†
-----	Wir wandelten	LH	EF-GF	†
-----	Komm, wir wandeln	H	FS-GS	SC
Franz	Dedication	HML	BF-C	†
-----	For music	ML	C-D	†
-----	Im Herbst	HM	A-F	†
-----	Mutter, o sing mich zur Ruh	HL	E-G	†
Haydn	O tuneful voice			
-----	She never told her love	HL	B-D	DIT

168

(Haydn)	With verdure clad (The Creation)	H	E-BF	†
Hindemith	Pietà from Marienleben			AMP
Lehar	Vilia (The Merry Widow)			CHA
Loewe	Canzonetta	MH	B-A	DIT
Marx	Hat dich die Liebe beruehrt	MH	EF-BF	AMP
-----	Nocturne	H	EF-AF	AMP
-----	Waldseligkeit	H	D-A	UNI
Mendelssohn	Der Mond	HL		†
-----	Hear ye, Israel (Elijah)	H	E-A	†
-----	Jerusalem, thou that killest (Saint Paul)	H	F-F	†
------	Minnelied	H	E-G	AUG
-----	Nachtlied			
-----	On wings of song			JCH
Mozart	Abendempfindung	M	E-F	
-----	Ach, ich fuehl's (Die Zauberfloete)	H	CS-BF	†
-----	Wiegenlied	MH	G-G	†
Reger	Friede	H	EF-G	UNI
Reichardt	In the time of roses			†
Schubert	Am Grabe Anselmos	HL	B-EF	†
-----	An die Musik	HL	A-DS	†
-----	Das Wirtshaus	HL	C-D	†
-----	Der Leiermann	ML	C-D	†
-----	Der Neugierige	HL	CS-EF	†
-----	Der Wegweiser	L	D-EF	†
-----	Des Maedchens Klage	LH	C-E	†
-----	Die Maenner sind mechant			PET
-----	Fruehlingsglaube	M	EF-F	†
-----	Ganymed	LH	EF-G	†
-----	Ihr Bild	HL	C-C	†
-----	Naehe des Geliebten	HL	D-EF	†
-----	Nur wer die Sehnsucht kennt	LH		†
-----	Wanderers Nachtlied 2	LH	F-F	†
-----	Wehmuth	HL	B-D	†
Schumann	An den Sonnenschein	HL	A-D	†
-----	Dein Angesicht	HL	B-EF	†
-----	Der Himmel hat eine Traene geweint			
-----	Die Lotusblume	HLM	BF-F	GSC
-----	Du bist wie eine Blume	HM	F-EF	†
-----	In der Fremde	HL		†
-----	Lied der Suleika			
-----	Mein schoener Stern			
-----	Stille Traenen	HL		†
-----	Wer machte dich so krank?			

Strauss	Ach Lieb, ich muss nun scheiden	H	D-G	
-----	Breit ueber mein Haupt	LH	GF-AF	HSC
-----	Kornblumen	LH	DF-AF	†
-----	Mit deinen blauen Augen	LH	C-GS	†
-----	Morgen	HML	E-F	†
Strauss	Seitdem dein Aug' in meines schaute			SC
Wolf	Anakreons Grab	HL	D-D	†
-----	An eine Aeolsharfe			†
-----	Auf eine Christblume	HL	C-F	†
-----	Bedeckt mich mit Blumen	HL	B-D	†
-----	Das verlassene Maegdlein	HL	D-EF	†
-----	Der Genesene an die Hoffnung	H	BF-AF	PET
-----	Gesang Weylas	HL	DF-F	†
-----	Heb auf dein blondes Haupt	HL	G-DF	†
-----	Herr, was traegt der Boden	HL	B-DS	INT
-----	Im Fruehling	HL	BF-F	†
-----	Lebe wohl	HL	BF-F	†

Italian Songs and Arias Employing Sustained Singing

Lyric Soprano

Boito	Morte di Margherita (L' altra notte) (Mefistofele)	H	D-B	GSC
Braga	Angel's serenade Violin	LH	D-G	†
Caccini	Amarilli, mia bella	ML	C-D	†
Caldara	Come raggio di sol	HL	D-F	†
Catalani	Ebben? Ne andrò lontana (La Wally)	H	E-B	RIC
Cesti	Che angoscia, che affanno (Il Pomo d'Oro)	HL	C-DF	DIT
-----	Lasciatemi in pace			
Cilea	Io son'l'umile ancella (Adriana Lecouvreur)	H		AMP
-----	Poveri fiori (Adriana Lecouvreur)			SON
Cimarosa	Bel nume che adoro			RIC
Donaudy	O del mio amato ben	M	EF-F	RIC
Durante	Vergin, tutta amor	LM	C-EF	†
Giordano	La mamma morta (Andrea Chenier)	H	CS-B	AMP

170

Gluck	Spiagge amate			†
	(Paride ed Elena)			
Handel	Ombre, piante	H	FS-A	CFI
	(Rodelinda)			
-----	Rendi'l sereno al ciglio	LH	EF-F	†
	(Sosarme)			
-----	V'adoro pupille			BOO
	(Julius Caesar)			
-----	Vieni o figlio caro e mi			†
	consola (Ottone)			
Haydn	Del mio core			GSC
	(Orfeo ed Euridice)			
-----	Pensi a me			
Mascagni	Son pochi fiori			GSC
	(L'Amico Fritz)			
Mozart	Bella mia fiamma, addio			BOO
-----	Ch' io mi scordi di te			BOO
-----	Non mi dir	H	F-B	†
	(Don Giovanni)			
-----	Parto, parto	H		AMP
	(La Clemenza di Tito)			
	B flat clarinet and piano			
-----	Per pietà, ben mio			†
	(Così Fan Tutte)			
-----	Porgi amor	H	D-AF	†
	(Le Nozze di Figaro)			
-----	Ridente la calma			BOS
-----	Se' il padre perdei			RIC
	(Idomeneo)			
Paisiello	Nel cor più non mi sento	HL	C-EF	†
Pergolesi	Nina	HL	CS-D	DIT
Puccini	In quelle trine morbide	H	DF-BF	RIC
	(Manon Lescaut)			
-----	Musetta's waltz	H	EF-BF	RIC
	(La Boeheme)			
-----	Signore, ascolta			RIC
	(Turandot)			
-----	Tu, che di gel sei cinta			RIC
	(Turandot)			
------	Un bel di vedremo	H	DF-BF	RIC
	(Madama Butterfly)			
-----	Vissi d'arte (Tosca)	MH	EF-BF	RIC
Respighi	Abbandono			BON
-----	Ballata			RIC
-----	Nebbie			†
-----	Nevicata	HM		BON
Sgambati	Separazione	LMH	FS-G	GSC
Sibella	O bocca dolorosa	HM	D-F	GSC
Stradella	Così, amor, mi fai languir	HL	F-G	DIT

171

(Stradella)	Per pietà (Il Floridoro)	HM	D-F	DIT
-----	Pietà, Signore	HM	C-F	GSC
Verdi	Caro nome (Rigoletto)	H	DS-DS	†
-----	D'amor sull'ali rosee (Il Trovatore)	H	C-DF	†
-----	Ecco l'orrido campo (Un Ballo in Maschera)	H	B-C	RIC

Miscellaneous Songs Employing
Sustained Singing

Lyric Soprano

Attey	Sweet was the song			BOO
Bach-Gounod	Ave Maria			†
Cherubini	Ave Maria	H	E-A	GSC
Dvořák	Hear my prayer, O Lord			AMP
-----	Lord thou art my refuge and shield			AMP
-----	Turn Thee to me			AMP
Falla	Vivan los que ríen (La Vida Breve)			AMP
Franck	O Lord most Holy	LM	A-FS	BOS
Granados	La maja dolorosa	M		INT
-----	The maja and the nightingale (Goyescas)	H	BS-A	GSC
Gretchaninoff	Over the steppe	LM	C-G	GSC
-----	Wounded birch	HL	B-EF	†
Grieg	I love thee	HML	E-F	†
Kjerulf	Synnove's song	M	C-F	GSC
Rachmaninoff	Oh cease thy singing, maiden fair	H	E-A	CFI
-----	O thou billowy harvest field	HL	CS-E	GSC
-----	The soldier's bride			BOO
-----	To the children	MH	F-G	DIT
-----	Vocalise	LH	CS-A	GSC
Rubinstein	Es blinkt der Thau	LH	EF-GF	GSC
Sibelius	Black roses	M	A-ES	AMP
-----	From the north	H	DS-G	GSC
-----	The first kiss	M		AMP
-----	Was it a dream			BRH
Tchaikovsky	A legend	M	D-E	GSC
-----	All for you			
-----	Complaint of the bride			
-----	None but the lonely heart	HLM	C-F	DIT
-----	Song of the gypsy girl			DIT
-----	Why	HL		†

172

American Songs Employing
Spirited Singing

Lyric Soprano

Bacon	Four songs	H	DF-G	MUP
Barber	I hear an army	LH	D-AF	GSC
Beach	The year's at the spring	MH	AF-AF	ASC
Boatner	Oh, what a beautiful city!	HL	D-E	GSC
Brown	Love is where you find it (The Kissing Bandit)			
Burleigh	Joshua fit de battle ob Jericho	LH	DS-E	RIC
-----	Little David play on you harp	HL		RIC
Buzzi-Peccia	Under the greenwood tree	LMH	EF-A	DIT
Carpenter	If	M	D-E	GSC
-----	Light, my light	M	C-G	GSC
-----	Serenade	LH	CS-A	GSC
Castelnuovo-Tedesco	O mistress mine			CHE
Charles	Let my song fill your heart	LH	EF-AF	GSC
Clough-Leighter	My lover he comes on the skee	HM	D-F	BOS
Crist	O come hither	HM	B-GS	CFI
Curran	Ho! Mr. Piper	LH	D-G	GSC
Deis	Come down to Kew			
Duke	I can't be talkin' of love	H	CS-G	GSC
-----	Just spring	M	B-FS	GSC
Elwell	The road not taken	M	B-FS	GSC
Giannini	Sing to my heart a song	H	D-B	ELV
Griffes	Elves	H	F-AF	GSC
-----	Time was, when I in anguish lay	H	E-GS	GSC
Hadley	My shadow			ASC
Hageman	At the well	LH	EF-AF	GSC
-----	Miranda	HL		GAL
Hindemith	The whistling thief	M	E-F	AMP
Hopkinson	O'er the hills	LH	C-G	†
Josten	Cupid's counsel	H	EF-AF	GSC
Kountz	The sleigh	HL	D-FS	GSC
La Forge	Song of the open	MH	EF-AF	DIT
Levitzki	Ah, thou beloved one	H	EF-AF	GSC
MacDowell	A maid sings light	H	F-G	ASC
Mitchell	Love is the wind	MHH	F-A	GAH
Nevin	One spring morning	MH	DS-F	BOS
Nordoff	There shall be more joy	M	CS-FS	AMP

Robyn	A heart that's free	MH	EF-AF	FEI
Rogers	The last song	MLH	E-AF	GSC
Rummel	Ecstasy	LMH	GF-AF	GSC
Saar	The little gray dove	MH	D-BF	GSC
Sacco	Mexican serenade	HL	D-EF	BOS
-----	Rapunzel	MH	FS-BF	GSC
Schneider	Flower rain			SUM
Schuman	Holiday song	M	C-F	GSC
Spross	Will o' the wisp			JCH
Taylor	The rivals	H	E-G	JFI
Warner	Hurdy gurdy	M	D-F	CFI
Warren	White horses of the sea	LH	F-G	GSC
Weaver	Moon-marketing	LMH	E-G	GSC

British Songs and Arias Employing
Spirited Singing

Lyric Soprano

Bantock	A feast of lanterns	HM	D-F	GAL
Bartlet	Whither runneth my sweetheart			BOO
Bax	Oh dear what can the matter be?	M	D-EF	CHE
-----	Shieling song	H	CS-A	CHE
Besley	Listening	H	E-AF	CUR
Bishop	Bid me discourse	H	B-A	†
-----	Lo! here the gentle lark Flute	H		†
-----	Love has eyes	M		†
-----	Should he upbraid	H		†
Bliss	The buckle			CUR
-----	Three jolly gentlemen	H		†
Brewer	The fairy pipers	HML		BOH
Carey	A pastoral			GSC
Dowland	Awake, sweet love	M	E-F	STB
-----	Come again! sweet love	M	D-E	STB
-----	Shall I sue?			STB
Elgar	Be not extreme, O Lord (Light of Life)			NOV
German	Charming Chloe	HML		NOV
-----	Waltz song (Tom Jones)	H	B-B	CHA
Gibbs	Five eyes	HL	D-D	BOS
Handel	From mighty Kings (Judas Maccabaeus)	H	D-A	†
-----	Hallelujah (Esther)	H	E-B	CFI
-----	Love's a dear deceitful jewel	LH	F-F	RBR

174

(Handel)	Rejoice greatly (The Messiah)	H	E-A	†
Head	A piper	HL		BOO
Hook	Softly waft, ye southern breezes			GSC
Jacob	Laughing song	H	D-G	OXF
Lehmann	The cukoo	HH	D-B	BOH
Linley	O, bid your faithful Ariel fly			BOO
Molloy	The Kerry dance	LH	C-G	GSC
Morley	It was a lover and his lass	HM		DIT
Novello	The little damozel	LHM	C-G	BOO
Purcell	Hark! The echoing (The Fairy Queen)			BAF
-----	Nymphs and shepherds (The Libertine)	HM	C-F	†
Quilter	Blow, blow, thou winter wind	HL	C-E	BOO
-----	It was a lover and his lass	HL	CS-E	BOO
-----	Love's philosophy	LMH	D-A	BOO
Ronald	Love, I have won you	HML	EF-EF	ENO
Warlock	Pretty ring time	H	D-G	CFI

French Songs and Arias Employing Spirited Singing

Lyric Soprano

Bizet	Chanson d'avril	H	BF-G	†
-----	Ouvre ton coeur	MH	DS-GS	†
Bruneau	Le sabot de frêne			CHO
Chabrier	Les cigales	HML		†
-----	L'île heureuse	M	B-F	†
-----	Villanelle des petits canards	HML	B-E	†
Chaminade	L'été	MH	E-A	†
Chausson	Les papillons	M	C-F	GSC
Dalcroze	Le petit oiseau			
Debussy	Chevaux de bois	H	C-G	†
-----	De grève	HL		†
-----	De soir	HL		†
-----	Fantoches	H	D-A	JOB
-----	Fêtes galantes	LH	CS-A	†
-----	La mer est plus belle	HL		†
-----	Le balcon			JOB
-----	Le faune			DUR

175

(Debussy)	Mandoline	HM	BF-F	†
-----	Noël des enfants qui n'ont plus de maisons			DUR
Delibes	Myrto	M	A-FS	GSC
Dupont	Mandoline			DUR
Fauré	Mandoline	HL	F-E	†
-----	Noël	LH	EF-AF	GSC
-----	Notre amour	H	DS-B	†
-----	Poème d'un jour			HAM
Fourdrain	Chanson norvégienne	H	E-G	RIC
Georges	La pluie	HL		INT
Gounod	Air des bijoux (Faust)	H	B-B	†
-----	Au printemps	LMH	DF-AF	GSC
-----	Je veux vivre (Roméo et Juliette)	H	F-C	†
-----	Vénise	HL		INT
Grétry	Je ne fais semblant de rein (L'Ami de la Maison)			LEM
-----	La fauvette avec ses petits (Zémire et Azor) Flute			LEM
Hahn	Fêtes galantes			
-----	Le printemps			
-----	Quand je fus pris au pavillon	M		HEU
-----	Si mes vers avaient des ailes	HLM	B-FS	†
Honegger	Les cloches			SEN
Koechlin	La lune	M	C-F	ROU
-----	Le thé	HM	C-E	BOS
-----	Si tu le veux	LH	FS-A	MAR
Laparra	Lettre à une espagnole			ENO
Massenet	Ouvre tes yeux bleus	MH	C-G	†
-----	Première danse	H	E-G	GSC
Pierné	Ils étaient trois petits chats blancs			MAR
-----	Le moulin	ML	C-E	BOS
Poldowski	Cortège	M	D-FS	CHE
Poulenc	Air champêtre			ROU
-----	Air vif	H	C-AF	ROU
Ravel	Manteau de fleurs	H		INT
-----	Nicolette	L	B-FS	ELK
-----	Quel galant!	M	D-F	DUR
-----	Tout gai	MH	EF-F	DUR
Saint-Saëns	Guitares et mandolines			DUR
Severac	Chanson pour le petit cheval			ROU
Thomas	Je connais un pauvre enfant (Mignon)	H	C-B	†

176

Vidal	Ariette	LH	F-A	GSC
Weckerlin	Chantons les amours de Jean	H	D-G	GSC

German Songs and Arias Employing Spirited Singing

Lyric Soprano

Bach, J. S.	Herr, der Du stark und maechtig bist (Cantata 10)			
-----	I follow Thee also (St. John Passion) Flute			†
-----	Jauchzet Gott in allen Landen (Cantata 51)			BRO
-----	Mein glaeubiges Herze (Cantata 68)	HML		†
-----	Mein Seelenschatz (Cantata 18) Flute and viola			BRO
-----	Patron, das macht der Wind (Phoebus and Pan)	M	C-G	GSC
-----	Wie zittern und wanken (Cantata 105) Oboe			BRO
Beethoven	Busslied			†
-----	Freudvoll und leidvoll	M	DS-E	†
-----	Mailied			RIC
-----	Neue Liebe, neues Leben			†
Brahms	Auf dem Schiffe	LH	GS-A	†
-----	Bei dir sind meine Gedanken	MH	E-FS	†
-----	Blinde Kuh			†
-----	Botschaft	HL	D-F	†
-----	Das Maedchen spricht	H	E-FS	†
-----	Der Gang zur Liebsten	HL		GSC
-----	Der Jaeger	HL		†
-----	Dort in den Weiden	LH	A-A	†
-----	Es liebt sich so lieblich im Lenze	LH	D-GS	†
-----	Juchhe!			†
-----	Mein wundes Herz verlangt			
-----	Meine Lieder	HL	D-DS	†
-----	O liebliche Wangen	MLH	E-G	†
-----	Salome			†
-----	Vergebliches Staendchen	LHM	E-FS	†
Eckert	Swiss echo song	H	A-B	GSC
Franz	Er ist gekommen	HL	EF-F	†
-----	Sonnenuntergang	HL	CS-FS	†

Haydn	O how pleasing to the senses (The Seasons)	H		†
-----	The mermaid's song	M	C-F	PRE
Hindemith	The moon	M	DS-EF	AMP
Jensen	Am Ufer des Flusses des Manzanares	H	D-FS	GSC
-----	Murmuring zephyrs	LH	E-AF	GSC
Loewe	Der Zahn			SC
-----	Des Glockenthuermers Tochterlein	H	CS-A	SC
-----	Niemand hat's gesehen	LM	DS-FS	†
Mahler	Das irdische Leben	HL	A-F	INT
-----	Rheinlegendchen	M	B-FS	BOH
-----	Wer hat dies Liedlein erdacht?	HL	BF-E	INT
Marx	Der bescheidene Schaefer			UNI
-----	Und gestern hat er mir Rosen gebracht	H	E-A	AMP
-----	Valse de Chopin	M	CS-GS	AMP
Mendelssohn	Fruehlingslied	H	DS-GS	†
-----	Im Gruenen	H	E-BF	AUG
-----	Neue Liebe	H	CS-A	†
-----	O Jugend	H	E-A	†
-----	Suleika	H	E-GS	†
Mozart	Ach, ich liebte (Abduction from Seraglio)			†
-----	An Chloe	LH	EF-AF	
-----	Die kleine Spinnerin			
-----	Martern aller Arten (Abduction from Seraglio)	H	B-D	†
-----	Sehnsucht nach dem Fruehling			
Nicolai	Now to my aid fun wit and humor (The Merry Wives)			
Schubert	Der Wachtelschlag	H	DS-FS	PET
-----	Die Forelle	MLH	EF-GF	†
-----	Die Post	HML	BF-EF	†
-----	Ellens zweiter Gesang			PET
-----	Erstarrung	HL	D-F	†
-----	Fruehlingssehnsucht	HL	B-E	†
-----	Halt!	HL	E-F	GSC
-----	Heidenroeslein			
-----	Mein!	HL		†
-----	Rastlose Liebe	M	B-F	†
-----	Suleika I	LH	DS-G	†
-----	Suleika II	LH	F-BF	†
-----	Wohin?	HL	B-E	†
Schulze	Staendchen			SIM
Schumann	Auftraege	HL	C-E	†

(Schumann)	Er ist's	HL	BF-EF	†
-----	Fruehlingsnacht	L	CS-E	†
-----	Geisternaehe			
-----	Widmung	HL	BF-F	†
Strauss, J.	Adele's laughing song (Die Fledermaus)	H	D-B	GSC
-----	So elend und so treu (The Gypsy Baron)			CRZ
-----	Tales from the Vienna Forest	H	EF-C	GSC
-----	Voci di primavera	LMH	EF-C	GSC
Strauss, R.	Heimliche Aufforderung	HL	B-E	†
-----	Kling			†
-----	Schlechtes Wetter			†
-----	Wie sollten wir geheim sie halten	LH	D-A	
Wolf	Ach, im Maien	HL	C-E	†
-----	Auf einer Wanderung	HL		†
-----	Die Zigeunerin			†
-----	Er ist's	H	D-G	†
-----	Ich hab' in Penna	LH		INT
-----	Liebe mir in Busen zuendet	M	E-F	†
-----	Lied vom Winde			†
-----	Nimmersatte Liebe	LH	CF-AF	†
-----	Nixe Binsefuss	H	E-G	†
-----	Waldmaedchen			PET
-----	Zum neuen Jahr			PET

Italian Songs and Arias Employing Spirited Singing

Lyric Soprano

Arditi	Il bacio	H	CS-B	†
Bellini	Ah! non credea mirarti (La Sonnambula)			GSC
-----	Casta diva (Norma)	H	F-C	†
Bononcini	L'esperto nocchiero (Astarte)	HL	B-E	†
Castelnuovo-Tedesco	Recuerdo			
Cavalli	Donzelle fuggite	HL	C-EF	†
Cimara	Canto di primavera		D-G	FRL
D'Astorga	Vo' cercando in queste valli	H	D-G	STB
Donaudy	Ah mai non cessate			RIC
-----	Spirate pur, spirate			RIC

179

Donizetti	Prendi, prendi per mei sei libero (L'Elisir d'Amore)			BRO
Falconieri	Non più d'amore	HL	C-D	DIT
-----	Nudo arciero	HL	AF-AF	DIT
Handel	Amor commanda (Floridante)	H		†
-----	Ch'io mai vi possa (Siroe)			†
-----	Dira che amor per me (Serse)	H	F-A	CFI
-----	Lusinghe più care (Alessandro)	H	D-G	†
-----	Mio caro bene (Rodelinda)			OXF
-----	Qual farfalletta (Partenope)	H	E-A	AUG
-----	Riportai gloriosa palma (Atalanta)			BOO
-----	Sei, mia gioja (Partenope)			CFI
-----	Spietati, io vi giurai (Rodelinda)			BOO
Legranzi	Che fiero costume	HML	C-D	†
Mozart	A questo seno, deh vieni			BOO
-----	Ah lo previdi			PET
-----	Dove sono (Le Nozze di Figaro)	H	D-A	†
-----	Mi tradi quell' alma ingrata (Don Giovanni)			†
-----	Non so più cosa son (Le Nozze di Figaro)	H	EF-G	†
-----	Un moto di gioja (Le Nozze di Figaro)			†
-----	Voi che sapete (Le Nozze di Figaro)	M	C-F	†
Paisiello	Chi vuol la zingarella	L	C-F	GSC
Paradies	M'ha preso alla sua ragna	M	EF-F	GSC
Pergolesi	A Serpina penserete (La Serva Padrona)	HLM	D-F	†
-----	Confusa, smarrita			GSC
------	Stizzoso, mio stizzoso (La Serva Padrona)	H	C-AF	†
Piccini	Se il ciel mi divide (Alessandro di Indie)	M	C-F	†
Porpora	Non più fra sassi			PET
Puccini	Ancora un passo (Madama Butterfly)			RIC
Respighi	Invito alla danza			BON
-----	Pioggia			BON
-----	Scherzo			BON
Rontani	Or ch'io non segno più	HL	CS-E	DIT

Rossini	La pastorella delle Alpi	H	E-C	CFI
-----	Una voce poco fa	HM	GS-E	GSC
	(Il Barbiere di Siviglia)			
Scarlatti, A.	All' acquisto di gloria	H	C-G	GSC
	(Tigrane)			
-----	Già il sole dal Gange	LH	EF-F	GSC
-----	Se Florindo è fedele	LM	EF-EF	GSC
Scarlatti, D.	Consolati e spara amante	L	BF-E	GSC
-----	Qual farfalletta			
Verdi	Ernani involami (Ernani)	H	AF-BF	GSC

Miscellaneous Songs Employing Spirited Singing

Lyric Soprano

Dvořák	The lark			
-----	Tune thy fiddle gypsy			SIM
Falla	El paño moruno	HL		AMP
-----	Seguidilla murciana	HL		AMP
-----	Siete canciones	HL		AMP
Glazounoff	La primavera d'or	H	D-BF	GSC
Granados	El majo discreto	H		INT
Gretchaninoff	The skylark			DIT
Grieg	My Johann	HL	BF-EF	GSC
Mozart	Alleluja	LMH	F-C	†
Mussorgsky	In the corner			INT
Rachmaninoff	Floods of spring	HL		DIT
-----	God took away from me			GSC
-----	Sorrow in spring	H	D-BF	DIT
Rubinstein	The lark	LH	EF-G	DIT
Sandoval	Sin tu amor	H	E-G	GSC
Stravinsky	The cloister (La novice)			DIT
Tchaikovsky	At the ball	MH		GSC
Turina	Cantares			UME
-----	Farruca	M	A-F	UME
-----	Las locas por amor			UME
-----	Madrigal	H	D-BF	UME
-----	Rima	H	A-A	AMP

Songs and Arias Employing Staccato

Lyric Soprano

Arne, M.	The lass with the delicate air	MH	D-G	†
Arne, T.	Polly Willis	H	D-G	†

181

(Arne, T.)	Where the bee sucks	HM		†
Bemberg	Il neige	H	FS-G	GRU
Delibes	Les filles de Cadix	HM	A-A	†
-----	Passepied	LH	DS-CS	GSC
Dupont	Chanson des noisettes			HEU
Fourdrain	Carnaval	M	C-F	RIC
Grieg	Solvejg's song	MH	E-A	†
Handel	Oh! had I Jubal's lyre (Joshua)	H	E-FS	†
-----	So shall the lute and harp awake (Judas Maccabaeus)			†
Haydn	My mother bids me bind hair	M	E-E	†
Hue	L'âne blanc	H	EF-G	HEU
La Forge	Come unto these yellow sands	H	FS-B	GSC
Liadoff	The musical snuff box	H	CS-D	GSC
Monsigny	Il regardait mon bouquet (Le Roi et le Fermier)	H	D-G	GSC
Mozart	Das Veilchen	LMH	F-G	†
-----	Vedrai carino (Don Giovanni)	H	G-G	†
Saminsky	Queen Estherka's laugh	H	D-A	CFI
Scarlatti, A.	Rugiadose odorose (Il Pirro e Demetrio)	HL	D-E	DIT
Schubert	Der Juengling an der Quelle	LH	E-A	†
Sibella	La Girometta	HML	D-E	GSC
-----	O bimba bimbetta	LMH	D-G	GSC
Strauss, R.	Zerbinetta's aria (Ariadne auf Naxos)			BOO
Verdi	Tacea la notte placida (Il Trovatore)	H	D-DF	†
Watts	The little shepherd's song	H	G-BF	RIC
Weckerlin	Maman, dietes-moi	M	E-FS	BOS

American and British Songs
of Popular Appeal

Lyric Soprano

Arne, M.	The lass with the delicate air	MH	D-G	†
Balfe	Killarney	H	D-E	GSC
Beach	Ah, love but a day			ASC
Besley	The second minuet	HL		BOO
Bishop	Lo! here the gentle lark Flute	H		†

182

(Bishop)	Love has eyes	M		†
-----	Pretty mocking bird Flute	H		†
Bliss	The buckle			CUR
Brahe	Bless this house	HML	A-EF	BOO
Buzzi-Peccia	Under the greenwood tree	LMH	EF-A	DIT
Cadman	From the land of the sky-blue water			WHI
-----	Joy	MH	E-A	GSC
Campbell-Tipton	A spirit flower	LHM	B-G	GSC
Carey	A pastoral			GSC
Charles	And so, goodbye	LH	EF-AF	GSC
-----	Let my song fill your heart	LH	EF-AF	GSC
-----	When I have sung my songs	HM	BF-EF	GSC
Clarke	Shy one	HL	BF-G	BOH
Coates	The green hills o' Somerset			
Curran	Dawn	LMH	E-BF	GSC
-----	Ho! Mr. Piper	LH	D-G	GSC
De Rose	I heard a forest praying	MH	EF-GF	CHA
Donaldson	My buddy			REM
Dougherty	Everyone sang			
-----	Love in the dictionary	M	C-G	GSC
-----	Weathers			
Duke	I can't be talkin' of love	H	CS-G	GSC
Edwards	By the bend of the river	HML	C-E	GSC
-----	Into the night	HML	C-DF	GSC
Elgar	Land of hope and glory			BOO
Firestone	You are the song in my heart			
Fox	The hills of home	HML	BF-DF	CFI
Friml	L'amour, toujours l'amour			HAR
Gaynor	May magic			
Geehl	For you alone			SHU
German	Who'll buy my lavender?	HML		BOO
Giannini	Sing to my heart a song	H	D-B	ELV
Griselle and Young	The cuckoo clock	LH	EF-G	GSC
Henschel	Morning-hymn	MH	DS-GS	†
Herbert	Summer serenade			SHU
Kountz	Prayer of the Norwegian child	ML	C-C	GSC
-----	The little French clock	LH	D-G	GAL
-----	The sleigh	HL	D-FS	GSC
La Forge	Song of the open	MH	EF-AF	DIT
Lehmann	The cuckoo	HH	D-B	BOH

183

Levitzki	Ah, thou beloved one	H	EF-AF	GSC
Lieurance	By the waters of Minnetonka			PRE
Malotte	A little song of life	LMH	DS-A	GSC
Manning	In the Luxembourg Gardens	HML	BF-D	GSC
-----	Shoes	M	EF-F	GSC
Mitchell	Love is the wind	MHH	F-A	GAH
Molloy	The Kerry dance	LH	C-G	GSC
Mopper	The lemon-colored dodo	H	F-BF	BOS
Nevin	Little boy blue			BOS
-----	Mighty lak' a rose			JCH
-----	The Rosary	HML	C-D	BOS
Novello	The little damozel	LHM	C-G	BOO
Poldini	Dance of the dolls			CHM
Porter	When love comes your way			HAR
Rasbach	April	LH	EF-G	GSC
-----	Mountains	LH	DF-AF	GSC
-----	Promise	LH	AF-BF	GSC
-----	Trees	LMH	CS-GS	GSC
Rich	American Lullaby	LH	C-F	GSC
Robyn	A heart that's free	MH	EF-AF	FEI
Rogers	At parting	LH	CS-FS	GSC
-----	The star	LH	C-AF	GSC
Ronald	Down in the forest	HML	C-D	ENO
-----	Drift down, drift down			BOO
-----	Love, I have won you	HML	EF-EF	ENO
-----	O, lovely night	HML		BOO
-----	Prelude	HML	B-D	ENO
Russell	Fulfillment	LH	EF-GF	BOS
Rybner	Pierrot	HL		GSC
Saar	The little gray dove	MH	D-BF	GSC
Sandoval	Theme and 3 variations on "Long ago"	H	CS-B	GSC
Schertzinger	March of the grenadiers			FAM
-----	One night of love			ROU
Schneider	Flower rain			SUM
Schuman	Holiday song	M	C-F	GSC
Scott	Blackbird's song			ELK
-----	Think on me	HML	D-EF	GAL
Speaks	In May time	HL	D-E	JCH
Spross	Will o' the wisp			JCH
Strelezki	Dreams	LMH	B-A	GSC
Taylor	A song for lovers	MH	D-F	JFI
Ware	This day is mine	MH	EF-AF	BOS
Warren	Fulfilment	H	D-BF	GAL
Weaver	Moon-marketing	LMH	E-G	GSC
Wilson	My lovely Celia	HL	B-E	BOO
Wolf	Jack in the box			
Wood	A brown bird singing	HLM	FS-G	CHA

| Woodman | Love's in my heart | LH | F-BF | GSC |
| Worth | Midsummer | LM | E-A | GSC |

(See also Humorous Songs, Negro Spirituals,
Folk Songs, Operetta Songs and Opera Arias.)

Miscellaneous Songs of Popular Appeal

Lyric Soprano

Acqua	Chanson provençale	H	D-BF	GSC
Alvarez	La partida	HL	DS-E	GSC
Arditi	Il bacio	H	CS-B	†
Bach-Gounod	Ave Maria			†
Berger	They all dance the samba	M	A-FS	GSC
Bizet	Agnus Dei	HLM	C-AF	†
-----	Chanson d'avril	H	BF-G	†
-----	Ouvre ton coeur	MH	DS-GS	†
Braga	Angel's serenade Violin	LH	D-G	†
Buzzi-Peccia	Colombetta			RIC
Cavalli	Donzelle fuggite	HL	C-EF	†
Cimara	Canto di primavera		D-G	FRL
Dalcroze	Le coeur de ma mie	HML		†
De Curtis	Torna al Surriento	HM	D-F	CFI
De Mejo	Bela bimba			
Delibes	Les filles de Cadix	HM	A-A	†
-----	Passepied	LH	DS-CS	GSC
Donaudy	O del mio amato ben	M	EF-F	RIC
Dvořák	Songs my mother taught me	HM	E-E	†
Eckert	Swiss echo song	H	A-B	GSC
Fontenailles	Obstination	MH	EF-GF	DUR
Franz	Dedication	HML	BF-C	†
Freire	Ay, ay, ay	LH		RIC
Glazounoff	La primavera d'or	H	D-BF	GSC
Gounod	Au printemps	LMH	DF-AF	GSC
-----	Sérenade	LMH	D-A	GSC
Grieg	A dream			†
------	I love thee	HML	E-F	†
------	My Johann	HL	BF-EF	GSC
------	Solvejg's song	MH	E-A	†
Hahn	Si mes vers avaient des ailes	HLM	B-FS	†
Hue	A des oiseaux	H	E-G	†
Leroux	Le nil Cello or Violin	LH	E-A	†
Liadoff	The musical snuff box	H	CS-D	GSC
Lilljebjorn	When I was seventeen			RIC
Marx, B.	Senhorinha Brasileira			

185

Massenet	Elégie	LM	C-GF	GSC
-----	Ouvre tes yeux bleus	MH	C-G	†
Mendelssohn	On wings of song			†
Moret	Le nélumbo	H	E-DF	HEU
Padilla	El relicario			GOL
-----	La violetera			HAR
Pestalozza	Ciribiribin			DIT
Poulenc	Les chemins de l'amour	M		AMP
Rabey	Tes yeux Violin and piano	H	EF-G	DUR
Rachmaninoff	To the children	MH	F-G	DIT
Reichardt	In the time of roses			†
Rimsky-Korsakov	The nightingale and the rose	H	FS-FS	DIT
Rossini	La danza	MH	E-A	†
-----	La pastorella delle Alpi	H	E-C	CFI
Rubinstein	Since first I met thee	H	D-G	DIT
Saint-Saëns	La libellule	H	C-D	DUR
Sandoval	Eres tú			
Schubert	An die Musik	HL	A-DS	†
-----	Ave Maria	LMH	F-F	†
-----	Hark! hark! the lark	LMH	F-G	†
-----	Staendchen			
Schumann	Widmung	HL	BF-F	†
Sibella	La Girometta	HML	D-E	GSC
Strauss, J.	Blue Danube waltz			GSC
-----	Tales from the Vienna forest	H	EF-C	GSC
-----	Voci di primavera	LMH	EF-C	GSC
-----	Wiener Blut			
Tchaikovsky	None but the lonely heart	HLM	C-F	DIT
Tosti	'A vucchella	LH	F-G	RIC
-----	Marechiare	M	D-FS	GSC
Weber	Invitation to the dance	H	FF-EF	GSC
Yradier	La paloma	HL	BF-EF	GSC

(See also Humorous Songs, Negro Spirituals, Folk Songs, Operetta Songs and Opera Arias.)

Arias from British Operas

Lyric Soprano

Arnold	Hist! hist! (Maid of the Mill)	M	D-G	STB
Balfe	I dream't I dwelt in marble halls (The Bohemian Girl)			†

Britten	Church Scene (Peter Grimes)			BOH
-----	Embroidery aria (Peter Grimes)			
Goossens	The fan song (Don Juan de Mahara)			
Handel	Spring is coming (Ottone)	M	D-F	CUR
-----	Trip, blithe streamlet (Serse)			
-----	With artful beguiling (Alessandro)			†
Purcell	Fairest isle (King Arthur)			NOV
-----	From rosy bow'rs (Don Quixote)			AUG
-----	Hark! the echoing air (The Fairy Queen)			BAF
-----	I attempt from love's sickness to fly (The Indian Queen)	MH	CS-E	
-----	Music for a while (Oedipus)	LH		SC
-----	Nymphs and shepherds (The Libertine)	HM	C-F	†
-----	Sweeter than roses (Pausanias)			SC
Vaughn Williams	Greensleeves (Sir John in Love)			OXF

Arias from French Operas

Lyric Soprano

Auber	Quel bonheur (Fra Diavolo)			BOO
Berlioz	Autrefois un roi de Thule (La Damnation de Faust)			CST
Bizet	Comme autrefois dans la nuit sombre (Les Pêcheurs des Perles)			CHO
-----	Je dis que rien ne m'épouvante (Carmen)	LH	D-B	†
-----	O dieu Brahma (Les Pêcheurs des Perles)	H	B-D	GSC
Campra	Charmant papillon (Les Fêtes Venitiennes)	MH	D-G	GSC
Charpentier	Depuis le jour (Louise)	MH	D-B	†

187

David	Charmant oiseau (La Perle du Brésil)	M	D-E	†
Delibes	Pourquoi dans les grands bois (Lakmé)	H	FS-AF	BRO
Dourlen	Je sais attacher des rubans (Le Frère Philippe)			
Gluck	Adieu, conservez dans votre âme (Iphigénie en Aulide)			†
-----	Grands dieux (Alceste)	H	E-BF	GSC
-----	Jamais dans ces beaux lieux (Armide)			PET
-----	L'ai-je bien entendu? (Iphigénie en Aulide)			†
-----	Non! ce n'est point (Alceste)	H	E-G	†
Godard	Cachés dans cet asile (Jocelyn)	MH	DF-F	GSC
Gounod	Ah, si je redevenais belle (Philémon et Baucis)	H	E-A	GSC
-----	Air des bijoux (Faust)	H	B-B	†
-----	Je veux vivre (Roméo et Juliette)	H	F-C	†
-----	Le jour se lève (Mireille)			CHO
-----	Mon coeur ne peut changer! (Mireille)			GSC
-----	Plus grand, dans son obscurité (La Reine de Saba)	MH	CS-B	†
Grétry	Je crains de lui (Richard Coeur de Lion)			LEM
-----	Je ne fais semblant de rein (L'Ami de la Maison)			LEM
-----	Je ne le dis qu'à vous (La Fausse Magie)			LEM
-----	La fauvette avec ses petits (Zémire et Azor) Flute			LEM
-----	Plus de dépit (Les deux Avares)			LEM
-----	Rose chérie (Zémire et Azor)			LEM
-----	Vous etiez, ce que vous n'êtes plus (Le Tableau Parlant)			JOB
Halévy	Il va venir (La Juive)	H	D-CF	†
Lully	Ariette de Cloris (Que soupirer) (Divertissement de Chambord)			
-----	Chant du Vénus (Revenez amours) (Thésée)			LEM

188

(Lully)	Fermez-vous pour jamais (Amadis)			LEM
-----	Par le secours (Roland)			
-----	Plus j'observe ces lieux (Armide)			LEM
Massé	Air du rossignol (Les Noces de Jeannette) Flute			
-----	Chanson du tigre (Paul et Virginie)			
Massenet	Adieu, notre petite table (Manon)			GSC
-----	Charmes des jours passés (Hérodiade)			HEU
-----	Dis-moi que je suis belle	H	D-B	HEU
	(Thaïs)			
-----	Gavotte (Manon)			†
-----	Il est doux, il est bon	MH	EF-BF	GSC
	(Hérodiade)			
-----	J'ai bien assez de mes tristesses (Don Quichotte)			
-----	Je suis encore tout étourdie (Manon)			HEU
-----	L'amour est une vertu rare (Thaïs)			HEU
-----	Sévillana (Don Cesar da Bazan)			HEU
-----	Tristesse de Dulcinée (Don Quichotte)			HEU
Messager	La maison grise (Fortuno)			CHO
Meyerbeer	Nobles Seigneurs, salut! (Les Huguenots)	LH	C-C	†
-----	O beau pays (Les Huguenots)	H	CS-D	GSC
-----	Roberto, o tu che adoro (Robert le Diable)	H	C-C	DEI
Monsigny	Il regardait mon bouquet (Le Roi et le Fermier)	H	D-G	GSC
-----	La sagesse est un trésor (Rose et Colas)			LEM
Offenbach	Couplets de l'aveu (La Périchole)			
-----	Elle a fui, la tourterelle (Tales of Hoffman)	H	D-A	GSC
Rameau	Air de Vénus (Dardanus)			LEM
-----	Dans ces doux asiles (Castor et Pollux)			LEM
-----	Rossignols amoureux (Hippolyte et Aricie)			†

(Rameau)	Tristes apprêts (Castor et Pollux)			CHE
Ravel	Concepcion's air (Oh la pitoyable adventure (L'Heure espagnole)			
Spontini	Toi que je laisse sur la terre (La Vestale)			
Thomas	Je connais un pauvre enfant H (Mignon)		C-B	†
-----	Me voice dans son boudoir (Mignon)			

Arias from German Operas

Lyric Soprano

Beethoven	O waer' ich schon mit dir vereint (Fidelio)			†
Humperdinck	Ein Maennlein steht im Walde (Haensel und Gretel)	M	C-F	SC
Korngold	Marietta's song (The Dead City)	MH	F-BF	AMP
Mozart	Ach, ich fuehl's (Die Zauberfloete)	H	CS-BF	†
-----	Ach, ich liebte (Abduction from Seraglio)			†
-----	Bester Juengling, mit Entzuecken (Der Schauspieldirector)			RIC
-----	Durch Zaertlichkeit (Abduction from Seraglio)			†
-----	Martern aller Arten (Abduction from Seraglio)	H	B-D	†
-----	Welche Wonne, welche Lust (Abduction from Seraglio)			†
Nicolai	Now to my aid fun wit and humor (The Merry Wives)			
Schubert	Liebe schwaermt auf allen Wegen (Claudine von Villa Bella)			PET
Strauss	Mein Elemer (Arabella)			BOO
-----	Zerbinetta's aria (Ariadne auf Naxos)			BOO
Weber	Truebe Augen (Der Freischuetz)			GSC
-----	Und ob die Wolke (Der Freischuetz)	H	EF-AF	†

Arias From Italian Operas

Lyric Soprano

Bellini	Ah! non credea mirarti (La Sonnambula)			GSC
-----	Casta diva (Norma)	H	F-C	†
Boito	Morte di Margherita (L'altra notte) (Mefistofele)	H	D-B	GSC
Catalani	Dove son (Loreley)	H		RIC
-----	Ebben? Ne andrò lontana (La Wally)	H	E-B	RIC
Cilea	Esser madre è un inferno (L'Arlesiana)			SON
-----	Io son'l'umile ancella (Adriana Lecouvreur)	H		AMP
-----	Poveri fiori (Adriana Lecouvreur)			SON
Donizetti	Chacun le sait (La Fille du Régiment)	H	C-A	RIC
-----	Il faut partir (La Fille du Régiment)	H	E-C	GSC
-----	O luce di quest' anima (Linda di Chamounix)	H	C-E	GSC
-----	Prendi, prendi per mei sei libero (L'Elisir d'Amore)			BRO
-----	Quel guardo (Don Pasquale)			BRO
Faccio	Sortita d'Ofelia (Amleto)			GSC
Flotow	Qui sola, vergin rosa (Martha)			BRO
Gagliano	Dormi amore (La Flora)	HL	CS-E	DIT
Giordano	La mamma morta (Andrea Chenier)	H	CS-B	AMP
Gluck	Che fiero momento (Orfeo ed Euridice			HEU
Handel	Dira che amor per me (Serse)	H	F-A	CFI
Leoncavallo	Ballatella! (I Pagliacci)	H	CS-AS	†
Mascagni	Non mi resta che (L'Amico Fritz)			GSC
-----	Son pochi fiori (L'Amico Fritz)			GSC
Monteverdi	Lasciatemi morire (Arianna)	ML	D-D	†
-----	Sento un certo non so che (L'Incoronazione di Poppea)			HEU

191

Mozart	Batti, batti, o bel Masetto (Don Giovanni)	H	C-BF	†
-----	Come scoglio (Così Fan Tutte)			†
-----	Deh vieni non tardar (Le Nozze di Figaro)	H	A-A	†
-----	Dove sono (Le Nozze di Figaro)	H	D-A	†
-----	Geme la tortorella (La Finta Giardiniera)			
-----	L'amero, saro costante (Il Re Pastore) Violin or flute	H	D-B	GSC
-----	Mi tradi quell' alma ingrata (Don Giovanni)			†
-----	Non mi dir (Don Giovanni)	H	F-B	†
-----	Non so più cosa son (Le Nozze di Figaro)	H	EF-G	†
-----	Or sai, chi l'onore (Don Giovanni)			GSC
-----	Parto, parto (La Clemenza di Tito) B flat clarinet and piano	H		AMP
-----	Per pietà, ben mio (Così Fan Tutte)			†
-----	Porgi amor (Le Nozze di Figaro)	H	D-AF	†
-----	Se' il padre perdei (Idomeneo)			RIC
-----	Un moto di gioja (Le Nozze di Figaro)			†
-----	Vedrai carino (Don Giovanni)	H	G-G	†
-----	Venite inginocchiatevi (Le Nozze di Figaro)	H	D-G	†
-----	Voi che sapete (Le Nozze di Figaro)	M	C-F	†
-----	Zeffiretti lusinghieri (Idomeneo)			†
Pergolesi	A Serpina penserete (La Serva Padrona)	HLM	D-F	†
-----	Stizzoso, mio stizzoso (La Serva Padrona)	H	C-AF	†
Pietri	Uno strano senso arcano (Maristella)			
Puccini	Ancora un passo (Madama Butterfly)			RIC

(Puccini)	Chi bel sogno di doretta (La Rondine)	H	C-G	SON
-----	Donde lieta usci̇́ (La Boheme)			
-----	In quelle trine morbide (Manon Lescaut)	H	DF-BF	RIC
-----	Musetta's waltz (La Boheme)	H	EF-BF	RIC
-----	O mio babbino caro (Gianni Schicchi)			RIC
-----	Ore dolci e divine (La Rondine)	H	E-A	SON
-----	Senza mamma (Suor Angelica)			RIC
-----	Signore, ascolta (Turandot)			RIC
-----	Solo perduta abbandonata (Manon Lescaut)			RIC
-----	Spira sul mare (Madama Butterfly)			RIC
-----	Tu, che di gel sei cinta (Turandot)			RIC
-----	Tu? tu? piccolo Iddio! (Madama Butterfly)			RIC
-----	Un bel di vedremo (Madama Butterfly)	H	DF-BF	RIC
-----	Vissi d'arte (Tosca)	MH	EF-BF	RIC
Rossini	Sombre forêt (Guillaume Tell)			
-----	Una voce poco fa (Il Barbiere di Siviglia)	HM	GS-E	GSC
Verdi	Addio del passato (La Traviata)			†
-----	Ah fors' è lui (La Traviata)	H	C-DF	†
-----	Anch' io dischiuso un giorno (Nabucco)			RIC
-----	Ave Maria (Otello)	H	EF-AF	GSC
-----	Caro Nome (Rigoletto)	H	DS-DS	†
-----	D'amor sull' ali rosee (Il Trovatore)	H	C-DF	†
-----	Ecco l'orrido campo (Un Ballo in Maschera)	H	B-C	RIC
-----	Ernani involami (Ernani)	H	AF-BF	GSC
-----	O madre del cielo (I Lombardi)			
-----	Salce, salce (Otello)	H	CS-FS	RIC

(Verdi)	Sul fil d'un soffio etesio (Falstaff)	H	DS-A	RIC
-----	Tacea la notte placida (Il Trovatore)	H	D-DF	†
-----	Volta la terrea (Un Ballo in Maschera)	H	D-BF	GSC
Wolf-Ferrari	Gioia, la nube leggera (Secret of Susanne)			BRO

Miscellaneous Opera Arias

Lyric Soprano

Dvořák	Armida's aria (Armida)			
-----	O lovely moon (Rusalka)			
Falla	Vivan los que ríen (La Vida Breve)			AMP
Gershwin	My man's gone now (Porgy and Bess)			CHA
-----	Summertime (Porgy and Bess)			CHA
Granados	Descúbrase el Pensamiento (Goyescas)			GSC
-----	The maja and the nightingale (Goyescas)	H	BS-A	GSC
Hanson	No witch am I (Merry Mount)			HAR
Janecek	Every now and then (Jenufa)			
Kodaly	I am poor (Hary Janos)			
-----	Two hens of mine (Hary Janos)			
Menotti	Laetitia's aria (Old Maid and the Thief)			RIC
-----	Lucy's arietta (The Telephone)			GSC
-----	Monica's waltz (The Medium)			GSC
-----	To this we've come (The Consul)			
Mussorgsky	Chanson de Parassia (The Fair at Sorotchinsk)	H		CHE
Rimsky-Korsakov	Hymn to the sun (Le Coq D'Or)	H	FS-B	GSC
-----	Little Snow Flake's arietta (The Snow Maiden)	H	C-AF	GSC
-----	Song of India (Sadko)	LH	D-G	GSC

(Rimsky-Korsakov)	Song of the shepherd lehl (Snegourotchka)	LM		DIT
Smetana	Carolina's aria (Two Widows)			
-----	Gladly do I trust you (The Bartered Bride)			BOO
-----	How strange and dead (The Bartered Bride)			BOO
Tchaikkvsky	Iolanthe's aria (Iolanthe)			

Arias from Oratorios and Latin Works

Lyric Soprano

Bach, J. S.	For love my Savior now is dying (St. Matthew Passion) Flute			†
-----	Bleed and break (St. Matthew Passion)			†
-----	I follow Thee also (St. John Passion) Flute			†
-----	Seele, deine Specereien (Easter Oratorio) Flute or violin			
Beethoven	O praise Him (Mount of Olives)			
Carissimi	Lamento della figlia de Jephte (Jepthe)			
Dvořák	O grant me in the dust to fall (St. Ludmilla)			
Elgar	Be not extreme, O Lord (Light of Life)			NOV
Fauré	Pie Jesu (The Requiem)			HAM
Gaul	Sun of my soul (Ten Virgins)			
-----	These are they (The Holy City)	H	E-GS	GSC
Handel	Angels ever bright and fair (Theodora)	H	E-F	†
-----	Ask if yon damask rose (Susanna)			†
-----	As when the dove (Acis and Galatea)	H	D-G	†
-----	Beneath the cypress (Susanna)			

195

(Handel)	But o what art can teach (Ode from St. Cecelia's Day)			
-----	Chi sprezzando il somo bene (La Passione)			
-----	Come unto Him (The Messiah)	MH	F-G	†
-----	Farewell, ye limpid springs and floods (Jephtha)	H	D-G	†
-----	From mighty Kings (Judas Maccabaeus)	H	D-A	†
-----	Hallelujah (Esther)	H	E-B	CFI
-----	How beautiful are the feet of them (The Messiah)	H		†
-----	If God be with us, who can be against us (The Messiah)			†
-----	Let me wander not unseen (L'Allegro)	M	D-G	†
-----	Let the bright seraphim (Samson) Trumpet	H	E-A	†
-----	Oh, had I Jubal's lyre (Joshua)	H	E-FS	†
-----	O King of Kings (Esther)	H		CHE
-----	O Liberty, thou choicest treasure (Judas Maccabaeus)			
-----	O sleep, why dost thou leave me (Semele)	H	DS-GS	†
-----	Pious orgies (Judas Maccabaeus)			
-----	Praise the Lord (Esther)	H	E-G	
-----	Rejoice greatly (The Messiah)	H	E-A	†
-----	So shall the lute and harp awake(Judas Maccabaeus)			†
-----	Sweet bird (L'Allegro) Flute			NOV
-----	Thou God most high (Belshazzer)			
-----	What's sweeter than a new-blown rose? (Joseph)	H	EF-AF	†
-----	What though I trace each herb and flower (Solomon)		CS-E	†
-----	With thee th' unsheltered moor (Solomon)			†
Haydn	O how pleasing to the senses (The Seasons)	H		†
-----	On mighty pens uplifted soars (The Creation)	H	E-A	†

(Haydn)	With verdure clad	H	E-BF	†
	(The Creation)			
Honegger	O had I wings like a dove			CHE
	(King David)			
Massenet	'Twas even here			
	(Mary Magdeline)			
Mendelssohn	Hear ye, Israel (Elijah)	H	E-A	†
- - - - -	I will sing of Thy great	H	E-F	†
	mercies (Saint Paul)			
- - - - -	Jerusalem, thou that	H	F-F	GSC
	killest (Saint Paul)			
Mozart	Et incarnatus est			PET
	(C Minor Mass)			
Parker	O country bright and fair			
	(Hora Novissima)			
Sullivan	My Redeemer and my Lord			
	(Golden Legend)			

Cantata Arias

Lyric Soprano

Bach, J. S.	Alleluja from (Cantata 51)	BRO
- - - - -	Auch mit gedaempften,	PET
	schwachen Stimmen	
	(Cantata 36) Violin	
- - - - -	Bereite Dir, Jesu	
	(Cantata 147) Violin	
- - - - -	Des Reichtums Glanz auf	
	weiter Erden (Von der	
	Vergnuegsamkeit) Violin	
- - - - -	Die Armen will der Herr	PET
	umarmen (Cantata 186)	
	Violin	
- - - - -	Die Seele ruht in Jesu	AUG
	Haenden (Cantata 127)	
	2 Flutes and oboe	
- - - - -	Eilt, ihr Stunden, kommt	RIC
	herbei (Cantata 30) Violin	
- - - - -	Erfuellet, ihr himmlischen,	NOV
	goettlichen Flammen	
	(Cantata 1) English horn	
- - - - -	Es halt' es mit der blinden	
	Welt (Cantata 94) Oboe d'amore	
- - - - -	Frische Schatten (Cantata 205)	
- - - - -	Genuegsamkeit ist ein Schatz	
	in diesem Leben (Cantata 144)	
	Oboe d'amore	

(Bach, J. S.)	Gerechter Gott, ach rechnest Du Cantata 89 (Oboe)			
-----	Gott versorget alles Leben (Cantata 187) Oboe			
-----	Herr, der Du stark und maechtig bist (Cantata 10)			
-----	Hoechster was ich habe (Cantata 39) Flute			NOV
-----	Hoert doch! der sanften Floeten (Cantata 206) 3 Flutes and continuo			
-----	Hoert, ihr Augen auf zu weinen (Cantata 98) Oboe			PET
-----	Hoert, ihr Voelker (Cantata 76) Violin			BRO
-----	Ich ende behende mein irdisches Leben (Cantata 57) Violin			
-----	Ich nehme mein Leiden (Cantata 75) Oboe d'amore			AUG
-----	Ich will auf den Herren schaun (Cantata 93) Oboe			NOV
-----	Jagen ist die Lust der Goetter (Cantata 208) 2 Waldenhorn			
-----	Jesus soll mein erstes Wort (Cantata 171) Violin			
-----	Liebster Jesu, mein verlangen (Cantata 32) Oboe			
-----	Mein glaeubiges Herze (Cantata 68)	HML		†
-----	Mein Seelenschatz (Cantata 18) Flute and viola			BRO
-----	Meine Seele, sei vergnuegt (Von der Vergnuegsamkeit) Flute			
-----	Meinem Hirten bleib' ich treu (Cantata 92) Oboe d'amore			
-----	Patron, das macht der Wind (Phoebus and Pan)	M	C-G	GSC
-----	Ruhet hie, matte Toene (Cantata 210) Oboe d'amore and violin			AUG
-----	Schweigt ihr Floeten, schweigt ihr Toene (Cantata 210) Flute			
-----	Seufzer, Traenen, Kummer, Noth (Cantata 21) Oboe			†
-----	Sheep may safely graze (Cantata 208) 2 Flutes and continuo	LM	EF-GF	GAL

(Bach, J.S.)	Suesser Trost, mein Jesus kommt (Cantata 151) Flute			
-----	Wie zittern und wanken (Cantata 105) Oboe			BRO
-----	Wirf, mein Herze (Cantata 155) Strings and continuo			
Debussy	Air de Lia (L'Enfant Prodigue)	H	E-A	DUR
Handel	Have mercy, Lord (Te Deum)	HM		†
Rameau	Quand le silence (Air tendre) (Diane et Acteon)			DUR
Scarlatti, D.	Tuo mi chiami (Tinto a Note di Sangue)			OXF

Operetta, Musical Comedy or Show Songs

Lyric Soprano

Arlen	Over the rainbow (The Wizard of Oz)			FEI
Brown	Love is where you find it (The Kissing Bandit)			
Caryll	By the Saskatchewan (The Pink Lady)			CHA
Christine	Do I love you (Naughty Marietta)			HAR
Coward	I'll follow my secret heart (Conversation Piece)	M	A-FS	CHA
-----	I'll see you again (Bitter Sweet)	M	C-F	HAR
-----	Kiss me (Bitter Sweet)			HAR
-----	Nevermore (Conversation Piece)			CHA
-----	Someday I'll find you (Private Lives)			CHA
-----	Zigeuner (Bitter Sweet)	H	CF-G	HAR
De Koven	Oh promise me (Robin Hood)	HML	C-D	†
Duke	April in Paris (Walk a Little Faster)			HAR
-----	The love I long for (Sadie Thompson)			PAR
Forrest-				
Grieg	Now (Song of Norway)			CHA
Friml	Donkey serenade (The Firefly)			WIT

199

(Friml)	Giannina mia (The Firefly)			GSC
-----	Indian love call (Rose Marie)			HAR
-----	Love is like a firefly (The Firefly)	H		GSC
-----	Love me tonight (The Vagabond King)			FAM
-----	Only a rose (The Vagabond King)			GSC
-----	Some day (The Vagabond King)			FAM
German	Waltz song (Tom Jones)	H	B-B	CHA
Gershwin	Bidin' my time (Girl Crazy)			
-----	Love walked in (Goldwyn Follies 1938)			CHA
-----	Somebody loves me (George White's Scandals)			CHA
-----	'S wonderful (Smarty)			CHA
-----	The man I love (Strike up the Band)			BRO
Goetz	So this is love (Little Miss Bluebeard)			HAR
Hahn	Air des adieux (Mozart)			HEU
-----	C'est sa banlieue (Ciboulette)			SAL
-----	Dans une charrette (Ciboulette)			HEU
-----	Etre adoré (Mozart)			HEU
-----	La dernière valse (Une Revue)			HEU
-----	Letter song (Mozart)			HEU
-----	Moi, je m'appelle Ciboulette (Ciboulette)			SAL
Herbert	A kiss in the dark (Orange Blossoms)			WIT
-----	Ah! sweet mystery of life (Naughty Marietta)	LMH	A-A	WIT
-----	Always do as people say you should (The Fortune Teller)			WIT
-----	Cupid tell me why (The Duchess)			WIT
-----	I can't do that sum (Babes in Toyland)			WIT
-----	I'd love to be a lady (Eileen)			WIT

(Herbert)	I list the trill in golden throat (Natoma)			GSC
-----	I'm falling in love with someone (Naughty Marietta)			WIT
-----	Indian Summer (An American Idyll)			HAR
-----	Italian Street song (Naughty Marietta)			WIT
-----	Kiss me again (Mlle. Modiste)	LHM	CS-A	WIT
-----	Make him guess (Princess Pat)			WIT
-----	Moonbeams (The Red Mill)			WIT
-----	Neapolitan love song (Princess Pat)			WIT
-----	'Neath the southern moon (Naughty Marietta)			
-----	Romany life (The Fortune Teller)			WIT
-----	Sweetheart waltz (Sweethearts)			GSC
-----	The commandereress in chief (It Happened in Nordland)			WIT
-----	The knot of blue (It Happened in Nordland)			WIT
-----	The mascot of the troop (Mlle. Modiste)			WIT
-----	Thine alone (Eileen)			WIT
-----	Twilight in Barakeesh (The Rose of Algeria)			WIT
-----	Two laughing Irish eyes (Princess Pat)			WIT
-----	When you're away (The Only Girl)			WIT
Herold	Air de Nicette (Le Pré aux Clercs)			BRA
Kern	All the things you are (Very Warm for May)	M	BF-F	HAR
-----	Dearly beloved (You Were Never Lovlier)			CHA
-----	Don't ever leave me (Sweet Adeline)			CHA
-----	I'm old fashioned (You Were Never Lovelier)			CHA
-----	I've told every little star (Music in the Air)			CHA
-----	Long ago (Cover Girl)			CHA

(Kern)	Look for the silver lining (Sally)			CHA
-----	Make Believe (Show Boat)	M	CS-FS	HAR
-----	Our song (When You're in Love)			CHA
-----	Smoke get in your eyes (Roberta)			HAR
-----	The song is you (Music in the Air)	M	C-F	HAR
-----	The touch of your hand (Roberta)			CHA
-----	They didn't believe me (Girl from Utah)			HAR
-----	Why do I love you (Show Boat)	M	C-F	HAR
-----	Why was I born (Sweet Adeline)			HAR
-----	Yesterdays (Roberta)			CHA
-----	You are love (Show Boat)			CHA
Kreisler	Stars in my eyes (The King Steps Out)			CHA
-----	What shall remain (The King Steps Out)			CHA
Lehar	Einer wird kommen (Zarewitsch)			GLO
-----	Ich bin verliebt (Schoen ist die Welt)			GLO
-----	Ich moecht wieder einmal die Heimat sehn (The Land of Smiles)			GLO
-----	Liebe, du Himmel auf Erde (Paganini)			GLO
-----	Lippen Schweigen (The Merry Widow)	LMH	D-A	CHA
-----	Love is like a breeze in May (Paganini)			SAL
-----	Meine Lippen, sie kuessen so heiss (Giuditta)			GLO
-----	My little nest of heavenly blue (Frasquita)	HML		MAR
-----	Vilia (The Merry Widow)			CHA
-----	War einst ein Maedel (Gypsy Love)			BRO
-----	Warum hast du mich aufgewacht gekuesst (Friederike)			SAL

(Lehar)	Wenn du bist das Herz der Welt (Lied)	
Loesser	Lovelier than ever (Where's Charley)	MOR
Luders	Message of the violet (The Prince of Pilsen)	WIT
Messager	Ma foi! pour venir de Provence (Veronique)	CHO
-----	Petite dinde: ah! quel outrage! (Véronique)	CHO
-----	Tu n'est pas beau (La Perichole)	
-----	Valse des cigales (Madame Chrysanthème)	
Milloecker	I give my heart (Mme. Dubarry)	CHA
Monckton	Arcady is ever young (The Arcadians)	CHA
-----	Bring me a rose (The Arcadians)	CHA
Monsigny	Adieu, chère Louise (Le Déserteur)	JOB
Porter	Easy to love (Born to Dance)	CHA
-- -----	Ev'rytime we say goodbye (Seven Lively Arts)	CHA
-----	I get a kick out of you (Anything Goes)	BRO
-----	Only another boy and girl (Seven Lively Arts)	CHA
-----	So in love (Kiss Me Kate)	CHA
-----	What is this thing called love (Wake Up and Dream)	HAR
Rodgers	Come home (Allegro)	BRO
-----	Falling in love with love (The Boys from Syracuse)	WIL
-----	If I loved you (Carousel)	WIL
-----	I'm in love with a wonderful guy (South Pacific)	CHA
-----	It's a grand night for singing (State Fair)	CHA
-----	Mr. Snow (Carousel)	WIL
-----	My heart stood still (Connecticut Yankee)	HAR
-----	Out of my dreams (Oklahoma)	CHA
-----	What's the use of wond'rin'? (Carousel)	WIL

(Rodgers)	You'll never walk alone (Carousel)			WIL
Romberg	Deep in my heart dear (The Student Prince)			HAR
-----	Lover come back to me	H	D-G	HAR
	(New Moon)			
-----	One kiss (New Moon)			HAR
-----	Romance (The Desert Song)	H	D-BF	HAR
-----	Serenade			HAR
	(The Student Prince)			
-----	Softly as in a morning sunrise (New Moon)			BRO
-----	Something new is in my heart			CHA
Schmidseder	Das ist das Geheimnis von Wien (Der Himmlische Walzer)			
-----	Himmlischer Walzer (Der Himmlische Walzer)			
Schubert	Arietta from Claudine von Villabella			SC
Schwartz	Dancing in the dark (The Band Wagon)			HAR
-----	You and the night and the music (Revenge with Music)			HAR
Strauss, O.	My hero (The Chocolate Soldier)	H	D-G	WIT
Strauss, J.	Adele's laughing song (Die Fledermaus)	H	D-B	GSC
-----	Czardas (Die Fledermaus)			BOO
-----	Ein Maedchen hat es gar nicht gut (The Gypsy Baron)			CRZ
-----	So elend und so treu (The Gypsy Baron)			CRZ
-----	Southern roses (Spitzentuch der Koenigin)			
-----	Spiel' ich die Unschuld vom Lande (Die Fledermaus)			BOO
Tierney	Alice Blue Gown (Irene)			FEI
Wehle	Ein glas Champagner (Anni)			
Weill	September song (Knickerbocker Holiday)			CHA
-----	Somehow I never could believe (Street Scene)			BRO
Youmans	I want to be happy (No, no Nanette)			HAR
Zeller	Sei nicht boes! (Der Obersteiger)			

Song Cycles (Or groups of songs)

Lyric Soprano

Alberti	Four sketches from the Far East	HM	C-F	GSC
Alfano	Three poems by Tagore			
Bacon	Four songs	H	DF-G	MUP
Berger	Villanescas	H	CS-B	GSC
Bergsma	Six songs	H	E-BF	CFI
Berlioz	Les nuits d'été			AUG
Bernstein	I hate music	H	C-A	WIT
-----	La bonne cuisine	H	B-B	GSC
Bliss	Lovelocks			GOT
Brahms	Five songs of Ophelia	HL	B-EF	†
Breville	Prières d'enfant	M	D-F	ROU
Britten	On this island			
Caplet	Les prières			DUR
Chanler	Epitaphs			ARR
-----	The children (9 songs)	M	C-G	GSC
Chausson	La mort de l'amour			
Cornelius	Bridal songs			INT
Crist	Chinese mother goose rhymes	H	C-G	CFI
Debussy	Ariettes oubliées	HL		†
-----	Chansons de Bilitis	M	C-FS	†
-----	Fêtes galantes	LH	CS-A	†
-----	Le promenoir des deux amants			DUR
-----	Proses lyriques	HL		JOB
-----	Trois ballades de François Villon			DUR
Fauré	La bonne chanson	HL		INT
-----	Le jardin clos	M	C-E	DUR
-----	Mirages			DUR
-----	Poème d'un jour			HAM
Finzi	Let us garlands bring (Shakesperian songs)	M		BOO
Granados	La maja dolorosa	M		INT
Grieg	Haugtussa	M	B-GF	PET
Gruenberg	Animals and insects	M	A-A	UNI
Head	Over the rim of the moon	LH	C-AF	BOO
Heise	Dyvekes sange			
Holst	Four songs for voice and violin	M	C-G	CHE
Honegger	Saluste du Bartas			LEM
-----	Trois chansons String quartet and flute			SEN
-----	Trois poèmes de Claudel			SAL

205

(Honegger)	Three psalms			SAL
Kilpinen	Lieder der Liebe			AMP
Korngold	Songs of farewell	H		AMP
-----	The Eternal			WIT
Leguerney	Je vous envoie	H	C-A	ROU
Manning	Sketches of Paris	HL	C-E	GSC
Martinu	Songs on one page			
Milhaud	Cinq chansons de Paul Vidrac			SAL
-----	Les soirées de Petrograde			DUR
Mussorgsky	The nursery	M	C-G	INT
Osma	Cantares de mi tierra	H	D-G	BOS
Poulenc	Airs chantés	H	C-AF	ROU
-----	Banalités			AMP
-----	Chansons polonaises			ROU
-----	Métamorphoses			SAL
Ravel	Chansons madécasses Flute, cello and piano			DUR
-----	Cinq mélodies populaires grecques			†
-----	Deux epigrammes de Clément Marot			AMP
-----	Deux mélodies hébraïques (Kaddisch) (Enigme eternelle)			DUR
-----	Histoires naturelles			DUR
-----	Shéhérazade	M	CS-G	DUR
Ronald	Cycle of life			ENO
Rorem	Cycle of holy songs			
Schubert	Songs of Mignon			PET
Schumann	Lieder der Braut	H	D-A	†
-----	Liederkreis			
Slonimsky	Gravestones at Hancock, New Hampshire	H	D-G	AXE
Strauss	Three songs of Ophelia			
Stravinsky	Three Japanese lyrics for Voice, piano, string quartet, 2 flutes, and 2 clarinets			RUM
-----	Trois histoires pour enfants			CHE
Wolf	Geistliche Lieder from Spanisches Liederbuch			PET
Woodford-Finden	Indian love lyrics			BOO

Solo Cantatas

Lyric Soprano

| Bach, J.S. | Ich bin vergnuegt in meinem Leiden | | | RIC |

(Bach, J.S.)	(Cantata 58) Violin			
-----	Jauchzet Gott in allen			BRO
	Landen (Cantata 51)			
-----	Mein Herze schwimmt			
	im Blut (Unnumbered)			
-----	Non sa che sia dolore			
	(Cantata 209)			
-----	O holder Tag (Cantata 210)			
-----	Weichet nur, betruebte			
	Schatten (Cantata 202) Oboe			
Finzi	Dies natalis			BOO
	(Cantata with orchestra)			
Foss	The song of songs	H		CFI
Handel	Preis der Tonkunst			KSS
Medtner	Sonata-Vocalise			DIT
Mozart	Exsultate jubilate			INT
	2 strings, 2 oboes,			
	2 horns and organ			
Pergolesi	Salve Regina 1			ROM
	2 Violins and cembalo			
-----	Salve Regina 4			ROM
Rameau	Le berger fidèle			DUR
-----	L'Impatience			
Scarlatti, A.	Cantata pastorale (for the			
	Nativity of our Lord			
	Jesus Christ)			
-----	Solitude Ameni apriche			
	Collinette			

See Solo Cantatas of Pergolesi, Handel and
Scarlatti, Kirchenkantaten of Buxtehude and
Symphoniae Sacrae of Schuetz.

Concert Arias

Lyric Soprano

Berg	Der wein (Concert aria)			
Mendelssohn	Infelice (Concert aria,	H	D-BF	GSC
	opus. 94)			
Mozart	A questo seno, deh vieni			BOO
-----	Ah, spiegarti, O Dio			
-----	Ah, lo previdi			PET
-----	Bella mia fiamma, addio			BOO
-----	Ch'io mi scordi di te			BOO
-----	Der Liebe himmlisches			
	Gefuehl			
-----	Misera, dove son			BOO

(Mozart)	Nehmt meinen Dank ihr holden Goenner!			
-----	No, no, che non sei capace			PET
-----	Non temer amato bene			BOO
-----	Popoli di Tessaglia			PET
-----	Schon lacht der holde Fruehling			
-----	Vado, ma dove?			
-----	Voi avete cor fedele			
-----	Vorrei spiegarvi, o Dio			

Christmas Songs

Lyric Soprano

Adam	O Holy Night	LMH		†
Attey	Sweet was the song			BOO
Bacon	Ancient Christmas carol			NEM
Bax	A Christmas carol	H	DF-A	CHE
Benjamin	Before dawn			CUR
Bergsma	Lullee, lullay	H	E-G	CFI
Black	In the sky a wondrous star	H	DF-AF	GRA
Bornschein	Babe of Bethlehem	H	EF-G	CFI
Busser	La salutation angélique	HM		DUR
-----	Le sommeil de l'enfant Jésus			
Carr	As on the night	M	E-FS	GSC
Chaminade	Christmas carol of the birds	MH	D-A	GSC
Clokey	No lullaby need Mary sing			JFI
Cottone	Ninna, nanna	H	FS-A	MCR
De Koven	The white Christ	L	C-D	GSC
Dickinson	The shepherds' story	H		GRA
Dougherty	The first Christmas	H	D-A	GSC
Dunhill	To the Queen of Heaven	M	C-G	GSC
Eakin	What of that midnight long ago	M	D-F	GAL
Fauré	Noël	LH	EF-AF	GSC
Forsyth	The Child Jesus	H	EF-B	GRA
France	A Christmas lullaby	M	DS-F	GAL
Hageman	Christmas eve	HML	BF-EF	GAL
Handel	How beautiful are the feet of them (The Messiah)	H		†
-----	Rejoice greatly (The Messiah)	H	E-A	†
Harker	A child is born in Bethlehem	LH	D-G	GSC

208

(Harker)	There's a song in the air	HL	BF-D	GSC
Harris	The holy infant	H	G-AF	GAL
Head	A slumber song of the Madonna			BOH
-----	Small Christmas tree	H	F-AF	BOO
-----	The little road to Bethlehem	MH	EF-AF	BOO
-----	The robin's carol	H	C-AF	BOH
-----	The three mummers			BOO
Ireland	The Holy Boy	MH	D-G	BOO
Jewell	The vision of the shepherds	HL	A-D	ASC
Kountz	The sleigh	HL	D-FS	GSC
Lynn	The magic night of Christmas	M	D-D	DIT
MacGimsey	Sweet little Jesus boy	ML	D-D	CFI
Martin	The Holy Child	HML	G-G	ENO
McKinney	The Holy Mother sings	MH	AF-AF	JFI
Neidlinger	The birthday of a King	LMH	C-F	GSC
-----	The manger cradle	L	EF-F	GSC
Niles	Our Lovely Lady singing	M	EF-F	GSC
Ohlson	The vigils of Mary	H		GSC
Pinkham	A partridge in a pear tree	H	D-BF	ROW
Ravel	Noël des jouets	M	BS-FS	MAT
Reger	The Virgin's slumber song	MMH	G-G	
Reimann	Joseph tender, Joseph mine	M	F-F	GRA
Sadero	Fa la nana, bambin			
Schubert	Ave Maria	LMH	F-F	†
-----	They sang that night in Bethlehem	LMH	EF-EF	GSC
Sevitzky	Christmas bells			
Strauss	Die heiligen drei Koenige	H	C-G	
Thiman	I saw three ships	L		NOV
Trunk	Mary	HM		AMP
Wagner	Schlaf, holdes Kind			
Warren	Christmas candle	HML	D-E	GSC
Wentzel	Lamkins			GRA
West	It came upon a midnight	MM	E-FS	SUM
Wolf	Die heilige Marie singt			
-----	Fuehr' mich, Kind	H	E-FS	
Yon	Gesu Bambino	HL	B-E	JFI

Easter Songs

Lyric Soprano

Bach, J. S.	Seele, deine Specereien			

(Bach)	(Easter Oratorio) Flute or violin			
Bantock	Easter hymn	M	FS-F	CHE
Barnes	Easter	HM	D-EF	GSC
Burleigh	Were you there?	HML		RIC
Chaffin	Easter message	MH	D-G	FLA
Curran	Crucifixion			
Dennee	Easter song	HM	B-F	ASC
Diack	All in the April evening	LMH	D-G	BOO
Gore	O sing unto the Lord a new song	H		JFI
Guion	At the cry of the first bird	H	D-G	GSC
-----	Mary alone	LH	D-GS	GSC
Hageman	Christ went up into the hills	LH	EF-AF	CFI
Handel	I know that my Redeemer liveth (The Messiah)	MH	E-GS	†
Huhn	Christ is risen	HM	C-E	ASC
Lekberg	A ballad of trees and the Master	H	E-A	GAL
Morris	Alleluja, joyeous Easter hymn			GSC
O'Hara	There is no death	LMH	EF-AF	CHA
Ohlson	The vigils of Mary	H		GSC
Parker	O country bright and fair (Hora Novissima)			
Schubert	Ave Maria	LMH	F-F	GSC
Scott	Angels roll the rock away	MH	E-G	HUN
Stainer	My hope is in the everlasting (The Daughter of Jairus)			
Tchaikovsky	A legend	M	D-E	GSC
Wolf	Herr, was traegt der Boden	HL	B-DS	†
Yon	Christ Triumphant	MH	E-A	JFI
-----	O faithful Cross	HM	C-EF	JFI
-----	Our Paschal Joy	LH	AF-AF	JFI

Patriotic Songs

Lyric Soprano

Alberti	A nation's prayer	H		ELV
Cadman	Glory	H	EF-G	GAL
Dungan	Eternal life	HL		PRE
Elgar	Land of hope and glory			BOO
Foster, F.	The Americans come	MH	F-BF	JFI
Howe	To the unknown soldier	H	D-G	GSC

Lester	Greater love hath no man	LH	B-E	CFI
O'Hara	There is no death	LMH	EF-AF	CHA
Steffe	Battle hymn of the Republic			
Ward				
Stephens	Phantom legions	MHH	EF-BF	CHA

Sacred Songs

Lyric Soprano

Allitsen	The Lord is my light	LMH	D-AF	BOO
Bach, C.P.E.	The last judgement			
Bach, J.S.	Draw near to me	HML		GSC
-----	Father what I proffer			
-----	God my shepherd walks beside me	H		GRA
-----	Sheep may safely graze (Cantata 208) 2 Flutes and continuo	LM	EF-GF	GAL
Beethoven	The worship of God in nature			
Bitgood	The greatest of these is love	M		GRA
Bone and Fenton	Thy word is a lamp	LH	C-F	ROW
Brahms	Ye now are sorrowful	H		GAL
Brown	The twenty third Psalm	LH	E-G	GRA
-----	What are these which are arrayed	HLM	C-F	ASC
Browning	For I am persuaded	LM	DF-G	CFI
-----	The beatitudes	HM	C-F	CFI
Buck	Fear not ye, O Israel	HLM		GSC
Campbell-Tipton	I will give thanks unto the Lord	LMH	DF-AF	GSC
Candlyn	Light at evening time	H	FS-GS	GRA
Chadwick	A ballad of trees and the Master	HML	A-F	DIT
Charles	Incline Thine ear	HL	BF-D	GSC
-----	Love is of God	H	D-G	GSC
Clokey	God is in everything	LH	D-G	JFI
Creston	Psalm 23	MH	F-AF	GSC
Davis	Let not your heart be troubled	HML		WOO
-----	Trust in the Lord	MH	CS-G	GAL
Diack	All in the April evening	LMH	D-G	BOO
Dungan	Eternal life	HL		PRE
Dvořák	God is my shepherd			AMP

211

(Dvořák)	Hear my prayer, O Lord			AMP
-----	Turn Thee to me			AMP
Edmunds	Praise we the Lord	HL	D-D	ROW
Gaul	These are they (The Holy City)	H	E-GS	GSC
Gore	O sing unto the Lord a new song	H		JFI
Gounod	O Divine Redeemer	LMH	C-G	GSC
-----	There is a green hill far away	LMH	E-F	GSC
Guion	Prayer	HL		GSC
Hageman	Christ went up into the hills	LH	EF-AF	CFI
Hamblen	Trust in Him	LH	D-G	GSC
Handel	Have mercy Lord (Te Deum)	HM		†
-----	How beautiful are the feet of them (The Messiah)	H		GSC
-----	I know that my Redeemer liveth (The Messiah)	MH	E-GS	†
-----	Let the bright seraphim (Samson) Trumpet	H	E-A	†
-----	Praise the Lord (Esther)	H	E-G	
-----	Thanks be to Thee	M	CS-E	†
Harker	How beautiful upon the mountains	MLH	EF-G	GSC
Haydn	With verdure clad (The Creation)	H	E-BF	†
Henschel	Morning-hymn	MH	DS-GS	†
Kountz	Lord bless the coming year			
Liddle	How lovely are Thy dwellings	HML		BOS
MacDermid	In my Father's house are many mansions	HML		FRS
MacGimsey	Sweet little Jesus boy	ML	D-D	CFI
Malotte	The beatitudes	LH	E-G	GSC
-----	The Lord's Prayer	MLH	EF-AF	GSC
-----	The twenty third Psalm	HLM	C-F	GSC
McGill	Thine eternal peace	HL	A-CS	GSC
Mendelssohn	Hear ye, Israel (Elijah)	H	E-A	†
Mendelssohn	I will sing of Thy great mercies (Saint Paul)	H	E-F	†
-----	O for the wings of a dove	MLH	D-G	†
Saint-Saëns	Thou, O Lord art my protector	MH	C-A	GSC
Sanderson	Green pastures	HL	BF-EF	BOO
Scott	Angels roll the rock away	MH	E-G	HUN
	Come ye blessed	LMH	EF-AF	GSC

212

(Scott)	Ride on, ride on	HML		FLA
Sowerby	O God of light	H		GRA
-----	O Jesus, Lord of mercy great	H		GRA
Speaks	The Lord is my light	HML		GSC
-----	Thou wilt keep him in perfect peace	HML		GSC
Stainer	My hope is in the everlasting (The Daughter of Jairus)			
Stevenson	I sought the Lord	HL	D-F	DIT
Stickles	Saith the Lord	LH	D-F	CHA
Thiman	My Master hath a garden	HL		NOV
-----	Thou wilt keep him in perfect peace	H	D-G	GRA
Thompson	My Master hath a garden	M		ECS
Timmings	In the evening it will be light Chimes	H		GRA
Voris	Song of mothers	LH	D-FS	GRA
Weaver	Assurance	H	EF-G	GAL
-----	Praise the Lord, His glories show	H	E-G	GAL
Widor	O Lord most holy			
Wolf	Give praise to Him through whom the world arose			
-----	Prayer (Gebet)			

Wedding Songs

Lyric Soprano

Barnby	O perfect love	M	C-G	DIT
Beethoven	Ich liebe dich	HL	BF-DF	†
Bond	I love you truly			BOS
Cough-Leighter	Possession	MH	DF-AF	GSC
De Koven	Oh promise me (Robin Hood)	HML	C-D	†
Dello Joio	How do I love thee?	H	D-G	CFI
Diggle	A wedding prayer	HM	EF-F	GSC
Franck	O Lord most Holy	LM	A-FS	BOS
Geehl	For you alone			SHU
Grieg	I love thee	HML	E-F	†
Lippe	How do I love you?			BOS
Marx	Hat dich die Liebe beruehrt	MH	EF-BF	AMP
Ronald	Love, I have won you	HML	EF-EF	ENO
Rosa	Wedding song	F	DF-GF	GSC

Rowley	Here at Thine altar, Lord			NOV
Schubert	Du bist die Ruh	LMH	EF-AF	†
-----	Ungeduld	HML		†
Schumann	Widmung	HL	BF-F	†
Sowerby	O perfect love	MH	EF-AF	GRA
Strauss	Seitdem dein Aug' in meines schaute			SC
Willan	O perfect love	HM	E-FS	GRA

Songs and Arias With Added Accompanying Instrument

Lyric Soprano

Bach, J.S.	Auch mit gedaempften, schwachen Stimmen (Cantata 36) Violin	PET
-----	For love my Savior now is dying (St. Matthew Passion) Flute	†
-----	Bereite Dir, Jesu (Cantata 147) Violin	
-----	Des Reichtums Glanz auf weiter Erden (Von der Vergnuegsamkeit) Violin	
-----	Die Armen will der Herr umarmen (Cantata 186) Violin	PET
-----	Eilt, ihr Stunden kommt herbei (Cantata 30) Violin	RIC
-----	Erfuellet, ihr himmlischen goettlichen Flammen (Cantata 1) English horn	NOV
-----	Genuegsamkeit ist ein Schatz in diesem Leben (Cantata 144) Oboe d'amore	
-----	Gerechter Gott, ach rechnest Du (Cantata 89) Oboe	
-----	Gott versorget alles Leben (Cantata 187) Oboe	
-----	Hoechster, was ich habe (Cantata 39) Flute	NOV
-----	Hoert doch! der sanften Floeten (Cantata 206) 3 Flutes and continuo	
-----	Hoert, ihr augen, auf zu weinen (Cantata 98) Oboe	PET

214

(Bach)	Hoert, ihr Voelker (Cantata 76) Violin			BRO
-----	Ich bin vergnuegt in meinem Leiden (Cantata 58) Violin			RIC
-----	Ich ende behende mein irdisches Leben (Cantata 57) Violin			
-----	Ich nehme mein Leiden (Cantata 75) Oboe d'amore			AUG
-----	Ich will auf den Herren schaun (Cantata 93) Oboe			NOV
-----	I follow thee also (St. John Passion) Flute			†
-----	Jagen ist die Lust der Goetter (Cantata 208) 2 Waldenhorn			
-----	Jesus soll mein erstes Wort (Cantata 171) Violin			
-----	Liebster Jesu, mein Verlangen (Cantata 32) Oboe			
-----	Meine Seele, sei vergnuegt (Von der Vergnuegsamkeit) Flute			
-----	Meinem Hirten bleib ich treu (Cantata 92) Oboe d'amore			
-----	Ruhet hie, matte Toene (Cantata 210) Oboe d'amore and violin			AUG
-----	Schweigt ihr Floeten, schweigt ihr Toene (Cantata 210) Flute			
-----	Seele, deine Specereien (Easter Oratorio) Flute or violin			
-----	Seufzer, Traenen, Kummer, Noth (Cantata 21) Oboe			†
-----	Suesser Trost, mein Jesus kommt (Cantata 151) Flute			†
-----	Weichet nur, betruebte Schatten (Cantata 202) Oboe			
-----	Wie zittern und wanken (Cantata 105) Oboe			BRO
Bishop	Lo! here the gentle lark Flute	H		†
-----	Pretty mocking bird Flute	H		†
Braga	Angel's serenade Violin	LH	D-G	†
Buxtehude	My Jesus is my lasting joy 2 Violins and organ	H	D-G	GRA
Chausson	Chanson perpétuelle String quartet	H	CS-GS	ROU

(Chausson)	Le colibri Violin or cello	M	F-GF	BOS
Couperin	Adolescentalus sum ego Organ, flute and strings			
Forsyth	The Child Jesus Organ	H	EF-B	GRA
-----	The stranger Organ	H	A-B	GRA
Godard	Cachés dans cet asile (Jocelyn) Violin or cello	MH	DF-F	GSC
Gretry	La fauvette avec ses petits (Zemire et Azor) Flute			LEM
Handel	Let the bright seraphim (Samson) Trumpet	H	E-A	†
-----	Nel dolce dell oblio Flute			
-----	Sweet bird (L'Allegro) Flute			NOV
Holst	Four songs for voice and violin	M	C-G	CHE
Honegger	Trois chansons String quartet and flute			SEN
Hue	Soir Païen Flutes			ROU
Kramer	Pleading String quartet	LH	D-GF	JFI
Leroux	Le nil Cello or violin	LH	E-A	†
Massé	Air du rossignol (Les Noces de Jeannette) Flute			
Mozart	Exsultate jubilate 2 Strings, 2 oboes, 2 horns and organ			INT
-----	L'amero, saro costante (Il Re Pastore) Violin or flute	H	D-B	GSC
-----	Parto, parto (La Clemenza di Tito) B Flat clarinet and piano	H		AMP
Pergolesi	Lontananza Cembalo			ROM
-----	Salve Regina 1 2 Violins and cembalo			ROM
Rabey	Tes yeux Violin and piano	H	EF-G	DUR
Ravel	Chansons madécasses Flute, cello and piano			DUR
Saint-Saëns	A swan's song Harp or piano and cello	H	D-G	GSC
-----	Le bonheur est une chose legere Violin and piano	H	C-A	CHO
Schubert	Auf dem Strom Horn or violoncello			PET
-----	Der Hirt auf dem Felsen Clarinet or violoncello	H	BF-B	†

Shepherd	Triptych String quartet	H	GSC
Timmings	In the evening it will be light Chimes	H	GRA
Villa-Lobos	Bachianas Brazileiras, no. 5 8 Celli and bass		AMP
Weinberger	The way to Emmaus Organ		GRA
Wentzel	Lamkins Cello and piano		GRA

Dramatic Soprano

Alberti	Oriental serenade	H	CS-A	CFI
-----	White swan of Samarkand			
Barber	A nun takes the veil	MH	G-G	GSC
-----	I hear an army	LH	D-AF	GSC
-----	Monks and raisons	M	DF-E	GSC
-----	Rain has fallen	HM	D-E	GSC
-----	Sure on this shining night	MH	D-G	GSC
-----	The daisies	M	C-F	GSC
Beach	Ah, love but a day			ASC
-----	The year's at the spring	MH	AF-AF	ASC
Bowles	Heavenly grass	ML	B-E	GSC
-----	Letter to Freddy	M	EF-EF	GSC
Braine	Dawn awakes	HML	A-D	ASC
Cadman	Joy	MH	E-A	GSC
Campbell- Tipton	A spirit flower	LHM	B-G	GSC
-----	Rhapsodie	LMH	DF-A	GSC
-----	The crying of water	LH	FS-GS	GSC
Carnevali	Come love, with me	LMH	E-A	JFI
Carpenter	Berceuse de guerre	M	C-G	GSC
-----	Don't ceare	M	C-D	GSC
-----	Go, lovely rose	M	DF-EF	GSC
-----	I am like a remnant of a cloud of autumn	L	BF-F	GSC
-----	If	M	D-E	GSC
-----	Light, my light	M	C-G	GSC
-----	On the seashore of endless worlds	M	C-FS	GSC
-----	Serenade	LH	CS-A	GSC
-----	The pools of peace	M	D-F	GSC
-----	The sleep that flits on baby's eyes	M	B-FS	GSC
-----	When I bring to you colour'd toys	LM	CS-FS	GSC
Chadwick	Allah	LH	CS-GS	ASC
Charles	And so, goodbye	LH	EF-AF	GSC
-----	Clouds	HML	C-EF	GSC
-----	Let my song fill your heart	LH	EF-AF	GSC
-----	Night	MH	F-AF	GSC
-----	When I have sung my songs	HM	BF-EF	GSC
Chasins	Dreams			JFI
Clough- Leighter	My lover he comes on the skee	HM	D-F	BOS

Cowles	The grasshopper			
Crist	Evening	H	C-G	GSC
-----	Knock on the door	H	EF-AF	GSC
-----	Nina, bobo	HL		CFI
-----	O come hither	HM	B-GS	CFI
-----	You will not come again	HML	BF-CS	CFI
Davis	Nancy Hanks	H	D-G	GAL
Deis	Come down to Kew			
Dittenhaver	Lady of the amber wheat	H		GAL
Dougherty	Heaven-haven			
-----	Love in the dictionary	M	C-G	GSC
-----	Madonna of the evening flowers	M		BOO
-----	Sonatina	M	E-FS	GSC
-----	Song for autumn			
Duke	Bells in the rain	H	E-GS	CFI
-----	The bird			GSC
-----	To Karen, singing	M	CS-G	ELV
Edmunds	Billy boy	ML	BF-EF	ROW
-----	Fare you well	MH	F-AF	ROW
Engel	Sea shell	M	EF-EF	GSC
Fairchild	A memory			BOS
Ferrata	Night and the curtains drawn			JFI
Gaines	My heart hath a mind			
Ganz	A memory	HM	B-D	GSC
Gaynor	May magic			
Giannini	Heart cry	H		RIC
-----	If I had known	H		RIC
-----	There were two swans	H	CS-G	ELV
Griffes	Elves	H	F-AF	GSC
-----	Evening song	H	DS-GS	GSC
-----	Sorrow of Mydath	M		GSC
-----	Somphony in yellow	M	D-GF	GSC
-----	The dreamy lake	H	BS-GS	GSC
-----	The lament of Ian the proud	MH	DS-AS	GSC
-----	The rose of the night	H	CS-A	GSC
-----	Thy dark eyes to mine	H	EF-AF	GSC
Guion	Wild geese	M	D-F	CFI
Hadley	My shadow			ASC
-----	The time of parting	HLM	E-G	CFI
Hageman	At the well	LH	EF-AF	GSC
-----	Do not go, my love	HL	B-EF	GSC
-----	Miranda	HL		GAL
-----	Music I heard with you	MH	E-A	GAL
Hindemith	The whistling thief	M	E-F	AMP
Hopkinson	My days have been so wondrous free	LH	EF-G	†

Horsman	The bird of the wilderness	LMH	DB-BF	GSC
Howe	Berceuse	HM	EF-F	GSC
Ilgenfritz	Blow, blow thou winter wind			
Josten	Cupid's counsel	H	EF-AF	GSC
Kernochan	We two together	H	EF-AF	GAL
Kingsford	Alas that spring should vanish			
Kramer	Invocation			DIT
-----	Now like a lantern	M		RIC
La Forge	Grieve not, beloved	H	FS-G	RIC
-----	Hills	HL		RIC
-----	Into the light	HL		RIC
-----	Song of love	LH		RIC
Levitzki	Ah, thou beloved one	H	EF-AF	GSC
MacDowell	Midsummer lullaby			AMP
-----	The swan bent low	LH		ELK
Malotte	Upstream	M	C-F	GSC
Manning	In the Luxembourg gardens	HML	BF-D	GSC
McArthur	Night	H	F-AF	GSC
-----	Spring came	HL	D-F	GSC
-----	We have turned again home	LMH	F-G	GSC
McDonald	Daybreak	H		ELV
Mopper	Men	M	D-FS	BOS
Naginski	Look down, fair moon			
-----	The pasture	M	BF-EF	GSC
Nevin	One spring morning	MH	DS-F	BOS
Nordoff	Music I heard with you	H	DS-FS	AMP
-----	Serenade	H	CS-FS	AMP
-----	Tell me, Thyrsis	H	E-G	AMP
-----	There shall be more joy	M	CS-FS	AMP
Olmstead	Thy sweet singing	HL	BF-EF	GSC
Powell	Heartsease	M	DF-G	GSC
Proctor	I light the blessed candles	H	DF-A	GSC
Protheroe	Ah, love but a day	LMH	F-AF	GAM
Rasbach	Mountains	LH	DF-AF	GSC
Rogers	The last song	MLH	E-AF	GSC
-----	Time for making songs	HM	CS-F	DIT
-----	Wind song	LM	C-G	GSC
Rummel	Ecstasy	LMH	GF-AF	GSC
Russell	Fulfillment	LH	EF-GF	BOS
-----	Harbor night	M	D-F	CFI
Rybner	Pierrot	HL		GSC
Sacco	The ragpicker	MH	C-AF	GSC
Sachs	The little worm	LH	CS-FS	FLA
Salter	The cry of Rachel	LH	C-AF	GSC
Sargent	File for future reference	M	CS-E	DIT

Schuman	Holiday Song	M	C-F	GSC
Spross	Will o' the wisp			JCH
Stein	The puffin	M		CFI
Taylor	A song for lovers	MH	D-F	JFI
Thompson	Velvet shoes	M	C-E	ECS
Tyson	Like barley bending	HL	C-EF	GSC
-----	Sea moods	LH	E-AF	GSC
Vene	Age and youth	H	E-A	RIC
Ware	This day is mine	MH	EF-AF	BOS
Warner	Hurdy gurdy	M	D-F	CFI
Warren	We two	LH	E-A	GSC
Watts	Nichavo			
-----	Ponts Vecchio, Florence			DIT
Weaver	A book of verses	H	D-AF	GAL
Wolf	Weather forecast	H	EF-GS	GSC
Worth	Midsummer	LM	E-A	GSC
Zimbalist	Lullaby, oh lullaby			

British Recital Songs

Dramatic Soprano

Arne, T.	Blow, blow thou winter	M	C-F	†
-----	In infancy			NOV
-----	The plague of love			BOO
-----	Where the bee sucks	HM		†
Bainton	Ring out, wild bells	M	C-EF	OXF
Bantock	A feast of lanterns	HM	D-F	GAL
-----	Silent strings	MH	F-G	BOO
Bax	A lullaby			
-----	Cradle song			CHA
-----	O, green grow the rushes	MH	EF-BF	OXF
-----	Rann of exile	H	D-G	CHE
-----	Shieling song	H	CS-A	CHE
Benjamin	Calm sea and mist			CUR
-----	Hedgerow			CUR
-----	The wasp			CUR
Besley	Listening	H	E-AF	CUR
Bishop	Love has eyes	M		†
Bliss	Three jolly gentlemen	H		†
Brewer	The fairy pipers	HML		BOH
Bridge	All things that we clasp	HL		BOS
-----	Love went a-riding	HL		BOS
-----	Mantle of blue	H	D-F	ROG
-----	O that it were so	LMH	D-G	CHA
Clarke	Eight o'clock			ROG
-----	Shy one	HL	BF-G	BOH

221

Coleridge-Taylor	Life and death	HML		ASC
-----	She rested by the broken brook	HL		DIT
Delius	Indian love song	H		†
-----	Love's philosophy			†
Dowland	Come again! sweet love	M	D-E	STB
Dunhill	The cloths of heaven	LM	EF-G	STB
Edmunds	I know my love	HL	BF-EF	ROW
Elgar	Where corals lie	HL		BOO
German	Charming Chloe	HML		NOV
Gibbs	Five eyes	HL	D-D	BOS
-----	Padraic the fidiler			CUR
Green	My lips shall speak the praise	M	E-F	OXF
-----	Salvatiion belongeth unto the Lord	M	F-EF	OXF
Gurney	Under the greenwood tree			ROG
Head	A piper	HL		BOO
-----	Sweet chance that led my steps abroad	LM	C-F	BOH
-----	The happy wanderer			
Hely-Hutchinson	Old mother Hubbard	HL	B-E	CFI
Henschel	Morning-hymn	MH	DS-GS	†
Holst	The heart worships	ML	BF-D	STB
Horn	Cherry ripe	M	D-G	GSC
-----	I've been roaming	L	B-E	†
Hughes	O men from the fields	M	F-F	BOO
Ireland	Bed in summer			CUR
Matthews	All suddenly the wind comes soft	H	C-A	ELV
Moeran	Bright cap			OXF
Morley	It was a lover and his lass	HM		DIT
Purcell	If music be the food of love	M	D-G	BOO
-----	Man is for woman made			
Quilter	Blow, blow thou winter wind	HL	C-E	BOO
-----	It was a lover and his lass	HL	CS-E	BOO
-----	Love's philosophy	LMH	D-A	BOO
-----	Take, o take those lips away			BOO
-----	The fuchsia tree			BOO
-----	Under the greenwood tree			
Ronald	Down in the forest	HML	C-D	ENO
-----	Love, I have won you	HML	EF-EF	ENO

222

Scott	Lullaby	MML	BF-DF	GAL
-----	Night song	ML	BF-EF	ELK
Sharp	My mother did so before me			MEU
-----	Whistle daughter, whistle			DIT
Shaw	Song of the palanquin bearers	LH	E-F	CUR
Stanford	I'll rock you to rest	HML		BOH
Stephenson	Love is a sickness	HML	C-D	BOO
-----	Ships that pass in the night	HML	DF-DF	BOO
Vaughan Williams	Silent noon			GSC

French Recital Songs

Dramatic Soprano

Bachelet	Chère nuit	H	DF-BF	GSC
Bemberg	Chant hindou	HML	A-EF	†
Berlioz	L'absence	H	CS-FS	GSC
-----	Le spectre de la rose			CST
Bernard	Ça fait peur aux oiseaux	H	GS-F	GSC
Bizet	Adieu de l'hôtesse arabe	H	BF-G	†
Chabrier	Espana waltz			ENO
-----	Villanelle des petits canards	HML	B-E	†
Chaminade	The silver ring	HM	BF-F	GSC
Charpentier	Trois sorcieres			
Chausson	Chanson perpétuelle String quartet	H	CS-GS	ROU
-----	La caravane	MH	CS-A	HAM
-----	Le colibri Violin or cello	M	F-GF	BOS
-----	Le temps des lilas	MH	D-GS	†
-----	Les papillons	M	C-F	GSC
Debussy	Beau soir	LH	C-FS	†
-----	C'est l'extase	LH	CS-A	†
-----	Chevaux de bois	H	C-G	†
-----	Colloque sentimental			DUR
-----	De fleurs	H	C-AF	†
-----	Fantoches	H	D-A	JOB
-----	La chevelure	M	CF-FS	†
-----	La flûte de Pan		B-B	†
-----	Mandoline	HM	BF-F	CFI
-----	Romance	HM	C-E	†
-----	Spleen			
Delibes	Le rossignol	M		GSC
Duni	Les temps passés			LEM

Duparc	Au pays où se fait la guerre			SAL
-----	Chanson triste	MH	FS-AF	†
-----	Extase	LMH	FS-A	†
-----	La vague et la cloche			ROU
-----	La vie antérieure	HL		†
-----	Lamento	ML	EF-EF	†
-----	La manoir de Rosamunde	HL	B-F	BOS
-----	L'invitation au voyage	HM	E-F	†
-----	Phidylé	MH	EF-AF	BOS
-----	Sérénade florentine	HL		INT
-----	Testament	HL		INT
Fauré	Après un rêve	HM	C-F	†
-----	Automne	MH	D-FS	GSC
-----	Clair de lune	MH	C-G	†
-----	Dans les ruines d'une abbaye	M	E-FS	†
-----	En prière	H	F-F	†
-----	Fleur jetée	HM	BF-FS	†
-----	L'hiver a cessé	HL		INT
-----	Lydia	MH	G-G	†
-----	Mandoline	HL	F-E	†
-----	Prison	LH		†
-----	Rencontre	H	EF-AF	MAR
-----	Soir	LH	D-GS	†
-----	Toujours	LH	F-AF	†
Fourdrain	Carnaval	M	C-F	RIC
-----	Chanson norvégienne	H	E-G	RIC
Franck	La procession	LH	E-GS	†
-----	Nocturne	HL		†
Georges	Hymne au soleil	LH	E-A	HOM
-----	La pluie	HL		INT
Godard	Florian's song	LMH	D-FS	GSC
Gounod	Au printemps	LMH	DF-AF	GSC
-----	Vénise	HL		INT
Hahn	D'une prison	L	BF-EF	HEU
-----	Infidélité	M		HEU
-----	L'enamourée			HEU
-----	L'heure exquise	M	DF-F	†
-----	Offrande	M	D-D	†
-----	Paysage	MH	EF-G	HEU
-----	Si mes vers avaient des ailes	HLM	B-FS	†
Honegger	Les cloches			SEN
Hue	J'ai pleuré en rêve	HL	D-E	BOS
-----	Sonnez les matines	H	FS-G	HEU
Laparra	La maison blanche			
Lenormand	Quelle souffrance	HM	AF-F	HAM
Liszt	Comment, disaient-ils?	H	C-AF	†
-----	Jeanne d'Arc au Bûcher			

(Liszt)	Oh! quand je dors	H	E-A	DIT
Lully	Au clair de la lune	H	E-D	CFI
Martini	Plaisir d'amour	M	BF-EF	GSC
Messiaen	Epouvante			DUR
-----	La maison			DUR
-----	Paysage			DUR
Milhaud	Chant d'amour	M	C-GF	ESC
-----	Chant de Forgeron	M	C-FS	SC
-----	Chant du laboureur	M	B-F	ESC
-----	La tourterelle	M	B-G	DUR
Paladilhe	Lamento provincal	M	CS-FS	HOM
-----	Les trois prières			
-----	Psyché	HM	BF-F	GSC
Parkyns	Le portrait			
Pesse	Chanson rêvée			
Pierné	Ils étaient trois petits chats blancs			MAR
Poldowski	Colombine	H	D-GF	CHE
-----	Dansons la gigue	M	EF-G	MAR
-----	L'heure exquise	LMH	DF-AF	CHE
Poulenc	Air vif	H	C-AF	ROU
-----	Bleuet	H	FS-GF	DUR
-----	Priez pour paix	ML		ROU
-----	Voyage à Paris			AMP
Rameau	Le grillon			DUR
Ravel	Kaddisch	H	C-G	DUR
-----	La flûte enchantée	M	DS-FS	DUR
-----	Tout gai!	MH	EF-F	
-----	Vocalise en forme de habanera	MH	BF-G	MAR
Saint-Saëns	Guitares et mandolines			DUR
-----	L'attente			DUR
-----	La cloche	LH	DF-AF	†
-----	Tristesse			
Satie	Le chapelier			ROU
Severac	Aubade			SAL

German Recital Songs

Dramatic Soprano

Bach, C.P.E.	Passionslied			SIM
Bach, J. S.	Bist du bei mir	HML	A-EF	†
-----	Dir, Dir Jehovah			†
-----	Komm suesser Tod	MH	C-G	†
-----	Willst du dein Herz mir schenken			BRH
Beethoven	Andenken			†

225

(Beethoven)	Die Ehre Gottes	HL	AF-EF	†
-----	Die Trommel geruehret			†
-----	Fruedvoll und Leidvoll	M	DS-E	†
-----	God is my song			
-----	Ich liebe dich	HL	BF-DF	†
-----	Mit einem gemalten Band			RIC
-----	Neue Liebe, neues Leben			†
-----	Wonne der Wehmut			†
Brahms	Ach, wende diesen Blick			†
-----	Am Sonntag Morgen	L	CS-FS	†
-----	An die Nachtigall	H	DS-G	†
-----	An eine Aeolsharfe	H	EF-AF	†
-----	Auf dem Kirchhofe	HL	BF-EF	†
-----	Auf dem Schiffe	LH	GS-A	†
-----	Auf dem See	HL	D-F	†
-----	Bei dir sind meine Gedanken	MH	E-FS	†
-----	Blinde Kuh			RIC
-----	Botschaft	HL	D-F	†
-----	Daemm' rung senkte sich von oben	LH	BF-G	†
-----	Das Maedchen spricht	H	E-FS	†
-----	Dein blaues Auge	MH	BF-G	†
-----	Der Jaeger	HL		†
-----	Der Kranz			†
-----	Der Schmied	HL	EF-EF	†
-----	Der Tod, das ist die kuehle Nacht	L	AF-F	†
-----	Die Mainacht	HL	BF-FF	†
-----	Dort in den Weiden	LH	A-A	†
-----	Eine gute, gute Nacht			†
-----	Erinnerung	H	E-G	†
-----	Es traeumte mir			†
-----	Feldeinsamkeit	HL	C-EF	†
-----	Fruehlingslied			†
-----	Fruehlingstrost	LH	E-A	†
-----	Geheimnis			†
-----	Gestillte Sehnsucht Viola and piano			†
-----	Immer leiser wird mein Schlummer	LH	DF-A	†
-----	In Waldeseinsamkeit	H	ES-G	†
-----	Juchhe!			†
-----	Klage	LH	FS-FS	†
-----	Lerchengesang	LH	FS-GS	CFI
-----	Liebestreu	ML	C-F	†
-----	Maedchenlied	HL		†
-----	Meine Liebe ist gruen	MLH	ES-A	†
-----	Mondenschein	LH	D-GF	†

(Brahms)	Muss es eine Trennung geben?	LH	FS-FS	†
-----	Nachtigall	MHL	BF-FS	†
-----	Nicht mehr zu dir zu gehen			†
-----	O kuehler Wald	MH	A-F	†
-----	O liebliche Wangen	MLH	E-G	†
-----	O wuesst' ich doch den Weg zurueck	H	E-FS	†
-----	Regenlied	HL	CS-F	†
-----	Salamander			†
-----	Salome			†
-----	Sandmaennchen	LH	F-G	†
-----	Schoen war, das ich dir weihte			†
-----	Schwesterlein			†
-----	Sehnsucht	H	EF-AF	†
-----	Sommerabend			†
-----	Sonntag	H	D-G	†
-----	Spanisches Lied			†
-----	Staendchen	HL	BF-E	†
-----	Therese	HL	B-D	†
-----	Unbewegte laue Luft			†
-----	Vergebliches Staendchen			†
-----	Von ewiger Liebe	LMH	B-AF	GSC
-----	Wie froh und frisch	HL	B-E	†
-----	Wiegenlied			
-----	Wie Melodien zieht es	HL	A-E	†
-----	Willst du, dass ich geh'?	L	C-G	†
-----	Wir wandelten	LH	EF-GF	†
Franck, J.W.	Auf, auf, zu Gottes Lob			SIM
-----	Sei nur still			
Franz	Dies und das			
-----	Ein Stuendlein wohl vor Tag			†
-----	Er ist gekommen	HL	EF-F	†
-----	For music	ML	C-D	†
-----	Gute Nacht	HL		†
-----	Im Herbst	HM	A-F	†
-----	Mutter, o sing mich zur Ruh	HL	E-G	†
-----	Sonnenuntergang	HL	CS-FS	†
-----	Staendchen	HL		†
-----	Sterne mit den gold' nen Fuesschen	HL	DS-E	†
-----	Weisst du noch	HL		GSC
Handel	Dank sei Dir, Herr (Added to Israel in Egypt)	M	CS-E	†
Haydn	She never told her love	HL	B-D	DIT
-----	The mermaid's song	M	C-F	PRE

227

Hindemith	Geburt Marias			AMP
Jensen	Am Ufer des Flusses des Manzanares	H	D-FS	GSC
-----	Waldesgespraech			
Konjovic	Lieder meiner Heimat			
Korngold	Love letter			AMP
Liszt	Freudvoll und leidvoll			DUR
Loehnor	O Ewigkeit			SIM
Loewe	Canzonetta	MH	B-A	DIT
-----	Des Glockenthuermers Tochterlein	H	CS-A	SC
-----	Walpurgisnacht	H	G-G	SC
Lohner	O Ewigkeit			
Mahler	Abloesung im Sommer	HL		INT
-----	Das Irdische Leben	HL	A-F	INT
-----	Erinnerung	HL		INT
-----	Fruehlingsmorgen	HL		INT
-----	Hans und Grethe	HL		INT
-----	Ich atmet' einen linden Duft	HL		INT
-----	Ich bin der Welt abbanden gekommen	HL		INT
-----	Ich ging mit Lust	HL		INT
-----	Liebst du um Schoenheit	HL		INT
-----	Nicht wiedersehen	HL		INT
-----	Scheiden und Meiden	HL		INT
-----	Starke Einbildungskraft	HL		INT
-----	Wer hat dies Liedlein erdacht?	HL	BF-E	INT
-----	Wo die schoenen Trompeten blasen	HL	GF-F	INT
Marx	Hat dich die Liebe beruehrt	MH	EF-BF	AMP
-----	Selige Nacht	M	DF-GF	AMP
-----	Und gestern hat er mir Rosen gebracht	H	E-A	AMP
-----	Valse de Chopin	M	CS-GS	AMP
Mendelssohn	An die Entfernte	M	F-F	
-----	And 'res Maienlied			AUG
-----	Bei der Wiege	M	DF-EF	†
-----	Der Mond	HL		†
-----	Die Liebende schreibt	HL		†
-----	Es weiss und raeth es doch keiner	H	D-G	
-----	Frage			†
-----	Gruss	M	DS-FS	†
-----	Im Gruenen	H	E-BF	AUG
-----	Keine von der Erde Schoenen			AUG

228

(Mendelssohn)	Lieblingsplaetzchen	LM	FS-E	†
-----	Morgengruss	M	D-E	AUG
-----	Nachtlied			
-----	Neue Liebe	H	CS-A	†
-----	On wings of song			†
-----	Pagenlied	M	E-E	†
-----	Schilflied	M	F-FS	
-----	Suleika	H	E-GS	†
Mozart	Abendempfindung	M	E-F	
-----	Als Luise die Briefe			GSC
-----	An Chloe	LH	EF-AF	
-----	Die Verschweigung			
-----	Warnung	HM	C-D	
-----	Wiegenlied	MH	G-G	†
Pfitzner	Gretel			BOO
Reger	Mit Rosen bestreut			UNI
-----	Waldeinsamkeit	HML	A-D	BOS
Schoeck	Herbstgefuehl			
-----	Mit einem getmaten Bande			
Schoenberg	Erhebung			GSC
Schubert	Am Feierabend	HL	BF-F	†
-----	Am Grabe Anselmos	HL	B-EF	†
-----	An den Mond	HL	F-GF	†
-----	An die Entfernte			PET
-----	An eine Quelle			PET
-----	An Emma			
-----	Auf dem Flusse	HL	F-E	†
-----	Auf dem Wasser zu singen	MH	EF-GF	†
-----	Aufenthalt	HLM	A-F	†
-----	Aufloesung	LH	D-A	†
-----	Ave Maria	LMH	F-F	†
-----	Das Echo	M	F-F	†
-----	Das Wandern	HLM	E-E	†
-----	Das Wirtshaus	HL	C-D	†
-----	Dass sie hier gewesen!			PET
-----	Dem Unendlichen	L	A-GF	DIT
-----	Der Atlas	HL	BF-F	†
-----	Der Doppelgaenger	HL	G-D	†
-----	Der Erlkoenig	HML	A-E	†
-----	Der Juengling an der Quelle	LH	E-A	†
-----	Der Juengling und der Tod	M	DF-FF	†
-----	Der Leiermann	ML	C-D	†
-----	Der Lindenbaum	HL	A-D	†
-----	Der Musensohn	LH	FS-G	†
-----	Der Neugierige	HL	CS-EF	†
-----	Der Wanderer	HML	FS-D	†
-----	Der Wegweiser	L	D-EF	†

(Schubert)	Des Maedchens Klage	LH	C-E	†
-----	Die Allmacht	HML	G-E	†
-----	Die Forelle	MLH	EF-GF	†
-----	Die junge Nonne	LH	C-GF	†
-----	Die Liebe hat gelogen	LM	G-F	†
-----	Die Maenner sind mechant			PET
-----	Die Nebensonnen	HL	F-D	†
-----	Die Post	HML	BF-EF	†
-----	Die Rose	M	G-FS	PET
-----	Die Unterscheidung	LH	D-G	†
-----	Du bist die Ruh	LMH	EF-AF	†
-----	Du liebst mich nicht	LH	E-FS	†
-----	Ellens zweiter Gesang			PET
-----	Erstarrung	HL	D-F	GSC
-----	Fruehlingsglaube	M	EF-F	†
-----	Fruehlingssehnsucht	HL	B-E	†
-----	Fruehlingstraum	HL	C-D	†
-----	Ganymed	LH	EF-G	†
-----	Gretchen am Spinnrade	H	F-A	†
-----	Gruppe aus dem Tartarus	L	CS-EF	†
-----	Heidenroeslein			
-----	Heimliches Lieben	LH	F-G	†
-----	Ihr Bild	HL	C-C	†
-----	Im Abendrot	HL	C-D	†
-----	Im Fruehling	LH	D-FS	†
-----	In der Ferne	HL		†
-----	Lachen und Weinen	HL	C-EF	†
-----	Letzte Hoffnung	HL		†
-----	Liebesbotschaft	H	E-G	†
-----	Lied der Mignon	HL		†
-----	Lied eines Schiffers an die Dioskuren	HL	A-C	†
-----	Litanei	HLM	C-EF	†
-----	Mein!	HL		†
-----	Mut	HL		†
-----	Nacht und Traeume	HL	C-DF	†
-----	Nur wer die Sehnsucht kennt	LH		†
-----	Schaefers Klagelied	HL	BF-D	†
-----	Schwanengesang			†
-----	Seligkeit			
-----	Staendchen	MH	B-E	†
-----	Traenenregen	HL		GSC
-----	Um Mitternacht	H	F-G	†
-----	Ungeduld	HML		†
-----	Vor meiner Wiege	HL	C-E	†
-----	Wanderers Nachtlied 2	LH	F-F	†
-----	Wiegenlied (Op. 98)			†

(Schubert)	Wohin?	HL	B-E	†
Schumann	Alte Laute	HL	DF-DF	†
-----	Auftraege	HL	C-E	†
-----	Aus den oestlichen Rosen			
-----	Aus den Hebraeischen Gesaengen			
-----	Der Nussbaum	LMH	D-FS	†
-----	Die Lotusblume	HLM	BF-F	†
-----	Die Soldatenbraut	HL	AF-EF	†
-----	Die Tochter Jephthas	HL	A-E	
-----	Du bist wie eine Blume	HM	F-EF	†
-----	Du Ring an meinem Finger	HL	C-F	†
-----	Er, der Herrlichste von Allen	HL	A-EF	†
-----	Er ist's	HL	BF-EF	†
-----	Fruehlingsnacht	L	CS-E	†
-----	Heiss' mich nicht reden			
-----	Hochlaendisches Wiegenlied			†
-----	Ihre Stimme	LH		†
-----	Im Westen	HL		†
-----	Lied der Suleika			
-----	Maerzveilchen	HL	C-C	†
-----	Marienwuermchen	HL	D-D	†
-----	Meine Rose			
-----	Mit Myrthen und Rosen	HL	A-D	†
-----	Mondnacht	M	E-FS	†
-----	O ihr Herren, o ihr Werthen	LH		†
-----	Provenzalisches Lied	LH		†
-----	Requiem			†
-----	Rose, Meer und Sonne			
-----	Schneegloeckchen	HL		†
-----	Seit ich ihn gesehen	HL	DF-DF	†
-----	Sitz' ich allein			
-----	Stille Traenen	HL		†
-----	Talismane			
-----	Volksliedchen	HL		†
-----	Waldesgespraech	HL	A-FS	†
-----	Wer machte dich so krank?			
-----	Widmung	HL	BF-F	†
Strauss	Ach Lieb, ich muss nun scheiden	H	D-G	
-----	Ah, du wolltest mich nicht deinem Mund			
-----	Allerseelen	HL	AS-E	†
-----	Befreit			HSC
-----	Breit ueber mein Haupt	LH	GF-AF	HSC
-----	Caecilie	MH	E-B	GSC
-----	Die Georgine	LH	B-A	†

(Strauss, R.)	Die Nacht	HL		†
-----	Du meines Herzens Kroenelein	HL	CS-E	†
-----	Fruendliche Vision	HL	C-F	†
-----	Hat gesagt bleibt s nicht dabei			†
-----	Heimkehr	HL	B-E	†
-----	Heimliche Aufforderung	HL	B-E	†
-----	Ich liebe dich			†
-----	Ich trage meine minne	M		†
-----	Kling			†
-----	Mein Herz ist stumm	LH	EF-AF	
-----	Mit deinen blauen Augen	LH	C-GS	†
-----	Morgen	HML	E-F	†
-----	Ruhe meine Seele			†
-----	Schoen sind doch kalt die Himmelssterne	H	F-BF	
-----	Traum durch die Daemmerung	HML	BF-EF	†
-----	Wiegenliedchen			†
-----	Zueignung	HL	CS-FS	†
Trunk	Der Feind			
-----	Die Nachtigallen			
Wagner	Der Engel	LH	CS-G	†
-----	Im Treibhaus	HL		†
-----	Schmerzen	HL		†
-----	Stehe still!	HL		GSC
-----	Traeume	HL		†
Wolf	Ach, im Maien	HL	C-E	†
-----	Alle gingen, Herz, zu Ruh	HL	C-EF	
-----	Anakreons Grab	HL	D-D	†
-----	An eine Aeolsharfe			†
-----	Auch kleine Dinge	HM	D-E	†
-----	Auf ein altes Bild	HL	E-DS	†
-----	Bedeckt mich mit Blumen	HL	B-D	†
-----	Blumengruss	HL	D-E	†
-----	Dank des Paria			PET
-----	Das Koehlerweib ist trunken			PET
-----	Das verlassene Maegdlein	HL	D-EF	†
-----	Denk' es, o Seele	LH	EF-F	†
-----	Der Freund	HM	BF-E	PET
-----	Der Gaertner	HL		†
-----	Der Knabe und das Immlein	L	CS-A	†
-----	Der Mond hat eine schwere Klag' erhoben	HL	BF-DF	†
-----	Die Bekehrte			PET
-----	Die ihr schwebet	HL	EF-EF	†

(Wolf)	Die Nacht			†
-----	Die Sproede			†
-----	Du denkst, mit einem Faedchen			†
-----	Elfenlied	HL	D-F	INT
-----	Er ist's	H	D-G	†
-----	Erstes Liebeslied eines Maedchens	H	EF-AF	†
-----	Fussreise	HL	D-E	†
-----	Gebet	HL		†
-----	Geh' Geliebter, geh' jetzt			PET
-----	Gleich und gleich			†
-----	Heimweh (Moerike Lieder)			†
-----	Ich hab' in Penna	LH		†
-----	In dem Schatten meiner Locken	M	C-EF	†
-----	In der Fruehe	HL	C-C	†
-----	Klinge, klinge, mein Pandero	HL	CF-EF	†
-----	Lebe wohl	HL	BF-F	†
-----	Liebe mir in Busen zuendet	M	E-F	†
-----	Lied vom Winde			†
-----	Mausfallen Spruechlein	HL	BF-E	†
-----	Mignon	LH		†
-----	Mir ward gesagt du reisest in die Ferne			†
-----	Morgenstimmung	LH	C-GS	†
-----	Mueh'voll komm' ich und beladen	H	D-G	†
-----	Nachtgruss			†
-----	Neue Liebe	LH	D-AF	†
-----	Nun wandre, Maria	HL	EF-D	†
-----	Peregrina I			†
-----	Sie blasen zum Abmarsch			
-----	Storchenbotschaft			†
-----	Ueber Nacht	LH	D-G	†
-----	Um Mitternacht	HL	G-EF	†
-----	Und willst du deinen Liebsten sterben	HL		†
-----	Verborgenheit	HL	B-E	†
-----	Verschwiegene Liebe	LH	DF-FS	†
-----	Wenn du, mein Liebster	LH	DF-GF	†
-----	Wenn du zu den Blumen gehst	HL	B-EF	†
-----	Wie glaenzt der helle Mond			†
-----	Wie lange schon war immer mein Verlangen			PET
-----	Wiegenlied			

(Wolf)	Zitronenfalter im April	HL		†
-----	Zur Ruh', zur Ruh'	HL	A-GF	†
Wolff	Alle Dinge haben Sprache	M	BF-GF	†
-----	Du bist so jung			HMP
-----	Stimme im Dunkeln	M	BF-GF	HMC

Italian Recital Songs

Dramatic Soprano

Bononcini	Deh, lascia			HEU
-----	L'esperto nocchiero (Astarte)	HL	B-E	†
-----	Per la gloria	HL	C-EF	†
Caccini	Amarilli, mia bella	ML	C-D	†
Caldara	Alma del core			GSC
-----	Come raggio di sol	HL	D-F	†
ᵣ-----	Sebben crudele	HML	E-DS	†
-----	Selve amiche, ombrose piante	HM	E-E	†
Carissimi	Vittoria, mio core	HLM	B-E	†
Casella	Amante sono vaghiccia di voi			RIC
Cavalli	Donzelle fuggite	HL	C-EF	†
Cesti	Intorno all' idol mio (Orontea)	MH	D-F	†
Cimara	Fiocca la neve	H	G-G	GSC
-----	Stornellata marinara	HM		RIC
Cimarosa	Bel nume che adoro			RIC
-----	Nel lasciarti (L'Olympiade)			RIC
D'Astorga	Vo' cercando in queste valli	H	D-G	STB
DeLuca	Non posso disperar	HL	C-E	GSC
Donaudy	O del mio amato ben	M	EF-F	RIC
Durante	Vergin, tutta amor	LM	C-EF	GSC
Falconieri	Non più d'amore	HL	C-D	DIT
-----	Nudo arciero	HL	AF-AF	DIT
-----	O bellissimi capelli	HL	B-D	†
Fasolo	Cangia, cangia tue voglie	H	C-G	GSC
Frescobaldi	Se l'aura spira	HL	C-EF	DIT
Galuppi	La pastorella (Il Filosoto di Campagna)			DUR
Giordani	Caro mio ben	HML	B-D	†
Gluck	Spiagge amate (Paride ed Elena)			†
Handel	Care selve (Atalanta)	MH	FS-A	†

(Handel)	Ch'io mai vi possa (Siroe)			†
-----	Lascia ch'io pianga (Rinaldo)			
-----	Ombra mai fu (Serse)	HM	BF-EF	†
-----	Rendi'l sereno al ciglio (Sosarme)	LH	EF-F	†
-----	Sommi Dei (Radimisto)			†
-----	V'adoro pupille (Julius Caesar)			BOO
Haydn	Un tetto umil			
Jommelli	Chi vuol comprar la bella	H	B-G	GSC
Legrenzi	Che fiero costume	HML	C-D	†
Lotti	Pur dicesti, o bocca bella	LMH	E-FS	GSC
Malipiero	Inno a Maria, Nostra Donna	H		CHE
Marcello	Il mio bel foco	LMH	C-G	GSC
-----	Non m' è grave morir per amore	L	C-E	GSC
Paisiello	Chi vuol la zingarella	L	C-F	GSC
Panizza	D'une prison	H	C-G	GSC
Paradies	M'ha preso alla sua ragna	M	EF-F	GSC
Pergolesi	Confusa, smarrita			GSC
-----	Dite ch' ogni momento			BOS
-----	Se tu m'ami	LMH	C-G	GSC
Quagliati	Apra il suo verde seno	HL	E-CS	DIT
Respighi	In alto mare			BON
-----	Mattinata			BON
-----	Nebbie			†
-----	Nevicata	HM		BON
-----	Pioggia			BON
Rontani	Or ch'io non segno più	HL	CS-E	DIT
Rosa	Selve, voi che le speranze	MH	D-G	DIT
Rossini	La danza	MH	E-A	†
Santoliguido	Riflessi			FOR
Scarlatti, A.	La fortuna			BOS
-----	Se Florindo è fedele	LM	EF-EF	GSC
Sibella	La Girometta	HML	D-E	GSC
Stradella	Così, amor, mi fai languir	HL	F-G	DIT
-----	Ragion sempre addita	H	E-G	GSC
-----	Se nel ben			CFI
Torelli	Tu lo sai	HL	BF-F	†
Tosti	Mattinata			RIC
Traetta	Ombra cara, amorosa	HL	B-F	†
Wolf-Ferrari	Un verde praticello			
Zandonai	Ultima rosa	M		RIC

Russian Recital Songs

Dramatic Soprano

Arensky	Autumn	H	CS-FS	GSC
-----	Revery	MH	DS-FS	DIT
Borodin	A dissonance	MH	E-F	†
Cui	The statue at Czarskoe-Selo	HM	DF-EF	†
Dargomijshky	I love you			
-----	The miller			
Gliere	Ah, twine no blossoms	HM	CS-F	DIT
Gretchaninoff	All along the highway			
-----	Hushed the song of the nightingale	MH	E-G	DIT
-----	Lullaby			
-----	Over the steppe	LM	C-G	GSC
-----	Snowflakes			AMP
-----	The snowdrop	HM	BF-F	DIT
Mednikoff	The hills of Gruzia	H	DS-A	LAC
Mussorgsky	Death the commander			
-----	Hopak	HM	CS-FS	GSC
-----	I love you			
-----	Night			GSC
-----	Star, you, will you tell me?			
-----	The miller			
-----	The orphan girl			GSC
-----	Tiny star where art thou	LH	DF-F	BOS
Rachmaninoff	All things depart			BOO
-----	Before my window	HM	C-G	GSC
-----	Daisies			†
-----	Floods of spring	HL		DIT
-----	God took away from me			GSC
-----	How fair this spot	MH		GSC
-----	In the silence of night	LH	D-A	GSC
-----	Lilacs	LH	EF-G	†
-----	Nuit de mai-fragment			
-----	Oh cease thy singing, maiden fair	H	E-A	CFI
-----	O, do not grieve	M	BF-AF	GSC
-----	Oh, no, I pray do not depart	H		DIT
-----	O thou billowy harvest field	HL	CS-E	GSC
-----	The coming of spring	LH	DF-AF	BOS
-----	The island	LH	DF-F	†
-----	The soldier's bride			†
-----	Vocalise	LH	CS-A	GSC
-----	When yesterday we met			BOH

236

| Tchaikovsky | All for you | | | |
| ----- | Regret | | | NOV |

Scandinavian Recital Songs

Dramatic Soprano

Alnaes	En morgen var din grav	M	CS-D	HAN
-----	Lykken mellem to mennesker	M	B-FS	HAN
-----	Nu brister i alle de kløfter	L	A-F	HAN
-----	Vaarlaengsler			
-----	Ved syrintid			
-----	A dream			†
-----	A swan			†
-----	By the brook			GSC
-----	Den Aergjerrige			
-----	Det syng	M	C-GF	HAN
-----	En fuglevise			
-----	Eros	LM	C-F	†
-----	From Monte Pincio			PET
-----	Formål			
-----	Greeting			PET
-----	Gutten			
-----	Heart wounds			
-----	Hope			
-----	I love thee	HML	E-F	†
-----	In the boat	LM	D-ES	†
-----	Prinsessen	HL	B-E	†
-----	Radiant night			
-----	Saint John's eve	L	DF-E	CFI
-----	Simpel sang			
-----	Snegl, Snegl	M	B-F	HAN
-----	Springtide	M		DIT
-----	The wounded heart			PET
-----	To Norway	M	E-F	DIT
-----	Udvandreren	M	EF-F	HAN
-----	Vaer hilset, I Damer	M	D-F	HAN
-----	With a primrose	H	DF-GF	GSC
-----	With a water lily	HM	CS-EF	†
Hakanson	Budbarerskan			
Jonsson	Under haeggarna			
Jordan	Es naht der Herbst			
-----	Og se hun kom			
Kjerulf	Synnove's song	M	C-F	GSC
Lie	Soft-footed snow	HM		DIT
Nielson	Aebleblomsten			HAN

(Nielson)	Sommersang			HAN
Sibelius	Black roses	M	A-ES	AMP
-----	Diamonds on the March snow			
-----	On a balcony by the sea			
Sinding	I hear the gull			JCH
Soderberg	Fågelns visa			
Thrane	Aagots fjeldsang			

Spanish Recital Songs

Dramatic Soprano

Alvarez	La partida	HL	DS-E	GSC
Falla	Siete canciones	HL		AMP
Ginastera	Canción al árbol del olvido			RIC
Ginastera	Triste			RIC
Nin	El amor es como un nino			ESC
-----	El vito			ESC
Obradors	Coplas de curro dulce			
-----	Del cabello mas sutil			RIC
-----	El tumba y le			

Miscellaneous Recital Songs

Dramatic Soprano

Bach-Gounod	Ave Maria			
Bizet	Agnus Dei	HLM	C-AF	
Chajes	Adarim			TRA
Dvořák	Clouds and darkness			
-----	God is my shepherd			AMP
-----	Hear my prayer, O Lord			AMP
-----	I will sing new songs of gladness	HL		†
-----	Lord, Thou art my refuge and shield			AMP
-----	Song my mother taught me	HM	E-E	†
-----	Turn Thee to me			AMP
Fisher	Eili, Eili	LMH	E-G	DIT
Franck	Panis angelicus	LM		
Konjovic	Bosnian song			
-----	Serbian song			
Mozart	Alleluia	LMH	F-C	
Schubert	Ave Maria			
Villa-Lobos	Cançao do carreiro			

British Songs For Opening Recitals

Dramatic Soprano

Green	My lips shall speak the praise	M	E-F	OXF
-----	Salvation belongeth unto the Lord	M	F-EF	OXF
Handel	Have mercy Lord (Te Deum)	HM		†
-----	Let me wander not unseen (L'Allegro)	M	D-G	†
-----	Trip, blithe streamlet (Serse)			
Purcell	If music be the food of love	M	D-G	BOO
-----	Music for a while (Oedipus)	LH		SC
-----	When I am laid in earth (Dido and Aeneas)	LH	C-G	†

German Songs For Opening Recitals

Dramatic Soprano

Bach, J. S.	Bist du bei mir	HML	A-EF	†
Beethoven	Andenken			†
-----	God is my song			
-----	Ich liebe dich	HL	BF-DF	†
Brahms	Nachtigall	MHL	BF-FS	†
Buxtehude	Singet dem Herrn Violin and piano			
Handel	Dank sei Dir, Herr	M	CS-E	†
Mozart	An Chloe	LH	EF-AF	
Schubert	Das Wandern	HLM	E-E	†
-----	Ganymed	LH	EF-G	†
-----	Liebesbotschaft	H	E-G	†
Schumann	Mit Myrthen und Rosen	HL	A-D	†
Wolf	Ueber Nacht	LH	D-G	†
Wolff	Stimme im Dunkeln	M	BF-GF	HMC

Italian Songs and Arias For Opening Recitals

Dramatic Soprano

Beethoven	Ah! Perfido	H		DIT

Caccini	Amarilli, mia bella	ML	C-D	†
Caldara	Sebben crudele	HML	E-DS	†
Carissimi	Vittoria, mio core	HLM	B-E	†
Cimara	Stornellata marinara	HM		RIC
Cimarosa	Nel lasciarti (L'Olympiade)			RIC
Durante	Vergin, tutta amor	LM	C-EF	†
Falconieri	O bellissimi capelli	HL	B-D	†
Gluck	Spiagge amate (Paride ed Elena)			†
Handel	Care selve (Atalanta)	MH	FS-A	†
-----	Ch'io mai vi possa (Siroe)			†
-----	Lascia ch'io pianga (Rinaldo)	HM	EF-F	†
-----	Ombra mai fu (Serse)	HM	BF-EF	†
-----	Rendi'l sereno al ciglio (Sosarme)	LH	EF-F	†
-----	V'adoro pupille (Julius Caesar)			BOO
Jommelli	Chi vuol comprar la bella	H	B-G	GSC
Lotti	Pur dicesti, o bocca bella	LMH	E-FS	GSC
Marcello	Il mio bel foco	LMH	C-G	GSC
Mozart	Ch'io mi scordi di te			BOO
-----	Non più di fiori (La Clemenza di Tito)			†
-----	Parto, parto (La Clemenza di Tito) B flat clarinet and piano	H		AMP
Paisiello	Chi vuol la zingarella	L	C-F	GSC
Pergolesi	Se tu m'ami	LMH	C-G	GSC
Stradella	Se nel ben			CFI
Traetta	Ombra cara, amorosa	HL	B-F	†

American Songs For Closing Recitals

Dramatic Soprano

Barber	I hear an army	LH	D-AF	GSC
-----	Sure on this shining night	MH	D-G	GSC
Bassett	Take joy home	LH	EF-BF	GSC
Cadman	Joy	MH	E-A	GSC
Carpenter	Light, my light	M	C-G	GSC
-----	Serenade	LH	CS-A	GSC
Charles	And so, goodbye	LH	EF-AF	GSC
-----	Let my song fill your heart	LH	EF-AF	GSC

(Charles)	Night	MH	F-AF	GSC
-----	When I have sung my songs	HM	BF-EF	GSC
Clough-Leighter	My lover he comes on the skee	HM	D-F	BOS
Crist	Knock on the door	H	EF-AF	GSC
Curran	Life	HM	BF-F	GSC
Dougherty	Everyone sang			
-----	Song for autumn			
Giannini	Sing to my heart a song	H	D-B	ELV
Hageman	At the well	LH	EF-AF	GSC
-----	Miranda	HL		GAL
Horsman	The bird of the wilderness	LMH	DF-BF	GSC
Ilgenfritz	Blow, blow thou winter wind			
Kernochan	We two together	H	EF-AF	GAL
La Forge	Hills	HL		RIC
-----	Into the light	HL		RIC
-----	Song of the open	MH	EF-AF	DIT
Levitzki	Ah, thou beloved one	H	EF-AF	GSC
Malotte	Upstream	M	C-F	GSC
McArthur	Night	H	F-AF	GSC
-----	Spring came	HL	D-F	GSC
McDonald	Daybreak	H		ELV
Nordoff	Tell me, Thyrsis	H	E-G	AMP
Rogers	The last song	MLH	E-AF	GSC
-----	Time for making songs	HM	CS-F	DIT
Rummel	Ecstasy	LMH	GF-AF	GSC
Salter	The cry of Rachel	LH	C-AF	GSC
Schuman	Holiday song	M	C-F	GSC
Speaks	Morning	HML	BF-D	GSC
Tyson	Sea moods	LH	E-AF	GSC
Ware	This day is mine	MH	EF-AF	BOS
Warren	We two	LH	E-A	GSC
Worth	Midsummer	LM	E-A	GSC

(See also Negro Spirituals and Folk Songs.)

Miscellaneous Songs For Closing Recitals

Dramatic Soprano

Besley	Listening	H	E-AF	CUR
Bizet	Adieu de l'hôtesse arabe	H	BF-G	†
Bliss	The buckle			CUR
-----	Three jolly gentlemen	H		†

Brahms	Feinsliebchen, du sollst nicht barfuss geh'n			†
-----	Juchhe!			†
-----	Meine Liebe ist gruen	MLH	ES-A	†
-----	Wie froh und frisch	HL	B-E	†
-----	Willst du, dass ich geh'?	L	C-G	†
Bridge	Love went a-riding	HL		BOS
Dargomijshky	The miller			
Debussy	Chevaux de bois	H	C-G	†
Delius	Love's philosophy			†
Falla	Jota	LH		AMP
Grieg	By the brook			GSC
-----	En fuglevise			
-----	Simpel sang			
-----	Vaer hilset, I Damer	M	D-F	HAN
Head	A piper	HL		BOO
Hely Hutchinson	Old mother Hubbard	HL	B-E	CFI
Henschel	Morning-hymn	MH	DS-GS	DIT
Konjovic	Bosnian song			
Nin	El vito			ESC
Obradors	Coplas de curro dulce			
-----	El tumba y le			
Poulenc	Air vif	H	C-AF	ROU
Quilter	Blow, blow thou winter wind	HL	C-E	BOO
-----	Love's philosophy	LMH	D-A	BOO
Rachmaninoff	Floods of spring	HL		DIT
-----	Oh, no, I pray do not depart	H		DIT
Respighi	Pioggia			BON
Ronald	Love, I have won you	HML	EF-EF	ENO
Schoenberg	Erhebung			GSC
Schubert	Aufloesung	LH	D-A	†
-----	Die Forelle	MLH	EF-GF	†
Schumann	Er ist's	HL	BF-EF	†
Strauss, J.	Blue Danube waltz			GSC
Trunk	Der Feind			
Villa-Lobos	Cançao do carreiro			
Wolf	Er ist's	H	D-G	†
-----	Morgenstimmung	LH	C-GS	†
-----	Wie lange schon war immer mein Verlangen			PET

Atmospheric Songs

Dramatic Soprano

Alnaes	Lykken mellem to mennesker	M	B-FS	HAN
Barber	Rain has fallen	HM	D-E	GSC
Benjamin	Calm sea and mist			CUR
Burleigh	Sometimes I feel like a motherless child	HML		RIC
Carpenter	Go, lovely rose	M	DF-EF	GSC
-----	On the seashore of endless worlds	M	C-FS	GSC
-----	The pools of peace	M	D-F	GSC
-----	When I bring to you colour'd toys	LM	CS-FS	GSC
Chaminade	The silver ring	HM	BF-F	GSC
Charles	Clouds	HML	C-EF	GSC
-----	When I have sung my songs	HM	BF-EF	GSC
Chausson	Les papillons	M	C-F	GSC
Cimara	Fiocca la neve	H	G-G	GSC
Cui	The statue at Czarskoe-Selo	HM	DF-EF	†
Curran	Nocturne Violin	HML	B-DS	GSC
Davis	Nancy Hanks	H	D-G	GAL
Debussy	C'est l'extase	LH	CS-A	†
Duke	Bells in the rain	H	E-GS	CFI
-----	The bird			GSC
Dunhill	The cloths of heaven	LM	EF-G	STB
Duparc	La vie antérieure	HL		†
Eakin	What of that midnight long ago	M	D-F	GAL
Elmore and Reed	Come all ye who weary	L	C-C	JFI
Ferrata	Night and the curtains drawn			JFI
Fourdrain	Chanson norvégienne	H	E-G	RIC
Franz	Sterne mit den gold'nen Fuesschen	HL	DS-E	†
Ganz	A memory	HM	B-D	GSC
Grieg	A dream			†
-----	A swan			†
-----	Det syng	M	C-GF	HAN
-----	In the boat	LM	D-ES	†
-----	Radiant night			
-----	Snegl, Snegl	M	B-F	HAN
-----	Udvandreren	M	EF-F	HAN
Griffes	Symphony in yellow	M	D-GF	GSC
-----	The dreamy lake	H	BS-GS	GSC
Guion	At the cry of the first bird	H	D-G	GSC

243

Hageman	Do not go, my love	HL	B-EF	GSC
Hahn	D'une prison	L	BF-EF	HEU
-----	L'heure exquise	M	DF-F	†
-----	Paysage	MH	EF-G	HEU
Haydn	She never told her love	HL	B-D	DIT
Holst	The heart worships	ML	BF-D	STB
Hughes	O men from the fields	M	F-F	BOO
Kjerulf	Synnove's song	M	C-F	GSC
Kramer	Now like a lantern	M		RIC
Lie	Soft-footed snow	HM		DIT
Lynn	Gently little Jesus	L	BF-BF	DIT
-----	The magic night of Christmas	M	D-D	DIT
MacGimsey	Sweet little Jesus boy	ML	D-D	CFI
Mahler	Ich ging mit Lust	HL		INT
Marx	Selige Nacht	M	DF-GF	AMP
McArthur	Night	H	F-AF	GSC
Mussorgsky	Tiny star where art thou	LH	DF-F	BOS
Naginski	Look down, fair moon			
Niles	I wonder as I wander	HL	BF-D	GSC
Nordoff	Music I heard with you	H	DS-FS	AMP
Paladilhe	Psyché	HM	BF-F	GSC
Poldowski	L'heure exquise	LMH	DF-AF	CHE
Proctor	I light the blessed candles	H	DF-A	GSC
Rachmaninoff	Lilacs	LH	EF-G	†
Reger	The Virgin's slumber song	MMH	G-G	†
Sacco	The ragpicker	MH	C-AF	GSC
Schubert	Nacht und Traeume	HL	C-DF	†
Schumann	Der Nussbaum	LMH	D-FS	†
Strauss, R.	Die Nacht	HL		†
-----	Traum durch die Daemmerung	HML	BF-EF	†
Tyson	Like barley bending	HL	C-EF	GSC
Vaughan Williams	Silent noon			GSC
Wolf	In dem Schatten meiner Locken	M	C-EF	GSC
-----	Verborgenheit	HL	B-E	†

American Dramatic Songs

Dramatic Soprano

Barber	I hear an army	LH	D-AF	GSC
Beach	Ah, love but a day			ASC
-----	The year's at the spring	MH	AF-AF	ASC

244

Campbell-Tipton				
Campbell-Tipton	A spirit flower	LHM	B-G	GSC
-----	The crying of water	LH	FS-GS	GSC
Carpenter	Berceuse de guerre	M	C-G	GSC
-----	I am like a remnant of a cloud of autumn	L	BF-F	GSC
-----	Light, my light	M	C-G	GSC
Crist	You will not come again	HML	BF-CS	CFI
Curran	Life	HM	BF-F	GSC
Giannini	Sing to my heart a song	H	D-B	ELV
Griffes	Evening song	H	DS-GS	GSC
-----	Sorrow of Mydath	M		GSC
-----	The lament of Ian the proud	MH	DS-AS	GSC
-----	The rose of the night	H	CS-A	GSC
-----	Thy dark eyes to mine	H	EF-AF	GSC
Guion	Wild geese	M	D-F	CFI
Hageman	Do not go, my love	HL	B-EF	GSC
-----	Music I heard with you	MH	E-A	GAL
Horsman	The bird of the wilderness	LMH	DF-BF	GSC
Kernochan	We two together	H	EF-AF	GAL
La Forge	Grieve not, beloved	H	FS-G	RIC
-----	Song of the open	MH	EF-AF	DIT
Nordoff	Tell me, Thyrsis	H	E-G	AMP
Protheroe	Ah, love but a day	LMH	F-AF	GAM
Rogers	The last song	MLH	E-AF	GSC
-----	Time for making songs	HM	CS-F	DIT
Salter	The cry of Rachel	LH	C-AF	GSC
Schuman	Holiday song	M	C-F	GSC
Speaks	Morning	HML	BF-D	GSC
Tyson	Sea moods	LH	E-AF	GSC
Vene	Age and youth	H	E-A	RIC
Ware	This day is mine	MH	EF-AF	BOS
Warren	We two	LH	E-A	GSC
Worth	Midsummer	LM	E-A	GSC

British Dramatic Songs and Arias

Dramatic Soprano

Bainton	Ring out, wild bells	M	C-EF	OXF
Bax	Rann of exile	H	D-G	CHE
Besley	Listening	H	E-AF	CUR
Bridge	O that it were so	LMH	D-G	CHA
Clarke	Eight o'clock			ROG
Coleridge-Taylor	Life and death	HML		ASC
Delius	Indian love song	H		†

Del Riego	Homing	HML	BF-E	CHA
Elgar	Be not extreme, O Lord			NOV
Henschel	Morning-hymn	MH	DS-GS	†
Purcell	When I am laid in earth (Dido and Aeneas)	LH	C-G	†
Quilter	Blow, blow thou winter wind	HL	C-E	BOO
Ronald	Down in the forest	HML	C-D	ENO
-----	Prelude	HML	B-D	ENO

French Dramatic Songs and Arias

Dramatic Soprano

Berlioz	D'amour l'ardente flamme (La Damnation de Faust)			NOV
-----	Le spectre de la rose			CST
Chausson	Chanson perpétuelle String quartet	H	CS-GS	ROU
-----	La caravane	MH	CS-A	HAM
-----	Poème de l'amour et de la mer	H		INT
Debussy	Air de Lia (L'Enfant Prodigue)	H	E-A	DUR
-----	Chevaux de bois	H	C-G	†
-----	Colloque sentimental			DUR
-----	De fleurs	H	C-AF	†
Duparc	Au pays où se fait la guerre			SAL
-----	La vague et la cloche			ROU
-----	La vie antérieure	HL		†
-----	Le manoir de Rosamunde	HL	B-F	BOS
-----	Phidylé	MH	EF-AF	BOS
-----	Testament	HL		INT
Fauré	Automne	MH	D-FS	GSC
-----	Fleur jetée	HM	BF-FS	†
-----	L'hiver a cessé	HL		INT
-----	Prison	LH		†
-----	Toujours	LH	F-AF	†
Fourdrain	Chanson norvégienne	H	E-G	RIC
Gluck	L'ai-je-bien entendu? (Iphigénie en Aulide)			JOB
-----	Le perfide Renaud me fuit (Armide)			PET
-----	Non! ce n'est point (Alceste)	H	E-G	†
Gounod	Plus grand, dans son obscurité (La Reine de Saba)	MH	CS-B	†

Hahn	D'une prison	L	BF-EF	HEU
-----	Offrande	M	D-D	†
Halévy	Il va venir (La Juive)	H	D-CF	†
Honegger	Les cloches			SEN
Hue	J'ai pleuré en rêve	HL	D-E	BOS
Lenormand	Quelle souffrance	HM	AF-F	HAM
Massenet	Charmes des jours passés (Hérodiade)			HEU
-----	Dis-moi que je suis belle (Thaïs)	H	D-B	HEU
-----	Il est doux, il est bon (Hérodiade)	MH	EF-BF	GSC
Meyerbeer	Ah! mon fils (Le Prophète)	M	B-AS	†
Milhaud	Chant du laboureur	M	B-F	ESC
Paladilhe	Lamento provinçal	M	CS-FS	HOM
Poldowski	Dansons la gigue	M	EF-G	MAR
-----	L'heure exquise	LMH	DF-AF	CHE
Saint-Saëns	L'attente			DUR
Spontini	Toi que j'implore (La Vestale)			LEM

German Dramatic Songs and Arias

Dramatic Soprano

Beethoven	Abscheulicher, wo eilst du hin? (Fidelio)		B-B	†
Brahms	Ach, wende diesen Blick			†
-----	Am Sonntag Morgen	L	CS-FS	†
-----	Nicht mehr zu dir zu gehen			†
-----	Von ewiger Liebe	LMH	B-AF	†
Bruch	Ave Maria (Das Feuerkreuz)	LH	D-BF	AMP
Franz	Im herbst	HM	A-F	†
Liszt	Freudvoll und Leidvoll			DUR
Loewe	Walpurgisnacht	H	G-G	SC
Mahler	Das Irdische Leben	HL	A-F	INT
-----	Um Mitternacht	HL		INT
Marx	Hat dich die Liebe beruehrt	MH	EF-BF	AMP
-----	Selige Nacht	M	DF-GF	AMP
Mendelssohn	Hear ye, Israel (Elijah)	H	E-A	†
-----	Schilflied	M	F-FS	
Schoenberg	Erhebung			GSC
Schubert	Am Feierabend	HL	BF-F	†
-----	Auf dem Flusse	HL	F-E	†
-----	Aufenthalt	HLM	A-F	†
-----	Dem Unendlichen	L	A-GF	†

247

(Schubert)	Der Atlas	HL	BF-F	†
-----	Der Doppelgaenger	HL	G-D	†
-----	Der Erlkoenig	HML	A-E	†
-----	Der Lindenbaum	HL	A-D	GSC
-----	Die Allmacht	HML	G-E	†
-----	Die junge Nonne	LH	C-GF	†
-----	Die Liebe hat gelogen	LM	G-F	†
-----	Du liebst mich nicht	LH	E-FS	†
-----	Erstarrung	HL	D-F	†
-----	Fruehlingstraum	HL	C-D	†
-----	Ganymed	LH	EF-G	†
-----	Gruppe aus dem Tartarus	L	CS-EF	†
-----	In der Ferne	HL		†
-----	Mut	HL		†
-----	Schaefers Klagelied	HL	BF-D	†
Schumann	Heiss' mich nicht reden			
-----	Mit Myrthen und Rosen	HL	A-D	†
-----	Talismane			
-----	Waldesgespraech	HL	A-FS	†
Strauss	Caecilie	MH	E-B	†
-----	Kling			†
-----	Ruhe meine Seele			†
-----	Zueignung	HL	CS-FS	†
Trunk	Der Feind			
Wagner	Dich theure Halle (Tannhaeuser)	H	DS-A	†
-----	Du bist der Lenz (Die Walkuere)			†
-----	Schmerzen	HL		†
-----	Senta's ballad (Der Fliegende Hollaender)			GSC
-----	Starke Scheite (Goetterdaemmerung)			GSC
Weber	Bethoerte, die an meine Liebe glaubt (Euryanthe)			PET
-----	Ozean, du Ungeheuer (Oberon)	H	C-C	GSC
Wolf	Alle gingen, herz, zu Ruh	HL	C-EF	†
-----	Das Koehlerweib ist trunken			PET
-----	Denk' es, o Seele	LH	EF-F	†
-----	Der Freund	HM	BF-E	PET
-----	Die ihr schwebet	HL	EF-EF	†
-----	Geh' Geliebter, geh' jetzt			PET
-----	Lebe wohl	HL	BF-F	†
-----	Liebe mir in Busen zuendet	M	E-F	†
-----	Ueber Nacht	LH	D-G	†
-----	Zur Ruh', zur Ruh'	HL	A-GF	†

Italian Dramatic Songs and Arias

Dramatic Soprano

Boito	Morte di Margherita (L'altra notte) (Mefistofele)	H	D-B	GSC
Casella	Amante sono vaghiccia di voi			RIC
Catalani	Ebben? Ne andro lontana (La Wally)	H	E-B	RIC
Donizetti	O mio Fernando (La Favorita)	M	B-A	†
Durante	Vergin, tutta amor	LM	C-EF	†
Mascagni	Un di ero piccina (Iris)			RIC
-----	Voi lo sapete (Cavalleria Rusticana)	H	B-A	†
Mozart	Or sai, chi l'onore (Don Giovanni)			†
Pergolesi	Confusa, smarrita			GSC
Ponchielli	Stella del marinar (La Gioconda)	M	B-A	RIC
-----	Suicidio! (La Gioconda)	HM	BF-AF	†
Puccini	In quelle trine morbide (Manon Lescaut)	H	DF-BF	RIC
-----	Tu, che di gel sei cinta (Turandot)			RIC
-----	Un bel di vedremo (Madama Butterfly)	H	DF-BF	RIC
-----	Vissi d'arte (Tosca)	MH	EF-BF	RIC
Respighi	In alto mare			BON
-----	Nebbie			†
Verdi	Ecco l'orrido campo (Un Ballo in Maschera)	H	B-C	RIC
-----	Madre, pietosa Vergine (La Forza del Destino)	H	B-B	RIC
-----	Morrò, ma prima in grazia (Un Ballo in Maschera)			RIC
-----	O don fatale (Don Carlos)	MH	CF-CF	†
-----	Pace, pace mio Dio (La Forza del Destino)	H	CS-BF	†
-----	Ritorna vincitor (Aida)	H	DF-BF	†
-----	Tu che la vanita (Don Carlos)			RIC

Miscellaneous Dramatic Songs and Arias

Dramatic Soprano

Alvarez	La partida	HL	DS-E	GSC

249

Borodin	A dissonance	MH	E-F	†
Dvořák	Hear my prayer, O Lord			AMP
Gliere	Ah, twine no blossoms	HM	CS-F	DIT
Granados	La maja dolorosa	M		INT
Gretchaninoff	Over the steppe	LM	C-G	GSC
Grieg	A dream			†
-----	A swan			†
-----	Den Aergjerrige			
-----	Eros	LM	C-F	†
-----	In the boat	LM	D-ES	†
-----	Prinsessen	HL	B-E	†
-----	Simpel sang			
-----	Vaer hilset, I Damer	M	D-F	HAN
Mussorgsky	Hopak	HM	CS-FS	GSC
-----	The orphan girl			GSC
Rachmaninoff	Christ is risen	LM	D-F	GAL
-----	Floods of spring	HL		DIT
-----	God took away from me			GSC
-----	O, do not grieve	M	BF-AF	GSC
-----	Oh, no, I pray, do not depart	H		DIT
-----	O thou billowy harvest field	HL	CS-E	GSC
-----	The soldier's bride			†
-----	To the children	MH	F-G	DIT
Sibelius	Black roses	M	A-ES	AMP
Tchaikovsky	Adieu forêts (Jeanne d'Arc)	HM	BF-FS	GSC
-----	All for you			
-----	Letter scene (Eugene Onegin)			GSC
-----	None but the lonely heart	HLM	C-F	DIT

Humorous Songs

Dramatic Soprano

Bax	Oh dear, what can the matter be?	M	D-EF	CHE
Bernstein	I hate music	H	C-A	WIT
Bliss	The buckle			CUR
-----	Three jolly gentlemen	H		†
Brahms	Der Kranz			†
-----	Vergebliches Staendchen	LHM	E-FS	†
Carpenter	Don't ceare	M	C-D	GSC
-----	If	M	D-E	GSC
Chabrier	Villanelle des petits canards	HML	B-E	†

Clarke	Shy one	HL	BF-G	BOH
Crist	Chinese mother goose rhymes	H	C-G	CFI
Dougherty	Love in the dictionary	M	C-G	GSC
Gibbs	Five eyes	HL	D-D	BOS
Grieg	My Johann	HL	BF-EF	GSC
Griselle and Young	The cuckoo clock	LH	EF-G	GSC
Hadley	My shadow			ASC
Hely-Hutchinson	Old Mother. Hubbard	HL	B-E	CFI
Hindemith	The whistling thief	M	E-F	AMP
Josten	Cupid's counsel	H	EF-AF	GSC
Lehmann	The cuckoo	HH	D-B	BOH
Loewe	Das Glockenthuermers Tochterlein	H	CS-A	SC
Mahler	Wer hat dies Liedlein erdacht?	HL	BF-E	INT
Mozart	Warnung	HM	C-D	
Nordoff	Serenade	H	CS-FS	AMP
-----	There shall be more joy	M	CS-FS	AMP
Paisiello	Chi vuol la zingarella	L	C-F	GSC
Pierné	Ils etaient trois petits chats blancs			MAR
Reger	Waldeinsamkeit	HML	A-D	BOS
Rich	American lullaby	LH	C-F	GSC
Rontani	Or ch'io non sengo più	HL	CS-E	DIT
Satie	Le chapelier			ROU
Schubert	Die Maenner sind mechant			PET
-----	Heidenroeslein			
Schuman	Holiday song	M	C-F	GSC
Slonimsky	Gravestones at Hancock, New Hampshire	H	D-G	AXE
Spross	Will o' the wisp			JCH
Stein	The puffin	M		CFI
Wolf	Weather forecast	H	EF-GS	GSC
-----	Der Knabe und das Immlein	L	CS-A	†
-----	Elfenlied	HL	D-F	†
-----	Ich hab' in Penna	LH		
-----	Storchenbotschaft			†

American Folk Songs (Arr.)

Dramatic Soprano

Brockway	Barbara Allen			GRA
-----	Frog went-a-courting			GRA

(Brockway)	The nightingale			GRA
-----	The old maid's song			GRA
Davis	Deaf old woman			GAL
Foster, S.C.	Sweetly she sleeps			
Hughes	Birds' courting song			GSC
Niles	Down in the valley			GSC
-----	I wonder as I wander	HL	BF-D	GSC
-----	The blue Madonna			GSC
Powell	The rich old woman	M		JFI
Siegmeister	He's gone away			

British Folk Songs (Arr.)

Dramatic Soprano

Bax	Oh, dear, what can the matter be?	M	D-EF	CHE
Beethoven	Irish songs			
-----	Scotch songs			
Britten	The Sally gardens			BOH
Gatty	Bendemeer's stream	LMH		BOO
Grainger	The sprig of thyme	LH	E-FS	GSC
Harty	The lowlands of Holland			OXF
Hopekirk	Coming through the rye			DIT
-----	Flow gently, sweet Afton			DIT
-----	Loch Lomond			DIT
Hughes	Down by the Sally gardens			BOO
-----	Hey diddle diddle			CRA
-----	I know my love			BOO
-----	The leprehaun			
Kennedy-Fraser	An Eriskay love lilt			BOO
-----	Land of heart's desire			BOO
-----	The Bens of Jura			BOO
-----	The road to the isles			BOO
Kreisler	Leezie Lindsay			
Page	The foggy dew			
-----	The harp that once through Tara's halls			DIT
Quilter	Ye banks and braes	M	DF-EF	BOH
Vaughan Williams	And all in the morning			STB
-----	Robin Hood and the pedlar	M	D-E	OXF
-----	Rolling in the dew			OXF
Welsh	All through the night			
-----	The ash grove			
Wilson	Come let's be merry			BOO

Miscellaneous Folk Songs (Arr.)

Dramatic Soprano

Brahms	Da unten in Thale			†
-----	Erlaube mir, fein's Maedchen			†
-----	Feinsliebchen, du sollst nicht barfuss geh'n			†
-----	Mein Maedel hat einen Rosenmund	M	F-F	†
Dvořák	Gypsy songs	LH	D-A	AMP
Falla	Jota	LH		AMP
-----	Siete canciones	HL		AMP
Ferrari	Le jardin d'amour	LM	EF-F	GSC
Liddle	An old French carol	LM	F-F	BOO
McFeeters	Gentle Mary	H	EF-AF	GSC
Ravel	Chanson italienne			DUR
-----	Là-bas vers l'église	MH	GS-E	DUR
-----	Tout gai	MH	EF-F	DUR
Weckerlin	Chantons les amours de Jean	H	D-G	GSC

Negro Spirituals

Dramatic Soprano

Boatner	Oh, what a beautiful city!	HL	D-E	GSC
-----	On mah journey	LH	EF-EF	RIC
-----	Trampin'(Tryin' to make Heaven my home	L	D-F	ELK
Burleigh	De gospel train	HL		RIC
-----	Deep river	HML		RIC
-----	Go down, Moses	HL		RIC
-----	Hard trials	M		RIC
-----	Joshua fit de battle ob Jericho	LH	DS-E	RIC
-----	Little David play on yo' harp	HL		RIC
-----	Oh, didn't it rain	LH		RIC
-----	Oh, Peter, go ring a dem bells			RIC
-----	Sometimes I feel like a motherless child	HML		RIC
-----	Swing low, sweet chariot	HL		RIC
-----	Were you there?	HML		RIC
Dett	Sit down servant			GSC
Johnson	City called Heaven			ROB
-----	Dere's no hidin' place down dere			

(Johnson)	Hold on			ROB
-----	Honor, honor	HM	C-E	CFI
-----	My good Lord done been here	HM	BF-F	CFI
-----	Witness	HM	D-F	CFI
Kerby-Forrest	He's got the whole world in His hands	M	G-E	MLS
MacGimsey	Sweet little Jesus boy	ML	D-D	CFI
Price	My soul's been anchored in the Lord			GAM
Ryder	Let us break bread together	LH	D-G	JFI
White	Wake up Jacob			PRE

American Songs Employing Agility

Dramatic Soprano

Charles	Let my song fill your heart	LH	EF-AF	GSC
Clough-Leighter	My lover he comes on the skee	HM	D-F	BOS
Crist	O come hither	HM	B-GS	CFI
Curran	Ho! Mr. Piper	LH	D-G	GSC
Gaines	My heart hath a mind			
Hageman	Miranda	HL		GAL
Nevin	One spring morning	MH	DS-F	BOS
Nordoff	There shall be more joy	M	CS-FS	AMP
Speaks	In May time	HL	D-E	JCH

British Songs Employing Agility

Dramatic Soprano

Arne, T.	Where the bee sucks	HM		†
Bax	Shieling song	H	CS-A	CHE
Besley	Listening	H	E-AF	CUR
Bishop	Love has eyes	M		†
Bliss	Three jolly gentlemen	H		†
German	Charming Chloe	HML		NOV
Green	My lips shall speak the praise	M	E-F	OXF
-----	Salvation belongeth unto the Lord	M	F-EF	OXF
Hely-Hutchinson	Old Mother Hubbard	HL	B-E	CFI

Moeran	Bright cap			OXF
Morley	It was a lover and his lass	HM		DIT
Purcell	Nymphs and shepherds	HM	C-F	†
	(The Libertine)			
Quilter	Love's philosophy	LMH	D-A	BOO
Scott	Blackbird's song			ELK
Wilson	Come let's be merry			BOO

French Songs Employing Agility

Dramatic Soprano

Bizet	Adieux de l'hôtesse arabe			
-----	Ouvre ton coeur	MH	DS-GS	†
Chausson	Le colibri			
-----	Les papillons	M	C-F	GSC
Delibes	Le rossignol	M		GSC
Fauré	Mandoline	HL	F-E	†
Ferrari	Le jardin d'amour	LM	EF-F	GSC
Georges	La pluie	HL		INT
Meyerbeer	Nobles Seigneurs, salut!			
	(Les Huguenots)			
Poulenc	Air vif	H	C-AF	ROU
Ravel	Kaddisch	H	C-G	DUR
Saint-Saëns	Guitares et mandolines			DUR
Spontini	Toi que j'implore			LEM
	(La Vestale)			

German Songs and Arias Employing Agility

Dramatic Soprano

Bach, J.S.	Mein glaeubiges Herze	HML		†
	(Cantata 68)			
Beethoven	Abscheulicher, wo eilst		B-B	†
	du hin? (Fidelio)			
Brahms	Botschaft	HL	D-F	†
-----	Das Maedchen spricht	H	E-FS	†
-----	O liebliche Wangen	MLH	E-G	†
Franz	Ein Stuendlein wohl vor Tag			†
Haydn	The mermaid's song	M	C-F	PRE
Jensen	Am Ufer des Flusses des	H	D-FS	GSC
	Manzanares			
Keiser	Von dem Landleben			SIM
Loewe	Des Glockenthuermers	H	CS-A	SC
	Tochterlein			
Mahler	Fruehlingsmorgen	HL		INT

255

(Mahler)	Ich bin der Welt abbanden gekommen	HL		INT
-----	Wer hat dies Liedlein erdacht?	HL	BF-E	INT
Marx	Und gestern hat er mir Rosen gebracht	H	E-A	AMP
Schubert	Auf dem Wasser zu singen	MH	EF-GF	†
-----	Das Wandern	HLM	E-E	†
-----	Liebesbotschaft	H	E-G	†
-----	Mein!	HL		†
-----	Ungeduld	HML		†
Schumann	Auftraege	HL	C-E	†
-----	Fruehlingsnacht	L	CS-E	GSC
-----	Mondnacht	M	E-FS	†
-----	Waldesgespraech	HL	A-FS	†
Strauss, J.	Blue Danube waltz			GSC
-----	Czardas (Die Fledermaus)			BOO
Weber	Wie nahte mir der Schlummer (Der Freischuetz)	H	B-B	†

Italian Songs and Arias Employing Agility

Dramatic Soprano

Bellini	Casta diva (Norma)	H	F-C	†
Bononcini	L'esperto nocchiero (Astarte)	HL	B-E	†
Carissimi	Vittoria, mio core	HLM	B-E	†
Cimarosa	Nel lasciarti (L'Olympiade)			RIC
Handel	Ch'io mai vi possa (Siroe)			†
Jommelli	Chi vuol comprar la bella	H	B-G	GSC
Lotti	Pur dicesti, o bocca bella	LMH	E-FS	GSC
Mozart	Come scoglio (Cosi Fan Tutte)			†
-----	Dove sono (Le Nozze di Figaro)	H	D-A	†
-----	Mi tradi quell' alma ingrata (Don Giovanni)			†
-----	Misera, dove son			BOO
Rossini	Bel raggio lusinghier (Semiramide)	H	CS-A	GSC
-----	La danza	MH	E-A	†
Scarlatti, A.	Se Florindo è fedele	LM	EF-EF	GSC
Stradella	Ragion sempre addita	H	E-G	†
Verdi	Ernani involami (Ernani)	H	AF-BF	GSC
-----	Merce, dilette amiche (I Vespri Siciliani)	MH	A-CS	GSC

Miscellaneous Songs Employing Agility

Dramatic Soprano

Alnaes	En morgen var din grav	M	CS–D	HAN
Alvarez	La partida	HL	DS–E	GSC
Falla	Nana			
-----	Vivan los que rien (La Vida Breve)			AMP
Granados	El majo discreto	H		INT
Mozart	Alleluja	LMH	F–C	†
-----	Et incarnatus est (C Minor Mass)			PET
Mussorgsky	Tiny star where art thou	LH	DF–F	BOS
Sibelius	From the north	H	DS–G	GSC
Stravinsky	Pastorale			GSC
Turina	Cantilena	M	C–EF	UME

American Songs Employing Crescendo and Diminuendo

Dramatic Soprano

Barber	Rain has fallen	HM	D–E	GSC
-----	The daisies	M	C–F	GSC
Beach	Ah, love but a day			ASC
Campbell-Tipton	A spirit flower	LHM	B–G	GSC
-----	The crying of water	LH	FS–GS	GSC
Carpenter	Go, lovely rose	M	DF–EF	GSC
-----	The pools of peace	M	D–F	GSC
-----	The sleep that flits on baby's eyes	M	B–FS	GSC
-----	When I bring to you colour'd toys	LM	CS–FS	GSC
Charles	Clouds	HML	C–EF	GSC
Duke	Bells in the rain	H	E–GS	CFI
Engel	Sea shell	M	EF–EF	GSC
Fairchild	A memory			BOS
Hopkinson	My days have been so wondrous free	LH	EF–G	†
Howe	Berceuse	HM	EF–F	GSC
La Forge	Hills	HL		RIC
Naginski	The pasture	M	BF–EF	GSC
Niles	I wonder as I wander	HL	BF–D	GSC
Nordoff	Serenade	H	CS–FS	AMP
Rogers	At parting	LH	CS–FS	GSC
Thompson	Velvet shoes	M	C–E	ECS

British Songs and Arias Employing
Crescendo and Diminuendo

Dramatic Soprano

Arne, T.	The plague of love			BOO
Bax	A lullaby			
-----	Cradle song			CHA
Benjamin	Calm sea and mist			CUR
-----	The wasp			CUR
Clarke	Shy one	HL	BF-G	BOH
Delius	Indian love song	H		†
Gurney	Under the greenwood tree			ROG
Handel	Angels ever bright and fair (Theodora)	H	E-F	†
-----	Let me wander not unseen (L'Allegro)	M	D-G	†
Horn	Cherry ripe	M	D-G	†
-----	I've been roaming	L	B-E	†
Ireland	Bed in summer			CUR
Purcell	I attempt from love's sickness to fly (The Indian Queen)	MH	CS-E	†
Quilter	The fuchsia tree			BOO
Scott	Night song	ML	BF-EF	ELK
Shaw	Song of the palanquin bearers	LH	E-F	CUR

French Songs and Arias Employing
Crescendo and Diminuendo

Dramatic Soprano

Bachelet	Chère nuit	H	DF-BF	GSC
Bernard	Ça fait peur aux oiseaux	H	GS-F	GSC
Chaminade	The silver ring	HM	BF-F	GSC
David	Charmant oiseau (La Perle du Brésil)	M	D-E	†
Debussy	Air de Lia (L'Enfant Prodigue)			DUR
-----	C'est l'extase	LH	CS-A	†
-----	La flûte de Pan		B-B	†
Duparc	Chanson triste	MH	FS-AF	†
-----	L'invitation au voyage	HM	E-F	†
-----	Phidylé	MH	EF-AF	BOS
-----	Sérénade florentine	HL		INT
Fauré	Clair de lune	MH	C-G	†
-----	En prière	H	F-F	†
-----	Lydia	MH	G-G	†

Liszt	Comment, disaient-ils?	H	C-AF	†
Martini	Plaisir d'amour	M	BF-EF	GSC
Meyerbeer	Nobles Seigneurs, salut!	LH	C-C	†
	(Les Huguenots)			
Paladilhe	Psyché	HM	BF-F	GSC
Rameau	Le grillon			DUR

German Songs Employing
Crescendo and Diminuendo

Dramatic Soprano

Beethoven	Andenken			†
-----	Mit einem gemalten Band			RIC
Brahms	Auf dem See	HL	D-F	†
-----	Geheimnis			†
-----	Sandmaennchen	LH	F-G	†
-----	Sonntag	H	D-G	†
-----	Spanisches Lied			†
-----	Therese	HL	B-D	†
-----	Wie Melodien zieht es	HL	A-E	†
Franz	Gute Nacht	HL		†
-----	Sterne mit den gold' nen	HL	DS-E	†
	Fuesschen			
Mahler	Fruehlingsmorgen	HL		INT
-----	Ich atmet einen linden	HL		INT
	Duft			
Mendelssohn	Lieblingsplaetzchen	LM	FS-E	†
-----	Pagenlied	M	E-E	†
Reger	Mit Rosen bestreut			UNI
-----	Waldeinsamkeit	HML	A-D	BOS
Schubert	An den Mond	HL	F-GF	†
-----	Auf dem Wasser zu singen	MH	EF-GF	†
-----	Der Musensohn	LH	FS-G	†
-----	Der Wanderer	HML	FS-D	†
-----	Fruehlingstraum	HL	C-D	GSC
-----	Gretchen am Spinnrade	H	F-A	†
-----	Im Fruehling	LH	D-FS	†
-----	Lachen und Weinen	HL	C-EF	†
-----	Liebesbotschaft	H	E-G	†
-----	Nacht und Traeume	HL	C-DF	†
-----	Wiegenlied (Op. 98)			†
Schumann	Aus den oestlichen Rosen			
-----	Der Nussbaum	LMH	D-FS	†
-----	Die Soldatenbraut	HL	AF-EF	†
-----	Maerzveilchen	HL	C-C	†
-----	Marienwuermchen	HL	D-D	†
-----	Provenzalisches Lied	LH		†

(Schumann)	Schneegloeckchen	HL		†
-----	Volksliedchen	HL		†
Strauss	Die Nacht	HL		†
Wolf	Auch kleine Dinge	HM	D-E	†
-----	Blumengruss	HL	D-E	†
-----	Der Gaertner	HL		†
-----	Der Knabe und das Immlein	L	CS-A	†
-----	Gleich und gleich			†
-----	In dem Schatten meiner Locken	M	C-EF	†
-----	Mausfallen Spruechlein	HL	BF-E	†
-----	Nun wandre, Maria	HL	EF-D	†
-----	Und willst du deinen Liebsten sterben	HL		†
-----	Verschwiegene Liebe	LH	DF-FS	GSC
-----	Wenn du zu den Blumen gehst	HL	B-EF	†

Italian Songs and Arias Employing Crescendo and Diminuendo

Dramatic Soprano

Bononcini	Per la gloria	HL	C-EF	†
Caldara	Alma del core			GSC
-----	Sebben crudele	HML	E-DS	†
-----	Selve amiche, ombrose piante	HM	E-E	†
Cesti	Intorno all'idol mio (Orontea)	MH	D-F	†
De Luca	Non posso disperar	HL	C-E	GSC
Falconieri	O bellissimi capelli	HL	B-D	†
Fasolo	Cangia, cangia tue voglie	H	C-G	GSC
Frescobaldi	Se l'aura spira	HL	C-EF	DIT
Handel	Ombra mai fu (Serse)	HM	BF-EF	†
Marcello	Non m'è grave morir per amore	L	C-E	GSC
Monteverdi	Lasciatemi morire (Arianna)	ML	D-D	†
Pergolesi	Se tu m'ami	LMH	C-G	GSC
Respighi	Mattinata			BON
Rosa	Selve, voi che le speranze	MH	D-G	DIT
Scarlatti, A.	La fortuna			BOS
Verdi	Ave Maria (Otello)	H	EF-AF	GSC

Miscellaneous Songs Employing
Crescendo and Diminuendo

Dramatic Soprano

Backer- Groendahl	In dreaming dance			
Gretchaninoff	The snowdrop	HM	BF-F	DIT
Grieg	En fuglevise			
-----	In the boat	LM	D-ES	†
-----	It was a lovely summer evening			
-----	Springtide	M		DIT
-----	With a water lily	HM	CS-EF	†
Rachmaninoff	Daisies			†
-----	Lilacs	LH	EF-G	†
-----	The island	LH	DF-F	†
Turina	Cantilena	M	C-EF	UME

American Songs Employing Piano Singing

Dramatic Soprano

Barber	Rain has fallen	HM	D-E	GSC
Campbell- Tipton	A spirit flower	LHM	B-G	GSC
-----	The crying of water	LH	FS-GS	GSC
Carpenter	Go, lovely rose	M	DF-EF	GSC
-----	On the seashore of endless worlds	M	C-FS	GSC
-----	The pools of peace	M	D-F	GSC
-----	The sleep that flits on baby's eyes	M	B-FS	GSC
-----	When I bring to you colour'd toys	LM	CS-FS	GSC
Charles	Clouds	HML	C-EF	GSC
-----	When I have sung my songs	HM	BF-EF	GSC
Crist	Evening	H	C-G	GSC
Davis	Nancy Hanks	H	D-G	GAL
Duke	Bells in the rain	H	E-GS	CFI
-----	The bird			GSC
-----	To Karen, singing	M	CS-G	ELV
Engel	Sea shell	M	EF-EF	GSC
Fairchild	A memory			BOS
Gaines	My heart hath a mind			
Ganz	A memory	HM	B-D	GSC
Griffes	Symphony in yellow	M	D-GF	GSC

(Griffes)	The dreamy lake	H	BS-GS	GSC
-----	Thy dark eyes to mine	H	EF-AF	GSC
Hageman	Do not go, my love	HL	B-EF	GSC
Howe	Berceuse	HM	EF-F	GSC
MacGimsey	Sweet little Jesus Boy	ML	D-D	CFI
Manning	In the Luxembourg gardens	HML	BF-D	GSC
Naginski	The pasture	M	BF-EF	GSC
Niles	I wonder as I wander	HL	BF-D	GSC
Nordoff	Music I heard with you	H	DS-FS	AMI
-----	Serenade	H	CS-FS	AMI
Taylor	A song for lovers	MH	D-F	JFI
Thompson	Velvet shoes	M	C-E	ECS

British Songs Employing Piano Singing

Dramatic Soprano

Bax	Cradle song			CHA
Benjamin	Calm sea and mist			CUR
Clarke	Shy one	HL	BF-G	BOH

Coleridge-
  Taylor
	She rested by the broken
	  brook
		HL		DIT

Dunhill	The cloths of Heaven	LM	EF-G	STB
Handel	Let me wander not unseen (L'Allegro)	M	D-G	†
Ronald	Down in the forest	HML	C-D	ENC
Scott	Lullaby	MML	BF-DF	GAL
Vaughan Williams	Silent noon			GSC

French Songs Employing Piano Singing

Dramatic Soprano

Bernard	Ça fait peur aux oiseaux	H	GS-F	GSC
Chaminade	The silver ring	HM	BF-F	GSC
Debussy	La flûte de Pan		B-B	†
Duparc	Extase	LMH	FS-A	†
Fauré	Après un rêve	HM	C-F	†
-----	Clair de lune	MH	C-G	†
-----	Dans les ruines d'une abbaye	M	E-FS	†
-----	En prière	H	F-F	†
-----	Lydia	MH	G-G	†
Hahn	D'une prison	L	BF-EF	HEU
-----	Infidélité	M		HEU

(Hahn)	L'heure exquise	M	DF-F	†
-----	Offrande	M	D-D	†
-----	Paysage	MH	EF-G	HEU
Liszt	Comment, disaient-ils?	H	C-AF	†
-----	Oh! quand je dors	H	E-A	†
Lully	Au clair de la lune	H	E-D	CFI
-----	Bois épais (Amadis)	ML	C-EF	†
Paladilhe	Psyché	HM	BF-F	GSC
Poldowski	L'heure exquise	LMH	DF-AF	CHE
Ravel	La flûte enchantée	M	DS-FS	DUR

German Songs and Arias Employing
Piano Singing

Dramatic Soprano

Beethoven	Ich liebe dich	HL	BF-DF	†
Brahms	Eine gute, gute Nacht			†
-----	Es traeumte mir			†
-----	Geheimnis			†
-----	In Waldeseinsamkeit	H	ES-G	†
-----	Lerchengesang	LH	FS-GS	†
-----	Sandmaennchen	LH	F-G	†
-----	Spanisches Lied			†
-----	Staendchen	HL	BF-E	†
Bruch	Ave Maria	LH	D-BF	AMP
	(Das Feuerkreuz)			
Franz	Ein Stuendlein wohl vor Tag			†
-----	Gute Nacht	HL		†
-----	Sterne mit den gold' nen	HL	DS-E	†
	Fuesschen			
Hindemith	Geburt Marias			AMP
Korngold	Marietta's song	MH	F-BF	AMP
	(The Dead City)			
Mahler	Erinnerung	HL		INT
-----	Fruehlingsmorgen	HL		INT
-----	Ich atmet' einen linden	HL		INT
	Duft			
-----	Ich bin der Welt abbanden	HL		INT
	gekommen			
-----	Ich ging mit Lust	HL		INT
-----	Liebst du um Schoenheit	HL		INT
-----	Wo die schoenen Trompeten	HL	GF-F	INT
	blasen			
Marx	Selige Nacht	M	DF-GF	AMP
Mendelssohn	Bei der Wiege	M	DF-EF	†
-----	Gruss	M	DS-FS	†
-----	Lieblingsplaetzchen	LM	FS-E	†

(Mendelssohn)	Pagenlied	M	E-E	†
Schubert	Auf dem Wasser zu singen	MH	EF-GF	†
-----	Ave Maria	LMH	F-F	†
-----	Du bist die Ruh	LMH	EF-AF	†
-----	Fruehlingstraum	HL	C-D	†
-----	Im Abendrot	HL	C-D	†
-----	Im Fruehling	LH	D-FS	†
-----	Lachen und Weinen	HL	C-EF	†
-----	Liebesbotschaft	H	E-G	†
-----	Nacht und Traeume	HL	C-DF	†
-----	Wiegenlied (Op. 98)			†
Schumann	Der Nussbaum	LMH	D-FS	†
-----	Marienwuermchen	HL	D-D	†
-----	Mondnacht	M	E-FS	†
-----	Requiem			†
-----	Volksliedchen	HL		†
Strauss, J.	Czardas (Die Fledermaus)			BOO
Strauss, R.	Allerseelen	HL	AS-E	†
-----	Die Nacht	HL		†
-----	Freundliche Vision	HL	C-F	†
-----	Heimkehr	HL	B-E	†
-----	Ich trage meine Minne	M		UNI
-----	Mein Herz ist stumm	LH	EF-AF	
-----	Traum durch die Daemmerung	HML	BF-EF	†
-----	Wiegenliedchen			†
Wagner	Der Engel	LH	CS-G	†
-----	Euch Lueften die mein Klagen (Lohengrin)			†
-----	Im Treibhaus	HL		†
Wolf	Auf ein altes Bild	HL	E-DS	†
-----	Der Gaertner	HL		†
-----	Du denkst, mit einem Faedchen			†
-----	Gleich und gleich			†
-----	In dem Schatten meiner Locken	M	C-EF	†
-----	Mausfallen Spruechlein	HL	BF-E	†
-----	Schlafendes Jesuskind	HL	AS-F	†
-----	Verborgenheit	HL	B-E	†
-----	Verschwiegene Liebe	LH	DF-FS	†
-----	Wie glaenzt der helle Mond			†

Italian Songs and Arias Employing Piano Singing

Dramatic Soprano

Bononcini   Deh più a me non v'ascondete

Cimara	Fiocca la neve	H	G-G	GSC
D'Astorga	Vo' cercando in queste valli			
Frescobaldi	Se l'aura spira	HL	C-EF	DIT
Gagliano	Dormi amore			DIT
Handel	Care selve (Atalanta)	MH	FS-A	†
Jommelli	Chi vuol comprar la bella	H	B-G	GSC
Monteverdi	Lasciatemi morire (Arianna)	ML	D-D	†
Respighi	Notte			BON
Verdi	Ave Maria (Otello)	H	EF-AF	GSC
-----	O cieli azzuri (Aida)	H	B-C	†
-----	Salce, salce (Otello)	H	CS-FS	RIC

Miscellaneous Songs Employing Piano Singing

Dramatic Soprano

Alnaes	En morgen var din grav	M	CS-D	HAN
-----	Lykken mellem to mennesker	M	B-FS	HAN
Arensky	Revery	MH	DS-FS	DIT
Cui	The statue at Czarskoe-Selo	HM	DF-EF	†
Dvořák	God is my shepherd			AMP
-----	Songs my mother taught me	HM	E-E	†
Gretchaninoff	Hushed the song of the nightingale	MH	E-G	DIT
Grieg	A dream			†
-----	A swan			†
-----	In the boat	LM	D-ES	†
-----	Radiant night			
-----	Snegl, Snegl	M	B-F	HAN
Lie	Soft-footed snow	HM		DIT
Mednikoff	The hills of Gruzia	H	DS-A	LAC
Rachmaninoff	Before my window	HM	C-G	†
-----	In the silence of night	LH	D-A	GSC

American Songs Employing Rapid Enunciation

Dramatic Soprano

Boatner	Oh, what a beautiful city!	HL	D-E	GSC

Burleigh	Joshua fit de battle ob Jericho	LH	DS-E	RIC
-----	Little David play on yo harp	HL		RIC
Carpenter	Don't ceare	M	C-D	GSC
Clough-Leighter	My lover he comes on the skee	HM	D-F	BOS
Curran	Ho! Mr. Piper	LH	D-G	GSC
Deis	Come down to Kew			
Griffes	Elves	H	F-AF	GSC
Hadley	My shadow			ASC
Hageman	At the well	LH	EF-AF	GSC
-----	Miranda	HL		GAL
Josten	Cupid's counsel	H	EF-AF	GSC
Kountz	The sleigh	HL	D-FS	GSC
Nevin	One spring morning	MH	DS-F	BOS
Spross	Will o' the wisp			JCH
Warner	Hurdy-gurdy	M	D-F	CFI

British Songs Employing Rapid Enunciation

Dramatic Soprano

Bantock	A feast of lanterns	HM	D-F	GAL
Bax	Oh dear, what can the matter be?	M	D-EF	CHE
Bishop	Love has eyes	M		†
Brewer	The fairy pipers	HML		BOH
German	Charming Chloe	HML		NOV
Gibbs	Five eyes	HL	D-D	BOS
Head	A piper	HL		BOO
Hughes	Hey diddle diddle			CRA
Morley	It was a lover and his lass	HM		DIT

French Songs Employing Rapid Enunciation

Dramatic Soprano

Bernard	Ça fait peur aux oiseaux	H	GS-F	GSC
Chabrier	Villanelle des petits canards	HML	B-E	†
Debussy	Chevaux de bois	H	C-G	†
-----	Fantoches	H	D-A	JOB
-----	La flûte de Pan		B-B	†

(Debussy)	Mandoline	HM	BF-F	†
Fauré	Dans les ruines d'une abbaye	M	E-FS	†
-----	Mandoline	H	F-E	†
-----	Toujours	LH	F-AF	†
Ferrari	Le jardin d'amour	LM	EF-F	GSC
Fourdrain	Carnaval	M	C-F	RIC
Milhaud	La tourterelle	M	B-G	DUR
Pierné	Ils étaient trois petits chats blancs			MAR
Poldowski	Dansons la gigue	M	EF-G	MAR
Ravel	Tout gai	MH	EF-F	DUR
Saint-Saëns	L'attente			DUR
Weckerlin	Chantons les amours de Jean	H	D-G	GSC

German Songs Employing Rapid Enunciation

Dramatic Soprano

Beethoven	Neue Liebe, neues Leben			†
Brahms	Blinde Kuh			†
-----	Das Maedchen spricht	H	E-FS	†
-----	Der Jaeger	HL		†
-----	Dort in den Weiden	LH	A-A	†
-----	Juchhe!			†
-----	Meine Liebe ist gruen	MLH	ES-A	†
-----	O liebliche Wangen	MLH	E-G	†
-----	Staendchen	HL	BF-E	†
-----	Vergebliches Staendchen	LHM	E-FS	†
Loewe	Walpurgisnacht	H	G-G	SC
Mendelssohn	An die Entfernte	M	F-F	
-----	Im Gruenen	H	E-BF	AUG
-----	Neue Liebe	H	CS-A	†
Mozart	Warnung	HM	C-D	
Schubert	Am Feierabend	HL	BF-F	†
-----	Das Wandern	HLM	E-E	†
-----	Die Forelle	MLH	EF-GF	†
-----	Die Post	HML	BF-EF	†
-----	Erstarrung	HL	D-F	†
-----	Fruehlingssehnsucht	HL	B-E	†
-----	Mein!	HL		†
-----	Ungeduld	HML		†
-----	Wohin?	HL	B-E	DIT
Schumann	Auftraege	HL	C-E	†
-----	Volksliedchen	HL		†
Wolf	Elfenlied	HL	D-F	†

267

Italian Songs and Arias Employing
Rapid Enuncation

Dramatic Soprano

Carissimi	Vittoria, mio core	HLM	B-E	†
Cavalli	Donzelle fuggite	HL	C-EF	†
Falconieri	Non più d'amore	HL	C-D	DIT
-----	Nudo arciero	HL	AF-AF	DIT
Handel	Ch'io mai vi possa (Siroe)			†
Legrenzi	Che fiero costume	HML	C-D	†
Mozart	Non so più cosa son (Le Nozze di Figaro)	H	EF-G	†
-----	Voi che sapete (Le Nozze di Figaro)	M	C-F	†
Paisiello	Chi vuol la zingarella	L	C-F	GSC
Paradies	M'ha preso alla sua ragna	M	EF-F	GSC
Rontani	Or ch'io non segno più	HL	CS-E	DIT
Rossini	La danza	MH	E-A	†
Stradella	Ragion sempre addita	H	E-G	†

Miscellaneous Songs Employing
Rapid Enunciation

Dramatic Soprano

Falla	Seguidilla murciana	HL		AMP
Grieg	In the boat	LM	D-ES	†
-----	My Johann	HL	BF-EF	GSC
-----	Simpel sang			
-----	The way of the world			DIT
-----	Til min dreng			
-----	With a waterlily			
Mussorgsky	The evening prayer	M	C-E	GSC
-----	The magpie and the gypsy dancer			GSC

American Songs Employing
Sustained Singing

Dramatic Soprano

Barber	A nun takes the veil	MH	G-G	GSC
-----	Sure on this shining night	MH	D-G	GSC

Burleigh	Deep river	HML		RIC
-----	Sometime I feel like a motherless child	HML		RIC
-----	Were you there?	HML		RIC
Chadwick	Allah	LH	CS–GS	ASC
Charles	And so, goodbye	LH	EF–AF	GSC
Curran	Nocturne Violin	HML	B–DS	GSC
Edwards	By the bend of the river	HML	C–E	GSC
-----	Into the night	HML	C–DF	GSC
Foster, S.C.	Sweetly she sleeps			
Griffes	Evening song	H	DS–GS	GSC
-----	The lament of Ian the proud	MH	DS–AS	GSC
-----	The rose of the night	H	CS–A	GSC
Hageman	Music I heard with you	MH	E–A	GAL
Horsman	The bird of the wilderness	LMH	DF–BF	GSC
Kernochan	We two together	H	EF–AF	GAL
Lieurance	By the waters of Minnetonka			PRE
MacDowell	The swan bent low	LH		ELK
McDonald	Daybreak	H		ELV
Metcalf	At nightfall	HML	C–DF	ASC
Powell	Heartsease	M	DF–G	GSC
Rogers	Wind song	LM	C–G	GSC
Scott	Think on me	HML	D–EF	GAL

British Songs and Arias Employing Sustained Singing

Dramatic Soprano

Arne, T.	Blow, blow thou winter wind	M	C–F	†
-----	In infancy			NOV
Bantock	Silent strings	MH	F–G	BOO
Bridge	All things that we clasp	HL		BOS
-----	O that it were so	LMH	D–G	CHA
Britten	The Sally gardens			BOH
Clarke	Eight o'clock			ROG
Coleridge-Taylor	Life and death	HML		ASC
Del Riego	Homing	HML	BF–E	CHA
Dunhill	To the Queen of Heaven	M	C–G	GSC
Grainger	The sprig of thyme	LH	E–FS	GSC
Handel	Come unto Him (The Messiah)	MH	F–G	†
-----	How beautiful are the feet of them (The Messiah)	H		†
-----	I know that my Redeemer liveth (The Messiah)	MH	E–GS	†

Henschel	Morning-hymn	MH	DS-GS	†
Holst	The heart worships	ML	BF-D	STB
Purcell	If music be the food of love	M	D-G	BOO
-----	Music for a while (Oedipus)	LH		SC
-----	When I am laid in earth (Dido and Aeneas)	LH	C-G	†
Ronald	O, lovely night	HML		BOO
-----	Prelude	HML	B-D	ENO
Stephenson	Love is a sickness	HML	C-D	BOO
Welsh	All through the night			
-----	The ash grove			

French Songs and Arias Employing Sustained Singing

Dramatic Soprano

Bemberg	Chant hindou	HML	A-EF	†
Berlioz	D'amour l'ardente flamme (La Damnation de Faust)			NOV
-----	Le spectre de la rose			CST
Bizet	Adieu de l'hôtesse arabe	H	BF-G	†
Chausson	Chanson perpétuelle	H	CS-GS	ROU
-----	Le colibri Violin or cello	M	F-GF	BOS
-----	Le temps des lilas	MH	D-GS	†
Debussy	Beau soir	LH	C-FS	†
-----	Chansons de Bilitis	M	C-FS	†
-----	Colloque sentimental			DUR
-----	De fleurs	H	C-AF	†
-----	La chevelure	M	CF-FS	†
-----	Romance	HM	C-E	†
Duparc	Au pays où se fait la guerre			SAL
-----	La vie antérieure	HL		†
-----	Lamento	ML	EF-EF	†
Fauré	Automne	MH	D-FS	GSC
-----	Le jardin clos	M	C-E	DUR
-----	Prison	LH		†
-----	Rencontre	H	EF-AF	†
-----	Soir	LH	D-GS	†
Franck	Nocturne	HL		INT
Georges	Hymne au soleil	LH	E-A	HOM
Gluck	Adieu, conservez dans votre âme (Iphigenie en Aulide)			†
-----	Divinités du Styx (Alceste)	MH	DF-AF	†
-----	Grands dieux (Alceste)	H	E-BF	GSC

270

(Gluck)	Non! ce n'est point (Alceste)	H	E-G	†
Godard	Florian's song	LMH	D-FS	GSC
Gossec	Ah! faut-il me venger (Thésée)			LEM
Gounod	Plus grand, dans son obscurité (La Reine de Saba)	MH	CS-B	†
Halévy	Il va venir (La Juive)	H	D-CF	†
Hue	J'ai pleuré en rêve	HL	D-E	BOS
Lenormand	Quelle souffrance	HM	AF-F	HAM
Massenet	Charmes des jours passés (Hérodiade)			HEU
-----	Elégie	LM	C-GF	GSC
-----	Il est doux, il est bon (Hérodiade)	MH	EF-BF	GSC
Meyerbeer	Ah! mon fils (Le Prophète)	M	B-AS	†
-----	O beau pays (Les Huguenots)	H	CS-D	GSC
Offenbach	Elle a fui, la tourterelle (Tales of Hoffman)	H	D-A	GSC
Paladilhe	Lamento provinçal	M	CS-FS	HOM
Poulenc	Bleuet	H	FS-GF	DUR
Ravel	Chanson italienne			DUR
-----	Kaddisch	H	C-G	DUR
-----	Là-bas vers l'église	MH	GS-E	DUR
-----	Vocalise en forme de habanera	MH	BF-G	MAR
Saint-Saëns	La cloche	LH	DF-AF	†

German Songs and Arias Employing Sustained Singing

Dramatic Soprano

Bach, C.P.E.	Passionslied			SIM
Bach, J.S.	Bist du bei mir	HML	A-EF	†
-----	Willst du dein Herz mir schenken			BRH
Beethoven	Die Ehre Gottes	HL	AF-EF	†
-----	Wonne der Wehmut			†
Bohm	Calm as the night	HML	A-EF	†
Brahms	An die Nachtigall	H	DS-G	†
-----	An eine Aeolsharfe	H	EF-AF	†
-----	Auf dem Kirchhofe	HL	BF-EF	†
-----	Daemm'rung senkte sich von oben	LH	BF-G	†
-----	Dein blaues Auge	MH	BF-G	†

(Brahms)	Der Tod, das ist die kuehle Nacht	L	AF–F	†
-----	Die Mainacht	HL	BF–FF	†
-----	Erinnerung	H	E–G	†
-----	Feldeinsamkeit	HL	C–EF	†
-----	Immer leiser wird mein Schlummer	LH	DF–A	†
-----	Liebestreu	ML	C–F	†
-----	Mondenschein	LH	D–GF	†
-----	Muss es eine Trennung geben?	LH	FS–FS	†
-----	Nachtigall	MHL	BF–FS	†
-----	O kuehler Wald	MH	A–F	†
-----	O wuesst' ich doch den Weg zurueck	H	E–FS	†
-----	Schoen war, das ich dir weihte			†
-----	Sommerabend			RIC
-----	Wir wandelten	LH	EF–GF	†
Franz	Dedication	HML	BF–C	†
-----	For music	ML	C–D	†
-----	Im Herbst	HM	A–F	†
-----	Mutter, o sing mich zur Ruh	HL	E–G	†
Haydn	She never told her love	HL	B–D	DIT
Korngold	Love letter			AMP
Lehar	Vilia (The Merry Widow)			CHA
Liszt	Freudvoll und leidvoll			DUR
Loewe	Canzonetta	MH	B–A	DIT
Lohner	O Ewigkeit			
Mahler	Um Mitternacht	HL		INT
Marx	Hat dich die Liebe beruehrt	MH	EF–BF	AMP
Mendelssohn	Der Mond	HL		†
-----	Hear ye, Israel (Elijah)	H	E–A	†
-----	Jerusalem, thou that killest (Saint Paul)	H	F–F	†
-----	Nachtlied			
-----	On wings of song			†
Mozart	Abendempfindung	M	E–F	
-----	Die ihr des unermesslichen Weltalls			
-----	Wiegenlied	MH	G–G	†
Schoenberg	Erhebung			GSC
Schubert	Am Grabe Anselmos	HL	B–EF	†
-----	An die Musik	HL	A–DS	†
-----	Auf dem Flusse	HL	F–E	†
-----	Das Wirtshaus	HL	C–D	†
-----	Der Doppelgaenger	HL	G–D	†

(Schubert)	Der Leiermann	ML	C-D	†
-----	Der Lindenbaum	HL	A-D	†
-----	Der Neugierige	HL	CS-EF	†
-----	Der Wegweiser	L	D-EF	†
-----	Des Maedchens Klage	LH	C-E	†
-----	Die Allmacht	HML	G-E	†
-----	Die Liebe hat gelogen	LM	G-F	†
-----	Die Maenner sind mechant			PET
-----	Die Nebensonnen	HL	F-D	†
-----	Du liebst mich nicht	LH	E-FS	†
-----	Fruehlingsglaube	M	EF-F	†
-----	Ganymed	LH	EF-G	†
-----	Ihr Bild	HL	C-C	†
-----	In der Ferne	HL		†
-----	Lied eines Schiffers an die Dioskuren	HL	A-C	†
-----	Litanei	HLM	C-EF	†
-----	Nur wer die Sehnsucht kennt	LH		†
-----	Schaefers Klagelied	HL	BF-D	†
-----	Staendchen	MH	B-E	†
-----	Wanderers Nachtlied 2	LH	F-F	GSC
Schumann	Aus den Hebraeischen Gesaengen			
-----	Die Lotusblume	HLM	BF-F	†
-----	Du bist wie eine Blume	HM	F-EF	†
-----	Du Ring an meine Finger	HL	C-F	†
-----	Ihre Stimme	LH		†
-----	Im Westen	HL		†
-----	Lied der Suleika			
-----	Mit Myrthen und Rosen	HL	A-D	†
-----	Seit ich ihn gesehen	HL	DF-DF	†
-----	Stille Traenen	HL		†
-----	Wer machte dich so krank?			
Strauss	Ach Lieb, ich muss nun scheiden	H	D-G	
-----	Befreit			HSC
-----	Breit ueber mein Haupt	LH	GF-AF	HSC
-----	Mit deinen blauen Augen	LH	C-GS	†
-----	Morgen	HML	E-F	†
-----	Ruhe meine Seele			†
Wagner	Elizabeth's prayer (Tannhaeuser)	LMH	DF-GF	†
------	Elsa's dream (Lohengrin)	MH	EF-AF	†
-----	Five Wesendonck songs			GSC
-----	Mild und leise (Tristan und Isolde)	H	E-A	GSC
-----	Schmerzen	HL		†

273

(Wagner)	Senta's ballad			GSC
	(Der Fliegende Hollaender)			
-----	Traeume	HL		†
-----	War es so schmaehlich			†
	(Die Walkuere)			
Weber	Und ob die Wolke	H	EF-AF	†
	(Der Freischuetz)			
Wolf	Alle gingen, herz, zu Ruh	HL	C-EF	†
-----	Anakreons Grab	HL	D-D	†
-----	An eine Aeolsharfe			†
-----	Bedeckt mich mit Blumen	HL	B-D	†
-----	Das verlassene Maegdlein	HL	D-EF	†
-----	Denk' es, o Seele	LH	EF-F	†
-----	Der Mond hat eine schwere	HL	BF-DF	†
	Klag' erhoben			
-----	Gebet	HL		†
-----	Herr, was traegt der	HL	B-DS	†
	Boden			
-----	In der Fruehe	HL	C-C	†
-----	Lebe wohl	HL	BF-F	†
-----	Morgenstimmung	LH	C-GS	†
-----	Mueh'voll komm' ich und	H	D-G	†
	beladen			
-----	Neue Liebe	LH	D-AF	†
-----	Um Mitternacht	HL	G-EF	†
-----	Zur Ruh', zur Ruh'	HL	A-GF	†
Wolff	Alle Dinge haben Sprache	M	BF-GF	†
-----	Du bist so jung			HMP

Italian Songs and Arias Employing Sustained Singing

Dramatic Soprano

Beethoven	Ah! perfido	H		DIT
Boito	Morte di Margherita	H	D-B	GSC
	(L'altra notte) (Mefistofele)			
Bononcini	Deh, lascia			HEU
Caccini	Amarilli, mia bella	ML	C-D	†
Caldara	Come raggio di sol	HL	D-F	†
Catalani	Ebben? Ne andrò lontana	H	E-B	RIC
	(La Wally)			
Cimara	Stornellata marinara	HM		RIC
Cimarosa	Bel nume che adoro			RIC
Donaudy	O del mio amato ben	M	EF-F	RIC
Donizetti	O mio Fernando	M	B-A	†
	(La Favorita)			
Durante	Vergin, tutta amor	LM	C-EF	†

Gluck	Spiagge amate (Paride ed Elena)			†
Handel	Lascia ch'io pianga (Rinaldo)	HM	EF-F	†
-----	Rendi 'l sereno al ciglio (Sosarme)	LH	EF-F	†
-----	V'adoro pupille (Julius Caesar)			BOO
Mascagni	Un di ero piccina (Iris)			RIC
-----	Voi lo sapete (Cavalleria Rusticana)	H	B-A	†
Mozart	Ch'io mi scordi di te			BOO
-----	Deh, se piacer mi vuoi (La Clemenza di Tito)			RIC
-----	Non mi dir (Don Giovanni)	H	F-B	†
-----	Non più di fiori (La Clemenza di Tito)			†
-----	Parto, parto (La Clemenza di Tito) B flat clarinet and piano	H		AMP
-----	Per pietà, ben mio (Cosi Fan Tutte)			†
-----	Porgi amor (Le Nozze di Figaro)	H	D-AF	†
Pergolesi	Dite ch'ogni momento			BOS
Ponchielli	Suicidio! (La Gioconda)	HM	BF-AF	†
Puccini	In quelle trine morbide (Manon Lescaut)	H	DF-BF	RIC
-----	Tu, che di gel sei cinta (Turandot)			RIC
-----	Un bel di vedremo (Madama Butterfly)	H	DF-BF	RIC
-----	Vissi d'arte (Tosca)	MH	EF-BF	RIC
Respighi	Nebbie			†
-----	Nevicata	HM		BON
Stradella	Così, amor, mi fai languir	HL	F-G	DIT
-----	Se nel ben			CFI
Torelli	Tu lo sai	HL	BF-F	†
Verdi	D'amor sull'ali rosee (Il Trovatore)	H	C-DF	†
-----	Ecco l'orrido campo (Un Ballo in Maschera)	H	B-C	RIC
-----	Madre, pietosa Vergine (La Forza del Destino)	H	B-B	RIC
-----	Morrò, ma prima in grazia (Un Ballo in Maschera)			RIC
-----	Tu che la vanita (Don Carlos)			RIC

Miscellaneous Songs and Arias
Employing Sustained Singing

Dramatic Soprano

Arensky	Autumn	H	CS-FS	GSC
Bach-Gounod	Ave Maria			†
Borodin	A dissonance	MH	EF	†
Dvořák	Hear my prayer, O Lord			AMP
-----	Lord thou art my refuge and shield			AMP
-----	Turn Thee to me			AMP
Falla	Vivan los que ríen (La Vida Breve)			AMP
Gliere	Ah, twine no blossoms	HM	CS-F	DIT
Granados	La maja dolorosa	M		INT
Gretchaninoff	Over the steppe	LM	C-G	GSC
Grieg	I love thee	HML	E-F	†
-----	To Norway	M	E-F	DIT
Kjerulf	Synnove's song	M	C-F	GSC
Rachmaninoff	Christ is risen	LM	D-F	GAL
-----	Oh cease thy singing, maiden fair	H	E-A	CFI
-----	O, do not grieve	M	BF-AF	GSC
-----	O thou billowy harvest field	HL	CS-E	GSC
-----	The soldier's bride			†
-----	To the children	MH	F-G	DIT
-----	Vocalise	LH	CS-A	GSC
Sibelius	Black roses	M	A-ES	AMP
Sinding	I hear the gull			JCH
Tchaikovsky	Adieu forêts (Jeanne d'Arc)	HM	BF-FS	GSC
-----	All for you			
-----	None but the lonely heart	HLM	C-F	DIT

American Songs Employing
Spirited Singing

Dramatic Soprano

Barber	I hear an army	LH	D-AF	GSC
Bassett	Take joy home	LH	EF-BF	GSC
Beach	The year's at the spring	MH	AF-AF	ASC
Boatner	Oh, what a beautiful city!	HL	D-E	GSC
Burleigh	Joshua fit de battle ob Jericho	LH	DS-E	RIC

(Burleigh)	Little David play on yo harp	HL		RIC
Carpenter	Don't ceare	M	C-D	GSC
-----	If	M	D-E	GSC
-----	Light, my light	M	C-G	GSC
-----	Serenade	LH	CS-A	GSC
Charles	Let my song fill your heart	LH	EF-AF	GSC
Clough-Leighter	My lover he comes on the skee	HM	D-F	BOS
Crist	O come hither	HM	B-GS	CFI
Curran	Ho! Mr. Piper	LH	D-G	GSC
-----	Life	HM	BF-F	GSC
Deis	Come down to Kew			
Giannini	Sing to my heart a song	H	D-B	ELV
Griffes	Elves	H	F-AF	GSC
Guion	Wild geese	M	D-F	CFI
Hadley	My shadow			ASC
Hageman	At the well	LH	EF-AF	GSC
-----	Miranda	HL		GAL
Hindemith	The whistling thief	M	E-F	AMP
Josten	Cupid's counsel	H	EF-AF	GSC
Kountz	The sleigh	HL	D-FS	GSC
LaForge	Song of the open	MH	EF-AF	DIT
Levitzki	Ah, thou beloved one	H	EF-AF	GSC
Mitchell	Love is the wind	MHH	F-A	GAH
Nevin	One spring morning	MH	DS-F	BOS
Nordoff	There shall be more joy	M	CS-FS	AMP
Rogers	The last song	MLH	E-AF	GSC
Rummel	Ecstasy	LMH	GF-AF	GSC
Saar	The little gray dove	MH	D-BF	GSC
Salter	The cry of Rachel	LH	C-AF	GSC
Schuman	Holiday song	M	C-F	GSC
Speaks	Morning	HML	BF-D	GSC
Spross	Will o' the wisp			JCH
Warner	Hurdy gurdy	M	D-F	CFI

British Songs and Arias Employing
Spirited Singing

Dramatic Soprano

Bantock	A feast of lanterns	HM	D-F	GAL
Bax	Oh dear what can the matter be?	M	D-EF	CHE
-----	Shieling song	H	CS-A	CHE
Benjamin	Hedgerow			CUR
Besley	Listening	H	E-AF	CUR

277

Bishop	Love has eyes	M		†
Bliss	The buckle			CUR
-----	Three jolly gentlemen	H		†
Brewer	The fairy pipers	HML		BOH
Bridge	Love went a-riding	HL		BOS
Dowland	Come again! sweet love	M	D-E	STB
Elgar	Be not extreme, O Lord (Light of Life)			NOV
German	Charming Chloe	HML		NOV
Gibbs	Five eyes	HL	D-D	BOS
-----	Padraic the fidiler			CUR
Head	A piper	HL		BOO
Lehmann	The cuckoo	HH	D-B	BOH
Moeran	Bright cap			OXF
Morley	It was a lover and his lass	HM		DIT
Purcell	Nymphs and shepherds (The Libertine)	HM	C-F	†
Quilter	Blow, blow, thou winter wind	HL	C-E	BOO
-----	It was a lover and his lass	HL	CS-E	BOO
-----	Love's philosophy	LMH	D-A	BOO
Ronald	Love, I have won you	HML	EF-EF	ENO

French Songs Employing Spirited Singing

Dramatic Soprano

Bizet	Ouvre ton coeur	MH	DS-GS	†
Chabrier	Villanelle des petits canards	HML	B-E	†
Chausson	La caravane	MH	CS-A	HAM
-----	Les papillons	M	C-F	GSC
Debussy	Chevaux de bois	H	C-G	†
-----	Fantoches	H	D-A	JOB
-----	Mandoline	HM	BF-F	†
Duni	Les temps passés			LEM
Duparc	Le manoir de Rosamunde	HL	B-F	BOS
-----	Testament	HL		INT
Fauré	Fleur jetée	HM	BF-FS	†
-----	L'hiver a cessé	HL		INT
-----	Mandoline	HL	F-E	†
-----	Toujours	LH	F-AF	†
Fourdrain	Chanson norvégienne	H	E-G	RIC
Georges	La pluie	HL		INT
Gounod	Au printemps	LMH	DF-AF	GSC
-----	Vénise	HL		INT
Hahn	Si mes vers avaient des ailes	HLM	B-FS	†

Honegger	Les cloches			SEN
Massenet	Ouvre tes yeux bleus	MH	C–G	†
Milhaud	Chant d'amour	M	C–GF	ESC
-----	Chant du laboureur	M	B–F	ESC
-----	La tourterelle	M	B–G	DUR
Pierné	Ils étaient trois petits chats blancs			MAR
Poldowski	Colombine	H	D–GF	CHE
-----	Dansons la gigue	M	EF–G	MAR
Poulenc	Air vif	H	C–AF	ROU
Ravel	Tout gai	MH	EF–F	DUR
Saint-Saëns	Guitares et mandolines			DUR
-----	L'attente			DUR
Weckerlin	Chantons les amours de Jean	H	D–G	GSC

German Songs and Arias Employing Spirited Singing

Dramatic Soprano

Bach, J.S.	Herr der Du stark und maechtig bist (Cantata 10)			
-----	Mein glaeubiges Herze (Cantata 68)	HML		†
Beethoven	Die Trommel geruehret			†
-----	Freudvoll und leidvoll	M	DS–E	†
-----	Neue Liebe, neues Leben			†
Brahms	Auf dem Schiffe	LH	GS–A	†
-----	Bei dir sind meine Gedanken	MH	E–FS	†
-----	Blinde Kuh			†
-----	Botschaft	HL	D–F	†
-----	Das Maedchen spricht	H	E–FS	†
-----	Der Gang zur Liebsten	HL		†
-----	Der Jaeger	HL		†
-----	Der Schmied	HL	EF–EF	†
-----	Dort in den Weiden	LH	A–A	†
-----	Juchhe!			†
-----	Klage	LH	FS–FS	†
-----	Meine Liebe ist gruen	MLH	ES–A	†
-----	O liebliche Wangen	MLH	E–G	†
-----	Salome			†
-----	Sehnsucht	H	EF–AF	†
-----	Vergebliches Staendchen	LHM	E–FS	GSC
-----	Wie froh und frisch	HL	B–E	†
Franz	Er ist gekommen	HL	EF–F	†
-----	Sonnenuntergang	HL	CS–FS	†

Haydn	The mermaid's song	M	C-F	PRE
Jensen	Am Ufer des Flusses des Manzanares	H	D-FS	GSC
Loewe	Des Glockenthuermers Tochterlein	H	CS-A	SC
-----	Walpurgisnacht	H	G-G	SC
Mahler	Das Irdische Leben	HL	A-F	INT
-----	Hans und Grethe	HL		INT
-----	Wer hat dies Liedlein erdacht?	HL	BF-E	INT
Marx	Und gestern hat er mir Rosen gebracht	H	E-A	AMP
-----	Valse de Chopin	M	CS-GS	AMP
Mendelssohn	An die Entfernte	M	F-F	
-----	Im Gruenen	H	E-BF	AUG
-----	Neue Liebe	H	CS-A	†
-----	Suleika	H	E-GS	†
Mozart	An Chloe	LH	EF-AF	
Schubert	Am Feierabend	HL	BF-F	†
-----	Aufenthalt	HLM	A-F	†
-----	Die Forelle	MLH	EF-GF	†
-----	Die Post	HML	BF-EF	†
-----	Ellens zweiter Gesang			PET
-----	Erstarrung	HL	D-F	†
-----	Fruehlingssehnsucht	HL	B-E	†
-----	Heidenroeslein			
-----	Mein!	HL		†
-----	Mut	HL		†
-----	Wohin?	HL	B-E	†
Schumann	Auftraege	HL	C-E	†
-----	Er, der Herrlichste von Allen	HL	A-EF	†
-----	Er ist's	HL	BF-EF	†
-----	Fruehlingsnacht	L	CS-E	†
-----	Waldesgespraech	HL	A-FS	†
-----	Widmung	HL	BF-F	†
Strauss	Caecilie	MH	E-B	†
-----	Heimliche Aufforderung	HL	B-E	†
-----	Kling			†
-----	Zuegnung	HL	CS-FS	†
Wagner	Dich theure Halle (Tannhaeuser)	H	DS-A	†
-----	Du bist der Lenz (Die Walkuere)			†
-----	Ho-jo-to-ho! (Die Walkuere)	H	DS-C	†
-----	Stehe still!	HL		†
Weber	Bethoerte, die an meine Liebe glaubt (Euryanthe)			PET

(Weber)	Wie nahte mir der Schlummer (Der Freischuetz)	H	B-B	†
Wolf	Ach, im Maien	HL	C-E	†
-----	Das Koehlerweib ist trunken			PET
-----	Die ihr schwebet	HL	EF-EF	†
-----	Er ist's	H	D-G	†
-----	Erstes Liebeslied eines Maedchens	H	EF-AF	DIT
-----	Fussreise	HL	D-E	†
-----	Geh' Geliebter, geh' jetzt			PET
-----	Ich hab' in Penna	LH		†
-----	Klinge, klinge, mein Pandero	HL	CF-EF	†
-----	Liebe mir in Busen zuendet	M	E-F	†
-----	Lied vom Winde			†

Italian Songs and Arias Employing Spirited Singing

Dramatic Soprano

Bellini	Casta diva (Norma)	H	F-C	†
Bononcini	L'esperto nocchiero (Astarte)	HL	B-E	†
Carissimi	Vittoria, mio core	HLM	B-E	†
Casella	Amante sono vaghiccia di voi			RIC
Cavalli	Donzelle fuggite	HL	C-EF	†
D'Astorga	Vo' cercando in queste valli	H	D-G	STB
Falconieri	Non più d'amore	HL	C-D	DIT
-----	Nudo arciero	HL	AF-AF	DIT
Handel	Ch'io mai vi possa (Siroe)			†
Legrenzi	Che fiero costume	HML	C-D	†
Marcello	Il mio bel foço	LMH	C-G	†
Mozart	Dove sono (Le Nozze di Figaro)	H	D-A	†
-----	Mi tradi quell' alma ingrata (Don Giovanni)			†
-----	Non so più cosa son (Le Nozze di Figaro)	H	EF-G	†
-----	Voi che sapete (Le Nozze di Figaro)	M	C-F	†
Paisiello	Chi vuol la zingarella	L	C-F	GSC
Paradies	M'ha preso alla sua ragna	M	EF-F	GSC
Pergolesi	Confusa, smarrita			GSC
Piccini	Se il ciel mi divide	M	C-F	†

(Piccini)	(Alessandro di Indie)			
Ponchielli	Stella del marinar (La Gioconda)	M	B–A	RIC
Respighi	In alto mare			BON
-----	Pioggia			BON
Rontani	Or ch'io non segno più	HL	CS–E	DIT
Rossini	Bel raggio lusinghier (Semiramide)	H	CS–A	GSC
Scarlatti, A.	Se Florindo è fedele	LM	EF–EF	GSC
Verdi	Ernani involami (Ernani)	H	AF–BF	GSC
-----	Merce, dilette amiche (I Vespri Siciliani)	MH	A–CS	GSC
-----	Pace, pace mio Dio (La Forza del Destino)	H	CS–BF	†

Miscellaneous Songs Employing Spirited Singing

Dramatic Soprano

Alnaes	Nu brister I alle de kløfter	L	A–F	HAN
Dvořák	I will sing new songs of gladness	HL		†
Falla	Siete canciones	HL		AMP
Grieg	My Johann	HL	BF–EF	GSC
-----	Simpel sang			
-----	Vaer hilset, I Damer	M	D–F	HAN
-----	With a water lily			
Mussorgsky	Hopak	HM	CS–FS	GSC
Rachmaninoff	Floods of spring	HL		DIT
-----	God took away from me			GSC
-----	Oh, no, I pray do not depart	H		DIT

Songs and Arias Employing Staccato

Dramatic Soprano

Arne, T.	Where the bee sucks	HM		†
Fourdrain	Carnaval	M	C–F	RIC
Handel	Oh! had I Jubal's lyre (Joshua)	H	E–FS	†
Mozart	Das Veilchen	LMH	F–G	GSC
-----	Vedrai carino (Don Giovanni)	H	G–G	†
Saminsky	Queen Estherka's laugh	H	D–A	CFI

Scarlatti, A.	Rugiadose odorose	HL	D-E	DIT
Schubert	Der Juengling an der Quelle	LH	E-A	†
Sibella	La Girometta	HML	D-E	GSC
Verdi	Tacea la notte placida (Il Trovatore)	H	D-DF	†

American and British Songs of Popular Appeal

Dramatic Soprano

Balfe	Killarney	H	D-E	GSC
Bassett	Take joy home	LH	EF-BF	GSC
Beach	Ah, love but a day			ASC
Bishop	Love has eyes	M		†
Bliss	The buckle			CUR
Brahe	Bless this house	HML	A-EF	BOO
Cadman	Joy	MH	E-A	GSC
Campbell-Tipton	A spirit flower	LHM	B-G	GSC
Carnevali	Come love, with me	LMH	E-A	JFI
Charles	And so, goodbye	LH	EF-AF	GSC
-----	Let my song fill your heart	LH	EF-AF	GSC
-----	When I have sung my songs	HM	BF-EF	GSC
Clarke ,	Shy one	HL	BF-G	BOH
Curran	Ho! Mr. Piper	LH	D-G	GSC
-----	Life	HM	BF-F	GSC
Del Riego	Homing	HML	BF-E	CHA
Dougherty	Everyone sang			
-----	Love in the dictionary	M	C-G	GSC
Edwards	By the bend of the river	HML	C-E	GSC
-----	Into the night	HML	C-DF	GSC
Elgar	Land of hope and glory			BOO
Fenner	Night song	L	BF-EF	FEN
Fox	The hills of home	HML	BF-DF	CFI
Gaynor	May magic			
German	Who'll buy my lavender?	HML		BOO
Giannini	Sing to my heart a song	H	D-B	ELV
Griselle and Clock	The cuckoo clock	LH	EF-G	GSC
Hely-Hutchinson	Old mother Hubbard	HL	B-E	CFI
Henschel	Morning-hymn	MH	DS-GS	†
La Forge	Song of love	LH		RIC
-----	Song of the open	MH	EF-AF	DIT
Lehmann	The cuckoo	HH	D-B	BOH
Levitzki	Ah, thou beloved one	H	EF-AF	GSC

283

Lieurance	By the waters of Minnetonka			PRE
Manning	In the Luxembourg gardens	HML	BF-D	GSC
Mitchell	Love is the wind	MHH	F-A	GAH
Rasbach	Mountains	LH	DF-AF	GSC
Rich	American Lullaby	LH	C-F	GSC
Rogers	At parting	LH	CS-FS	GSC
Ronald	Down in the forest	HML	C-D	ENO
-----	Love, I have won you	HML	EF-EF	ENO
-----	O, lovely night	HML		BOO
-----	Prelude	HML	B-D	ENO
Russell	Fulfillment	LH	EF-GF	BOS
Rybner	Pierrot	HL		GSC
Saar	The little gray dove	MH	D-BF	GSC
Sachs	The little worm	LH	CS-FS	FLA
Schuman	Holiday song	M	C-F	GSC
Scott	Blackbird's song	M	C-F	GSC
Scott	Think on me	HML	D-EF	GAL
Speaks	In may time	HL	D-E	JCH
-----	Morning	HML	BF-D	GSC
Spross	Will o' the wisp			JCH
Strelezki	Dreams	LMH	B-A	GSC
Taylor	A song for lovers	MH	D-F	JFI
Ware	This day is mine	MH	EF-AF	BOS
Wilson	My lovely Celia	HL	B-E	BOO
Worth	Midsummer	LM	E-A	GSC

(See also Humorous Songs, Negro Spirituals,
Folk songs, Operetta Songs and Opera Arias.)

Miscellaneous Songs Of Popular Appeal

Dramatic Soprano

Alvarez	La partida	HL	DS-E	GSC
Bach-Gounod	Ave Maria			†
Bizet	Agnus Dei	HLM	C-AF	†
-----	Ouvre ton coeur	MH	DS-GS	†
Bohm	Calm as the night	HML	A-EF	†
Cavalli	Donzelle fuggite	HL	C-EF	†
Donaudy	O del mio amato ben	M	EF-F	RIC
Dvořák	Songs my mother taught me	HM	E-E	†
Franz	Dedication	HML	BF-C	†
Gounod	Au printemps	LMH	DF-AF	GSC
Grieg	A dream			†
-----	I love thee	HML	E-F	†
-----	My Johann	HL	BF-EF	GSC

284

Hahn	Si mes vers avaient des ailes	HLM	B-FS	†
Massenet	Elégie	LM	C-GF	GSC
-----	Ouvre tes yeux bleus	MH	C-G	†
Mendelssohn	On wings of song			†
Mozart	Alleluja	LMH	F-C	†
Ponce	Estrellita	LH		†
Rachmaninoff	To the children	MH	F-G	DIT
Reichardt	In the time of roses			†
Rossini	La danza	MH	E-A	GSC
Schubert	An die Musik	HL	A-DS	†
-----	Ave Maria	LMH	F-F	GSC
-----	Staendchen			
Schumann	Widmung	HL	BF-F	†
Sibella	La Girometta	HML	D-E	GSC
Sieczynski	Vienna, city of my dreams			HAR
Stolz	Im Prater blueh'n die Baeume			
Strauss, J.	Blue Danube waltz			GSC
Strauss, R.	Zueignung	HL	CS-FS	†
Tchaikovsky	None by the lonely heart	HLM	C-F	DIT

(See also Humorous Songs, Negro Spirituals,
Folk Songs, Operetta Songs and Opera Arias.)

Arias From British Operas

Dramatic Soprano

Britten	Church scene (Peter Grimes)			
-----	Embroidery aria (Peter Grimes)			
Handel	Trip, blithe streamlet (Serse)			
Purcell	I attempt from love's sickness to fly (The Indian Queen)	MH	CS-E	†
-----	Music for a while (Oedipus)	LH		SC
-----	Nymphs and shepherds (The Libertine)	HM	C-F	†
-----	The Plaint (The Fairy Queen)			
-----	When I am laid in earth (Dido and Aeneas)	LH	C-G	†

Arias From French Operas

Dramatic Soprano

Berlioz	D'amour l'ardente flamme (La Damnation de Faust)			NOV
David	Charmant oiseau (La Perle du Brésil)	M	D-E	†
Gaveaux	Dieu d'Israel (L'Enfant Prodigue)			
Gluck	Adieu, conservez dans votre âme (Iphigénie en Aulide)			†
-----	Ah, malgré moi (Alceste)			†
-----	Divinités du Styx (Alceste)	MH	DF-AF	†
-----	Grands dieux (Alceste)	H	E-BF	GSC
-----	L'ai-je bien entendu? (Iphigenie en Aulide)			†
-----	Le perfide Renaud me fuit (Armide)			PET
-----	Non! ce n'est point (Alceste)	H	E-G	†
Gossec	Ah! faut-il me venger (Thésée)			LEM
Gounod	Plus grand, dans son obscurité (La Reine de Saba)	MH	CS-B	†
Halévy	Il va venir (La Juive)	H	D-CF	†
Lully	Bois épais (Amadis)	ML	C-EF	†
-----	Chant du Vénus (Revenez amours) (Thésée)			LEM
Massenet	Charmes des jours passés (Hérodiade)			HEU
-----	Dis-moi que je suis belle (Thaïs)	H	D-B	HEU
-----	Il est doux, il est bon (Hérodiade)	MH	EF-BF	GSC
-----	Pleurez, mes yeux (Le Cid)			HEU
-----	Plus de tourments (Le Cid)	H	F-BF	HEU
Meyerbeer	Ah! mon fils (Le Prophète)	M	B-AS	†
-----	Nobles Seigneurs, salut! (Les Huguenots)	LH	C-C	†
-----	O beau pays (Les Huguenots)	H	CS-D	GSC
Offenbach	Couplets de l'aveu (La Périchole)			
-----	Elle a fui, la tourterelle (Tales of Hoffman)	H	D-A	GSC
Reyer	O palais radieux (Sigurd)			HEU

(Reyer)	Salut, splendeur du jour (Sigurd)			HEU
Spontini	O nume tutelar (La Vestale)			
-----	Toi que je laisse sur la terre (La Vestale)			LEM
-----	Toi que j'implore (La Vestale)			LEM

Arias From German Operas

Dramatic Soprano

Beethoven	Abscheulicher, wo eilst du hin? (Fidelio)		B-B	†
Korngold	Marietta's song (The Dead City)	MH	F-BF	AMP
Strauss	Composer's song (Ariadne auf Naxos)			BOO
-----	Da geht er hin (Der Rosenkavalier)			BOO
-----	Es gibt ein Reich (Ariadne auf Naxos)			BOO
Wagner	Dich theure Halle (Tannhaeuser)	H	DS-A	†
-----	Du bist der Lenz (Die Walkuere)			†
-----	Elizabeth's prayer (Tannhaeuser)	LMH	DF-GF	†
-----	Elsa's dream (Lohengrin)	MH	EF-AF	†
-----	Euch Lueften die mein Klagen (Lohengrin)			†
-----	Ho-jo-to-ho! (Die Walkuere)	H	DS-C	†
-----	Mild und leise (Tristan und Isolde)	H	E-A	†
-----	O Sachs! mein Freund! (Die Meistersinger)			GSC
-----	Senta's ballad (Der Fliegende Hollaender)			GSC
-----	Starke Scheite (Goetterdaemmerung)			†
-----	War es so schmaehlich (Die Walkuere)			†
Weber	Bethoerte die an meine Liebe glaubt (Euryanthe)			DIT
-----	Ozean, du Ungeheur (Oberon)	H	C-C	GSC

287

| (Weber) | Und ob die Wolke (Der Freischuetz) | H | EF-AF | † |
| ----- | Wie nahte mir der Schlummer (Der Freischuetz) | H | B-B | † |

Arias From Italian Operas

Dramatic Soprano

Bellini	Casta diva (Norma)	H	F-C	†
Boito	Morte di Margherita (L'Altra notte) (Mefistofele)	H	D-B	GSC
Catalani	Dove son (Loreley)			SON
-----	Ebben? Ne andrò lontana (La Wally)	H	E-B	RIC
Donizetti	O mio Fernando (La Favorita)	M	B-A	†
Mascagni	Un di ero piccina (Iris)			RIC
-----	Voi lo sapete (Cavalleria Rusticana)	H	B-A	†
Monteverdi	Lasciatemi morire (Arianna)	ML	D-D	†
Mozart	Al desio di chi t'adora (Appendix, Nozze di Figaro)			
-----	Come scoglio (Così Fan Tutte)			†
-----	Deh, se piacer mi vuoi (La Clemenza di Tito)			RIC
-----	Dove sono (Le Nozze di Figaro)	H	D-A	†
-----	Mi tradi quell' alma ingrata (Don Giovanni)			†
-----	Non mi dir (Don Giovanni)	H	F-B	†
-----	Non più di fiori (La Clemenza di Tito)			†
-----	Non so più cosa son (Le Nozze di Figaro)	H	EF-G	†
-----	Or sai, chi l'onore (Don Giovanni)			GSC
-----	Parto, parto (La Clemenza di Tito) B flat clarinet and piano	H		AMP
-----	Per pietà, ben mio (Cosi Fan Tutte)			†
-----	Porgi amor (Le Nozze di Figaro)	H	D-AF	†
-----	Vedrai carino (Don Giovanni)	H	G-B	†

(Mozart)	Voi che sapete (Le Nozze di Figaro)	M	C-F	†
Ponchielli	Stella del marinar (La Gioconda)	M	B-A	RIC
-----	Suicidio! (La Gioconda)	HM	BF-AF	†
Puccini	Donde lieta uscì (La Boheme)			
-----	In quelle trine morbide (Manon Lescaut)	H	DF-BF	RIC
-----	Laggiù nel soledad (La Fanciulla del West)			RIC
-----	Non la sospiri (Tosca)			RIC
-----	Tu, che di gel sei cinta (Turandot)			RIC
-----	Un bel di vedremo (Madama Butterfly)	H	DF-BF	RIC
-----	Vissi d'arte (Tosca)	MH	EF-BF	RIC
Rossini	Bel raggio lusinghier (Semiramide)	H	CS-A	GSC
Verdi	Ave Maria (Otello)	H	EF-AF	GSC
-----	D'amor sull'ali rosee (Il Trovatore)	H	C-DF	†
-----	Ecco l'orrido campo (Un Ballo in Maschera)	H	B-C	RIC
-----	Ernani involami (Ernani)	H	AF-BF	GSC
-----	Madre, pietosa Vergine (La Forza del Destino)	H	B-B	RIC
-----	Merce, dilette amiche (I Vespri Siciliani)	MH	A-CS	GSC
-----	Morrò, ma prima in grazia (Un Ballo in Maschera)			RIC
-----	O cieli azzuri (Aida)	H	B-C	†
-----	O don fatale (Don Carlos)	MH	CF-CF	†
-----	Oh patria mia (Aida)	H	B-C	GSC
-----	Pace, pace mio Dio (La Forza del Destino)	H	CS-BF	†
-----	Ritorna vincitor (Aida)	H	DF-BF	†
-----	Salce, salce (Otello)	H	CS-FS	RIC
-----	Tu che la vanita (Don Carlos)			RIC
-----	Un macchia è qui tuttora (Macbeth)			

Miscellaneous Opera Arias

Dramatic Soprano

Borodin	Arioso of Jaroslavna (Prince Igor)			BOO

Falla	Vivan los que ríen			AMP
	(La Vida Breve)			
Menotti	To this we've come			
	(The Consul)			
Rimsky-				
Korsakov	Song of the shepherd	LM		DIT
	lehl (Snegourotchka)			
Tchaikovsky	Adieu forêts	HM	BF-FS	GSC
-----	Letter scene			GSC
	(Eugene Onegin)			

Arias From Oratorios and Latin Works

Dramatic Soprano

Elgar	Be not extreme, O Lord			NOV
	(Light of Life)			
Gaul	These are they	H	E-GS	GSC
	(The Holy City)			
Handel	Angels ever bright and	H	E-F	†
	fair (Theodora)			
-----	Come unto Him	MH	F-G	†
	(The Messiah)			
-----	How beautiful are the feet	H		†
	of them (The Messiah)			
-----	I know that my Redeemer	MH	E-GS	†
	liveth (The Messiah)			
-----	Let me wander not unseen	M	D-G	†
	(L'Allegro)			
-----	Recitative and aria of			BOO
	Nitocris (Belshazzer)			
Mendelssohn	Hear ye, Israel (Elijah)	H	E-A	†
-----	I will sing of Thy great	H	E-F	†
	mercies (Saint Paul)			
-----	Jerusalem, thou that	H	F-F	†
	killest (Saint Paul)			
Mozart	Et incarnatus est			PET
	(C Minor Mass)			

Cantata Arias

Dramatic Soprano

| Bach, J.S. | Herr, der Du stark und |
| | maechtig bist (Cantata 10) |

(Bach)	Mein glaeubiges Herze (Cantata 68)	HML		†
-----	Sheep may safely graze (Cantata 208) 2 Flutes and continuo	LM	EF-GF	GAL
Bruch	Ave Maria (Das Feuerkreuz)	LH	D-BF	AMP
Debussy	Air de Lia (L'Enfant Prodigue)	H	E-A	DUR
Handel	Have mercy Lord (Te Deum)	HM		†
Tchaikovsky	Prayer (Moscow Cantata)	M	A-GF	GAL

Operetta, Musical Comedy or Show Songs

Dramatic Soprano

De Koven	Oh promise me (Robin Hood)	HML	C-D	†
Herbert	Ah! sweet mystery of life (Naughty Marietta)	LMH	A-A	WIT
-----	I can't do that sum (Babes in Toyland)			WIT
-----	Kiss me again (Mlle. Modiste)	LHM	CS-A	WIT
-----	'Neath the southern moon (Naughty Marietta)			
Kern	All the things you are (Very Warm for May)	M	BF-F	HAR
-----	My Bill (Show Boat)			BRO
-----	The song is you (Music in the Air)	M	C-F	HAR
-----	You are love (Show Boat)			CHA
Lehar	Lippen Schweigen (The Merry Widow)	LMH	D-A	CHA
-----	Vilia (The Merry Widow)			CHA
Porter	Begin the Beguine (Jubilee)	L	BF-F	HAR
-----	Night and day (Gay Divorcee)	M	BF-EF	HAR
Rodgers	Out of my dreams (Oklahoma)			CHA
Romberg	Lover come back to me (New Moon)	H	D-G	HAR
Strauss, J.	Love's roundelay (A Waltz Dream)			MAR
-----	Czardas (Die Fledermaus)			BOO

291

| Youmans | Through the years (Through the Years) | HML | A-F | MLR |

Song Cycles (Or groups of songs)

Dramatic Soprano

Bax	Celtic song cycle	MH	BF-A	CHE
Beethoven	Irish songs Piano, violin and cello			
-----	Scotch songs Piano, violin and cello			
-----	Sechs geistliche Lieder			
Bernstein	I hate music	H	C-A	WIT
Brahms	Five songs of Ophelia	HL	B-EF	†
-----	Two songs for alto, viola and piano			
Carpenter	Gitanjali	M	B-G	GSC
Chanler	The children (9 songs)	M	C-G	GSC
Chausson	Poème de l'amour et de la mer	H		INT
Cornelius	Bridal songs			INT
-----	Six Christmas songs	HL		BOS
Crist	Chinese mother goose rhymes	H	C-G	CFI
Debussy	Chansons de Bilitis	M	C-FS	†
Fauré	Le jardin clos	M	C-E	DUR
Granados	La maja dolorosa	M		INT
Grieg	Haugtussa	M	B-GF	PET
Holst	Four songs for voice and violin	M	C-G	CHE
Mussorgsky	The nursery	M	C-G	INT
Poulenc	Tel jour, telle nuit	M	B-A	DUR
Ravel	Shéhérazade	M	CS-G	DUR
Schubert	Die schoene Muellerin	HL		†
-----	Die Winterreise			GSC
-----	Songs of Mignon			PET
Schumann	Frauenliebe und Leben	HL		†
-----	Lieder der Braut	H	D-A	†
-----	Liederkreis			
Slonimsky	Gravestones at Hancock, New Hampshire	H	D-G	AXE
Strauss	Four last songs			
Wagner	Five Wesendonck songs			GSC
Woodford-Finden	Indian love lyrics			BOO

Solo Cantatas

Dramatic Soprano

Foss	The song of songs	H		CFI
Pergolesi	Salve Regina 5			

(See Solo Cantatas of Pergolesi, Handel and
Scarlatti, Kirchenkantaten of Buxtehude and
Symphoniae Sacrae of Schuetz)

Concert Arias

Dramatic Soprano

Beethoven	Ah! Perfido	H		DIT
Mendelssohn	Infelice (concert aria, opus 94)	H	D-BF	GSC
Mozart	Ch'io mi scordi di te			BOO
-----	Misera, dove son			BOO

Christmas Songs

Dramatic Soprano

Adam	O holy night	LMH		†
Bax	A Christmas carol	H	DF-A	CHE
Bergsma	Lulee, lullay	H	E-G	CFI
Brahms	Geistliches Wiegenlied Piano and viola			†
Branscombe	Hail ye time of holidays			
Carr	As on the night	M	E-FS	GSC
Clokey	No lullaby need Mary sing			JFI
Dunhill	To the Queen of Heaven	M	C-G	GSC
Eakin	What of that midnight long ago	M	D-F	GAL
Elmore and Reed	Come all ye who weary	L	C-C	JFI
France	A Christmas lullaby	M	DS-F	GAL
Hageman	Christmas eve	HML	BF-EF	GAL
Handel	How beautiful are the feet of them (The Messiah)	H		†
Harker	A child is born in Bethlehem	LH	D-G	GSC
-----	Theres a song in the air	HL	BF-D	GSC
Head	A slumber song of the Madonna			BOH

(Head)	The little road to Bethlehem	MH	EF-AF	BOO
-----	The three mummers			BOO
Ireland	The Holy Boy	MH	D-G	BOO
Kountz	The sleigh	HL	D-FS	GSC
Lehmann	No candle was there and no fire	MH	EF-G	CHA
Lynn	Gently little Jesus	L	BF-BF	DIT
-----	The magic night of Christmas	M	D-D	DIT
Martin	The Holy Child	HML	G-G	ENO
McKinney	The Holy Mother sings	MH	AF-AF	JFI
Niles	Our lovely Lady singing	M	EF-F	GSC
Reger	The Virgin's slumber song	MMH	G-G	†
Schubert	Ave Maria	LMH	F-F	†
Strauss	Die heiligen drei Koenige	H	C-G	
Thiman	I saw three ships	L		NOV
Thorp	Come, Mary, take courage	M	DS-FS	GAL
Trunk	The Christ child in the manger	HM		AMP
Warren	Christmas candle	HML	D-E	GSC
Wentzel	Lamkins Cello and piano			GRA
Wolf	Schlafendes Jesuskind	HL	AS-F	†
Wright	A Babe lies in His cradle warm	MD	D-D	GSC
Yon	Gesu Bambino	HL	B-E	JFI

Easter Songs

Dramatic Soprano

Bantock	Easter hymn	M	FS-F	CHE
Barnes	Easter	HM	D-EF	GSC
Chaffin	Easter message	MH	D-G	FLA
Curran	Crucifixion			
Davis	Christ is risen today	M		GAL
Diack	All in the April evening	LMH	D-G	BOO
Granier	Hosanna	HH	F-BF	DIT
Guion	At the cry of the first bird	H	D-G	GSC
Hageman	Christ went up into the hills	LH	EF-AF	CFI
Handel	I know that my Redeemer liveth (The Messiah)	MH	E-GS	†
Huhn	Christ is risen	HM	C-E	ASC
LaForge	Before the Crucifix	HML	BF-EF	GSC
Lekberg	A ballad of tree and the Master	H	E-A	GAL

Mahler	Um Mitternacht	HL		INT
O'Connor	Alleluia	ML	D-D	BOO
O'Hara	There is no death	LMH	EF-AF	CHA
Rachmaninoff	Christ is risen	LM	D-F	GAL
Schubert	Ave Maria	LMH	F-F	†
Scott	Angels roll the rock away	MH	E-G	HUN
-----	The first Easter morn	LH	F-G	GSC
Wolf	Herr, was traegt der Boden	HL	B-DS	†
Yon	Christ triumphant	MH	E-A	JFI
-----	O faithful Cross	HM	C-EF	JFI
-----	Our Paschal Joy	LH	AF-AF	JFI

Patriotic Songs

Dramatic Soprano

Alberti	A nation's prayer	H		ELV
Cadman	Glory	H	EF-G	GAL
Dungan	Eternal life	HL		PRE
Elgar	Land of hope and glory			BOO
Foster, F.	The Americans come	MH	F-BF	JFI
Howe	To the unknown soldier	H	D-G	GSC
Lester	Greater love hath no man	LH	B-E	CFI
O'Hara	There is no death	LMH	EF-AF	CHA
Steffe	Battle hymn of the Republic			
Ward				
Stephens	Phantom legions	MHH	EF-BF	CHA

Sacred Songs

Dramatic Soprano

Allitsen	The Lord is my light	LMH	D-AF	BOO
Bach, J.S.	Draw near to me	HML		GSC
-----	Sheep may safely graze (Cantata 208) 2 Flutes and continuo	LM	EF-GF	GAL
Beethoven	The worship of God in nature			
Bitgood	Be still and know that I am God	ML		GRA
-----	The greatest of these is love	M		GRA
Bizet	O Lord be merciful	HL		GSC
Bone and Fenton	Thy word is a lamp	LH	C-F	ROW
Buck	Fear not ye, O Israel	HLM		GSC

Campbell- Tipton	I will give thanks unto the Lord	LMH	DF-AF	GSC
Chadwick	A ballad of trees and the Master	HML	A-F	DIT
Charles	Love is of God	H	D-G	GSC
Clokey	God is in everything	LH	D-G	JFI
Creston	Psalm 23	MH	F-AF	GSC
Davis	Let not your heart be troubled	HML		WOO
-----	Trust in the Lord	MH	CS-G	GAL
Dvořák	God is my shepherd			AMP
-----	Hear my prayer, O Lord			AMP
-----	Turn Thee to me			AMP
Edmunds	Praise we the Lord	HL	D-D	ROW
Gaul	These are they (The Holy City)	H	E-GS	GSC
Goodhall	The mountain	M	D-E	GAL
Gounod	O Divine Redeemer	LMH	C-G	GSC
Guion	Prayer	HL		GSC
Handel	Have mercy Lord (Te Deum)	HM		†
-----	How beautiful are the feet of them (The Messiah)	H		†
-----	I know that my Redeemer liveth (The Messiah)	MH	E-GS	†
-----	Thanks be to Thee	M	CS-E	†
Harker	How beautiful upon the mountains	MLH	EF-G	GSC
Henschel	Morning-hymn	MH	DS-GS	†
Holst	The heart worships	ML	BF-D	STB
Liddle	How lovely are Thy dwellings	HML		BOS
MacDermid	In my Father's house are many mansions	HML		FRS
Malotte	The Lord's Prayer			GSC
-----	The twenty-third Psalm	HLM	C-F	GSC
Mendelssohn	Hear ye, Israel (Elijah)	H	E-A	†
-----	I will sing of Thy great mercies (Saint Paul)	H	E-F	†
Schubert	The Omnipotent			
Scott	Come ye blessed	LMH	EF-AF	GSC
-----	Ride on, ride on	HML		FLA
Sowerby	Thou art my strength	H	E-G	GRA
Speaks	The Lord is my light	HML		GSC
-----	Thou wilt keep him in perfect peace	HML		GSC
Stevenson	Praise	M	F-F	CFI
Stickles	Saith the Lord	LH	D-F	CHA

Tchaikovsky	Lord, Almight God (Moscow Cantata)	M		GRA
Thiman	Thou wilt keep him in perfect peace	H	D-G	GRA
Thompson	My Master hath a garden	M		ECS
Ware	The greatest of these	LH	EF-AF	BOS
Weaver	Assurance	H	EF-G	GAL
-----	Build thee more stately mansions	M	C-E	GAL
-----	Praise the Lord his glories show	H	E-G	GAL
Wolf	Morning prayer (Morgenstimme)			
-----	Prayer (Gebet)			

Wedding Songs

Dramatic Soprano

Barnby	O perfect love	M	C-G	DIT
Beethoven	Ich liebe dich	HL	BF-DF	†
Cough-Leighter	Possession	MH	DF-AF	GSC
DeKoven	Oh promise me (Robin Hood)	HML	C-D	†
Dello Joio	How do I love thee?	H	D-G	CFI
Franck	O Lord most holy	LM	A-FS	BOS
Grieg	I love thee	HML	E-F	†
Lippe	How do I love you?			BOS
Manney	Consecration	MHH	E-A	DIT
Marx	Hat dich die Liebe beruehrt	MH	EF-BF	AMP
Ronald	Love, I have won you	HML	EF-EF	ENO
Rowley	Here at thine altar, Lord			NOV
Sacco	With this ring	M	F-F	BVC
Saxe	Wedded souls			
Schubert	Du bist die Ruh	LMH	EF-AF	†
-----	Ungeduld	HML		†
Schumann	Du Ring an meinem Finger	HL	C-F	†
-----	Widmung	HL	BF-F	†
Sowerby	O perfect love	MH	EF-AF	GRA
Strauss	Ich liebe dich			†
Thiman	The God of love my shepherd is	ML	A-D	NOV
Willan	O perfect love	HM	E-FS	GRA

297

Songs and Arias With Added
Accompanying Instrument

Dramatic Soprano

Beethoven	Irish songs Piano, violin and cello			
-----	Scotch songs Piano, violin and cello			
Brahms	Geistliches Wiegenlied Piano and viola			†
-----	Gestillte Sehnsucht Viola and piano			†
Buxtehude	Singet dem Herrn Violin and piano			
Chausson	Chanson perpétuelle String quartet	H	CS–GS	ROU
-----	Le colibri Violin or cello	M	F–GF	BOS
Curran	Nocturne Violin	HML	B–DS	GSC
Holst	Four songs for voice and violin	M	C–G	CHE
Mozart	Parto, parto (La Clemenza di Tito) B flat clarinet and piano	H		AMP
Thomson	Stabat mater aria String quartet	H	D–BF	COS
Wentzel	Lamkins Cello and piano			GRA

Elementary Songs

Dramatic Soprano

Braine	Dawn awakes	HML	A–D	ASC
Chadwick	Allah	LH	CS–GS	ASC
Curran	Ho! Mr. Piper	LH	D–G	GSC
Del Riego	Homing	HML	BF–E	CHA
Fox	The hills of home	HML	BF–DF	CFI
Giordani	Caro mio ben	HML	B–D	†
Grieg	A swan			†
Kjerulf	Synnove's song	M	C–F	GSC
Lully	Bois épais (Amadis)	ML	C–EF	†
Manning	In the Luxembourg gardens	HML	BF–D	GSC
Monteverdi	Lasciatemi morire (Arianna)	ML	D–D	†
Ponce	Estrellita	LH		†
Rogers	Cloud shadows	M	C–E	GSC

(Rogers)	Wind song	LM	C-G	GSC
Rosa	Selve voi che le speranze	MH	D-G	DIT
Scott	Lullaby	MML	BF-DF	GAL
Speaks	In May time	HL	D-E	JCH
Stephenson	Love is a sickness	HML	C-D	BOO
-----	Ships that pass in the night	HML	DF-DF	BOO
Wright	A Babe lies in His cradle	MD	D-D	GSC

American Recital Songs

Mezzo Soprano

Alberti	My lady sleeps			
Bacon	Is there such a thing as day?	M	DS-FS	AMP
-----	Let down the bars			
-----	Lonesome grove	HM	C-E	CFI
Barber	A nun takes the veil	MH	G-G	GSC
-----	Dover Beach String quartet	M	BF-F	GSC
-----	I hear an army	LH	D-AF	GSC
-----	Monks and raisons	M	DF-E	GSC
-----	Nocturne	HM	CS-FS	GSC
-----	Rain has fallen	HM	D-E	GSC
-----	Sleep now	MH	EF-AF	GSC
-----	Sure on this shining night	MH	D-G	GSC
-----	The daisies	M	C-F	GSC
-----	The Queen's face on the summery coin	L	C-E	GSC
Barnett	Music, when soft voices die	M	C-E	GSC
Bartholomew	When we are parted	M	CS-E	GAL
Beach	Ah, love but a day			ASC
-----	Wouldn't that be queer?	HM		ASC
Bernstein	Afterthought			
Bibb	A rondel of spring	HL	BF-D	GSC
Bone and Fenton	Blue water	MH	DF-AF	CFI
Bowles	Heavenly grass	ML	B-E	GSC
-----	Letter to Freddy	M	EF-EF	GSC
-----	On a quiet conscience	M	C-F	MUP
-----	Sugar in the cane	M	D-FS	GSC
Braine	Dawn awakes	HML	A-D	ASC
Branscombe	Across the blue Aegean	M	G-G	GAL
-----	At the postern gate	MH	DF-AF	ASC
Browning	Phoenix			
Campbell-Tipton	A spirit flower	LHM	B-G	GSC

299

(Campbell-Tipton)	After sunset	HM	DS-A	GSC
-----	Invocation	L	C-FS	GSC
-----	The crying of water	LH	FS-GS	GSC
Carpenter	Berceuse de guerre	M	C-G	GSC
-----	Dansons la gigue	M	B-E	GSC
-----	Don't ceare	M	C-D	GSC
-----	Go, lovely rose	M	DF-EF	GSC
-----	I am like a remnant of a cloud of autumn	L	BF-F	GSC
-----	If	M	D-E	GSC
-----	Light, my light	M	C-G	GSC
-----	May the maiden			DIT
-----	On the seashore of endless worlds	M	C-FS	GSC
-----	Serenade	LH	CS-A	GSC
-----	Slumber song	ML	BF-F	GSC
-----	The cock shall crow	M	B-E	GSC
-----	The day is no more	M	GS-DS	GSC
-----	The green river	M	B-E	GSC
-----	The Lawd is smilin' through the do'	L	B-E	GSC
-----	The player Queen	M	BF-EF	GSC
-----	The pools of peace	M	D-F	GSC
-----	The sleep that flits on baby's eyes	M	B-FS	GSC
-----	To a young gentleman	M	C-F	GSC
-----	To one unknown	M	A-DS	GSC
-----	When I bring to you colour'd toys	LM	CS-FS	GSC
Carter	Dust of snow	M	D-E	AMP
Castelnuovo-Tedesco	Springtime	M		CHE
-----	The daffodils	M	BF-F	GAL
Chadwick	Allah	LH	CS-GS	ASC
Chanler	The doves	M	C-F	AMP
-----	Wind			GSC
Charles	Clouds	HML	C-EF	GSC
-----	Song of exaltation	M		GSC
-----	Sweet song of long ago	HML	A-D	GSC
-----	The white swan	HL	C-F	GSC
-----	When I have sung my songs	HM	BF-EF	GSC
Clough-Leighter	My lover he comes on the skee	HM	D-F	BOS
-----	Who knows?	M		GSC
Cowell	St. Agnes morning	M	C-G	MER
-----	The donkey	M	D-F	MER

Creston	Joy			
-----	Out of the dusk			
Crist	Into a ship dreaming	LMH	EF-GS	CFI
-----	Love's offering			
-----	Nina Bobo	HL		CFI
-----	O come hither	HM	B-GS	CFI
Davis	Nancy Hanks	H	D-G	GAL
Dello Joio	Mill doors	M	D-E	CFI
-----	New born	M	C-D	CFI
-----	The assassination			CFI
-----	There is a lady sweet and kind	M	C-F	CFI
Diamond	Let nothing disturb thee	M	C-F	AMP
-----	The shepherd boy	M		SOU
Dobson	Yasmin	M		GSC
Dougherty	Declaration of independence	L	C-C	GSC
-----	Love in the dictionary	M	C-G	GSC
-----	Loveliest of trees	HM	C-E	BOH
-----	Serenader			
-----	Song for autumn			
-----	The K' e	M	D-F	GSC
-----	The taxi			
Duke	Evening			
-----	I can't be talkin' of love	H	CS-G	GSC
-----	I've dreamed of sunsets	M	C-G	GSC
-----	Loveliest of trees	L	C-D	GSC
-----	Luke Havergal	M	BF-F	CFI
-----	On a March day	M	B-GF	BOH
-----	To Karen, singing	M	CS-G	ELV
-----	XXth century	M		VLP
-----	Viennese waltz	H	C-GF	ROW
-----	Voices	H	FS-A	BOH
-----	White in the moon the long road lies	M		VLP
Dukelsky	The ladies of St. James			
Edmunds	Billy boy	ML	BF-EF	ROW
-----	Fare you well	MH	F-AF	ROW
-----	Milk maids	M	DF-F	MER
Edwards	Awake beloved	ML	C-F	GSC
-----	Little shepherd's song			MLS
-----	Sometimes at close of day	HML	C-E	GSC
Elwell	Music I heard	M		AMP
-----	Renouncement	M	G-G	GSC
-----	The road not taken	M	B-FS	GSC
Engel	A decade	M	F-F	GSC
-----	A sprig of rosemary	M	EF-F	GSC
-----	Sea shell	M	EF-EF	GSC
Fairchild	A memory			BOS

Foote	On the way to Kew			ASC
Gaines	My heart hath a mind			
Ganz	A memory	HM	B-D	GSC
Giannini	Be still my heart			ELV
-----	Tell me, o blue, blue sky	H		RIC
Gilberte	Two roses	LMH	CS-G	CFI
Golde	Calls	HL	BF-EF	GSC
-----	O beauty, passing beauty	MH	CS-GS	GSC
-----	Sudden light	HL		RIC
-----	Who knows	HM	BF-F	GSC
Griffes	By a lonely forest pathway	HML	A-EF	GSC
-----	Night on ways unknown has fallen	L	GS-F	GSC
-----	O'er the Tarn's unruffled mirror	HL	G-E	GSC
-----	Sorrow of Mydath	M		GSC
-----	The dreamy lake	H	BS-GS	GSC
-----	The lament of Ian the proud	MH	DS-AS	GSC
-----	We'll to the woods and gather May	M	D-F	GSC
Hadley	Make me a song	H	C-AF	GSC
-----	My shadow			ASC
-----	The time of parting	HLM	E-G	CFI
Hageman	Animal crackers	HL	C-D	GSC
-----	At the well	LH	EF-AF	GSC
-----	Charity	LMH	DF-AF	GSC
-----	Do not go, my love	HL	B-EF	GSC
-----	Evening	HL		RIC
-----	Miranda	HL		GAL
-----	Music I heard with you	MH	E-A	GAL
-----	Voices			
Harris	Agatha Morley	M	C-D	CFI
-----	Someone came knocking at my door	M		GAL
-----	Fog	M	D-F	CFI
-----	Vanished summer	M	C-E	GAL
Hindemith	Echo	H	D-FS	AMP
-----	Envoy	M	EF-F	AMP
-----	The wildflower's song	MH	E-G	AMP
Hopkinson	Beneath a weeping willow's shade	H	D-G	†
-----	Give me thy heart			
-----	My days have been so wondrous free	LH	EF-G	†
Horsman	In the yellow dusk	MH	FS-A	GSC
Howe	Berceuse	HM	EF-F	GSC
Kagen	Upstream	H	CS-F	WTR

302

Kingsford	Command	HLM	EF-G	GSC
-----	Courage	M	C-F	GSC
-----	Wallpaper for a little girl's room	M	BF-F	GSC
Kramer	Allah			
-----	For a dream's sake	HL		JFI
-----	Our lives together	HL	D-E	GAL
-----	Swans	HL		RIC
La Forge	To a messenger	HLM	CF-G	GSC
Lamont	Music			
Levitzki	Ah, thou beloved one	H	EF-AF	GSC
Lockwood	O, lady, let the sad tears fall	M		MER
MacDowell	The swan bent low	LH		ELK
Mana-Zucca	Rachem Trumpet	HML		CHA
-----	Speak to me			
Manning	Chinoise			
Metcalf	At nightfall	HML	C-DF	ASC
Mopper	Men	M	D-FS	BOS
Naginski	Look down, fair moon			
-----	Night song at Amalfi	M	D-EF	GSC
-----	The pasture	M	BF-EF	GSC
Nevin	One spring morning	MH	DS-F	BOS
Nordoff	Serenade	H	CS-FS	AMP
-----	There shall be more joy	M	CS-FS	AMP
-----	This is the shape of the leaf	M	B-E	SC
-----	Willow River	H	D-G	AMP
Olmstead	Thy sweet singing	HL	BF-EF	GSC
Ormond	Pierrot	HM		RIC
Parker	The lark now leaves her watery nest	LH	D-BF	JCH
Porter, Q.	Music, when soft voices die	HM	D-C	MUP
Protheroe	Ah love, but a day	LMH	F-AF	GAM
Rawls	The balloon man	L	A-FS	AMP
Rogers	Requiem			
-----	The last song	MLH	E-AF	GSC
-----	Time for making songs	HM	CS-F	DIT
-----	Wind song	LM	C-G	GSC
Rorem	The lordly Hudson	M	DF-G	MER
Rummel	Ecstasy	LMH	GF-AF	GSC
Sacco	Jabberwock from through the looking glass			
-----	Mexican serenade	HL	D-EF	BOS
-----	Rapunzel	MH	FS-BF	GSC
-----	The ragpicker	MH	C-AF	GSC
Saint Leger	April			
Salter	The cry of Rachel	LH	C-AF	GSC

303

Sargent	File for future reference	M	CS-E	DIT
-----	Manhattan joy ride	M	D-F	GSC
-----	Twentieth Century	H	EF-GS	LEE
Schuman	Holiday song	M	C-F ·	GSC
-----	Orpheus with his lute	M	C-FS	GSC
Silberta	You shall have your red rose			
Smith	An ocean idyl			
Spencer	For whom the bell tolls	MH	F-AF	BOS
Spross	Will o' the wisp			JCH
Stein	The puffin	M		CFI
Still	If you should go			LEE
Swanson	Joy	M	BF-EF	LEE
-----	The valley	L	BF-DF	LEE
Taylor	As love a sleeping lay			
Thompson	Velvet shoes	M	C-E	ECS
Thomson	Dirge	M	D-F	GSC
-----	Preciosilla	H	EF-A	GSC
Tureman	A winter sunset	L	BF-E	GSC
Tyson	Noon and night	LH	F-AF	GSC
-----	Sea moods	LH	E-AF	GSC
Wagenaar	I stood in dreams of darkness	M	CS-FS	GSC
-----	Look, Edwin!	M	C-F	GSC
Ware	This day is mine	MH	EF-AF	BOS
Warner	Hurdy gurdy	M	D-F	CFI
Warren	Snow towards evening	LH	EF-AF	GSC
-----	We two	LH	E-A	GSC
-----	When you walk through woods			
Watts	Green branches	HM		DIT
-----	Joy	HL	D-F	GSC
-----	Like music on the waters	H		GSC
-----	Transformation	ML	AS-DS	GSC
-----	Wild tears	L	A-F	GSC
Weaver	A book of verses	H	D-AF	GAL
Weill	In autumn			
Worth	Midsummer	LM	E-A	GSC

British Recital Songs

Mezzo Soprano

Arne, T.	Come away, death	M	C-AF	AUG
-----	In infancy			NOV
-----	Where the bee sucks	HM		†
-----	Why so pale and wan?			GSC
Bainton	Ring out, wild bells	M	C-EF	OXF
Bantock	A feast of lanterns	HM	D-F	GAL
-----	Evening song			

(Bantock)	Hymn to Aphrodite			
-----	I loved thee once, Atthis			
-----	Silent strings	MH	F-G	BOO
-----	The celestial weaver			
-----	Yung Yang	MH	E-G	GAL
Bax	A lullaby			
-----	Cradle song			CHA
Benjamin	Calm sea and mist			CUR
-----	Hedgerow			CUR
Besley	Time, you old gipsy man!	L	A-E	BOO
Brewer	The fairy pipers	HML		BOH
Bridge	All things that we clasp	HL		BOS
-----	Love went a-riding	HL		BOS
-----	Mantle of blue	H	D-F	ROG
-----	O that it were so	LMH	D-G	CHA
Butterworth	Loveliest of trees			AUG
-----	When I was one and twenty			AUG
Clarke	Eight o'clock			ROG
-----	Shy one	HL	BF-G	BOH
-----	The seal man	M		BOH
Coleridge-Taylor	Big lady moon			BOO
-----	Life and death	HML		ASC
-----	She rested by the broken brook	HL		DIT
Delius	Love's philosophy			†
-----	Twilight fancies	M	D-FS	CFI
Dowland	Come again! sweet love	M	D-E	STB
-----	Come away			BOO
-----	Deare, if you change			BOO
-----	Flow, my tears	M	D-E	STB
-----	Sorrow, sorrow stay	M	D-D	BOS
Dunhill	The cloths of Heaven	LM	EF-G	STB
Edmunds	I know my love	HL	BF-EF	ROW
-----	The faucon	M	D-F	MER
Elgar	Like to the damask rose			FOX
-----	Pleading	HML		NOV
-----	Shepherd's song			AHC
-----	The swimmer			BOO
-----	Where corals lie	HL		BOO
German	Charming Chloe	HML		NOV
Gibbs	Five eyes	HL	D-D	BOS
Goossens	Melancholy	M		CHE
Green	My lips shall speak the praise	M	E-F	OXF
-----	Salvation belongeth unto the Lord	M	F-EF	OXF
Gurney	Under the greenwood tree			ROG
Handel	Pack clouds away			PAT

305

Harty	Across the door			NOV
Head	A piper	HL		BOO
-----	Sweet chance that led my steps abroad	LM	C-F	BOH
-----	The ships of Arcady	ML	BF-EF	BOH
-----	Why have you stolen my delight?	LH		BOH
Henschel	Morning-hymn	MH	DS-GS	†
Holst	Creation			GSC
-----	Indra (God of storm and battle)	M	B-F	CHE
-----	The heart worships	ML	BF-D	STB
-----	Weep ye no more	M		STB
Horn	Cherry ripe	M	D-G	†
-----	I've been roaming	L	B-E	†
Ireland	Bed in summer			CUR
Johnson	Dear, do not your fair beauty wrong			DIT
Milford	So sweet love seemed Cello	HL	D-D	GRA
Morley	It was a lover and his lass	HM		DIT
Murray	The wandering player	M	C-F	CFI
Peterkin	A curse on a closed gate Voice and viola	M	D-É	OXF
-----	The garden of bamboos	M	EF-F	OXF
Pilkington	Rest, sweet nymphs			STB
Purcell	Ah, how pleasant 'tis to love			AUG
-----	Hark! how all things with one sound rejoice			NOV
-----	If music be the food of love	M	D-G	BOO
-----	Man is for woman made			
-----	Not all my torments			NOV
-----	There's not a swain on the plain	M	B-G	BAF
Quilter	Blow, blow thou winter wind	HL	C-E	BOO
-----	Dream valley	H	EF-GF	ROG
-----	Drink to me only	LMH	GF-GF	BOH
-----	Fairy lullaby			
-----	Music and moonlight	L	C-EF	CUR
-----	O mistress mine	HML		BOO
-----	The fuchsia tree			BOO
Ronald	Love, I have won you	HML	EF-EF	ENO
-----	Southern song			ENO
-----	The dove			ENO
Rosseter	When Laura smiles	LM	D-E	STB
Sanderson	Jewels			
-----	Quiet	ML	AF-EF	BOH

Scott	Lullaby	MML	BF-DF	GAL
-----	The unforeseen	HML		GAL
Sharp	My mother did so before me			MEU
-----	Whistle daughter, whistle			DIT
Shaw	Song of the Palanquin bearers	LH	E-F	CUR
Somervell	A song of sleep			
Stephenson	Love is a sickness	HML	C-D	BOO
-----	Ships that pass in the night	HML	DF-DF	BOO
Sullivan	Orpheus with his lute			BOO
Vaughn Williams	A piper			OXF
-----	Bright is the ring of wordsL			BOH
-----	How can the tree but wither			OXF
-----	Linden-Lea	HML	C-D	BOS
-----	Silent noon			GSC
-----	The call	M	D-F	STB
-----	The twilight people	L	BF-EF	OXF
-----	The water mill	L	C-D	OXF
Walton	Lay of the silver Persian			
Warlock	Sleep			OXF
Wilson	Phillis has such charming graces	ML	CS-EF	BOO

French Recital Songs

Mezzo Soprano

Anon	Lamentation napolitaine			
Aubert	Le vaincu			DUR
-----	Le visage penché			DUR
-----	Vieille chanson espagnole			DUR
Bemberg	Chant hindou	HML	A-EF	†
Berlioz	La captive	HL		GSC
-----	Le spectre de la rose			CST
-----	L'isle inconnue			CST
-----	Villanelle	H	E-FS	†
Berton	Hymne d'amour	HM	B-DS	LRO
Bizet	Adieu de l'hôtesse arabe	H	BF-G	†
-----	Eglogue			
-----	Pastorale	H	C-FS	GSC
Chabrier	Les cigales	HML		†
-----	Romance de l'étoile			ENO
-----	Villanelle des petits canards	HML	B-E	†
Chaminade	Chant slave			GSC
-----	The silver ring	HM	BF-F	GSC

308

(Duparc)	L'invitation au voyage	HM	E-F	†
-----	Phidylé	MH	EF-AF	BOS
-----	Testament	HL		INT
Dupont	Cendrillon	M		
Fauré	Adieu	MH	F-F	†
-----	Après un rêve	HM	C-F	GSC
-----	Arpège	MH	E-FS	HAM
-----	Au cimetière	LH	D-F	†
-----	Automne	MH	D-FS	GSC
-----	C'est l'extase	HL	C-FF	GSC
-----	Clair de lune	MH	C-G	†
-----	Dans les ruines d'une abbaye	M	E-FS	†
-----	En prière	H	F-F	†
-----	La fée aux chansons	LH	F-F	†
-----	Le parfum impérissable	LH	GF-GF	
-----	Le secret	LH	F-G	†
-----	Les berceaux	LMH	BF-G	†
-----	Mandoline	HL	F-E	†
-----	Nocturne	H	F-A	MAR
-----	Notre amour	H	DS-B	†
-----	Prison	LH		†
-----	Rencontre	H	EF-AF	†
-----	Serenade Toscane	MH	G-AF	HAM
-----	Soir	LH	D-GS	†
-----	Spleen	H	E-FS	MAR
-----	Toujours	LH	F-AF	†
Ferrari	Le miroir	M	E-F	GSC
Février	L'intruse	M	B-DF	HEU
Fourdrain	Alger le soir	M		RIC
-----	Carnaval	M	C-F	RIC
-----	Il neige des fleurs			
Franck	Le mariage des roses	M	E-FS	BOS
-----	Lied	LH	FS-FS	†
-----	Nocturne	LH		†
Garat	Dans le printemps de mes années	M		DUR
Georges	Hymne au soleil	LH	E-A	HOM
-----	La pluie	HL		INT
Godard	Florian's song	LMH	D-FS	GSC
Gounod	Adore and be still	HL		GSC
-----	Au printemps	LMH	DF-AF	GSC
-----	Au rossignol	LMH	D-G	CHO
-----	Vénise	HL		INT
Hahn	A Chloris	H	DS-FS	HEU
-----	D'une prison	L	BF-EF	HEU
-----	L'heure exquise	M	DF-F	†
-----	Les cygnes			HEU
-----	Offrande	M	D-D	†

(Hahn)	Paysage	MH	EF-G	HEU
-----	Si mes vers avaient des ailes	HLM	B-FS	†
Honegger	Chanson (Ronsard)			SEN
-----	Les cloches			SEN
-----	Psalm 130 (Mimaamaquim)			SAL
Hue	Berceuse triste			
-----	J'ai pleuré en rêve	HL	D-E	BOS
-----	Sur l'eau			HEU
Indy	Lied maritime	LH	B-G	†
Koechlin	L'hiver	H	E-G	†
-----	La lune	M	C-F	ROU
Lalo	Chant breton	M	E-E	HAM
Leguerney	L'adieu	M	B-FS	DUR
Lenormand	Quelle souffrance	HM	AF-F	HAM
Liszt	Jeanne d'Arc au Bucher			
Lully	Au clair de la lune	H	E-D	CFI
Martini	Plaisir d'amour	M	BF-EF	GSC
Massenet	Crépuscule	M	D-E	GSC
-----	Marquise			
Messiaen	Le sourire	H		DUR
-----	Pourquoi	H		DUR
Milhaud	Chansons de négresse			SAL
-----	La tourterelle	M	B-G	DUR
Paladilhe	Lamento provinçal	M	CS-FS	HOM
-----	Les trois prières			
-----	Psyché	HM	BF-F	GSC
Paulin	Que deviennent les roses			
Pessard	L'adieu du matin	ML	BF-D	GSC
Pierné	Ils étaient trois petits chats blancs			MAR
-----	Le moulin	ML	C-E	BOS
Poldowski	Colombine	H	D-GF	CHE
-----	Dansons la gigue	M	EF-G	MAR
-----	Spleen	M	D-F	CHE
Poulenc	A sa guitare	M	D-FS	DUR
-----	Air grave			ROU
-----	Air vif	H	C-AF	ROU
-----	Amoureuse	M	BS-F	DUR
-----	Avant le cinéma	M		ROU
-----	Fleurs	M	DF-F	ROU
-----	Hôtel			AMP
-----	Miroirs brulants			DEI
-----	Rodeuse au front de verre	M	BF-F	DUR
-----	Violon			ROU
-----	Voyage à Paris			AMP
Ravel	Asie	M	BF-G	DUR
-----	Chanson francaise			
-----	D'Anne qui me jecta	HM	CS-FS	GSC

310

(Ravel)	Kaddisch	H	C-G	DUR
-----	La flûte enchantée	M	DS-FS	DUR
-----	La pintade			DUR
-----	Le martin-pêcheur			DUR
-----	Le paon	M	C-F	DUR
-----	Manteau de fleurs	H		INT
-----	Nicolette	L	B-FS	ELK
-----	Sainte	M	C-G	ELV
-----	Sur l'herbe	MH	C-G	DUR
-----	Tout gai!	MH	EF-F	
-----	Trois beaux oiseaux du paradis			DUR
-----	Vocalise en forme de habanera	MH	BF-G	MAR
Rhené-Baton	Berceuse			DUR
-----	Sérénade mélancolique			
Rousseau	Arpèges			
Roussel	A un jeune gentilhomme			
-----	Le jardin mouillé	M	C-FS	ROU
Saint-Saëns	Aimons-nous			DUR
-----	L'attente			DUR
-----	La cloche	LH	DF-AF	†
-----	Le lever de la lune			DUR
-----	Mai	H	G-FS	DUR
-----	Tristesse			
-----	Tournoiement			DUR
Satie	Daphénéo			ROU
-----	Je te veux			SAL
-----	La statue de bronze			ROU
-----	Le chapelier			ROU
Severac	Chanson de Blaisine			
-----	Chanson pour le petit cheval			ROU
-----	Ma poupée chérie			ROU
Tremisot	Novembre			ENO
-----	Nuit d'été			
Widor	Contemplation	HL	BF-AF	
-----	Je ne veux pas autre chose	HL	C-EF	HAM
-----	Non credo			DUR

German Recital Songs

Mezzo Soprano

Ahle	Bruenstiges Verlangen	M	E-E	GSC
Bach, J.S.	Bist du bei mir	HML	A-EF	†
-----	Come Christians greet this day	L	BF-F	CFI

311

(Bach, J.S.)	Dir, Dir Jehovah			†
-----	Komm suesser Tod	MH	C-G	†
-----	Liebster Herr Jesu			BRH
-----	O Jesulein suess			
Bach, W.F.	No blade of grass can flourish			DIT
Beethoven	An die Geliebte	M	E-E	†
-----	Andenken			†
-----	Busslied			†
-----	Das Geheimnis			
-----	Die Ehre Gottes	HL	AF-EF	†
-----	Die Trommel geruehret			†
-----	Faithfu' Johnie			
-----	Ich liebe dich	HL	BF-DF	†
-----	Mignon (Kennst du das land)	M	E-FS	AUG
-----	Vom Tode	L	A-EF	GSC
-----	Wonne der Wehmut			†
Brahms	Ach, wende diesen Blick			†
-----	Alte Liebe	HL	C-F	†
-----	Am Sonntag Morgen	L	CS-FS	†
-----	An eine Aeolsharfe	H	EF-AF	†
-----	Auf dem Kirchhofe	HL	BF-EF	CFI
-----	Auf dem See	HL	D-F	†
-----	Bei dir sind meine Gedanken	MH	E-FS	†
-----	Blinde Kuh			†
-----	Botschaft	HL	D-F	†
-----	Das Maedchen spricht	H	E-FS	†
-----	Dein blaues Auge	MH	BF-G	†
-----	Der Jaeger	HL		†
-----	Der Kranz			†
-----	Der Schmied	HL	EF-EF	†
-----	Der Tod, das ist die kuehle Nacht	L	AF-F	†
-----	Die Mainacht	HL	BF-FF	†
-----	Dort in den Weiden	LH	A-A	†
-----	Es traeumte mir			†
-----	Feldeinsamkeit	HL	C-EF	†
-----	Fruehlingstrost	LH	E-A	†
-----	Gestillte Sehnsucht Viola and piano			†
-----	Immer leiser wird mein Schlummer	LH	DF-A	†
-----	In Waldeseinsamkeit	H	ES-G	†
-----	Klage	LH	FS-FS	†
-----	Lerchengesang	LH	FS-GS	†
-----	Liebestreu	ML	C-F	†
-----	Maedchenlied	HL		†

(Brahms)	Meine Liebe ist gruen	MLH	ES-A	†
-----	Mit vierzig Jahren	HL	FS-D	CFI
-----	Mondenschein	LH	D-GF	†
-----	Muss es eine Trennung geben?	LH	FS-FS	†
-----	Nachtigall	MHL	BF-FS	†
-----	Nicht .mehr zu dir zu gehen			†
-----	O komm holde Sommernacht			†
-----	O kuehler Wald	MH	A-F	†
-----	O liebliche Wangen	MLH	E-G	†
-----	O wuesst' ich doch den Weg zurueck	H	E-FS	†
-----	Salamander			†
-----	Salome			†
-----	Sapphische Ode	HML		†
-----	Sehnsucht	H	EF-AF	†
-----	Sommerabend			†
-----	Sonntag	H	D-G	†
-----	Spanisches Lied			†
-----	Staendchen	HL	BF-E	†
-----	Steig' auf, geliebter Schatten	HL	BF-EF	†
-----	Tambourliedchen			†
-----	Therese	HL	B-D	†
-----	Treue Liebe	LMH	DS-E	†
-----	Ueber die Haide			†
-----	Vergebliches Staendchen	LMH	E-FS	†
-----	Verzagen	MH	CS-FS	†
-----	Von ewiger Liebe	LMH	B-AF	†
-----	Wehe, so willst du mich wieder			PET
-----	Wenn du nur zuweilen laechelst			†
-----	Wie froh und frisch	HL	B-E	†
-----	Wiegenlied			
-----	Wie Melodien zieht es	HL	A-E	†
-----	Willst du, dass ich geh'?	L	C-G	†
-----	Wir wandelten	LH	EF-GF	†
Franz	Abends	HM	C-EF	†
-----	Das macht das dunkel-gruene Laub	HL		†
-----	Die blauen Fruehlingsaugen	HL		†
-----	Die helle Sonne leuchtet			
-----	Ein Stuendlein wohl vor Tag			†
-----	Er ist gekommen	HL	EF-F	†
-----	Es hat die Rose sich beklagt	LH	DF-F	†

(Franz)	Es ragt ins Meer der Runenstein	HL	G-F	†
-----	For music	ML	C-D	†
-----	Fruehling und Liebe	HL		†
-----	Im Herbst	HM	A-F	†
-----	Mutter, o sing mich zur Ruh	HL	E-G	†
-----	Sonnenuntergang	HL	CS-FS	†
-----	Staendchen	HL		GSC
-----	Sterne mit den gold'nen Fuesschen	HL	DS-E	†
Handel	Dank sei Dir, Herr	M	CS-E	†
Hassler	Gagliarda			SIM
-----	Tanzlied			SIM
Haydn	My mother bids me bind my hair	M	E-E	†
-----	She never told her love	HL	B-D	DIT
-----	The mermaid's song	M	C-F	PRE
-----	The spirit's song	M	B-GF	†
-----	The wanderer			
Himmel	Die Sendung			SIM
Hindemith	Pietà from Marienleben			AMP
Jensen	Am Ufer des Flusses des Manzanares	H	D-FS	GSC
-----	Wie so bleich			
Kahn	Es geht ein Wehen durch den Wald Violin, cello and piano			
-----	Mein Herzblut geht in Spruengen Violin, cello and piano			
-----	Waldesnacht, du wunderkuehle Violin, cello and piano			
-----	Wie bin ich nun in kuehler Nacht Violin, cello and piano			
Korngold	Love letter			AMP
Liszt	Die drei Zigeuner	LM	B-G	GSC
-----	Die Lorelei	LH	BF-BF	†
-----	Freudvoll und leidvoll			DUR
-----	Gestorben war ich			
-----	Hohe Liebe			DUR
-----	O lieb' so lang du lieben kannst	HML	B-F	†
Loewe	Canzonetta	MH	B-A	DIT
-----	Der heilige Franziskus	L	A-E	SC
-----	Die Uhr	HML	AF-EF	†
-----	Walpurgisnacht	H	G-G	SC
Mahler	Das Irdische Leben	HL	A-F	INT

(Mahler)	Des Antonius von Padua Fischpredigt	HL	GF-F	†
-----	Die zwei blauen Augen	M	A-G	†
-----	Ging heut Morgen uebers Feld	M	A-FS	INT
-----	Hans und Grethe	HL		INT
-----	Ich atmet' einen linden Duft	HL		INT
-----	Ich bin der Welt abbanden gekommen	HL		INT
-----	Ich hab' ein gluehend Messer	M	BF-GF	WEI
-----	Liebst du um Schoenheit	HL		INT
-----	Rheinlegendchen	M	B-FS	†
-----	Scheiden und Meiden	HL		INT
-----	Urlicht	L	DF-E	†
-----	Wenn mein Schatz Hochzeit macht			WEI
-----	Wer hat dies Liedlein erdacht?	HL	BF-E	INT
-----	Wo die schoenen Trompeten blasen	HL	GF-F	INT
Marx	An einen Herbstwald	M	CS-FS	UNI
-----	Der bescheidene Schaefer			UNI
-----	Der Rauch			UNI
-----	Der Ton	M	C-F	AMP
-----	Ein junger Dichter			AMP
-----	Hat dich die Liebe beruehrt	MH	EF-BF	AMP
Mendelssohn	An die Entfernte	M	F-F	
-----	Bei der Wiege	M	DF-EF	†
-----	Die Liebende schreibt	HL		†
-----	Nachtlied			
-----	Neue Liebe	H	CS-A	†
-----	On wings of song			†
-----	Schilflied	M	F-FS	
-----	Suleika	H	E-GS	†
-----	Volkslied	M	E-A	†
Mozart	Abendempfindung	M	E-F	
-----	Als Luise die Briefe			GSC
-----	Die Alte			
-----	Verdankt sei es dem Glanz			DIT
-----	Warnung	HM	C-D	
-----	Wiegenlied	MH	G-G	†
Pfitzner	Gretel			BOO
-----	Venus Mater			
-----	Verrat			
Reger	Am Bruennele			
-----	Des Kindes Gebet	H	F-G	BOT

(Reger)	Mit Rosen bestreut			UNI
-----	Waldeinsamkeit	HML	A-D	BOS
Reichardt	Rhapsodie			MOS
Ries	Die blauen Fruehlingsaugen	HM	CS-E	GSC
Schoenberg	Song of the wood dove			AMP
-----	Traumleben			UNI
Schubert	Am Bach im Fruehling			PET
-----	Am Feierabend	HL	BF-F	†
-----	Am Grabe Anselmos	HL	B-EF	†
-----	An den Mond	HL	F-GF	†
-----	An die Leier	LM	BF-F	†
-----	An Schwager Kronos	HL	G-E	†
-----	Auf dem Wasser zu singen	MH	EF-GF	†
-----	Aufenthalt	HLM	A-F	†
-----	Aufloesung	LH	D-A	†
-----	Aus Heliopolis			PET
-----	Ave Maria	LMH	F-F	†
-----	Bei dir allein			PET
-----	Das Wandern	HLM	E-E	†
-----	Das Wirtshaus	HL	C-D	†
-----	Dem Unendlichen	L	A-GF	†
-----	Der Atlas	HL	BF-F	†
-----	Der Doppelgaenger	HL	G-D	†
-----	Der Einsame	LH	D-G	GSC
-----	Der Erlkoenig	HML	A-E	†
-----	Der Fluss			
-----	Der Juengling an der Quelle	LH	E-A	†
-----	Der Leiermann	ML	C-D	†
-----	Der Lindenbaum	HL	A-D	†
-----	Der Musensohn	LH	FS-G	†
-----	Der Neugierige	HL	CS-EF	†
-----	Der Schmetterling	LH	E-F	†
-----	Der stuermische Morgen	HL		
-----	Der Tod und das Maedchen	HL	A-EF	†
-----	Der Wanderer	HML	FS-D	†
-----	Der Wanderer an den Mond	LM	D-F	PET
-----	Der Wegweiser	L	D-EF	†
-----	Der Zwerg	M	A-GF	PET
-----	Des Maedchens Klage	LH	C-E	†
-----	Die Allmacht	HML	G-E	†
-----	Die boese Farbe	HL	CS-F	†
-----	Die Forelle	MLH	EF-GF	†
-----	Die junge Nonne	LH	C-GF	†
-----	Die Kraehe	HL	A-E	†
-----	Die liebe Farbe			

(Schubert)	Die Liebe hat gelogen	LM	G-F	†
-----	Die Maenner sind mechant			PET
-----	Die Mutter Erde			PET
-----	Die Nebensonnen	HL	F-D	GSC
-----	Die Post	HML	BF-EF	†
-----	Die Stadt	HL	A-E	†
-----	Die Taubenpost	HL	D-EF	†
-----	Dithyrambe	L	A-D	†
-----	Du bist die Ruh	LMH	EF-AF	†
-----	Du liebst mich nicht	LH	E-FS	†
-----	Ellens zweiter Gesang			PET
-----	Erstarrung	HL	D-F	†
-----	Fahrt zum Hades	HL	G-DF	PET
-----	Fischerweise	L	C-D	†
-----	Fragment aus dem Aeschylus			PET
-----	Fruehlingstraum	HL	C-D	†
-----	Ganymed	LH	EF-G	†
-----	Geheimes	HL	BF-EF	†
-----	Gretchen am Spinnrade	H	F-A	†
-----	Gruppe aus dem Tartarus	L	CS-EF	†
-----	Heidenroeslein			
-----	Ihr Bild	HL	C-C	†
-----	Im Abendrot	HL	C-D	†
-----	Im Fruehling	LH	D-FS	†
-----	In der Ferne	HL		†
-----	Irrlicht			
-----	Klaerchens Lied			
-----	Lachen und Weinen	HL	C-EF	†
-----	Letzte Hoffnung	HL		†
-----	Liebsebotschaft	H	E-G	†
-----	Liebhaber in allen Gestalten			PET
-----	Lied der Mignon	HL		†
-----	Lied eines Schiffers an die Dioskuren	HL	A-C	†
-----	Litanei	HLM	C-EF	†
-----	Mut	HL		†
-----	Nachtgesang			PET
-----	Nacht und Traeume	HL	C-DF	†
-----	Nur wer die Sehnsucht kennt	LH		†
-----	Rastlose Liebe	M	B-F	†
-----	Romanze aus Rosamunde			PET
-----	Schaefers Klagelied	HL	BF-D	†
-----	Sei mir gegruesst	LH	G-G	†
-----	Seligkeit			
-----	Staendchen			
-----	Suleika I	LH	DS-G	†
-----	Suleika II	LH	F-BF	†

317

(Schubert)	Thekla	HL	B-E	PET
-----	Ungeduld	HML		†
-----	Wehmuth	HL	B-D	†
-----	Wiegenlied (Op. 105)			PET
-----	Wohin?	HL	B-E	†
Schuetz	Aus dem 119th Psalm			
Schumann	Abends am Strande			
-----	An den Sonnenschein	HL	A-D	†
-----	Aus den Hebraeischen Gesaengen			
-----	Dein Angesicht	HL	B-EF	DIT
-----	Der Himmel hat eine Traene geweint			
-----	Der Nussbaum	LMH	D-FS	†
-----	Der Sandmann	HL	AF-DF	†
-----	Die Kartenlegerin			
-----	Die Lotusblume	HLM	BF-F	†
-----	Die Soldatenbraut	HL	AF-EF	†
-----	Die Tochter Jephthas	HL	A-E	
-----	Du bist wie eine Blume	HM	F-EF	†
-----	Du Ring an meinem Finger	HL	C-F	†
-----	Er, der Herrlichste von Allen	HL	A-EF	†
-----	Er ist's	HL	BF-EF	†
-----	Erstes Gruen	HL	D-D	†
-----	Fruehlingsfahrt	HL	B-E	†
-----	Fruehlingsnacht	L	CS-E	†
-----	Heiss' mich nicht reden			
-----	Hoch, hoch sind die Berge			
-----	Ihre Stimme	LH		†
-----	Im Walde	HL	A-D	†
-----	Im Westen	HL		†
-----	Ins freie			
-----	Liebeslied			
-----	Lied der Suleika			
-----	Lust der Sturmnacht			
-----	Marienwuermchen	HL	D-D	GSC
-----	Melancholie			
-----	Mit Myrthen und Rosen	HL	A-D	†
-----	Mondnacht	M	E-FS	†
-----	Requiem			†
-----	Schoene Wiege meiner Leiden	HL	C-EF	†
-----	Seit ich ihn gesehen	HL	DF-DF	†
-----	Stille Traenen	HL		†
-----	Waldesgespraech	HL	A-FS	†
-----	Was soll ich sagen!			†
-----	Wer machte dich so krank?			

(Schumann)	Widmung	HL	BF-F	†
Strauss	Allerseelen	HL	AS-E	†
-----	Befreit			HSC
-----	Caecilie	MH	E-B	†
-----	Dem Herzen sehnlich			
-----	Die Georgine	LH	B-A	†
-----	Die Nacht	HL		†
-----	Freundliche Vision	HL	C-F	†
-----	Fuer fuenfzehn Pfennige			†
-----	Hat gesagt bleibt's nicht dabei			†
-----	Heimkehr	HL	B-E	†
-----	Heimliche Aufforderung	HL	B-E	†
-----	Ich trage meine Minne	M		UNI
-----	Liebeshymnus			†
-----	Meinem Kinde			†
-----	Mit deinen blauen Augen	LH	C-GS	†
-----	Morgen	HML	E-F	†
-----	Nichts	LH	E-A	†
-----	Ruhe meine Seele			†
-----	Seitdem dein Aug' in meines schaute			SC
-----	Traum durch die Daemmerung	HML	BF-EF	†
-----	Wiegenliedchen			†
Trunk	In meiner Heimat			
Wagner	Der Tannenbaum			
-----	Im Treibhaus	HL		†
-----	Schmerzen	HL		†
-----	Stehe still!	HL		†
Wolf	Ach, des Knaben Augen	HL		†
-----	Ach, im Maien	HL	C-E	†
-----	Agnes	HL		†
-----	Alle gingen, Herz, zu Ruh	HL	C-EF	†
-----	An die Geliebte			†
-----	An eine Aeolsharfe			†
-----	Auch kleine Dinge	HM	D-E	†
-----	Auf dem gruenen Balkon	HL		†
-----	Auf einer Wanderung	HL		DIT
-----	Bedeckt mich mit Blumen	HL	B-D	†
-----	Bei einer Trauung			PET
-----	Cophtisches Lied 2			†
-----	Dank des Paria			PET
-----	Das Koehlerweib ist trunken			PET
-----	Das Staendchen	HL		†
-----	Das verlassene Maegdlein	HL	D-EF	†
-----	Denk' es, o Seele	LH	EF-F	†
-----	Der Freund	HM	BF-E	PET
-----	Der Gaertner	HL		†

(Wolf)	Der Mond hat eine schwere Klag' erhoben	HL	BF-DF	†
-----	Die ihr schwebet	HL	EF-EF	†
-----	Die Zigeunerin			†
-----	Du denkst, mit einem Faedchen			†
-----	Elfenlied	HL	D-F	†
-----	Er ist's	H	D-G	†
-----	Erstes Liebeslied eines Maedchens	H	EF-AF	†
-----	Fussreise	HL	D-E	†
-----	Ganymed	HL	CS-D	†
-----	Gebet	HL		†
-----	Geh' Geliebter, geh' jetzt			PET
-----	Gesang Weylas	HL	DF-F	†
-----	Heimweh (Moerike Lieder)			†
-----	Herbstentschluss			
-----	Ich hab' in Penna	LH		†
-----	Im Fruehling	HL	BF-F	†
-----	In dem Schatten meiner Locken	M	C-EF	†
-----	In der Fruehe	HL	C-C	†
-----	Kennst du das Land			†
-----	Klinge, klinge, mein Pandero	HL	CF-EF	†
-----	Liebe mir in Busen zuendet	M	E-F	†
-----	Lied vom Winde			†
-----	Mausfallen Spruechlein	HL	BF-E	†
-----	Mignon	LH		†
---᠇---	Morgenstimmung	LH	C-GS	†
-----	Morgentau	HL	D-D	†
-----	Neue Liebe	LH	D-AF	†
-----	Nimmersatte Liebe	LH	CF-AF	†
-----	Nun wandre, Maria	HL	EF-D	†
-----	Rat einer Alten			†
-----	Sie blasen zum Abmarsch			
-----	Sterne mit den goldnen Fuesschen			
-----	Tretet ein, hoher Krieger	HL	B-F	†
-----	Ueber Nacht	LH	D-G	†
-----	Um Mitternacht	HL	G-EF	†
-----	Und willst du deinen Liebsten sterben	HL		†
-----	Verborgenheit	HL	B-E	†
-----	Verschling' der Abgrund			PET
-----	Verschwiegene Liebe	LH	DF-FS	†
-----	Wenn du, mein Liebster	LH	DF-GF	†

(Wolf)	Wenn du zu den Blumen gehst	HL	B-EF	†
-----	Wie glaenzt der helle Mond			†
-----	Zur ruh', zur Ruh'	HL	A-GF	†
Wolff	Alle Dinge haben Sprache	M	BF-GF	†
-----	Bekenntnis			
-----	Die heisse schwuele Sommernacht			HMP
-----	Die Lor' sitzt im Garten	M	C-FS	HMP
-----	Ewig			
-----	Ich bin eine Harfe			HMP
-----	Knabe und Veilchen	M	D-D	HMP
-----	Since you're near	M	BF-GF	†
-----	Voegleins Schwermut			

Italian Recital Songs

Mezzo Soprano

Alfano	Felicità			
-----	Melodia			RIC
Bimboni	Sospiri miei	M	EF-EF	GAL
Bononcini	Deh, lascia			HEU
-----	Per la gloria	HL	C-EF	†
-----	Pietà, mio caro bene	HL	C-EF	DIT
Brogi	Mattinata			
Caccini	Amarilli, mia bella	ML	C-D	†
Caldara	Alma del core			GSC
-----	Come raggio di sol	HL	D-F	†
-----	Mirti, faggi			PET
-----	Sebben crudele	HML	E-DS	†
-----	Selve amiche, ombrose piante	HM	E-E	†
Carissimi	A morire!	ML	C-D	
-----	Vittoria, mio core	HLM	B-E	†
Castelnuovo-Tedesco	Ninna Nanna			
-----	Recuerdo			
Cavalli	Donzelle fuggite	HL	C-EF	†
Cesti	Ah, quanto è vero (Il Pomo d'Oro)	HL	F-F	DIT
-----	Che angoscia, che affanno (Il Pomo d'Oro)	HL	C-DF	DIT
-----	E dove t'aggiri (Il Pomo d'Oro)	HM	D-EF	DIT
Cherubini	Ahi, che forse ai miei di (Demofonte)			RIC

Cimara	Fiocca la neve	H	G-G	GSC
-----	Stornellata marinara	HM		RIC
Cimarosa	Nel lasciarti (L'Olympiade)			RIC
Del Leuto	Dimmi, amor	M	C-F	GSC
De Luca	Non posso disperar	HL	C-E	GSC
Donaudy	Quando ti rivedrò			RIC
-----	Spirate pur, spirate			RIC
Durante	Danza, danza fanciulla gentile	HM	BF-F	†
-----	Vergin, tutta amor	LM	C-EF	†
Falconieri	Non più d'amore	HL	C-D	DIT
-----	Nudo arciero	HL	AF-AF	DIT
Gagliano	Dormi, amore	HL	CS-E	DIT
-----	Valli profonde (Il Dannato)			HEU
Galuppi	La pastorella (Il Filosoto di Campagna)			DUR
Ghedini	La tortora			
Giordani	Caro mio ben	HML	B-D	†
Gluck	Di questa cetra (Il Parnasso Confuso)			LEM
-----	O del mio dolce ardor (Paride ed Elena)	LH	D-FS	GSC
-----	Spiagge amate (Paride ed Elena)			†
-----	Vieni che poi sereno (La Semiramide)	M	D-G	†
Guarnieri	Caro, caro il mio bambin			RIC
Handel	Affani del pensier (Ottone)			GSC
-----	Amor commanda (Floridante)	H		†
-----	Cangio d'aspetto (Admeto)			†
-----	Cara sposa (Radamisto)	M	CS-D	†
-----	Ch'io mai vi possa (Siroe)			†
-----	Crude furie de gl'orri diubissi (Serse)			
-----	Dove sei, amato bene (Rodelinda)	L	BF-EF	†
-----	Furibondo spira (Partenope)			KIS
-----	Lascia chio pianga (Rinaldo)			
-----	O rendetemi, il mio bene (Amadigi)	L	CS-EF	CFI
-----	Ombra mai fu (Serse)	HM	BF-EF	†
-----	Piangero la (Julius Caesar)			CFI
-----	Qual farfalletta (Partenope)	H	E-A	†

322

(Handel)	V'adoro pupille (Julius Caesar)			BOO
-----	Verdi prati (Alcina)			†
Haydn	Cara speme (Orfeo ed Euridice)			
Legrenzi	Che fiero costume	HML	C-D	†
Lotti	Pur dicesti, o bocca bella	LMH	E-FS	GSC
Malipiero	Ballata	H		CHE
Marcello	Non m'è grave morir per amore	L	C-E	GSC
Paisiello	Chi vuol la zingarella	L	C-F	GSC
-----	Nel cor più non mi sento	HL	C-EF	†
Panizza	D'une prison	H	C-G	GSC
Paradies	M'ha preso alla sua ragna	M	EF-F	GSC
Pergolesi	Confusa, smarrita			GSC
-----	Ogni pena più spietata	L	B-E	GSC
-----	Se tu m'ami	LMH	C-G	GSC
Peri	Funeste piaggie (Euridice)			GSC
Piccini	O nuit, dresse du mystere (Le Faux Lord)			GSC
-----	Se il ciel mi divide (Alessandro di Indie)	M	C-F	†
Pignatta	Cieco si finse amor			
Pizzetti	La madre al figlio lontano			FRL
Porpora	Come la luce è tremola			
Quagliati	Apra il suo verde seno	HL	E-CS	DIT
Recli	La luna prigioniera	H		RIC
Respighi	Abbandono			BON
-----	Ballata			RIC
-----	Contrasto	M		RIC
-----	E se un giorno tornasse	M		RIC
-----	Il tramonto			RIC
-----	In alto mare			BON
-----	Invito alla danza			BON
-----	Io sono la madre	L		RIC
-----	Mattino di luce	M		RIC
-----	Nebbie			†
-----	Notte			BON
-----	Pioggia			BON
-----	Scherzo			BON
Rontani	Or ch'io non segno più	HL	CS-E	DIT
-----	Se bel rio	ML	D-C	†
Rosa	Selve, voi che le speranze	MH	D-G	DIT
-----	Vado ben spesso	ML	C-EF	†
Rossi	Ah, rendimi (Mitrane)	L	GS-FS	GSC
Rossini	La danza	MH	E-A	†
-----	La regatta Veneziana			

Sadero	I battitori di grano	M		CHE
Santoliquido	I canti della sera			RIC
-----	Le domandai			
Sarti	Lungi dal caro bene (Armide)	HL	G-D	GSC
Scarlatti, A.	O cessate di piagarmi	HL	DS-E	GSC
-----	Rugiadose odorose (Il Pirro e Demetrio)	HL	D-E	DIT
-----	Se Florindo è fedele	LM	EF-EF	GSC
-----	Sento nel core	M	E-F	†
Scarlatti, D.	Consolati e spara amante	L	BF-E	GSC
-----	Qual farfalletta			
Secchi	Love me or not			BOO
-----	Lungi dal caro bene	HL	A-FS	DIT
Sibella	Sotto il ciel	HM	C-F	GSC
Stradella	Col mio sangue comprenderei (Il Floridoro)	HL	E-F	DIT
-----	Per pietà (Il Floridoro)	HM	D-F	DIT
-----	Pietà, Signore	HM	C-F	GSC
Torelli	Tu lo sai	HL	BF-F	†
Tosti	Dopo!			RIC
-----	La serenata	HLM	D-EF	GSC
-----	Mattinata			RIC
Vivaldi	Da du venti (Ercole)			
-----	Onde chiare			
-----	Un certo no so che	HL	BF-EF	†

Russian Recital Songs

Mezzo Soprano

Arensky	Autumn	H	CS-FS	GSC
-----	Revery	MH	DS-FS	DIT
-----	Valse	H	DF-GF	GSC
Cui	The statue at Czarskoe-Selo	HM	DF-EF	†
Dargomijshky	I still love him			
-----	My darling girls			
Gliere	Ah, twine no blossoms	HM	CS-F	DIT
-----	Sweetly sang the nightingale			
Glinka	How sweet it is to be with you	HM		GSC
Gretchaninoff	Declaration of love			
-----	Dewdrop			
-----	Hushed the song of the nightingale	MH	E-G	DIT
-----	Il s'est tu, le charmant rossignol	H	EF-G	†

(Gretchaninoff)	L'amour eternel			
-----	Lullaby			
-----	My native land	L	C-EF	GSC
-----	Over the steppe	LM	C-G	GSC
-----	Wounded birch	HL	B-EF	†
Mednikoff	The hills of Gruzia	H	DS-A	LAC
Mussorgsky	After the battle			GSC
-----	Cradle song of the poor	M	B-DS	GSC
-----	Death the commander			
-----	Hopak	HM	CS-FS	GSC
-----	In the corner			INT
-----	On the Dnieper			GSC
-----	Peasant cradle song	M		GSC
-----	Serenade			BES
-----	Sphinx			BRH
-----	The classic			BRH
-----	The orphan girl			GSC
Prokofieff	Snowdrops			GSC
-----	Snowflakes			GSC
Rachmaninoff	A dream	H		BOO
-----	All things depart			BOO
-----	April			
-----	As fair is she as noonday light			GSC
-----	Floods of spring	HL		DIT
-----	In the silence of night	LH	D-A	GSC
-----	Into my open window	HL	B-FS	BOS
-----	Like blossom dew	M		BOO
-----	Lilacs	LH	EF-G	†
-----	Morning	ML	B-DS	GSC
-----	My heart trembles again			
-----	Oh cease thy singing, maiden fair	H	E-A	CFI
-----	O, do not grieve	M	BF-AF	GSC
-----	Oh, no, I pray do not depart	H		DIT
-----	O thou billowy harvest field	HL	CS-E	GSC
-----	The answer	H		BOO
-----	The island	LH	DF-F	†
-----	The raising of Lazarus			BRH
-----	The soldier's bride			†
-----	Vocalise	LH	CS-A	GSC
Rimsky-Korsakov	Clearer is the skylark's singing			
-----	On the Georgian hills	HM		GSC
Rubinstein	Der Asra	HM	B-F	GSC
Stravinsky	Pastorale			GSC
-----	The cloister (La Novice)			DIT
Tchaikovsky	At the ball	MH		GSC

(Tchaikovsky)	Evening	HM		GSC
-----	If you would only know			
-----	Lizochek			
-----	One word			
-----	The terrible moment			

Scandinavian Recital Songs

Mezzo Soprano

Alnaes	Der du gjekk fyre			
-----	En morgen var din grav	M	CS-D	HAN
-----	Lykken mellem to mennesker	M	B-FS	HAN
-----	Nu brister i all de kløfter	L	A-F	HAN
Backer-Gröndahl	In dreaming dance			
Grieg	A dream			†
-----	A swan			†
-----	Autumnal gale	HL	A-F	CFI
-----	By the brook			GSC
-----	Den Aergjerrige			
-----	Den blonde pige			HAN
-----	Det syng	M	C-GF	HAN
-----	Eros	LM	C-F	†
-----	From Monte Pinci			PET
-----	Goat dance			
-----	Good morning			†
-----	Hjemkomst	M	B-F	HAN
-----	I love thee	HML	E-F	†
-----	In the boat	LM	D-ES	†
-----	Jeg giver mit digt til våren.	M	CS-G	HAN
-----	Jeg lever et liv i laengsel	L	BF-E	HAN
-----	Når jeg vil dø	L	CS-EF	HAN
-----	Nu er aftenen lys og lang	L	C-E	HAN
-----	På Hamars ruiner	M	BF-G	HAN
-----	På Norges nøgne fjelde	M	D-F	HAN
-----	På skogstien	H	E-G	HAN
-----	Radiant night			
-----	Saint John's eve	L	DF-E	CFI
-----	Snegl, Snegl	M	B-F	HAN
-----	Solvejgs' cradle song	M	CS-FS	GSC
-----	Spring rain			PET
-----	Thanks for thy counsel			DIT
-----	The mother sings			DIT
-----	The tryst			DIT
-----	The wounded heart			PET

(Grieg)	Til en I	L	B-CS	HAN
-----	Til en II	M	E-F	HAN
-----	Til min dreng		C-E	
-----	Turisten	M	CS-F	HAN
-----	Udvandreren	M	EF-F	HAN
-----	Vaer hilset, I Damer	M	D-F	HAN
-----	Ved Moders grav	M	C-F	HAN
-----	Verse for an album			
-----	With a water lily	HM	CS-EF	†
Heise	Arnes sang			
-----	Sol deroppe ganger under lide			
Henriques	Vaaren er kommen			
Kjerulf	Synnove's song	M	C-F	GSC
-----	The cuckoo calls	M		AMP
Lange- Mueller	Gjenboens først vise			
-----	Himlen ulmer svagt i flammerødt			
Lie	Soft-footed snow	HM		DIT
Nielson	Pigen højt i taarnet sad			
Rangstroem	Melodie			
Sibelius	Black roses	M	A-ES	AMP
-----	Diamonds on the March snow			
-----	Hymn to Thais the unforgettable			
-----	In the field a maiden sings			
-----	On a balcony by the sea			
-----	Reeds, reeds rustle			
-----	Song of the Jewish girl			
-----	Spring is fleeting			DIT
-----	The first kiss	M		AMP
-----	The silent town			AMP
-----	The tryst	M		AMP
-----	The young huntsman			
-----	Was it a dream?			BRH
Sinding	I hear the gull			JCH
-----	The daisies secret			
Sjoeberg	Visions	MH	F-AF	GAL
Soderberg	Fågelns visa			
Vehanen	Cantilena			
Weyse	I skovens dybe, stille ro			
-----	Natten er saa stille			
-----	Pigen paa gjaerdet			

Spanish Recital Songs

Mezzo Soprano

Alvarez	La partida	HL	DS-E	GSC
Falla	Psyché String quartet, harp and flute	M		CHE
Ferrazzano	El lago			
Ginastera	Chacarera			RIC
-----	Triste			RIC
Granados	El majo discreto	H		INT
Guastavino	Encantamiento			
-----	La rose y la sauce			RIC
Nin	Cloris hermosa			
-----	El amor es como un niño			ESC
-----	El vito			ESC
-----	Paño murciano			ESC
-----	Villancico vasco			ESC
Obradors	Coplas de curro dulce			
-----	El vito			
-----	Malagueña de la magruga			
-----	Romance de los pelegrinitos			
Ravel	Chanson espagnole			DUR
Turina	Farruca	M	A-F	UME

Miscellaneous Recital Songs

Mezzo Soprano

Bach-Gounod	Ave Maria			
Bartok	Tears of autumn	M	C-F	GSC
Bizet	Agnus Dei	HLM	C-AF	
Chajes	Adarim			TRA
Chopin	Lithuanian song	ML	C-C	GSC
-----	Melancholy	HL		GSC
-----	My beloved	HL		GSC
-----	The maiden's wish	LM	CS-E	GSC
Dvořák	Clouds and darkness			
-----	God is my shepherd			AMP
-----	Hear my prayer, O Lord			AMP
-----	I will sing new songs of gladness	HL		
-----	Lord, Thou art my refuge and shield			AMP
-----	Sing ye a joyful song			AMP
-----	Songs my mother taught me	HM	E-E	
-----	Tune thy fiddle gypsy			SIM
-----	Turn Thee to me			AMP

Enesco	Aux demoiselles paresseuses			
-----	Etienne à Anne			
Fisher	Eili, Eili	LMH	E-G	DIT
Franck	Panis angelicus	LM		
Luzzi	Ave Maria	HL	BF-EF	GSC
Mignone	Cantiga de ninar			SUM
-----	Dona janaina			
Ravel	Mayerke mein suhn			RAV
Saint-Saëns	Ave Maria	HM		DIT
-----	Ave Verum			DUR
Villa-Lobos	Abril			
-----	Adeus Ema			AMP
-----	Bachianas Brazileiras, no. 5 8 Celli and bass			AMP
-----	Canção do carreiro			
-----	Canção do marinheiro			
-----	Desejo			
-----	Evocacao			
-----	Miau (A gatinha parda)			
-----	Modinha (Love song)			
-----	No paz do outono			
-----	Nozani-na			AMP
-----	Papae curumiassu			AMP
-----	Saudades da minha vida			
-----	Sino da aldeia			
-----	Xango			AMP

British Songs and Arias for Opening Recitals

Mezzo Soprano

Green	My lips shall speak the praise	M	E-F	OXF
-----	Salvation belongeth unto the Lord	M	F-EF	OXF
Handel	Art thou troubled (Rodelinda)	M	F-F	GSC
-----	Have mercy, Lord (Te Deum)	HM		†
-----	Let me wander not unseen (L'Allegro)	M	D-G	†
-----	Lord to Thee each night and day (Theodora)	L	C-E	†
-----	O sleep why dost thou leave me (Semele)	H	DS-GS	†
Purcell	Ah, how pleasant 'tis to love			AUG
-----	Hark, the echoing air (The Fairy Queen)			BAF
-----	If music be the food of love	M	D-G	BOO

329

(Purcell)	Music for a while (Oedipus)	LH		SC
-----	Not all my torments			NOV
-----	There's not a swain on on the plain	M	B-G	BAF
-----	When I am laid in earth (Dido and Aeneas)	LH	C-G	†

German Songs For Opening Recitals

Mezzo Soprano

Bach, J.S.	Bist du bei mir	HML	A-EF	†
-----	O Jesulein suess			
Beethoven	Andenken			†
-----	Bonnie laddie, highland laddie			†
-----	Ich liebe dich	HL	BF-DF	†
Brahms	Nachtigall	MHL	BF-FS	†
-----	Verzagen	MH	CS-FS	†
Buxtehude	Singet dem Herrn Violin and piano			
Handel	Dank sei dir, Herr	M	CS-E	†
Haydn	She never told her love	HL	B-D	DIT
-----	The mermaid's song	M	C-F	PRE
Schubert	Das Wandern	HLM	E-E	†
-----	Ganymed	LH	EF-G	†
-----	Liebesbotschaft	H	E-G	†
Schumann	Mit Myrthen und Rosen	HL	A-D	†
Wolf	Ueber Nacht	LH	D-G	†

Italian Songs and Arias For Opening Recitals

Mezzo Soprano

Caccini	Amarilli, mia bella	ML	C-D	†
Caldara	Sebben crudele	HML	E-DS	†
Carissimi	Vittoria, mio core	HLM	B-E	†
Cavalli	Donzelle fuggite	HL	C-EF	†
Cesti	Ah, quanto è vero (Il Pomo d'Oro)	HL	F-F	DIT
-----	Che angoscia, che affanno (Il Pomo d'Oro)	HL	C-DF	DIT
Cherubini	Ahi, che forse ai miei di (Demofonte)			RIC
Cimara	Stornellata marinara	HM		RIC

330

Cimarosa	Nel lasciarti (L'Olympiade)			RIC
Donaudy	Quando ti rivedrò			RIC
Durante	Vergin, tutta amor	LM	C-EF	†
Gluck	O del mio dolce ardor (Paride ed Elena)	LH	D-FS	GSC
-----	Spiagge amate (Paride ed Elena)			†
Handel	Affani del pensier (Ottone)			†
-----	Cangio d'aspetto (Admeto)			†
-----	Cara sposa (Radamisto)	M	CS-D	†
-----	Ch'io mai vi possa (Siroe)			†
-----	Dove sei, amato bene (Rodelinda)	L	BF-EF	CFI
-----	Furibondo spira (Partenope)			KIS
-----	Lascia ch'io pianga (Rinaldo)	HM	EF-F	†
-----	O rendetemi il mio bene (Amadigi)	L	CS-EF	CFI
-----	Ombra mai fu (Serse)	HM	BF-EF	†
-----	Piangero la sorte mia (Julius Caesar)			CFI
-----	V'adoro pupille (Julius Caesar)			BOO
Haydn	Cara speme (Orfeo ed Euridice)			
Lotti	Pur dicesti, o bocca bella	LMH	E-FS	GSC
Mozart	Ch'io mi scordi di te			BOO
-----	Non più di fiori (La Clemenza di Tito)			†
-----	Parto, parto (La Clemenza di Tito) B flat clarinet and piano	H		AMP
Paisiello	Chi vuol la zingarella	L	C-F	GSC
-----	Nel cor più non mi sento	HL	C-EF	†
Pergolesi	Se tu m'ami	LMH	C-G	GSC
Piccini	O nuit, dresse du mystere (Le Faux Lord)			GSC
Pignatta	Cieco si finse amor			
Rosa	Vado ben spesso	ML	C-EF	BOO
Sarti	Lungi dal caro bene (Armide)	HL	G-D	GSC
Scarlatti, A.	Sento nel core	M	E-F	†
Stradella	Per pietà (Il Floridoro)	HM	D-F	DIT
-----	Pietà, Signore	HM	C-F	GSC
Vivaldi	Un certo no so che	HL	BF-EF	†

Mezzo Soprano

Barber	I hear an army	LH	D-AF	GSC
-----	Sure on this shining night	MH	D-G	GSC
Bassett	Take joy home	LH	EF-BF	GSC
Bernstein	La bonne cuisine	H	B-B	GSC
Bibb	A rondel of spring	HL	BF-D	GSC
Bowles	Sugar in the cane	M	D-FS	GSC
Branscombe	At the postern gate	MH	DF-AF	ASC
Browning	Phoenix			
Carpenter	Light, my light	M	C-G	GSC
-----	Serenade	LH	CS-A	GSC
Castelnuovo-				
Tedesco	Springtime	M		CHE
Clough-				
Leighter	My lover he comes on the skee	HM	D-F	BOS
Diack	Little Jack Horner			CFI
Dougherty	Everyone sang			
-----	Song for autumn			
Duke	Evening			
-----	On a March day	M	B-GF	BOH
-----	XXth century	M		VLP
Dukelsky	The ladies of St. James			
Enders	Russian picnic	HM	C-G	GSC
Giannini	Sing to my heart a song	H	D-B	ELV
Golde	Who knows?	HM	BF-F	GSC
Hageman	At the well	LH	EF-AF	GSC
-----	Miranda	HL		GAL
Kingsford	Command	HLM	EF-G	GSC
-----	Courage	M	C-F	GSC
Kramer	Allah			
La Forge	Song of the open	MH	EF-AF	DIT
-----	To a messenger	HLM	CF-G	GSC
Levitzki	Ah, thou beloved one	H	EF-AF	GSC
Mana-Zucca	Rachem	HML		CHA
Rogers	The last song	MLH	E-AF	GSC
-----	Time for making songs	HM	CS-F	DIT
Rummel	Ecstasy	LMH	GF-AF	GSC
Sacco	Rapunzel	MH	FS-BF	GSC
Salter	The cry of Rachel	LH	C-AF	GSC
Sargent	Twentieth century	H	EF-GS	LEE
Schuman	Holiday song	M	C-F	GSC
Silberta	You shall have your red rose			
Speaks	Morning	HML	BF-D	GSC
Swanson	Joy	M	BF-EF	Lee

Tyson	Sea moods	LH	E-AF	GSC
Ware	This day is mine	MH	EF-AF	BOS
Warren	Fulfilment	H	D-BF	GAL
-----	We two	LH	E-A	GSC
Watts	Green branches	HM		DIT
-----	Joy	HL	D-F	GSC
Worth	Midsummer	LM	E-A	GSC

(See also Negro Spirituals and Folk Songs.)

Miscellaneous Songs For
Closing Recitals

Mezzo Soprano

Bizet	Adieu de l'hôtesse arabe	H	BF-G	†
Bliss	The buckle			CUR
Brahms	Meine Liebe ist gruen	MLH	ES-A	†
-----	Wenn du nur zuweilen laechelst			†
-----	Wie froh und Frisch	HL	B-E	†
-----	Willst du, dass ich geh'?	L	C-G	†
Bridge	Love went a-riding	HL		BOS
Britten	A charm	L	AS-E	BOO
-----	Oliver Cromwell			BOH
Cimara	Canto di primavera		D-G	FRL
Debussy	Chevaux de bois	H	C-G	†
Delius	Love's philosophy			†
Elgar	The swimmer			BOO
Falla	Jota	LH		AMP
-----	Polo	HL		AMP
Gretchaninoff	My native land	L	C-EF	GSC
Grieg	By the brook			GSC
-----	Good morning			†
-----	Jeg lever et liv i laengsel	L	BF-E	HAN
-----	Vaer hilset, I Damer	M	D-F	HAN
Head	A piper	HL		BOO
Hely Hutchinson	Old mother Hubbard	HL	B-E	CFI
Henschel	Morning-hymn	MH	DS-GS	†
Kennedy-Fraser	Song of the sea-reivers			
Marx	Der Ton	M	C-F	AMP
Nin	El vito			ESC
Obradors	Coplas de curro dulce			
-----	El vito			
Poulenc	Air vif	H	C-AF	ROU

333

Quilter	Blow, blow, thou winter wind	HL	C-E	BOO
Rachmaninoff	Floods of spring	HL		DIT
-----	Oh, no, I pray do not depart	H		DIT
Respighi	Pioggia			BON
Ronald	Southern song			ENO
Schubert	Aufloesung	LH	D-A	†
-----	Die Forelle	MLH	EF-GF	†
Schumann	Er ist's	HL	BF-EF	†
Shaw	Romance			
Sibelius	The tryst	M		AMP
-----	Was it a dream			BRH
Turina	Farruca	M	A-F	UME
Villa-Lobos	Canção do carreiro			
Wolf	Er ist's	H	D-G	†
-----	Morgenstimmung	LH	C-GS	†

American Atmospheric Songs

Mezzo Soprano

Barber	Rain has fallen	HM	D-E	GSC
-----	Sleep now	MH	EF-AF	GSC
Burleigh	Sometimes I feel like a motherless child	HML		RIC
Carpenter	Go, lovely rose	M	DF-EF	GSC
-----	On the seashore of endless worlds	M	C-FS	GSC
-----	Slumber song	ML	BF-F	GSC
-----	The day is no more	M	GS-DS	GSC
-----	The green river	M	B-E	GSC
-----	The pools of peace	M	D-F	GSC
-----	When I bring to you colour'd toys	LM	CS-FS	GSC
Carter	Dust of snow	M	D-E	AMP
Charles	Clouds	HML	C-EF	GSC
-----	When I have sung my songs	HM	BF-EF	GSC
Crist	Into a ship dreaming	LMH	EF-GS	CFI
Davis	Nancy Hanks	H	D-G	GAL
Dello Joio	New born	M	C-D	CFI
Dougherty	Loveliest of trees	HM	C-E	BOH
Duke	I can't be talkin' of love	H	CS-G	GSC
-----	Loveliest of trees	L	C-D	GSC
Ganz	A memory	HM	B-D	GSC
Griffes	Night on ways unknown has fallen	L	GS-F	GSC

(Griffes)	The dreamy lake	H	BS-GS	GSC
Hageman	Do not go, my love	HL	B-EF	GSC
Harris	Fog	M	D-F	CFI
-----	Vanished summer	M	C-E	GAL
Kramer	Our lives together	HL	D-E	GAL
-----	Swans	HL		RIC
MacGimsey	Sweet little Jesus boy	ML	D-D	CFI
Naginski	Look down, fair moon			
-----	Night song at Amalfi	M	D-EF	GSC
Niles	I wonder as I wander	HL	BF-D	GSC
-----	Jesus, Jesus rest your head	HL	A-D	GSC
Sacco	The ragpicker	MH	C-AF	GSC
Silberta	Aylia, dancer of Kashmir	M	B-F	GSC
Tureman	A winter sunset	L	BF-E	GSC
Tyson	Noon and night	LH	F-AF	GSC

British Atmospheric Songs

Mezzo Soprano

Benjamin	Calm sea and mist			CUR
Dunhill	The cloths of heaven	LM	EF-G	STB
Elgar	Sea pictures	L	A-A	BOO
Handel	O sleep why dost thou leave me (Semele)	H	DS-GS	†
Harty	My lagan love	ML	BF-EF	BOO
Holst	The heart worships	ML	BF-D	STB
Hughes	A Ballynure ballad	L	BF-D	BOH
-----	O men from the fields	M	F-F	BOO
Quilter	Dream valley	H	EF-GF	ROG
Sanderson	Quiet	ML	AF-EF	BOH
Vaughan Williams	Bright is the ring of words	L		BOH
Warlock	Sleep			OXF

French Atmospheric Songs

Mezzo Soprano

Chaminade	The silver ring	HM	BF-F	GSC
Chausson	Les papillons	M	C-F	GSC
Debussy	C'est l'extase	LH	CS-A	†
Duparc	La vie antérieure	HL		†
Ferrari	Le miroir	M	E-F	GSC
Février	L'intruse	M	B-DF	HEU
Gounod	Sérénade	LMH	D-A	GSC

Hahn	A Chloris	H	DS-FS	HEU
-----	D'une prison	L	BF-EF	HEU
-----	L'heure exquise	M	DF-F	†
-----	Paysage	MH	EF-G	HEU
Leguerney	L'adieu	M	B-FS	DUR
Paladilhe	Psyché	HM	BF-F	GSC
Poulenc	Fleurs	M	DF-F	ROU
Ravel	Sainte	M	C-G	ELV
-----	Sur l'herbe	MH	C-G	DUR
Roussel	Le jardin mouillé	M	C-FS	ROU

German Atmospheric Songs

Mezzo Soprano

Brahms	Steig' auf, geliebter Schatten	HL	BF-EF	†
Franz	Sterne mit den gold'nen Fuesschen	HL	DS-E	†
Haydn	She never told her love	HL	B-D	DIT
Schubert	Der Tod und das Maedchen	HL	A-EF	†
-----	Nacht und Traeume	HL	C-DF	†
Schumann	Dein Angesicht	HL	B-EF	†
-----	Der Nussbaum	LMH	D-FS	†
-----	Im Walde	HL	A-D	†
Strauss	Die Nacht	HL		†
-----	Traum durch die Daemmerung	HML	BF-EF	†
Wolf	In dem Schatten meiner Locken	M	C-EF	†
-----	Verborgenheit	HL	B-E	†

Miscellaneous Atmospheric Songs

Mezzo Soprano

Alnaes	Lykken mellem to mennesker	M	B-FS	HAN
Cimara	Fiocca la neve	H	G-G	GSC
Cui	The statue at Czarskoe-Selo	HM	DF-EF	†
Grieg	A dream			†
-----	A swan			†
-----	Det syng	M	C-GF	HAN
-----	Digte af Vilhelm Krag			HAN
-----	In the boat	LM	D-ES	†
-----	Julens vuggesang			

(Grieg)	Når jeg vil dø	L	CS-EF	HAN
-----	På Norges nøgne fjelde	M	D-F	HAN
-----	På skogstien	H	E-G	HAN
-----	Radiant night			
-----	Snegl, Snegl	M	B-F	HAN
-----	Spring rain			PET
-----	Til En I	L	B-CS	HAN
-----	Til En II	M	E-F	HAN
-----	Udvandreren	M	EF-F	HAN
Kjerulf	Synnove's song	M	C-F	GSC
Lie	Soft-footed snow	HM		DIT
Rachmaninoff	Lilacs	LH	EF-G	BOS
-----	Morning	ML	B-DS	GSC
Sibelius	Reeds, reeds rustle			

American Dramatic Songs

Mezzo Soprano

Barber	I hear an army	LH	D-AF	GSC
Beach	Ah, love but a day			ASC
Campbell- Tipton	A spirit flower	LHM	B-G	GSC
-----	The crying of water	LH	FS-GS	GSC
Carpenter	Berceuse de guerre	M	C-G	GSC
-----	I am like a remnant of a cloud of autumn	L	BF-F	GSC
-----	Light, my light	M	C-G	GSC
-----	Slumber song	ML	BF-F	GSC
-----	The green river	M	B-E	GSC
-----	To one unknown	M	A-DS	GSC
Duke	Evening			
-----	On a March day	M	B-GF	BOH
Elwell	Renouncement	M	G-G	GSC
Enders	Russian picnic	HM	C-G	GSC
Giannini	Sing to my heart a song	H	D-B	ELV
Griffes	Sorrow of Mydath	M		GSC
-----	The lament of Ian the proud	MH	DS-AS	GSC
-----	We'll to the woods and gather May	M	D-F	GSC
Hageman	Do not go, my love	HL	B-EF	GSC
-----	Music I heard with you	MH	E-A	GAL
Hindemith	Envoy	M	EF-F	AMP
Johnson	Roll Jerd'n roll	M	EF-F	GSC
La Forge	Song of the open	MH	EF-AF	DIT
Parker	Gens duce splendida (Hora Novissima)			NOV

337

Protheroe	Ah, love but a day	LMH	F-AF	GAM
Rogers	The last song	MLH	E-AF	GSC
-----	Time for making songs	HM	CS-F	DIT
Salter	The cry of Rachel	LH	C-AF	GSC
Schuman	Holiday song	M	C-F	GSC
Silberta	Aylia, dancer of Kashmir	M	B-F	GSC
Speaks	Morning	HML	BF-D	GSC
Tyson	Sea moods	LH	E-AF	GSC
Ware	This day is mine	MH	EF-AF	BOS
Warren	Fulfilment	H	D-BF	GAL
-----	We two	LH	E-A	GSC
Worth	Midsummer	LM	E-A	GSC

British Dramatic Songs

Mezzo Soprano

Bainton	Ring out, wild bells	M	C-EF	OXF
Bridge	O that it were so	LMH	D-G	CHA
Clarke	Eight o'clock			ROG
-----	The seal man	M		BOH
Coleridge-Taylor	Life and death	HML		ASC
Delius	Twilight fancies	M	D-FS	CFI
Del Riego	Homing	HML	BF-E	CHA
Elgar	Sea pictures	L	A-A	BOO
-----	The swimmer			BOO
Henschel	Morning-hymn	MH	DS-GS	†
Purcell	When I am laid in earth (Dido and Aeneas)	LH	C-G	†
Quilter	Blow, blow, thou winter wind	HL	C-E	BOO

French Dramatic Songs and Arias

Mezzo Soprano

Berlioz	Le spectre de la rose			CST
-----	Les nuits d'été			AUG
Bizet	Habanera (Carmen)	HM	D-F	†
Chausson	Chanson perpétuelle String quartet	H	CS-GS	ROU
-----	Poème de l'amour et de la mer	H		INT
Debussy	Air de Lia (L'Enfant Prodigue)	H	E-A	DUR
-----	Chevaux de bois	H	C-G	†

(Debussy)	Colloque sentimental			DUR
-----	Noël des enfants qui n'ont plus de maisons			DUR
Duparc	Au pays où se fait la guerre			SAL
-----	La vague et la cloche			ROU
-----	La vie antérieure	HL		†
-----	Le manoir de Rosamunde	HL	B-F	BOS
-----	Phidylé	MH	EF-AF	BOS
-----	Testament	HL		INT
Fauré	Automne	MH	D-FS	GSC
-----	Poème d'un jour			HAM
-----	Prison	LH		†
-----	Toujours	LH	F-AF	†
Février	L'intruse	M	B-DF	HEU
Gounod	O ma lyre immortelle (Sappho)	M	C-G	†
Hahn	D'une prison	L	BF-EF	HEU
-----	Offrande	M	D-D	†
Halévy	Humble fille des champs (Charles VI)			GSC
Honegger	Les cloches			SEN
Hue	J'ai pleuré en Rêve	HL	D-E	BOS
Indy	Lied maritime	LH	B-G	†
Lenormand	Quelle souffrance	HM	AF-F	HAM
Massenet	Il est doux, il est bon (Hérodiade)	MH	EF-BF	GSC
-----	Werther! qui m'aurait dit (Air de lettres) (Werther)			HEU
Meyerbeer	Ah! mon fils (Le Prophète)	M	B-AS	†
Paladilhe	Lamento provinçal	M	CS-FS	HOM
Poldowski	Dansons la gigue	M	EF-G	MAR
Saint-Saëns	Amour, viens aider (Samson et Dalila)	HM	AF-G	†
-----	L'attente			DUR
Severac	Chanson pour le petit cheval			ROU

German Dramatic Songs

Mezzo Soprano

Brahms	Ach, wende diesen Blick			†
-----	Am Sonntag Morgen	L	CS-FS	†
-----	Nicht mehr zu dir zu gehen			†
-----	Treue Liebe	LMH	DS-E	†
-----	Von ewiger Liebe	LMH	B-AF	†
Franz	Im Herbst	HM	A-F	†
Liszt	Die drei Zigeuner	LM	B-G	GSC
-----	Die Lorelei	LH	BF-BF	†

339

Loewe	Walpurgisnacht	H	G–G	SC
Mahler	Das Irdische Leben	HL	A–F	INT
-----	Ich hab' ein gluehend Messer	M	BF–GF	WEI
-----	Lieder eines fahrenden Gesellen	M		INT
Marx	An einen Herbstwald	M	CS–FS	UNI
-----	Hat dich die Liebe beruehrt	MH	EF–BF	AMP
Mendelssohn	Schilflied	M	F–FS	
Schubert	Am Feierabend	HL	BF–F	†
-----	An Schwager Kronos	HL	G–E	†
-----	Aufenthalt	HLM	A–F	†
-----	Dem Unendlichen	L	A–GF	†
-----	Der Atlas	HL	BF–F	†
-----	Der Doppelgaenger	HL	G–D	GSC
-----	Der Erlkoenig	HML	A–E	†
-----	Der Lindenbaum	HL	A–D	†
-----	Der Tod und das Maedchen	HL	A–EF	†
-----	Der Zwerg	M	A–GF	PET
-----	Die Allmacht	HML	G–E	†
-----	Die junge Nonne	LH	C–GF	†
-----	Die Kraehe	HL	A–E	†
-----	Die Liebe hat gelogen	LM	G–F	†
-----	Die Stadt	HL	A–E	†
-----	Du liebst mich nicht	LH	E–FS	†
-----	Erstarrung	HL	D–F	†
-----	Fahrt zum Hades	HL	G–DF	PET
-----	Fragment aus dem Aeschylus			PET
-----	Fruehlingstraum	HL	C–D	†
-----	Ganymed	LH	EF–G	†
-----	Gruppe aus dem Tartarus	L	CS–EF	†
-----	In der Ferne	HL		†
-----	Mut	HL		†
-----	Schaefers Klagelied	HL	BF–D	†
Schumann	Der arme Peter	HL	B–G	†
-----	Fruehlingsfahrt	HL	B–E	†
-----	Heiss' mich nicht reden			
-----	Mit Myrthen und Rosen	HL	A–D	†
-----	Schoene Wiege meiner Leiden	HL	C–EF	GSC
-----	Waldesgespraech	HL	A–FS	†
Strauss	Caecilie	MH	E–B	†
-----	Ruhe meine Seele			†
Wagner	Schmerzen	HL		†
Wolf	Alle gingen, Herz zu Ruh	HL	C–EF	†
-----	Das Koehlerweib ist trunken			PET
-----	Denk' es, o Seele	LH	EF–F	†

(Wolf)	Der Freund	HM	BF-E	PET
-----	Die ihr schwebet	HL	EF-EF	†
-----	Geh' Geliebter, geh' jetzt			PET
-----	Liebe mir in Busen zuendet	M	E-F	†
-----	Ueber Nacht	LH	D-G	†
-----	Zur Ruh', zur Ruh'	HL	A-GF	†

Italian Dramatic Songs and Arias

Mezzo Soprano

Cimara	Canto di primavera		D-G	FRL
Donizetti	O mio Fernando	M	B-A	†
	(La Favorita)			
Durante	Vergin, tutta amor	LM	C-EF	†
Mascagni	Voi lo sapete	H	B-A	†
	(Cavalleria Rusticana)			
Pergolesi	Confusa, smarrita			GSC
Piccini	O nuit, dresse du mystere			GSC
	(Le Faux Lord)			
Pizzetti	La madre al figlio lontano			FRL
Ponchielli	Stella del marinar	M	B-A	RIC
	(La Gioconda)			
-----	Voce di donna (La Gioconda)			
Respighi	In alto mare			BON
-----	Io sono la madre	L		RIC
-----	Nebbie			†
Verdi	Condotta ell' era in ceppi			GSC
	(Il Trovatore)			
-----	O don fatale (Don Carlos)	MH	CF-CF	†
-----	Stride la vampa	M	B-G	†
	(Il Trovatore)			

Miscellaneous Dramatic Songs and Arias

Mezzo Soprano

Alvarez	La partida	HL	DS-E	GSC
Dvořák	Hear my prayer, O Lord			AMP
Gliere	Ah, twine no blossoms	HM	CS-F	DIT
Granados	La maja dolorosa	M		INT
Gretchaninoff	Over the steppe	LM	C-G	GSC
-----	Wounded birch	HL	B-EF	†
Grieg	A dream			†
-----	A swan			†
-----	Autumnal gale	HL	A-F	CFI
-----	Den Aergjerrige			

(Grieg)	Digte af Vilhelm Krag			HAN
-----	Eros	LM	C-F	†
-----	Hjemkomst	M	B-F	HAN
-----	In the boat	LM	D-ES	†
-----	Jeg lever et liv i laengsel	L	BF-E	HAN
-----	Vaer hilset, I damer	M	D-F	HAN
-----	Verse for an album			
Mussorgsky	After the battle			GSC
-----	Divination by water (Khovantchina)	L	GS-FS	GSC
-----	Hopak	HM	CS-FS	GSC
-----	Matha's song (Khovantchina)	ML		GSC
-----	On the Dnieper			GSC
-----	The orphan girl			GSC
Rachmaninoff	As fair is she as noonday light			GSC
-----	Christ is risen	LM	D-F	GAL
-----	Floods of spring	HL		DIT
-----	O, do not grieve	M	BF-AF	GSC
-----	Oh, no, I pray do not depart	H		DIT
-----	O thou billowy harvest field	HL	CS-E	GSC
-----	The soldier's bride			†
-----	To the children	MH	F-G	DIT
Rimsky-Korsakov	On the Georgian hills	HM		GSC
Sibelius	Black Roses	M	A-ES	AMP
-----	The tryst	M		AMP
-----	Was it a dream			BRH
Stravinsky	The cloister (La novice)			DIT
Tchaikovsky	Adieu forêts (Jeanne D'Arc)	HM	BF-FS	GSC
-----	None but the lonely heart	HLM	C-F	DIT
-----	Pauline's romance (Pique Dame)	M	BF-AF	GSC

American Humorous Songs

Mezzo Soprano

Bernstein	I hate music	H	C-A	WIT
-----	La bonne cuisine	H	B-B	GSC
Carpenter	Don't ceare	M	C-D	GSC
-----	If	M	D-E	GSC
-----	To a young gentleman	M	C-F	GSC
Crist	Chinese mother goose rhymes	H	C-G	CFI

Davis	Deaf old woman			GAL
Diack	Little Jack Horner			CFI
-----	Little Polly Flinders			CFI
Dougherty	Declaration of independence	L	C-C	GSC
-----	Love in the dictionary	M	C-G	GSC
Duke	I can't be talkin' of love	H	CS-G	GSC
Enders	Russian picnic	HM	C-G	GSC
Griselle and Young	The cuckoo clock	LH	EF-G	GSC
Hadley	My shadow			ASC
Hageman	Animal crackers	HL	C-D	GSC
Kountz	The little French clock	LH	D-G	GAL
Nordoff	Serenade	H	CS-FS	AMP
-----	There shall be more joy	M	CS-FS	AMP
Rawls	The balloon man	L	A-FS	AMP
Rich	American lullaby	LH	C-F	GSC
Sacco	Mexican serenade	HL	D-EF	BOS
Schuman	Holiday song	M	C-F	GSC
Slonimsky	Gravestones at Hancock, New Hampshire	H	D-G	AXE
Spross	Will o' the wisp			JCH
Stein	The puffin	M		CFI
Wolf	Jack in the box			

British Humorous Songs

Mezzo Soprano

Arne, T.	Why so pale and wan			GSC
Bax	Oh dear, what can the matter be?	M	D-EF	CHE
Bliss	The buckle			CUR
Britten	Oliver Cromwell			BOH
Clarke	Shy one	HL	BF-G	BOH
Gibbs	Five eyes	HL	D-D	BOS
Hely-Hutchinson	Old mother Hubbard	HL	B-E	CFI
Hughes	A Ballynure ballad	L	BF-D	BOH
Johnston	Because I were shy	L	B-E	CRA
Lehmann	The cuckoo	HH	D-B	BOH
Novello	The little damozel	LHM	C-G	BOO

343

French Humorous Songs

Mezzo Soprano

Chabrier	Villanelle des petits canards	HML	B-E	†
Debussy	Ballade des femmes de Paris			DUR
Pierné	Ils etaient trois petits chats blancs			MAR
Poulenc	Le bestiaire String quartet, flute, clarinet and bassoon	M		AMP
Ravel	Sur l'herbe	MH	C-G	DUR
Satie	La statue de bronze			ROU
-----	Le chapelier			ROU

German Humorous Songs and Arias

Mezzo Soprano

Bach, J.S.	Patron, das macht der Wind (Phoebus and Pan)	M	C-G	GSC
Brahms	Der Kranz			†
-----	Vergebliches Staendchen	LHM	E-FS	†
Mahler	Des Antonius von Padua Fischpredigt	HL	GF-F	†
-----	Rheinlegendchen	M	B-FS	†
-----	Wer hat dies Liedlein erdacht?	HL	BF-E	INT
Marx	Der bescheidene Schaefer			UNI
Mozart	Die Alte			
-----	Warnung	HM	C-D	
Reger	Waldeinsamkeit	HML	A-D	BOS
Reichardt	Rhapsodie			MOS
Schubert	Die Maenner sind mechant			PET
-----	Heidenroeslein			
Strauss	Fuer fuenfzehn Pfennige			†
Wolf	Elfenlied	HL	D-F	†
-----	Ich hab' in Penna	LH		†
-----	Nimmersatte Liebe	LH	CF-AF	†
-----	Tretet ein, hoher Krieger	HL	B-F	†

Miscellaneous Humorous Songs

Mezzo Soprano

Grieg	My Johann	HL	BF-EF	GSC
-----	Til min dreng		C-E	
Paisiello	Chi vuol la zingarella	L	C-F	GSC
Rontani	Or ch'io non segno più	HL	CS-E	DIT

American Folk Songs (Arr.)

Mezzo Soprano

Bacon	Adam and Eve	M	B-D	CFI
-----	Common Bill			
Bartholomew	Dearest Billie	M	E-E	GSC
Brockway	Barbara Allen			
-----	Frog went-a-courting			
-----	Sourwood Mountain			
-----	The nightingale			GRA
-----	The old maid's song			GRA
Davis	Deaf old woman			GAL
-----	He's gone away	M	C-E	GAL
Hughes	Birds' courting song			GSC
Matteson	The blue eyed boy			GSC
Niles	Down in the valley			GSC
-----	Go 'way from my window	MH	C-G	GSC
-----	Hi, ho the preacher man			GSC
-----	I wonder as I wander	HL	BF-D	GSC
-----	If I had a ribbon bow			GSC
-----	Jesus, Jesus rest your head	M		JFI
Powell	The rich old woman	M		JFI
Scott	Wailie, wailie	M	D-E	JCH
Shaw	Black is the color of my true love's hair	M	C-F	DIT
-----	He's gone away	M	C-E	DIT
Taylor	Twenty, eighteen	HM	D-E	JFI
Young	Red rosey bush	M		CFI

British Folk Songs (Arr.)

Mezzo Soprano

Bax	Oh dear, what can the matter be?	M	D-EF	CHE
Benjamin	Linstead market	M		BOO

Britten	A charm	L	AS-E	BOO
-----	O waly, waly			
-----	Oliver Cromwell			BOH
-----	The ash grove			BOH
-----	The miller of Dee			
-----	The Sally gardens			BOH
-----	The trees they grow so high			
Butterworth	Roving in the dew			AUG
Clayton	O men from the fields	M	C-F	BOS
Harty	My lagan love	ML	BF-EF	BOO
-----	The lowlands of Holland			OXF
Hopekirk	Coming through the rye			DIT
-----	Loch Lomond			DIT
Hughes	A Ballynure ballad	L	BF-D	BOH
-----	Down by the Sally gardens			BOO
-----	Hey diddle diddle			CRA
-----	I know my love			BOO
Johnson	Because I were shy	L	B-E	CRA
Kennedy-Fraser	An Eriskay love lilt			BOO
-----	Kishmul's galley			BOO
-----	Song of the sea reivers			
-----	The bens of Jura			BOO
Kreisler	Loch Lomond			
Lawson	Turn ye to me	M	B-E	GSC
McGill	Lord Randall			BOO
-----	Lord Thomas			BOO
Page	The harp that once through Tara's halls			DIT
Peterkin	I wish and I wish	M	B-E	OXF
Quilter	Ye banks and braes	M	DF-EF	BOH
Reid	Turn ye to me			BOO
Shaw	The land of heart's desire	M	C-E	CUR
Stevens	Early one morning			
Vaughan Williams	And all in the morning	L	D-E	GAL
-----	King William	L	D-D	OXF
-----	Lullaby of the Madonna	L	BF-D	GRA
-----	Robin Hood and the pedlar	M	D-E	OXF
-----	Rolling in the dew			OXF
Welsh	All through the night			
Wilson	Come let's be merry			BOO

Miscellaneous Folk Songs (Arr.)

Mezzo Soprano

Beethoven	Bonnie laddie, Highland laddie			†
-----	Enchantress farewell			
-----	Sally in our alley			
-----	Sunset			
-----	The lovely lass of Inverness			
Brahms	Mein Maedel hat einen Rosenmund	M	F-F	†
Canteloube	Baïlèro			HEU
-----	Brezaviola			HEU
-----	L'aïo de rotso			HEU
-----	L'antouèno			HEU
-----	Malurous qu'o uno fenno			HEU
-----	Passo pel prat			HEU
Dvořák	Gypsy songs	LH	D-A	AMP
Falla	Asturiana	HL		AMP
-----	El paño moruno	HL		AMP
-----	Jota	LH		AMP
-----	Nana	HL		AMP
-----	Polo	HL		AMP
-----	Seguidilla murciana	HL		AMP
-----	Siete canciones	HL		AMP
Greek Folk	Neranzula			
Obradors	Con amores a mi madre			RIC
Ravel	Chanson espagnole	LH	D-BF	DUR
-----	Cinq mélodies populaires grecques			CUR
-----	Quel galant!	M	D-F	DUR
-----	Tout gai	MH	EF-F	DUR
Schumann	Drei Gesaenge (Hebrew melodies) Harp or piano			
Weckerlin	Maman, dites-moi	M	E-FS	BOS
-----	Menuet d'Exaudet	H	D-G	GSC
-----	O,ma tendre musette	LM	A-E	GSC
-----	Venez, agréable printemps	M	C-F	

Negro Spirituals

Mezzo Soprano

Boatner	Oh, what a beautiful city!	HL	D-E	GSC
-----	On mah journey	LH	EF-EF	RIC
-----	Trampin', tryin' to make Heaven my home	L	D-F	ELK

Brown	Dere's no hidin' place down dere			CFI
-----	Every time I feel de spirit	L		AMP
-----	Sometimes I feel like a motherless child	L		AMP
Burleigh	Balm in Gilead	HL		RIC
-----	De gospel train	HL		RIC
-----	Deep river	HML		RIC
-----	Go down, Moses	HL		RIC
-----	Hard trials	M		RIC
-----	Joshua fit de battle ob Jericho	LH	DS-E	RIC
-----	My Lord what a mornin'?			
-----	Nobody knows de trouble I've seen	HL		RIC
-----	Oh Peter, go ring-a-dem bells			RIC
-----	Ride on, King Jesus	H		RIC
-----	Sometimes I feel like a motherless child	HML		RIC
-----	Were you there?	HML		RIC
Dett	Sit down servant			GSC
Fisher	He's de lily of de valley			
Johnson	At the feet of Jesus	L		
-----	City called Heaven			ROB
-----	Dere's no hidin' place down dere			
-----	Hold on			ROB
-----	Honor, honor	HM	C-E	CFI
-----	My good Lord done been here	HM	BF-F	CFI
-----	Ride on, King Jesus			CFI
-----	Roll Jerd'n roll	M	EF-F	GSC
-----	Witness	HM	D-F	CFI
Kerby-Forrest	He's got the whole world in His hands	M	G-E	MLS
Lawrence	Let us break bread together	HML	BF-EF	MCR
MacGimsey	Sweet little Jesus boy	ML	D-D	CFI
Niles	Does you call dat religion?			GSC
-----	Hold on			GSC
-----	My little black star			GSC
Payne	Crucifixion	L	C-C	GSC
Price	My soul's been anchored in the Lord			GAM
Ryder	Let us break bread together	LH	D-G	JFI

| Saunders | The Lord's prayer | L | BF-C | BOH |
| White | Wake up, Jacob | | | PRE |

American Songs Employing Agility

Mezzo Soprano

Bernstein	La bonne cuisine	H	B-B	GSC
Cough- Leighter	My lover he comes on the skee	HM	D-F	BOS
Crist	O come hither	HM	B-GS	CFI
Curran	Ho! Mr. Piper	LH	D-G	GSC
Diack	Little Jack Horner			CFI
Griffes	We'll to the woods and gather May	M	D-F	GSC
Hageman	Miranda	HL		GAL
Nevin	One spring morning	MH	DS-F	BOS
Nordoff	There shall be more joy	M	CS-FS	AMP
Parker	The lark now leaves her watery nest	LH	D-BF	JCH
Speaks	In May time	HL	D-E	JCH

British Songs and Arias Employing Agility

Mezzo Soprano

Arne, T.	Where the bee sucks	HM		†
German	Charming Chloe	HML		NOV
Green	My lips shall speak the praise	M	E-F	OXF
-----	Salvation belongeth unto the Lord	M	F-EF	OXF
Handel	In the battle, fame pursuing (Deborah)	L	A-D	†
-----	Lord, to thee each night and day (Theodora)	L	C-E	†
-----	O thou that tellest good tidings to Zion (The Messiah)	L	A-C	†
Hely- Hutchinson	Old mother Hubbard	HL	B-E	CFI
Morley	It was a lover and his lass	HM		DIT
Purcell	From rosy bow'rs (Don Quixote)			AUG
-----	Hark! how all things with one sound rejoice			NOV

(Purcell)	Hark! the echoing air (The Fairy Queen)			BAF
-----	Nymphs and shepherds (The Libertine)	HM	C-F	†
Wilson	Come let's be merry			BOO
-----	Phillis has such charming graces	ML	CS-EF	BOO

French Songs and Arias Employing Agility

Mezzo Soprano

Bizet	Adieu de l'hotesse arabe			
-----	Ouvre ton coeur	MH	DS-GS	†
-----	Seguidilla (Carmen)	HM	B-FS	†
Campra	Charmant papillon (Les Fêtes Venitiennes)	MH	D-G	GSC
Chausson	Les papillons	M	C-F	GSC
Debussy	Fêtes galantes	LH	CS-A	†
Delibes	Le rossignol	M		GSC
-----	Passepied	LH	DS-CS	GSC
Dupont	Cendrillon	M		
Falla	Polo	HL		AMP
Fauré	Mandoline	HL	F-E	†
Georges	La pluie	HL		INT
Gounod	Que fais-tu blanche tourterelle? (Roméo et Juliette)			JCH
Meyerbeer	O prêtres de Baal (Le Prophète)			BRO
Poulenc	Air vif	H	C-AF	ROU
Thomas	Je connais un pauvre enfant (Mignon)	H	C-B	†

German Songs and Arias Employing Agility

Mezzo Soprano

Bach, J.S.	Gelobet sei der Herr (Cantata 129) Oboe d'Amore			AUG
-----	Hochgelobter Gottessohn (Cantata 6) English horn or viola or violin			NOV
-----	It is finished (St. John Passion)	L	B-D	†
-----	Mein glaeubiges Herze (Cantata 68)	HML		†
Brahms	Botschaft	HL	D-F	†

(Brahms)	Das Maedchen spricht	H	E-FS	†
-----	O liebliche Wangen	MLH	E-G	†
Haydn	My mother bids me bind my hair	M	E-E	†
-----	The mermaid's song	M	C-F	PRE
Jensen	Am Ufer des Flusses des Manzanares	H	D-FS	GSC
Mahler	Des Antonius von Padua Fischpredigt	HL	GF-F	†
-----	Rheinlegendchen	M	B-FS	†
-----	Wer hat dies Liedlein erdacht?	HL	BF-E	INT
Schubert	Das Wandern	HLM	E-E	†
-----	Irrlicht			
-----	Ungeduld	HML		†
Schumann	Fruehlingsnacht	L	CS-E	†
-----	Waldesgespraech	HL	A-FS	†
Strauss	Fuer fuenfzehn Pfennige			†
Wolf	Die Zigeunerin			PET

Italian Songs and Arias Employing Agility

Mezzo Soprano

Carissimi	Vittoria, mio core	HLM	B-E	†
Cimara	Canto di primavera		D-G	FRL
Cimarosa	Nel lasciarti (L'Olympiade)			RIC
Donaudy	Spirate pur, spirate			RIC
Donizetti	Il segreto per esser felici (Lucrezia Borgia)	M	C-G	†
Durante	Danza, danza fanciulla gentile	HM	BF-F	†
Handel	Amor commanda (Floridante)	H		†
-----	Ch'io mai vi possa (Siroe)			†
-----	Furibondo spira (Partenope)			KIS
-----	Qual farfalletta (Partenope)	H	E-A	†
Lotti	Pur dicesti, o bocca bella	LMH	E-FS	GSC
Pergolesi	Ogni pena più spietata	L	B-E	GSC
Rossini	Bel raggio lusinghier (Semiramide)	H	CS-A	GSC
-----	La danza	MH	E-A	†
-----	Non più mesta (La Cenerentola)	M	A-B	GSC
-----	Una voce poco fa (Il Barbiere di Siviglia)	HM	GS-E	GSC

351

Scarlatti, A.	Rugiadose odorose	HL	D-E	DIT
	(Il Pirro e Demetrio)			
-----	Se Florindo è fedele	LM	EF-EF	GSC
Scarlatti, D.	Consolati e spara amante	L	BF-E	GSC
-----	Qual farfalletta			
Vivaldi	Un certo no so che	HL	BF-EF	†

Miscellaneous Songs and Arias
Employing Agility

Mezzo Soprano

Alvarez	La partida	HL	DS-E	GSC
Bach, J.S.	Qui sedes ad dexteram			†
	Patris (Mass in B Minor)			
	Oboe d'amore			
Chopin	The maiden's wish	LM	CS-E	GSC
Falla	Nana	HL		AMP
-----	Seguidilla murciana	HL		AMP
Granados	El majo discreto	H		INT
Grieg	Good morning			†
Mozart	Laudamus Te			PET
	(C Minor Mass)			
Stravinsky	The cloister (La novice)			DIT
Turina	Farruca	M	A-F	UME

American Songs Employing
Crescendo and Diminuendo

Mezzo Soprano

Bacon	Is there such a thing as day?	M	DS-FS	AMP
Barber	Rain has fallen	HM	D-E	GSC
-----	Sleep now	MH	EF-AF	GSC
-----	The daisies	M	C-F	GSC
Beach	Ah, love but a day			ASC
Branscombe	Across the blue Aegean	M	G-G	GAL
Cadman	From the land of the sky-blue water			WHI
Campbell-Tipton	A spirit flower	LHM	B-G	GSC
-----	The crying of water	LH	FS-GS	GSC
Carpenter	Go, lovely rose	M	DF-EF	GSC
-----	The day is no more	M	GS-DS	GSC
-----	The pools of peace	M	D-F	GSC

352

(Carpenter)	The sleep that flits on baby's eyes	M	B-FS	GSC
-----	Watercolors	M	C-F	GSC
-----	When I bring to you colour'd toys	LM	CS-FS	GSC
Charles Clough- Leighter	Clouds	HML	C-EF	GSC
	Who knows?	M		GSC
Duke	Loveliest of trees	L	C-D	GSC
Engel	Sea shell	M	EF-EF	GSC
Fairchild	A memory			BOS
Hopkinson	Beneath a weeping willow's shade	H	D-G	†
-----	My days have been so wondrous free	LH	EF-G	
Howe	Berceuse	HM	EF-F	GSC
Naginski	The pasture	M	BF-EF	GSC
Niles	I wonder as I wander	HL	BF-D	GSC
-----	Jesus, Jesus rest your head	HL	A-D	GSC
Nordoff	Serenade	H	CS-FS	AMP
Rogers	At parting	LH	CS-FS	GSC
Silberta	Aylia, dancer of Kashmir	M	B-F	GSC
Thompson	Velvet shoes	M	C-E	ECS

British Songs and Arias Employing Crescendo and Diminuendo

Mezzo Soprano

Bantock	Yung Yang	MH	E-G	GAL
Bax	A lullaby			
-----	Cradle song			CHA
Benjamin	Calm sea and mist			CUR
Clarke	Shy one	HL	BF-G	BOH
Goossens	Melancholy	M		CHE
Gurney	Under the greenwood tree			ROG
Handel	Art thou troubled (Rodelinda)	M	F-F	GSC
-----	He shall feed His (The Messiah)	L	C-D	†
-----	He was despised (The Messiah)	L	B-D	†
-----	Let me wander not unseen (L'Allegro)	M	D-G	†
-----	O sleep why dost thou leave me (Semele)	H	DS-GS	†
Head	The ships of Arcady	ML	BF-EF	BOH

353

Horn	Cherry ripe	M	D-G	†
-----	I've been roaming	L	B-E	†
Ireland	Bed in summer			CUR
Peterkin	The garden of bamboos	M	EF-F	OXF
Purcell	I attempt from love's sickness to fly (The Indian Queen)	MH	CS-E	†
Quilter	Dream valley	H	EF-GF	ROG
-----	The fuchsia tree			BOO
Shaw	Song of the Palanquin bearers	LH	E-F	CUR

French Songs and Arias Employing Crescendo and Diminuendo

Mezzo Soprano

Berlioz	Villanelle	H	E-FS	†
Chabrier	Romance de l'étoile			ENO
Chaminade	The silver ring	HM	BF-F	GSC
David	Charmant oiseau (La Perle du Brésil)	M	D-E	†
Debussy	Air de Lia (L'Enfant Prodigue)	H	E-A	DUR
-----	C'est l'extase	LH	CS-A	†
-----	En sourdine	M	C-FS	†
-----	La flûte de Pan		B-B	†
-----	Le tombeau des Naïades			JOB
-----	Les ingénus			DUR
Duparc	Chanson triste	MH	FS-AF	†
-----	L'invitation au voyage	HM	E-F	†
-----	Phidylé	MH	EF-AF	BOS
Fauré	Adieu	MH	F-F	†
-----	Arpège	MH	E-FS	HAM
-----	Clair de lune	MH	C-G	†
-----	En prière	H	F-F	†
-----	Le secret	LH	F-G	†
-----	Spleen	H	E-FS	MAR
Koechlin	L'hiver	H	E-G	†
Martini	Plaisir d'amour	M	BF-EF	GSC
Meyerbeer	Nobles Seigneurs, salut! (Les Huguenots)	LH	C-C	†
Mouret	Doux plaisirs (Pirithous)			CHE
Paladilhe	Psyché	HM	BF-F	GSC
Rameau	A l'amour rendez les armes (Hippolyte et Aricie)			CHO
-----	Dans ces doux asiles (Castor et Pollux)			LEM

Rhené-Baton	Berceuse			DUR
Satie	Daphénéo			ROU

German Songs Employing Crescendo and Diminuendo

Mezzo Soprano

Beethoven	Andenken			†
Brahms	Auf dem See	HL	D-F	†
-----	Sonntag	H	D-G	†
-----	Spanisches Lied			†
-----	Therese	HL	B-D	†
-----	Wie Melodien zieht es	HL	A-E	†
Franz	Die blauen Fruehlingsaugen	HL		†
-----	Es hat die Rose sich beklagt	LH	DF-F	†
-----	Fruehling und Liebe	HL		†
-----	Sterne mit den gold'nen Fuesschen	HL	DS-E	†
Mahler	Ich atmet' einen linden Duft	HL		INT
Reger	Des Kindes Gebet	H	F-G	BOT
-----	Mit Rosen bestreut			UNI
-----	Waldeinsamkeit	HML	A-D	BOS
Schubert	An den Mond	HL	F-GF	†
-----	Auf dem Wasser zu singen	MH	EF-GF	†
-----	Der Einsame	LH	D-G	†
-----	Der Musensohn	LH	FS-G	†
-----	Der Schmetterling	LH	E-F	†
-----	Der Wanderer	HML	FS-D	GSC
-----	Der Wanderer an den Mond	LM	D-F	PET
-----	Die Taubenpost	HL	D-EF	†
-----	Fruehlingstraum	HL	C-D	†
-----	Geheimes	HL	BF-EF	†
-----	Gretchen am Spinnrade	H	F-A	†
-----	Im Fruehling	LH	D-FS	†
-----	Lachen und Weinen	HL	C-EF	†
-----	Liebesbotschaft	H	E-G	†
-----	Nacht und Traeume	HL	C-DF	†
Schumann	Der Nussbaum	LMH	D-FS	†
-----	Der Sandmann	HL	AF-DF	†
-----	Die Soldatenbraut	HL	AF-EF	†
-----	Erstes Gruen	HL	D-D	†
-----	Lieder der Braut	H	D-A	†

(Schumann)	Marienwuermchen	HL	D-D	†
Strauss	Die Nacht	HL		†
Wolf	Auch kleine Dinge	HM	D-E	†
-----	Der Gaertner	HL		†
-----	In dem Schatten meiner Locken	M	C-EF	†
-----	Mausfallen Spruechlein	HL	BF-E	†
-----	Morgentau	HL	D-D	†
-----	Nun wandre, Maria	HL	EF-D	†
-----	Und willst du deinen Liebsten sterben	HL		†
-----	Verschwiegene Liebe	LH	DF-FS	†
-----	Wenn du zu den Blumen gehst	HL	B-EF	DIT
Wolff	Knabe und Veilchen	M	D-D	HMP

Italian Songs and Arias Employing Crescendo and Diminuendo

Mezzo Soprano

Bononcini	Per la gloria	HL	C-EF	†
Caldara	Alma del core			GSC
-----	Sebben crudele	HML	E-DS	†
-----	Selve amiche, ombrose piante	HM	E-E	†
De Luca	Non posso disperar	HL	C-E	GSC
Gluck	Vieni che poi sereno (La Semiramide)	M	D-G	†
Handel	Affani del pensier (Ottone)			†
-----	Cangio d'aspetto (Admeto)			†
-----	Ombra mai fu (Serse)	HM	BF-EF	†
Marcello	Non m'è grave morir per amore	L	C-E	GSC
Monteverdi	Lasciatemi morire (Arianna)	ML	D-D	†
Pergolesi	Se tu m'ami	LMH	C-G	GSC
Respighi	Contrasto	M		RIC
Rontani	Se bel rio	ML	D-C	†
Rosa	Selve, voi che le speranze	MH	D-G	DIT
-----	Vado ben spesso	ML	C-EF	†
Scarlatti, A.	Sento nel core	M	E-F	†
Secchi	Love me or not			BOO

Miscellaneous Songs and Arias Employing
Crescendo and Diminuendo

Mezzo Soprano

Bach, J.S.	Esurientes implevit bonis			†
	(Magnificat in D Major)			
Backer-Grondahl	In dreaming dance			
Gretchaninoff	My native land	L	C-EF	GSC
Grieg	In the boat	LM	D-ES	†
-----	Nu er aftenen lys og lang	L	C-E	HAN
-----	With a water lily	HM	CS-EF	†
Mussorgsky	Oriental chant	ML	BF-E	GSC
	(Josua Navine Cantata)			
Rachmaninoff	Lilacs	LH	EF-G	†
-----	The island	LH	DF-F	†
Stravinsky	Pastorale			GSC

American Songs Employing
Piano Singing

Mezzo Soprano

Barber	Rain has fallen	HM	D-E	GSC
-----	Sleep now	MH	EF-AF	GSC
Campbell-Tipton	A spirit flower	LHM	B-G	GSC
-----	The crying of water	LH	FS-GS	GSC
Carpenter	Go, lovely rose	M	DF-EF	GSC
-----	May the maiden			DIT
-----	On the seashore of endless worlds	M	C-FS	GSC
-----	The day is no more	M	GS-DS	GSC
-----	The green river	M	B-E	GSC
-----	The pools of peace	M	D-F	GSC
-----	The sleep that flits on baby's eyes	M	B-FS	GSC
-----	Watercolors	M	C-F	GSC
-----	When I bring to you colour'd toys	LM	CS-FS	GSC
Charles	Clouds	HML	C-EF	GSC
-----	When I have sung my songs	HM	BF-EF	GSC
Clough-Leighter	Who knows?	M		GSC
Davis	Nancy Hanks	H	D-G	GAL
Duke	To Karen, singing	M	CS-G	ELV

Engel	A sprig of rosemary	M	EF-F	GSC
-----	Sea shell	M	EF-EF	GSC
Fairchild	A memory			BOS
Gaines	My heart hath a mind			
Ganz	A memory	HM	B-D	GSC
Giannini	Tell me, o blue, blue sky	H		RIC
Griffes	O'er the Tarn's unruffled mirror	HL	G-E	GSC
-----	The dreamy lake	H	BS-GS	GSC
Guion	Mam'selle Marie	M	D-E	GSC
Hageman	Do not go, my love	HL	B-EF	GSC
Howe	Berceuse	HM	EF-F	GSC
Kingsford	Wallpaper for a little girl's room	M	BF-F	GSC
Kramer	Swans	HL		RIC
MacGimsey	Sweet little Jesus boy	ML	D-D	CFI
Manning	In the Luxembourg gardens	HML	BF-D	GSC
-----	Shoes	M	EF-F	GSC
Menotti	Lullaby (The Consul)			GSC
Naginski	Night song at Amalfi	M	D-EF	GSC
-----	The pasture	M	BF-EF	GSC
Niles	I wonder as I wander	HL	BF-D	GSC
-----	Jesus, Jesus rest your head	HL	A-D	GSC
Nordoff	Serenade	H	CS-FS	AMP
Schuman	Orpheus with his lute	M	C-FS	GSC
Thompson	Velvet shoes	M	C-E	ECS

British Songs Employing
Piano Singing

Mezzo Soprano

Bax	Cradle song			CHA
Benjamin	Calm sea and mist			CUR
Clarke	Shy one	HL	BF-G	BOH
Coleridge-Taylor	She rested by the broken brook	HL		DIT
Delius	Twilight fancies	M	D-FS	CFI
Dunhill	The cloths of heaven	LM	EF-G	STB
Elgar	Sea pictures	L	A-A	BOO
Handel	Let me wander not unseen (L'Allegro)	M	D-G	†
Harty	My lagan love	ML	BF-EF	BOO
Head	The ships of Arcady	ML	BF-EF	BOH
Peterkin	The garden of bamboos	M	EF-F	OXF

Pilkington	Rest, sweet nymphs			STB
Quilter	Dream valley	H	EF-GF	ROG
Sanderson	Quiet	ML	AF-EF	BOH
Scott	Lullaby	MML	BF-DF	GAL
Shaw	The land of heart's desire	M	C-E	CUR
Vaughn Williams	Silent noon			GSC
-----	The twilight people	L	BF-EF	OXF

French Songs and Arias Employing
Piano Singing

Mezzo Soprano

Berlioz	Villanelle	H	E-FS	†
Bizet	Pastorale	H	C-FS	GSC
Chabrier	Romance de l'étoile			ENO
Chaminade	The silver ring	HM	BF-F	GSC
Chausson	Dans la forêt	HL		INT
Debussy	En sourdine	M	C-FS	†
-----	Il pleure dans mon coeur	LH	CS-GS	†
-----	L'ombre des arbres			†
-----	La flûte de Pan		B-B	†
-----	La grotte			DUR
-----	La mort des amants			†
-----	Le tombeau des naïades			JOB
-----	Recueillement			DUR
Fauré	Adieu	MH	F-F	†
-----	Après un rêve	HM	C-F	†
-----	C'est l'extase	HL	C-FF	GSC
-----	Clair de lune	MH	C-G	†
-----	Dans les ruines d'une abbaye	M	E-FS	†
-----	En prière	H	F-F	†
-----	Le secret	LH	F-G	†
Ferrari	Le miroir	M	E-F	GSC
Fevrier	L'intruse	M	B-DF	HEU
Franck	Le mariage des roses	M	E-FS	BOS
Godard	Cachés dans cet asile (Jocelyn) Violin or cello	MH	DF-F	GSC
Gossec	Dors, mon enfant (Rosine)	L		CHE
Gounod	Au rossignol	LMH	D-G	CHO
-----	Sérénade	LMH	D-A	GSC
Hahn	A Chloris	H	DS-FS	HEU
-----	D'une prison	L	BF-EF	HEU
-----	L'heure exquise	M	DF-F	†
-----	Offrande	M	D-D	†
-----	Paysage	MH	EF-G	HEU

Lully	Au clair de la lune	H	E-D	CFI
-----	Bois épais (Amadis)	ML	C-EF	†
Massenet	Crépuscule	M	D-E	GSC
Mouret	Doux plaisirs (Pirithous)			CHE
Paladilhe	Psyché	HM	BF-F	GSC
Pessard	L'adieu du matin	ML	BF-D	GSC
Rameau	Dans ces doux asiles (Castor et Pollux)			LEM
Ravel	D'Anne qui me jecta	HM	CS-FS	GSC
-----	La flûte enchantée	M	DS-FS	DUR
-----	Noël des jouets	M	BS-FS	MAT
-----	Sainte	M	C-G	ELV
-----	Sur l'herbe	MH	C-G	DUR
-----	Trois beaux oiseaux du paradis			DUR
-----	Trois poemes de Mallarme 2 Flutes, 2 clarients, 4 strings and piano	M	BF-G	DUR
Roussel	Le jardin mouillé	M	C-FS	ROU
Saint-Saëns	Mai	H	G-FS	DUR
Severac	Ma poupée chérie			ROU
Weckerlin	Menuet d'Exaudet	H	D-G	GSC
-----	O ma tendre musette	LM	A-E	GSC
Widor	Je ne veux pas autre chose	HL	C-EF	HAM

German Songs and Arias Employing
Piano Singing

Mezzo Soprano

Bach, J.S.	Jesus schlaeft (Cantata 81)	L	A-D	GSC
Beethoven	Ich liebe dich	HL	BF-DF	†
Brahms	Es traeumte mir			†
-----	Five songs of Ophelia	HL	B-EF	†
-----	In Waldeseinsamkeit	H	ES-G	†
-----	Lerchengesang	LH	FS-GS	†
-----	Sapphische Ode	HML		†
-----	Spanisches Lied			†
-----	Staendchen	HL	BF-E	†
-----	Steig, auf geliebter Schatten	HL	BF-EF	†
Franz	Abends	HM	C-EF	†
-----	Die blauen Fruelingsaugen	HL		†
-----	Ein Stuendlein wohl vor Tag			†
-----	Es hat die Rose sich beklagt	LH	DF-F	†

(Franz)	Sterne mit den gold'nen Fuesschen	HL	DS-E	†
Hassler	Tanzlied			SIM
Mahler	Die zwei blauen Augen	M	A-G	†
-----	Ich atmet' einen linden Duft	HL		INT
-----	Ich bin der Welt abbanden gekommen	HL		INT
-----	Liebst du um Schoenheit	HL		INT
-----	Wo die schoenen Trompeten blasen	HL	GF-F	INT
Marx	Der Rauch			UNI
Mendelssohn	Bei der Wiege	M	DF-EF	†
-----	O rest in the Lord (Elijah)	L	B-D	†
Reger	Des Kindes Gebet	H	F-G	BOT
Schubert	Auf dem Wasser zu singen	MH	EF-GF	†
-----	Ave Maria	LMH	F-F	†
-----	Der Einsame	LH	D-G	†
-----	Der Schmetterling	LH	E-F	†
-----	Der Tod und das Maedchen	HL	A-EF	†
-----	Der Wanderer an den Mond	LM	D-F	PET
-----	Die Taubenpost	HL	D-EF	†
-----	Du bist die Ruh	LMH	EF-AF	†
-----	Fruehlingstraum	HL	C-D	†
-----	Geheimes	HL	BF-EF	†
-----	Im Abendrot	HL	C-D	†
-----	Im Fruehling	LH	D-FS	†
-----	Lachen und Weinen	HL	C-EF	†
-----	Liebesbotschaft	H	E-G	†
-----	Nacht und Traeume	HL	C-DF	†
Schumann	Der Nussbaum	LMH	D-FS	†
-----	Der Sandmann	HL	AF-DF	†
-----	Marienwuermchen	HL	D-D	†
-----	Mondnacht	M	E-FS	†
-----	Requiem			†
Strauss	Allerseelen	HL	AS-E	†
-----	Die Nacht	HL		DIT
-----	Freundliche Vision	HL	C-F	†
-----	Heimkehr	HL	B-E	†
-----	Ich trage meine Minne	M		†
-----	Meinem Kinde			†
-----	Traum durch die Daemmerung	HML	BF-EF	†
-----	Wiegenliedchen			†
Trunk	In meiner Heimat			
Wagner	Im Treibhaus	HL		†

Wolf	Ach, des Knaben Augen	HL		†
-----	An die Geliebte			†
-----	Der Gaertner	HL		†
-----	Du denkst, mit einem Faedchen			†
-----	In dem Schatten meiner Locken	M	C-EF	†
-----	Mausfallen Spruechlein	HL	BF-E	†
-----	Morgentau	HL	D-D	†
-----	Schlafendes Jesuskind	HL	AS-F	†
-----	Verborgenheit	HL	B-E	†
-----	Verschwiegene Liebe	LH	DF-FS	†
-----	Wie glaenzt der helle Mond			†
Wolff	Ich bin eine Harfe			HMP
-----	Knabe und Veilchen	M	D-D	HMP

Italian Songs and Arias Employing Piano Singing

Mezzo Soprano

Castelnuovo-Tedesco	Ninna Nanna			
Cimara	Fiocca la neve	H	G-G	GSC
Gagliano	Dormi, amore (La Flora)	HL	CS-E	DIT
Gluck	O del mio dolce ardor (Paride ed Elena)	LH	D-FS	GSC
Monteverdi	Lasciatemi morire (Arianna)	ML	D-D	†
Respighi	Mattino di luce	M		RIC
-----	Notte			BON
Rontani	Se bel rio	ML	D-C	†
Secchi	Lungi dal caro bene	HL	A-FS	DIT

Miscellaneous Songs Employing Piano Singing

Mezzo Soprano

Alnaes	En morgen var din grav	M	CS-D	HAN
-----	Lykken mellem to mennesker	M	B-FS	HAN
Arensky	Revery	MH	DS-FS	DIT
-----	Valse	H	DF-GF	GSC
Cui	The statue at Czarskoe-Selo	HM	DF-EF	†
Dvořák	God is my shepherd			AMP

362

(Dvořák)	Songs my mother taught me	HM	E-E	†
Gretchaninoff	Hushed the song of the nightingale	MH	E-G	DIT
Grieg	A dream			†
-----	A swan			†
-----	In the boat	LM	D-ES	†
-----	Radiant night			
-----	Snegl, Snegl	M	B-F	HAN
-----	Til En II	M	E-F	HAN
Lie	Soft-footed snow	HM		DIT
Mednikoff	The hills of Gruzia	H	DS-A	LAC
Rachmaninoff	In the silence of night	LH	D-A	GSC
-----	Into my open window	HL	B-FS	BOS
Sibelius	The tryst	M		AMP
Tchaikovsky	Evening	HM		GSC

American Songs Employing
Rapid Enunciation

Mezzo Soprano

Bernstein	La bonne cuisine	H	B-B	GSC
Boatner	Oh, what a beautiful city!	HL	D-E	GSC
Burleigh	Joshua fit de battle ob Jericho	LH	DS-E	RIC
Carpenter	Don't ceare	M	C-D	GSC
-----	The cock shall crow	M	B-E	GSC
Clough-Leighter	My lover he comes on the skee	HM	D-F	BOS
Curran	Ho! Mr. Piper	LH	D-G	GSC
Deis	Come down to Kew			
Hadley	My shadow			ASC
Hageman	At the well	LH	EF-AF	GSC
-----	Miranda	HL		GAL
Kountz	The sleigh	HL	D-FS	GSC
Nevin	One spring morning	MH	DS-F	BOS
Sacco	Mexican serenade	HL	D-EF	BOS
Spross	Will o' the wisp			JCH
Warner	Hurdy gurdy	M	D-F	CFI

British Songs Employing
Rapid Enunciation

Mezzo Soprano

Bantock	A feast of lanterns	HM	D-F	GAL
Bax	Oh dear, what can the matter be?	M	D-EF	CHE
Brewer	The fairy pipers	HML		BOH
Britten	Oliver Cromwell			BOH
German	Charming Chloe	HML		NOV
Gibbs	Five eyes	HL	D-D	BOS
Head	A piper	HL		BOO
Hughes	Hey diddle diddle			CRA
Morley	It was a lover and his lass	HM		DIT
Purcell	There's not a swain on the plain	M	B-G	BAF
Vaughn Williams	A piper			OXF
-----	The water mill	L	C-D	OXF

French Songs and Arias Employing
Rapid Enunciation

Mezzo Soprano

Bizet	Habanera (Carmen)	HM	D-F	†
Chabrier	Les cigales	HML		†
-----	Villanelle des petits canards	HML	B-E	†
Debussy	Ballade des femmes de Paris			DUR
-----	Chevaux de bois	H	C-G	†
-----	Fantoches	H	D-A	JOB
-----	Fêtes galantes	LH	CS-A	†
-----	Le temps a laissié son manteau			DUR
-----	Mandoline	HM	BF-F	†
-----	Placet futile			DUR
Fauré	Mandoline	HL	F-E	†
-----	Notre amour	H	DS-B	†
-----	Poème d'un jour			HAM
-----	Toujours	LH	F-AF	†
Fourdrain	Carnaval	M	C-F	RIC
Gounod	Flower song (Faust)			†
Koechlin	La lune	M	C-F	ROU
Milhaud	La tourterelle	M	B-G	DUR

Pierné	Ils étaient trois petits chats blancs			MAR
Poldowski	Dansons la gigue	M	EF-G	MAR
Ravel	Manteau de fleurs	H		INT
-----	Nicolette	L	B-FS	ELK
-----	Tout gai	MH	EF-F	DUR
Saint-Saëns	L'attente			DUR
-----	Tournoiement			DUR
Severac	Chanson pour le petit cheval			ROU
Weckerlin	Maman, dites-moi	M	E-FS	BOS

German Songs Employing Rapid Enunciation

Mezzo Soprano

Bach, J.S.	Patron, das macht der Wind (Phoebus and Pan)	M	C-G	GSC
Brahms	Blinde Kuh			†
-----	Das Maedchen spricht	H	E-FS	†
-----	Der Jaeger	HL		†
-----	Dort in den Weiden	LH	A-A	†
-----	Meine Liebe ist gruen	MLH	ES-A	†
-----	O liebliche Wangen	MLH	E-G	†
-----	Tambourliedchen			†
-----	Vergebliches Staendchen	LHM	E-FS	†
Loewe	Walpurgisnacht	H	G-G	SC
Mendelssohn	An die Entfernte	M	F-F	
-----	Neue Liebe	H	CS-A	†
Mozart	Warnung	HM	C-D	
Schubert	Am Feierabend	HL	BF-F	†
-----	Das Wandern	HLM	E-E	†
-----	Die Forelle	MLH	EF-GF	†
-----	Die Post	HML	BF-EF	†
-----	Erstarrung	HL	D-F	†
-----	Fischerweise	L	C-D	†
-----	Ungeduld	HML		†
-----	Wohin?	HL	B-E	†
Schumann	Die Kartenlegerin			
Strauss	Fuer fuenfzehn Pfennige			†
Wolf	Elfenlied	HL	D-F	INT
-----	Ich hab' in Penna	LH		†

Italian Songs and Arias Employing
Rapid Enunciation

Mezzo Soprano

Carissimi	Vittoria, mio core	HLM	B-E	†
Cavalli	Donzelle figgite	HL	C-EF	†
Donizetti	Il segreto per esser felici (Lucrezia Borgia)	M	C-G	†
Durante	Danza, danza fanciulla gentile	HM	BF-F	†
Falconieri	Non più d'amore	HL	C-D	DIT
-----	Nudo arciero	HL	AF-AF	DIT
Handel	Ch'io mai vi possa (Siroe)			†
Legrenzi	Che fiero costume	HML	C-D	†
Leoncavallo	Da quel suon soavemento (La Boheme)			SON
Malipiero	Ballata	H		CHE
Mozart	Non so più cosa son (Le Nozze di Figaro)	H	EF-G	†
-----	Voi che sapete (Le Nozze di Figaro)	M	C-F	†
Paisiello	Chi vuol la zingarella	L	C-F	GSC
Paradies	M'ha preso alla sua ragna	M	EF-F	GSC
Rontani	Or ch'io non segno più	HL	CS-E	DIT
Rossini	La danza	MH	E-A	†

Miscellaneous Songs Employing
Rapid Enunciation

Mezzo Soprano

Falla	Cancion del amor dolido			CHE
-----	Seguidilla murciana	HL		AMP
Grieg	My Johann	HL	BF-EF	GSC
-----	Simpel sang			
-----	With a water lily			GSC
-----	Til min dreng		C-E	
Mussorgsky	The evening prayer		MC-E	GSC
-----	The magpie and the gypsy dancer			GSC

American Songs Employing
Sustained Singing

Mezzo Soprano

Barber	A nun takes the veil	MH	G-G	GSC
-----	Sure on this shining night	MH	D-G	GSC
Burleigh	Deep river	HML		RIC
-----	Sometimes I feel like a motherless child	HML		RIC
-----	Were you there?	HML		RIC
Carpenter	Slumber song	ML	BF-F	GSC
-----	The player queen	M	BF-EF	GSC
-----	To one unknown	M	A-DS	GSC
Chadwick	Allah	LH	CS-GS	ASC
Dello Joio	New born	M	C-D	CFI
Edwards	By the bend of the river	HML	C-E	GSC
-----	Into the night	HML	C-DF	GSC
Foote	On the way to Kew			ASC
Giannini	Be still my heart			ELV
Golde	O beauty, passing beauty	MH	CS-GS	GSC
Griffes	By a lonely forest pathway	HML	A-EF	GSC
-----	The lament of Ian the proud	MH	DS-AS	GSC
Hageman	Music I heard with you	MH	E-A	GAL
Harris	Fog	M	D-F	CFI
Hindemith	Envoy	M	EF-F	AMP
-----	The wildflower's song	MH	E-G	AMP
Horsman	In the yellow dusk	MH	FS-A	GSC
Kramer	For a dream's sake	HL		JFI
MacDowell	The swan bent low	LH		ELK
Metcalf	At nightfall	HML	C-DF	ASC
Porter, Q.	Music, when soft voices die	HM	D-C	MUP
Rasbach	Trees	LMH	CS-GS	GSC
Rogers	Wind song	LM	C-G	GSC
Scott	Think on me	HML	D-EF	GAL
Tyson	Noon and night	LH	F-AF	GSC
Watts	Transformation	ML	AS-DS	GSC

British Songs and Arias Employing
Sustained Singing

Mezzo Soprano

Arne, T.	In infancy			NOV
Bantock	Silent strings	MH	F-G	BOO

Bridge	All things that we clasp	HL		BOS
-----	O that it were so	LMH	D-G	CHA
Britten	The Sally gardens			BOH
Butterworth	Loveliest of trees			AUG
Clarke	Eight o'clock			ROG
Coleridge-Taylor	Life and death	HML		ASC
Del Riego	Homing	HML	BF-E	CHA
Dowland	Flow, my tears	M	D-E	STB
-----	Sorrow, sorrow stay	M	D-D	BOS
Dunhill	To the Queen of Heaven	M	C-G	GSC
Elgar	Pleading	HML		NOV
Handel	In gentle murmurs will I mourn (Jephtha)	L	B-E	†
-----	Thou shalt bring them in (Israel in Egypt)	L	B-D	†
Henschel	Morning-hymn	MH	DS-GS	†
Holst	The heart worships	ML	BF-D	STB
Johnson	Dear, do not your fair beauty wrong			DIT
Milford	So sweet love seemed Cello	HL	D-D	GRA
Murray	I'll walk beside you			CHA
Purcell	If music be the food of love	M	D-G	BOO
-----	Music for a while (Oedipus)	LH		SC
-----	When I am laid in earth (Dido and Aeneas)	LH	C-G	†
Quilter	Drink to me only	LMH	GF-GF	BOH
Ronald	The dove			ENO
Scott	The unforeseen	HML		GAL
Stephenson	Love is a sickness	HML	C-D	BOO
Vaughn Williams	Bright is the ring of words	L		BOH
-----	Linden Lea	HML	C-D	BOS
Warlock	Sleep			OXF
Welsh	All through the night			

French Songs and Arias Employing Sustained Singing

Mezzo Soprano

Bemberg	Chant hindou	HML	A-EF	†
Berlioz	La captive	HL		GSC
-----	Le spectre de la rose			CST
-----	Les nuits d'été			AUG

368

Bizet	Adieu de l'hôtesse arabe	H	BF-G	†
Caplet	Les prières			DUR
Chaminade	Chant slave			GSC
Chausson	Chanson perpétuelle	H	CS-GS	ROU
-----	Le charme	HM	BF-EF	HAM
-----	Le colibri	M	F-GF	BOS
-----	Le temps des lilas	MH	D-GS	†
Debussy	Ballade que fait Villon à la requeste de sa mère			DUR
-----	Beau soir	LH	C-FS	†
-----	Chansons de Bilitis	M	C-FS	†
-----	Colloque sentimental			DUR
-----	Je tremble en voyant ton visage			DUR
-----	La chevelure	M	CF-FS	†
-----	Le son du cor	HL		†
Duparc	Au pays où se fait la guerre			SAL
-----	La vie antérieure	HL		†
-----	Lamento	ML	EF-EF	†
Fauré	Au cimetière	LH	D-F	
-----	Automne	MH	D-FS	GSC
-----	Le jardin clos	M	C-E	DUR
-----	Le parfum impérissable	LH	GF-GF	
-----	Les berceaux	LMH	BF-G	†
-----	Nocturne	H	F-A	MAR
-----	Prison	LH		†
-----	Rencontre	H	EF-AF	†
-----	Soir	LH	D-GS	†
Franck	Nocturne	HL		†
Georges	Hymne au soleil	LH	E-A	HOM
Gluck	Divinités du Styx (Alceste)	MH	DF-AF	†
Godard	Florian's song	LMH	D-FS	GSC
Gounod	O ma lyre immortelle (Sappho)	M	C-G	†
Honegger	Chanson (Ronsard) Flute and string quartet			SEN
Hue	J'ai pleuré en rêve	HL	D-E	BOS
Indy	Lied maritime	LH	B-G	†
Lalo	Chant breton	M	E-E	HAM
Leguerney	L'adieu	M	B-FS	DUR
Lenormand	Quelle souffrance	HM	AF-F	HAM
Leroux	Le nil Cello or violin	LH	E-A	†
Lully	Fermez-vous pour jamais (Amadis)			LEM
Massenet	Elégie	LM	C-GF	GSC
-----	Il est doux, il est bon (Hérodiade)	MH	EF-BF	GSC

369

Meyerbeer	Ah! mon fils (Le Prophète)	M	B-AS	GSC
Paladilhe	Lamento provinçal	M	CS-FS	HOM
Poulenc	A sa guitare	M	D-FS	DUR
-----	Air grave			ROU
-----	Fleurs	M	DF-F	ROU
-----	Violon			ROU
Ravel	Kaddisch	H	C-G	DUR
-----	Le martin-pêcheur			DUR
-----	Le paon	M	C-F	DUR
-----	Vocalise en forme de habanera	MH	BF-G	MAR
Saint-Saëns	Aimons-nous			DUR
-----	Amour, viens aider (Samson et Dalila)	HM	AF-G	†
-----	La cloche	LH	DF-AF	†
-----	Le lever de la lune			DUR
-----	Mon coeur s'ouvre à ta voix (Samson et Dalila)	HLM	BF-GF	†
-----	Printemps qui commence (Samson et Dalila)	M	B-E	†
Thomas	Connais-tu le pays? (Mignon)	HML	C-F	†
Tremisot	Nuit d'été			
Weckerlin	Venez, agréable printemps	M	C-F	

German Songs and Arias Employing Sustained Singing

Mezzo Soprano

Ahle	Bruenstiges Verlangen	M	E-E	GSC
Bach, J.S.	Bist du bei mir	HML	A-EF	†
Beethoven	Das Geheimnis			
-----	Die Ehre Gottes	HL	AF-EF	†
-----	Faithfu' Johnie			
-----	Vom Tode	L	A-EF	GSC
-----	Wonne der Wehmut			†
Bohm	Calm as the night	HML	A-EF	†
Brahms	An eine Aeolsharfe	H	EF-AF	†
-----	Auf dem Kirchhofe	HL	BF-EF	†
-----	Dein blaues Auge	MH	BF-G	†
-----	Der Tod, das ist die kuehle Nacht	L	AF-F	†
-----	Die Mainacht	HL	BF-FF	†
-----	Feldeinsamkeit	HL	C-EF	†
-----	Immer leiser wird mein Schlummer	LH	DF-A	†

(Brahms)	Liebestreu	ML	C-F	†
-----	Mit vierzig Jahren	HL	FS-D	†
-----	Mondenschein	LH	D-GF	†
-----	Muss es eine Trennung geben?	LH	FS-FS	†
-----	Nachtigall	MHL	BF-FS	†
-----	O kuehler Wald	MH	A-F	†
-----	O wuesst' ich doch den Weg zurueck	H	E-FS	†
-----	Sommerabend			†
-----	Treue Liebe	LMH	DS-E	GSC
-----	Ueber die Haide			†
-----	Verzagen	MH	CS-FS	†
-----	Wenn du nur zuweilen laechelst			†
-----	Wir wandelten	LH	EF-GF	†
Bruch	Penelope's sorrow (Odysseus)			SIM
Franz	Dedication	HML	BF-C	†
-----	Es ragt ins Meer der runenstein	HL	G-F	†
-----	For music	ML	C-D	†
-----	Im Herbst	HM	A-F	†
-----	Mutter, o sing mich zur Ruh	HL	E-G	†
Haydn	She never told her love	HL	B-D	DIT
Himmel	Die Sendung			SIM
Hindemith	Pietà from Marienleben			AMP
Jensen	Wie so bleich			
Korngold	Love letter			AMP
Lehar	Vilia (The Merry Widow)			CHA
Liszt	Freudvoll und leidvoll			DUR
Loewe	Canzonetta	MH	B-A	DIT
-----	Der heilige Franziskus	L	A-E	SC
Mahler	Wenn mein Schatz Hochzeit macht			WEI
Marx	Der Ton	M	C-F	AMP
-----	Hat dich die Liebe beruehrt	MH	EF-BF	AMP
Mendelssohn	But the Lord is mindful of His own (Saint Paul)	L	A-D	GSC
-----	Nachtlied			
-----	On wings of song			†
-----	Woe unto them who forsake him (Elijah)	L	B-E	†
Mozart	Abendempfindung	M	E-F	
-----	Verdankt sei es dem Glanz			DIT
-----	Wiegenlied	MH	G-G	†
Reichardt	In the time of roses			†

371

Schoenberg	Song of the wood dove			AMP
Schubert	Am Bach im Fruehling			PET
-----	Am Grabe Anselmos	HL	B-EF	†
-----	An die Leier	LM	BF-F	†
-----	An die Musik	HL	A-DS	†
-----	Das Wirtshaus	HL	C-D	†
-----	Der Doppelgaenger	HL	G-D	†
-----	Der Leiermann	ML	C-D	†
-----	Der Lindenbaum	HL	A-D	†
-----	Der Neugierige	HL	CS-EF	†
-----	Der Wegweiser	L	D-EF	†
-----	Des Maedchens Klage	LH	C-E	†
-----	Die Allmacht	HML	G-E	†
-----	Die Kraehe	HL	A-E	†
-----	Die Liebe hat gelogen	LM	G-F	†
-----	Die Maenner sind mechant			PET
-----	Die Nebensonnen	HL	F-D	†
-----	Die Stadt	HL	A-E	†
-----	Du liebst mich nicht	LH	E-FS	†
-----	Ganymed	LH	EF-G	†
-----	Ihr Bild	HL	C-C	†
-----	In der Ferne	HL		†
-----	Lied eines Schiffers an die Dioskuren	HL	A-C	†
-----	Litanei	HLM	C-EF	†
-----	Nachtgesang			PET
-----	Nur wer die Sehnsucht kennt	LH		†
-----	Schaefers Klagelied	HL	BF-D	†
-----	Sei mir gegruesst	LH	G-G	†
-----	Thekla	HL	B-E	PET
-----	Wehmuth	HL	B-D	†
Schuetz	Aus dem 119th Psalm			
Schumann	An den Sonnenschein	HL	A-D	†
-----	Aus den Hebraeischen Gesaengen			
-----	Dein Angesicht	HL	B-EF	†
-----	Der Himmel hat eine Traene geweint			
-----	Die Lotusblume	HLM	BF-F	†
-----	Du bist wie eine Blume	HM	F-EF	†
-----	Du ring an meinem Finger	HL	C-F	†
-----	Hoch, hoch sind die Berge			
-----	Ihre Stimme	LH		†
-----	Im Westen	HL		†
-----	Lied der Suleika			
-----	Mit Myrthen und Rosen	HL	A-D	†
-----	Seit ich ihn gesehen	HL	DF-DF	†
-----	Stille Traenen	HL		†

372

(Schumann)	Wer machte dich so krank?			
Strauss	Befreit			HSC
-----	Liebeshymnus			†
-----	Mit deinen blauen Augen	LH	C–GS	†
-----	Morgen	HML	E–F	†
-----	Ruhe meine Seele			†
-----	Seitdem dein Aug' in meines schaute			SC
Wagner	Five Wesendonck songs			GSC
-----	Schmerzen	HL		†
Wolf	Agnes	HL		†
-----	Alle gingen, Herz, zu Ruh	HL	C–EF	†
-----	An eine Aeolsharfe			†
-----	Bedeckt mich mit Blumen	HL	B–D	†
-----	Das Staendchen	HL		†
-----	Das verlassene Maegdlein	HL	D–EF	†
-----	Denk' es, o Seele	LH	EF–F	INT
-----	Der Mond hat eine schwere Klag' erhoben	HL	BF–DF	†
-----	Gebet	HL		†
-----	Gesang Weylas	HL	DF–F	†
-----	Herr, was traegt der Boden	HL	B–DS	†
-----	Im Fruehling	HL	BF–F	†
-----	In der Fruehe	HL	C–C	†
-----	Morgenstimmung	LH	C–GS	†
-----	Neue Liebe	LH	D–AF	†
-----	Um Mitternacht	HL	G–EF	†
-----	Zur ruh', zur Ruh'	HL	A–GF	†
Wolff	Alle Dinge haben Sprache	M	BF–GF	†
-----	Ewig			

Italian Songs and Arias Employing Sustained Singing

Mezzo Soprano

Bellini	Scombra è la sacra selva (Norma)			RIC
Bimboni	Sospiri miei	M	EF–EF	GAL
Bononcini	Deh, lascia			HEU
-----	Pietà, mio caro bene	HL	C–EF	DIT
Caccini	Amarilli, mia bella	ML	C–D	†
Caldara	Come raggio di sol	HL	D–F	†
Cesti	Che angoscia, che affanno (Il Pomo d'Oro)	HL	C–DF	DIT

373

Cherubini	Ahi, che forse ai miei di (Demofonte)			RIC
Cimara	Stornellata marinara	HM		RIC
Del Leuto	Dimmi, amor	M	C-F	GSC
Donaudy	Quando ti rivedrò			RIC
Donizetti	O mio Fernando (La Favorita)	M	B-A	†
Durante	Vergin, tutta amor	LM	C-EF	†
Giordano	O grandi occhi lucenti (Fedora)			BRO
Gluck	Che farò senza Euridice (Orphée)	ML	BF-F	†
-----	Spiagge amate (Paride ed Elena)			†
Handel	Dove sei, amato bene (Rodelinda)	L	BF-EF	†
-----	Lascia ch'io pianga (Rinaldo)	HM	EF-F	DIT
-----	O rendetemi il mio bene (Amadigi)	L	CS-EF	CFI
-----	V'adoro pupille (Julius Caesar)			BOO
-----	Verdi prati (Alcina)			†
Mascagni	Voi lo sapete (Cavalleria Rusticana)	H	B-A	†
Monteverdi	Tu se' morta (Orfeo)	M	C-E	GSC
Mozart	Ch'io mi scordi di te			BOO
-----	Deh, se piacer mi vuoi (La Clemenza di Tito)			RIC
-----	Non più di fiori (La Clemenza di Tito)			†
-----	Parto, parto (La Clemenza di Tito) B flat clarinet and piano	H		AMP
Paisiello	Nel cor più non mi sento	HL	C-EF	†
Peri	Funeste piaggie (Euridice)			GSC
Piccini	O nuit, dresse du mystere (Le Faux Lord)			GSC
Pizzetti	La madre al figlio lontano			FRL
Ponchielli	Voce di donna (La Gioconda)	HM	A-G	GSC
Respighi	Abbandono			BON
-----	Ballata			RIC
-----	Io sono la madre	L		RIC
-----	Nebbie			GSC
Scarlatti, A.	O cessate di piagarmi	HL	DS-E	†
Stradella	Col mio sangue comprenderei (Il Floridoro)	HL	E-F	DIT

(Stradella)	Per pietà (Il Floridoro)	HM	D-F	DIT
-----	Pietà Signore	HM	C-F	GSC
Torelli	Tu lo sai	HL	BF-F	†

Miscellaneous Songs Employing Sustained Singing

Mezzo Soprano

Arensky	Autumn	H	CS-FS	GSC
Bach-Gounod	Ave Maria			†
Dvořák	Hear my prayer, O Lord			AMP
-----	Lord thou art my refuge and shield			AMP
-----	Turn Thee to me			AMP
Gliere	Ah, twine no blossoms	HM	CS-F	DIT
Granados	La maja dolorosa	M		INT
Gretchaninoff	Over the steppe	LM	C-G	GSC
-----	Wounded birch	HL	B-EF	†
Grieg	I love thee	HML	E-F	†
-----	The mother sings			DIT
Kjerulf	Synnove's song	M	C-F	GSC
Mussorgsky	Cradle-song of the poor	M	B-DS	GSC
-----	Martha's song (Khovantchina)	ML		GSC
-----	On the Dnieper			GSC
-----	Sphinx			BRH
Rachmaninoff	As fair is she as noonday light			GSC
-----	Christ is risen	LM	D-F	GAL
-----	Oh cease thy singing, maiden fair	H	E-A	CFI
-----	O, do not grieve	M	BF-AF	GSC
-----	O thou billowy harvest field	HL	CS-E	GSC
-----	The soldier's bride			†
-----	To the children	MH	F-G	DIT
-----	Vocalise	LH	CS-A	GSC
Rimsky-Korsakov	On the Georgian hills	HM		GSC
Sibelius	Black roses	M	A-ES	AMP
-----	The first kiss	M		AMP
-----	Was it a dream			BRH
Sinding	I hear the gull			JCH
-----	The daisies secret			
Tchaikovsky	A legend	M	D-E	GSC
-----	Adieu forêts (Jeanne d'Arc)	HM	BF-FS	GSC

(Tchaikovsky)	None but the lonely heart	HLM	C-F	DIT
-----	Pauline's romance	M	BF-AF	GSC
	(Pique Dame)			

American Songs Employing
Spirited Singing

Mezzo Soprano

Barber	I hear an army	LH	D-AF	GSC
Bassett	Take joy home	LH	EF-BF	GSC
Boatner	Oh, what a beautiful city!	HL	D-E	GSC
Burleigh	Joshua fit de battle ob Jericho	LH	DS-E	RIC
Carpenter	Dansons la gigue	M	B-E	GSC
-----	Don't ceare	M	C-D	GSC
-----	If	M	D-E	GSC
-----	Light, my light	M	C-G	GSC
-----	Serenade	LH	CS-A	GSC
-----	The cock shall crow	M	B-E	GSC
-----	To a young gentleman	M	C-F	GSC
Clough-Leighter	My lover he comes on the skee	HM	D-F	BOS
Crist	O come hither	HM	B-GS	CFI
Curran	Ho! Mr. Piper	LH	D-G	GSC
Deis	Come down to Kew			
Duke	I can't be talkin' of love	H	CS-G	GSC
-----	On a March day	M	B-GF	BOH
Elwell	The road not taken	M	B-FS	GSC
Enders	Russian picnic	HM	C-G	GSC
Giannini	Sing to my heart a song	H	D-B	ELV
Griffes	We'll to the woods, and gather May	M	D-F	GSC
Hadley	My shadow			ASC
Hageman	At the well	LH	EF-AF	GSC
-----	Miranda	HL		GAL
-----	Voices			
Johnson	Roll Jerd'n roll	M	EF-F	GSC
Kountz	The sleigh	HL	D-FS	GSC
La Forge	Song of the open	MH	EF-AF	DIT
Levitzki	Ah, thou beloved one	H	EF-AF	GSC
Nevin	One spring morning	MH	DS-F	BOS
Nordoff	There shall be more joy	M	CS-FS	AMP
Rawls	The balloon man	L	A-FS	AMP
Rogers	The last song	MLH	E-AF	GSC
Rummel	Ecstasy	LMH	GF-AF	GSC

Sacco	Mexican serenade	HL	D-EF	BOS
-----	Rapunzel	MH	FS-BF	GSC
Salter	The cry of Rachel	LH	C-AF	GSC
Schuman	Holiday song	M	C-F	GSC
Speaks	Morning	HML	BF-D	GSC
Spross	Will o' the wisp			JCH
Warner	Hurdy gurdy	M	D-F	CFI

British Songs and Arias Employing
Spirited Singing

Mezzo Soprano

Arne, T.	Why so pale and wan			GSC
Bantock	A feast of lanterns	HM	D-F	GAL
Bax	Oh dear what can the matter be?	M	D-EF	CHE
Benjamin	Hedgerow			CUR
Bliss	The buckle			CUR
Brewer	The fairy pipers	HML		BOH
Bridge	Love went a-riding	HL		BOS
Butterworth	When I was one and twenty			AUG
Dowland	Come again! sweet love	M	D-E	STB
Elgar	The swimmer			BOO
German	Charming Chloe	HML		NOV
Gibbs	Five eyes	HL	D-D	BOS
Harty	Across the door			NOV
Head	A piper	HL		BOO
Johnston	Because I were shy	L	B-E	CRA
Lehmann	The cuckoo	HH	D-B	BOH
Morley	It was a lover and his lass	HM		DIT
Novello	The little damozel	LHM	C-G	BOO
Purcell	Hark! how all things with one sound rejoice			NOV
-----	Hark! the echoing air (The Fairy Queen)			BAF
-----	Nymphs and shepherds (The Libertine)	HM	C-F	†
-----	There's not a swain on the plain	M	B-G	BAF
Quilter	Blow, blow, thou winter wind	HL	C-E	BOO
-----	O mistress mine	HML		BOO
Ronald	Love, I have won you	HML	EF-EF	ENO
Vaughn Williams	A piper			OXF

French Songs and Arias Employing
Spirited Singing

Mezzo Soprano

Bizet	Habanera (Carmen)	HM	D-F	†
-----	Ouvre ton coeur	MH	DS-GS	†
-----	Seguidilla (Carmen)	HM	B-FS	†
Chabrier	Les cigales	HML		†
-----	Villanelle des petits canards	HML	B-E	†
Chausson	Les papillons	M	C-F	GSC
Debussy	Ballade des femmes de Paris			DUR
-----	Chevaux de bois	H	C-G	†
-----	De grève	HL		†
-----	De soir	HL		†
-----	Fantoches	H	D-A	JOB
-----	Fêtes galantes	LH	CS-A	†
-----	La mer est plus belle	HL		†
-----	Le faune			DUR
-----	Le temps a laissié son manteau			DUR
-----	Mandoline	HM	BF-F	†
-----	Noël des enfants qui n'ont plus de maisons			DUR
Duparc	Le manoir de Rosamunde	HL	B-F	BOS
-----	Testament	HL		INT
Fauré	Mandoline	HL	F-E	†
-----	Noël	LH	EF-AF	GSC
-----	Notre amour	H	DS-B	†
-----	Poème d'un jour			HAM
-----	Toujours	LH	F-AF	MAR
Georges	La pluie	HL		INT
Gluck	Amours, sors pour jamais (Armide)			PET
Gounod	Au printemps	LMH	DF-AF	GSC
-----	Flower song (Faust)			†
-----	Que fais-tu blanche tourterelle? (Romeo et Juliette)			JCH
-----	Vénise	HL		INT
Hahn	Si mes vers avaient des ailes	HLM	B-FS	†
Honegger	Les cloches			SEN
Koechlin	La lune	M	C-F	ROU
Milhaud	La tourterelle	M	B-G	DUR
Pierné	Ils étaient trois petits chats blancs			MAR
-----	Le moulin	ML	C-E	BOS

Poldowski	Colombine	H	D-GF	CHE
-----	Dansons la gigue	M	EF-G	MAR
Poulenc	Air vif	H	C-AF	ROU
Ravel	Chanson espagnole	LH	D-BF	DUR
-----	Manteau de fleurs	H		INT
-----	Nicolette	L	B-FS	ELK
-----	Quel galant!	M	D-F	DUR
-----	Tout gai	MH	EF-F	DUR
Saint-Saëns	L'attente			DUR
-----	Tournoiement			DUR
Severac	Chanson pour le petit cheval			ROU
Thomas	Je connais un pauvre enfant (Mignon)	H	C-B	GSC

German Songs and Arias Employing
Spirited Singing

Mezzo Soprano

Bach, J.S.	Mein glaebiges Herze (Cantata 68)	HML		†
-----	Patron, das macht der Wind (Phoebus and Pan)	M	C-G	GSC
Beethoven	An die Geliebte	M	E-E	†
-----	Busslied			†
-----	Die Trommel geruehret			†
-----	Mignon (Kennst du das Land)	M	E-FS	AUG
Brahms	Alte Liebe	HL	C-F	†
-----	Bei dir sind meine Gedanken	MH	E-FS	†
-----	Blinde Kuh			†
-----	Botschaft	HL	D-F	†
-----	Das Maedchen spricht	H	E-FS	†
-----	Der Gang zur Liebsten	HL		†
-----	Der Jaeger	HL		†
-----	Der Schmied	HL	EF-EF	†
-----	Dort in den Weiden	LH	A-A	†
-----	Klage	LH	FS-FS	†
-----	Meine Liebe ist gruen	MLH	ES-A	†
-----	O komm holde Sommernacht			†
-----	O liebliche Wangen	MLH	E-G	†
-----	Salome			†
-----	Sehnsucht	H	EF-AF	GSC
-----	Tambourliedchen			†
-----	Vergebliches Staendchen	LHM	E-FS	†
-----	Wie froh und frisch	HL	B-E	†

Franz	Er ist gekommen	HL	EF-F	†
-----	Sonnenuntergang	HL	CS-FS	†
Hassler	Gagliarda			SIM
Haydn	The mermaid's song	M	C-F	PRE
Jensen	Am Ufer des Flusses des Manzanares	H	D-FS	GSC
Loewe	Walpurgisnacht	H	G-G	SC
Mahler	Das Irdische Leben	HL	A-F	INT
-----	Ging heut Morgen uebers Feld	M	A-FS	INT
-----	Hans und Grethe	HL		INT
-----	Ich hab' ein gluehend Messer	M	BF-GF	WEI
-----	Lieder eines fahrenden Gesellen	M		INT
-----	Rheinlegendchen	M	B-FS	†
-----	Wer hat dies Liedlein erdacht?	HL	BF-E	INT
Marx	Der bescheidene Schaefer			UNI
Mendelssohn	An die Entfernte	M	F-F	
-----	Neue Liebe	H	CS-A	†
-----	Suleika	H	E-GS	†
Schubert	Am Feierabend	HL	BF-F	†
-----	Aufenthalt	HLM	A-F	†
-----	Die Forelle	MLH	EF-GF	†
-----	Die Post	HML	BF-EF	GSC
-----	Ellens zweiter Gesang			PET
-----	Erstarrung	HL	D-F	†
-----	Fischerweise	L	C-D	†
-----	Heidenroeslein			
-----	Mut	HL		†
-----	Rastlose Liebe	M	B-F	†
-----	Suleika I	LH	DS-G	†
-----	Suleika II	LH	F-BF	†
-----	Wohin?	HL	B-E	†
Schumann	Er, der Herrlichste von Allen	HL	A-EF	†
-----	Er ist's	HL	BF-EF	†
-----	Fruehlingsnacht	L	CS-E	†
-----	Im Walde	HL	A-D	†
-----	Schoene Wiege meiner Leiden	HL	C-EF	†
-----	Waldesgespraech	HL	A-FS	†
-----	Widmung	HL	BF-F	†
Strauss	Caecilie	MH	E-B	†
-----	Fuer fuenfzehn Pfennige			†
-----	Heimliche Aufforderung	HL	B-E	†
Wagner	Stehe still!	HL		†

Weber	Bethoerte, die an meine Liebe glaubt (Euryanthe)			PET
Wolf	Ach, im Maien	HL	C-E	†
-----	Auf dem gruenen Balkon	HL		†
-----	Auf einer Wanderung	HL		DIT
-----	Das Koehlerweib ist trunken			PET
-----	Die ihr schwebet	HL	EF-EF	†
-----	Die Zigeunerin			†
-----	Er ist's	H	D-G	†
-----	Erstes Liebeslied eines Maedchens	H	EF-AF	†
-----	Fussreise	HL	D-E	†
-----	Geh' Geliebter, geh' jetzt			PET
-----	Ich hab' in Penna	LH		†
-----	Klinge, klinge, mein Pandero	HL	CF-EF	†
-----	Liebe mir in Busen zuendet	M	E-F	†
-----	Lied vom Winde			†
-----	Nimmersatte Liebe	LH	CF-AF	†

Italian Songs and Arias Employing Spirited Singing

Mezzo Soprano

Carissimi	Vittoria, mio core	HLM	B-E	†
Castelnuovo-Tedesco	Recuerdo			
Cavalli	Donzelle fuggite	HL	C-EF	†
Cimara	Canto di primavera		D-G	FRL
Donaudy	Spirate pur, spirate			RIC
Donizetti	Il segreto per esser felici (Lucrezia Borgia)	M	C-G	†
Durante	Danza, danza fanciulla gentile	HM	BF-F	†
Falconieri	Non più d'amore	HL	C-D	DIT
-----	Nudo arciero	HL	AF-AF	DIT
Handel	Amor commanda (Floridante)	H		†
-----	Ch'io mai vi possa (Siroe)			†
-----	Furibondo spira (Partenope)			KIS
-----	Piangero la sorte mia (Julius Caesar)			CFI
-----	Qual farfalletta (Partenope)	H	E-A	†
Legrenzi	Che fiero costume	HML	C-D	†
Leoncavallo	Da quell suon soavemento (La Boheme)			SON
Mozart	Non so più cosa son	H	EF-G	†

	(Le Nozze di Figaro)			
(Mozart)	Voi che sapete	M	C-F	†
	(Le Nozze di Figaro)			
Paisiello	Chi vuol la zingarella	L	C-F	GSC
Paradies	M'ha preso alla sua ragna	M	EF-F	GSC
Pergolesi	Confusa, smarrita			GSC
Piccini	Se il ciel mi divide	M	C-F	†
	(Alessandro di Indie)			
Ponchielli	Stella del marinar	M	B-A	RIC
	(La Gioconda)			
Respighi	In alto mare			BON
-----	Invito alla danza			BON
-----	Pioggia			BON
-----	Scherzo			BON
Rontani	Or ch'io non segno più	HL	CS-E	DIT
Rossi	Ah, rendimi (Mitrane)	L	GS-FS	GSC
Rossini	Bel raggio lusinghier	H	CS-A	GSC
	(Semiramide)			
-----	Una voce poco fa (Il	HM	GS-E	GSC
	Barbiere di Siviglia)			
Scarlatti, A.	Se Florindo è fedele	LM	EF-EF	GSC
Scarlatti, D.	Consolati e spara amante	L	BF-E	GSC
-----	Qual farfalletta			

Miscellaneous Songs Employing
Spirited Singing

Mezzo Soprano

Alnaes	Nu brister i alle de kløfter	L	A-F	HAN
Dvořák	I will sing new songs of gladness	HL		†
-----	Sing ye a joyful song			AMP
-----	Tune thy fiddle gypsy			SIM
Falla	El paño moruno	HL		AMP
-----	Seguidilla murciana	HL		AMP
-----	Siete canciones	HL		AMP
Granados	El majo discreto	H		INT
Grieg	Good morning			†
-----	Jeg lever et liv i laengsel	L	BF-E	HAN
-----	My Johann	HL	BF-EF	GSC
-----	På Hamars ruiner	M	BF-G	HAN
-----	7 children's songs			HAN
-----	Til min dreng		C-E	
-----	Turisten	M	CS-F	HAN
-----	Vaer hilset, I damer	M	D-F	HAN
Mussorgsky	Hopak	HM	CS-FS	GSC

(Mussorgsky)	In the corner			INT
Rachmaninoff	Floods of spring	HL		DIT
-----	Oh, no, I pray do not depart	H		DIT
Stravinsky	The cloister (La novice)			DIT
Tchaikovsky	At the ball	MH		GSC
Turina	Farruca	M	A-F	UME

Songs and Arias Employing Staccato

Mezzo Soprano

Arne, T.	Where the bee sucks	HM		†
Delibes	Passepied	LH	DS-CS	GSC
Fourdrain	Carnaval	M	C-F	RIC
Haydn	My mother bids me bind my hair	M	E-E	†
Rossini	Non più mesta (La Cenerentola)	M	A-B	GSC
Scarlatti, A.	Rugiadose odorose (Il Pirro e Demetrio)	HL	D-E	DIT
Schubert	Der Juengling an der Quelle	LH	E-A	
Weckerlin	Maman, dites-moi	M	E-FS	BOO

American and British Songs of Popular Appeal

Mezzo Soprano

Bassett	Take joy home	LH	EF-BF	GSC
Beach	Ah, love but a day			ASC
Besley	The second minuet	HL		BOO
Bliss	The buckle			CUR
Brahe	Bless this house	HML	A-EF	BOO
Cadman	From the land of the sky-blue water			WHI
Campbell-Tipton	A spirit flower	LHM	B-G	GSC
Charles	When I have sung my songs	HM	BF-EF	GSC
Clarke	Shy one	HL	BF-G	BOH
Curran	Ho! Mr. Piper	LH	D-G	GSC
Del Riego	Homing	HML	BF-E	CHA
D'Hardelot	My message			
Diack	Little Jack Horner			CFI
-----	Little Polly Flinders			CFI

Dougherty	Everyone sang			
-----	Love in the dictionary	M	C-G	GSC
Duke	I can't be talkin' of love	H	CS-G	GSC
Edwards	By the bend of the river	HML	C-E	GSC
-----	Into the night	HML	C-DF	GSC
Enders	Russian picnic	HM	C-G	GSC
Fox	The hills of home	HML	BF-DF	CFI
Friml	L'amour, toujours l'amour			HAR
Gade	Jalousie			HAR
German	Who'll buy my lavender	HML		BOO
Giannini	Sing to my heart a song	H	D-B	ELV
Goulding	The lovely song my heart is singing	ML	A-D	GSC
Griffes	We'll to the woods and gather May	M	D-F	GSC
Grisell and Young	The cuckoo clock	LH	EF-G	GSC
Guion	Mam'selle Marie	M	D-E	GSC
Hely-Hutchinson	Old mother Hubbard	HL	B-E	CFI
Henschel	Morning-hymn	MH	DS-GS	†
Kountz	Prayer of the Norwegian child	ML	C-C	GSC
-----	The little French clock	LH	D-G	GAL
LaForge	Song of the open	MH	EF-AF	DIT
-----	To a messenger	HLM	CF-G	GSC
Lehmann	The cuckoo	HH	D-B	BOH
Levitzki	Ah, thou beloved one	H	EF-AF	GSC
Manning	In the Luxembourg gardens	HML	BF-D	GSC
-----	Shoes	M	EF-F	GSC
Murray	I'll walk beside you			CHA
Novello	The little damozel	LHM	C-G	BOO
Quilter	Drink to me only	LMH	GF-GF	BOH
Rasbach	Trees	LMH	CS-GS	GSC
Rich	American lullaby	LH	C-F	GSC
Rodgers	Lover			FAM
Rogers	At parting	LH	CS-FS	GSC
Ronald	Love, I have won you	HML	EF-EF	ENO
Schuman	Holiday song	M	C-F	GSC
Scott	Think on me	HML	D-EF	GAL
Silberta	Aylia, dancer of Kashmir	M	B-F	GSC
Speaks	In May time	HL	D-E	JCH
-----	Morning	HML	BF-D	GSC
Spross	Will o' the wisp			JCH
Strelezki	Dreams	LMH	B-A	GSC
Tyson	Noon and night	LH	F-AF	GSC
Ware	This day is mine	MH	EF-AF	BOS
Warren	Fulfilment	H	D-BF	GAL

Weatherly	Danny boy	LMH		BOO
Wolf	Jack in the box			
Wood	A brown bird singing	HLM	FS-G	CHA
Woodford-				
Finden	Kashmiri song			BOO
Worth	Midsummer	LM	E-A	GSC

(See also Humorous Songs, Negro Spirituals,
Folk Songs, Operetta Songs and Opera Arias.)

Miscellaneous Songs of Popular Appeal

Mezzo Soprano

Alvarez	La partida	HL	DS-E	GSC
Bach-				
Gounod	Ave Maria			†
Bizet	Agnus Dei	HLM	C-AF	†
-----	Ouvre ton coeur	MH	DS-GS	†
Bohm	Calm as the night	HML	A-EF	†
Cavalli	Donzelle fuggite	HL	C-EF	†
Cimara	Canto di primavera		D-G	FRL
Delibes	Passepied	LH	DS-CS	GSC
Denza	Funiculi, funicula			†
Dvořák	Songs my mother taught me	HM	E-E	†
Franz	Dedication	HML	BF-C	†
Gounod	Au printemps	LMH	DF-AF	GSC
-----	Sérénade	LMH	D-A	GSC
Grieg	A dream			†
-----	I love thee	HML	E-F	†
-----	My Johann	HL	BF-EF	GSC
Hahn	Si mes vers avaient des ailes	HLM	B-FS	†
Lara	Novillero			
Lecuona	Siboney			FEI
Leroux	Le nil Cello or violin	LH	E-A	†
Louiquy	La vie en rose			
Massenet	Elégie	LM	C-GF	GSC
Mendelssohn	On wings of song			†
Pestalozza	Ciribiribin			Dit
Ponce	Estrellita	LH		†
Poulenc	Les chemins de l'amour	M		AMP
Rachmaninoff	To the children	MH	F-G	DIT
Reichardt	In the time of roses			†
Rossini	La danza	MH	E-A	†
Roy	How do I love thee	HM	C-G	GSC
Schubert	An die Musik	HL	A-DS	†

(Schubert)	Ave Maria	LMH	F-F	†
-----	Staendchen			
Schumann	Widmung	HL	BF-F	†
Sieczynski	Vienna, city of my dreams			HAR
Sjoberg	Visions	MH	F-AF	GAL
Tchaikovsky	None but the lonely heart	HLM	C-F	DIT
Tosti	Marechiare	M	D-FS	GSC
Velázquez	Bésame mucho	M	CS-D	SOU

(See also Humorous Songs, Negro Spirituals,
Folk Songs, Operetta Songs and Opera Arias.)

Arias From British Operas

Mezzo Soprano

Handel	Art thou troubled	M	F-F	GSC
	(Rodelinda)			
Purcell	Celia has a thousand charms			
	(The Rival Sisters)			
-----	From rosy bow'rs			AUG
	(Don Quixote)			
-----	Hark! the echoing air			BAF
	(The Fairy Queen)			
-----	I attempt from love's	MH	CS-E	†
	sickness to fly			
	(The Indian Queen)			
-----	Music for a while	LH		SC
	(Oedipus)			
-----	Nymphs and shepherds	HM	C-F	†
	(The Libertine)			
-----	When I am laid in earth	LH	C-G	†
	(Dido and Aeneas)			
Vaughn				
Williams	Greensleeves			OXF
	(Sir John in Love)			

Arias From French Operas

Mezzo Soprano

Bizet	Card scene (Carmen)			
-----	Habanera (Carmen)	HM	D-F	†
-----	Seguidilla (Carmen)	HM	B-FS	†
Campra	Charmant papillon (Les	MH	D-G	GSC
	Fêtes Venitiennes)			

David	Charmant oiseau (La Perle du Brésil)	M	D-E	†
Debussy	Voici ce qu'il ecrit (Pelléas et Mélisande)			BRO
Gluck	Amours, sors pour jamais (Armide)			PET
-----	Divinités du Styx (Alceste)	MH	DF-AF	†
Godard	Cachés dans cet asile (Jocelyn) Violin or cello	MH	DF-F	GSC
Gossec	Dors, mon enfant (Rosine)	L		CHE
Gounod	Flower song (Faust)			†
-----	O ma lyre immortelle (Sappho)	M	C-G	†
-----	Que fais-tu blanche tourterelle? (Romeo and Juliette)			JCH
-----	Si le bonheur (Faust)			†
Grétry	La danse n'est pas ce que j'aime (Richard Coeur-de-Lion)			JOB
Halévy	Humble fille des champs (Charles VI)			GSC
Lully	Air de Persée (Persée)			
-----	Ariette de Cloris (Divertissement de Chambord)			
-----	Bois épais (Amadis)	ML	C-EF	†
-----	Fermez-vous pour jamais (Amadis)			LEM
Massenet	Il est doux, il est bon (Hérodiade)	MH	EF-BF	GSC
-----	Ne me refuse pas (Hérodiade)			HEU
-----	Va laisse, les couler (Werther)			
-----	Werther! qui m'aurait dit (Air de lettres) (Werther)			
Meyerbeer	Ah! mon fils (Le Prophète)	M	B-AS	B †
-----	Nobles Seigneurs, salut! (Les Huguenots)	LH	C-C	†
-----	O prêtres de Baal (Le Prophete)			BRO
Mouret	Doux plaisirs (Pirithous)			CHE
Offenbach	Ah, quel dîner (La Périchole)			
-----	Couplets de l'aveu (La Périchole)			
-----	Mon Dieu, que les hommes sont bêtes (La Périchole)			
-----	O mon cher amant, je te jure (La Périchole)			
Rameau	A l'amour rendez les armes (Hippolyte et Aricie)			CHO

(Rameau)	Air de Vénus (Dardanus)			LEM
-----	Dans ces doux asiles (Castor et Pollux)			LEM
Saint-Saëns	Amour, viens aider (Samson et Dalila)	HM	AF-G	†
-----	Mon coeur s'ouvre à ta voix (Samson et Dalila)	HLM	BF-GF	†
-----	Printemps qui commence (Samson et Dalila)	M	B-E	†
Thomas	Connais-tu le pays? (Mignon)	HML	C-F	†
-----	Je connais un pauvre enfant (Mignon)	H	C-B	†

Arias From German Operas

Mezzo Soprano

Bruch	Penelope's sorrow (Odysseus)		SIM
-----	Einsam wachend in der Nacht (Tristan und Isolde)	FS-FS	PET
Wagner			
-----	Entweihte Goetter! Helft jetzt meiner Rache! (Lohengrin)	FS-AS	GSC
-----	Geliebter, komm', sieh' dort die Grotte (Tannhaeuser)	F-A	PET
-----	Hoere mit Sinn, was ich dir sage (Die Goetterdaemmerung)	G-G	PET
-----	In seiner Bluete bleicht mein Leben (Rienzi)		PET
-----	So ist es denn aus mit den ewigen Goettern (Die Walkuere)	CS-GS	GSC
Weber	Bethoerte! Die an meine Liebe glaubt (Euryanthe)		

Arias From Italian Operas

Mezzo Soprano

Bellini	Scombra è la sacra selva (Norma)			RIC
Cilea	O vagabonda stella d'oriente (Adriana Lecouvreur)			AMP
Donizetti	Il segreto per esser felici (Lucrezia Borgia)	M	C-G	†
-----	O mio Fernando (La Favorita)	M	B-A	†

Giordano	O grandi occhi lucenti (Fedora)			BRO
Gluck	Che farò senza Euridice (Orphée)	ML	BF-F	†
Leoncavallo	Da quel suon soavemento (La Boheme)			
Mascagni	Lacere miseri (L'Amico Fritz)			GSC
-----	O pallida che un giorno (L'Amico Fritz)			
-----	Voi lo sapete (Cavalleria Rusticana)	H	B-A	†
Monteverdi	Lasciatemi morire (Arianna)	ML	D-D	†
-----	Tu se' morta (Orfeo)	M	C-E	GSC
Mozart	Al desio di chi t'adora (Appendix, Nozze di Figaro)			
-----	Deh, se piacer mi vuoi (La Clemenza di Tito)			RIC
-----	Non più di fiori (La Clemenza di Tito)			†
-----	Non so più cosa son (Le Nozze di Figaro)	H	EF-G	GSC
-----	Parto, parto (La Clemenza di Tito) B flat clarinet and piano	H		AMP
-----	Voi che sapete (Le Nozze di Figaro)	M	C-F	†
Pittaluga	Romanza de solita (La Romeria de los Cornudos)			
Ponchielli	Stella del marinar (La Gioconda)	M	B-A	RIC
-----	Voce di donna (La Gioconda)	HM	A-G	GSC
Respighi	Maria Egiziaca-Prelude and aria (Maria Egiziaca)			RIC
Rossini	Bel raggio lusinghier (Semiramide)	H	CS-A	GSC
-----	Cruda sorte, amor tiranno! (L'Italiana in Algeri)			
-----	Non più mesta (La Cenerentola)	M	A-B	GSC
-----	Pensa alla patria (L'Italiana in Algeri)			RIC
-----	Una voce poco fa (Il Barbiere di Siviglia)	HM	GS-E	GSC
Verdi	Aria of Abigail (Nabucco)			RIC
-----	Condotta ell'era in ceppi (Il Trovatore)			GSC

(Verdi)	Giunta all' albergo della Giarettiera (Falstaff)	L	G–G	RIC
-----	O don fatale (Don Carlos)	MH	CF–CF	†
-----	Stride la vampa (Il Trovatore)	M	B–G	GSC

Miscellaneous Opera Arias

Mezzo Soprano

Cadman	Song of the Robin Woman (Shanewis)	MH	CS–GS	MOR
Gershwin	A woman is a sometime thing (Porgy and Bess)			GER
Menotti	Lullaby (The Consul)			GSC
-----	The black swan (The Medium)	M	D–G	GSC
Mussorgsky	Divination by water (Khovantchina)	L	GS–FS	GSC
-----	Martha's song (Khovantchina)	ML		GSC
-----	Song of Khivria (The Fair at Sorotchinsk)			GSC
Rimsky-Korsakov	Song of the shepherd lehl (Snegourotchka)	LM		DIT
Stravinsky	Jacasta's aria (Oedipus Rex)			BOO
Tchaikovsky	Adieu forêts (Jeanne d'Arc)	HM	BF–FS	GSC
-----	It is near to midnight (Pique Dame)			GSC
-----	Pauline's romance (Pique Dame)	M	BF–AF	GSC

Arias From Oratorios and Latin Works

Mezzo Soprano

Bach, J.S.	Agnus Dei (Mass in B Minor) Violin			†
-----	Esurientes implevit bonis (Magnificat in D Major)		.	†
-----	Et exultavit spiritus meus (Magnificat in D)			
-----	It is finished (St. John Passion)	L	B–D	†

(Bach, J.S.)	Prepare thyself, Zion (Christmas Oratorio)			
-----	Qui sedes ad dexteram Patris (Mass in B Minor) Oboe d'amore			†
Bennett	O Lord, thou hast searched (Woman of Samaria)			
Gaul	Thou art the guide (Ten Virgins)			
Handel	Chi sprezzando il somo bene (La Passione)			
-----	Come and trip it (L'Allegro)	M	C-F	†
-----	Father, whose blessing (Ode from St. Cecelia's Day)			
-----	He shall feed His flock (The Messiah)	L	C-D	†
-----	He was despised (The Messiah)	L	B-D	†
-----	In gentle murmurs will I mourn (Jephtha)	L	B-E	†
-----	In the battle, fame pursuing (Deborah)	L	A-D	GSC
-----	Let me wander not unseen (L'Allegro)	M	D-G	†
-----	Lord, to thee each night and day (Theodora)	L	C-E	†
-----	O sleep why dost thou leave me (Semele)	H	DS-GS	†
-----	O thou that tellest good tidings to Zion (The Messiah)	L	A-C	†
-----	Return, O God of hosts (Samson)	L	B-E	GSC
-----	The parent bird in search of food (Susanna)			
-----	The smiling hours a joyful train (Hercules)			
-----	Thou shalt bring them in (Israel in Egypt)	L	B-D	†
-----	Weep no more (Hercules)			†
Hindemith	Sing on there in the swamp (When Lilacs in the Dooryard Bloomed)			
Mendelssohn	But the Lord is mindful of His own (Saint Paul)	L	A-D	†
-----	I will sing of Thy great mercies (Saint Paul)	H	E-F	†

(Mendelssohn)	O rest in the Lord (Elijah)	L	B-D	†
-----	Woe unto them who forsake him (Elijah)	L	B-E	†
Mozart	Laudamus Te (C Minor Mass)			PET
Parker	Gens duce splendida (Hora Novissima)			NOV
Rossini	Fac ut portem (Stabat Mater)	L	B-G	DIT
Saint-Saëns	Expectans Dominum (Christmas Oratorio)			GSC
-----	Patiently (Christmas Oratorio)			
Sullivan	Love not the world (The Prodigal Son)	L		GSC
Verdi	Liber scriptus (The Requiem)			GSC

Cantata Arias

Mezzo Soprano

Bach, J.S.	Christi Glieder, ach bedenket (Cantata 132) Violin			
-----	Gelobet sei der Herr (Cantata 129) Oboe d'amore			AUG
-----	Jesu lass Dich finden (Cantata 154)			
-----	Jesus macht mich geistlich reich (Cantata 75) Violin			
-----	Jesus schlaeft (Cantata 81)	L	A-D	GSC
-----	Mein glaeubiges Herze (Cantata 68)	HML		†
-----	Oh, yes, just so (Phoebus and Pan)			NOV
-----	Patron, das macht der Wind (Phoebus and Pan)	M	C-G	GSC
-----	Sheep may safely graze (Cantata 208) 2 Flutes and continuo	LM	EF-GF	GAL
Debussy	Air de Lia (L'Enfant Prodigue)	H	E-A	DUR
Gaul	Eye hath not seen (The Holy City)	ML	B-D	GSC
Gretchaninov	Credo from Liturgica Domestica			BOO

Handel	Have mercy, Lord (Te Deum)	HM		†
Mussorgsky	Oriental chant (Josua Navine Cantata)	ML	BF-E	GSC
Prokofieff	Song after the battle (Alexander Nevsky)	M		AMP
Tchaikovsky	Prayer (Moscow Cantata)	M	A-GF	GAL

Operetta, Musical Comedy
or Show Songs

Mezzo Soprano

Arlen	Right as the rain (Bloomer Girl)			CHA
Berlin	It's a lovely day tomorrow (Louisiana Purchase)			BER
Bowers	Chinese lullaby (East is West)			FFI
Brown	Temptation (Going Hollywood)			ROB
Coward	I'll see you again (Bitter Sweet)	M	C-F	HAR
-----	Zigeuner (Bitter Sweet)	H	CF-G	HAR
De Koven	Oh promise me (Robin Hood)	HML	C-D	†
Forrest- Grieg	Strange music (Song of Norway)			CHA
Friml	Give me one hour (The White Eagle)			MRT
Gershwin	The man I love (Strick Up the Band)			BRO
Herbert	A kiss in the dark (Orange Blossoms)			WIT
-----	Ah! sweet mystery of life (Naughty Marietta)	LMH	A-A	WIT
-----	I can't do that sum (Babes in Toyland)			WIT
-----	I'm falling in love with someone (Naughty Marietta)			WIT
-----	If only you were mine (The Singing Girl)			WIT
-----	Kiss me again (Mlle. Modiste)	LHM	CS-A	WIT
-----	Moonbeams (The Red Mill)			WIT
-----	'Neath the southern moon (Naughty Marietta)			

(Herbert)	Rose of the world (The Rose of Algeria)			WIT
-----	Sweetheart waltz (Sweethearts)			GSC
-----	Tell it all over again (The Only Girl)			WIT
-----	Thine alone (Eileen)			WIT
Kern	Can't help lovin' dat man (Show Boat)	L	BF-EF	HAR
-----	Look for the silver lining (Sally)			CHA
-----	Smoke gets in your eyes (Roberta)			HAR
-----	The night was made for love (The Cat and the Fiddle)	M	C-F	HAR
-----	The song is you (Music in the Air)	M	C-F	HAR
-----	The touch of your hand (Roberta)			CHA
-----	They didn't believe me (Girl from Utah)			HAR
-----	Yesterdays (Roberta)			CHA
Lehar	Meine Lippen, sie kuessen so heiss (Giuditta)			GLO
-----	My little nest of heavenly blue (Frasquita)	HML		MAR
-----	Vilia (The Merry Widow)			CHA
Milloecker	I give my heart (Mme. Dubarry)			CHA
Porter	Ev'rything I love (Let's Face It)			CHA
-----	Begin the Beguine (Jubilee)	L	BF-F	HAR
-----	I love you (Mexican Hayride)			CHA
-----	In the still of the night (Rosalie)			CHA
-----	I've got you under my skin (Born to Dance)			CHA
-----	Night and Day (Gay Divorcee)	M	BF-EF	HAR
-----	What is this thing called love? (Wake Up and Dream)			HAR
Rodgers	Bali ha'i (South Pacific)			CHA
-----	Fallin in love with love (The Boys from Syracuse)			WIL
-----	It might as well be spring (State Fair)			CHA
-----	My heart stood still (Connecticut Yankee)			HAR

(Rodgers)	People will say we're in love (Oklahoma)			CHA
-----	What's the use of wond'rin'? (Carousel)			WIL
-----	Where or when? (Babes in Arms)			CHA
Romberg	Lover come back to me (New Moon)	H	D-G	HAR
-----	Mother (My Maryland)			HAR
-----	When I grow too old to dream (The Night is Young)	HLM	C-G	ROB
Schwarz	Dancing in the dark (The Band Wagon)			HAR
-----	You and the night and the music (Revenge with Music)			HAR
Tierney	Alice Blue Gown (Irene)			FEI
Weill	September song (Knickerbocker Holiday)			CHA
Youmans	Through the years (Through the Years)	HML	A-F	MLR
-----	Time on my hands you in my arms (Smiles)	M	C-E	MLR
-----	You're everywhere (Through the Years)			MLR

Song Cycles (Or Groups of Songs)

Mezzo Soprano

Bantock	Muse of the golden throne			
-----	Sappho			
Bax	Celtic song cycle	MH	BF-A	CHE
Beethoven	Sechs geistliche Lieder			
Berger	Four sonnets Piano or string quartet	M	A-G	GSC
Berlioz	Les nuits d'été			AUG
Bernstein	I hate music	H	C-A	WIT
-----	La bonne cuisine	H	B-B	GSC
Bloch	Poèmes d'automne	M	B-G	GSC
Brahms	Five songs of Ophelia	HL	B-EF	†
-----	Two songs for alto, viola and piano	L		AMP
Caplet	Les prieres			DUR
Carpenter	Gitanjali	M	B-G	GSC
-----	Watercolors	M	C-F	GSC
Chanler	The children (9 songs)	M	C-G	GSC
Chausson	Poème de l'amour et de la mer	H		INT

395

Cornelius	Bridal songs			INT
-----	Six Christmas songs	HL		BOS
Crist	Chinese mother goose rhymes	H	C-G	CFI
-----	Coloured stars	HM		CFI
Debussy	Chansons de Bilitis	M	C-FS	†
-----	Fêtes galantes	LH	CS-A	†
-----	Proses lyriques	HL		JOB
Dvořák	Biblical songs	HL		AMP
Elgar	Sea pictures	L	A-A	BOO
Falla	El amor brujo	M		BRO
Fauré	Le jardin clos	M	C-E	DUR
-----	Poème d'un jour			HAM
Granados	La maja dolorosa	M		INT
Grieg	Digte af Vilhelm Krag			HAN
-----	Elegiske digte af John Paulsen			HAN
-----	Haugtussa	M	B-GF	PET
-----	7 children's songs			HAN
Hindemith	Das Marienleben	H		AMP
Holst	Four songs for voice and violin	M	C-G	CHE
Honegger	Quatre chansons pour voix grave			SAL
-----	Trois chansons String quartet and flute			SEN
Kabelevsky	Seven merry songs			
Kilpinen	Lieder um den Tod	M		AMP
Mahler	Kindertotenlieder	L	G-GF	INT
-----	Lieder eines fahrenden Gesellen	M		INT
Milhaud	Trois poèmes de Jean Cocteau			SIR
Mussorgsky	Songs and dances of death			INT
-----	Sunless			CHE
-----	The nursery	M	C-G	INT
Poulenc	Chansons villageoises	M	C-G	ESC
-----	Cinq poèmes de Ronsard			HEU
-----	Le bestiaire	M		AMP
-----	Tel jour, telle nuit	M	B-A	DUR
Ravel	Chansons madécasses Flute, cello and piano			DUR
-----	Cinq mélodies populaires grecques			CUR
-----	Quatre chants populaires	M		DUR
-----	Shéhérazade	M	CS-G	DUR
-----	Trois poèmes de Mallarmé 2 flutes, 2 clarinets, 4 strings and piano	M	BF-G	DUR

396

Schumann	Der arme Peter	HL	B-G	†
-----	Frauenliebe und Leben	HL		†
-----	Lieder der Braut	H	D-A	†
Slonimsky	Gravestones at Hancock, New Hampshire	H	D-G	AXE
Still	Songs of separation			LEE
Stravinsky	Trois histoires pour enfants			CHE
Villa-Lobos	Serestas			
Wagner	Five Wesendonck songs			GSC
Woodford-Finden	Indian love lyrics			BOO

Solo Cantatas

Mezzo Soprano

Pergolesi	Salve Regina			
Stradella	Se amor m'annoda	L	BF-F	

(See Solo Cantatas of Pergolesi, Handel and
Scarlatti, Kirchenkantaten of Buxtehude and
Symphoniae Sacrae of Schuetz.)

Conçert Aria

Mezzo Soprano

Mozart	Ch'io mi scordi di te			BOO

Christmas Songs

Mezzo Soprano

Adam	O Holy night			†
Andrews	I heard the bells on Christmas day	L	A-E	GAL
Bach, J.S.	Prepare thyself, Zion (Christmas Oratorio)			
-----	Schlafe mein Liebster (Christmas Oratorio)			
Bacon	Ancient Christmas carol			NEM
Baldwin	Little Lordeen	L	BF-EF	WIT
Bax	A Christmas carol	H	DF-A	CHE
Berlin	White Christmas (Holiday Inn)			BER

Brahms	Geistliches Wiegenlied Piano and viola			†
Branscombe	Hail ye time of holidays			
Bush	I saw a maiden fair	L	C-DF	GRA
Candlyn	The song of Mary	M	B-D	GRA
Carr	As on the night	M	E-FS	GSC
Chaminade	Christmas carol of the birds	MH	D-A	GSC
De Koven	The white Christ	L	C-D	GSC
Dickinson	Joseph, tender Joseph	M		GRA
Dunhill	To the Queen of Heaven	M	C-G	GSC
Elmore and Reed	Come all ye who weary	L	C-C	JFI
Evans	The Virgin had a baby	L	C-EF	BOH
Fauré	Noël	LH	EF-AF	GSC
France	A Christmas lullaby	M	DS-F	GAL
Grieg	Christmas song			AUG
-----	Jule Sne	M	C-G	HAN
-----	Julens Vuggesang			
Handel	O thou that tellest good tidings to Zion (The Messiah)	L	A-C	†
Harker	A child is born in Bethlehem	LH	D-G	GSC
-----	There's a song in the air	HL	BF-D	GSC
Harris	The feast of Christmas	M	C-F	OXF
Head	Slumber song of the Madonna	HL		BOO
-----	The little road to Bethlehem	MH	EF-AF	BOO
-----	The robin's carol	H	C-AF	BOH
-----	The three mummers			BOO
Herbert	Toyland (Babes in Toyland)			WIT
Holmes	Noël d'Irlande	HL		DIT
Ireland	The Holy boy	MH	D-G	BOO
Ives	A Christmas carol			NEM
Jewell	The vision of the shepherds	HL	A-D	ASC
Lehmann	No candle was there and no fire	MH	EF-G	CHA
Lynn	Gently little Jesus	L	BF-BF	DIT
-----	The magic night of Christmas	M	D-D	DIT
MacGimsey	A new Christmas morning hallelujah	M	DF-F	CFI
Martin	The Holy Child	HML	G-G	ENO
Matthews	Voices of the sky	HL	BF-D	GSC
McKinney	The Holy Mother sings	MH	AF-AF	JFI

Murphy	O little town of Bethlehem	M	D-F	SUM
Neidlinger	The birthday of a king	LMH	C-F	GSC
-----	The manger cradle	L	EF-F	GSC
Niles	Our lovely Lady singing	M	EF-F	GSC
-----	The cherry tree			GSC
Nin	Jesus de Nazareth			ESC
Prokoff	Christmas cradle song	LM	D-E	CHA
Ravel	Noël des jouets	M	BS-FS	MAT
Reger	The Virgin's slumber song	MMH	G-G	†
Reimann	Joseph tender Joseph mine	M	F-F	GRA
Rodney	A dream of Bethlehem	MML	G-DF	ENO
Russell	Child Redeemer	HL		GAL
Sadero	Fa la nana, bambin			RIC
Saint-Saëns	Expectans Dominum (Christmas Oratorio)			GSC
Schubert	Ave Maria	LMH	F-F	†
-----	They sang that night in Bethlehem	LMH	EF-EF	GSC
Taylor	Christmas folk song	L	BF-EF	GRA
Thiman	I saw three ships	L		NOV
-----	In the bleak midwinter	L	A-E	NOV
Thorp	Come, Mary take courage	M	DS-FS	GAL
Trunk	The Christ child in the manger	HM		AMP
Warlock	The first mercy	M	F-F	BOO
Warren	Christmas candle	HML	D-E	GSC
Wentzel	Lamkins Cello and piano			GRA
West	It came upon a midnight	MM	E-FS	SUM
Wild	The Christ child	M	EF-EF	CFI
Wolf	Schlafendes Jesuskind	HL	AS-F	†
Wright	A Babe lies in His cradle warm	MD	D-D	GSC
Yon	Gesu Bambino	HL	B-E	JFI

Easter Songs

Mezzo Soprano

Bach, J.S.	Hochgelobter Gottessohn (Cantata 6) English horn or viola or violin			NOV
-----	Jesus from the grave is risen	M	F-EF	CFI
Bantock	Easter hymn	M	FS-F	CHE
Barnes	Easter	HM	D-EF	GSC
Chaffin	Easter message	MH	D-G	FLA
Curran	Crucifixion			
Davis	Christ is risen today	M		GAL

Dennee	Easter song	HM	B-F	ASC
Diack	All in the April evening	LMH	D-G	BOO
Granier	Hosanna	HH	F-BF	DIT
Gretchaninoff	The Christ is risen			
Guion	At the cry of the first bird	H	D-G	GSC
Hageman	Christ went up into the hills	LH	EF-AF	CFI
Huhn	Christ is risen	HM	C-E	ASC
Kountz	Palm Sunday	HL		GAL
La Forge	Before the Crucifix	HML	BF-EF	GSC
MacFarlane	On wings of living light	MH	D-G	GSC
O'Hara	There is no death	LMH	EF-AF	CHA
Rachmaninoff	Christ is risen	LM	D-F	GAL
Rorem	The resurrection			
Scott	Angels roll the rock away	MH	E-G	HUN
-----	The first Easter morn	LH	F-G	GSC
Tchaikovsky	A legend	M	D-E	GSC
Turner	Hail your risen Lord	HL	C-D	GSC
Wolf	Herr, was traegt der Boden	HL	B-DS	†
Yon	Christ triumphant	MH	E-A	JFI
-----	O faithful Cross	HM	C-EF	JFI
-----	Our Paschal joy	LH	AF-AF	JFI

Patriotic Songs

Mezzo Soprano

Bone and Fenton	Prayer for a waiting world	L		CFI
Bowles	An American hero	M	E-E	AXE
Cadman	Glory	H	EF-G	GAL
Chadwick	He maketh wars to cease	ML		ASC
Dungan	Eternal life	HL		PRE
Foster, F.	The Americans come	MH	F-BF	JFI
Lester	Greater love hath no man	LH	B-E	CFI
O'Hara	There is no death	LMH	EF-AF	CHA
Steffe	Battle hymn of the Republic			
Ward-Stephens	Phantom legions	MHH	EF-BF	CHA

Sacred Songs

Mezzo Soprano

Bach, J.S.	Come, Christians, greet this day	L	BF-F	CFI

400

(Bach, J.S.)	Draw near to me	HML		GSC
Beethoven	The worship of God in nature			
Bitgood	Be still and know that I am God	ML		GRA
-----	The greatest of these is love	M		GRA
Bizet	O Lord be merciful	HL		GSC
Bone and Fenton	First Psalm	LM	DF-F	CFI
-----	Thy word is a lamp	LH	C-F	ROW
Brown	The twenty third Psalm	LH	E-G	GRA
Browning	For I am persuaded	LM	DF-G	CFI
-----	The beatitudes	HM	C-F	CFI
Buck	Fear not ye, O Israel	HLM		GSC
Campbell-Tipton	I will give thanks unto the Lord	LMH	DF-AF	GSC
Candlyn	God that madest earth and heaven	M	C-F	GRA
Chadwick	A ballad of trees and the Master	HML	A-F	DIT
Charles	Incline Thine ear	HL	BF-D	GSC
Clokey	God is in everything	LH	D-G	JFI
Davis	Be ye kind, one to another	L		GAL
-----	Let not your heart be troubled	HML		WOO
-----	Trust in the Lord	MH	CS-G	GAL
Dickinson	Roads	L		GRA
Dvořák	God is my shepherd			AMP
-----	Hear my prayer, O Lord			AMP
-----	Sing ye a joyful song			AMP
-----	Turn Thee to me			AMP
Edmunds	Praise we the Lord	HL	D-D	ROW
Goodhall	The mountain	M	D-E	GAL
Gounod	O Divine Redeemer	LMH	C-G	GSC
Guion	Prayer	HL		GSC
-----	The cross bearer	HM	B-DS	GSC
Hamblen	Trust in Him	LH	D-G	GSC
Handel	Thanks be to Thee	M	CS-E	†
Harker	How beautiful upon the mountains	MLH	EF-G	GSC
Henschel	Morning-hymn	MH	DS-GS	†
Hinchliffe	Tranquillity	M	E-F	CFI
Holst	The heart worships	ML	BF-D	STB
Kountz	What shall I ask?	L		GAL
La Forge	They that trust in the Lord	HL	BF-EF	GAL

401

Lederer	Psalm 104	L	A-E	CFI
Liddle	How lovely are Thy dwellings	HML		BOS
MacDermid	In my Father's house are many mansions	HML		FRS
MacGimsey	Think on these things	LM	BF-EF	CFI
Malotte	The beatitudes	LH	E-G	GSC
-----	The Lord's prayer			
-----	The twenty-third Psalm	HLM	C-F	GSC
McFeeters	A Psalm of praise	M		CFI
Mendelssohn	But the Lord is mindful of His own (Saint Paul)	L	A-D	†
-----	I will sing of Thy great mercies (Saint Paul)	H	E-F	†
-----	O rest in the Lord (Elijah)	L	B-D	†
-----	Woe unto them who forsake him (Elijah)	L	B-E	†
Noble	Souls of the righteous	M		GRA
O'Connor-Morris	Fill thou my life, O Lord	L	BF-EF	CFI
Rorem	Song of David	M		AMP
Sanderson	Green pastures	HL	BF-EF	BOO
Schubert	The Omnipotent			
-----	To the Infinite			
Scott	Come ye blessed	LMH	EF-AF	GSC
-----	Ride on, ride on	HML		FLA
Speaks	The Lord is my light	HML		GSC
-----	Thou wilt keep him in perfect peace	HML		GSC
Stevenson	I sought the Lord	HL	D-F	DIT
-----	Praise	M	F-F	CFI
Stickles	Saith the Lord	LH	D-F	CHA
Sullivan	Love not the world (The Prodigal Son)	L		GSC
Tchaikovsky	Lord, Almighty God (Moscow Cantata)	M		GRA
Thiman	My Master hath a garden	HL		NOV
Thompson	My Master hath a garden	M		ECS
Voris	Song of mothers	LH	D-FS	GRA
Watts	Intreat me not to leave thee	L	A-F	GSC
Weaver	Build thee more stately mansions	M	C-E	GAL
Wilder	Psalm 137			
Wolf	Morning prayer (Morgenstimme)			
-----	Prayer (Gebet)			

Wedding Songs

Mezzo Soprano

Barnby	O perfect love	M	C-G	DIT
Beethoven	Ich liebe dich	HL	BF-DF	†
Bond	I love you truly			BOS
Clough- Leighter	Possession	MH	DF-AF	GSC
Cornelius	Bridal songs			INT
De Koven	Oh promise me (Robin Hood)	HML	C-D	†
Grieg	I love Thee	HML	E-F	†
La Forge	How much I love you	HM	DF-F	GSC
Lippe	How do I love you?			BOS
Manney	Consecration	MHH	E-A	DIT
Marx	Hat dich die Liebe beruehrt	MH	EF-BF	AMP
Ronald	Love, I have won you	HML	EF-EF	ENO
Rowley	Here at thine altar, Lord			NOV
Roy	How do I love thee	HM	C-G	GSC
Sacco	With this ring	M	F-F	BVC
Schubert	Du bist die Ruh	LMH	EF-AF	†
-----	Ungeduld	HML		†
Schumann	Du Ring an meinem Finger	MHL	C-F	†
-----	Widmung	HL	BF-F	†
Sowerby	O perfect love	MH	BF-F	†
Strauss	Seitdem dein Aug' in meines Schaute			SC
Thiman	The God of love my . Shepherd is	ML	A-D	NOV
Willan	O perfect love	HM	E-FS	GRA
Youmans	Through the Years (Through the Years)	HML	A-F	MLR

Songs and Arias With Added
Accompanying Instrument

Mezzo Soprano

Bach, J.S.	Christi Glieder ach bedenket (Cantata 132) Violin	
-----	Gelobet sei der Herr (Cantata 129) Oboe d'amore	AUG
-----	Hochgelobter Gottessohn (Cantata 6) English horn or viola or violin	NOV

(Bach, J.S.)	Jesus macht mich geistlich reich (Cantata 75) Violin	M	BF-F	GSC
Barber	Dover Beach String quartet			†
Brahms	Geistliches Wiegenlied Piano and viola			†
-----	Gestillte Sehnsucht Viola and piano			
Buxtehude	Singet dem Herrn (Violin)			
Chausson	Chanson perpétuelle String quartet	H	CS-GS	ROU
-----	Le colibri Violin or cello	M	F-GF	BOS
Falla	Psyché String quartet, harp and flute	M		CHE
Godard	Cachés dans cet asile (Jocelyn) Violin or cello	MH	DF-F	GSC
Honegger	Chanson (Ronsard) Flute and string quartet			SEN
Kahn	Es geht ein Wehen durch den Wald Violin, cello and piano			
-----	Mein Herzblut geht in Spruengen Violin, cello and piano			
-----	Waldesnacht, du wunderkuehle Violin, cello and piano			
-----	Wie bin ich nun in kuehler Nacht Violin, cello and piano			
Leroux	Le nil Cello or violin	LH	E-A	†
Mana-Zucca	Rachem Trumpet	HML		CHA
Milford	So sweet love seemed Cello	HL	D-D	GRA
Mozart	Parto, parto (La Clemenza di Tito) B flat clarinet and piano	H		AMP
Rorem Peterkin	Music for voice and strings A curse on a closed gate Voice and viola	M	D-E	OXF
Rorem Villa-Lobos	Music for voice and strings Bachianas Brazileiras, no. 5 8 Celli and bass			AMP
Wentzel	Lamkins Cello and piano			GRA

American Recital Songs

Contralto

Alberti	The gypsy			
Bacon	A clear midnight			NEM
Barber	A nun takes the veil	MH	G-G	GSC
-----	Dover Beach	M	BF-F	GSC
	String quartet			
-----	I hear an army	LH	D-AF	GSC
-----	Nocturne	HM	DS-FS	GSC
-----	Sleep now	MH	EF-AF	GSC
-----	Sure on this shining night	MH	D-G	GSC
Bauer	Swan	M		AMP
-----	The harp			AMP
Beach	Ah, love but a day			ASC
Bellini	My Persian garden	HL	EF-EF	GSC
Bone and				
Fenton	Everything that I can spy	M	E-GF	CFI
Bowles	Once a lady was here	ML	C-EF	GSC
Braine	Dawn awakes	HML	A-D	ASC
Buchhauser	Beyond the stars			
Bucky	Hear the wind whispering			BOO
Campbell				
Tipton	The crying of water	LH	FS-GS	GSC
Carpenter	Don't ceare	M	C-D	GSC
-----	Go, lovely rose	M	DF-EF	GSC
-----	Highway men	M	C-F	GSC
-----	If	M	D-E	GSC
-----	Light, my light	M	C-G	GSC
-----	May the maiden			DIT
-----	Odalisque	M	EF-EF	GSC
-----	On a screen	L	BF-DF	GSC
-----	Serenade	LH	CS-A	GSC
-----	Slumber song	ML	BF-F	GSC
-----	The cock shall crow	M	B-E	GSC
-----	The day is no more	M	GS-DS	GSC
-----	The green river	M	B-E	GSC
-----	The Lawd is smilin'	L	B-E	GSC
	through the do'			
-----	The player queen	M	BF-EF	GSC
-----	The sleep that flits on	M	B-FS	GSC
	baby's eyes			
-----	To a young gentleman	M	C-F	GSC
-----	To one unknown	M	A-DS	GSC
-----	When I bring to you	LM	CS-FS	GSC
	colour'd toys			
Castelnuovo-				
Tedesco	Am Teetisch			

(Castelnuovo-Tedesco)	Apemantus grace			CHE
-----	New York			
Chadwick	The danza	HM		ASC
Chanler	Once upon a time	M	C-G	GSC
Charles	Clouds	HML	C-EF	GSC
-----	The white swan	HL	C-F	GSC
-----	When I have sung my songs	HM.	BF-EF	GSC
Clokey	The storke	M	C-D	JFI
Crist	Nina Bobo	HL		CFI
Dello Joio	Mill doors	M	D-E	CFI
-----	New born	M	C-D	CFI
Dougherty	Love in the dictionary	M	C-G	GSC
-----	Loveliest of trees	HM	C-E	BOH
-----	Pianissimo	M	C-G	GSC
-----	Portrait	HM	BF-G	GSC
-----	Sonatina	M	E-FS	GSC
-----	The bird and the beast			
Duke	Calvary	L	G-F	CFI
-----	Loveliest of trees	L	C-D	GSC
-----	Luke Havergal	M	BF-F	CFI
-----	On a March day	M	B-GF	BOH
-----	Wild swans	H	D-A	MER
Edmunds	Billy boy	ML	BF-EF	ROW
Elwell	Music I heard	M		AMP
-----	Renouncement	M	G-G	GSC
Engel	Sea shell	M	EF-EF	GSC
Fairchild	A memory			BOS
Farwell	These saw visions			GAL
Ferrata	Night and the curtains drawn			JFI
Foote	Tranquillity	HL	BF-E	ASC
Foster, S.C.	Ah, may the red rose live always			GSC
Ganz	A memory	HM	B-D	GSC
Giannini	I did not know	H		ELV
Golde	Calls	HL	BF-EF	GSC
-----	The deeper love			
Griffes	By a lonely forest pathway	HML	A-EF	GSC
-----	Evening song	H	DS-GS	GSC
-----	Night on ways unknown has fallen	L	GS-F	GSC
-----	We'll to the woods and gather May	M	D-F	GSC
Guion	When you go			
-----	Wild geese	M	D-F	CFI
Hadley	My shadow			ASC
Hageman	Do not go, my love	HL	B-EF	GSC
-----	Miranda	HL		GAL

406

(Hageman)	Music I heard with you	MH	E-A	GAL
Harris	Agatha Morley	M	C-D	CFI
-----	Fog	M	D-F	CFI
Hawley	Ah, 'tis a dream	L	G-C	JCH
Helm	Prairie waters by night			
Hindemith	The wildflower's song	MH	E-G	AMP
Horsman	The bird of the wilderness	LMH	DF-BF	GSC
Huhn	O that it were so	HLM	D-E	GSC
Ilgenfritz	As we part			SCH
Ives	Evening			CSC
Kettering	The turtle			
Kingsford	Command	HLM	EF-G	GSC
Kramer	Faltering dusk			DIT
Kurstiner	Invocation to Eros			
La Forge	Hills	HL		RIC
-----	Into the light	HL		RIC
-----	The sand			
Lockwood	O, lady, let the sad tears fall	M		MER
Malotte	One, two, three	M	C-F	GSC
-----	Upstream	M	C-F	GSC
Mana-Zucca	Mirror of my soul			
-----	Rachem Trumpet	HML		CHA
-----	Speak to me			
-----	Today is mine			CNG
Metcalf	At nightfall	HML	C-DF	ASC
Moore	Sigh no more, ladies			BOO
Mopper	Men	M	D-FS	BOS
Naginski	The buckle			
-----	The pasture	M	BF-EF	GSC
Nordoff	Serenade	H	CS-FS	AMP
-----	There shall be more joy	M	CS-FS	AMP
Olmstead	Thy sweet singing	HL	BF-EF	GSC
Parker	The south wind	LH	DF-GF	GAL
Price	Songs to the dark virgin	HL	BF-EF	GSC
Protheroe	Ah, love but a day	LMH	F-AF	GAM
-----	What is there hid in the heart of a rose?	ML		DIT
Rawls	The baloon man	L	A-FS	AMP
-----	Sail forth			
-----	The last song	MLH	E-AF	GSC
-----	Time for making songs	HM	CS-F	DIT
Rummel	Ecstasy	LMH	GF-AF	GSC
Rupp	Sweet nightingale			
Salter	The cry of Rachel	LH	C-AF	GSC
Saminsky	Mary Stuart's farewell to France			
Sargent	Manhattan joy ride	M	D-F	GSC
-----	River road			

(Sargent)	Stopping by woods	M	D-E	GSC
-----	Three a.m.	M	DF-E	GSC
Schuman	Orpheus with his lute	M	C-FS	GSC
Silberta	I met dame fate	L	BF-E	GSC
Spross	Will o' the wisp			JCH
Swanson	Pierrot	L	B-D	WTR
-----	The negro speaks of rivers	M		LEE
Thompson	Velvet shoes	M	C-E	ECS
Thomson	Dirge	M	D-F	GSC
Tureman	A winter sunset	L	BF-E	GSC
Tyson	Noon and night	LH	F-AF	GSC
-----	Sea moods	LH	E-AF	GSC
Warren	Heather	LH	FS-G	GSC
-----	Light the lamps up	HM	C-F	GSC
-----	Through my open window	HL	C-E	GSC
-----	We two	LH	E-A	GSC
Watts	Transformation	ML	AS-DS	GSC
-----	Wild tears	L	A-F	GSC
-----	Wings of night	LH	CS-G	GSC
Wolf	Weather forecast	H	EF-GS	GSC
Zimbalist	O take me to your breathing heart			

British Recital Songs

Contralto

Arne, T.	Come away death	M	C-AF	AUG
-----	Where the bee sucks	HM		†
-----	Why so pale and wan?			GSC
Bantock	Lament of Isis	L		AMP
-----	Silent strings	MH	F-G	BOO
Bax	I heard a piper piping	LH	D-G	CFI
Brewer	The fairy pipers	HML		BOH
Bridge	Love went a-riding	HL		BOS
-----	O that it were so	LMH	D-G	CHA
Brown	Shepherd thy demeanor vary			BOO
Clarke	The seal man	M		BOH
Dowland	Deare, if you change			BOO
-----	My thoughs are filled with hope			
-----	Sorrow, sorrow stay	M	D-D	BOS
-----	Woeful heart with grief oppressed			KEE
Dunhill	The cloths of heaven	LM	EF-G	STB
Edmunds	How should I my true love know?			

408

(Edmunds)	I know my love	HL	BF-EF	ROW
Elgar	The swimmer			BOO
-----	Where corals lie	HL		BOO
German	Charming Chloe	HML		NOV
Gibb	By a bier side			CUR
Gibbs	Five eyes	HL	D-D	BOS
Goossens	Melancholy	M		CHE
Green	I will lay me down in peace			
-----	Praised be the Lord	M	C-F	OXF
Head	A piper	HL		BOO
-----	Nocturne	HL		BOO
-----	Sweet chance that led my steps abroad	LM	C-F	BOH
-----	The ships of Arcady	ML	BF-EF	BOH
Hely-Hutchinson	Old mother Hubbard	HL	B-E	CFI
Henschel	Morning-hymn	MH	DS-GS	†
-----	There was an ancient king			ASC
Holst	Creation			GSC
-----	Hymn to the waters	M	B-FS	CHE
-----	Indra, God of storm and battle	M	B-F	CHE
-----	Speech	M	BF-F	CHE
-----	The heart worships	ML	BF-D	STB
Hook	Bright Phoebus	M	EF-F	GSC
Horn	I've been roaming	L	B-E	†
Hughes	O men from the fields	M	F-F	BOO
-----	The terrible robber men			
Ireland	Bed in summer			CUR
-----	Santa Chiara	ML	C-EF	AUG
Johnson	Care-charming sleep			
Morley	It was a lover and his lass	HM		DIT
Parry	Love is a bauble			NOV
-----	Why so pale and wan, fond lover	L		NOV
Peterkin	Advice to girls	H	CS-FS	CFI
Pilkington	Rest, sweet nymphs			STB
Purcell	Ah, how pleasant tis to love			AUG
-----	Bess of Bedlam			BOO
-----	Evening hymn	M	C-F	OXF
-----	Hark! how all things with one sound rejoice			NOV
-----	If music be the food of love	M	D-G	BOO
-----	Man is for woman made			
-----	Not all my torments			NOV
-----	Sweet, be no longer sad			NOV

409

(Purcell)	There's not swain on the plain	M	B-G	BAF
-----	Venus' song			AUG
Quilter	Blow, blow thou winter wind	HL	C-E	BOO
-----	Damask roses			BOO
-----	Love's philosophy	LMH	D-A	BOO
-----	Music and moonlight	L	C-EF	CUR
Rosseter	When Laura smiles	LM	D-E	STB
Rowley	Grieve not my heart			BOH
-----	The toll gate house			ROG
Sanderson	Quiet	ML	AF-EF	BOH
Scott	Lullaby	MML	BF-DF	GAL
Sharp	Whistle daughter, whistle			DIT
Shaw	Song of the Palanquin bearers	LH	E-F	CUR
Somervell	Shepherd's cradle song	HM		GSC
Stephenson	Ships that pass in the night	HML	DF-DF	BOO
Vaughn Williams	Boy Jonny	LH		BOH
-----	Four nights	L	AF-EF	OXF
-----	Linden Lea	HML	C-D	BOS
-----	Silent noon			GSC
-----	The new ghost			
-----	The water mill	L	C-D	OXF
Warlock	A prayer to St. Anthony of Padua	M	C-EF	CFI
-----	Consider	M	C-G	CFI
-----	In an arbour green	H	D-G	CFI
-----	Peterisms	H		CHE
-----	Rest, sweet nymphs	M	F-F	CFI
-----	Sleep			OXF

French Recital Songs

Contralto

Aubert	Vieille chanson espagnole			DUR
Bax	Femmes battez vos marys			
-----	Me suis en danse			
Bemberg	Chant hindou	HML	A-EF	†
Berlioz	La captive	HL		GSC
Bizet	Adieu de l'hôtesse arabe	H	BF-G	†
-----	Aubade			
-----	La sirène			
-----	Ma vie a son secret	L	AF-F	CHU
Caplet	La ronde	M		DUR

Chaminade	Chant slave			GSC
Chausson	Le colibri Violin or cello	M	F-GF	BOS
-----	Le temps des lilas	MH	D-GS	†
Debussy	Ballade des femmes de Paris			DUR
-----	Ballade que fait Villon à la requeste de sa mère			DUR
-----	Beau soir	LH	C-FS	†
-----	Chevaux de bois	H	C-G	†
-----	Je tremble en voyant ton visage			DUR
-----	La chevelure	M	CF-FS	†
-----	La flûte de Pan		B-B	†
-----	La mer est plus belle	HL		INT
-----	Le faune			DUR
-----	Mandoline	HM	BF-F	†
Duparc	Au pays où se fait la guerre			SAL
-----	Chanson triste	MH	FS-AF	†
-----	Lamento	ML	EF-EF	†
-----	Le manoir de Rosamunde	HL	B-F	BOS
-----	L'invitation au voyage	HM	E-F	†
-----	Phidylé	MH	EF-AF	BOS
Dupont	Mandoline			DUR
Fauré	Après un rêve	HM	C-F	†
-----	Automne	MH	D-FS	GSC
-----	Clair de lune	MH	C-G	†
-----	Fleur jetée	HM	BF-FS	†
-----	Le parfum impérissable	LH	GF-GF	
-----	Les berceaux	LMH	BF-G	†
-----	Nocturne	H	F-A	MAR
-----	Prison	LH		†
-----	Rencontre	H	EF-AF	†
-----	Toujours	LH	F-AF	†
Ferrari	Le miroir	M	E-F	GSC
Fontenailles	Souffrance			
Fourdrain	Carnaval	M	C-F	RIC
-----	Chevauchée cosaque	H	D-G	RIC
-----	Impression basque	M		RIC
Franck	La procession	LH	E-GS	†
-----	Le mariage des roses	M	E-FS	BOS
Georges	La pluie	HL		INT
Gounod	Au rossignol	LMH	D-G	CHO
Hahn	D'une prison	L	BF-EF	HEU
-----	L'heure exquise	M	DF-F	†
-----	Les cygnes			HEU
-----	Mai			HEU
-----	Offrande	M	D-D	†

411

(Hahn)	Paysage	MH	EF-G	HEU
Holmès	L'heure de pourpre			HEU
Honegger	Chanson (Ronsard) Flute and string quartet			SEN
-----	Les cloches			SEN
-----	Oh my love take my hand			SEN
-----	Psalm 130 (Mimaamaquim)			SAL
Hue	J'ai pleuré rêve	HL	D-E	BOS
Indy	Lied maritime	LH	B-G	†
Koechlin	L'hiver	H	E-G	†
Lalo	Chant breton	M	E-E	HAM
Martini	Plaisir d'amour	M	BF-EF	GSC
Massenet	Rose de mai			
Paladilhe	Lamento provinçal	M	CS-FS	HOM
-----	Psyché	HM	BF-F	GSC
Pessard	L'adieu du matin	ML	BF-D	GSC
Pierné	Le moulin	ML	C-E	BOS
Poldowski	Dansons la gigue	M	ÈF-G	MAR
-----	L'heure exquise	LMH	DF-AF	CHE
-----	Spleen	M	D-F	CHE
Poulenc	A sa guitare	M	D-FS	DUR
-----	Avant le cinéma	M		ROU
-----	Hôtel			AMP
-----	Le tombeau			HEU
-----	Priez pour paix	ML		ROU
-----	Voyage à Paris			AMP
Ravel	Chanson francaise			
-----	Kaddisch	H	C-G	DUR
-----	Nicolette	L	B-FS	ELK
-----	Tout gai!	MH	EF-F	
-----	Vocalise en forme de habanera	MH	BF-G	MAR
Rhené-Baton	Il pleut des pétales de fleurs	M	CS-E	DUR
Rosenthal	Grammaire			
-----	Le marabout			ESC
Saint-Saëns	L'attente			DUR
-----	La cloche	LH	DF-AF	†
Tremisot	Novembre			ENO
Vidal	Ariette	LH	F-A	GSC
Widor	Je ne veux pas autre chose	HL	C-EF	HAM

German Recital Songs

Contralto

Ahle	Bruenstiges Verlangen	M	E-E	GSC

412

Bach, C.P.E.	Suscepit Israel			
Bach, J.S.	Bist due bei mir	HML	A-EF	†
-----	Komm, suesser Tod	MH	C-G	†
-----	Kommt, Seelen, dieser Tag			
-----	Liebster Herr Jesu			BRH
Bach, P.E.	Bitten			
Beethoven	An die Geliebte	M	E-E	†
-----	Bitten			†
-----	Busslied			†
-----	Das Geheimnis			
-----	Die Ehre Gottes	HL	AF-EF	†
-----	Die Liebe des Naechsten			
-----	Die Trommel geruehret			†
-----	Faithfu' Johnie			
-----	God is my song			
-----	Ich liebe dich	HL	BF-DF	†
-----	Vom Tode	L	A-EF	GSC
-----	Wonne der Wehmut			†
Brahms	Ach, wende diesen Blick			†
-----	Am Sonntag Morgen	L	CS-FS	CFI
-----	An die Nachtigall	H	DS-G	†
-----	An eine Aeolsharfe	H	EF-AF	†
-----	Auf dem Kirchhofe	HL	BF-EF	†
--·--	Botschaft	HL	D-F	†
-----	Bratschenlieder			†
-----	Dein blaues Auge	MH	BF-G	†
-----	Der Kranz			†
-----	Der Schmied	HL	EF-EF	†
-----	Der Tod, das ist die kuehle Nacht	L	AF-F	†
-----	Die Mainacht	HL	BF-FF	†
-----	Die Schnur, die Perl an Perle			†
-----	Ein Wanderer	LH	E-AF	†
-----	Feldeinsamkeit	HL	C-EF	†
-----	Gestillte Sehnsucht Viola and piano			†
-----	Immer leiser wird mein Schlummer	LH	DF-A	†
-----	In Waldeseinsamkeit	H	ES-G	†
-----	Juchhe!			†
-----	Komm bald	HM	CS-F	†
-----	Kommt dir manchmal in den Sinn	H	DS-GS	†
-----	Liebestreu	ML	C-F	†
-----	Maedchenlied	HL		†
-----	Meine Liebe ist gruen	MLH	ES-A	†
-----	Mit vierzig Jahren	HL	FS-D	CFI
-----	Muss es eine Trennung geben?	LH	FS-FS	†

413

(Brahms)	Nachtigall	MHL	BF-FS	†
-----	Nicht mehr zu dir zu gehen			†
-----	O kuehler Wald	MH	A-F	†
-----	O liebliche Wangen	MLH	E-G	†
-----	O wuesst' ich doch den Weg zurueck	H	E-FS	†
-----	Roeslein drei			†
-----	Sapphische Ode	HML		†
-----	Schwermut			†
-----	Sehnsucht	H	EF-AF	†
-----	Sonntag	H	D-G	†
-----	Spanisches Lied			†
-----	Staendchen	HL	BF-E	†
-----	Steig' auf, geliebter Schatten	HL	BF-EF	†
-----	Trueue Liebe	LMH	DS-E	†
-----	Vergebliches Staendchen	LMH		†
-----	Verzagen	MH	CS-FS	†
-----	Von ewiger Liebe	LMH	B-AF	†
-----	Wehe, so willst du mich wieder			†
-----	Wie die Wolke			†
-----	Wiegenlied			
-----	Wie Melodien zieht es	HL	A-E	†
-----	Willst du, dass ich geh'?	L	C-G	†
-----	Wir wandelten	LH	EF-GF	GSC
-----	Wisst ihr wann			†
Buxtehude	Lord save me			
Cornelius	Komm wir wandeln	H	FS-GS	SC
Franz	Er ist gekommen	HL	EF-F	†
-----	Es ragt ins Meer der Runenstein	HL	G-F	†
-----	For music	ML	C-D	†
-----	Im Fruhling	HL		GSC
-----	Im Herbst	HM	A-F	†
-----	Mutter, o sing mich zur Ruh	HL	E-G	†
-----	Sterne mit den gold'nen Fuesschen	HL	DS-E	†
Grosz	Rondel			
Handel	Begruessung			
-----	Dank sei Dir, Herr	M	CS-E	†
Haydn	Das Leben ist ein Traum			GSC
-----	Die Seejungfer			
-----	Ein kleines Haus			
-----	My mother bids me bind my hair	M	E-E	†
-----	Schaeferlied			

414

(Haydn)	She never told her love	HL	B-D	DIT
-----	The spirit's song	M	B-GF	†
-----	The wanderer			
Himmel	Die Sendung			SIM
Jensen	Wie so bleich			
Liszt	Am Rhein			
-----	Die Lorelei	LH	BF-BF	†
-----	Freudvoll und leidvoll			DUR
Loewe	Der heilige Franziskus	L	A-E	SC
-----	Die Uhr	HML	AF-EF	†
-----	Edward	HL	F-E	†
-----	Maedchen sind wie der Wind			SC
-----	Walpurgisnacht	H	G-G	SC
Mahler	Das Irdische Leben	HL	A-F	INT
-----	Der Schildwache Nachtlied	L	A-G	†
-----	Des Antonius von Padua Fischpredigt	HL	GF-F	†
-----	Ging heut Morgen uebers Feld	M	A-FS	INT
-----	Ich bin der Welt abbanden gekommen	HL		INT
-----	Ich hab' ein gluehend Messer	M	BF-GF	WEI
-----	Liebst du um Schoenheit	HL		INT
-----	Wer hat dies Liedlein erdacht?	HL	BF-E	INT
-----	Wo die schoenen Trompeten blasen	HL	GF-F	INT
Marx	Der Denker			
-----	Italienisches Wiegenlied			
-----	Venetianisches Wiegenlied			AMP
Mendelssohn	And'res Maienlied			AUG
-----	Schlafloser Augen Leuchte			AUG
Mozart	Als Luise die Briefe			GSC
-----	Die Alte			
-----	Warnung	HM	C-D	
-----	Wiegenlied	MH	C-G	†
Ott	Leichte Wahl			
Pfitzner	Der Einsame			BOO
-----	Im tiefen Wald verborgen			
-----	Nachts			BOO
Raff	Keine Sorg' um den Weg			
Reger	Am Bruennele			
-----	Das Dorf			AMP
-----	Mit Rosen bestreut			UNI
-----	Morgengesang			PET
-----	Volkslied			AMP
-----	Waldeinsamkeit	HML	A-D	BOS

Reichardt	Rhapsodie			MOS
Schoenberg	Song of the wood dove			AMP
Schubert	Am Bach, im Fruehling			PET
-----	An die Leier	LM	BF-F	†
-----	An Schwager Kronos	HL	G-E	†
-----	Auf dem Wasser zu singen	MH	EF-GF	†
-----	Auf der Bruecke	HL		†
-----	Aufenthalt	HLM	A-F	GSC
-----	Aufloesung	LH	D-A	†
-----	Aus Heliopolis			PET
-----	Ave Maria	LMH	F-F	†
-----	Dem Unendlichen	L	A-GF	†
-----	Der Atlas	HL	BF-F	†
-----	Der Doppelgaenger	HL	G-D	†
-----	Der Erlkoenig	HML	A-E	†
-----	Der Geistertanz	L	G-EF	†
-----	Der Juengling an der Quelle	LH	E-A	†
-----	Der Juengling auf dem Huegel	L	G-F	†
-----	Der Juengling und der Tod	M	DF-FF	†
-----	Der Koenig in Thule	L	F-F	PET
-----	Der Leiermann	ML	C-D	†
-----	Der Lindenbaum	HL	A-D	†
-----	Der Musensohn	LH	FS-G	†
-----	Der Neugierige	HL	CS-EF	†
-----	Der stuermische Morgen	HL		
-----	Der Tod und das Maedchen	HL	A-EF	†
-----	Der Wanderer	HML	FS-D	†
-----	Der Wanderer an den Mond	LM	D-F	PET
-----	Der Wegweiser	L	D-EF	†
-----	Der Zwerg	M	A-GF	PET
-----	Des Maedchens Klage	LH	C-E	†
-----	Die Allmacht	HML	G-E	GSC
-----	Die boese Farbe	HL	CS-F	†
-----	Die Forelle	MLH	EF-GF	†
-----	Die Hoffnung	HM	E-E	†
-----	Die junge Nonne	LH	C-GF	†
-----	Die Kraehe	HL	A-E	†
-----	Die liebe Farbe			
-----	Die Liebe hat gelogen	LM	G-F	†
-----	Die Maenner sind mechant			PET
-----	Die Nebensonnen	HL	F-D	†
-----	Die Post	HML	BF-EF	†
-----	Die Unterscheidung	LH	D-G	†
-----	Du bist die Ruh	LMH	EF-AF	†
-----	Du liebst mich nicht	LH	E-FS	†
-----	Ellens zweiter Gesang			PET
-----	Erstarrung	HL	D-F	†
-----	Fahrt zum Hades	HL	G-DF	PET

(Schubert)	Fischerweise	L	C-D	†
-----	Fragment aus dem			PET
	Aeschylus			
-----	Fruehlingstraum	HL	C-D	†
-----	Gott im Fruehling			PET
-----	Gretchen am Spinnrade	H	F-A	†
-----	Gruppe aus dem Tartarus	L	CS-EF	†
-----	Heidenroeslein			
-----	Im Abendrot	HL	C-D	†
-----	Im Freien	HL	C-F	†
-----	In der Ferne	HL		GSC
-----	Iphigenia			PET
-----	Irrlicht			
-----	Lachen und Weinen	HL	C-EF	†
-----	Liebesbotschaft	H	E-G	†
-----	Lied der Mignon	HL		†
-----	Litanei	HLM	C-EF	†
-----	Meeresstille	HL	B-D	†
-----	Nachtgesang			PET
-----	Nacht und Traeume	HL	C-DF	†
-----	Rastlose Liebe	M	B-F	†
-----	Romanze aus Rosamunde			PET
-----	Schaefers Klagelied	HL	BF-D	†
-----	Seligkeit			
-----	Staendchen			
-----	Suleika I	LH	DS-G	†
-----	Thekla	HL	B-E	PET
-----	Ungeduld	HML		†
-----	Verklaerung			PET
-----	Wanderers Nachtlied 1	HL		†
-----	Wehmuth	HL	B-D	†
-----	Widerschein			PET
-----	Wohin?	HL	B-E	†
Schuetz	Aus dem 119th Psalm			
-----	O clap your hands			
Schumann, C.	Liebst du um Schoenheit			
Schumann, R.	Abends am Strande			
-----	Alte Laute	HL	DF-DF	†
-----	An den Sonnenschein	HL	A-D	†
-----	Auf das Trinkglas eines			
	verstorbenen Freundes			
-----	Aus den Hebraeischen Gesaengen			
-----	Der Himmel hat eine Traene			
	geweint			
-----	Der Nussbaum	LMH	D-FS	†
-----	Die Kartenlegerin			
-----	Die Lotusblume	HLM	BF-F	†
-----	Die Soldatenbraut	HL	AF-EF	†
-----	Die Tochter Jephthas	HL	A-E	

417

(Schumann)	Du bist wie eine Blume	HM	F-EF	†
-----	Du Ring an meinem Finger	HL	C-F	†
-----	Er, der Herrlichste von Allen	HL	A-EF	†
-----	Fruehlingsfahrt	HL	B-E	†
-----	Fruehlingsnacht	L	CS-E	†
-----	Heiss' mich nicht reden			
-----	Hoch, hoch sind die Berge			
-----	Im Walde	HL	A-D	†
-----	Im Westen	HL		†
-----	Kaeuzlein			
-----	Lied der Suleika			
-----	Lust der Sturmnacht			
-----	Mit Myrthen und Rosen	HL	A-D	DIT
-----	Mondnacht	M	E-FS	†
-----	O ihr Herren, o ihr Werthen	LH		†
-----	Schoene Wiege meiner Leiden	HL	C-EF	†
-----	Seit ich ihn gesehen	HL	DF-DF	†
-----	Talismane			
-----	Waldesgespraech	HL	A-FS	†
-----	Wehmut			†
-----	Wer machte dich so krank?			
-----	Widmung	HL	BF-F	†
Strauss	Allerseelen	HL	AS-E	†
-----	Befreit			HSC
-----	Caecilie	MH	E-B	†
-----	Die Georgine	LH	B-A	†
-----	Die Nacht	HL		†
-----	Freundliche Vision	HL	C-F	†
-----	Fruehlingsfeier			
-----	Geduld	LH	C-G	
-----	Heimliche Aufforderung	HL	B-E	†
-----	Im Spaetboot			
-----	In goldener Fuelle			†
-----	Liebeshymnus			†
-----	Maria ging hinaus			
-----	Mit deinen blauen Augen	LH	C-GS	†
-----	Morgen	HML	E-F	GSC
-----	Ruhe meine Seele			†
-----	Traum durch die Daemmerung	HML	BF-EF	†
-----	Wiegenliedchen			†
-----	Winterliebe			†
-----	Zueignung	HL	CS-FS	†
Trunk	Das Hemd			
-----	Fruehlingssonne			

(Trunk)	Suleika			
Wagner	Der Engel	LH	CS-G	†
-----	Schmerzen	HL		†
-----	Traeume	HL		†
Wolf	Agnes	HL		†
-----	Alle gingen, Herz, zu Ruh	HL	C-EF	†
-----	Als ich auf dem Euphrat schiffte			†
-----	An eine Aeolsharfe			†
-----	Auf einer Wanderung	HL		†
-----	Bedeckt mich mit Blumen	HL	B-D	†
-----	Bescheidene Liebe	MH	D-G	
-----	Cophtisches Lied I			†
-----	Dank des Paria			PET
-----	Das verlassene Maegdlein	HL	D-EF	†
-----	Die ihr schwebet	HL	EF-EF	INT
-----	Die Sproede			†
-----	Die Zigeunerin			†
-----	Dies zu deuten			PET
-----	Epiphanias	HL	B-D	†
-----	Er ist's	H	D-G	†
-----	Fussreise	HL	D-E	†
-----	Gebet	HL		†
-----	Geh' Geliebter, geh' jetzt			PET
-----	Gesang Weylas	HL	DF-F	†
-----	Hatt ich irgend wohl Bedenken			PET
-----	Ich hab' in Penna	LH		†
-----	Im Fruehling	HL	BF-F	†
-----	In dem Schatten meiner Locken	M	C-EF	†
-----	In der Fruehe	HL	C-C	†
-----	Kennst du das Land			†
-----	Klinge, klinge, mein Pandero	HL	CF-EF	†
-----	Mausfallen Spruechlein	HL	BF-E	†
-----	Mignon	LH		†
-----	Nachtzauber	HL	B-E	†
-----	Nimmersatte Liebe	LH	CF-AF	†
-----	Nun lass uns Frieden schliessen	HL		†
-----	Nun wandre, Maria	HL	EF-D	†
-----	Nur wer die Sehnsucht kennt			†
-----	Rat einer Alten			PET
-----	Ueber Nacht	LH	D-G	†
-----	Um Mitternacht	HL	G-EF	†
-----	Verborgenheit	HL	B-E	†
-----	Wenn du zu den Blumen gehst	HL	B-EF	†

419

(Wolf)	Wie glaenzt der helle Mond			†
-----	Zur Ruh', zur Ruh'	HL	A-GF	†
Wolff	Alle Dinge haben Sprache	M	BF-GF	†
-----	Die Heisse schwuele Sommernacht			HMP
-----	Ein solcher ist mein Freund	M	DS-F	†
-----	Ewig			
-----	Ich bin eine Harfe			HMP
-----	Maerchen	M	D-E	†
-----	Reim			
-----	Seidenschuh' ueber Leisten von Gold			
-----	Sommernacht			
-----	Wie Melodien aus reiner Sphaere hoer' ich			

Italian Recital Songs

Contralto

Arditi	Leggiero, invisibile			
Benati	Credi nell' alma mia			
Bononcini	Deh, più a me non v'ascondete	LH	EF-F	†
Caccini	Amarilli, mia bella	ML	C-D	†
Caldara	Come raggio di sol	HL	D-F	†
-----	Mirti, faggi			PET
-----	Sebben crudele	HML	E-DS	†
-----	Selve amiche, ombrose piante	HM	E-E	†
Carissimi	A morire!	ML	C-D	
-----	Vittoria, mio core	HLM	B-E	†
Cavalli	Beato chi può (Serse)			HEU
-----	Donzelle fuggite	HL	C-EF	†
Cesti	Ah, quanto è vero (Il Pomo d'Oro)	HL	F-F	DIT
-----	Che angoscia, che affanno (Il Pomo d'Oro)	HL	C-DF	DIT
-----	E dove t'aggiri (I' Pomo d'Oro)	HM	D-EF	DIT
-----	Intorno all'idol mio (Orontea)	MH	D-F	†
Cherubini	Ahi, che forse ai miei di (Demofonte)			RIC
Cimara	Fiocca la neve	H	G-G	GSC
-----	Stornellata marinara	HM		RIC
Cimarosa	Bel nume che adoro			RIC

De Luca	Non posso disperar	HL	C-E	GSC
Donaudy	Quando ti rivedrò			RIC
Durante	Danza, danza fanciulla gentile	HM	BF-F	†
-----	Vergin, tutta amor	LM	C-EF	†
Falconieri	Non più d'amore	HL	C-D	DIT
-----	Nudo arciero	HL	AF-AF	DIT
-----	O bellissimi capelli	HL	B-D	†
Frescobaldi	Se l'aura spira	HL	C-EF	DIT
Gagliano	Dormi, amore	HL	CS-E	DIT
Gasparini	Caro laccio, dolce nodo	M	EF-EF	GSC
Giordani	Caro mio ben	HML	B-D	†
Giordano	E l'Aprile che torna a me	H		RIC
Gluck	Spiagge amate (Paride ed Elena)			†
Handel	Ah! mio cor (Alcina)			†
-----	Ah! spietato (Amadigi)			
-----	Ben io sento l'ingrata spietata furio (Atalanta)	L	B-D	CFI
-----	Care selve (Atalanta)	MH	FS-A	†
-----	Ch'io mai vi possa (Siroe)			CFI
-----	Con rauco mormorio (Rodelinda)			
-----	Dove sei, amato bene (Rodelinda)	L	BF-EF	†
-----	Empio dirò tu sei (Julius Caesar)			
-----	Furibondo spira (Partenope)			KIS
-----	La speranza è giunto in porto (Ottone)			
-----	Lascia ch'io pianga (Rinaldo)			
-----	Notte cara (Floridante)			
-----	Ombra mai fu (Serse)	HM	BF-EF	†
-----	Piangero la (Julius Caesar)			CFI
-----	Rendi'l sereno al ciglio (Sosarme)	LH	EF-F	†
-----	Si, tra i ceppi (Berenice)	L	B-D	†
-----	Stille amare (Tolomeo)			MUP
-----	Tutta raccolta (Scipione)			CFI
-----	Un cenno leggia dretto (Serse)			
-----	V'adoro pupille (Julius Caesar)			BOO
-----	Verdi prati (Alcina)			
-----	Vieni o figlio caro e mi consola (Ottone)			CFI
Legrenzi	Che fiero costume	HML	C-D	†
Leoni	A little china figure	HM	DF-EF	GSC

421

Lotti	Pur dicesti, o bocca bella	LMH	E-FS	GSC
Malipiero	Inno a Maria Nostra Donna	H		CHE
Marcello	Il mio bel foco	LMH	C-G	†
-----	Non m'è grave morir per amore	L	C-E	GSC
Monteverdi	Illustatevi o cieli			
Paisiello	Chi vuol la zingarella	L	C-F	GSC
Pergolesi	Confusa, smarrita			GSC
-----	Se tu m'ami	LMH	C-G	GSC
Peri	Funeste piaggie (Euridice)			GSC
-----	Invocazione di Orfeo (Euridice)	HL	E-CS	DIT
Provenzale	Deh, rendetemi	ML	D-D	DIT
Recli	Anda			
-----	Nenia popolare			
Respighi	E se un giorno tornasse	M		RIC
-----	Il tramonto			RIC
-----	Io sono la madre	L		RIC
-----	Nebbie			†
-----	Pioggia			BON
-----	Scherzo			BON
Rontani	Or ch'io non segno più	HL	CS-E	DIT
-----	Se bel rio	ML	D-C	GSC
Rosa	Selve, voi che le speranze	MH	D-G	DIT
-----	Star vicino	HL	D-E	†
-----	Vado ben spesso	ML	C-EF	†
Rossi	Ah, rendimi (Mitrane)	L	GS-FS	GSC
Rossini	La danza	MH	E-A	†
Sadero	Amuri, Amuri	M		CHE
Santoliquido	I canti della sera			RIC
Sarti	Lungi dal caro bene (Armide)	HL	G-D	GSC
Scarlatti, A.	Chi vuole innamorarsi	HL	D-EF	DIT
-----	La fortuna			BOS
-----	O cessate di piagarmi	HL	DS-E	†
-----	Rugiadose odorose (Il Pirro e Demetrio)	HL	D-E	DIT
-----	Se Florindo è fedele	LM	EF-EF	GSC
-----	Sento nel core	M	E-F	†
Scarlatti, D.	Consolati e spara amante	L	BF-E	GSC
-----	Qual farfalletta			
Secchi	Lungi dal caro bene	HL	A-FS	DIT
Stradella	Col mio sangue comprenderei (Il Floridoro)	HL	E-F	DIT
-----	Per pietà (Il Floridoro)	HM	D-F	DIT
-----	Se nel ben			CFI
Strozzi	Amor dormiglione	HL	B-E	DIT

Torelli	Tu lo sai	HL	BF-F	†
Vivaldi	Un certo no so che	HL	BF-EF	†
Wolf- Ferrari	Rispetto			HSC

Russian Recital Songs

Contralto

Arensky	Valse	H	DF-GF	GSC
Borodin	A dissonance	MH	E-F	†
-----	Requiem of love			
Gliere	Ah, twine no blossoms	HM	CS-F	DIT
Gretchaninoff	Freedom			
-----	Hushed the song of the nightingale	MH	E-G	DIT
-----	In exile			
-----	Lullaby			
-----	Over the steppe	LM	C-G	GSC
-----	Rosy reflections			
-----	The snowdrop	HM	BF-F	DIT
-----	Wounded birch	HL	B-EF	†
Mednikoff	The hills of Gruzia	H	DS-A	LAC
Medtner	The angel			
-----	Waltz			
Mussorgsky	After the battle			GSC
-----	Death the commander			
-----	Fairy tales			
-----	Hopak	HM	CS-FS	GSC
-----	Gathering mushrooms			
-----	In the corner			INT
-----	On the Dnieper			GSC
-----	Peasant cradle song	M		GSC
-----	Serenade			BES
-----	Sphinx			BRH
-----	The banks of the Don			GSC
-----	The classic			BRH
-----	The forgotten one			
-----	The magpie and the gypsy dancer			GSC
-----	The orphan girl			GSC
Rachmaninoff	Child, lovely blossom			
-----	Fate	L		BOO
-----	Floods of spring	HL		DIT
-----	In the silence of night	LH	D-A	GSC
-----	Lilacs	LH	EF-G	†
-----	Oh, no, I pray do not depart	H		DIT

(Rachmaninoff)	O thou billowy harvest field	HL	CS-E	GSC
-----	Solitude			
-----	The island	LH	DF-F	†
-----	The raising of Lazarus			BRH
-----	'Tis time	L		BOO
Stravinsky	Song of the dew			JUR
-----	The cloister (La novice)			DIT
Tchaikovsky	Complaint of the bride			
-----	He loved me so dear	HL		GSC
-----	Speak not, O beloved			
-----	Why	HL		†

Scandinavian Recital Songs

Contralto

Grieg	A dream			†
-----	A swan			†
-----	Autumnal gale	HL	A-F	CFI
-----	By the brook			GSC
-----	Digtervise	L	A-EF	HAN
-----	Eros	LM	C-F	†
-----	Good morning			†
-----	Henrik Wergeland			PET
-----	Hjemkomst	M	B-F	HAN
-----	Hunter's song	L	DS-E	GSC
-----	I love thee	HML	E-F	†
-----	In the boat	LM	D-ES	†
-----	Jeg lever et liv i laengsel	L	BF-E	HAN
-----	Love			PET
-----	Poesien			
-----	Rock, O wave			
-----	Spillemand			
-----	Spring rain			PET
-----	Springtide	M		DIT
-----	The first meeting			PET
-----	The return			
-----	There screamed a bird			PET
-----	Turisten	M	CS-F	HAN
-----	Vandring i skoven	M	D-FS	HAN
-----	Verse for an album			
-----	With a primrose	H	DF-GF	GSC
-----	With a water lily	HM	CS-EF	†
Heise	Arnes sang			
Jonsson	Under haeggarna			
Kilpinen	Die Fusswaschung			
-----	En vårmelodi			

424

(Kilpinen)	Ring, ring			
Lasson, P.	Were I the flaming sun	HL	DF-G	GSC
Lindberg	Hur skall man bruden klaeda?			
Lundvik	Sov i sommarsus			
Nordquist	Kunde jag dikta en visa			
Palmgren	Autumn	HL		BOS
Peterson- Berger	Aftonstaemming			
-----	Swedish folk song			
-----	Titania			
Rangstroem	En gammal Danstrym			
-----	Night			
-----	Pan			
-----	Tragedie			
Sibelius	Astray			AMP
-----	Black roses	M	A-ES	AMP
-----	But my bird is long in homing			
-----	Come away death			AMP
-----	Coming of spring			HAN
-----	Diamonds on the March snow			
-----	Die Liebelle			
-----	Driftwood			AMP
-----	From the north	H	DS-G	GSC
-----	In the field a maiden sings			
-----	O wert thou here			AMP
-----	Reeds, reeds rustle			
-----	Slow as the colors			
-----	Speedwell			
-----	Spring is fleeting			DIT
-----	The first kiss	M		AMP
-----	The question			
-----	The tryst	M		AMP
-----	Was it a dream			BRH
Sinding	I hear the gull			JCH
Sjoegren	Jeg giver mit digt			
Vehanen	The girl the boys all love			

Spanish Recital Songs

Contralto

Berger	No jardín			
Falla	Canción del amor dolido			CHE
-----	Chanson du feu follet	L	B-B	CHE
Granados	Andalusia			
-----	Elegie eterna			
Grever	Rataplán	HL	BF-D	GSC

425

Guastavino	Cita			
-----	La rose y la sauce			RIC
Nin	Canción gallega			ESC
-----	El vito			ESC
-----	Paño murciano			ESC
Obrados	Cantos populares			
-----	Coplas de curro dulce			
-----	Del cabello mas sutil			RIC
-----	Dos cantares populares			
-----	El majo celoso			
-----	El tumba y le			
-----	El vito			
-----	La guitarra sin primo			
-----	La mi sola laureola			
Ravel	Chanson espagnole			DUR
Sandoval	Chafrinita			
-----	Madrigal	HL	A-E	GSC
Tavares	Funeral of King Naga			
Turina	Farruca	M	A-F	UME
-----	Rima	H	A-A	AMP

Miscellaneous Recital Songs

Contralto

Bach-Gounod	Ave Maria			
Bartok	Tears of autumn	M	C-F	GSC
Berger	Lonely people			
Binder	Emathay			
-----	Hineh mahtov			
-----	Shir shomrim			
Bizet	Agnus Dei	HLM	C-AF	
Bruckner	Ave Maria			AMP
Chajes	Adarim			TRA
-----	By the rivers of Babylon			
-----	Old Jerusalem			
Dessau	Al sefat jam kinareth			
Dvořák	By the waters of Babylon			AMP
-----	Clouds and darkness			
-----	God is my shepherd			AMP
-----	Hear my prayer, O Lord			AMP
-----	I will life mine eyes			AMP
-----	I will sing new songs of gladness	HL		
-----	Lord, Thou art my refuge and shield			AMP
-----	Sing ye a joyful song			AMP

426

(Dvořák)	Songs my mother taught me	HM	E-E	
-----	Turn Thee to me			AMP
Fisher	Eili, eili	LMH	E-G	DIT
Franck	Panis angelicus	LM		
Hasse	Salve Regina			BRH
Lotti	Miserere			
Luzzi	Ave Maria	HL	BF-EF	GSC
Mignone	A sombre			
-----	Janaina			
Mozart	Alleluia	LMH	F-C	
Ravel	Mayerke mein suhn			RAV
Sakelariou	Pentozalis			
Schwadren	Wetov li			
Stakianaki	Duru duru			
Villa-Lobos	Nhapope			
Weiner	Der shelem zecher			

British Songs and Arias
For Opening Recitals

Contralto

Handel	Art thou troubled (Rodelinda)	M	F-F	GSC
-----	Let me wander not unseen (L'Allegro)	M	D-G	†
-----	Lord, to Thee each night and day (Theodora)	L	C-E	†
-----	The land of dreams			
Purcell	Ah, how pleasant 'tis to love			AUG
-----	Evening hymn	M	C-F	OXF
-----	If music be the food of love	M	D-G	BOO
-----	Not all my torments			NOV
-----	There's not a swain on the plain	M	B-G	BAF
-----	When I am laid in earth (Dido and Aeneas)	LH	C-G	†

German Songs for Opening Recitals

Contralto

| Bach, J.S. | Bist du bei mir | HML | A-EF | † |
| Beethoven | God is my song | | | |

427

(Beethoven)	Ich liebe dich	HL	BF-DF	†
Brahms	Ein Wanderer	LH	E-AF	†
-----	Nachtigall	MHL	BF-FS	†
-----	Verzagen	MH	CS-FS	†
Buxtehude	Singet dem Herrn			
	Violin and piano			
Handel	Begruessung			
Haydn	She never told her love	HL	B-D	DIT
Schubert	Gott im Fruehling			PET
-----	Liebesbotschaft	H	E-G	†
-----	Verklaerung			PET
Schuetz	Bringt her dem Herren			
Schumann	Mit Myrthen und Rosen	HL	A-D	†
Wolf	Ueber Nacht	LH	D-G	†

Italian Songs and Arias
For Opening Recitals

Contralto

Benati	Credi nell' alma mia			
Bononcini	Deh, più a me non	LH	EF-F	†
	v'ascondete			
Caccini	Amarilli, mia bella	ML	C-D	†
Caldara	Sebben crudele	HML	E-DS	†
Carissimi	Vittoria, mio core	HLM	B-E	†
Cavalli	Beato chi può (Serse)			HEU
-----	Donzelle fuggite	HL	C-EF	†
Cesti	Ah, quanto è vero	HL	F-F	DIT
	(Il Pomo d'Oro)			
-----	Che angoscia, che affanno	HL	C-DF	DIT
	(Il Pomo d'Oro)			
-----	E dove t'aggiri			DIT
	(Il Pomo d'Oro)			
Cherubini	Ahi, che forse ai miei di			RIC
	(Demofonte)			
Cimara	Stornellata marinara	HM		RIC
Donaudy	Quando ti rivedrò			RIC
Durante	Vergin, tutta amor	LM	C-EF	†
Falconieri	O bellissimi capelli	HL	B-D	†
Gluck	Spiagge amate			†
	(Paride ed Elena)			
Handel	Ah! mio cor (Alcina)			†
-----	Ah! spietato (Amadigi)			
-----	Care selve (Atalanta)	MH	FS-A	BOO
-----	Ch'io mai vi possa (Siroe)			†
-----	Dove sei, amato bene	L	BF-EF	†
	(Rodelinda)			

428

(Handel)	Furibondo spira (Partenope)			KIS
-----	Lascia ch'io pianga (Rinaldo)	HM	EF-F	†
-----	Notte cara (Floridante)			
-----	Ombra mai fu (Serse)	HM	BF-EF	†
-----	Piangero la sorte mia (Julius Caesar)			CFI
-----	Rendi'l sereno al ciglio (Sosarme)	LH	EF-F	†
-----	Si, tra i ceppi (Berenice)	L	B-D	†
-----	Tutta raccolta (Scipione)			CFI
-----	V'adoro pupille (Julius Caesar)			BOO
Lotti	Pur dicesti, o bocca bella	LMH	E-FS	GSC
Marcello	Il mio bel foco	LMH	C-G	†
Paisiello	Chi vuol la zingarella	L	C-F	GSC
Pergolesi	Salve Regina			
-----	Se tu m'ami	LMH	C-G	GSC
Peri	Invocazione di Orfeo (Euridice)	HL	E-CS	DIT
Rosa	Star vicino	HL	D-E	RIC
-----	Vado ben spesso	ML	C-EF	†
Sarti	Lungi dal caro bene (Armide)	HL	G-D	GSC
Scarlatti, A.	Sento nel core	M	E-F	†
Stradella	Per pietà (Il Floridoro)	HM	D-F	DIT
-----	Se nel ben			CFI
Vivaldi	Un certo no so che	HL	BF-EF	

American Songs For Closing Recitals

Contralto

Barber	I hear an army	LH	D-AF	GSC
-----	Sure on this shining night	MH	D-G	GSC
Carpenter	Light, my light	M	C-G	GSC
-----	Serenade	LH	CS-A	GSC
Castelnuovo-Tedesco	New York			
Charles	When I have sung my songs	HM	BF-EF	GSC
Dougherty	Portrait	HM	BF-G	GSC
Duke	On a March day	M	B-GF	BOH
Enders	Russian picnic	HM	C-G	GSC
Giannini	Sing to my heart a song	H	D-B	ELV
Guion	When you go			
Hageman	Miranda	HL		GAL

Horsman	The bird of the wilderness	LMH	DF-BF	GSC
Ilgenfritz	As we part			SCH
Kingsford	Command	HLM	EF-G	GSC
La Forge	Hills	HL		RIC
-----	Into the light	HL		RIC
-----	Song of the open	MH	EF-AF	DIT
Malotte	Upstream	M	C-F	GSC
Mana-Zucca	Rachem Trumpet	HML		C HA
Rogers	Sail forth			
-----	The last song	MLH	E-AF	GSC
-----	Time for making songs	HM	CS-F	DIT
Rummel	Ecstasy	LMH	GF-AF	GSC
Salter	The cry of Rachel	LH	C-AF	GSC
Silberta	I met dame fate	L	BF-E	GSC
Speaks	Morning	HML	BF-D	GSC
Swanson	Pierrot	L	B-D	WTR
Tyson	Sea moods	LH	E-AF	GSC
Warren	Heather	LH	FS-G	GSC
-----	We two	LH	E-A	GSC

(See also Negro Spirituals and Folk Songs.)

Miscellaneous Songs for Closing Recitals

Contralto

Binder	Emathay			
-----	Hineh mahtov			
Bizet	Adieu de l'hôtesse arabe	H	BF-G	†
Brahms	Juchhe!			†
-----	Meine liebe ist Gruen	MLH	ES-A	†
-----	Willst du, dass ich geh'?	L	C-G	†
Bridge	Love went a-riding	HL		BOS
Britten	Oliver Cromwell			BOH
Debussy	Chevaux de bois	H	C-G	†
Elgar	The swimmer			BOO
Falla	Jota	LH		AMP
-----	Polo	HL		AMP
Grever	Rataplán	HL	BF-D	GSC
Grieg	By the brook			GSC
-----	Digtervise	L	A-EF	HAN
-----	Good morning			†
-----	Hunter's song	L	DS-E	GSC
-----	Jeg lever et liv i laengsel	L	BF-E	HAN
Head	A piper	HL		BOO

Hely-Hutchinson	Old mother Hubbard	HL	B-E	CFI
Henschel	Morning-hymn	MH	DS-GS	DIT
Holst	Speech	M	BF-F	CHE
Korngold	Much ado about nothing			
Lasson	Were I the flaming sun	HL	DF-G	GSC
Mussorgsky	The forgotten one			
Nin	El vito			ESC
Obradors	Coplas de curro dulce			
-----	El tumba y le			
-----	El vito			
Quilter	Blow, blow thou winter wind	HL	C-E	BOO
-----	Love's philosophy	LMH	D-A	BOO
-----	Over the mountains			BOS
Rachmaninoff	Floods of spring	HL		DIT
-----	Oh, no, I pray do not depart	H		DIT
Respighi	Pioggia			BON
Schubert	Aufloesung	LH	D-A	†
-----	Die Forelle	MLH	EF-GF	†
Shaw	Romance			
Sibelius	The tryst	M		AMP
-----	Was it a dream?			BRH
Turina	Farruca	M	A-F	UME
Warlock	Yarmouth Fair	HL	B-E	CFI
Wolf	Er ist's	H	D-G	†

Atmospheric Songs

Contralto

Barber	Sleep now	MH	EF-AF	GSC
Brahms	Steig' auf, geliebter Schatten	HL	BF-EF	†
Burleigh	Sometimes I feel like a motherless child	HML		RIC
Carpenter	Go, lovely rose	M	DF-EF	GSC
-----	Odalisque	M	EF-EF	GSC
-----	Slumber song	ML	BF-F	GSC
-----	The day is no more	M	GS-DS	GSC
-----	The green river	M	B-E	GSC
-----	When I bring to you colour'd toys	LM	CS-FS	GSC
Charles	Clouds	HML	C-EF	GSC
-----	When I have sung my songs	HM	BF-EF	GSC
Cimara	Fiocca la neve	H	G-G	GSC
Dello Joio	New born	M	C-D	CFI

Dougherty	Loveliest of trees	HM	C-E	BOH
Duke	Loveliest of trees	L	C-D	GSC
Dunhill	The cloths of heaven	LM	EF-G	STB
Elgar	Sea pictures	L	A-A	BOO
Elmore and				
Reed	Come all ye who weary	L	C-C	JFI
Ferrari	Le miroir	M	E-F	GSC
Ferrata	Night and the curtains drawn			JFI
Franz	Sterne mit den gold'nen Fuesschen	HL	DS-E	†
Ganz	A memory	HM	B-D	GSC
Grieg	A dream			†
-----	A swan			†
-----	In the boat	LM	D-ES	†
-----	Spring rain			PET
Griffes	Night on ways unknown has fallen	L	GS-F	GSC
Hageman	Do not go, my love	HL	B-EF	GSC
Hahn	D'une prison	L	BF-EF	HEU
-----	L'heure exquise	M	DF-F	†
-----	Paysage	MH	EF-G	HEU
Harris	Fog	M	D-F	CFI
Haydn	She never told her love	HL	B-D	DIT
Holst	The heart worships	ML	BF-D	STB
Hughes	O men from the fields	M	F-F	BOO
Lynn	Gently little Jesus	L	BF-BF	DIT
-----	The magic night of Christmas	M	D-D	DIT
MacGimsey	Sweet little Jesus boy	ML	D-D	CFI
Niles	I wonder as I wander	HL	BF-D	GSC
-----	Jesus, Jesus rest your head	HL	A-D	GSC
Paladilhe	Psyché	HM	BF-F	GSC
Poldowski	L'heure exquise	LMH	DF-AF	CHE
Rachmaninoff	Lilacs	LH	EF-G	†
Reger	The Virgin's slumber song	MMH	G-G	†
Sanderson	Quiet	ML	AF-EF	BOH
Schubert	Der Tod und das Maedchen	HL	A-EF	†
-----	Nacht und Traeume	HL	C-DF	†
Schumann	Der Nussbaum	LMH	D-FS	†
-----	Im Walde	HL	A-D	†
Sibelius	Reeds, reeds rustle			
Strauss	Die Nacht	HL		†
-----	Traum durch die Daemmerung	HML	BF-EF	†
Tureman	A winter sunset	L	BF-E	GSC

432

Tyson	Noon and night	LH	F-AF	GSC
Vaughan				
Williams	Four nights	L	AF-EF	OXF
-----	Silent noon			GSC
Warlock	Sleep			OXF
Watts	Wings of night	LH	CS-G	GSC
Wolf	In dem Schatten meiner Locken	M	C-EF	†
-----	Verborgenheit	HL	B-E	†

American Dramatic Songs

Contralto

Barber	I hear an army	LH	D-AF	GSC
Beach	Ah, love but a day			ASC
Campbell-				
Tipton	The crying of water	LH	FS-GS	GSC
Carpenter	Light, my light	M	C-G	GSC
-----	Slumber song	ML	BF-F	GSC
-----	The green river	M	B-E	GSC
-----	To one unknown	M	A-DS	GSC
Duke	Calvary	L	G-F	CFI
-----	On a March day	M	B-GF	BOH
-----	Wild swans	H	D-A	MER
Elwell	Renouncement	M	G-G	GSC
Enders	Russian picnic	HM	C-G	GSC
Giannini	Sing to my heart a song	H	D-B	ELV
Griffes	Evening song	H	DS-GS	GSC
-----	We'll to the woods and gather May	M	D-F	GSC
Guion	Wild geese	M	D-F	CFI
Hageman	Do not go, my love	HL	B-EF	GSC
-----	Music I heard with you	MH	E-A	GAL
Horsman	The bird of the wilderness	LMH	DF-BF	GSC
Johnson	Roll Jerd'n roll	M	EF-F	GSC
La Forge	Song of the open	MH	EF-AF	DIT
Protheroe	Ah, love but a day	LMH	F-AF	GAM
Rogers	The last song	MLH	E-AF	GSC
-----	Time for making songs	HM	CS-F	DIT
Salter	The cry of Rachel	LH	C-AF	GSC
Speaks	Morning	HML	BF-D	GSC
Tyson	Sea moods	LH	E-AF	GSC
Warren	We two	LH	E-A	GSC

British Dramatic Songs and Arias

Contralto

Bridge	O that it were so	LMH	D-G	CHA
Clarke	The seal man	M		BOH
Del Riego	Homing	HML	BF-E	CHA
Elgar	Sea pictures	L	A-A	BOO
-----	The swimmer			BOO
Head	Nocturne	HL		BOO
Henschel	Morning-hymn	MH	DS-GS	†
Parry	Love is a bauble			NOV
Purcell	When I am laid in earth (Dido and Aeneas)	LH	C-G	†
Quilter	Blow, blow thou winter wind	HL	C-E	BOO
Ronald	Prelude	HML	B-D	ENO
Sullivan	The lost chord	HL	C-F	GSC

French Dramatic Songs and Arias

Contralto

Bemberg	Du Christ avec ardeur (La Mort de Jeanne d'Arc	M	DF-AF	†
Bizet	Habanera (Carmen)	HM	D-F	†
Debussy	Chevaux de bois	H	C-G	†
Duparc	Au pays où se fait la guerre			SAL
-----	Le manoir de Rosamunde	HL	B-F	BOS
-----	Phidylé	MH	EF-AF	BOS
Fauré	Automne	MH	D-FS	GSC
-----	Fleur jetée	HM	BF-FS	†
-----	Prison	LH		†
-----	Toujours	LH	F-AF	†
Gounod	O ma lyre immortelle (Sappho)	M	C-G	†
Hahn	D'une prison	L	BF-EF	HEU
-----	Offrande	M	D-D	†
Halévy	Humble fille des champs (Charles VI)			GSC
Honegger	Les cloches			SEN
Hue	J'ai pleuré en rêve	HL	D-E	BOS
Indy	Lied maritime	LH	B-G	†
Lesuer	Hélas sans m'entendre (Ossian ou les Bardes)			CHE
Massenet	Werther! qui m'aurait dit (Air de lettres) (Werther)			HEU

Meyerbeer	Ah! mon fils (Le Prophéte)	M	B-AS	†
Paladilhe	Lamento provincal	M	CS-FS	HOM
Poldowski	Dansons la gigue	M	EF-G	MAR
-----	L'heure exquise	LMH	DF-AF	CHE
Rhené-Baton	Il pleut des pétales de fleurs	M	CS-E	DUR
Saint-Saëns	Amour, viens aider (Samson et Dalila)	HM	AF-G	†
-----	L'attente			DUR

German Dramatic Songs and Arias

Contralto

Brahms	Ach, wende diessen Blick			†
-----	Am Sonntag Morgen	L	CS-FS	†
-----	Nich mehr zu dir zu gehen			†
-----	Treue Liebe	LMH	DS-E	†
-----	Von ewiger Liebe	LMH	B-AF	†
Franz	Im Herbst	HM	A-F	†
Liszt	Die Lorelei	LH	BF-BF	†
-----	Freudvoll und leidvoll			DUR
Loewe	Edward	HL	F-E	†
-----	Walpurgisnacht	H	G-G	SC
Mahler	Das Irdische Leben	HL	A-F	INT
-----	Ich hab' ein gluehend Messer	M	BF-GF	WEI
Schubert	An Schwager Kronos	HL	G-E	†
-----	Aufenthalt	HLM	A-F	†
-----	Dem Unendlichen	L	A-GF	†
-----	Der Atlas	HL	BF-F	†
-----	Der Doppelgaenger	HL	G-D	†
-----	Der Erlkoenig	HML	A-E	†
-----	Der Lindenbaum	HL	A-D	†
-----	Der Tod und das Maedchen	HL	A-EF	†
-----	Der Zwerg	M	A-GF	PET
-----	Die Allmacht	HML	G-E	†
-----	Die junge Nonne	LH	C-GF	†
-----	Die Kraehe	HL	A-E	GSC
-----	Die Liebe hat gelogen	LM	G-F	†
-----	Du liebst mich nicht	LH	E-FS	†
-----	Erstarrung	HL	D-F	†
-----	Fahrt zum Hades	HL	G-DF	PET
-----	Fragment aus dem Aeschylus			PET

(Schubert)	Fruehlingstraum	HL	C-D	†
-----	Gruppe aus dem Tartarus	L	CS-EF	†
-----	In der Ferne	HL		†
-----	Schaefers Klagelied	HL	BF-D	†
Schumann	Fruehlingsfahrt	HL	B-E	†
-----	Heiss' mich nicht reden			
-----	Mit Myrthen und Rosen	HL	A-D	†
-----	Schoene Wiege meiner Leiden	HL	C-EF	†
-----	Talismane			
-----	Waldesgespraech	HL	A-FS	†
Strauss	Caecilie	MH	E-B	†
-----	Ruhe meine Seele			†
-----	Zueignung	HL	CS-FS	†
Wagner	Schmerzen	HL		†
-----	So ist es denn aus mit den ewigen Goettern (Die Walkuere)			GSC
-----	Weiche, Wotan! (Das Rheingold)			GSC
Wolf	Alle gingen, Herz, zu Ruh	HL	C-EF	†
-----	Die ihr schwebet	HL	EF-EF	INT
-----	Epiphanias	HL	B-D	†
-----	Geh' Geliebter, geh' jetzt			PET
-----	Nachtzauber	HL	B-E	†
-----	Ueber Nacht	LH	D-G	†
-----	Zur Ruh', zur Ruh'	HL	A-GF	†

Italian Dramatic Songs and Arias

Contralto

Donizetti	O mio Fernando (La Favorita)	M	B-A	†
Durante	Vergin, tutta amor	LM	C-EF	†
Giordano	Temer? perche? (Andrea Chenier)			BRO
Pergolesi	Confusa, smarrita			GSC
Ponchielli	Voce di donna (La Gioconda)	HM	A-G	GSC
Respighi	Io sono la madre	L		RIC
-----	Nebbie			†
Verdi	Re dell' abisso (Un Ballo in Maschera)			RIC
-----	Stride la vampa (Il Trovatore)	M	B-G	†

436

Contralto

Borodin	A dissonance	MH	E-F	†
Dvořák	By the waters of Babylon			AMP
-----	Hear my prayer, O Lord			AMP
Gliere	Ah, twine no blossoms	HM	CS-F	DIT
Granados	La maja dolorosa	M		INT
Gretchaninoff	Over the steppe	LM	C-G	GSC
-----	Wounded birch	HL	B-EF	†
Grieg	A dream			†
-----	A swan			†
-----	Autumnal gale	HL	A-F	CFI
-----	Digtervise	L	A-EF	HAN
-----	Eros	LM	C-F	†
-----	Henrik Wergeland			PET
-----	Hjemkomst	M	B-F	HAN
-----	In the boat	LM	D-ES	†
-----	Jeg lever et liv i laengsel	L	BF-E	HAN
-----	Poesien			
-----	Verse for an album			
Mussorgsky	After the battle			GSC
-----	Divination by water (Khovantchina)	L	GS-FS	GSC
-----	Hopak	HM	CS-FS	GSC
-----	Martha's song (Khovantchina)	ML		GSC
-----	On the Dnieper			GSC
-----	The orphan girl			GSC
Rachmaninoff	Christ is risen	LM	D-F	GAL
-----	Floods of spring	HL		DIT
-----	Oh, no, I pray do not depart	HL		DIT
-----	O thou billowy harvest field	HL	CS-E	GSC
-----	To the children	MH	F-G	DIT
Sibelius	Black roses	M	A-ES	AMP
-----	The tryst	M		AMP
-----	Was it a dream?			BRH
Stravinsky	Song of the dew			JUR
-----	The cloister (La novice)			DIT
Tchaikovsky	Adieu forêts (Jeanne d'Arc)	HM	BF-FS	GSC
-----	Complaint of the bride			
-----	None but the lonely heart	HLM	C-F	DIT
-----	Pauline's romance (Pique Dame)	M	BF-AF	GSC

| (Tchaikovsky) | Why | HL | | † |
| Turina | Rima | H | A-A | AMP |

Humorous Songs

Contralto

Arne, T.	Why so pale and wan			GSC
Bernstein	I hate music	H	C-A	WIT
Brahms	Der Kranz			†
-----	Vergebliches Staendchen	LHM	E-FS	†
Britten	Oliver Cromwell			BOH
Carpenter	Don't ceare	M	C-D	GSC
-----	If	M	D-E	GSC
-----	To a young gentleman	M	C-F	GSC
Davis	Deaf old woman			GAL
Debussy	Ballade des femmes de Paris			DUR
Dougherty	Love in the dictionary	M	C-G	GSC
Enders	Russian picnic	HM	C-G	GSC
Gibbs	Five eyes	HL	D-D	BOS
Grieg	My Johann	HL	BF-EF	GSC
Hadley	My shadow			ASC
Hely-Hutchinson	Old mother Hubbard	HL	B-E	CFI
Johnston	Because I were shy	L	B-E	CRA
Lehmann	The cuckoo	HH	D-B	BOH
Mahler	Des Antonius von Padua Fischpredigt	HL	GF-F	†
-----	Wer hat dies Liedlein erdacht?	HL	BF-E	INT
Mozart	Die Alte			
-----	Warnung	HM	C-D	
Nordoff	Serenade	H	CS-FS	AMP
-----	There shall be more joy	M	CS-FS	AMP
Paisiello	Chi vuol la zingarella	L	C-F	GSC
Parry	Love is a bauble			NOV
Rawls	The balloon man	L	A-FS	AMP
Reger	Waldeinsamkeit	HML	A-D	BOS
Reichardt	Rhapsodie			MOS
Rich	American lullaby	LH	C-F	GSC
Rontani	Or ch'io non segno più	HL	CS-E	DIT
Rosenthal	Le marabout			ESC
Scarlatti, A.	Chi vuole innamorarsi	HL	D-EF	DIT
Schubert	Die Maenner sind mechant			PET
-----	Heidenroeslein			
Spross	Will o' the wisp			JCH
Wolf	Weather forecast	H	EF-GS	GSC

438

(Wolf)	Epiphanias	HL	B-D	†
-----	Ich hab' in Penna	LH		
-----	Nimmersatte Liebe	LH	CF-AF	†

American Folk Songs (Arr.)

Contralto

Bacon	Adam and Eve	M	B-D	CFI
Bartholomew	Dearest Billie	M	E-E	GSC
Brockway	Barbara Allen			GRA
-----	Frog went-a-courting			GRA
-----	Sourwood mountain			GRA
Davis	Deaf old woman			GAL
-----	He's gone away	M	C-E	GAL
Hughes	Birds' courting song			GSC
Matteson	The blue eyed boy			GSC
Niles	Down in the valley			GSC
-----	Go 'way from my window	MH	C-G	GSC
-----	I wonder as I wander	HL	BF-D	GSC
-----	Jesus, Jesus rest your head	HL	A-D	GSC
-----	Sing we the Virgin Mary			
Schindler	Mother dearest	M	A-G	GSC
Shaw	He's gone away	M	C-E	DIT

British Folk Songs (Arr.)

Contralto

Britten	Little Sir William			BOH
-----	O can ye sew cushions			BOH
-----	Oliver Cromwell			BOH
-----	The ash grove			BOH
-----	The Bonny Earl O' Moray			BOH
-----	The plough boy			BOH
-----	The Sally gardens			BOH
-----	The trees they grow so high			BOH
Clayton	O men from the fields	M	C-F	GAL
Gatty	Bendemeer's stream	LMH		BOO
Harty	The lowlands of Holland			OXF
Hopekirk	Coming through the rye			DIT
-----	Loch Lomond			DIT
Hughes	Down by the Sally gardens			BOO
-----	I know my love			BOO
-----	The lover's curse			BOO
Johnston	Because I were shy	L	B-E	CRA

439

Kennedy-Fraser	A fairy's love song			BOO
-----	An Eriskay love lilt			BOO
-----	Kishmul's galley			BOO
-----	Land of heart's desire			BOO
-----	The mull fisher's love song			BOO
Kreisler	Loch Lomond			
Lawson	Turn ye to me	M	B-E	GSC
Liddle	Friar John			
Page	The foggy dew			DIT
-----	The harp that once through Tara's halls			DIT
Quilter	Barbara Allen			BOO
-----	Over the mountains			BOS
-----	Ye banks and braes	M	DF-EF	BOH
Reid	Turn ye to me			BOO
Vaughan Williams	King William	L	D-D	OXF
-----	Lullaby of the Madonna	L	BF-D	GRA
-----	Rolling in the dew			OXF
Warlock	Willow, willow			OXF
-----	Yarmouth Fair	HL	B-E	CFI
Welsh	All through the night			
Wilson	Come let's be merry			BOO

Miscellaneous Folk Songs (Arr.)

Contralto

Bakaleinikoff	Pozhalieh (Russian Gypsy Air)			
Brahms	In stiller Nacht			†
Falla	Asturiana	HL		AMP
-----	El paño moruno	HL		AMP
-----	Jota	LH		AMP
-----	Nana	HL		AMP
-----	Polo	HL		AMP
-----	Seguidilla murciana	HL		AMP
-----	Siete canciones	HL		AMP
Lefkowitz	Korobooshka (Russian gypsy air)			
Liddle	An old French carol	LM	F-F	BOO
Obradors	Con amores a mi madre			RIC
Poniridis	Lullaby			
Ravel	Chanson espagnole	LH	D-BF	DUR
-----	Cinq mélodies populaires grecques			CUR
Respighi	Three Armenian folk songs			
Sfakianaki	Duru duru			
Vehanen	Tuku, tuku lampaitani			GAL

Weckerlin	O ma tendre musette	LM	A-E	GSC
-----	Menuet d'Exaudet	H	D-G	GSC
-----	Venez, agreable printemps	M	C-F	

Negro Spirituals

Contralto

Boatner	Oh, what a beautiful city!	HL	D-E	GSC
-----	On mah journey	LH	EF-EF	RIC
-----	Trampin' (Tryin' to make heaven my home)	L	D-F	ELK
Brown	Dere's no hidin' place down dere			CFI
-----	Every time I feel de spirit	L		AMP
-----	Hammer song	L	A-C	AMP
-----	Hear de lam's a cryin'			SC
-----	Sometimes I feel like a motherless child	L		AMP
Burleigh	Balm in Gilead	HL		RIC
-----	De gospel train	HL		RIC
-----	Deep river	HML		RIC
-----	Go down, Moses	HL		RIC
-----	Hard trials	M		RIC
-----	Heav'n Heav'n	HL		RIC
-----	I don't feel no-ways tired	M		RIC
-----	Joshua fit de battle ob Jericho	LH	DS-E	RIC
-----	Nobody knows de trouble I've seen	HL		RIC
-----	Oh, Peter, go ring-a-dem bells			RIC
-----	Ride on, King Jesus	H		RIC
-----	Sinner, please doan let dis harves' pass	M		RIC
-----	Sometimes I feel like a motherless child	HML		RIC
-----	Swing low, sweet chariot	HL		RIC
-----	Were you there?	HML		RIC
-----	Wide river			
Dawson	Talk about a chile that do love Jesus			
Dett	A man goin' roun'			
-----	Sit down servant			GSC
Fisher	Little wheel a-turnin' in my heart			

441

Hayes	I can't stay away			
Johnson	At the feet of Jesus	L		
-----	City called Heaven			ROB
-----	Crucifixion			
-----	Dere's no hidin' place down dere			
-----	Fix me, Jesus	L	BF-DF	GSC
-----	Hold on			ROB
-----	Honor, honor	HM	C-E	CFI
-----	My good Lord done been here	HM	BF-F	CFI
-----	Nobody knows the trouble I see			
-----	Ride on, King Jesus			CFI
-----	Roll, Jerd'n roll	M	EF-F	GSC
-----	Take my mother home	M	BF-EF	CFI
-----	Witness	HM	D-F	CFI
Kerby-Forrest	Glory ina mah soul			
-----	He's got the whole world in his hands	M	G-E	MLS
Lawrence	Let us break bread together	HML	BF-EF	MCR
MacGimsey	If he change my name			
-----	Sweet little Jesus boy	ML	D-D	CFI
McFeeters	Redeemed	L	BF-F	MLS
Payne	Crucifixion	L	C-C	GSC
Price	My soul's been anchored in the Lord			GAM
Ryder	He ain't coming here to die no more			
-----	Let us break bread together	LH	D-G	JFI
Saunders	The Lord's Prayer	L	BF-C	BOH

American Songs Employing Agility

Contralto

Buzzi-Peccia	Under the greenwood tree	LMH		DIT
Charles	Let my song fill your heart	LH		GSC
Curran	Ho! Mr. Piper	LH	D-G	GSC
Griffes	We'll to the woods and gather May	M	D-F	GSC
Hageman	Miranda	HL		GAL
Hopkinson	O'er the hills	LH	C-G	†
Nordoff	There shall be more joy	M	CS-FS	AMP

442

Speaks	In May time	HL	D-E	JCH

British Songs and Arias
Employing Agility

Contralto

Arne, T.	Where the bee sucks	HM		†
German	Charming Chloe	HML		NOV
Handel	Hence, Iris, hence away (Semele)	L		NOV
-----	In the battle, fame pursuing (Deborah)	L	A-D	†
-----	Lord, to Thee each night and day (Theodora)	L	C-E	†
-----	O thou that tellest good tidings to Zion (The Messiah)	L	A-C	†
Hely-Hutchinson	Old mother Hubbard	HL	B-E	CFI
Hook	Bright Phoebus	M	EF-F	GSC
Morley	It was a lover and his lass	HM		DIT
Parry	Love is a bauble			NOV
Purcell	From rosy bow'rs (Don Quixote)			AUG
-----	Hark! how all things with one sound rejoice			NOV
-----	Nymphs and shepherds (The Libertine)	HM	C-F	†
Quilter	Love's philosophy	LMH	D-A	BOO
Wilson	Come let's be merry			BOO

French Songs and Arias
Employing Agility

Contralto

Berlioz	La captive	HL		GSC
Bizet	Adieu de l'hôtesse arabe			†
-----	Ouvre ton coeur	MH	DS-GS	†
Campra	Charmant papillon (Les Fêtes Venitiennes)	MH	D-G	GSC
Chausson	Le colibri			BOS
Falla	Polo	HL		AMP
Ferrari	Le jardin d'amour	LM	EF-F	GSC
Georges	La pluie	HL		INT

443

Massé	Chanson du tigre (Paul et Virginie)			
Meyerbeer	Nobles seigneurs, salut! (Les Huguenots)			†
-----	O pretres de Baal (Le Prophète)			BRO
Vidal	Ariette	LH	F-A	GSC

German Songs and Arias Employing Agility

Contralto

Bach, J.S.	From the bondage (St. John Passion)	L	BF-EF	†
-----	Gelobet sei der Herr (Cantata 129) Oboe d'amore			AUG
-----	Hochgelobter Gottessohn (Cantata 6) English horn or viola or violin			NOV
-----	In Jesu Demut (Cantata 151) Oboe d'amore or violin			AUG
-----	It is finished (St. John Passion)	L	B-D	†
-----	Mein glaeubiges Herze (Cantata 68)	HML		†
Brahms	Botschaft	HL	D-F	†
-----	O liebliche Wangen	MLH	E-G	†
Haydn	My mother bids me bind my hair	M	E-E	†
Mahler	Des Antonius von Padua Fischpredigt	HL	GF-F	†
-----	Wer hat dies Liedlein erdacht?	HL	BF-E	INT
Schubert	Irrlicht			
-----	Ungeduld	HML		†
Schumann	Fruehlingsnacht	L	CS-E	†
-----	Waldesgespraech	HL	A-FS	†
Wolf	Die Zigeunerin			†

Italian Songs and Arias Employing Agility

Contralto

Arditi	Leggiero, invisible			
Carissimi	Vittoria, mio core	HLM	B-E	†

444

Donizetti	Il segreto per esser felici (Lucrezia Borgia)	M	C-G	†
Durante	Danza, danza fanciulla gentile	HM	BF-F	†
Handel	Ben io sento l'ingrata spietata furio (Atalanta)	L	B-D	CFI
-----	Ch'io mai vi possa (Siroe)			†
-----	Furibondo spira (Partenope)			KIS
-----	Si, tra i ceppi (Berenice)	L	B-D	†
Lotti	Pur dicesti, o bocca bella	LMH	E-FS	GSC
Rossini	Bel raggio lusinghier (Semiramide)	H	CS-A	GSC
-----	La danza	MH	E-A	†
-----	Non più mesta (La Cenerentola)	M	A-B	GSC
Sadero	Amuri, Amuri	M		CHE
Scarlatti, A.	Rugiadose odorose (Il Pirro e Demetrio)	HL	D-E	DIT
-----	Se Florindo è fedele	LM	EF-EF	GSC
Scarlatti, D.	Consolati e spara amante	L	BF-E	GSC
-----	Qual farfalletta			
Vivaldi	Un certo no so che	HL	BF-EF	†

Miscellaneous Songs and Arias
Employing Agility

Contralto

Bach, J.S.	Qui sedes ad dexteram Patris (Mass in B Minor) Oboe d'amore			†
Falla	Canción del amor dolido			CHE
-----	Chanson du feu follet	L	B-B	CHE
-----	Nana	HL		AMP
-----	Seguidilla murciana	HL		AMP
Grieg	Good morning			†
Mozart	Alleluja	LMH	F-C	†
-----	Laudamus Te (C Minor Mass)			PET
Pergolesi	Fac ut portem (Stabat Mater)			DES
Stravinsky	The cloister (La novice)			DIT
Turina	Farruca	M	A-F	UME

American Songs Employing
Crescendo and Diminuendo

Contralto

Bacon	A clear midnight			NEM
Barber	Sleep now	MH	EF-AF	GSC
Beach	Ah, love but a day			ASC
Cadman	From the land of the sky-blue water			WHI
Campbell-Tipton	The crying of water	LH	FS-GS	GSC
Carpenter	Go, lovely rose	M	DF-EF	GSC
-----	Odalisque	M	EF-EF	GSC
-----	The day is no more	M	GS-DS	GSC
-----	The sleep that flits on baby's eyes	M	B-FS	GSC
-----	Watercolors	M	C-F	GSC
-----	When I bring to you colour'd toys	LM	CS-FS	GSC
Charles	Clouds	HML	C-EF	GSC
Duke	Loveliest of trees	L	C-D	GSC
Engel	Sea shell	M	EF-EF	GSC
Fairchild	A memory			BOS
La Forge	Hills	HL		RIC
Naginski	The pasture	M	BF-EF	GSC
Niles	I wonder as I wander	HL	BF-D	GSC
-----	Jesus, Jesus rest your head	HL	A-D	GSC
Nordoff	Serenade	H	CS-FS	AMP
Rogers	At parting	LH	CS-FS	GSC
Thompson	Velvet shoes	M	C-E	ECS
Watts	Wings of night	LH	CS-G	GSC

British Songs and Arias Employing
Crescendo and Diminuendo

Contralto

Goossens	Melancholy	M		CHE
Handel	Art thou troubled (Rodelinda)	M	F-F	GSC
-----	He shall feed His flock (The Messiah)	L	C-D	†
-----	He was despised (The Messiah)	L	B-D	†
-----	Let me wander not unseen (L'Allegro)	M	D-G	†

Head	The ships of Arcady	ML	BF-EF	BOH
Horn	I've been roaming	L	B-E	†
Ireland	Bed in summer			CUR
Purcell	I attempt from love's sickness to fly (The Indian Queen)	MH	CS-E	†
Shaw	Song of the Palanquin bearers	LH	E-F	CUF
Warlock	Rest, sweet nymphs	M	F-F	CFI

French Songs and Arias Employing Crescendo and Diminuendo

Contralto

Debussy	C'est l'extase	LH	CS-A	†
-----	La flûte de Pan		B-B	†
-----	Voici que le printemps	LH	CS-G	BOS
Duparc	Chanson triste	MH	FS-AF	†
-----	L'invitation au voyage	HM	E-F	†
-----	Phidylé	MH	EF-AF	BOS
Fauré	Au bord de l'eau	HL	C-F	†
-----	Clair de lune	MH	C-G	†
-----	Green	HL	CS-GF	†
Koechlin	L'hiver	H	E-G	†
Liszt	S'il est un charmant gazon	HL		†
Martini	Plaisir d'amour	M	BF-EF	GSC
Meyerbeer	Nobles Seigneurs, salut! (Les Huguenots)	LH	C-C	†
Paladilhe	Psyché	HM	BF-F	GSC

German Songs and Arias Employing Crescendo and Diminuendo

Contralto

Bach, J.S.	Ach, lege das Sodom (Cantata 48) Oboe or violin			
-----	Ich sehe schon im Geist (Cantata 43) 2 Oboes and continuo			NOV
-----	Schlafe, mein Liebster (Christmas Oratorio)			
Brahms	Komm bald	HM	CS-F	†
-----	Sonntag	H	D-G	†
-----	Spanisches Lied			†
-----	Therese	HL	B-D	†
-----	Wie Melodien zieht es	HL	A-E	†

447

Franz	Sterne mit den gold'nen Fuesschen	HL	DS-E	†
Reger	Mit Rosen bestreut			UNI
-----	Waldeinsamkeit	HML	A-D	BOS
Schubert	Auf dem Wasser zu singen	MH	EF-GF	†
-----	Der Juengling auf dem Huegel	L	G-F	†
-----	Der Musensohn	LH	FS-G	†
-----	Der Wanderer	HML	FS-D	†
-----	Der Wanderer an den Mond	LM	D-F	PET
-----	Fruehlingstraum	HL	C-D	†
-----	Gott im Fruehling			PET
-----	Gretchen am Spinnrade	H	F-A	†
-----	Hark! hark! the lark	LMH	F-G	GSC
-----	Lachen und Weinen	HL	C-EF	†
-----	Liebesbotschaft	H	E-G	†
-----	Nacht und Traeume	HL	C-DF	†
Schumann	Der Nussbaum	LMH	D-FS	†
-----	Die Soldatenbraut	HL	AF-EF	†
Strauss	Die Nacht	HL		†
Wolf	In dem Schatten meiner Locken	M	C-EF	†
-----	Mausfallen Spruechlein	HL	BF-E	†
-----	Nun lass uns Frieden schliessen	HL		†
-----	Nun wandre, Maria	HL	EF-D	†
-----	Wenn du zu den Blumen gehst	HL	B-EF	†
Wolff	Maerchen	M	D-E	†

Italian Songs and Arias Employing Crescendo and Diminuendo

Contralto

Caldara	Sebben crudele	HML	E-DS	†
-----	Selve amiche, ombrose piante	HM	E-E	†
Cesti	Intorno all' idol mio (Orontea)	MH	D-F	†
De Luca	Non posso disperar	HL	C-E	GSC
Falconieri	O bellissimi capelli	HL	B-D	†
Frescobaldi	Se l'aura spira	HL	C-EF	DIT
Handel	Ombra mai fu (Serse)	HM	BF-EF	†
Marcello	Non m'è grave morir per amore	L	C-E	GSC
Monteverdi	Lasciatemi morire (Arianna)	ML	D-D	†

448

Pergolesi	Se tu m'ami	LMH	C-G	GSC
Rontani	Se bel rio	ML	D-C	†
Rosa	Selve, voi che le speranze	MH	D-G	DIT
-----	Vado ben spesso	ML	C-EF	†
Scarlatti, A.	La fortuna			BOS
-----	Sento nel core	M	E-F	†

Miscellaneous Songs and Arias Employing Crescendo and Diminuendo

Contralto

Gretchaninoff	The snowdrop	HM	BF-F	DIT
Grieg	In the boat	LM	D-ES	†
-----	Springtide	M		DIT
-----	With a water lily	HM	CS-EF	†
Mussorgsky	Oriental chant (Josua Navine Cantata)	ML	BF-E	GSC
-----	The banks of the Don			GSC
Rachmaninoff	Lilacs	LH	EF-G	†
-----	The island	LH	DF-F	†

American Songs and Arias Employing Piano Singing

Contralto

Bacon	A clear midnight			NEM
Barber	Sleep now	MH	EF-AF	GSC
Campbell-Tipton	The crying of water	LH	FS-GS	GSC
Carpenter	Go, lovely rose	M	DF-EF	GSC
-----	May the maiden			DIT
-----	Odalisque	M	EF-EF	GSC
-----	On a screen	L	BF-DF	GSC
-----	The day is no more	M	GS-DS	GSC
-----	The green river	M	B-E	GSC
-----	The sleep that flits on baby's eyes	M	B-FS	GSC
-----	Watercolors	M	C-F	GSC
-----	When I bring to you colour'd toys	LM	CS-FS	GSC
Charles	Clouds	HML	C-EF	GSC
-----	When I have sung my songs	HM	BF-EF	GSC
Engel	Sea shell	M	EF-EF	GSC

Fairchild	A memory			BOS
Farwell	These saw visions			GAL
Foote	Tranquillity	HL	BF-E	ASC
Ganz	A memory	HM	B-D	GSC
Hageman	Do not go, my love	HL	B-EF	GSC
Ives	Evening			GSC
MacGimsey	Sweet little Jesus boy	ML	D-D	CFI
Manning	Shoes	M	EF-F	GSC
Menotti	Lullaby (The Consul)			GSC
Naginski	The pasture	M	BF-EF	GSC
Nevin	Mighty lak' a rose			JCH
Niles	I wonder as I wander	HL	BF-D	GSC
-----	Jesus, Jesus rest your head	HL	A-D	GSC
Nordoff	Serenade	H	CS-FS	AMP
Schuman	Orpheus with his lute	M	C-FS	GSC
Thompson	Velvet shoes	M	C-E	ECS
Watts	Wings of night	LH	CS-G	GSC

British Songs and Arias Employing Piano Singing

Contralto

Bax	I heard a piper piping	LH	D-G	CFI
Dunhill	The cloths of heaven	LM	EF-G	STB
Elgar	Sea pictures	L	A-A	BOO
Handel	Let me wander not unseen L'Allegro	M	D-G	†
Head	Nocturne	HL		BOO
-----	The ships of Arcady	ML	BF-EF	BOH
Pilkington	Rest, sweet nymphs			STB
Sanderson	Quiet	ML	AF-EF	BOH
Scott	Lullaby	MML	BF-DF	GAL
Vaughan Williams	Silent noon			GSC

French Songs and Arias Employing Piano Singing

Contralto

Debussy	La flûte de Pan		B-B	†
Fauré	Après un rêve	HM	C-F	†
-----	Clair de lune	MH	C-G	†
Ferrari	Le miroir	M	E-F	GSC
Franck	Le mariage des roses	M	E-FS	BOS

Gounod	Au rossignol	LMH	D-G	CHO
Hahn	D'une prison	L	BF-EF	HEU
-----	L'heure exquise	M	DF-F	†
-----	Offrande	M	D-D	†
-----	Paysage	MH	EF-G	HEU
Lully	Bois épais (Amadis)	ML	C-EF	†
Paladilhe	Psyché	HM	BF-F	GSC
Pessard	L'adieu du matin	ML	BF-D	GSC
Poldowski	L'heure exquise	LMH	DF-AF	CHE
Weckerlin	Menuet d'Exaudet	H	D-G	GSC
-----	O ma tendre musette	LM	A-E	GSC
Widor	Je ne veux pas autre chose	HL	C-EF	HAM

German Songs and Arias Employing Piano Singing

Contralto

Bach, J.S.	Jesus schlaeft (Cantata 81)	L	A-D	GSC
Beethoven	Ich liebe dich	HL	BF-DF	†
Brahms	In Waldeseinsamkeit	H	ES-G	†
-----	Komm bald	HM	CS-F	†
-----	Sapphische Ode	HML		†
-----	Spanisches Lied			†
-----	Staendchen	HL	BF-E	†
-----	Steig' auf, geliebter Schatten	HL	BF-EF	†
Franz	Sterne mit den gold'nen Fuesschen	HL	DS-E	†
Mahler	Ich bin der Welt abbanden gekommen	HL		INT
-----	Liebst du um Schoenheit	HL		INT
-----	Wo die schoenen Trompeten blasen	HL	GF-F	INT
Mendelssohn	O rest in the Lord (Elijah)	L	B-D	†
Schubert	Auf dem Wasser zu singen	MH	EF-GF	†
-----	Ave Maria	LMH	F-F	†
-----	Der Tod und das Maedchen	HL	A-EF	†
-----	Der Wanderer an den Mond	LM	D-F	PET
-----	Du bist die Ruh	LMH	EF-AF	†
-----	Fruehlingstraum	HL	C-D	†
-----	Gott im Fruehling			PET

451

(Schubert)	Im Abendrot	HL	C-D	GSC
-----	Lachen und Weinen	HL	C-EF	†
-----	Liebesbotschaft	H	E-G	†
-----	Nacht und Traeume	HL	C-DF	†
Schumann	Der Nussbaum	LMH	D-FS	†
-----	Mondnacht	M	E-FS	†
Strauss	Allerseelen	HL	AS-E	†
-----	Die Nacht	HL		†
-----	Fruendliche Vision	HL	C-F	†
-----	Traum durch die Daemmerung	HML	BF-EF	†
-----	Wiegenliedchen			†
Wagner	Der Engel	LH	CS-G	†
Wolf	In dem Schatten meiner Locken	M	C-EF	†
-----	Mausfallen Spruechlein	HL	BF-E	†
-----	Nachtzauber	HL	B-E	†
-----	Schlafendes Jesuskind	HL	AS-F	†
-----	Verborgenheit	HL	B-E	†
-----	Wie glaenzt der helle Mond			†
Wolff	Ich bin eine Harfe			HMP
-----	Maerchen	M	D-E	†

Italian Songs and Arias Employing
Piano Singing

Contralto

Bononcini	Deh, più a me non v'ascondete	LH	EF-F	†
Cimara	Fiocca la neve	H	G-G	GSC
Frescobaldi	Se l'aura spira	HL	C-EF	DIT
Gagliano	Dormi, amore (La Flora)	HL	CS-E	DIT
Gluck	O del mio dolce ardor (Paride ed Elena)			
Handel	Care selve (Atalanta)	MH	FS-A	†
Monteverdi	Lasciatemi morire (Arianna)	ML	D-D	†
Paradies	M'ha preso alla sua ragna	M		GSC
Rontani	Se bel rio	ML	D-C	†
Secchi	Lungi dal caro bene	HL	A-FS	DIT

Miscellaneous Songs Employing
Piano Singing

Contralto

Arensky	Valse	H	DF-GF	GSC
Dvořák	God is my shepherd			AMP
-----	I will lift mine eyes			AMP
-----	Songs my mother taught me	HM	E-E	†
Gretchaninoff	Hushed the song of the nightingale	MH	E-G	DIT
Grieg	A dream			†
-----	A swan			†
-----	In the boat	LM	D-ES	†
Mednikoff	The hills of Gruzia	H	DS-A	LAC
Rachmaninoff	In the silence of night	LH	D-A	GSC
Sibelius	The tryst	M		AMP

American Songs Employing
Rapid Enunciation

Contralto

Boatner	Oh, what a beautiful city!	HL	D-E	GSC
Burleigh	Joshua fit de battle ob Jericho	LH	DS-E	RIC
Carpenter	Don't ceare	M	C-D	GSC
-----	The cock shall crow	M	B-E	GSC
Hadley	My shadow			ASC
Hageman	Miranda	HL		GAL
Manning	Shoes	M	EF-F	GSC
Spross	Will o' the wisp			JCH

British Songs Employing
Rapid Enunciation

Contralto

Brewer	The fairy pipers	HML		BOH
Britten	Oliver Cromwell			BOH
Elgar	Sea pictures	L	A-A	BOO
German	Charming Chloe	HML		NOV
Gibbs	Five eyes	HL	D-D	BOS
Head	A piper	HL		BOO
Molloy	The Kerry dance	LH	C-G	GSC

Morley	It was a lover and his lass	HM		DIT
Purcell	There's not a swain on the plain	M	B-G	BAF
Vaughan Williams	The water mill	L	C-D	OXF

French Songs and Arias Employing
Rapid Enunciation

Contralto

Bizet	Habanera (Carmen)	HM	D-F	†
Caplet	La ronde	M		DUR
Debussy	Ballade des femmes de Paris			DUR
-----	Chevaux de bois	H	C-G	†
-----	La flûte de Pan		B-B	†
-----	Mandoline	HM	BF-F	†
Fauré	Toujours	LH	F-AF	†
Fourdrain	Carnaval	M	C-F	RIC
Pessard	L'adieu du matin	ML	BF-D	GSC
Poldowski	Dansons la gigue	M	EF-G	MAR
Ravel	Nicolette	L	B-FS	ELK
Saint-Saëns	L'attente			DUR

German Songs Employing
Rapid Enunciation

Contralto

Brahms	Juchhe!			†
-----	Meine Liebe ist gruen	MLH	ES-A	†
-----	O liebliche Wangen	MLH	E-G	†
-----	Staendchen	HL	BF-E	†
-----	Vergebliches Staendchen	LHM	E-FS	†
Loewe	Walpurgisnacht	H	G-G	SC
Mozart	Warnung	HM	C-D	
Schubert	Die Forelle	MLH	EF-GF	†
-----	Die Post	HML	BF-EF	†
-----	Erstarrung	HL	D-F	†
-----	Fischerweise	L	C-D	†
-----	Ungeduld	HML		†
-----	Wohin?	HL	B-E	†
Schumann	Die Kartenlegerin			
Wolf	Ich hab' in Penna	LH		†

Italian Songs and Arias Employing
Rapid Enunciation

Contralto

Carissimi	Vittoria, mio core	HLM	B-E	†
Cavalli	Donzelle fuggite	HL	C-EF	†
Donizetti	Il segreto per esser felici (Lucrezia Borgia)	M	C-G	†
Durante	Danza, danza fanciulla gentile	HM	BF-F	†
Falconieri	Non più d'amore	HL	C-D	DIT
-----	Nudo arciero	HL	AF-AF	DIT
Handel	Ch'io mai vi possa (Siroe)			†
Legrenzi	Che fiero costume	HML	C-D	†
Paisiello	Chi vuol la zingarella	L	C-F	GSC
Rontani	Or ch'io non segno più	HL	CS-E	DIT
Rossini	La danza	MH	E-A	†
Scarlatti, A.	Chi vuole innamorarsi	HL	D-EF	DIT

Miscellaneous Songs Employing
Rapid Enunciation

Contralto

Falla	Canción del amor dolido			CHE
-----	Chanson du feu follet	L	B-B	CHE
-----	Seguidilla murciana	HL		AMP
Grieg	Digtervise	L	A-EF	HAN
-----	In the boat	LM	D-ES	†
-----	My Johann	HL	BF-EF	GSC
-----	With a water lily			†
Mussorgsky	The magpie and the gypsy dancer			GSC

American Songs Employing
Sustained Singing

Contralto

Barber	A nun takes the veil	MH	G-G	GSC
-----	Sure on this shining night	MH	D-G	GSC
Burleigh	Deep river	HML		RIC
-----	Sometimes I feel like a motherless child	HML		RIC
-----	Were you there?	HML		RIC

455

Carpenter	Highway men	M	C-F	GSC
-----	Slumber song	ML	BF-F	GSC
-----	The player queen	M	BF-EF	GSC
-----	To one unknown	M	A-DS	GSC
Dello Joio	New born	M	C-D	CFI
Edwards	By the bend of the river	HML	C-E	GSC
-----	Into the night	HML	C-DF	GSC
Foster, S.C.	Ah, may the red rose live always!			GSC
Griffes	By a lonely forest pathway	HML	A-EF	GSC
-----	Evening song	H	DS-GS	GSC
Hageman	Music I heard with you	MH	E-A	GAL
Harris	Fog	M	D-F	CFI
Hawley	Ah, 'tis a dream	L	G-C	JCH
Hindemith	The wildflower's song	MH	E-G	AMP
Horsman	The bird of the wilderness	LMH	DF-BF	GSC
Metcalf	At nightfall	HML	C-DF	ASC
Moore	Sigh no more, ladies			BOO
Scott	Think on me	HML	D-EF	GAL
Tyson	Noon and night	LH	F-AF	GSC
Watts	Transformation	ML	AS-DS	GSC

British Songs and Arias Employing Sustained Singing

Contralto

Bantock	Silent strings	MH	F-G	BOO
Bridge	O that it were so	LMH	D-G	CHA
Britten	The Sally gardens			BOH
Del Riego	Homing	HML	BF-E	CHA
Dowland	Sorrow, sorrow stay	M	D-D	BOS
-----	Woeful heart with grief oppressed			KEE
Dunhill	To the Queen of Heaven	M	C-G	GSC
Handel	Thou shalt bring them in (Israel in Egypt)	L	B-D	†
-----	Vouchsafe, O Lord (Dettingen Te Deum)	HM		ELV
Henschel	Morning-hymn	MH	DS-GS	†
-----	There was an ancient king			ASC
Holst	The heart worships	ML	BF-D	STB
Purcell	If music be the food of love	M	D-G	BOO
-----	Sweet, be no longer sad			NOV

456

(Purcell)	When I am laid in earth (Dido and Aeneas)	LH	C-G	†
Ronald	Prelude	HML	B-D	ENO
Sullivan	The lost chord	HL	C-F	GSC
Vaughan Williams	Four nights	L	AF-EF	OXF
-----	Linden-Lea	HML	C-D	BOS
Warlock	Sleep			OXF
Welsh	All through the night			

French Songs and Arias Employing
Sustained Singing

Contralto

Bemberg	Chant hindou	HML	A-EF	†
-----	Du Christ avec ardeur (La Mort de Jeanne d'Arc)	M	DF-AF	†
Berlioz	La captive	HL		GSC
Bizet	Adieu de l'hôtesse arabe	H	BF-G	†
-----	Ma vie a son secret	L	AF-F	CHU
Chaminade	Chant slave			GSC
Chausson	Le colibri Violin or cello	M	F-GF	BOS
-----	Le temps des lilas	MH	D-GS	†
Debussy	Ballade que fait Villon à la requeste de sa mère			DUR
-----	Beau soir	LH	C-FS	†
-----	Je tremble en voyant ton visage			DUR
-----	La chevelure	M	CF-FS	†
Duparc	Au pays où se fait la guerre			SAL
-----	Lamento	ML	EF-EF	†
Fauré	Automne	MH	D-FS	GSC
-----	Le parfum impérissable	LH	GF-GF	
-----	Les berceaux	LMH	BF-G	†
-----	Nocturne	H	F-A	MAR
-----	Prison	LH		†
-----	Rencontre	H	EF-AF	†
Gluck	Divinités du Styx (Alceste)	MH	DF-AF	†
-----	Je n'ai jamais chéri la vie (Alceste)	L	A-F	GSC
Gounod	O ma lyre immortelle (Sappho)	M	C-G	†
Honegger	Chanson (Ronsard) Flute and string quartet			SEN

457

(Honegger)	Oh my love take my hand			SEN
Hue	J'ai pleuré en rêve	HL	D-E	BOS
Indy	Lied maritime	LH	B-G	†
Lalo	Chant breton	M	E-E	HAM
Leroux	Le nil	LH	E-A	†
Massenet	Elégie	LM	C-GF	GSC
Meyerbeer	Ah! mon fils (Le Prophète)	M	B-AS	†
Paladilhe	Lamento provincal	M	CS-FS	HOM
Poulenc	A sa guitare	M	D-FS	DUR
Ravel	Kaddisch	H	C-G	DUR
-----	Vocalise en forme de habanera	MH	BF-G	MAR
Rhene-Baton	Il pleut des pétales de fleurs	M	CS-E	DUR
Saint-Saëns	Amour, viens aider (Samson et Dalila)	HM	AF-G	†
-----	La cloche	LH	DF-AF	†
-----	Mon coeur s'ouvre à ta voix (Samson et Dalila)	HLM	BF-GF	†
-----	Printemps qui commence (Samson et Dalila)	M	B-E	†
Weckerlin	Venez, agréable printemps	M	C-F	

German Songs and Arias Employing Sustained Singing

Contralto

Ahle	Bruenstiges Verlangen	M	E-E	GSC
Bach, J.S.	Ach Herr! was ist ein Menschenkind (Cantata 110) Oboe d'amore			AUG
-----	Ach, schlaefrige Seele (Cantata 115)			AUG
-----	Bist du bei mir	HML	A-EF	†
-----	Geist und Seele wird verwirret (Cantata 35)			
-----	Schlage doch, gewuenschte Stunde (Cantata 53)			RIC
-----	Weh der Seele (Cantata 102) Oboe			BRO
Beethoven	Das Geheimnis			
-----	Die Ehre Gottes	HL	AF-EF	†
-----	Faithfu' Johnie			
-----	Vom Tode	L	A-EF	GSC
-----	Wonne der Wehmut			†
Bohm	Calm as the night	HML	A-EF	†

458

Brahms	An die Nachtigall	H	DS-G	†
-----	An eine Aeolsharfe	H	EF-AF	†
-----	Auf dem Kirchhofe	HL	BF-EF	†
-----	Dein blaues Auge	MH	BF-G	†
-----	Der Tod, das ist die kuehle Nacht	L	AF-F	†
-----	Die Mainacht	HL	BF-FF	†
-----	Feldeinsamkeit	HL	C-EF	†
-----	Immer leiser wird mein Schlummer	LH	DF-A	GSC
-----	Liebestreu	ML	C-F	†
-----	Mit vierzig Jahren	HL	FS-D	†
-----	Muss es eine Trennung geben?	LH	FS-FS	†
-----	Nachtigall	MHL	BF-FS	†
-----	O kuehler Wald	MH	A-F	†
-----	O wuesst' ich doch den Weg zurueck	H	E-FS	†
-----	Schwermut			†
-----	Treue Liebe	LMH	DS-E	†
-----	Verzagen	MH	CS-FS	†
-----	Wir wandelten	LH	EF-GF	†
Bruch	Penelope's sorrow (Odysseus)			SIM
Cornelius	Komm, wir wandeln	H	FS-GS	SC
Franz	Es ragt ins Meer der Runenstein	HL	G-F	†
-----	Im Herbst	HM	A-F	†
-----	Mutter, o sing mich zur Ruh	HL	E-G	†
Haydn	She never told her love	HL	B-D	DIT
Himmel	Die Sendung			SIM
Jensen	Wie so bleich			
Liszt	Freudvoll und leidvoll			DUR
Loewe	Der heilige Franziskus	L	A-E	SC
Mendelssohn	But the Lord is mindful of His own (Saint Paul)	L	A-D	†
-----	Woe unto them who forsake him (Elijah)	L	B-E	GSC
Mozart	Wiegenlied	MH	G-G	†
Schoenberg	Song of the wood dove			AMP
Schubert	Am Bach im Fruehling			PET
-----	An die Leier	LM	BF-F	†
-----	An die Musik	HL	A-DS	†
-----	Der Doppelgaenger	HL	G-D	†
-----	Der Leiermann	ML	C-D	†
-----	Der Lindenbaum	HL	A-D	†
-----	Der Neugierige	HL	CS-EF	†
-----	Der Wegweiser	L	D-EF	†

(Schubert)	Des Maedchens Klage	LH	C-E	†
-----	Die Allmacht	HML	G-E	†
-----	Die Kraehe	HL	A-E	†
-----	Die Liebe hat gelogen	LM	G-F	†
-----	Die Maenner sind mechant			PET
-----	Die Nebensonnen	HL	F-D	†
-----	Du liebst mich nicht	LH	E-FS	†
-----	In der Ferne	HL		†
-----	Litanei	HLM	C-EF	†
-----	Nachtgesang			PET
-----	Schaefers Klagelied	HL	BF-D	†
-----	Thekla	HL	B-E	PET
-----	Wanderers Nachtlied 1	HL		†
-----	Wehmuth	HL	B-D	†
Schuetz	Aus dem 119th Psalm			
Schumann	An den Sonnenschein	HL	A-D	†
-----	Aus den Hebraeischen Gesaengen			
-----	Der Himmel hat eine Traene geweint			
-----	Die Lotusblume	HLM	BF-F	†
-----	Du bist wie eine Blume	HM	F-EF	†
-----	Du Ring an meinem Finger	HL	C-F	†
-----	Hoch, hoch sind die Berge			
-----	Im Westen	HL		†
-----	Lied der Suleika			
-----	Mit Myrthen und Rosen	HL	A-D	†
-----	Seit ich ihn gesehen	HL	DF-DF	†
-----	Wehmut			†
-----	Wer machte dich so krank?			
Strauss	Befreit			HSC
-----	Im Spaetboot			
-----	Liebeshymnus			†
-----	Mit deinen blauen Augen	LH	C-GS	†
-----	Morgen	HML	E-F	†
-----	Ruhe meine Seele			†
Wagner	Schmerzen	HL		GSC
-----	Traeume	HL		†
Wolf	Agnes	HL		†
-----	Alle gingen, Herz, zu Ruh	HL	C-EF	†
-----	An eine Aeolsharfe			†
-----	Bedeckt mich mit Blumen	HL	B-D	†
-----	Das verlassene Maegdlein	HL	D-EF	†
-----	Gebet	HL		†
-----	Gesang Weylas	HL	DF-F	†
-----	Im Fruehling	HL	BF-F	†
-----	In der Fruehe	HL	C-C	†

(Wolf)	Um Mitternacht	HL	G-EF	†
-----	Zur Ruh', zur Ruh'	HL	A-GF	†
Wolff	Alle Dinge haben Sprache	M	BF-GF	†
-----	Ewig			

Italian Songs and Arias Employing Sustained Singing

Contralto

Bellini	Scombra è la sacra selva (Norma)			RIC
Caccini	Amarilli, mia bella	ML	C-D	†
Caldara	Come raggio di sol	HL	D-F	†
Cavalli	Beato chi può (Serse)			HEU
Cesti	Che angoscia, che affanno (Il Pomo d'Oro)	HL	C-DF	DIT
-----	E dove t'aggiri (Il Pomo d'Oro)			DIT
Cherubini	Ahi, che forse ai miei di (Demofonte)			RIC
Cimara	Stornellata marinara	HM		RIC
Cimarosa	Bel nume che adoro			RIC
Donaudy	Quando ti rivedrò			RIC
Donizetti	O mio Fernando (La Favorita)	M	B-A	†
Durante	Vergin, tutta amor	LM	C-EF	†
Giordano	O grandi occhi lucenti (Fedora)			BRO
Gluck	Che farò senza Euridice (Orphée)	ML	BF-F	†
-----	Spiagge amate (Paride ed Elena)			†
Handel	Dove sei, amato bene (Rodelinda)	L	BF-EF	†
-----	Lascia ch'io pianga (Rinaldo)	HM	EF-F	DIT
-----	Rend'l sereno al ciglio (Sosarme)	LH	EF-F	†
-----	Stille amare (Tolomeo)			MUP
-----	Tutta raccolta (Scipione)			CFI
-----	V'adoro pupille (Julius Caesar)			BOO
-----	Verdi prati (Alcina)			†
-----	Vieni o figlio caro e mi consola (Ottone)			†
Monteverdi	Tu se' morta (Orfeo)	M	C-E	GSC
Peri	Funeste piaggie (Euridice)			GSC

(Peri)	Invocazione di Orfeo (Euridice)	HL	E-CS	DIT
Ponchielli	Voce di donna (La Gioconda)	HM	A-G	GSC
Respighi	Io sono la madre	L		RIC
-----	Nebbie			†
Rosa	Star vicino	HL	D-E	†
Scarlatti, A.	O cessate di piagarmi	HL	DS-E	†
Stradella	Col mio sangue comprenderei (Il Floridoro)	HL	E-F	DIT
-----	Per pietà (Il Floridoro)	HM	D-F	DIT
-----	Se nel ben			CFI
Torelli	Tu lo sai	HL	BF-F	†
Verdi	Re dell' abisso (Un Ballo in Maschera)			RIC

Miscellaneous Songs and Arias Employing Sustained Singing

Contralto

Bach-Gounod	Ave Maria			†
Borodin	A dissonance	MH	E-F	†
Dvořák	By the waters of Babylon			AMP
-----	Hear my prayer, O Lord			AMP
-----	Inflammatus et accensus (Stabat Mater)	L	A-EF	NOV
-----	Lord, thou art my refuge and shield			AMP
-----	Turn Thee to me			AMP
Gliere	Ah, twine no blossoms	HM	CS-F	DIT
Granados	La maja dolorosa	M		INT
Gretchaninoff	Over the steppe	LM	C-G	GSC
-----	Wounded birch	HL	B-EF	†
Grieg	I love thee	HML	E-F	†
Hasse	Salve regina			BRH
Mussorgsky	Martha's song (Khovantchina)	ML		GSC
-----	On the Dnieper			GSC
-----	Sphinx			BRH
Rachmaninoff	Christ is risen	LM	D-F	GAL
-----	O thou billowy harvest field	HL	CS-E	GSC
-----	To the children	MH	F-G	DIT
Sibelius	Black roses	M	A-ES	AMP
-----	From the north	H	DS-G	GSC
-----	The first kiss	M		AMP
-----	Was it a dream			BRH

Sinding	I hear the gull			JCH
Tchaikovsky	Complaint of the bride			
-----	None but the lonely heart	HLM	C-F	DIT
-----	Pauline's romance	M	BF-AF	GSC
	(Pique Dame)			
-----	Why	HL		†

American Songs Employing
Spirited Singing

Contralto

Barber	I hear an army	LH	D-AF	GSC
Boatner	Oh, what a beautiful city!	HL	D-E	GSC
Burleigh	Joshua fit de battle ob Jericho	LH	DS-E	RIC
Carpenter	Don't ceare	M	C-D	GSC
-----	If	M	D-E	GSC
-----	Light, my light	M	C-G	GSC
-----	Serenade	LH	CS-A	GSC
-----	The cock shall crow	M	B-E	GSC
-----	To a young gentleman	M	C-F	GSC
Duke	On a March day	M	B-GF	BOH
Enders	Russian picnic	HM	C-G	GSC
Giannini	Sing to my heart a song	H	D-B	ELV
Griffes	We'll to the woods and gather May	M	D-F	GSC
Guion	Wild geese	M	D-F	CFI
Hadley	My shadow			ASC
Hageman	Miranda	HL		GAL
Johnson	Roll Jerd'n roll	M	EF-F	GSC
La Forge	Song of the open	MH	EF-AF	DIT
Nordoff	There shall be more joy	M	CS-FS	AMP
Rawls	The balloon man	L	A-FS	AMP
Rogers	The last song	MLH	E-AF	GSC
Rummel	Ecstasy	LMH	GF-AF	GSC
Salter	The cry of Rachel	LH	C-AF	GSC
Speaks	Morning	HML	BF-D	GSC
Spross	Will o' the wisp			JCH
Weaver	Moon-marketing	LMH	E-G	GSC

British Songs and Arias Employing
Spirited Singing

Contralto

Arne, T.	Why so pale and wan?			GSC
Brewer	The fairy pipers	HML		BOH
Bridge	Love went a-riding	HL		BOS
Elgar	The swimmer			BOO
German	Charming Chloe	HML		NOV
Gibbs	Five eyes	HL	D-D	BOS
Handel	Hence, Iris, hence away (Semele)	L		NOV
-----	Lord, to thee each night and day (Theodora)	L	C-E	†
Head	A piper	HL		BOO
Hook	Bright Phoebus	M	EF-F	GSC
Johnston	Because I were shy	L	B-E	CRA
Lehmann	The cuckoo	HH	D-B	BOH
Molloy	The Kerry dance	LH	C-G	GSC
Morley	It was a lover and his lass	HM		DIT
Parry	Love is a bauble			NOV
Purcell	Hark! how all things with one sound rejoice			NOV
-----	Nymphs and shepherds (The Libertine)	HM	C-F	†
-----	There's not a swain on the plain	M	B-G	BAF
Quilter	Blow, blow thou winter wind	HL	C-E	BOO
-----	Love's philosophy	LMH	D-A	BOO
Rowley	The toll gate house			ROG
Warlock	Consider	M	C-G	CFI
-----	In an arbour green	H	D-G	CFI

French Songs and Arias Employing
Spirited Singing

Contralto

Bizet	Habanera (Carmen)	HM	D-F	†
-----	Ouvre ton coeur	MH	DS-GS	†
Caplet	La ronde	M		DUR
Debussy	Ballade des femmes de Paris			DUR
-----	Chevaux de bois	H	C-G	†
-----	La mer est plus belle	HL		†

(Debussy)	Le faune			DUR
-----	Mandoline	HM	BF-F	†
Duparc	Le manoir de Rosamunde	HL	B-F	BOS
Dupont	Mandoline			DUR
Fauré	Fleur jetée	HM	BF-FS	†
-----	Toujours	LH	F-AF	†
Georges	La pluie	HL		INT
Gluck	Amours, sors pour jamais (Armide)			PET
Honegger	Les cloches			SEN
Pierné	Le moulin	ML	C-E	BOS
Poldowski	Dansons la gigue	M	EF-G	MAR
Ravel	Chanson espagnole	LH	D-BF	DUR
-----	Nicolette	L	B-FS	ELK
Saint-Saëns	L'attente			DUR
Vidal	Ariette	LH	F-A	GSC

German Songs Employing Spirited Singing

Contralto

Bach, J.S.	Mein glaeubiges Herze (Cantata 68)	HML		†
Beethoven	An die Geliebte	M	E-E	†
-----	Busslied			†
-----	Die Trommel geruehret			†
Brahms	Botschaft	HL	D-F	†
-----	Der Schmied	HL	EF-EF	†
-----	Juchhe!			†
-----	Meine Liebe ist gruen	MLH	ES-A	†
-----	O liebliche Wangen	MLH	E-G	†
-----	Sehnsucht	H	EF-AF	†
-----	Vergebliches Staendchen	LHM	E-FS	†
Franz	Er ist gekommen	HL	EF-F	†
Loewe	Maedchen sind wie der Wind			SC
-----	Walpurgisnacht	H	G-G	SC
Mahler	Das Irdische Leben	HL	A-F	INT
-----	Ging heut Morgen uebers Feld	M	A-FS	INT
-----	Ich hab' ein gluehend Messer	M	BF-GF	WEI
-----	Wer hat dies Liedlein erdacht?	HL	BF-E	INT
Schubert	Aufenthalt	HLM	A-F	†
-----	Die Forelle	MLH	EF-GF	†
-----	Die Post	HML	BF-EF	†

465

(Schubert)	Ellens zweiter Gesang			PET
-----	Erstarrung	HL	D-F	†
-----	Fischerweise	L	C-D	†
-----	Heidenroeslein			
-----	Rastlose Liebe	M	B-F	†
-----	Suleika I	LH	DS-G	†
-----	Wohin?	HL	B-E	†
Schumann	Er, der Herrlichste von Allen	HL	A-EF	†
-----	Fruehlingsnacht	L	CS-E	†
-----	Im Walde	HL	A-D	†
-----	Schoene Wiege meiner Leiden	HL	C-EF	†
-----	Waldesgespraech	HL	A-FS	†
-----	Widmung	HL	BF-F	†
Strauss	Caecilie	MH	E-B	†
-----	Heimliche Aufforderung	HL	B-E	†
-----	Zueignung	HL	CS-FS	†
Wolf	Auf einer Wanderung	HL		†
-----	Die ihr schwebet	HL	EF-EF	†
-----	Die Zigeunerin			†
-----	Er ist's	H	D-G	†
-----	Fussreise	HL	D-E	†
-----	Geh' Geliebter, geh' jetzt			PET
-----	Ich hab' in Penna	LH		†
-----	Klinge, klinge, mein Pandero	HL	CF-EF	†
-----	Nimmersatte Liebe	LH	CF-AF	DIT

Italian Songs and Arias Employing Spirited Singing

Contralto

Carissimi	Vittoria, mio core	HLM	B-E	†
Cavalli	Donzelle fuggite	HL	C-EF	†
Donizetti	Il segreto per esser felici (Lucrezia Borgia)	M	C-G	†
Durante	Danza, danza fanciulla gentile	HM	BF-F	†
Falconieri	Non più d'amore	HL	C-D	DIT
-----	Nudo arciero	HL	AF-AF	DIT
Giordano	Temer? perche? (Andrea Chenier)			BRO
Handel	Ch'io mai vi possa (Siroe)			†
-----	Furibondo spira (Partenope)			KIS

466

(Handel)	Piangero la sorte mia (Julius Caesar)			CFI
-----	Si, tra i ceppi (Berenice)	L	B-D	†
Legrenzi	Che fiero costume	HML	C-D	†
Leoncavallo	Mattinata	MLH	C-AF	†
Marcello	Il mio bel foco	LMH	C-G	†
Paisiello	Chi vuol la zingarella	L	C-F	GSC
Pergolesi	Confusa, smarrita			GSC
Respighi	Pioggia			BON
-----	Scherzo			BON
Rontani	Or ch'io non segno più	HL	CS-E	DIT
Rossi	Ah, rendimi (Mitrane)	L	GS-FS	GSC
Rossini	Bel raggio lusinghier (Semiramide)	H	CS-A	GSC
Scarlatti, A.	Chi vuole innamorarsi	HL	D-EF	DIT
-----	Se Florindo è fedele	LM	EF-EF	GSC
Scarlatti, D.	Consolati e spara amante	L	BF-E	GSC
-----	Qual farfalletta			

Miscellaneous Songs and Arias Employing Spirited Singing

Contralto

Dvořák	I will sing new songs of gladness	HL		†
-----	Sing ye a joyful song			AMP
Falla	Canción del amor dolido			CHE
-----	Chansón du feu follet	L	B-B	CHE
-----	El paño moruno	HL		AMP
-----	Seguidilla murciana	HL		AMP
-----	Siete canciones	HL		AMP
Grieg	Good morning			†
-----	Hunter's song	L	DS-E	GSC
-----	Jeg lever et liv i laengsel	L	BF-E	HAN
-----	My Johann	HL	BF-EF	GSC
-----	Poesien			
-----	Turisten	M	CS-F	HAN
Mozart	Alleluja	LMH	F-C	†
Mussorgsky	Hopak	HM	CS-FS	GSC
-----	In the corner			INT
-----	The magpie and the gypsy dancer			GSC
Rachmaninoff	Floods of spring	HL		DIT
-----	Oh, no, I pray do not depart	H		DIT
Stravinsky	The cloister (La novice)			DIT

Turina	Farruca	M	A–F	UME
-----	Rima	H	A–A	AMP

Songs and Arias Employing Staccato

Contralto

Arne, T.	Where the bee sucks	HM		†
Fourdrain	Carnaval	M	C–F	RIC
Haydn	My mother bids me bind my hair	M	E–E	
Rossini	Non più mesta (La Cenerentola)	M	A–B	GSC
Scarlatti, A.	Rugiadose odorose (Il Pirro e Demetrio)	HL	D–E	DIT
Schubert	Der Juengling an der Quelle	LH	E–A	†

American and British Songs of Popular Appeal

Contralto

Beach	Ah, love but a day			ASC
Besley	The second minuet	HL		BOO
Brahe	Bless this house	HML	A–EF	BOO
Cadman	From the land of the sky-blue water			WHI
-----	The moon drops low	HL		ASC
Charles	When I have sung my songs	HM	BF–EF	GSC
Del Riego	Homing	HML	BF–E	CHA
Dougherty	Love in the dictionary	M	C–G	GSC
— Edwards	By the bend of the river	HML	C–E	GSC
-----	Into the night	HML	C–DF	GSC
Enders	Russian picnic	HM	C–G	GSC
Foster	The Americans come	MH	F–BF	JFI
Fox	The hills of home	HML	BF–DF	CFI
Friml	L'amour, toujours l'amour			HAR
German	Who'll buy my lavender	HML		BOO
Giannini	Sing to my heart a song	H	D–B	ELV
Griffes	We'll to the woods and gather May	M	D–F	GSC
Hely-Hutchinson	Old mother Hubbard	HL	B–E	CFI
Henschel	Morning-hymn	MH	DS–GS	†
La Forge	Song of the open	MH	EF–AF	DIT

Lehmann	The cuckoo	HH	D-B	BOH
Manning	Shoes	M	EF-F	GSC
Molloy	The Kerry Dance	LH	C-G	GSC
Nevin	Mighty lak' a rose			JCH
Rich	American lullaby	LH	C-F	GSC
Rogers	At parting	LH	CS-FS	GSC
Romberg	Faithfully yours			HAR
Ronald	Prelude	HML	B-D	ENO
Scott	Think on me	HML	D-EF	GAL
Speaks	Morning	HML	BF-D	GSC
Spross	Will o' the wisp			JCH
Strelezki	Dreams	LMH	B-A	GSC
Sullivan	The lost chord	HL	C-F	GSC
Tyson	Noon and night	LH	F-AF	GSC
Weatherly	Danny boy	LMH		BOO
Weaver	Moon-marketing	LMH	E-G	GSC
Wilson	O sing a new song			
Wood	A brown bird singing	HLM	FS-G	CHA

(See also Humorous Songs, Negro Spirituals,
 Folk Songs, Operetta Songs and Opera Arias.)

Miscellaneous Songs of Popular Appeal

Contralto

Bach-Gounod	Ave Maria			†
Berger	They all dance the Samba	M	A-FS	GSC
Bizet	Agnus Dei	HLM	C-AF	†
-----	Ouvre ton coeur	MH	DS-GS	†
Bohm	Calm as the night	HML	A-EF	†
Cavalli	Donzelle fuggite	HL	C-EF	†
Dvořák	Songs my mother taught me	HM	E-E	†
Grieg	A dream			†
-----	I love thee	HML	E-F	†
-----	My Johann	HL	BF-EF	GSC
Korngold	Much ado about nothing			
Leoncavallo	Mattinata	MLH	C-AF	†
Leroux	Le nil Cello or violin	LH	E-A	†
Massenet	Elégie	LM	C-GF	GSC
Mozart	Alleluja	LMH	F-C	†
Ponce	Estrellita	LH		†
Rachmaninoff	To the children	MH	F-G	DIT
Reichardt	In the time of roses			†
Rossini	La danza	MH	E-A	†
Sadero	Amuri, Amuri	M		CHE
Schubert	An die Musik	HL	A-DS	†

<table>
<tr><td>(Schubert)</td><td>Ave Maria</td><td>LMH</td><td>F-F</td><td>GSC</td></tr>
</table>

(Schubert)	Ave Maria	LMH	F-F	GSC
-----	Hark! hark! the lark	LMH	F-G	†
-----	Staendchen			
Schumann	Widmung	HL	BF-F	†
Sieczynski	Vienna, city of my dreams			HAR
Strauss, R.	Zueignung	HL	CS-FS	†
Tchaikovsky	None but the lonely heart	HLM	C-F	DIT
Velazquez	Bésame mucho	M	CS-D	SOU

(See also Humorous Songs, Negro Spirituals,
Folk Songs, Operetta Songs and Opera Arias.)

Arias From British Operas

Contralto

Britten	Flower song (Rape of Lucretia)			BOH
Purcell	Celia has a thousand charms (The Rival Sisters)			
-----	From rosy bow'rs (Don Quixote)			AUG
-----	I attempt from love's sickness to fly (The Indian Queen)	MH	CS-E	†
-----	Nymphs and shepherds (The Libertine)	HM	C-F	†
-----	Retired from any mortal's sight (King Richard II)			NOV
-----	When I am laid in earth (Dido and Aeneas)	LH	C-G	†

Arias From French Operas

Contralto

Bizet	Card Scene (Carmen)			†
-----	Habanera (Carmen)	HM	D-F	†
Campra	Charmant papillon (Les Fêtes Venitiennes)	MH	D-G	GSC
Gluck	Amours, sors pour jamais (Armide)			PET
-----	Divinités du Styx (Alceste)	MH	DF-AF	†
-----	Je n'ai jamais chéri la vie (Alceste)	L	A-F	GSC
Gounod	O ma lyre immortelle (Sappho)	M	C-G	†

470

(Gounod)	Si le bonheur (Faust)			†
Halévy	Humble fille des champs (Charles VI)			GSC
Lesueur	Hélas sans m'entendre (Ossian ou les Bardes)			CHE
Lully	Bois épais (Amadis)	ML	C-EF	†
-----	J'ai perdu la beauté (Persée)			
-----	Je porte l'épouvante (Persée)			
Massé	Chanson du tigre (Paul et Virginie)			
Massenet	Ne me refuse pas (Hérodiade)			HEU
-----	Va! laisse couler mes larmes (Werther)			
-----	Werther! qui m'aurait dit (Air de lettres) (Werther)			
Meyerbeer	Ah! mon fils (Le Prophète)	M	B-AS	†
-----	Nobles seigneurs, salut! (Les Huguenots)	LH	C-C	GSC
-----	O prêtres de Baal (Le Prophète)			BRO
Saint-Saëns	Amour, viens aider (Samson et Dalila)	HM	AF-G	†
-----	Mon coeur s'ouvre à ta voix (Samson et Dalila)	HLM	BF-GF	†
-----	Printemps qui commence (Samson et Dalila)	M	B-E	†

Arias From German Operas

Contralto

Bruch	Penelope's sorrow (Odysseus)			SIM
Wagner	Gerechtiger Gott (Rienzi)	H	C-A	PET
-----	Hoere mit Sinn (Goetterdaemmerung)			
-----	So ist es denn aus mit den ewigen Goettern (Die Walkuere)			GSC
-----	Weiche, wotan! (Das Rheingold)			GSC
Weber	Hier dicht am Quell (Euryanthe)			PET

Arias From Italian Operas

Contralto

Bellini	Scombra è la sacra selva (Norma)			RIC
Boito	Padre nostro (Nerone)			
Cilea	Acerba volutta (Adriana Lecouvreur)			SON
-----	O vagabonda stella d'oriente (Adriana Lecouvreur)			AMP
Donizetti	Deh, non voler (Anna Bolena)			
-----	Il segreto per esser felici (Lucrezia Borgia)	M	C-G	†
-----	O mio Fernando (La Favorita)	M	B-A	†
Giordano	O grandi occhi lucenti (Fedora)			BRO
-----	Temer? perche? (Andrea Chenier)			BRO
Gluck	Che farò senza Euridice (Orphée)	ML	BF-F	†
Monteverdi	Lasciatemi morire (Arianna)	ML	D-D	†
-----	Oblivian soave (L'Incoronazione di Poppea)			HEU
-----	Tu se morta (Orfeo)	M	C-E	GSC
Ponchielli	Voce di donna (La Gioconda)	HM	A-G	GSC
Rossini	Ah quel giorno (Semiramide)			
-----	Bel raggio lusinghier (Semiramide)	H	CS-A	GSC
-----	Non più mesta (La Cenerentola)	M	A-B	GSC
-----	Re dell' abisso (Un Ballo in Maschera)			RIC
-----	Stride la vampa (Il Trovatore)	M	B-G	†

Miscellaneous Opera Arias

Contralto

Cadman	Song of the Robin Woman (Shanewis)	MH	CS-GS	MOR
Kodaly	Czardas (Hary Janos)			
Menotti	Lullaby (The Consul)			GSC
-----	The black swan (The Medium)	M	D-G	GSC

472

Mussorgsky	Divination by water (Khovantchina)	L	GS-FS	GSC
------	Martha's song (Khovantchina)	ML		GSC
-----	Song of Khivria (The Fair at Sorotchinsk)			GSC
Tchaikovsky	Adieu forêts (Jeanne d'Arc)	HM	BF-FS	GSC
-----	Pauline's romance (Pique Dame)	M	BF-AF	GSC

Arias From Oratorios
and Latin Works

Contralto

Bach, J.S.	Agnus Dei (Mass in B Minor) Violin			†
-----	Esurientes implevit bonis (Magnificat in D Major)			†
-----	Et exultavit spiritus meus (Magnificat in D)			
-----	From the bondage (St. John Passion)	L	BF-EF	†
-----	It is finished (St. John Passion)	L	B-D	†
-----	Prepare thyself Zion (Christmas Oratorio)			
-----	Qui sedes ad dexteram Patris (Mass in B Minor) Oboe d'amore			†
Bemberg	Du Christ avec ardeur (La Mort de Jeanne d'Arc)	M	DF-AF	†
Bennett	O Lord, thou hast searched (Woman of Samaria)			
Dvořák	Inflammatus et accensus (Stabat Mater)	L	A-EF	NOV
Gaul	Thou art the guide (Ten Virgins)			
Handel	Daughter of Zion (Brocke's Passion)			
-----	Father, whose blessing (Ode from St. Cecelia's Day)			
-----	Hence, Iris, hence away (Semele)	L		NOV
-----	He shall feed His flock (The Messiah)	L	C-D	GSC

473

(Handel)	He was despised (The Messiah)	L	B-D	†
-----	In the battle, fame pursuing (Deborah)	L	A-D	†
-----	Let me wander not unseen (L'Allegro)	M	D-G	†
-----	Lord, to thee each night and day (Theodora)	L	C-E	†
-----	O Lord whose mercies numberless (Saul)			
-----	O thou that tellest good tidings to Zion (The Messiah)	L	A-C	†
-----	Peaceful rest (Hercules)			
-----	Return, O God of hosts (Samson)	L	B-E	GSC
-----	Thou shalt bring them in (Israel in Egypt)	L	B-D	†
-----	What though I trace each herb and flower (Solomon)		CS-E	†
-----	Where shall I fly? (Hercules)			†
Mendelssohn	But the Lord is mindful of His own (Saint Paul)	L	A-D	†
-----	O rest in the Lord (Elijah)	L	B-D	†
-----	Woe unto them who forsake (Elijah)	L	B-E	†
Mozart	Laudamus Te (C Minor Mass)			PET
Parker	Gens duce splendida (Hora Novissima)			NOV
Pergolesi	Fac ut portem (Stabat Mater)			DES
Rossini	Fac ut portem (Stabat Mater)	L	B-G	DIT
Saint-Saëns	Expectans Dominum (Christmas Oratorio)			GSC
-----	Patiently (Christmas Oratorio)			
Sullivan	God shall wipe away all tears (The Light of the World)	L	B-E	GSC
-----	Love not the world (The Prodigal Son)	L		GSC
Verdi	Liber scriptus (The Requiem)			GSC

Cantata Arias

Contralto

| Bach, J.S. | Ach, bleibe doch, mein liebstes Leben (Cantata 11) Violin | | | NOV |

474

(Bach, J.S.)	Ach, es bleibt in meiner Liebe (Cantata 77) Trumpet	
-----	Ach Herr! was ist ein Menschenkind (Cantata 110) Oboe d'amore	AUG
-----	Ach, lege das Sodom (Cantata 48) Oboe or violin	
-----	Ach, schlaefrige Seele (Cantata 115)	AUG
-----	Ach, unaussprechlich ist die Not (Cantata 116) Oboe d'amore	NOV
-----	Betoerte Welt (Cantata 94) Flute	
-----	Christen muessen auf der Erden (Cantata 44) Oboe	
-----	Christi Glieder ach bedenket (Cantata 132) Violin	
-----	Die Obrigkeit ist Gottes Gabe (Cantata 119) Flute or Violin	NOV
-----	Ein ungefaerbt Gemuete (Cantata 24) Violin or viola	
-----	Ermuntert euch (Cantata 176) Oboe	BRO
-----	Es kommt ein Tag, so das Verborgne richtet (Cantata 136) Oboe d'amore	
-----	Gelobet sei der Herr (Cantata 129) Oboe d'amore	AUG
-----	Ich sehe schon im Geist (Cantata 43) 2 Oboes and continuo	NOV
-----	Ich traue seiner Gnaden (Cantata 97) Violin	PET
-----	Ich will doch wohl Rosen brechen (Cantata 86) Violin	
-----	In Jesu Demut (Cantata 151) Oboe d'amore or violin	
-----	Kein Arzt ist ausser Dir zu finden (Cantata 103) Violin or flute	
-----	Koennen nicht die roten Wangen (Cantata 205) Oboe d'amore	
-----	Kreuz und Krone (Cantata 12) Oboe	NOV
-----	Leget euch dem Heiland unter (Cantata 182) Flute or violin	BRO
-----	Mein glaeubiges Herze HML (Cantata 68)	†

(Bach, J.S.)	Schaeme dich, o Seele, nicht (Cantata 147) Oboe d'amore			
-----	Was Gott tut, das ist wohlgethan (Cantata 100, verse 5) Oboe d'amore			AUG
-----	Weh der Seele (Cantata 102) Oboe			BRO
-----	Willkommen! will ich sagen (Cantata 27) English horn			NOV
Bruch	Andromache's lament (Achilles)			
Gaul	Eye hath not seen (The Holy City)	ML	B-D	GSC
Handel	Dell bell' idolo mio (Cantata 2)			
-----	Vouchsafe, O Lord (Dettingen Te Deum)	HM		ELV
Mussorgsky	Oriental chant (Josua Navine Cantata)	ML	BF-E	GSC
Tunder	Wachet auf, ruft uns die Stimme (Tunder's Cantata)			BAR

Operetta, Musical Comedy or Show Songs

Contralto

Coward	If love were all (Bitter Sweet)			HAR
De Koven	Oh promise me	HML	C-D	†
Friml	Huguette Waltz (The Vagabond King)			FAM
-----	Totem tom-tom (Rose Marie)			HAR
Herbert	I can't do that sum (Babes in Toyland)			WIT
-----	Moonbeams (The Red Mill)			WIT
-----	'Neath the southern moon (Naughty Marietta)			
Kern	Can't help lovin' dat man (Show Boat)	L	BF-EF	HAR
-----	Smoke gets in your eyes (Roberta)			HAR
Kreisler	Stars in my eyes (The King Steps Out)			CHA
Luders	The tale of the seashell (The Prince of Pilsen)			WIT

Porter	Begin the Beguine (Jubilee)	L	BF-F	HAR
-----	I've got you under my skin (Born to Dance)			CHA
-----	Night and day (Gay Divorcee)	M	BF-EF	HAR
-----	So in love (Kiss Me Kate)			CHA
Rodgers	I could write a book (Pal Joey)			CHA
-----	I'm falling in love with love (South Pacific)			BRO
-----	I'm in love with a wonderful guy (South Pacific)			CHA
-----	It might as well be spring (State Fair)			CHA
-----	June is bustin' out all over (Carousel)			WIL
-----	So far (Allegro)			CHA
Romberg	Mother (My Maryland)			HAR
Schwartz	Something to remember you by (Three's a Crowd)			HAR
Sullivan	I'm called Little Buttercup (H.M.S. Pinafore)			GSC
Wickham	Time for love (Rosalind)			
Youmans	Through the years (Through the Years)	HML	A-F	MLR
Yvain	My man (Ziegfeld Follies)			FEI

Song Cycles (or groups of songs)

Contralto

Bantock	Sappho			
Berger	Three songs on poems of Langston Hughes			
Bernstein	I hate music	H	C-A	WIT
Brahms	Two songs for alto, viola and piano	L		AMP
-----	Zigeuner Lieder			
Carpenter	Gitanjali	M	B-G	GSC
-----	Watercolors	M	C-F	GSC
Cornelius	Six Christmas songs	HL		BOS
Dvořák	Biblical songs	HL		AMP
Elgar	Sea pictures	L	A-A	BOO
Falla	El amor brujo	M		BRO
Granados	La maja dolorosa	M		INT
Grieg	Five poems of Otto Benson			HAN

477

Griffes	Five poems of ancient China and Japan	M	AS–EF	GSC
Honegger	Quatre chansons pour voix grave			SAL
Kilpinen	Lieder um den Tod	M		AMP
Mahler	Kindertotenlieder	L	G–GF	INT
Mussorgsky	Songs and dances of death			INT
Poulenc	Le bestiaire String quartet, flute, clarinet and bassoon	M		AMP
Ravel	Cinq mélodies populaires grecques			
-----	Quatre chants populaires	M		DUR
Santoliquido	Three poesie persiane			FOR
Schoenberg	Das Buch der haengenden Gaerten			AMP
Schubert	Gesaenge des Harfners 1, 2 and 3			PET
Schumann	Frauenliebe und Leben	HL		GSC
Still	Songs of separation			LEE
Tchaikovsky	Three songs after Tolstoi Op. 38, 1, 2 and 3			
Villa-Lobos	Serestas			
Woodford-Finden	Indian love lyrics			BOO

Solo Cantatas

Contralto

Bach, J.S.	Geist und Seele wird verwirret (Cantata 35)	
-----	Schlage doch, gewuenschte Stunde (Cantata 53)	RIC
-----	Widerstehe doch der Suende (Cantata 54) Strings and continuo	
Bassani	Cantata for one voice	
Pergolesi	Salve Regina	

See Solo Cantatas of Pergolesi, Handel and Scarlatti, Kirchenkantaten of Buxtehude and Symphoniae Sacrae of Schuetz.

Concert Arias

Contralto

Haydn	Ariadne auf Naxos (Concert Aria)			
Mozart	Ombra felice			INT

Christmas Songs

Contralto

Adam	O Holy night			†
Andrews	I heard the bells on Christmas day	L	A-E	GAL
Bach, J.S.	Prepare thyself Zion (Christmas Oratorio)			
-----	Schlafe, mein Liebster (Christmas Oratorio)			
-----	Von der Welt verlang ich nichts (Cantata 64) Oboe d'amore			
Bacon	Ancient Christmas carol			NEM
Baldwin	Little Lordeen	L	BF-EF	WIT
Bax	A Christmas carol	H	DF-A	CHE
Berlin	White Christmas (Holiday Inn)			BER
Brahms	Geistliches Wiegenlied Piano and viola			†
Branscombe	Hail ye time of holidays			
Bush	I saw a maiden fair	L	C-DF	GRA
Candlyn	The song of Mary	M	B-D	GRA
Coerne	A rhyme for Christmas-tide	L	CS-CS	DIT
De Koven	The white Christ	L	C-D	GSC
Dunhill	To the Queen of Heaven	M	C-G	GSC
Elmore and Reed	Come all ye who weary	L	C-C	JFI
Evans	The Virgin had a baby	L	C-EF	BOH
Grieg	Christmas song			AUG
Handel	O thou that tellest good tidings to Zion (The Messiah)	L	A-C	†
Harker	A child is born in Bethlehem	LH	D-G	GSC
Head	Slumber song of the Madonna	HL		BOO
Herbert	Toyland (Babes in Toyland)			WIT
Holmès	Noël d'Irlande	HL		DIT

Humperdinck	Weihnachten			
Ives	A Christmas carol			NEM
Liddle	An old French carol	LM		BOO
Lynn	Gently little Jesus	L	BF-BF	DIT
-----	The magic night of Christmas	M	D-D	DIT
Martin	The Holy Child	HML	G-G	ENO
McKinney	The Holy Mother sings	MH	AF-AF	JFI
Neidlinger	The manger cradle	L	EF-F	GSC
Niles	The cherry tree			GSC
Owen	Lute book lullaby	L	A-D	GRA
Prokoff	Christmas cradle song	LM	D-E	CHA
Reger	The Virgin's slumber song	MMH	G-G	†
Rodney	A dream of Bethlehem	MML	G-DF	ENO
Saint-Saëns	Expectans Dominum (Christmas Oratorio)			GSC
Taylor	Christmas folk song	L	BF-EF	GRA
Thiman	In the bleak midwinter	L	A-E	NOV
Warren	Christmas candle	HML	D-E	GSC
Wentzel	Lamkins Cello and piano			GRA
Wolf	Schlafendes Jesuskind	HL	AS-F	†
Yon	Gesu Bambino	HL	B-E	JFI

Easter Songs

Contralto

Bach, J.S.	Hochgelobter Gottessohn (Cantata 6) English horn or viola or violin			NOV
-----	Ich will nach dem Himmel zu (Cantata 146) Violin			BRO
-----	Jesus from the grave is risen	M	F-EF	CFI
-----	Zum reinen Wasser (Cantata 112) Oboe d'amore			NOV
Barnes	Easter	HM	D-EF	GSC
Cadman	Hail joyous morn	HL	BF-DF	WIL
Coleridge-Taylor	Easter morn	MH	DF-AF	BOO
Curran	Crucifixion			
Diack	All in the April evening	LMH	D-G	BOO
Duke	Calvary	L	G-F	CFI
Harker	As it began to dawn	ML	G-DF	GSC
La Forge	Before the Crucifix	HML	BF-EF	GSC
Mac Farlane	On wings of living light	MH	D-G	GSC

480

MacGimsey	I was there when they crucified my Lord	HL		CFI
O'Hara	There is no death	LMH	EF-AF	CHA
Parker	Come see the place	HL		GSC
Rachmaninoff	Christ is risen	LM	D-F	GAL
Schubert	Ave Maria	LMH	F-F	†
Turner	Hail your risen Lord	HL	C-D	GSC
Yon	O faithful Cross	HM	C-EF	JFI
-----	Our Paschal Joy	LH	AF-AF	JFI

Patriotic Songs

Contralto

Bone and Fenton	Prayer for a waiting world	L		CFI
Bowles	An American hero	M	E-E	AXE
Chadwick	He maketh wars to cease	ML		ASC
Dungan	Eternal life	HL		PRE
Foster, F.	The Americans come	MH	F-BF	JFI
Lester	Greater love hath no man	LH	B-E	CFI
O'Hara	There is no death	LMH	EF-AF	CHA
Steffe	Battle hymn of the Republic			
Ward-Stephens	Phantom legions	MHH	EF-BF	CHA

Sacred Songs

Contralto

Bach, J.S.	Draw near to me	HML		GSC
Beethoven	The worship of God in nature			
Bitgood	Be still and know that I am God	ML		GRA
-----	The greatest of these is love	M		GRA
Bizet	O Lord be merciful	HL		GSC
Bone and Fenton	First Psalm	LM	DF-F	CFI
-----	They word is a lamp	LH	C-F	ROW
Brown	What are these which are arrayed	HLM	C-F	ASC
Buck	Fear not ye, O Israel	HLM		GSC
-----	Until God's day	L	BF-EF	GSC

Campbell–Tipton	I will give thanks unto the Lord	LMH	DF–AF	GSC
Candlyn	God that madest earth and heaven	M	C–F	GRA
Chadwick	A ballad of trees and the Master	HML	A–F	DIT
Charles	Incline Thine ear	HL	BF–D	GSC
Clokey	God is in everything	LH	D–G	JFI
Davis	Be ye kind, one to another	L		GAL
-----	Let not your heart be troubled	HML		WOO
Dickinson	Roads	L		GRA
Dvořák	By the waters of Babylon			AMP
-----	God is my shepherd			AMP
-----	Hear my prayer, O Lord			AMP
-----	I will life mine eyes			AMP
-----	Sing ye a joyful song			AMP
-----	Turn Thee to me			AMP
Edmunds	Praise we the Lord	HL	D–D	ROW
Goodhall	The mountain	M	D–E	GAL
Gounod	O Divine Redeemer	LMH	C–G	GSC
Green	Praised be the Lord	M	C–F	OXF
Guion	Prayer	HL		GSC
-----	The cross bearer	HM	B–DS	GSC
Handel	Thanks be to Thee	M	CS–E	†
Henschel	Morning-hymn	MH	DS–GS	†
Holst	The heart worships	ML	BF–D	STB
Kountz	What shall I ask?	L		GAL
La Forge	They that trust in the Lord	HL	BF–EF	GAL
-----	What shall I render unto the Lord?	HL	C–D	GSC
Lederer	Psalm 104	L	A–E	CFI
Liddle	How lovely are Thy dwellings	HML		BOS
MacDermid	In my Father's house are many mansions	HML		FRS
MacGimsey	Think on these things	LM	BF–EF	CFI
Malotte	The Lord's prayer			
-----	The twenty-third Psalm	HLM	C–F	GSC
McGill	Thine eternal peace	HL	A–CS	GSC
Mendelssohn	But the Lord is mindful of His own (Saint Paul)	L	A–D	†
-----	O rest in the Lord (Elijah)	L	B–D	†
-----	Woe unto them who forsake him (Elijah)	L	B–E	†

O'Connor and Morris	Fill thou my life, O Lord	L	BF-EF	CFI
O'Hara	Art thou the Christ?	HML	A-D	GSC
Rogers	Out of the depths	HL		ASC
Sanderson	Green pastures	HL	BF-EF	BOO
Schubert	The Omnipotent			
-----	To the Infinite			
Scott	Consider the lilies	HL	C-E	GSC
-----	Ride on, ride on	HML		FLA
Speaks	Thou wilt keep him in perfect peace	HML		GSC
Stickles	Saith the Lord	LH	D-F	CHA
Sullivan	Love not the world (The Prodigal Son)	L		GSC
Tchaikovsky	Lord, Almighty God (Moscow Cantata)	M		GRA
Thompson	My Master hath a garden	M		ECS
Voris	Song of mothers	LH	D-FS	GRA
Watts	Intreat me not to leave thee	L	A-F	GSC
Weaver	Build Thee more stately mansions	M	C-E	GAL
Wolf	Gebet	HL		†

Wedding Songs

Contralto

Beethoven	Ich liebe dich	HL	BF-DF	†
Bond	I love you truly			BOS
De Koven	Oh promise me (Robin Hood)	HML	C-D	†
Franck	O Lord most Holy	LM	A-FS	BOS
Grieg	I love thee	HML	E-F	†
Lippe	How do I love you?			BOS
Luzzi	Ave Maria	HL	BF-EF	GSC
Sacco	With this ring	M	F-F	BVC
Schubert	Du bist die Ruh	LMH	EF-AF	†
-----	Ungeduld	HML		†
Schumann	Du Ring an meinem Finger	HL	C-F	†
-----	Widmung	HL	BF-F	†
Thiman	The God of love my Shepherd is	ML	A-D	NOV
Youmans	Through the years (Through the Years)	HML	A-F	MLR

Contralto

Bach, J.S.	Ach, bleibe doch, mein liebstes Leben (Cantata 11) Violin	NOV
-----	Ach, es bleibt in meiner Liebe (Cantata 77) Trumpet	
-----	Ach Herr! was ist ein Menschenkind (Cantata 110) Oboe d'amore	AUG
-----	Ach, lege das Sodom (Cantata 48) Oboe or violin	
-----	Ach, unaussprechlich ist die Not (Cantata 116) Oboe d'amore	NOV
-----	Betoerte Welt (Cantata 94) Flute	
-----	Christen muessen auf der Erden (Cantata 44) Oboe	
-----	Christi Glieder, ach bedenket (Cantata 132) Violin	
-----	Die Obrigkeit ist Gottes Gabe (Cantata 119) Flute or violin	NOV
-----	Ein ungefaerbt Gemuete (Cantata 24) Violin or viola	
-----	Ermuntert euch (Cantata 176) Oboe	BRO
-----	Es kommt ein Tag so das Verborgne richtet (Cantata 136) Oboe d'amore	
-----	Gelobet sei der Herr (Cantata 129) Oboe d'amore	AUG
------	Hochgelobter Gottessohn (Cantata 6) English horn or viola or violin	NOV
-----	Ich will doch wohl Rosen brechen (Cantata 86) Violin	
-----	Ich will nach dem Himmel zu (Cantata 146) Violin	BRO
-----	In Jesu Demut (Cantata 151) Oboe d'amore or violin	AUG
-----	Jesus ist ein guter Hirt (Cantata 85) Violin or cello	RIC
-----	Kein Arzt ist ausser Dir zu finden (Cantata 103) Violin or flute	
-----	Kreuz und Krone (Cantata 12) Oboe	NOV

(Bach, J.S.)	Leget euch dem Heiland unter (Cantata 182) Flute or violin			BRO
-----	Schaeme dich, o Seele, nicht (Cantata 147) Oboe d'amore			
-----	Von der Welt verlang ich nichts (Cantata 64) Oboe d'amore			
-----	Was Gott tut, das ist wohlgethan (Cantata 100, verse 5) Oboe d'amore			AUG
-----	Weh der Seele (Cantata 102) Oboe			BRO
-----	Widerstehe doch der Suende (Cantata 54) Strings and continuo			
-----	Willkommen! will ich sagen (Cantata 27) English horn			NOV
-----	Zum reinen Wasser (Cantata 112) Oboe d'amore			NOV
Barber	Dover Beach String quartet	M	BF-F	GSC
Brahms	Geistliches Wiegenlied Piano and viola			†
-----	Gestillte Sehnsucht Viola and piano			†
Buxtehude	Jubilate domino Viola di gamba and harpsichord			UGR
-----	Singet dem Herrn Violin and piano			
Chausson	Le colibri Violin or cello	M	F-GF	BOS
Honegger	Chanson (Ronsard) Flute and string quartet			SEN
Leroux	Le nil Cello or violin	LH	E-A	†
Mana-Zucca	Rachem Trumpet	HML		CHA
Poulenc	Le bestiaire String quartet, flute, clarinet and bassoon	M		AMP
Wentzel	Lamkins Cello and piano			GRA

American Recital Songs

Lyric Tenor

Alberti	Oriental serenade	H	CS-A	CFI
Ames	Judgement	M	BF-G	MER
Baçon	Is there such a thing as day?	M	DS-FS	AMP
Barber	I hear an army	LH	D-AF	GSC

485

(Barber)	Rain has fallen	HM	D-E	GSC
-----	Sleep now	MH	EF-AF	GSC
-----	Sure on this shining night	MH	D-G	GSC
-----	The daisies	M	C-F	GSC
-----	With rue my heart is laden	HL	CS-D	GSC
Barnett	Serenade	H	F-G	GSC
Beach	Ah, love but a day			ASC
-----	Fairy lullaby			ASC
-----	The year's at the spring	MH	AF-AF	ASC
Bellini	Ninna nanna a liana	LH	G-G	GSC
Bone and Fenton	Captain Kidd	MH	B-G	CFI
-----	Finnegan's wake			
-----	Green fields	MH	E-A	PRE
-----	Tryst	MH	FS-G	CFI
-----	Wind in the tree tops			
Bowles	Night without sleep			
-----	Three			
Braine	Dawn awakes	HML	A-D	ASC
Branscombe	At the postern gate	MH	DF-AF	ASC
-----	I send my heart up to thee			
Burleigh	By the pool at the third roses	H		RIC
Campbell-Tipton	A spirit flower	LHM	B-G	GSC
-----	Darkness	H	D-A	GSC
-----	Requies	H	E-A	GSC
Carpenter	If	M	D-E	GSC
-----	Serenade	LH	CS-A	GSC
Carter	The rose family	M		AMP
Castelnuovo-Tedesco	Roundel	H		CHE
Chadwick	Allah	LH	CS-GS	ASC
Chanler	I rise when you enter	M	CS-G	GSC
-----	The doves	M	C-F	AMP
Charles	Clouds	HML	C-EF	GSC
-----	My lady walks in loveliness	HM	C-EF	GSC
-----	Sweet song of long ago	HML	A-D	GSC
-----	When I have sung my songs	HM	BF-EF	GSC
Copland	Long time ago			
-----	Simple gifts			
-----	The boatman			
Crist	Evening	H	C-G	GSC
-----	Girl of the red mouth	MH	E-BF	CFI
-----	Into a ship dreaming	LMH	EF-GS	CFI
-----	Knock on the door	H	EF-AF	GSC

(Crist)	White hours like snow	HL	CS-BF	CFI
-----	You will not come again	HML	BF-CS	CFI
Davis	Nancy Hanks	H	D-G	GAL
Deis	Ask nothing more	LMH	CS-AF	GSC
-----	Come down to Kew			
Dello Joio	Lament	M	C-F	CFI
-----	The assassination			CFI
-----	There is a lady sweet and kind	M	C-F	CFI
Diamond	Brigid's song	H	D-G	MER
Dougherty	Loveliest of trees	HM	C-E	BOH
-----	Primavera	H	C-BF	GSC
Duke	Bells in the rain	H	E-GS	CFI
-----	To Karen, singing	M	CS-G	ELV
-----	Voices	H	FS-A	BOH
Edmunds	Fare you well	MH	F-AF	ROW
Elwell	In the mountains	M	DF-F	BMI
-----	Palatine			
-----	The road not taken	M	B-FS	GSC
-----	The sound of the trees	M		AMP
Fairchild	The red cockatoo			
Foote	I'm wearing awa'	HL		ASC
Fox	By the short cut to the rosses			BOO
Gabrilowitsch	Goodbye			DIT
Ganz	A memory	HM	B-D	GSC
Giannini	Far above the purple hills	LH	CS-A	RIC
-----	It is a spring night	H	EF-A	RIC
-----	Longing	M	CS-GF	ELV
-----	Tell me, o blue, blue sky	H		RIC
-----	Zompa llari llira	H		RIC
Golde	Love was with me yesterday	LMH	E-A	CFI
-----	O beauty, passing beauty	MH	CS-GS	GSC
Grant	Looking across	H	D-G	AMP
Griffes	An old song resung	LM	EF-F	GSC
-----	Elves	H	F-AF	GSC
-----	In a myrtle shade	H	FS-A	GSC
-----	La fuite de la lune	M	CS-F	GSC
-----	Symphony in yellow	M	D-GF	GSC
-----	The lament of Ian the proud	MH	DS-AS	GSC
-----	Waikiki	H	DS-GS	GSC
Hadley	My shadow			ASC
Hageman	At the well	LH	EF-AF	GSC
-----	Do not go, my love	HL	B-EF	GSC
-----	Me company along	LH	F-BF	CFI
-----	Miranda	HL		GAL

(Hageman)	Music I heard with you	MH	E-A	GAL
-----	The night has a thousand eyes	M	C-FS	BOO
-----	Voices			
Harris	Winter	H	F-A	GAL
Haubiel	To you			CMP
Hindemith	The whistling thief	M	E-F	AMP
Hopkinson	My days have been so wondrous free	LH	EF-G	†
-----	My generous heart disdains			
-----	O'er the hills	LH	C-G	†
Horsman	The dream	H	F-G	GSC
-----	Thus wisdom sings	H	EF-A	GSC
Ilgenfritz	Blow, blow thou winter wind			
Kagen	All day I hear	H	F-FS	WTR
-----	The junkman			
-----	Upstream	H	CS-F	WTR
-----	War is kind			
Kernochan	Smuggler's song			GAL
-----	We two together	H	EF-AF	GAL
Klemm	Love magic			DIT
Kramer	At sunset	H		GAL
-----	I have seen dawn	M	DS-F	GSC
-----	Pleading	LH	D-GF	JFI
-----	Swans	HL		RIC
-----	The last hour	HML		JCH
-----	There is a garden in her face			DIT
La Forge	Hills	HL		RIC
-----	Retreat	LMH	E-G	GSC
-----	To a messenger	HLM	CF-G	GSC
Lang	Irish love song	HML	A-E	ASC
Levitzki	Ah, thou beloved one	H	EF-AF	GSC
-----	Do you remember?	HML	BF-EF	GSC
Loeffler	The fiddler of Dooney	H	E-A	GSC
-----	To Helen	M	DF-F	GSC
Luening	A farm picture	M	F-F	AMP
MacDowell	A maid sings light	H	F-G	ASC
-----	The sea	HL	D-D	BRH
-----	Thy beaming eyes	ML	BF-EF	ASC
Manning	In the Luxembourg gardens	HML	BF-D	GSC
Marsh	The urn	M	ES-FS	GSC
McArthur	Night	H	F-AF	GSC
-----	Spring came	HL	D-F	GSC
McDonald	Daybreak	H		ELV
Nordoff	Music I heard with you	H	DS-FS	AMP
-----	Tell me, Thyrsis	H	E-G	AMP

(Nordoff)	There shall be more joy	M	CS-FS	AMP
Olmstead	Thy sweet singing	HL	BF-EF	GSC
Proctor	I light the blessed candles	H	DF-A	GSC
Robb	Cradle song	MH	F-G	GSC
Rogers	The last song	MLH	E-AF	GSC
-----	Time for making songs	HM	CS-F	DIT
-----	Wind song	LM	C-G	GSC
Rorem	The lordly Hudson	M	DF-G	MER
Rummel	Ecstasy	LMH	GF-AF	GSC
Russell	Fulfillment	LH	EF-GF	BOS
-----	Harbor night	M	D-F	CFI
Sacco	Brother Will, brother John	M	C-F	GSC
-----	Mexican serenade	HL	D-EF	BOS
-----	Never the nightingale	H	EF-GF	GAL
-----	Spanish Johnny	HL	BF-F	GSC
-----	The ragpicker	MH	C-AF	GSC
Silberta	You shall have your red rose			
Spencer	For whom the bell tolls	MH	F-AF	BOS
Spross	Let all my life be music			JCH
Swanson	Night song			
Taylor	A song for lovers	MH	D-F	JFI
-----	The rivals	H	E-G	JFI
Thomson	Dirge	M	D-F	GSC
Tyson	Noon and night	LH	F-AF	GSC
-----	Sea moods	LH	E-AF	GSC
Walther	Sometimes	MH	EF-AF	GSC
Warner	Hurdy gurdy	M	D-F	CFI
Warren	King Arthur's farewell			GRA
-----	We two	LH	E-A	GSC
-----	White horses of the sea	LH	F-G	GSC
Watts	Blue are her eyes	H	FS-FS	DIT
-----	Stresa	H	EF-BF	DIT
-----	Wings of night	LH	CS-G	GSC
Weaver	A book of verses	H	D-AF	GAL
-----	Dream dawn			GAL
Weill	In autumn			
Wolf	Iris	LMH	F-BF	FLA
-----	Weather forecast	H	EF-GS	GSC

British Recital Songs

Lyric Tenor

Aiken	Sigh no more	HML		STB
Anon	False Phillis			

(Anon)	Have you seen but a white lily grow?	H	E-F	GSC
Arne, T.	Blow, blow thou winter wind	M	C-F	†
-----	Peggy			GSC
-----	Under the greenwood tree			
Attey	On a time			BOO
Balfe	Come into the garden, Maud	H	FS-G	GSC
Bantock	A dream of spring	H	E-G	CHE
-----	Desolation	M	C-GF	CHE
-----	Silent strings	MH	F-G	BOO
Bartlet	What thing is love			BOO
-----	Whither runneth my sweetheart			BOO
Bax	The enchanted fiddle			
-----	The white peace			CHE
Benjamin	The wasp			CUR
Besley	Listening	H	E-AF	CUR
-----	Siesta			
Bliss	Madame Noy	H	B-AF	CHE
-----	Three jolly gentlemen	H		
Bridge	Adoration	H		ROG
-----	Come to me in my dreams	HL	C-EF	BOH
-----	E'en as a lovely flower	HM	FS-E	BOH
-----	O that it were so	LMH	D-G	CHA
-----	So perverse			BOS
Britten	Fish in the unruffled lakes			BOH
-----	Nocturne			BOH
Bury	There is a lady	HM	CS-E	CFI
Butterworth	Loveliest of trees			AUG
Campion	Follow thy fair sun			STB
-----	There is a garden in her face			DIT
-----	When to her lute Corinna sings			STB
Clarke	Shy one	HL	BF-G	BOH
Coleridge-Taylor	Eleanore	HML		NOV
-----	Life and death	HML		ASC
-----	Onaway! Awake beloved	MH	FS-BF	†
-----	She rested by the broken brook	HL		DIT
-----	Unmindful of the roses			
Davies	Hame			
-----	When childher plays	HML		BOO
Delius	Love's philosophy			†
-----	Song of the hills			†

(Delius)	To the queen of my heart			†
Dowland	Awake, sweet love	M	E-F	STB
-----	Come again! sweet love	M	D-E	STB
-----	Come away			BOO
-----	Come, heavy sleep			STB
-----	Deare, if you change			BOO
-----	Fine knacks for ladies	M	E-F	STB
-----	Flow, my tears	M	D-E	STB
-----	In darkness let me dwell			STB
-----	I saw my lady weep	M	E-E	STB
-----	Lady, if you so spite me			STB
-----	Now, cease my wandering eyes			STB
-----	Say love, if ever thou didst find			STB
-----	Shall I sue?			STB
-----	What if I never speede	M	D-D	BOS
Dunhill	The cloths of heaven	LM	EF-G	STB
Eden	What's in the air today?	M	D-F	ELK
Elgar	Is she not passing fair			BOO
Finzi	Budmouth dears			
Ford	A prayer to our lady			
-----	Now I see thy looks were feigned			BOO
-----	Since first I saw your face			DIT
Forsyth	The bell man			DIT
German	Charming Chloe	HML		NOV
-----	Kangaroo and dingo			
Gibbs	Five eyes	HL	D-D	BOS
-----	To one who passed whistling H through the night		F-G	CUR
Green	My lips shall speak the praise	M	E-F	OXF
Gurney	Hawk and buckle			OXF
-----	Under the greenwood tree			ROG
Handel	Love and friendship			RBR
-----	Love's a dear deceitful jewel	LH	F-F	RBR
-----	Tell fair Irene			
Head	Sea gipsy	LM	E-GS	BOO
-----	Sweet chance that led my steps abroad	LM	C-F	BOH
-----	The ships of Arcady	ML	BF-EF	BOH
-----	When I think upon the maidens	LM	D-G	BOO
Henschel	Morning-hymn	MH	DS-GS	†
Holbrooke	Come not when I am dead			ENO
Holst	Things lovelier	M	D-G	AUG
Hook	Bright Phoebus	M	EF-F	GSC
Humphrey	I pass all my hours			DIT

491

Ireland	Great things			AUG
-----	Hope the hornblower			BOO
-----	Santa Chiara	ML	C-EF	AUG
Johnson	As I walked forth one summer day			DIT
Jones	What if I speede?			BOO
Keel	Bonny George Campbell			CRA
-----	Trade winds	HL	BF-EF	BOH
Lambert	She is far from the land	HML		CHA
Leveridge	When dull care			BOO
Linley	O, bid your faithful Ariel fly			BOO
Milford	Elegy	H	C-G	NOV
-----	Love on my heart	H	FS-FS	NOV
-----	The colour	H	D-G	OXF
Moeran	Diaphenia			BOO
-----	The sweet o' the year			AUG
Morgan	Clorinda	HM	C-EF	ENO
Morley	It was a lover and his lass	HM		DIT
Munro	My lovely Celia			BIR
Pilkington	Rest, sweet nymphs			STB
Purcell	An ode to Cynthia walking Richmond Hill			
-----	Cease, o my sad soul			POT
-----	Come unto these yellow sands			AUG
-----	Had I but love			DUN
-----	If music be the food of love	M	D-G	BOO
-----	I'll sail upon the dog star	HL	A-E	†
-----	Sylvia, now your scorn give over			FSY
-----	There's not a swain on the plain	M	B-G	BAF
Quilter	Blow, blow thou winter wind	HL	C-E	BOO
-----	Dream valley	H	EF-GF	ROG
-----	Go, lovely rose	LHM	F-GF	CHA
-----	It was a lover and his lass	HL	CS-E	BOO
-----	I will go with my father a-plowing	MH	D-G	ELK
-----	Love's philosophy	LMH	D-A	BOO
-----	Now sleeps the crimson petal	LMH	EF-GF	BOO
-----	When daffodils begin to peer			BOO
Ronald	Down in the forest	HML	C-D	ENO
-----	Drift down, drift down			BOO
Rosseter	What then is love but mourning			STB
-----	When Laura smiles	LM	D-E	STB

Rowley	The toll gate house			ROG
Russell	Poor man's garden	HML	A-D	BOO
Sanderson	Oh joy be thine			
Shaw	Song of the Palanquin bearers	LH	E-F	CUR
Stanford	The fairy lough	ML	A-EF	BOO
Stephenson	Love is a sickness	HML	C-D	BOO
-----	Ships that pass in the night	HML	DF-DF	BOO
Thiman	The silver swan	MH	EF-G	NOV
Toye	The inn	L	C-E	CUR
Vaughan Williams	Linden Lea	HML	C-D	BOS
-----	Orpheus with his lute			PRO
-----	See the chariot at hand			
-----	Silent noon			GSC
-----	The roadside fire	HML	BF-EF	BOO
Warlock	A prayer to St. Anthony of Padua	M	C-EF	CFI
-----	As ever I saw	MH	DF-GF	ROG
-----	Good ale			AUG
-----	Mr. Belloc's fancy	LM	D-G	AUG
-----	The sick heart			
Wilson	Phillis has such charming graces	ML	CS-EF	BOO

French Recital Songs

Lyric Tenor

Bemberg	Il neige	H	FS-G	GRU
Berlioz	L'absence	H	CS-FS	GSC
-----	L'isle inconnue			CST
Bizet	Après l'hiver			†
-----	Chanson d'avril	H	BF-G	†
-----	Douce mer			GSC
-----	Vielle chanson	H	EF-A	GSC
Busser	Notre père qui êtes aux cieux			
Campra	Air de Musette Flute, cello and harps			
Caplet	Le forêt			DUR
Chabrier	Villanelle des petits canards	HML	B-E	†
Chaminade	Madrigal	LH	E-GS	GSC
-----	Sombrero			
Charpentier	A mules			
-----	Les chevaux de bois	H	E-A	HEU

493

Chausson	Apaisement	MH	EF-G	HAM
-----	Le charme	HM	BF-EF	HAM
-----	L'amour d'Antan	HL		INT
-----	Le colibri	M	F-GF	BOS
-----	Le temps des lilas	MH	D-GS	†
-----	Nocturne	HL		INT
-----	Sérénade			
Dalayrac	Hélas! c'est près de vous			
Debussy	Ballade des femmes de Paris			DUR
-----	Beau soir	LH	C-FS	†
-----	C'est l'extase	LH	CS-A	†
-----	Chevaux de bois	H	C-G	†
-----	Clair de lune	M	CS-FS	JOB
-----	Colloque sentimental			DUR
-----	De fleurs	H	C-AF	†
-----	En sourdine	M	C-FS	†
-----	Green	H	C-AF	†
-----	Harmonie du soir			DUR
-----	Il pleure dans mon coeur	LH	CS-GS	†
-----	L'échelonnement des haies			HAM
-----	L'ombre des arbres			†
-----	La mer est plus belle	HL		†
-----	Le balcon			JOB
-----	Le faune			DUR
-----	Le jet d'eau			DUR
-----	Le voyageur			DUR
-----	Les angélus			HAM
-----	Les cloches	LH	E-GS	†
-----	Les ingénus			DUR
-----	Mandoline	HM	BF-F	†
-----	Noël des enfants qui n'ont plus de maisons			DUR
-----	Nuits d'etoiles	LH	E-A	MAR
-----	Placet futile			DUR
-----	Recueillement			DUR
-----	Romance	HM	C-E	CFI
-----	Voici que le printemps	LH	CS-G	BOS
De Fay	Dans la forêt			
Delibes	Bonjours, Suzon	LM	C-F	GSC
-----	Jours passés			GSC
-----	Myrto	M	A-FS	GSC
Duparc	Chanson triste	MH	FS-AF	†
-----	Extase	LMH	FS-A	†
-----	Lamento	ML	EF-EF	†
-----	L'invitation au voyage	HM	E-F	†
-----	Phidylé	MH	EF-AF	BOS
-----	Soupir	HL	CS-F	BOS
Dupont	Chanson des noisettes			HEU

(Dupont)	Mandoline			DUR
Fauré	Adieu	MH	F-F	†
-----	Après un rêve	HM	C-F	†
-----	Au bord de l'eau	HL	C-F	†
-----	C'est l'extase	HL	C-FF	GSC
-----	Chanson de Shylock			HAM
-----	Chanson du pêcheur	H	E-A	HAM
-----	Clair de lune	MH	C-G	†
-----	Green	HL	CS-GF	†
-----	Ici-bas!	H	FS-G	†
-----	L'hiver a cessé	HL		INT
-----	La lune blanche	HL		INT
-----	Le parfum impérissable	LH	GF-GF	
-----	Le secret	LH	F-G	†
-----	Le voyageur	H	F-G	MAR
-----	Les roses d'Ispahan	HM	D-FS	†
-----	Lydia	MH	G-G	†
-----	Madrigal	MH	F-F	HAM
-----	Mandoline	HL	F-E	†
-----	Nell	LH	FS-AF	†
-----	Notre amour	H	DS-B	†
-----	Rencontre	H	EF-AF	†
-----	Sérénade toscane	MH	G-AF	HAM
-----	Soir	LH	D-GS	†
-----	Spleen	H	E-FS	MAR
-----	Sylvie	HL	E-F	†
-----	Toujours	LH	F-AF	†
-----	Vocalise	H		LED
Ferrari	Le miroir	M	E-F	GSC
Fourdrain	Carnaval	M	C-F	RIC
-----	Celle que je préfère	H		RIC
-----	Chanson norvégienne	H	E-G	RIC
-----	Chevauchée cosaque	H	D-G	RIC
-----	Le papillon			RIC
-----	Madrigal	H		RIC
-----	Promenade au mule			
Franck	Aimer			BOS
-----	Le mariage des roses	M	E-FS	BOS
-----	Les cloches du soir	H	F-AF	
-----	Lied	LH	FS-FS	†
-----	Ninon			BOS
-----	Nocturne	HL		†
-----	S'il est un charmant gazon			
Gounod	Adore and be still	HL		GSC
-----	Aimons-nous			
-----	Au printemps	LMH	DF-AF	GSC
-----	Au rossignol	LMH	D-G	CHO
-----	Medjé Chanson arabe	MH	G-G	BOO
-----	Vénise	HL		INT

495

Grovlez	Guitares et mandolines			DUR
Hahn	A Chloris	H	DS-FS	HEU
-----	Je me metz en vostre mercy			HEU
-----	L'heure exquise	M	DF-F	†
-----	La barcheta			HEU
-----	Fêtes galantes			
-----	Le plus beau présent			HEU
-----	Le printemps			
-----	Le rossignol des lilas			
-----	Offrande	M	D-D	GSC
-----	Paysage	MH	EF-G	HEU
-----	Paysage triste			HEU
Hindemith	La belle dame sans merci	MH		SC
Holmès	Au pays	HM	C-F	CFI
Hue	D'avoir tenu vos chères mains			ROU
-----	Il a neigé des fleurs	H	EF-AF	
-----	J'ai pleuré en rêve	HL	D-E	BOS
-----	L'âne blanc	H	EF-G	HEU
-----	La fille du roi de Chine	H	FS-GS	HEU
-----	Le passant	H	D-G	†
-----	Les clochettes des muguets	HL	E-GF	INT
-----	Mon coeur est comme un arbre en fleurs			ROU
-----	Sonnez les matines	H	FS-G	HEU
Koechlin	L'air	M	F-FS	ROU
-----	L'hiver	H	E-G	†
-----	Le thé	HM	C-E	BOS
-----	Si tu le veux	LH	FS-A	MAR
Leguerney	Au sommeil			ROU
-----	Genièvres hérissés	H	D-G	ROU
Martini	Plaisir d'amour	M	BF-EF	GSC
Massenet	Crépuscule	M	D-E	GSC
-----	Noël païen			HEU
-----	Nuit d'Espagne			
-----	Pensée d'automne	HML	B-E	GSC
Mehul	Chant du départ			SEN
Milhaud	Chant d'amour	M	C-GF	ESC
Monteclair	Comme une hirondelle			
Mouret	Hymne à l'amour			ROU
Mozart	Dans un bois	H	EF-AF	
-----	Oiseaux, si tous les ans	H	C-G	KAL
Nerini	Rose ne croyez pas			
Paladilhe	Psyché	HM	BF-F	GSC
-----	Sonnet de Pétrarque			
Pessard	L'adieu du matin	ML	BF-D	GSC
-----	Requiem du coeur			LED
Pierné	En barque	L	D-DF	GSC

(Pierné)	Ils étaient trois petits chats blancs			MAR
-----	Le moulin	ML	C-E	BOS
-----	Provence			
Poldowski	Cortège	M	D-FS	CHE
-----	Dansons la gigue	M	EF-G	MAR
-----	L'heure exquise	LMH	DF-AF	CHE
Poulenc	A sa guitare	M	D-FS	DUR
-----	Air champêtre			ROU
-----	Air grave			ROU
-----	Air romantique			SAL
-----	Air vif	H	C-AF	ROU
-----	Bleuet	H	FS-GF	DUR
-----	C (J'ai traversé les ponts de C.)			ROU
-----	La dame d'André			
-----	Montparnasse	H	EF-G	ESC
-----	Priez pour paix	ML		ROU
-----	Violon			ROU
Rameau	Le grillon			DUR
Ravel	Chanson à boire			DUR
-----	Chanson romanesque			DUR
-----	D'Anne jouant de l'espinette	H	CS-GS	GSC
-----	D'Anne qui me jecta	HM	CS-FS	GSC
-----	Kaddisch	H	C-G	DUR
-----	Le grillon	H	E-G	DUR
-----	Le paon	M	C-F	DUR
-----	Manteau de fleurs	H		INT
-----	Nicolette	L	B-FS	ELK
-----	Ronde			
-----	Sainte	M	C-G	ELV
-----	Sur l'herbe	MH	C-G	DUR
-----	Tout gai!	MH	EF-F	DUR
-----	Trois beaux oiseaux du paradis			DUR
Roussel	Jazz dans la nuit	H	C-A	DUR
-----	Le bachelier de Salamanque			DUR
-----	Le jardin mouillé	M	C-FS	ROU
Saint-Saëns	Aimons-nous			DUR
-----	Guitares et mandolines			DUR
-----	La cloche	LH	DF-AF	
-----	Mai	H	G-FS	DUR
-----	Thou, O Lord art my protector	MH	C-A	GSC
-----	Tournoiement			DUR
Satie	Le chapelier			ROU
Severac	Chanson de Blaisine			
-----	Les hiboux			ROU

Staub	L'heure silencieuse	H	EF-G	DUR
Szulc	Claire de lune	H	E-G	AXE
-----	Hantise d'amour	H	D-BF	GSC

German Recital Songs

Lyric Tenor

Bach, C.P.E.	Das Gebet			SIM
-----	Passionslied			SIM
-----	The last judgement			
Bach, J.S.	Bist due bei mir	HML	A-EF	†
-----	God, my shepherd, walks beside me	H		GRA
-----	Meiner allerliebsten schoenen			
-----	O Jesulein suess			
Beethoven	Adelaide	HML	BF-E	†
-----	Andenken			†
-----	A song of penitence			
-----	Das Geheimnis			
-----	Der Kuss			†
-----	Die Ehre Gottes	HL	AF-EF	†
-----	Ich liebe dich	HL	BF-DF	†
-----	Lied aus der Ferne			
-----	Mailied			RIC
-----	Mit einem gemalten Band			RIC
-----	Neue Liebe, neues Leben			†
-----	Trocknet nicht			†
-----	Wonne der Wehmut			UNI
Blech	Heimkehr vom Feste			
Blume	Gruen ist die Heide			
Brahms	Ach, wende diesen Blick			†
-----	An die Nachtigall	H	DS-G	†
-----	An ein Veilchen	H	DS-GS	†
-----	Auf dem See	HL	D-F	†
-----	Bei dir sind meine Gedanken	MH	E-FS	†
-----	Blinde Kuh			†
-----	Botschaft	HL	D-F	†
-----	Der Tod, das ist die kuehle Nacht	L	AF-F	†
-----	Der Ueberlaeufer			†
-----	Die Sonne scheint nicht mehr			†
-----	Erinnerung	H	E-G	†
-----	Es liebt sich so lieblich im Lenze	LH	D-GS	†

498

(Brahms)	Es traeumte mir			†
-----	Feldeinsamkeit	HL	C-EF	†
-----	Fruehlingslied			†
-----	Geheimnis			†
-----	In Waldeseinsamkeit	H	ES-G	†
-----	Juchhe!			†
-----	Keinen hat es noch gereut	L	B-F	†
-----	Klage	LH	FS-FS	†
-----	Komm bald	HM	CS-F	†
-----	Lerchengesang	LH	FS-GS	†
-----	Liebe kam aus fernen Landen	HL	C-E	†
-----	Meine Liebe ist gruen	MLH	ES-A	GSC
-----	Minnelied	MHL	C-EF	†
-----	Mondenschein	LH	D-GF	†
-----	O liebliche Wangen	MLH	E-G	†
-----	O wuesst' ich doch den Weg zurueck	H	E-FS	†
-----	Ruhe Suessliebchen	HL	BS-E	†
-----	Salamander			†
-----	Schoen war, das ich dir weihte			†
-----	Sind es Schmerzen	HL	BF-F	†
-----	Sommerabend			†
-----	Sonntag	H	D-G	†
-----	So willst du des Armen	HL	C-E	†
-----	Staendchen	HL	BF-E	†
-----	Unueberwindlich			†
-----	Vergebliches Staendchen	LMH		†
-----	Wenn du nur zuweilen laechelst			†
-----	Wie bist du meine Koenigin	HL	C-E	†
-----	Wie Melodien zieht es	HL	A-E	†
-----	Willst du, dass ich geh'?	L	C-G	†
-----	Wir wandelten	LH	EF-GF	†
Franck, J.W.	Auf, auf, zu Gottes Lob			SIM
Franz	For music	ML	C-D	†
-----	Marie	HL	D-F	†
-----	Stille Sicherheit	M	E-F	†
Handel	Dank sei Dir, Herr	M	CS-E	JFI
-----	Gruene Matten, kuehle Haine			
Hassler	Gagliarda			SIM
Haydn	Das Leben ist ein Traum			GSC
-----	Der erste Kuss			
-----	Heller Blick			
-----	Liebes Maedchen, hoer' mir zu			HSC
-----	Matrosenlied			

(Haydn)	Serenade			
-----	She never told her love	HL	B-D	DIT
-----	The sailor's song			
Hildach	Der Lenz			HSC
Jensen	Am Ufer des Flusses des Manzanares	H	D-FS	GSC
-----	Margreta	M	F-F	PET
-----	Murmuring zephyr	LH	E-AF	GSC
Kaun	Der Sieger			
Korngold	Das Staendchen	M		SC
Liszt	Du bist wie eine Blume	H	E-G	†
-----	Es muss ein Wunderbares sein	HM	C-EF	DUR
-----	O lieb' so lang du lieben kannst	HML	B-F	†
Loewe	Canzonetta	MH	B-A	DIT
-----	Des fremden Kindes Heil'ger Christ			SC
-----	Des Glockenthuermers Tochterlein	H	CS-A	SC
Mahler	Ich atmet' einen linden Duft	HL		INT
-----	Ich ging mit Lust	HL		INT
Marx	Hat dich die Liebe beruehrt	MH	EF-BF	AMP
-----	Marienlied	MH	EF-AF	AMP
-----	Nocturne	H	EF-AF	AMP
-----	Waldseligkeit	H	D-A	UNI
-----	Wie einst			UNI
Mendelssohn	An die Entfernte	M	F-F	
-----	Die Sterne schau'n in stiller Nacht	L	A-E	
-----	Gestaendnis	M	CS-FS	AUG
-----	Im Gruenen	H	CS-BF	
-----	Jagdlied	HL	BF-EF	†
-----	Nachtlied			
-----	Neue Liebe	H	CS-A	†
-----	O Jugend	H	E-A	†
-----	On wings of song			†
-----	Pagenlied	M	E-E	†
-----	Venetianisches Gondellied	LM	E-FS	AUG
Mozart	Abendempfindung	M	E-F	
-----	An Chloe	LH	EF-AF	
-----	Das Traumbild			
-----	Das Veilchen	LMH	F-G	†
-----	Die Verschweigung			
-----	Die Zufriedenheit			
-----	Unglueckliche Liebe			
-----	Warnung	HM	C-D	

500

Reger	Des Kindes Gebet	H	F-G	BOT
-----	Friede	H	EF-G	UNI
Schoeck	Nachruf			
Schoenberg	Erhebung			GSC
Schubert	Abschied	HL	BF-F	†
-----	Am Meer	HML	B-D	†
-----	Am See			PET
-----	An den Mond	HL	F-GF	†
-----	An die Laute	LH	D-F	†
-----	An die Nachtigall	H	C-G	†
-----	An die Tueren	HL		†
-----	An Silvia			†
-----	Auf dem Wasser zu singen	MH	EF-GF	†
-----	Ave Maria	LMH	F-F	†
-----	Bei dir allein			PET
-----	Danksagung an den Bach	HL	E-F	†
-----	Das Fischermaedchen	L	A-EF	†
-----	Das Lied im Gruenen			PET
-----	Das Rosenband			PET
-----	Das Wandern	HLM	E-E	†
-----	Das Wirtshaus	HL	C-D	†
-----	Dass sie hier gewesen!			PET
-----	Der Einsame	LH	D-G	†
-----	Der Juengling an der Quelle	LH	E-A	†
-----	Der Juengling und der Tod	M	DF-FF	GSC
-----	Der Leiermann	ML	C-D	†
-----	Der Lindenbaum	HL	A-D	†
-----	Der Mondabend			PET
-----	Der Musensohn	LH	FS-G	†
-----	Der Neugierige	HL	CS-EF	†
-----	Der Schmetterling	LH	E-F	†
-----	Der Wachtelschlag	H	DS-FS	PET
-----	Der Wanderer an den Mond	LM	D-F	PET
-----	Der Wegweiser	L	D-EF	†
-----	Des Fischers Liebesglueck	LH	F-A	†
-----	Die boese Farbe	HL	CS-F	†
-----	Die Entzueckung			
-----	Die Forelle	MLH	EF-GF	†
-----	Die Hoffnung	HM	E-E	†
-----	Die liebe Farbe			
-----	Die liebe hat Gelogen	LM	G-F	†
-----	Die Nebensonnen	HL	F-D	†
-----	Die Post	HML	BF-EF	†
-----	Die Rose	M	G-FS	PET
-----	Die Taubenpost	HL	D-EF	†
-----	Du bist die Ruh	LMH	EF-AF	†
-----	Erlafsee	H	E-G	†

501

(Schubert)	Erstarrung	HL	D-F	†
-----	Erster Verlust	M	C-F	†
-----	Fischerweise	L	C-D	†
-----	Fruehlingsglaube	M	EF-F	†
-----	Fruehlingssehnsucht	HL	B-E	
-----	Fruehlingstraum	HL	C-D	†
-----	Geheimes	HL	BF-EF	†
-----	Heidenroeslein			†
-----	Ihr Bild	HL	C-C	†
-----	Ihr Grab			PET
-----	Im Abendrot	HL	C-D	†
-----	Laura am Klavier			
-----	Lebensmuth			PET
-----	Liebesbotschaft	H	E-G	†
-----	Lob der Thraenen	LM	F-F	†
-----	Memnon •	LM	AF-F	PET
-----	Nachtstueck	LH	D-G	†
-----	Nacht und Traeume	HL	C-DF	†
-----	Nachtviolen			PET
-----	Rastlose Liebe	M	B-F	†
-----	Schwanengesang			†
-----	Staendchen			
-----	Ueber Wildemann			PET
-----	Ungeduld	HML		†
-----	Wanderers Nachtlied, 2	LH	F-F	†
-----	Wehmuth	HL	B-D	†
-----	Widerschein			PET
-----	Wohin?	HL	B-E	†
Schuetz	Eile mich, Gott, zu erretten			BAR
-----	Hallelujah			
-----	Herr, unser Herrscher!			BAR
-----	Ich werde nicht sterben			BAR
-----	Vom namen Jesu			
-----	Staendchen			SIM
Schumann	Abendlied	HL	B-F	†
-----	Alte Laute	HL	DF-DF	†
-----	An den Sonnenschein	HL	A-D	†
-----	Auftraege	HL	C-E	†
-----	Dein Angesicht	HL	B-EF	†
-----	Der Hidalgo	HL	BF-F	†
-----	Der Nussbaum	LMH	D-FS	†
-----	Der Sandmann	HL	AF-DF	†
-----	Der Soldat			
-----	Die Lotusblume	HLM	BF-F	†
-----	Die Meerfee			
-----	Du bist wie eine Blume	HM	F-EF	†
-----	Fruehlingslust	HL		†

(Schumann)	Geisternaehe			
-----	Ich grolle nicht	HL	BF-D	†
-----	Ich hab' im Traum geweinet	HL	B-D	†
-----	Ihre Stimme	LH		†
-----	Intermezzo	HL	C-D	†
-----	Lieb' Liebchen	HL	B-E	†
-----	Mein schoener Stern			
-----	Meine Rose			
-----	Mit Myrthen und Rosen	HL	A-D	†
-----	Mondnacht	M	E-FS	GSC
-----	O wie lieblich ist das Maedchen			
-----	Provenzalisches Lied	LH		†
-----	Romanze	HL	C-E	†
-----	Roeselein, Roeselein			
-----	Staendchen			
-----	Stille Traenen	HL		†
-----	Wanderlied	HL	A-E	†
-----	Was soll ich sagen!			†
-----	Wenn ich in deine Augen seh'	HL	EF-FF	†
-----	Wer machte dich so krank?			
-----	Widmung	HL	BF-F	†
Silcher	Die Loreley			GSC
-----	Gut' Nacht			
-----	In der Ferne			
Strauss	Ach Lieb, ich muss nun scheiden	H	D-G	
-----	Allerseelen	HL	AS-E	†
-----	All' mein' Gedanken	H	CS-GS	
-----	Barcarolle	H	DF-BF	†
-----	Die Nacht	HL		†
-----	Freundliche Vision	HL	C-F	†
-----	Fruehlingsgedraenge			
-----	Heimkehr	HL	B-E	†
-----	Heimliche Aufforderung	HL	B-E	†
-----	Ich trage meine minne	M		UNI
-----	Kling			†
-----	Kornblumen	LH	DF-AF	†
-----	Madrigal	LH	EF-GF	
-----	Mein Herz ist stumm	LH	EF-AF	
-----	Mit deinen blauen Augen	LH	C-GS	†
-----	Morgen	HML	E-F	†
-----	Nichts	LH	E-A	†
-----	Schlagende Herzen			†
-----	Schoen sind doch kalt die Himmelssterne	H	F-BF	

(Strauss)	Seitdem dein Aug' in meines schaute			SC
-----	Traum durch die Daemmerung	HML	BF-EF	†
-----	Winterliebe			†
-----	Wozu noch, Maedchen	H	FS-A	
Trunk	An die Liebe			
-----	Der Feind			
-----	In meiner Heimat			
-----	Tanzlied			
Tunder	Ein kleines Kindelein			KIS
Weber	Staendchen			
Weingartner	Liebesfeier			
Wolf	Ach, im Maien	HL	C-E	†
-----	Auch kleine Dinge	HM	D-E	†
-----	Auf dem gruenen Balkon	HL		†
-----	Auf ein altes Bild	HL	E-DS	DIT
-----	Auftrag	HL		†
-----	Bedeckt mich mit Blumen	HL	B-D	†
-----	Beherzigung			PET
-----	Denk' es, o Seele	LH	EF-F	†
-----	Der Gaertner	HL		†
-----	Der Knabe und das Immlein	L	CS-A	†
-----	Der Musikant	HL	CS-D	†
-----	Der Scholar			PET
-----	Der verzweifelte Liebhaber			†
-----	Ein Staendchen euch zu bringen	HL		†
-----	Elfenlied	HL	D-F	†
-----	Er ist's	H	D-G	†
-----	Frage und Antwort			PET
-----	Frohe Botschaft			
-----	Fruehling uebers Jahr			†
-----	Fussreise	HL	D-E	†
-----	Ganymed	HL	CS-D	†
-----	Gebet	HL		†
-----	Gesellenlied			
-----	Gleich und gleich			†
-----	Heb' auf dein blondes Haupt	HL	G-DF	†
-----	Heimweh (Eichendorff Lieder)	M		†
-----	Im Fruehling	HL	BF-F	†
-----	Jaegerlied			PET
-----	Lied vom Winde			PET
-----	Mein Liebchen, wir sassen beisammen			
-----	Morgentau	HL	D-D	†
-----	Nimmersatte Liebe	LH	CF-AF	†

(Wolf)	Storchenbotschaft			†
-----	Unfall			PET
-----	Verborgenheit	HL	B-E	†
-----	Verschwiegene Liebe	LH	DF-FS	†
-----	Wenn du zu den Blumen gehst	HL	B-EF	†
-----	Wer sein holdes Lieb verloren			
-----	Zum neuen Jahr			PET
Wolff	Dann loesch' das Licht			HMP
-----	Faeden			
-----	Und alles gehoeret uns			HMP

Italian Recital Songs

Lyric Tenor

Arcadelt	Il bianco e dolce cigno			
Barthelemy	Pesca d'amore			
Bassani	Dormi, bella, dormi tu	L	EF-F	GSC
-----	Posate, dormite (La Serenata)	H	EF-F	GSC
Bimboni	Sospiri miei	M	EF-EF	GAL
Bononcini	Deh, più a me non v'ascondete	LH	EF-F	†
-----	L'esperto nocchiero (Astarte)	HL	B-E	†
-----	Lungi di te			
-----	Per la gloria	HL	C-EF	†
-----	Vado ben spesso			JCH
Caccini	Amarilli, mia bella	ML	C-D	†
-----	Fere, selvagge	HL	CS-GS	DIT
Caldara	Alma del core			GSC
-----	Come raggio di sol	HL	D-F	†
-----	Sebben crudele	HML	E-DS	†
-----	Selve amiche, ombrose piante	HM	E-E	†
Carissimi	Deh, contentatevi	LH	E-G	†
-----	Filli, non t'amo più	HL	B-D	†
-----	No, no, non si speri!	HL	C-EF	†
-----	Vittoria, mio core	HLM	B-E	†
Castelnuovo-Tedesco	La ermita de San Simon			
-----	L'Infinito			
Cavalli	Donzelle fuggite	HL	C-EF	†
Cesti	Ah quanto è vero (Il Pomo D'Oro)	HL	F-F	DIT

(Cesti)	Che angoscia, che affanno (Il Pomo d'Oro)	HL	C-DF	DIT
-----	Intorno all'idol mio (Orontea)	MH	D-F	†
-----	Tu mancavi a tormentarmi	H	D-G	GSC
Chopin	Io son un fior che muore			
Cimara	Fiocca la neve	H	G-G	GSC
-----	Non più			
-----	Stornello			BON
Cimarosa	Brillar mi sento il core (Il Matrimonio Segreto)			RIC
-----	Pria che spunti in ciel (Il Matrimonió Segreto)			RIC
Crescenzo	Notte d'amore			RIC
-----	Quann' a femmena vo			RIC
-----	Rondine al nido	HM	DS-FS	CAR
-----	Tarantella sincera	HM	DS-FS	CAR
-----	Triste Maggio			RIC
D'Astorga	Vo' cercando in queste valli	H	D-G	STB
Del Moral	El camino canta			
De Luca	Non posso disperar	HL	C-E	GSC
Denza	Si tu m'aimais	LMH	D-GS	CFI
Donaudy	Ah mai non cessate			RIC
-----	Freschi luoghi			RIC
-----	O bei nidi d'amore			RIC
-----	O del mio amato ben	M	EF-F	RIC
-----	Quando ti rivedrò			RIC
-----	Spirate pur, spirate			RIC
-----	Vaghissima sembianza	H	E-A	RIC
Durante	Danza, danza fanciulla gentile	HM	BF-F	†
-----	Vergin, tutta amor	LM	C-EF	†
Falconieri	Bella Porta di Rubini	LH	E-EF	DIT
Fasolo	Cangia, cangia tue voglie	H	C-G	GSC
Gaffi	Luci vezzose	HL	D-E	DIT
Gagliano	Dormi, Amore	HL	CS-E	DIT
Gargiulo	Ninna nanna	M	D-F	GSC
Giordani	Caro mio ben	HML	B-D	†
Gluck	O del mio dolce ardor (Paride ed Elena)	LH	D-FS	GSC
-----	Spiagge amate (Paride ed Elena)			†
Handel	Allor che sorge astro lucente (Rodrigo)			BOO
-----	Alma mia (Floridante)	HM	CS-E	†
-----	Care selve (Atalanta)	MH	FS-A	BOO
-----	Due bell' alme (Deidamia)			BOO
-----	No, oh Dio			

(Handel)	Non lo dirò (Tolomeo)			
-----	Ombra mai fu (Serse)	HM	BF-EF	†
-----	Rendi'l sereno al ciglio (Sosarme)	LH	EF-F	†
-----	Sei, mia gioja (Partenope)			CFI
Haydn	Pensi a me			
-----	Un tetto umil			
Legrenzi	Che fiero costume	HML	C-D	†
Leoncavallo	Sérénade francaise			
Lotti	Pur dicesti, o bocca bella	LMH	E-FS	GSC
Malipiero	Ballata	H		CHE
Manzolo	Quando tu mi guardi e ridi			
-----	Se vedeste le piaghe			
Mazzaferrata	Presto, presto io m'innamoro	HL	CS-E	DIT
Monteverdi	Maledetto sia l'aspetto			PET
-----	Ohime, ch'io cado			
Paisiello	Nel cor più non mi sento	HL	C-EF	†
Paradies	M'ha preso alla sua ragna	M	EF-F	GSC
Pergolesi	Dite ch'ogni momento			BOS
-----	Nina	HL	CS-D	DIT
Peri	Bellissima Regina			
-----	Invocazione di Orfeo (Euridice)	HL	E-CS	DIT
Piccini	L'amour fait verser trop de pleurs (Atys)			LEM
Porpora	Non più fra sassi			PET
Quagliati	Apra il suo verde seno	HL	E-CS	DIT
Respighi	Abbandono			BON
-----	Invito alla danza			BON
-----	Nebbie			†
Rontani	Or ch'io non segno più	HL	CS-E	DIT
Rosa	Selve, voi che le speranze	MH	D-G	DIT
-----	Star vicino	HL	D-E	†
Rossini	La danza	MH	E-A	†
Sadero	Amuri, Amuri	M		CHE
Santoliquido	I canti della sera			RIC
-----	Io mi levai			
-----	Riflessi			FOR
Sarti	Lungi dal caro bene (Armide)	HL	G-D	GSC
Scarlatti, A.	All' acquisto di gloria (Tigrane)	H	C-G	GSC
-----	Chi vuole innamorarsi	HL	D-EF	DIT
-----	Già il sole dal Gange	LH	EF-F	GSC
-----	Già mai la lontananza			DUR
-----	Ingrata quanto sei			

507

(Scarlatti, A.)	Rugiadose odorose	HL	D-E	DIT
	(Il Pirro e Demetrio)			
-----	Sento nel core	M	E-F	†
-----	Son tutta duolo	M	D-EF	GSC
Scarlatti, D.	Qual farfalletta			
Secchi	Lungi dal caro bene	HL	A-FS	DIT
Sibella	La Girometta	HML	D-E	GSC
-----	O bocca dolorosa	HM	D-F	GSC
Stradella	Pietà, Signore	HM	C-F	GSC
-----	Ragion sempre addita	H	E-G	†
-----	Se nel ben			CFI
Torelli	Tu lo sai	HL	BF-F	†
-----	Serenade			HEU
Tosti	'A vucchella	LH	F-G	RIC
-----	Addio	MH		RIC
-----	Aprile	LMH		RIC
-----	La serenata	HLM	D-EF	GSC
-----	Luna d'estate			
-----	Mattinata			RIC
-----	My dreams	LMH		CHA
-----	Parted			RIC
-----	Pour un baiser			
-----	The last song	HL		RIC
Willaert	Con lagrime e sospir			
Wolf-Ferrari	Rispetto			HSC

Russian Recital Songs

Lyric Tenor

Arensky	Autumn	H	CS-FS	GSC
-----	But lately in dance I embraced her	HM	C-EF	BOS
-----	Revery	MH	DS-FS	DIT
-----	Valse	H	DF-GF	GSC
Borodin	Homeward you went			
-----	The sleeping princess	M	DF-F	†
Cui	Dusk fallen	LH	E-GS	DIT
-----	The statue at Czarskoe-Selo	HM	DF-EF	†
Dargomijshky	O thou rose maiden	H	E-G	DIT
Gliere	O that thou couldst know			
Glinka	Barcarolle			BES
-----	I remember			LÉE
-----	The lark			JFI

Gretchaninoff	Hushed the song of the nightingale	MH	E-G	DIT
-----	The skylark			DIT
-----	The song of Alloscha			
-----	Wounded birch	HL	B-EF	†
Mednikoff	The hills of Gruzia	H	DS-A	LAC
Mussorgsky	Ballade			
-----	Hopak	HM	CS-FS	GSC
-----	Gathering mushrooms			
-----	In my attic			GSC
-----	Night			GSC
-----	On the Dnieper			GSC
-----	Savishna			BES
-----	Serenade			BES
-----	Star, you, will you tell me?			
-----	The goat	HL	C-E	CFI
-----	The seminarian			GSC
-----	Tiny star where art thou	LH	DF-F	BOS
-----	Yeremushka's cradle song			
Rachmaninoff	A persian poem			
-----	Before my window	HM	C-G	†
-----	Daisies			†
-----	Drooping corn	LH	E-G	CFI
-----	Floods of spring	HL		DIT
-----	Here beauty dwells	H	D-B	CFI
-----	In the silence of night	LH	D-A	GSC
-----	Into my open window	HL	B-FS	BOS
-----	It cannot be			
-----	Morning	ML	B-DS	GSC
-----	Oh cease thy singing, maiden fair	H	E-A	CFI
-----	O, do not grieve	M	BF-AF	GSC
-----	Oh, no, I pray do not depart	H		DIT
-----	O thou billowy harvest field	HL	CS-E	GSC
-----	Sorrow in spring	H	D-BF	DIT
-----	The cherry tree			
-----	The island	LH	DF-F	†
-----	What joy			
Rimsky-Korsakov	It is not the wind blowing			
-----	Oh if you could			
-----	On the Georgian hills	HM		GSC
-----	The night	M	CS-E	CHE
-----	The nightingale and the rose	M	FS-FS	DIT
-----	The wind			
Rubinstein	Come back my love			

Taneieff	The fountains			
-----	Through the haze of the summer night			
Tchaikovsky	A child's song			
-----	At the ball	MH		GSC
-----	At the open window			GSC
-----	If you would only know			
-----	In this hour of the night	H		GSC
-----	Night	H		GSC
-----	One word			
-----	Pimpinella			
-----	Speak not, O beloved			
-----	The cuckoo			
-----	The nightingale			
-----	Why	HL		†

Scandinavian Recital Songs

Lyric Tenor

Agerby	Havren			
-----	Lilje Konval			
-----	Majnatt			
Alfven	Skogen sover			LUN
Bellman	Bufferflies at Haga			
-----	Ulla min Ulla			
Gade	Aprilsvise			
Grieg	A dream			†
-----	A swan			†
-----	By the brook			GSC
-----	Eros	LM	C-F	†
-----	Heart wounds			
-----	I love thee	HML	E-F	†
-----	It was a lovely summer evening			
-----	Outward bound			PET
-----	På Norges nøgne fjelde	M	D-F	HAN
-----	På skogstien	H	E-G	HAN
-----	Ragna			†
-----	Springtide	M		DIT
-----	The poet's last song			PET
-----	The way of the world			DIT
-----	The wounded heart			PET
-----	Til En II	M	E-F	HAN
-----	Two brown eyes	LM	EF-F	GSC
-----	With a water lily	HM	CS-EF	†
Hartmann	Du som har song I sinde			
-----	Flyv fugl, flyv			

510

(Hartmann)	Laer mig			
Heise	Arnes sang			
-----	Dengang jeg var kun saa			
-----	Der var en svend med sin pigelil			
-----	Kongesønnens romance			
-----	Liden Karen			
-----	Skovensomhed			
Kjerulf	Alt laegger for din fod jeg ned			
-----	Blanchefleur			
-----	My heart and lute	H		DIT
Lange-Mueller	Alle klokker bringe fjernt			
-----	Himlen ulmer svagt i flammerødt			
Larsson	Tills det blir sista gang			
Lassen	Thine eyes so blue	LH	C-G	CFI
Laub	Aldrig, Herre, du forglemme			
Nielson	Den Danske sang			
-----	Grøn er vaarens haek			
-----	Havet omkring Danmark			
-----	Havren			
-----	Irmelin rose			HAN
-----	Jaegersangen			
-----	Jens Vejmand			
-----	Pigen højt i taarnet sad			
-----	Sommersang			HAN
-----	Vi sletternes sønner			
Peterson-Berger	Titania			
Rangstroem	Old rhythms of dance			
Rung	Hvor Nilen vande Aegypterens jord			
Sibelius	Autumn night			
-----	Black roses	M	A-ES	AMP
-----	Reeds, reeds rustle			
-----	The spider			
-----	The tryst	M		AMP
-----	Was it a dream			BRH
Sinding	May night			DIT
-----	Sylvelin	M	E-E	GSC
Sjoeberg	Visions	MH	F-AF	GAL
Sjoegren	I drømmen du är mig nära			
-----	The Seraglio's garden	HL		GSC
Weyse	Der staar et slott i Vesterled			
-----	En skaal for den mö			
-----	Julen har bragt velsignet bud			
-----	Natten er saa stille			

(Weyse)   Skjön jomfru

Alvarez	A granada	M	D-FS	GSC
-----	La partida	HL	DS-E	GSC
Esteve	Alma sintamos			
Ginastera	Arrorro			RIC
-----	Gato			
Granados	Andalusia			
Grever	Atardecer en España			
-----	Bolero			
Huarte	Madrigal español	LH	D-G	GSC
Lara	Granada			SOU
Lecuona	Pregón de las flores			SOU
Longas	Ronda	H		MAR
Nin	Alma sintamos			ESC
-----	Canto andaluz			AMP
-----	Granadina			AMP
-----	Minué cantado			ESC
-----	Montañesa			AMP
Obradors	A quel sombrero de monte			
-----	Del cabello mas sutil			RIC
-----	El vito			
-----	La guitarra sin primo			
Padilla	Princesita	M		BOS
-----	Valenica			SHU
Piccinelli	Canción moresca			
Ravel	Chanson espagnole			DUR
Sandoval	Sin tu amor	H	E-G	GSC
Serrano	El trust de los tenorios			
Turina	Madrigal	H	D-BF	UME
-----	Poème en forma de canciones			
-----	Rima	H	A-A	AMP
Valverde	Clavelitos	MH	E-F	GSC

Miscellaneous Recital Songs

Lyric Tenor

Bach-Gounod	Ave Maria		
Bartok	Parosito		
Bizet	Agnus Dei	HLM	C-AF
Carr	Ave Maria		

Chausson	Ave verum corpus			
Cherubini	Ave Maria	H	E-A	GSC
Cornelius	Ave Maria			SC
Couperin	Ostende nobis domine			
Dvořák	God is my shepherd			AMP
-----	Hear my prayer, O Lord			AMP
-----	I will sing new songs of gladness	HL		
-----	Lord, Thou art my refuge and shield			AMP
-----	Songs my mother taught me	HM	E-E	
-----	Turn Thee to me			AMP
Fisher	Eili, Eili	LMH	E-G	DIT
Franck	Panis angelicus	LM		
Janacek	Alone			
-----	Music makers			
-----	Witchcraft			
Kodaly	Verbunk			
Ravel	Mayerke mein suhn			RAV
Saint-Saëns	Ave Maria	HM		DIT
Schuetz	Fili mi Absalom			
	4 Trombones and harpsichord			
Tomasi	Rengaine			
Villa-Lobos	Chant de mukumba (Zango)			
-----	Suite (Voice and violin)			AMP
Weinberg	Chazak Veemats			

British Songs and Arias
For Opening Recitals

Lyric Tenor

Anon	Have you seen but a white lily grow?	H	E-F	GSC
Attey	On a time			BOO
Dowland	I saw my lady weep	M	E-E	STB
Green	My lips shall speak the praise	M	E-F	OXF
Handel	Have mercy, Lord (Te Deum)	HM		†
-----	Let me wander not unseen (L'Allegro)	M	D-G	†
-----	O sleep why dost thou leave me (Semele)	H	DS-GS	†
-----	Silent worship (Tolomeo)	LM	D-E	CUR

(Handel)	Wher'er you walk (Semele)	HML	C–D	†
Purcell	An ode to Cynthia walking on Richmond Hill			
-----	Fairest isle (King Arthur)			NOV
-----	Hark, the echoing air (The Fairy Queen)			BAF
-----	If music be the food of love	M	D–G	BOO
-----	Music for a while (Oedipus)	LH		SC
-----	There's not a swain on the plain	M	B–G	BAF

German Songs and Arias
For Opening Recitals

Lyric Tenor

Bach, J.S.	Bist du bei mir	HML	A–EF	†
-----	O Jesulein suess			
-----	Only be still (Cantata 93) 2 Violins, viola and cello			NOV
-----	Pan is master (Phoebus and Pan)			NOV
Beethoven	Adelaide	HML	BF–E	†
-----	Andenken			†
-----	Ich liebe dich	HL	BF–DF	†
Handel	Dank sei Dir, Herr	M	CS–E	†
Haydn	She never told her love	HL	B–D	DIT
Mozart	An Chloe	LH	EF–AF	
Schubert	Das Wandern	HLM	E–E	†
-----	Der Wachtelschlag	H	DS–FS	PET
-----	Liebesbotschaft	H	E–G	†
Schuetz	Bringt her dem Herren			
-----	Eile mich, Gott, zu erretten			BAR
-----	Give ear, Oh Lord			
Schumann	Mit Myrthen und Rosen	HL	A–D	†

Italian Songs and Arias
For Opening Recitals

Lyric Tenor

Bassani	Posate, dormite (La Serenata)	H	EF–F	GSC

514

Bononcini	Deh più a me non v'ascondete	LH	EF-F	†
Caccini	Amarilli, mia bella	ML	C-D	†
-----	Fere, selvagge	HL	CS-GS	DIT
Caldara	Sebben crudele	HML	E-DS	†
Carissimi	Vittoria, mio core	HLM	B-E	†
Cavalli	Donzelle fuggite	HL	C-EF	†
Cesti	Ah, quanto è vero (Il Pomo d'Oro)	HL	F-F	DIT
-----	Che angoscia, che affanno (Il Pomo d'Oro)	HL	C-DF	DIT
-----	Tu mancavi a tormentarmi	H	D-G	GSC
Donaudy	Quando ti rivedrò			RIC
Durante	Vergin, tutta amor	LM	C-EF	†
Gluck	O del mio dolce ardor (Paride ed Elena)	LH	D-FS	GSC
-----	Spiagge amate (Paride ed Elena)			†
Handel	Allor che sorge astro lucente (Rodrigo)			BOO BOO
-----	Care selve (Atalanta)	MH	FS-A	†
-----	Ombra mai fu (Serse)	HM	BF-EF	†
-----	Rendi'l sereno al ciglio (Sosarme)	LH	EF-F	†
-----	Sei, mia gioja (Partenope)			CFI
Lotti	Pur dicesti, o bocca bella	LMH	E-FS	GSC
Manzolo	Quando tu mi guardi e ridi			
Mascagni	Ed anche Beppe amo (L'Amico Fritz)			JCH
Monteverdi	Ahi, troppo è duro (Il Balletto delle Ingrate)	HL	C-EF	DIT
Mozart	Dalla sua pace (Don Giovanni)	H	D-G	†
-----	Misero! o sogno	H	EF-AF	BOO
Paisiello	Nel cor più non mi sento	HL	C-EF	†
Peri	Invocazione di Orfeo (Euridice)	HL	E-CS	DIT
Porpora	Non più fra sassi			PET
Rosa	Star vicino	HL	D-E	†
Sarti	Lungi dal caro bene (Armide)	HL	G-D	GSC
Scarlatti, A.	All' acquisto di gloria (Tigrane)	H	C-G	GSC
-----	Già il sole dal Gange	LH	EF-F	GSC
-----	Già mai la lontananza			DUR
-----	Sento nel core	M	E-F	†
Stradella	Pietà, Signore	HM	C-F	GSC
-----	Se nel ben			CFI

American Songs for Closing Recitals

Lyric Tenor

Barber	I hear an army	LH	D-AF	GSC
-----	Sure on this shining night	MH	D-G	GSC
Bassett	Take joy home	LH	EF-BF	GSC
Branscombe	At the postern gate	MH	DF-AF	ASC
Carpenter	Serenade	LH	CS-A	GSC
Chanler	I rise when you enter	M	CS-G	GSC
Charles	When I have sung my songs	HM	BF-EF	GSC
Copland	I bought me a cat			
Crist	Girl of the red mouth	MH	E-BF	CFI
-----	Knock on the door	H	EF-AF	GSC
Curran	Life	HM	BF-F	GSC
Dougherty	Primavera	H	C-BF	GSC
Enders	Russian picnic	HM	C-G	GSC
Foster	My journey's end	HLM	DF-G	GSC
Hageman	At the well	LH	EF-AF	GSC
-----	Me company along	LH	F-BF	CFI
-----	Miranda	HL		GAL
-----	Voices			
Ilgenfritz	Blow, blow thou winter wind			
Kernochan	We two together	H	EF-AF	GAL
La Forge	Hills	HL		RIC
-----	Song of the open	MH	EF-AF	DIT
-----	To a messenger	HLM	CF-G	GSC
Levitzki	Ah, thou beloved one	H	EF-AF	GSC
Malotte	Blow me eyes	MH	C-G	GSC
McArthur	Night	H	F-AF	GSC
-----	Spring came	HL	D-F	GSC
Mc Donald	Daybreak	H		ELV
Nordoff	Tell me, Thyrsis	H	E-G	AMP
Rogers	The last song	MLH	E-AF	GSC
-----	Time for making songs	HM	CS-F	DIT
Rummel	Ecstasy	LMH	GF-AF	GSC
Russell	The way to the town	H	F-AF	GAL
Silberta	You shall have your red rose			
Speaks	Morning	HML	BF-D	GSC
Tyson	Sea moods	LH	E-AF	GSC
Warren	Fulfilment	H	D-BF	GAL
-----	We two	LH	E-A	GSC
-----	White horses of the sea	LH	F-G	GSC
Watts	Stresa	H	EF-BF	DIT
Wolf	Iris	LMH	F-BF	FLA
Wolfe	Who's gonna mourn for me	LMH	D-A	ROB

(See also Negro Spirituals and Folk Songs.)

Miscellaneous Songs for Closing Recitals

Lyric Tenor

Besley	Listening	H	E-AF	CUR
Bliss	Three jolly gentlemen	H		†
Brahms	Juchhe!			†
-----	Meine Liebe ist gruen	MLH	ES-A	†
-----	Wenn du nur zuweilen laechelst			†
-----	Willst du, dass ich geh'?	L	C-G	†
Cowen	Border ballad	LM	D-E	BOO
Debussy	Chevaux de bois	H	C-G	†
Delius	Love's philosophy			†
Durante	Danza, danza fanciulla gentile	HM	BF-F	†
Eden	What's in the air today?	M	D-F	ELK
Falla	Jota	LH		AMP
Grieg	By the brook			GSC
Head	When I think upon the maidens	LM	D-G	BOO
Henschel	Morning-hymn	MH	DS-GS	†
Huarte	Madrigal español	LH	D-G	GSC
Ireland	Great things			AUG
Keel	Trade winds	HL	BF-EF	BOH
Obradors	Chiquitita la novia			
-----	El vito			
Poulenc	Air vif	H	C-AF	ROU
Quilter	Blow, blow thou winter wind	HL	C-E	BOO
-----	Love's philosophy	LMH	D-A	BOO
Rachmaninoff	Floods of spring	HL		DIT
-----	Oh, no, I pray do not depart	H		DIT
-----	What joy			
Schoenberg	Erhebung			GSC
Schubert	Die Forelle	MLH	EF-GF	†
-----	Ueber Wildemann			PET
Sibelius	The tryst	M		AMP
-----	Was it a dream?			BRH
Strauss, J.	Blue Danube waltz			GSC
Trunk	Der Feind			
Vaughan Williams	The roadside fire	HML	BF-EF	BOO
Villa-Lobos	Chant de mukumba (Zango)			
Warlock	Yarmouth Fair	HL	B-E	CFI
Wolf	Er ist's	H	D-G	†
-----	Gesellenlied			

American Atmospheric Songs

Lyric Tenor

Barber	Rain has fallen	HM	D-E	GSC
-----	Sleep now	MH	EF-AF	GSC
Barnett	Serenade	H	F-G	GSC
Bone and Fenton	Green fields	MH	E-A	PRE
-----	Tryst	MH	FS-G	CFI
Burleigh	Sometimes I feel like a motherless child	HML		RIC
Charles	Clouds	HML	C-EF	GSC
-----	My lady walks in loveliness	HM	C-EF	GSC
-----	When I have sung my songs	HM	BF-EF	GSC
Crist	Into a ship dreaming	LMH	EF-GS	CFI
Davis	Nancy Hanks	H	D-G	GAL
Dougherty	Loveliest of trees	HM	C-E	BOH
Duke	Bells in the rain	H	E-GS	CFI
Ganz	A memory	HM	B-D	GSC
Giannini	Longing	M	CS-GF	ELV
Griffes	Symphony in yellow	M	D-GF	GSC
Kramer	Pleading	LH	D-GF	JFI
-----	Swans	HL		RIC
-----	The last hour	HML		JCH
MacGimsey	Sweet little Jesus boy	ML	D-D	CFI
McArthur	Night	H	F-AF	GSC
Niles	I wonder as I wander	HL	BF-D	GSC
-----	The gambler's lament	HL	B-E	GSC
Nordoff	Music I heard with you	H	DS-FS	AMP
Proctor	I light the blessed candles	H	DF-A	GSC
Robinson	Water boy	M	B-E	BOS
Sacco	The ragpicker	MH	C-AF	GSC
Tyson	Noon and night	LH	F-AF	GSC
Watts	Blue are her eyes	H	FS-FS	DIT
-----	Wings of night	LH	CS-G	GSC

British Atmospheric Songs

Lyric Tenor

Anon	Have you seen but a white lily grow?	H	E-F	GSC
Bantock	A dream of spring	H	E-G	CHE
Bax	The white peace			CHE
Bridge	E'en as a lovely flower	HM	FS-E	BOH

518

Del Riego	O dry those tears	LMH	E-GS	CHA
Dunhill	The cloths of Heaven	LM	EF-G	STB
Forsyth	The bell man			DIT
Handel	O sleep why dost thou leave me (Semele)	H	DS-GS	†
Harty	My lagan love	ML	BF-EF	BOO
Hughes	A Ballynure ballad	L	BF-D	BOH
-----	Open the door softly	LMH	G-G	ENO
-----	The bard of Armagh			BOO
Milford	Elegy	H	C-G	NOV
Quilter	Dream valley	H	EF-GF	ROG
-----	Now sleeps the crimson petal	LMH	EF-GF	BOO
Ronald	Drift down, drift down			BOO
Stanford	The fairy lough	ML	A-EF	BOO
Vaughn Williams	Silent noon			GSC

French Atmospheric Songs

Lyric Tenor

Bizet	Douce mer			GSC
Breville	Prières d'enfant	M	D-F	ROU
Chausson	Apaisement	MH	EF-G	HAM
Debussy	C'est l'extase	LH	CS-A	†
-----	Les cloches	LH	E-GS	†
-----	Nuits d'etoiles	LH	E-A	MAR
Duparc	Soupir	HL	CS-F	BOS
Ferrari	Le miroir	M	E-F	GSC
Gounod	Sérénade	LMH	D-A	GSC
Hahn	À Chloris	H	DS-FS	HEU
-----	L'heure exquise	M	DF-F	
-----	Paysage	MH	EF-G	HEU
Leguerney	Genièvres herisses	H	D-G	ROU
-----	Je vous envoie	H	C-A	ROU
Paladilhe	Psyché	HM	BF-F	GSC
Ravel	D'Anne jouant de l'espinette	H	CS-GS	GSC
-----	Le réveil de la mariée	MH	G-F	DUR
-----	Sainte	M	C-G	ELV
-----	Sur l'herbe	MH	C-G	DUR
Roussel	Le jardin mouillé	M	C-FS	ROU
Staub	L'heure silencieuse	H	EF-G	DUR
Szulc	Claire de lune	H	E-G	AXE

519

German Atmospheric Songs

Lyric Tenor

Haydn	She never told her love	HL	B-D	DIT
Mahler	Ich ging mit Lust	HL		INT
Marx	Marienlied	MH	EF-AF	AMP
Schubert	An die Nachtigall	H	C-G	†
-----	Nacht und Traeume	HL	C-DF	†
-----	Nachtviolen			PET
Schumann	Dein Angesicht	HL	B-EF	†
-----	Der Nussbaum	LMH	D-FS	†
-----	Ich hab' im Traum geweinet	HL	B-D	†
Strauss	Die Nacht	HL		†
-----	Traum durch die Daemmerung	HML	BF-EF	†
Wolf	Verborgenheit	HL	B-E	†

Italian Atmospheric Songs and Arias

Lyric Tenor

Bassani	Posate dormite (La Serenata)	H		GSC
Cimara	Fiocca la neve	H	G-G	GSC
-----	Non più			
Donizetti	Una furtiva legrima (L'Elisir d'Amore)	H	F-AF	†
Frescobaldi	Se l'aura spira	HL	C-EF	DIT
Giordano	Vedi, io piango (Fedora)			SON
Gluck	O del mio dolce ardor (Paride ed Elena)			GSC
Handel	Care selve (Atalanta)			†
Rossini	Se il mio nome (Il Barbiere di Siviglia)			†
Sarti	Lungi dal caro bene			
Tosti	Ideale			GSC

Miscellaneous Atmospheric Songs

Lyric Tenor

Cui	The statue at Czarskoe-Selo	HM	DF-EF	†
Grieg	På Norges nøgne fjelde	M	D-F	HAN
-----	På skogstien	H	E-G	HAN

(Grieg)	Ragna			†
-----	Til En II	M	E-F	HAN
Mussorgsky	Tiny star where art thou	LH	DF-F	BOS
Rachmaninoff	Morning	ML	B-DS	GSC
Sibelius	Reeds, reeds, rustle			
Sinding	Sylvelin	M	E-E	GSC

American Dramatic Songs

Lyric Tenor

Barber	I hear an army	LH	D-AF	GSC
Beach	Ah, love but a day			ASC
-----	The year's at the spring	MH	AF-AF	ASC
Burleigh	By the pool at the third roses	H		RIC
Campbell-Tipton .	A spirit flower	LHM	B-G	GSC
Crist	You will not come again	HML	BF-CS	CFI
Curran	Life	HM	BF-F	GSC
Dello Joio	Lament	M	C-F	CFI
Dougherty	Primavera	H	C-BF	GSC
Enders	Russian picnic	HM	C-G	GSC
Foster	My journey's end	HLM	DF-G	GSC
Geehl	For you alone			SHU
Giannini	Far above the purple hills	LH	CS-A	RIC
Griffes	An old song resung	LM	EF-F	GSC
-----	The lament of Ian the proud	MH	DS-AS	GSC
-----	Waikiki	H	DS-GS	GSC
Hageman	Do not go, my love	HL	B-EF	GSC
-----	Music I heard with you	MH	E-A	GAL
Kernochan	We two together	H	EF-AF	GAL
La Forge	Song of the open	MH	EF-AF	DIT
Loeffler	To Helen	M	DF-F	GSC
MacDowell	The sea	HL	D-D	BRH
Mana-Zucca	I love life	LM	F-F	PRE
Nordoff	Tell me, Thyrsis	H	E-G	AMP
Rogers	The last song	MLH	E-AF	GSC
-----	Time for making songs	HM	CS-F	DIT
Sacco	Never the nightingale	H	EF-GF	GAL
Speaks	Morning	HML	BF-D	GSC
Tyson	Sea moods	LH	E-AF	GSC
Warren	Fulfilment	H	D-BF	GAL
-----	We two	LH	E-A	GSC
-----	White horses of the sea	LH	F-G	GSC
Wolf	Iris	LMH	F-BF	FLA
Wolfe	Who's gonna mourn for me	LMH	D-A	ROB

British Dramatic Songs and Arias

Lyric Tenor

Arne, T.	Preach not me your musty rules (Comus)	HML		ROW
Besley	Listening	H	E-AF	CUR
Bridge	O that it were so	LMH	D-G	CHA
Coleridge-Taylor	Life and death	HML		ASC
Cowen	Border ballad	LM	D-E	BOO
Delius	To the queen of my heart			†
Dix	The trumpeter	HML	A-C	BOH
Dowland	Fine knacks for ladies	M	E-F	STB
Handel	Sound an alarm! (Judas Maccabaeus)	H		†
-----	Total eclipse (Samson)			†
Head	Sea gipsy	LM	E-GS	BOO
Henschel	Morning-hymn	MH	DS-GS	†
Holbrooke	Come not when I am dead			ENO
Ireland	Great things			AUG
-----	Hope the hornblower			BOO
Leveridge	When dull care			BOO
Milford	The colour	H	D-G	OXF
Purcell	I'll sail upon the dog star	HL	A-E	†
Quilter	Blow, blow thou winter wind	HL	C-E	BOO
Ronald	Down in the forest	HML	C-D	ENO
-----	Prelude	HML	B-D	ENO
Sanderson	Shipmates of mine	LL	G-D	BOO
Sullivan	The lost chord	HL	C-F	GSC

French Dramatic Songs and Arias

Lyric Tenor

Berlioz	Nature immense (La Damnation de Faust)			NOV
-----	Les nuits d'été			AUG
Bizet	Flower song (Carmen)	H	E-BF	†
Caplet	Le forêt			DUR
Debussy	Air d'Azaël (L'Enfant Prodigue)	H	C-A	GSC
-----	Chevaux de bois	H	C-G	†
-----	Colloque sentimental			DUR
-----	De fleurs	H	C-AF	†

(Debussy)	Noël des enfants qui n'ont plus de maisons			DUR
Duparc	Phidylé	MH	EF-AF	BOS
Fauré	L hiver a cessé	HL		INT
-----	Poème d'un jour			HAM
-----	Toujours	LH	F-AF	†
Fourdrain	Chanson norvégienne	H	E-G	RIC
Gounod	Ah! lève-toi, soleil! (Roméo et Juliette)	H	F-BF	†
Hahn	Offrande	M	D-D	†
Holmès	Au pays	HM	C-F	CFI
Hue	J'ai pleuré en rêve	HL	D-E	BOS
Massenet	Ah! fuyez, douce image (Manon)	H	F-BF	GSC
-----	J'aurais sur ma poitrine (Werther)			HEU
-----	Je ne sais si je veille (Werther)			HEU
-----	O souverain! ô juge! ô père! (Le Cid)			HEU
-----	Pourquoi me reveiller (Werther)	H	FS-AS	HEU
Meyerbeer	O paradis (L'Africaine)	H	F-BF	†
Pessard	Requiem du coeur			LED
Poldowski	Dansons la gigue	M	EF-G	MAR
-----	L'heure exquise	LMH	DF-AF	CHE

German Dramatic Songs and Arias

Lyric Tenor

Brahms	Ach, wende diesen Blick			†
Marx	Hat dich die Liebe beruehrt	MH	EF-BF	AMP
Mendelssohn	The sorrows of death (Hymn of Praise)			†
Schoenberg	Erhebung			GSC
Schubert	Am Meer	HML	B-D	†
-----	Der Lindenbaum	HL	A-D	†
-----	Die Liebe hat gelogen	LM	G-F	†
-----	Erstarrung	HL	D-F	†
-----	Fruehlingstraum	HL	C-D	†
Schumann	Der Soldat			
-----	Ich grolle nicht	HL	BF-D	†
-----	Mit Myrthen und Rosen	HL	A-D	†
Strauss	Kling			†
-----	Madrigal	LH	EF-GF	
Trunk	Der Feind			

| Wagner | Mein lieber Schwan (Lohengrin) | | | † |
| Wolf | Denk' es, o Seele | LH | EF-F | † |

Italian Dramatic Songs and Arias

Lyric Tenor

Bellini	Meco all' altar di venere (Norma)	H	D-C	RIC
Boito	Dai campi, dai prati (Mefistofele)			RIC
-----	Giunto sul passo estremo (Epilogue) (Mefistofele)			RIC
Cilea	La dolcissima effigie (Adriana Lecouvreur)	H		AMP
-----	L'anima ho stanca (Adriana Lecouvreur)	H		AMP
Durante	Vergin, tutta amor	LM	C-EF	†
Giordano	Amor ti vieta (Fedora)	H		AMP
-----	Come un bel di (Andrea Chenier)	H	E-BF	AMP
-----	Mia madre, la mia vecchia madre (Fedora)			BRO
-----	Un di all'azzurro spazio (Andrea Chenier)	H	F-BF	SON
-----	Vedi, io piango (Fedora)			SON
Leoncavallo	Testa adorata (La Boheme)			SON
-----	Vesti la giubba (I Pagliacci)	H	D-A	†
Mascagni	Addio alla madre (Cavalleria Rusticana)			GSC
-----	Ed anche Beppe amo (L'Amico Fritz)			JCH
-----	O amore, o bella luce (L'Amico Fritz)			GSC
Ponchielli	Cielo e mar (La Gioconda)	H	D-BF	†
Puccini	Nessun dorma (Turandot)			RIC
Respighi	Nebbie			†
Verdi	Giorno di pianto (I Vespri Siciliani)			RIC
-----	O tu che in seno agli angeli (La Forza del Destino)	H	DF-BF	RIC
-----	Quando le sere al placido (Luisa Miller)			RIC

Wolf-Ferrari	Benedicimi tu (Jewels of the Madonna)	H	AF-AF	GSC

Miscellaneous Dramatic Songs

Lyric Tenor

Alvarez	La partida	HL	DS-E	GSC
Dvořák	Hear my prayer, O Lord			AMP
Gretchaninoff	The skylark			DIT
-----	Wounded birch	HL	B-EF	†
Grieg	A dream			†
-----	A swan			†
-----	Eros	LM	C-F	†
Mussorgsky	Hopak	HM	CS-FS	GSC
-----	On the Dnieper			GSC
Rachmaninoff	Christ is risen	LM	D-F	GAL
-----	Floods of spring	HL		DIT
-----	O, do not grieve	M	BF-AF	GSC
-----	Oh, no, I pray do not depart	H		DIT
-----	O thou billowy harvest field	HL	CS-E	GSC
-----	Sorrow in spring	H	D-BF	DIT
-----	To the children	MH	F-G	DIT
Rimsky-Korsakov	On the Georgian hills	HM		GSC
Sibelius	Black roses	M	A-ES	AMP
-----	The tryst	M		AMP
-----	Was it a dream			BRH
Tchaikovsky	None but the lonely heart	HLM	C-F	DIT
-----	Why	HL		†
Turina	Madrigal	H	D-BF	UME
-----	Rima	H	A-A	AMP

American Humorous Songs

Lyric Tenor

Bergsma	Six songs	H	E-BF	CFI
Bone and Fenton	Captain Kidd	MH	B-G	CFI
Brockway	The swapping song			GSC
Carpenter	If	M	D-E	GSC
Chanler	I rise when you enter	M	CS-G	GSC
Davis	Deaf old woman			GAL

Diack	Sing a song of sixpence			
Enders	Russian picnic	HM	C-G	GSC
Hadley	My shadow			ASC
Hindemith	The whistling thief	M	E-F	AMP
MacDowell	A maid sings light	H	F-G	ASC
Malotte	Blow me eyes	MH	C-G	GSC
Mana Zucca	The big brown bear	HML	C-F	GSC
Niles	The gambler's lament	HL	B-E	GSC
Nordoff	There shall be more joy	M	CS-FS	AMP
Powell	The deaf woman's courtship	M		JFI
Rodgers	Soliloquy (Carousel)			CHA
Sacco	Brother Will, Brother John	M	C-F	GSC
-----	Mexican serenade	HL	D-EF	BOS
Slonimsky	Gravestones at Hancock, New Hampshire	H	D-G	AXE
Wolf	Weather forecast	H	EF-GS	GSC
Wolfe	Short'nin' bread	LHM	D-D	FLA

British Humorous Songs

Lyric Tenor

Arden and Wille	Cockles and mussels	HM	E-E	ROW
Bliss	Three jolly gentlemen	H		†
Bridge	So perverse			BOS
Britten	Oliver Cromwell			BOH
Clarke	Shy one	HL	BF-G	BOH
Gibbs	Five eyes	HL	D-D	BOS
Head	When I think upon the maidens	LM	D-G	BOO
Hughes	A Ballynure ballad	L	BF-D	BOH
-----	Kitty, my love will you marry me?	M	C-F	BOH
-----	The stuttering lovers	MH	E-FS	CHA
Liddle	The garden where the praties grow	LMH	E-FS	STB
Lohr	The little Irish girl	HLM	C-E	CHA
Purcell	Sylvia, now your scorn give over			FSY
Torrence	Smilin Kitty O' Day	ML	CS-D	BOO

French Humorous Songs

Lyric Tenor

Chabrier	Villanelle des petits canards	HML	B-E	†
Debussy	Ballade des femmes de Paris			DUR
-----	Voici que le printemps	LH	CS-G	BOS
Delibes	Bonjours, Suzon	LM	C-F	GSC
Pierné	Ils étaient trois petits chats blancs			MAR
Ravel	Sur l'herbe	MH	C-G	DUR
Satie	Le chapelier			ROU

German Humorous Songs and Arias

Lyric Tenor

Beethoven	Der Kuss			†
Blech	Heimkehr vom Feste			UNI
Brahms	Vergebliches Staendchen	LHM	E-FS	†
Loewe	Des Glockenthuermers Tochterlein	H	CS-A	SC
Mozart	Alles fuehlt der Liebe Freuden (Die Zauberfloete)			†
-----	Warnung	HM	C-D	
Schubert	Heidenroeslein			
Strauss, J.	Open road, open sky (The Gypsy Baron)			GSC
Wolf	Der Knabe und das Immlein	L	CS-A	†
-----	Der Musikant	HL	CS-D	†
-----	Elfenlied	HL	D-F	†
-----	Nimmersatte Liebe	LH	CF-AF	†
-----	Storchenbotschaft			†

Miscellaneous Humorous Songs

Lyric Tenor

Castelnuovo-Tedesco	La ermita de San Simon			
Grieg	The way of the world			DIT
Mussorgsky	The seminarian			GSC
Rontani	Or ch'io non segno più	HL	CS-E	DIT
Scarlatti, A.	Chi vuole innamorarsi	HL	D-EF	DIT

Smetana	Ma-ma-mama so dear (The Bartered Bride)			BOO

American Folk Songs (Arr.)

Lyric Tenor

Bacon	Careless love			
-----	The Erie canal	L	D-C	CFI
Brockway	An inconstant lover			
-----	No, sir, no			
-----	The barnyard song			GRA
-----	The swapping song			GSC
Copland	I bought me a cat			
Davis	Deaf old woman			GAL
Endicott	He stole my tender heart away			BRO
Guion	All day on the prarie	M	EF-F	GSC
Hughes	Birds' courting song			GSC
La Forge	Las gaviotas	LH		RIC
Niles	Black is the color of my true love's hair			
-----	I wonder as I wander	HL	BF-D	GSC
-----	See Jesus the Savior			GSC
-----	The gambler's lament	HL	B-E	GSC
-----	The rovin' gambler	HL	BF-EF	GSC
Powell	The deaf woman's courtship	M		JFI
-----	The rich old woman	M		JFI
Robinson	Water boy	M	B-E	BOS
Russell	The way to the town	H	F-AF	GAL
Siegmeister	He's gone away			
-----	Poor way faring stranger			

British Folk Songs (Arr.)

Lyric Tenor

Arden and Wille	Cockles and mussels	HM	E-E	ROW
Balfe	The harp that once through Tara's halls			BOO
Beethoven	Irish songs			
-----	Scotch songs			
Benjamin	Jan (Creole melody)	M		BOO
-----	Linstead market	M		BOO
Britten	Come ye not from Newcastle			BOH

528

(Britten)	Heigh ho, heigh hi!			BOH
-----	Little Sir William			BOH
-----	Oliver Cromwell			BOH
-----	The ash grove			BOH
-----	The bonny Earl O' Moray			BOH
-----	The foggy, foggy dew			BOH
-----	The plough boy			BOH
Broadwood	Some rival has stolen my true love	LM	D-E	BOO
Gatty	Bendemeer's stream	LMH		BOO
Grainger	Brigg fair			GSC
-----	The sprig of thyme	LH	E-FS	GSC
Harty	My lagan love	ML	BF-EF	BOO
Hatton	The minstrel boy			BOO
Hook	Mary of Allendale			BOO
Hopekirk	Annie Laurie			DIT
-----	Flow gently, sweet Afton			DIT
-----	Loch Lomond			DIT
Hughes	A Ballynure ballad	L	BF-D	BOH
-----	Down by the Sally gardens			BOO
-----	Kitty, my love will you marry me?	M	C-F	BOH
-----	Oft in the stilly night			
-----	Open the door softly	LMH	G-G	ENO
-----	She moved thro' the fair			BOO
-----	The bard of Armagh			BOO
-----	The lark in clear air	ML	BF-D	BOO
-----	The leprehaun			
-----	The old turf fire			BOO
-----	The Palatine's daughter			ENO
-----	The stuttering lovers	MH	E-FS	CHA
Kennedy-Fraser	An Eriskay love lilt			BOO
-----	Land of heart's desire			BOO
-----	The bens of Jura			BOO
-----	The mull fisher's love song			BOO
-----	The road to the isles			BOO
Liddle	The garden where the praties grow	LMH	E-FS	STB
McGill	Lord Randall			BOO
Miller	Ye banks and braes			OXF
Page	The harp that once through Tara's halls			DIT
-----	The meeting of the waters			DIT
Peel	In summertime on Bredon	ML	BF-EF	CHA
Peterkin	The fiddler	H	F-AF	OXF
Schneider	Meeting of the waters			
Somervell	All through the night			CRA
Taylor	May Day carol			JFI

| Vaughan Williams | Rolling in the dew | | | OXF |
| Warlock | Yarmouth Fair | HL | B-E | CFI |

Miscellaneous Folk Songs (Arr.)

Lyric Tenor

Bartok	Feketeföd			BOH
-----	I set out from my country			BOO
Beethoven	Morning a cruel turmoiler is			
-----	The morning air plays on my face			
-----	The pulse of an Irishman			
Brahms	Da unten in Thale			†
-----	Erlaube mir, fein's Maedchen			†
-----	Mein Maedel hat einen Rosenmund	M	F-F	†
Dvořák	Gypsy songs	LH	D-A	AMP
Falla	Asturiana	HL		AMP
-----	El paño moruno	HL		AMP
-----	Jota	LH		AMP
-----	Nana	HL		AMP
-----	Seguidilla murciana	HL		AMP
Landen	Tientos gitanos			
Mc Feeters	Gentle Mary	H	EF-AF	GSC
Obradors	Chiquitita la novia			
Ravel	Le réveil de la mariée	MH	G-F	DUR
Tiersot	Briolage			
-----	L'amours de moi	M	EF-F	HEU
-----	Tambourin			
Weckerlin	Aminte	M	C-D	†
-----	Chantons les amours de Jean	H	D-G	GSC
-----	Je connais un berger discret	M	EF-EF	BOS
-----	Jeune fillette	M	G-E	GSC
-----	L'amour s'envole	H	E-G	GSC
-----	Menuet d'Exaudet	H	D-G	GSC
-----	O ma tendre musette	LM	A-E	GSC
-----	Trop aimable Sylvia	M	D-E	GSC

Negro Spirituals

Lyric Tenor

Boatner	Oh, what a beautiful city!	HL	D-E	GSC
-----	On mah journey	LH	EF-EF	RIC
Burleigh	Balm in Gilead	HL		RIC
-----	De gospel train	HL		RIC
-----	Hard trials	M		RIC
-----	Joshua fit de battle ob Jericho	LH	DS-E	RIC
-----	Scandalize my name	M		RIC
-----	Swing low, sweet chariot	HL		RIC
-----	Were you there?	HML		RIC
Dett	Sit down servant			GSC
Johnson	City called Heaven			ROB
-----	John Henry			CFI
-----	Ride on, King Jesus			CFI
-----	Witness	HM	D-F	CFI
Kerby-Forrest	He's got the whole world in His hands	M	G-E	MLS
Lawrence	Let us break bread together	HML	BF-EF	MCR
MacGimsey	Sweet little Jesus boy	ML	D-D	CFI
Ryder	Let us break bread together	LH	D-G	JFI

British Songs and Arias
Employing Agility

Lyric Tenor

Aiken	Sigh no more	HML		STB
Arne, T.	Preach not me your musty rules (Comus)	HML		ROW
Besley	Listening	H	E-AF	CUR
Bliss	Three jolly gentlemen	H		†
German	Charming Chloe	HML		NOV
Green	My lips shall speak the praise	M	E-F	OXF
Handel	Evr'y valley (The Messiah)			†
-----	How vain is man (Judas Maccabaeus)			†
-----	Say to Irene (Atalanta)	H	D-AF	CFI
-----	Sound an alarm! (Judas Maccabaeus)	H		†

531

(Handel)	The enemy said (Israel in Egypt)	H	D-A	NOV
-----	Thou shalt dash them (The Messiah)	H		†
-----	Why does the God of Israel sleep? (Samson)			†
-----	Would you gain the tender creature (Acis and Galatea)			†
Hook	Bright Phoebus	M	EF-F	GSC
Linley	O, bid your faithful Ariel fly			BOO
Morgan	Clorinda	HM	C-EF	ENO
Morley	It was a lover and his lass	HM		DIT
Purcell	Come unto these yellow sands			AUG
-----	Hark! the echoing air (The Fairy Queen)			BAF
-----	I'll sail upon the dog star	HL	A-E	†
Quilter	Love's philosophy	LMH	D-A	BOO
Wilson	Phillis has such charming graces	ML	CS-EF	BOO

French Songs Employing Agility

Lyric Tenor

Debussy	Fêtes galantes	LH	CS-A	†
Delibes	Bonjours, Suzon	LM	C-F	GSC
Dupont	Chanson des noisettes			HEU
Falla	Polo	HL		AMP
Fauré	Mandoline	HL	F-E	†
Grétry	Si l'univers entier m'oublie (Richard Couer-de-Lion)			
Poulenc	Air vif	H	C-AF	ROU
Ravel	Chanson à boire			DUR
Saint-Saëns	Guitares et mandolines			DUR
Vidal	Ariette	LH	F-A	GSC
Weckerlin	L'amour s'envole	H	E-G	GSC

German Songs and Arias Employing Agility

Lyric Tenor

Bach, J.S.	Ja, tausendmal (Cantata 43) Violin			NOV

532

(Bach, J.S.)	Nimm mich Dir zu eigen hin (Cantata 65)			NOV
Beethoven	Mailied			RIC
Brahms	Botschaft	HL	D-F	†
-----	O liebliche Wangen	MLH	E-G	†
Jensen	Am Ufer des Flusses des Manzanares	H	D-FS	GSC
Loewe	Des Glockenthuermers Tochterlein	H	CS-A	SC
Schubert	Das Wandern	HLM	E-E	†
-----	Der Wachtelschlag	H	DS-FS	PET
-----	Ungeduld	HML		†
Schumann	Auftraege	HL	C-E	†
Strauss, J.	Blue Danube waltz			GSC
-----	Tales from the Vienna forest	H	EF-C	GSC

Italian Songs and Arias
Employing Agility

Lyric Tenor

Bononcini	L'esperto nocchiero (Astarte)	HL	B-E	†
Carissimi	Filli, non t'amo più	HL	B-D	†
-----	Vittoria, mio core	HLM	B-E	†
Castelnuovo-Tedesco	La ermita de San Simon			
Cimarosa	Brillar mi sento il core (Il Matrimonio Segreto)			RIC
-----	Pria che spunti in ciel (Il Matrimonio Segreto)			RIC
Donaudy	Ah mai non cessate			RIC
-----	Spirate pur, spirate			RIC
Durante	Danza, danza fanciulla gentile	HM	BF-F	†
Handel	Sei, mia gioja (Partenope)			CFI
Lotti	Pur dicesti, o bocca bella	LMH	E-FS	GSC
Porpora	Non più fra sassi			PET
Rossini	La danza	MH	E-A	†
Sadero	Amuri, Amuri	M		CHE
Scarlatti, A.	All' acquisto di gloria (Tigrane)	H	C-G	GSC
-----	Già il sole dal Gange	LH	EF-F	GSC
-----	Rugiadose odorose (Il Pirro e Demetrio)	HL	D-E	DIT

Scarlatti, D.	Qual farfalletta			
Stradella	Ragion sempre addita	H	E-G	GSC
Verdi	La donna è mobile (Rigoletto)	LMH	FS-AS	†

Miscellaneous Songs Employing Agility

Lyric Tenor

Alvarez	La partida	HL	DS-E	GSC
Falla	Nana	HL		AMP
-----	Seguidilla murciana	HL		AMP
Grieg	Good morning			†
Hageman	Miranda	HL		GAL
Hopkinson	O'er the hills	LH	C-G	†
Mussorgsky	Tiny star where art thou	LH	DF-F	BOS
Nordoff	There shall be more joy	M	CS-FS	AMP
Speaks	In May time	HL	D-E	JCH

American Songs Employing Crescendo and Diminuendo

Lyric Tenor

Bacon	Is there such a thing as day?	M	DS-FS	AMP
Barber	Rain has fallen	HM	D-E	GSC
-----	Sleep now	MH	EF-AF	GSC
-----	The daisies	M	C-F	GSC
Beach	Ah, love but a day			ASC
-----	Fairy lullaby			ASC
Cadman	From the land of the sky-blue water			WHI
Campbell-Tipton	A spirit flower	LHM	B-G	GSC
Charles	Clouds	HML	C-EF	GSC
Duke	Bells in the rain	H	E-GS	CFI
Elwell	In the mountains	M	DF-F	BMI
Hopkinson	My days have been so wondrous free	LH	EF-G	†
La Forge	Hills	HL		RIC
Loeffler	To Helen	M	DF-F	GSC
Niles	I wonder as I wander	HL	BF-D	GSC
Rogers	At parting	LH	CS-FS	GSC
Watts	Wings of night	LH	CS-G	GSC

British Songs and Arias Employing
Crescendo and Diminuendo

Lyric Tenor

Arne, T.	Peggy			GSC
Bantock	A dream of spring	H	E–G	CHE
Benjamin	The wasp			CUR
Bliss	Lovelocks			GOT
Bridge	E'en as a lovely flower	HM	FS–E	BOH
Clarke	Shy one	HL	BF–G	BOH
Gibbs	To one who passed whistling through the night	H	F–G	CUR
Gurney	Under the greenwood tree			ROG
Handel	Ask if yon damask rose (Susanna)			†
-----	Let me wander not unseen (D'Allegro)	M	D–G	†
-----	Love in her eyes sits playing (Acis and Galatea)			†
-----	O sleep why dost thou leave me (Semele)	H	DS–GS	†
Head	The ships of Arcady	ML	BF–EF	BOH
Purcell	I attempt from love's sickness to fly (The Indian Queen)	MH	CS–E	†
-----	Sylvia, now your scorn give over			FSY
Quilter	Dream valley	H	EF–GF	ROG
-----	Now sleeps the crimson petal	LMH	EF–GF	BOO
Shaw	Song of the Palanquin bearers	LH	E–F	CUR

French Songs and Arias Employing
Crescendo and Diminuendo

Lyric Tenor

Berlioz	Le repos de la Ste. Famille (L'Enfance du Christ)	MH		CST
Bizet	Après l'hiver			†
-----	Vielle chanson	H	EF–A	GSC
Debussy	C'est l'extase	LH	CS–A	†
-----	En sourdine	M	C–FS	†
-----	Green	H	C–AF	†
-----	Les angélus			HAM

(Debussy)	Les cloches	LH	E–GS	†
-----	Les ingénus			DUR
-----	Voici que le printemps	LH	CS–G	BOS
Duparc	Chanson triste	MH	FS–AF	†
-----	L'invitation au voyage	HM	E–F	†
-----	Phidylé	MH	EF–AF	BOS
Fauré	Adieu	MH	F–F	†
-----	Au bord de l'eau	HL	C–F	†
-----	Clair de lune	MH	C–G	†
-----	Green	HL	CS–GF	†
-----	Le secret	LH	F–G	†
-----	Les roses d'Ispahan	HM	D–FS	†
-----	Lydia	MH	G–G	†
-----	Nell	LH	FS–AF	†
-----	Spleen	H	E–FS	MAR
-----	Sylvie	HL	E–F	†
Franck	Ninon			BOS
Gounod	Medjé (Chanson arabe)	MH	G–G	BOO
Hahn	Le rossignol des lilas			
Koechlin	L'hiver	H	E–G	†
Lalo	Aubade (Le Roe d'Ys)			†
Martini	Plaisir d'amour	M	BF–EF	GSC
Paladilhe	Psyché	HM	BF–F	GSC
Rameau	A l'amour rendez les armes (Hippolyte et Aricie)			CHO
-----	Dans ces doux asiles (Castor et Pollux)			LEM
-----	Le grillon			DUR
Ravel	Le grillon	H	E–G	DUR
Rousseau	Je vais revoir ma charmante maîtresse (Le Devin du Village)			CHE

German Songs Employing
Crescendo and Diminuendo

Lyric Tenor

Beethoven	Andenken			†
-----	Mit einem gemalten Band			RIC
Brahms	Auf dem See	HL	D–F	†
-----	Geheimnis			†
-----	Komm bald	HM	CS–F	†
-----	Sonntag	H	D–G	†
-----	Wie Melodien	HL	A–E	†
Franz	Stille Sicherheit	M	E–F	†
Haydn	Der erste Kuss			
-----	Liebes Maedchen, hoer' mir zu			HSC

Mahler	Ich atmet' einen linden Duft	HL		INT
Marx	Wie einst			UNI
Mendelssohn	Pagenlied	M	E-E	†
-----	Venetianisches Gondellied	LM	E-FS	AUG
Reger	Des Kindes Gebet	H	F-G	BOT
Schubert	Abschied	HL	BF-F	†
-----	Am See			PET
-----	An den Mond	HL	F-GF	†
-----	An die Laute	LH	D-F	†
-----	An die Nachtigall	H	C-G	†
-----	Auf dem Wasser zu singen	MH	EF-GF	†
-----	Das Lied im Gruenen			PET
-----	Das Rosenband			PET
-----	Der Einsame	LH	D-G	†
-----	Der Musensohn	LH	FS-G	†
-----	Der Schmetterling	LH	E-F	†
-----	Der Wanderer an den Mond	LM	D-F	PET
-----	Die Taubenpost	HL	D-EF	†
-----	Fruehlingstraum	HL	C-D	†
-----	Geheimes	HL	BF-EF	†
-----	Hark! hark! the lark	LMH	F-G	
-----	Liebesbotschaft	H	E-G	†
-----	Nacht und Traeume	HL	C-DF	†
Schumann	Der Nussbaum	LMH	D-FS	†
-----	Der Sandmann	HL	AF-DF	†
-----	Die Meerfee			
-----	Fruehlingslust	HL		†
-----	Intermezzo	HL	C-D	†
-----	Provenzalisches Lied	LH		†
-----	Romanze	HL	C-E	†
-----	Roeselein, Roeselein			
-----	Staendchen			
Strauss	All' mein' Gedanken	H	CS-GS	
-----	Barcarolle	H	DF-BF	†
-----	Die Nacht	HL		†
-----	Schlagende Herzen			†
Wolf	Auch kleine Dinge	HM	D-E	†
-----	Der Gaertner	HL		INT
-----	Der Knabe und das Immlein	L	CS-A	†
-----	Fruehling uebers Jahr			†
-----	Gleich und gleich			†
-----	Morgentau	HL	D-D	†
-----	Verschwiegene Liebe	LH	DF-FS	†
-----	Wenn du zu den Blumen gehst	HL	B-EF	†
Wolff	Faeden			

Italian Songs and Arias Employing
Crescendo and Diminuendo

Lyric Tenor

Bononcini	Per la gloria	HL	C-EF	†
-----	Vado ben spesso			JCH
Caldara	Alma del core			GSC
-----	Sebben crudele	HML	E-DS	†
-----	Selve amiche, ombrose piante	HM	E-E	†
Carissimi	No, no, non si speri	HL	C-EF	†
Cesti	Intorno all'idol (Orontea)	MH	D-F	†
De Luca	Non posso disperar	HL	C-E	GSC
Donaudy	Freschi luoghi			RIC
Donizetti	Com'è gentil (Don Pasquale)			RIC
Fasolo	Cangia, cangia tue voglie	H	C-G	GSC
Handel	Ombra mai fu (Serse)	HM	BF-EF	†
Monteverdi	Lasciatemi morire (Arianna)	ML	D-D	†
Mozart	Il mio tesoro (Don Giovanni)	H	D-A	†
Piccini	L'amour fait verser trop de pleurs (Atys)			LEM
Rosa	Selve, voi che le speranze	MH	D-G	DIT
Scarlatti, A.	Sento nel core	M	E-F	†

Miscellaneous Songs Employing
Crescendo and Diminuendo

Lyric Tenor

Borodin	The sleeping princess	M	DF-F	†
Grieg	En fuglevise			
-----	In the boat			†
-----	It was a lovely summer evening			
-----	Springtide	M		DIT
-----	With a water lily	HM	CS-EF	†
Nin	Minué cantabo			ESC
Rachmaninoff	Daisies			†
-----	Lilacs			†
-----	The island	LH	DF-F	†

Lyric Tenor

Barber	Rain has fallen	HM	D-E	GSC
-----	Sleep now	MH	EF-AF	GSC
-----	With rue my heart is laden	HL	CS-D	GSC
Barnett	Serenade	H	F-G	GSC
Burleigh	By the pool at the third roses	H		RIC
-----	Jean	HML		PRE
Campbell-Tipton	A spirit flower	LHM	B-G	GSC
Carpenter	If	M	D-E	GSC
Charles	Clouds	HML	C-EF	GSC
-----	My lady walks in loveliness	HM	C-EF	GSC
-----	When I have sung my songs	HM	BF-EF	GSC
Crist	Evening	H	C-G	GSC
-----	White hours like snow	HL	CS-BF	CFI
Davis	Nancy Hanks	H	D-G	GAL
De Rose	I heard a forest praying	MH	EF-GF	CHA
Duke	Bells in the rain	H	E-GS	CFI
-----	To Karen, singing	M	CS-G	ELV
Elwell	In the mountains	M	DF-F	BMI
Ganz	A memory	HM	B-D	GSC
Giannini	Tell me, O blue, blue sky	H		RIC
Griffes	In a myrtle shade	H	FS-A	GSC
-----	Symphony in yellow	M	D-GF	GSC
Hageman	Do not go, my love	HL	B-EF	GSC
Kramer	Pleading	LH	D-GF	JFI
-----	Swans	HL		RIC
Mac Dowell	A maid sings light	H	F-G	ASC
-----	The sea	HL	D-D	BRH
MacGimsey	Sweet little Jesus Boy	ML	D-D	CFI
Manning	In the Luxembourg gardens	HML	BF-D	GSC
-----	Shoes	M	EF-F	GSC
Nevin	Little boy blue			BOS
-----	Mighty lak' a rose			JCH
Niles	I wonder as I wander	HL	BF-D	GSC
Nordoff	Music I heard with you	H	DS-FS	AMP
Taylor	A song for lovers	MH	D-F	JFI
Watts	Blue are her eyes	H	FS-FS	DIT
-----	Stresa	H	EF-BF	DIT
-----	Wings of night	LH	CS-G	GSC

British Songs and Arias Employing
Piano Singing

Lyric Tenor

Anon	Have you seen but a white lily grow?	H	E-F	GSC
Arden and Wille	Cockles and mussels	HM	E-E	ROW
Bartlet	Whither runneth my sweetheart			BOO
Bliss	Lovelocks			GOT
Bridge	E'en as a lovely flower	HM	FS-E	BOH
Clarke	Shy one	HL	BF-G	BOH
Coleridge-Taylor	Onaway! Awake beloved	MH	FS-BF	†
-----	She rested by the broken brook	HL		DIT
Del Riego	O dry those tears	LMH	E-GS	CHA
Dunhill	The cloths of Heaven	LM	EF-G	STB
Forsyth	The bell man			DIT
Gibbs	To one who passed whistling through the night	H	F-G	CUR
Handel	Let me wander not unseen (L'Allegro)	M	D-G	†
-----	Silent worship (Tolomeo)	LM	D-E	CUR
Harty	My lagan love	ML	BF-EF	BOO
Head	The ships of Arcady	ML	BF-EF	BOH
Hook	Mary of Allendale			BOO
Hughes	Open the door softly	LMH	G-G	ENO
-----	The bard of Armagh			BOO
Lehmann	Ah, moon of my delight			BOS
Liddle	The garden where the praties grow	LMH	E-FS	STB
Pilkington	Rest sweet nymphs			STB
Quilter	Dream valley	H	EF-GF	ROG
-----	Now sleeps the crimson petal	LMH	EF-GF	BOO
Ronald	Down in the forest	HML	C-D	ENO
-----	Drift down, drift down			BOO
Rowley	The toll gate house			ROG
Vaughan Williams	Orpheus with his lute			PRO
-----	Silent noon			GSC

Lyric Tenor

Bemberg	Il neige	H	FS-G	GRU
Berlioz	Merci, doux crepuscule			NOV
	(La Damnation de Faust)			
Bizet	Chanson d'avril	H	BF-G	†
-----	Douce mer			GSC
-----	Je crois entendre encore	H	D-A	GSC
	(Les Pecheurs des Perles)			
Breville	Prières d'enfant	M	D-F	ROU
Chausson	Nocturne	HL		INT
Debussy	Clair de lune	M	CS-FS	JOB
-----	En sourdine	M	C-FS	†
-----	Green	H	C-AF	†
-----	Harmonie du soir			DUR
-----	Il pleure dans mon coeur	LH	CS-GS	†
-----	L'ombre des arbres			†
-----	La mer est plus belle	HL		†
-----	Le jet d'eau			DUR
-----	Les angélus			HAM
-----	Les cloches	LH	E-GS	†
-----	Mandoline	HM	BF-F	†
-----	Nuits d'etoiles	LH	E-A	MAR
-----	Recueillement			DUR
-----	Voici que le printemps	LH	CS-G	BOS
Delibes	Bonjours, Suzon	LM	C-F	GSC
Duparc	Extase	LMH	FS-A	†
-----	Soupir	HL	CS-F	BOS
Dupont	Mandoline			DUR
Fauré	Adieu	MH	F-F	†
-----	Après un rêve	HM	C-F	†
-----	Au bord de l'eau	HL	C-F	†
-----	C'est l'extase	HL	C-FF	GSC
-----	Clair de lune	MH	C-G	†
-----	Ici-bas!	H	FS-G	†
-----	La lune blanche	HL		†
-----	Le secret	LH	F-G	†
-----	Les mélodies de Venise			HAM
-----	Lydia	MH	G-G	†
-----	Mandoline	HL	F-E	†
-----	Notre amour	H	DS-B	†
-----	Poème d'un jour			HAM
-----	Sylvie	HL	E-F	†
Ferrari	Le miroir	M	E-F	GSC
Franck	Le mariage des roses	M	E-FS	BOS
-----	Les cloches du soir	H	F-AF	

541

Godard	Cachés dans cet asile (Jocelyn) Violin or cello	MH	DF-F	GSC
Gounod	Au rossignol	LMH	D-G	CHO
-----	Sérénade	LMH	D-A	GSC
Hahn	À Chloris	H	DS-FS	HEU
-----	L'heure exquise	M	DF-F	†
-----	Fêtes galantes			
-----	Le rossignol des lilas			
-----	Offrande	M	D-D	GSC
-----	Paysage	MH	EF-G	HEU
Hue	L'âne blanc	H	EF-G	HEU
Koechlin	L'air	M	F-FS	ROU
-----	Le thé	HM	C-E	BOS
-----	Si tu le veux	LH	FS-A	MAR
Lalo	Aubade (Le Roi D'Ys)			†
Leguerney	Je vous envoie	H	C-A	ROU
Lully	Bois épais (Amadis)	ML	C-EF	†
Massenet	Crépuscule	M	D-E	GSC
-----	Le rêve de Des Grieux (Manon)	H	E-A	†
Mozart	Oiseaux, si tous les ans	H	C-G	KAL
Paladilhe	Psyché	HM	BF-F	GSC
Pessard	L'adieu du matin	ML	BF-D	GSC
Pierné	Ils etaient trois petits chats blancs			MAR
Poldowski	L'heure exquise	LMH	DF-AF	CHE
Poulenc	Air champêtre			ROU
-----	C (J'ai traversé les ponts de C)			ROU
-----	Montparnasse	H	EF-G	ESC
Rabey	Tes yeux Violin and piano	H	EF-G	DUR
Rameau	Dans ces doux asiles (Castor et Pollux)			LEM
Ravel	D'Anne jouant de l'espinette	H	CS-GS	GSC
-----	D'Anne qui me jecta	HM	CS-FS	GSC
-----	Don Quichotte à Dulcinée	HM	A-F	DUR
-----	Sainte	M	C-G	ELV
-----	Sur l'herbe	MH	C-G	DUR
-----	Trois beaux oiseaux du paradis			DUR
Roussel	Le jardin mouillé	M	C-FS	ROU
Saint-Saëns	Guitares et mandolines			DUR
-----	Mai	H	G-FS	DUR
Staub	L'heure silencieuse	H	EF-G	DUR
Szulc	Claire de lune	H	E-G	AXE

Thomas	Elle ne croyait pas (Mignon)	H	G-A	†
Weckerlin	Aminte	M	C-D	†
-----	Je connais un berger discret	M	EF-EF	BOS
-----	Menuet d' Exaudet	H	D-G	GSC
-----	O ma tendre musette	LM	A- E	GSC
-----	Trop aimable Sylvia	M	D-E	GSC

German Songs and Arias Employing
Piano Singing

Lyric Tenor

Beethoven	Ich liebe dich	HL	BF-DF	†
Blech	Heimkehr vom Feste			UNI
Brahms	An ein Veilchen	H	DS-GS	†
-----	Bei dir sind meine Gedanken	MH	E-FS	†
-----	Botschaft	HL	D-F	†
-----	Der Gang zur Liebsten	HL		†
-----	Es traeumte mir			†
-----	Geheimnis			†
-----	In Waldeseinsamkeit	H	ES-G	†
-----	Komm bald	HM	CS-F	†
-----	Lerchengesang	LH	FS-GS	†
-----	Staendchen	HL	BF-E	†
-----	Vergebliches Staendchen	LHM	E-FS	†
Franz	Marie	HL	D-F	†
Haydn	Liebes Maedchen, hoer' mir zu			HSC
Jensen	Am Ufer des Flusses des Manzanares	H	D-FS	GSC
-----	Margreta	M	F-F	PET
-----	Murmuring zephyr	LH	E-AF	GSC
Mahler	Ich atmet' einen linden Duft	HL		INT
-----	Ich ging mit Lust	HL		INT
Marx	Marienlied	MH	EF-AF	AMP
Mendelssohn	An die Entfernte	M	F-F	
-----	Pagenlied	M	E-E	†
Mozart	Alles fuehlt der Liebe Freuden (Die Zauberfloete)			RIC
-----	An Chloe	LH	EF-AF	
-----	Das Veilchen	LMH	F-G	†
-----	Im Mohrenland (Abduction from Seraglio)			†
Reger	Des Kindes Gebet	H	F-G	BOT

Schubert	Abschied	HL	BF–F	†
-----	An die Laute	LH	D–F	†
-----	Auf dem Wasser zu singen	MH	EF–GF	†
-----	Ave Maria	LMH	F–F	†
-----	Danksagung an den Bach	HL	E–F	†
-----	Das Fischermaedchen	L	A–EF	†
-----	Das Rosenband			PET
-----	Der Einsame	LH	D–G	†
-----	Der Schmetterling	LH	E–F	†
-----	Der Wachtelschlag	H	DS–FS	PET
-----	Der Wanderer an den Mond	LM	D–F	PET
-----	Die Taubenpost	HL	D–EF	†
-----	Du bist die Ruh	LMH	EF–AF	†
-----	Erlafsee	H	E–G	†
-----	Fruehlingstraum	HL	C–D	†
-----	Geheimes	HL	BF–EF	†
-----	Im Abendrot	HL	C–D	†
-----	Liebesbotschaft	H	E–G	†
-----	Lob der Thraenen	LM	F–F	†
-----	Nacht und Traeume	HL	C–DF	†
-----	Nachtviolen			PET
-----	Wohin?	HL	B–E	†
Schumann	Auftraege	HL	C–E	†
-----	Der Nussbaum	LMH	D–FS	†
-----	Der Sandmann	HL	AF–DF	†
-----	Die Meerfee			
-----	Fruehlingslust	HL		†
-----	Mondnacht	M	E–FS	†
-----	Staendchen			
Strauss	Allerseelen	HL	AS–E	†
-----	All' mein' Gedanken	H	CS–GS	
-----	Barcarolle	H	DF–BF	†
-----	Die Nacht	HL		†
-----	Fruendliche Vision	HL	C–F	†
-----	Heimkehr	HL	B–E	†
-----	Ich trage meine Minne	M		†
-----	Mein Herz ist stumm	LH	EF–AF	
-----	Traum durch die Daemmerung	HML	BF–EF	†
Trunk	In meiner Heimat			
-----	Tanzlied			
Wolf	Ach, im Maien	HL	C–E	†
-----	Auf dem gruenen Balkon	HL		†
-----	Auf ein altes Bild	HL	E–DS	†
-----	Der Gaertner	HL		†
-----	Ein Staendchen euch zu bringen	HL		†

544

(Wolf)	Frage und Antwort			PET
-----	Fruehling uebers Jahr			†
-----	Gleich und gleich			†
-----	Jaegerlied			PET
-----	Morgentau	HL	D-D	†
-----	Schlafendes Jesuskind	HL	AS-F	†
-----	Verborgenheit	HL	B-E	†
-----	Verschwiegene Liebe	LH	DF-FS	†

Italian Songs and Arias Employing
Piano Singing

Lyric Tenor

Bassani	Posate, dormite (La Serenata)	H	EF-F	GSC
Bononcini	Deh, più a me non v'ascondete	LH	EF-F	†
Castelnuovo-Tedesco	L'Infinito			
Cimara	Fiocca la neve	H	G-G	GSC
-----	Non più			
D'Astorga	Vo' cercando in queste valli	H	D-G	STB
Donizetti	Una furtiva lagrima (L'Elisir d'Amore)	H	F-AF	†
Gagliano	Dormi, amore (La Flora)	HL	CS-E	DIT
Giordano	Vedi, io piango (Fedora)			SON
Gluck	O del mio dolce ardor (Paride ed Elena)	LH	D-FS	GSC
Handel	Care selve (Atalanta)	MH	FS-A	†
Leoncavallo	Harlequin's serenade (I Pagliacci)	H	E-A	CFI
Mascagni	Apri la tua finestra (Iris)			RIC
Monteverdi	Lasciatemi morire (Arianna)	ML	D-D	†
Paradies	M'ha preso alla sua ragna	M	EF-F	GSC
Rossini	Se il mio nome (Il Barbiere di Siviglia)	H	GS-B	†
Secchi	Lungi dal caro bene	HL	A-FS	DIT
Tosti	Ideale			GSC
Verdi	Dal labbro il canto (Falstaff)	H	DS-AF	RIC
-----	La mia letizia infondere (I Lombardi)	H		RIC

Miscellaneous Songs Employing
Piano Singing

Lyric Tenor

Arensky	Revery	MH	DS–FS	DIT
-----	Valse	H	DF–GF	GSC
Borodin	The sleeping princess	M	DF–F	†
Cui	Dusk fallen	LH	E–GS	DIT
-----	The statue at Czarskoe-Selo	HM	DF–EF	†
Dvořák	God is my shepherd			AMP
-----	Songs my mother taught me	HM	E–E	†
Gretchaninoff	Hushed the song of the nightingale	MH	E–G	DIT
Grieg	A dream			†
-----	A swan			†
-----	Ragna			†
-----	Til En II	M	E–F	HAN
Mednikoff	The hills of Gruzia	H	DS–A	LAC
Rachmaninoff	Before my window	HM	C–G	†
-----	Here beauty dwells	H	D–B	CFI
-----	In the silence of night	LH	D–A	GSC
-----	Into my open window	HL	B–FS	BOS
Sibelius	The tryst	M		AMP
Sinding	Sylvelin	M	E–E	GSC

American Songs Employing
Rapid Enunciation

Lyric Tenor

Boatner	Oh, what a beautiful city!	HL	D–E	GSC
Brockway	The swapping song			GSC
Burleigh	Joshua fit de battle ob Jericho	LH	DS–E	RIC
Deis	Come down to Kew			
Griffes	Elves	H	F–AF	GSC
Hadley	My shadow			ASC
Hageman	At the well	LH	EF–AF	GSC
-----	Miranda	HL		GAL
Kernochan	Smuggler's song			GAL
Kountz	The sleigh	HL	D–FS	GSC
Leoni	Tally-ho!	LH	E–F	GSC
Mac Dowell	A maid sings light	H	F–G	ASC
Mana-Zucca	The big brown bear	HML	C–F	GSC

Sacco	Brother Will, Brother John	M	C-F	GSC
-----	Mexican serenade	HL	D-EF	BOS
Warner	Hurdy gurdy	M	D-F	CFI
Wolfe	Short'nin' bread	LHM	D-D	FLA

British Songs Employing
Rapid Enunciation

Lyric Tenor

Bartlet	Whither runneth my sweetheart			BOO
Bax	The enchanted fiddle			
Britten	Oliver Cromwell			BOH
Cowen	Border ballad	LM	D-E	BOO
Dowland	Shall I sue?			STB
German	Charming Chloe	HML		NOV
Gibbs	Five eyes	HL	D-D	BOS
Head	When I think upon the maidens	LM	D-G	BOO
Hughes	Kitty, my love, will you marry me?	M	C-F	BOH
-----	The stuttering lovers	MH	E-FS	CHA
Liddle	The garden where the praties grow	LMH	E-FS	STB
Molloy	The Kerry Dance	LH	C-G	GSC
Morgan	Clorinda	HM	C-EF	ENO
Morley	It was a lover and his lass	HM		DIT
Purcell	There's not a swain on the plain	M	B-G	BAF
Sanderson	Susan is her name	LM	D-E	BOH
Warlock	Good ale			AUG

French Songs Employing
Rapid Enunciation

Lyric Tenor

Bemberg	Il neige	H	FS-G	GRU
Bizet	Chanson d'avril	H	BF-G	†
Chabrier	Villanelle des petits canards	HML	B-E	†
Debussy	Ballade des femmes de Paris			DUR
-----	Chevaux de bois	H	C-G	†

547

(Debussy)	Fêtes galantes	LH	CS-A	†
-----	Mandoline	HM	BF-F	†
-----	Placet futile			DUR
Delibes	Bonjours, Suzon	LM	C-F	GSC
Dupont	Chanson des noisettes			HEU
Fauré	Mandoline	HL	F-E	†
-----	Notre amour	H	DS-B	†
-----	Poème d'un jour			HAM
-----	Toujours	LH	F-AF	†
Fourdrain	Carnaval	M	C-F	RIC
Pierné	Ils étaient trois petits chats blancs			MAR
Poldowski	Cortège	M	D-FS	CHE
-----	Dansons la gigue	M	EF-G	MAR
Ravel	Manteau de fleurs	H		INT
-----	Nicolette	L	B-FS	ELK
Roussel	Le bachelier de Salamanque			DUR
Saint-Saëns	Tournoiement			DUR
Weckerlin	Chantons les amours de Jean	H	D-G	GSC

German Songs Employing Rapid Enunciation

Lyric Tenor

Beethoven	Mailied			RIC
-----	Neue Liebe, neues Leben			†
Brahms	Blinde Kuh			†
-----	Juchhe!			†
-----	Meine Liebe ist gruen	MLH	ES-A	†
-----	O liebliche Wangen	MLH	E-G	†
-----	Vergebliches Staendchen	LHM	E-FS	†
Jensen	Margreta	M	F-F	PET
Mendelssohn	An die Entfernte	M	F-F	
-----	Neue Liebe	H	CS-A	†
Mozart	Warnung	HM	C-D	
Schubert	Das Wandern	HLM	E-E	†
-----	Die Forelle	MLH	EF-GF	†
-----	Die Post	HML	BF-EF	†
-----	Erstarrung	HL	D-F	†
-----	Fischerweise	L	C-D	†
-----	Fruehlingssehnsucht	HL	B-E	†
-----	Ueber Wildemann			PET
-----	Ungeduld	HML		†
-----	Wohin?	HL	B-E	†
Schumann	Auftraege	HL	C-E	†
Strauss	Wozu noch, Maedchen	H	FS-A	

548

Wolf	Ein Staendchen euch zu bringen	HL		INT
-----	Elfenlied	HL	D-F	†

Italian Songs and Arias Employing
Rapid Enunciation

Lyric Tenor

Buzzi-Peccia	Povero pulcinella	H	E-A	GSC
Carissimi	Vittoria, mio core	HLM	B-E	†
Cavalli	Donzelle fuggite	HL	C-EF	†
Cimarosa	Pria che spunti in ciel (Il Matrimonio Segreto)			RIC
Donaudy	Ah mai non cessate			RIC
Durante	Danza, danza fanciulla gentile	HM	BF-F	†
Legrenzi	Che fiero costume	HML	C-D	†
Leoncavallo	Harlequin's serenade (I Pagliacci)	H	E-A	CFI
Malipiero	Ballata	H		CHE
Paradies	M'ha preso alla sua ragna	M	EF-F	GSC
Puccini	Tra voi belle (Manon Lescaut)			RIC
Rontani	Or ch'io non segno più	HL	CS-E	DIT
Rossini	La danza	MH	E-A	†
Scarlatti, A.	Chi vuole innamorarsi	HL	D-EF	DIT
Stradella	Ragion sempre addita	H	E-G	†
Tosti	A vucchella	LH	F-G	RIC
Verdi	Di tu se fedele (Un Ballo in Maschera)			RIC
-----	Questa o quella (Rigoletto)	H	EF-AF	†

Miscellaneous Songs Employing
Rapid Enunciation

Lyric Tenor

Falla	Seguidilla murciana	HL		AMP
Grieg	In the boat			†
-----	The way of the world			DIT
-----	With a water lily			†
Mussorgsky	The magpie and the gypsy dancer			GSC
-----	The seminarian			GSC
Smetana	Ma-ma-mama so dear (The Bartered Bride)			BOO

American Songs Employing
Sustained Singing

Lyric Tenor

Barber	Sure on this shining night	MH	D-G	GSC
Burleigh	Sometimes I feel like a motherless child	HML		RIC
-----	Were you there?	HML		RIC
Chadwick	Allah	LH	CS-GS	ASC
Clay	I'll sing thee songs of Araby	MH	EF-AF	†
Dunn	The bitterness of love			JFI
Edwards	By the bend of the river	HML	C-E	GSC
-----	Into the night	HML	C-DF	GSC
Foote	I'm wearing awa'	HL		ASC
Foster, S.C.	Jeanie with the light brown hair	LH	D-G	CFI
Giannini	Far above the purple hills	LH	CS-A	RIC
Golde	Love was with me yesterday	LMH	E-A	CFI
-----	O beauty, passing beauty	MH	CS-GS	GSC
Griffes	La fuite de la lune	M	CS-F	GSC
-----	The lament of Ian the proud	MH	DS-AS	GSC
Hageman	Music I heard with you	MH	E-A	GAL
Kernochan	We two together	H	EF-AF	GAL
La Forge	Retreat	LMH	E-G	GSC
Lang	Irish love song	HML	A-E	ASC
Levitzki	Do you remember?	HML	BF-EF	GSC
Mac Dowell	Thy beaming eyes	ML	BF-EF	ASC
Manning	Sketches of Paris	HL	C-E	GSC
Mc Donald	Daybreak	H		ELV
Rasbach	Trees	LMH	CS-GS	GSC
Robinson	Water boy	M	B-E	BOS
Rogers	The star	LH	C-AF	GSC
-----	Wind song	LM	C-G	GSC
Sacco	Never the nightingale	H	EF-GF	GAL
Scott	Think on me	HML	D-EF	GAL
Skiles	You will know my love			CFI
Speaks	Sylvia	HML	AF-DF	GSC
Tyson	Noon and night	LH	F-AF	GSC

British Songs and Arias Employing
Sustained Singing

Lyric Tenor

Arne, T.	Blow, blow thou winter wind	M	C-F	†
Attey	On a time			BOO
Balfe	Then you'll remember me (The Bohemian Girl)	M	E-F	†
Bantock	Silent strings	MH	F-G	BOO
Bax	The white peace			CHE
Bridge	O that it were so	LMH	D-G	CHA
Bury	There is a lady	HM	CS-E	CFI
Butterworth	Loveliest of trees			AUG
Campion	Follow thy fair sun			STB
-----	There is a garden in her face			DIT
-----	When to her lute Corinna sings			STB
Coates	Bird songs at eventide	LM		CHA
Coleridge-Taylor	Life and death	HML		ASC
Dowland	Come, heavy sleep			STB
-----	Flow, my tears	M	D-E	STB
-----	In darkness let me dwell			STB
-----	I saw my lady weep	M	E-E	STB
Dunhill	To the Queen of Heaven	M	C-G	GSC
Ford	Now I see thy looks were feigned			BOO
-----	Since first I saw your face			DIT
Glover	Rose of Tralee	LMH	E-G	MOV
Grainger	The sprig of thyme	LH	E-FS	GSC
Handel	Comfort ye (The Messiah)	H	E-GS	†
-----	Thus when the sun (Samson)	H	D-G	†
-----	Total eclipse (Samson)			†
-----	Waft her, angels (Jephtha)	H	D-A	†
-----	Wher'er you walk (Semele)	HML	C-D	†
Henschel	Morning-hymn	MH	DS-GS	†
Holbrooke	Come not when I am dead			ENO
Humphrey	I pass all my hours			DIT
Johnson	As I walked forth one summer day			DIT
McGill	Duna	HML	BF-D	BOO
Milford	The colour	H	D-G	OXF
Purcell	Cease, o my sad soul			POT
-----	Had I but love			DUN

551

(Purcell)	If music be the food of love	M	D-G	BOO
-----	Music for a while (Oedipus)	LH		SC
Quilter	Go, lovely rose	LHM	F-GF	CHA
Ronald	Prelude	HML	B-D	ENO
Stephenson	Love is a sickness	HML	C-D	BOO
Sullivan	The lost chord	HL	C-F	GSC
Thiman	The silver swan	MH	EF-G	NOV
Vaughan Williams	Linden Lea	HML	C-D	BOS
Wood	I look into your garden	LMH	F-AF	CHA

French Songs and Arias Employing Sustained Singing

Lyric Tenor

Berlioz	Nature immense (La Damnation de Faust)			NOV
-----	Les nuits d'été			AUG
Bizet	Flower song (Carmen)	H	E-BF	†
Caplet	Le forêt			DUR
-----	Les prières			DUR
Chausson	Apaisement	MH	EF-G	HAM
-----	Le charme	HM	BF-EF	HAM
-----	L'amour d'Antan	HL		INT
-----	Le colibri Violin or cello	M	F-GF	BOS
-----	Le temps des lilas	MH	D-GS	†
Dalayrac	Hélas! c'est près de vous			
Debussy	Air d'Azaël (L'Enfant Prodigue)	H	C-A	GSC
-----	Beau soir	LH	C-FS	†
-----	Colloque sentimental			DUR
-----	De fleurs	H	C-AF	†
-----	Romance	HM	C-E	†
Delibes	Fantaisie aux divins mensonges (Lakmé)			BRO
-----	Jours passés			GSC
Duparc	Lamento	ML	EF-EF	†
Fauré	Le parfum impérissable	LH	GF-GF	
-----	Rencontre	H	EF-AF	†
-----	Soir	LH	D-GS	†
-----	Vocalise	H		LED
Franck	Nocturne	HL		†
Gluck	S'il était vrai (Iphigénie en Aulide)			

(Gluck)	Unis dès la plus tendre enfance (Iphigénie en Aulide)			NOV
Gounod	Ah! lève-toi, soleil! (Roméo et Juliette)	H	F-BF	†
-----	Salut! demeure chaste et pure (Faust)	H	EF-C	†
Herold	Ce soir, j'arrive donc (Le Pré aux Clercs)			BRA
Hue	J'ai pleuré en rêve	HL	D-E	BOS
Leguerney	Au sommeil			ROU
Leroux	Le nil Cello or violin	LH	E-A	†
Lully	Air du grand prêtre (Persée)	M	E-E	ROU
-----	Plus j'observe ces lieux (Armide)			LEM
Massenet	Ah! fuyez, douce image (Manon)	H	F-BF	GSC
-----	Elégie	LM	C-GF	GSC
-----	Je ne sais si je veille (Werther)			HEU
-----	O souverain! ô juge! ô père (Le Cid)			HEU
-----	Pourquoi me reveiller (Werther)	H	FS-AS	HEU
Mehul	A peine sortir (Joseph)			
Messager	La maison grise (Fortuno)			CHO
Meyerbeer	O paradis (L'Africaine)	H	F-BF	†
Mozart	Dans un bois	H	EF-AF	
Poulenc	A sa guitare	M	D-FS	DUR
-----	Air grave			ROU
-----	Bleuet	H	FS-GF	DUR
-----	Violon			ROU
Rameau	Tristes apprêts (Castor et Pollux)			CHE
Ravel	Kaddisch	H	C-G	DUR
-----	Le paon	M	C-F	DUR
Saint-Saëns	Aimons-nous			DUR
-----	La cloche	LH	DF-AF	†
Severac	Les hiboux			ROU
Tiersot	L'amours de moi	M	EF-F	HEU

German Songs and Arias Employing
Sustained Singing

Lyric Tenor

Bach, C.P.E.	Das Gebet			SIM
-----	Passionslied			SIM

553

Bach, J.S.	Ah, my soul (St. John Passion)			†
-----	Bist du bei mir	HML	A-EF	†
-----	Erbarme dich (Cantata 55) Flute			RIC
-----	Handle nicht nach deinen Rechten (Cantata 101) Violin			
-----	Ich will leiden (Cantata 87) 2 Violins, viola and continuo			DIT
-----	Man halte nur ein wenig stille (Cantata 93)			NOV
-----	O Seelen Paradies (Cantata 172) Violin or viola			AUG
Beethoven	Adelaide	HML	BF-E	†
-----	An die ferne Geliebte	HL	C-E	†
-----	Das Geheimnis			
-----	Die Ehre Gottes	HL	AF-EF	†
-----	Wonne der Wehmut			†
Brahms	An die Nachtigall	H	DS-G	†
-----	Der Tod, das ist die kuehle Nacht	L	AF-F	†
-----	Der Ueberlaeufer			†
-----	Erinnerung	H	E-G	†
-----	Feldeinsamkeit	HL	C-EF	†
-----	Minnelied	MHL	C-EF	†
-----	Mondenschein	LH	D-GF	CFI
-----	O wuesst' ich doch den Weg zurueck	H	E-FS	†
-----	Ruhe Suessliebchen	HL	BS-E	†
-----	Schoen war, das ich dir weihte			†
-----	Sommerabend			†
-----	Wenn du nur zuweilen laechelst			†
-----	Wie bist du meine Koenigin	HL	C-E	†
-----	Wir wandelten	LH	EF-GF	†
Franz	Dedication	HML	BF-C	†
-----	For music	ML	C-D	†
Haydn	She never told her love	HL	B-D	DIT
Liszt	Du bist wie eine Blume	H	E-G	†
-----	Es muss ein Wunderbares sein	HM	C-EF	DUR
Loewe	Canzonetta	MH	B-A	DIT
Marx	Hat dich die Liebe beruehrt	MH	EF-BF	AMP
-----	Nocturne	H	EF-AF	AMP
-----	Waldseligkeit	H	D-A	UNI

Mendelssohn	Be thou faithful unto death (Saint Paul)	MH	D-G	†
-----	He counteth all your sorrows (Hymn of Praise)	H	D-G	†
-----	If with all your hearts (Elijah)	MH	F-AF	†
-----	Nachtlied			
-----	On wings of song			JCH
-----	Then shall the righteous shine forth (Elijah)	H	EF-AF	†
-----	The sorrows of death (Hymn of Praise)			†
Mozart	Abendempfindung	M	E-F	
-----	Die ihr des unermessliechen Weltalls			
-----	Dies Bildnis ist bezaubernd schoen (Die Zauberfloete)			†
-----	Hier soll ich dich denn sehen (Abduction from Seraglio)			†
Reger	Friede	H	EF-G	UNI
Schoenberg	Erhebung			GSC
Schubert	Am Meer	HML	B-D	†
-----	An die Musik	HL	A-DS	†
-----	An die Tueren	HL		†
-----	Das Wirtshaus	HL	C-D	†
-----	Der Leiermann	ML	C-D	†
-----	Der Lindenbaum	HL	A-D	†
-----	Der Neugierige	HL	CS-EF	†
-----	Der Wegweiser	L	D-EF	†
-----	Die Liebe hat gelogen	LM	G-F	†
-----	Die Nebensonnen	HL	F-D	†
-----	Erster Verlust	M	C-F	†
-----	Fruehlingsglaube	M	EF-F	†
-----	Ihr Bild	HL	C-C	†
-----	Memnon	LM	AF-F	PET
-----	Wanderers Nachtlied, 2	LH	F-F	†
-----	Wehmuth	HL	B-D	
Schumann	An den Sonnenschein	HL	A-D	†
-----	Dein Angesicht	HL	B-EF	†
-----	Die Lotusblume	HLM	BF-F	†
-----	Du bist wie eine Blume	HM	F-EF	†
-----	Ich grolle nicht	HL	BF-D	†
-----	Ich hab' im Traum geweinet	HL	B-D	†
-----	Ihre Stimme	LH		†
-----	Mein schoener Stern			
-----	Mit Myrthen und Rosen	HL	A-D	†
-----	Stille Traenen	HL		†
-----	Wenn ich in deine Augen seh'	HL	EF-FF	†

(Schumann)	Wer machte dich so krank?			
Strauss	Ach Lieb, ich muss nun scheiden	H	D-G	
-----	Kornblumen	LH	DF-AF	†
-----	Madrigal	LH	EF-GF	
-----	Mit deinen blauen Augen	LH	C-GS	†
-----	Morgen	HML	E-F	†
Strauss	Seitdem dein Aug' in meines schaute			SC
Wagner	Atmest du nich mit mir die suessen Duefte (Lohengrin)			GSC
-----	In fernem Land (Lohengrin)	H	E-A	†
-----	Mein lieber Schwan (Lohengrin)			†
Wolf	Bedeckt mich mit Blumen	HL	B-D	INT
-----	Denk' es, o Seele	LH	EF-F	†
-----	Gebet	HL		†
-----	Heb' auf dein blondes Haupt	HL	G-DF	†
-----	Heimweh (Eichendorff Lieder)	M		†
-----	Herr, was traegt der Boden	HL	B-DS	
-----	Im Fruehling	HL	BF-F	†

Italian Songs and Arias Employing Sustained Singing

Lyric Tenor

Bellini	Meco all' altar di venere (Norma)	H	D-C	RIC
Bimboni	Sospiri miei	M	EF-EF	GAL
Boito	Dai campi, dai prati (Mefistofele)			RIC
-----	Giunto, sul passo estremo (Epilogue) (Mefistofele)			RIC
Braga	Angel's serenade Violin	LH	D-G	†
Caccini	Amarilli, mia bella	ML	C-D	†
-----	Fere, selvagge	HL	CS-GS	DIT
Caldara	Come raggio di sol	HL	D-F	†
Carissimi	Deh, contentatevi	LH	E-G	†
Cesti	Che angoscia, che affanno (Il Pomo d'Oro)	HL	C-DF	DIT
-----	Tu mancavi a tormentarmi	H	D-G	GSC
Cilea	La dolcissima effigie (Adriana Lecouvreur)	H		AMP

556

(Cilea)	L'anima ho stanca (Adriana Lecouvreur)	H		AMP
Donaudy	O bei nidi d'amore			RIC
-----	O del mio amato ben	M	EF-F	RIC
-----	Quando ti rivedrò			RIC
-----	Vaghissima sembianza	H	E-A	RIC
Donizetti	Quanto è bella (L'Elisir d'Amore)			BRO
-----	Spirto gentil (La Favorita)	H	G-C	†
-----	Tombe degl'avi miei (Lucia di Lammermoor)	H	F-BF	BRO
-----	Una vergine, un angiol (La Favorita)	H	E-C	BRO
Durante	Vergin, tutta amor	LM	C-EF	†
Flotow	M'appari (Martha)	HLM	EF-AF	†
Giordano	Amor ti vieta (Fedora)	H		AMP
-----	Come un bel di (Andrea Chenier)	H	E-BF	AMP
-----	Un di all' azzurro spazio (Andrea Chenier)	H	F-BF	SON
Gluck	Spiagge amate (Paride ed Elena)			†
Handel	Allor che sorge astro lucente (Rodrigo)			BOO
-----	Due bell'alme (Deidamia)			BOO
-----	Rendi'l sereno al ciglio (Sosarme)	LH	EF-F	†
Haydn	Pensi a me			
Leoncavallo	Testa adorata (La Boheme)			SON
-----	Vesti la giubba (I Pagliacci)	H	D-A	†
Mascagni	Addio alla madre (Cavalleria Rusticana)			GSC
-----	Ed anche Beppe amo (L'Amico Fritz)			JCH
-----	O amore, o bella luce (L'Amico Fritz)			GSC
-----	Siciliana: (O Lola) (Cavalleria Rusticana)	H	AF-AF	†
Mattei	Non è ver	HML		DIT
Monteverdi	Ahi, troppo è duro (Il Balletto delle Ingrate)	HL	C-EF	DIT
Mozart	Dalla sua pace (Don Giovanni)	H	D-G	†
-----	Misero! o sogno	H	EF-AF	BOO
-----	Un aura amorosa (Cosi Fan Tutte)			†

557

Paisiello	Nel cor più non mi sento	HL	C-EF	†
Pergolesi	Dite ch'ogni momento			BOS
-----	Nina	HL	CS-D	DIT
Peri	Invocazione di Orfeo (Euridice)	HL	E-CS	DIT
Ponchielli	Cielo e mar (La Gioconda)	H	D-BF	†
Respighi	Abbandono			BON
-----	Nebbie			†
Rosa	Star vicino	HL	D-E	†
Rossini	Ecco ridente in cielo (Il Barbiere di Siviglia)	H	FS-B	†
Scarlatti, A.	Son tutta duolo	M	D-EF	GSC
Sibella	O bocca dolorosa	HM	D-F	GSC
Stradella	Pietà, Signore	HM	C-F	GSC
-----	Se nel ben			CFI
Torelli	Tu lo sai	HL	BF-F	DIT
Tosti	Aprile	LMH		RIC
Verdi	De' miei bollenti spiriti (La Traviata)	H	F-AF	†
-----	O tu che in seno agli angeli (La Forza del Destino)	H	DF-BF	RIC
-----	Parmi veder le lagrime (Rigoletto)	H	F-AF	GSC
-----	Quando le sere al placido (Luisa Miller)			RIC
Wolf-Ferrari	Benedicimi tu (Jewels of the Madonna)	H	AF-AF	GSC

Miscellaneous Songs and Arias Employing Sustained Singing

Lyric Tenor

Arensky	Autumn	H	CS-FS	GSC
Dvořák	Hear my prayer, O Lord			AMP
-----	Lord, Thou art my refuge and shield			AMP
-----	Turn Thee to me			AMP
Granados	The maja and the nightingale (Goyescas)	H	BS-A	GSC
Gretchaninoff	Wounded birch	HL	B-EF	†
Grieg	I love thee	HML	E-F	†
-----	Two brown eyes	LM	EF-F	GSC
Mussorgsky	In my attic			GSC
-----	On the Dnieper			GSC

Nin	Alma sintamos			ESC
Rachmaninoff	Christ is risen	LM	D-F	GAL
-----	Oh cease thy singing, maiden fair	H	E-A	CFI
-----	O, do not grieve	M	BF-AF	GSC
-----	O thou billowy harvest field	HL	CS-E	GSC
-----	To the children	MH	F-G	DIT
Rimsky-Korsakov	On the Georgian hills	HM		GSC
Sibelius	Black roses	M	A-ES	AMP
-----	Was it a dream?			BRH
Sinding	May night			DIT
Sjoegren	The Seraglio's garden	HL		GSC
Tchaikovsky	A legend	M	D-E	GSC
-----	None but the lonely heart	HLM	C-F	DIT
-----	Why	HL		†

American Songs Employing Spirited Singing

Lyric Tenor

Bacon	The Erie canal	L	D-C	CFI
Barber	I hear an army	LH	D-AF	GSC
Bassett	Take joy home	LH	EF-BF	GSC
Beach	The year's at the spring	MH	AF-AF	ASC
Boatner	Oh, what a beautiful city!	HL	D-E	GSC
Burleigh	Joshua fit de battle ob Jericho	LH	DS-E	RIC
Carpenter	If	M	D-E	GSC
-----	Serenade	LH	CS-A	GSC
Chanler	I rise when you enter	M	CS-G	GSC
Crist	Girl of the red mouth	MH	E-BF	CFI
Curran	Life	HM	BF-F	GSC
Deis	Come down to Kew			
Elwell	The road not taken	M	B-FS	GSC
Enders	Russian picnic	HM	C-G	GSC
Griffes	An old song resung	LM	EF-F	GSC
-----	Elves	H	F-AF	GSC
Guion	All day on the prarie	M	EF-F	GSC
Hadley	My shadow			ASC
Hageman	At the well	LH	EF-AF	GSC
-----	Me company along	LH	F-BF	CFI
-----	Miranda	HL		GAL
-----	Voices			
Hindemith	The whistling thief	M	E-F	AMP
Hopkinson	O'er the hills	LH	C-G	

Kountz	The sleigh	HL	D-FS	GSC
La Forge	Song of the open	MH	EF-AF	DIT
Levitzki	Ah, thou beloved one	H	EF-AF	GSC
Mac Dowell	A maid sings light	H	F-G	ASC
Mana-Zucca	I love life	LM	F-F	PRE
Margetson	Tommy, lad	HML	A-D	BOH
Niles	The rovin' gambler	HL	BF-EF	GSC
Nordoff	There shall be more joy	M	CS-FS	AMP
Porter	Begin the Beguine (Jubilee)	L	BF-F	HAR
Rodgers	Falling in love with love (The Boys from Syracuse)			WIL
Rogers	The last song	MLH	E-AF	GSC
Rummel	Ecstasy	LMH	GF-AF	GSC
Sacco	Brother Will, Brother John	M	C-F	GSC
-----	Mexican serenade	HL	D-EF	BOS
Speaks	Morning	HML	BF-D	GSC
Taylor	The rivals	H	E-G	JFI
Warner	Hurdy gurdy	M	D-F	CFI
Warren	White horses of the sea	LH	F-G	GSC
Wolfe	Short'nin' bread	LHM	D-D	FLA

British Songs and Arias Employing
Spirited Singing

Lyric Tenor

Arne, T.	Preach not me your musty rules (Comus)	HML		ROW
Bartlet	Whither runneth my sweetheart			BOO
Bax	The enchanted fiddle			
Besley	Listening	H	E-AF	CUR
Bliss	Three jolly gentlemen	H		†
Bridge	So perverse			BOS
Cowen	Border ballad	LM	D-E	BOO
Delius	To the queen of my heart			†
Dowland	Awake, sweet love	M	E-F	STB
-----	Come again! sweet love	M	D-E	STB
-----	Say love, if ever thou didst find			STB
-----	Shall I sue?			STB
-----	What if I never speede	M	D-D	BOS
Eden	What's in the air today?	M	D-F	ELK
German	Charming Chloe	HML		NOV
Gibbs	Five eyes	HL	D-D	BOS
Handel	Evr'y valley (The Messiah)			†

(Handel)	Love and friendship			RBR
-----	Love's a dear deceitful jewel	LH	F-F	RBR
-----	Say to Irene (Atalanta)	H	D-AF	CFI
-----	The enemy said (Israel in Egypt)	H	D-A	NOV
-----	Why does the God of Israel sleep? (Samson)			†
Head	Sea gipsy	LM	E-GS	BOO
-----	When I think upon the maidens	LM	D-G	BOO
Hook	Bright Phoebus	M	EF-F	GSC
Hughes	The stuttering lovers	MH	E-FS	CHA
Ireland	Great things			AUG
-----	Hope the hornblower			BOO
Jones	What if I speede?			BOO
Keel	Trade winds	HL	BF-EF	BOH
Leveridge	When dull care			BOO
Liddle	The garden where the praties grow	LMH	E-FS	STB
Linley	O, bid your faithful Ariel fly			BOO
Molloy	The Kerry Dance	LH	C-G	GSC
Morgan	Clorinda	HM	C-EF	ENO
Morley	It was a lover and his lass	HM		DIT
Purcell	Hark! the echoing air (The Fairy Queen)			BAF
-----	I'll sail upon the dog star	HL	A-E	†
-----	There's not a swain on the plain	M	B-G	BAF
Quilter	Blow, blow thou winter wind	HL	C-E	BOO
-----	It was a lover and his lass	HL	CS-E	BOO
-----	I will go with my father a-plowing	MH	D-G	ELK
-----	Love's philosophy	LMH	D-A	BOO
Rowley	The toll gate house			ROG
Toye	The inn	L	C-E	CUR
Vaughan Williams	The roadside fire	HML	BF-EF	BOO
Warlock	As ever I saw	MH	DF-GF	ROG
-----	Good ale			AUG

French Songs and Arias Employing
Spirited Singing

Lyric Tenor

Bizet	Chanson d'avril	H	BF-G	†
Chabrier	Villanelle des petits canards	HML	B-E	†
Charpentier	Les chevaux de bois	H	E-A	HEU
Debussy	Ballade des femmes de Paris			DUR
-----	Chevaux de bois	H	C-G	†
-----	Fêtes galantes	LH	CS-A	†
-----	La mer est plus belle	HL		†
-----	Le balcon			JOB
-----	Le faune			DUR
-----	Mandoline	HM	BF-F	†
-----	Noël des enfants qui n'ont plus de maisons			DUR
Delibes	Bonjours, Suzon	LM	C-F	GSC
-----	Myrto	M	A-FS	GSC
Dupont	Mandoline			DUR
Fauré	L'hiver a cessé	HL		INT
-----	Mandoline	HL	F-E	†
-----	Noël	LH	EF-AF	GSC
-----	Notre amour	H	DS-B	†
-----	Poème d'un jour			HAM
-----	Toujours	LH	F-AF	†
Fourdrain	Chanson norvégienne	H	E-G	RIC
Gluck	Bannis la crainte (Alceste)			†
Gounod	Au printemps	LMH	DF-AF	GSC
-----	Vénise	HL		INT
Hahn	Fêtes galantes			
-----	Le printemps			
Koechlin	Le thé	HM	C-E	BOS
-----	Si tu le veux	LH	FS-A	MAR
Massenet	J'aurais sur ma poitrine (Werther)			HEU
-----	Ouvre tes yeux bleus	MH	C-G	†
Milhaud	Chant d'amour	M	C-GF	ESC
Pierné	Ils étaient trois petits chats blancs			MAR
-----	Le moulin	ML	C-E	BOS
Poldowski	Cortège	M	D-FS	CHE
-----	Dansons la gigue	M	EF-G	MAR
Poulenc	Air champêtre			ROU
-----	Air vif	H	C-AF	ROU
Ravel	Chanson à boire			DUR
-----	Manteau de fleurs	H		INT

(Ravel)	Nicolette	L	B-FS	ELK
Roussel	Le bachelier de Salamanque			DUR
Saint-Saëns	Guitares et mandolines			DUR
-----	Tournoiement			DUR
Weckerlin	Chantons les amours de Jean	H	D-G	GSC

German Songs and Arias Employing
Spirited Singing

Lyric Tenor

Bach, J.S.	Ja, tausendmal (Cantata 43) Violin			NOV
-----	Nimm mich Dir zu eigen hin (Cantata 65)			NOV
Beethoven	Der Kuss			†
-----	Mailied			RIC
-----	Neue Liebe, neues Leben			†
Brahms	Bei dir sind meine Gedanken	MH	E-FS	†
-----	Blinde Kuh			†
-----	Botschaft	HL	D-F	†
-----	Der Gang zur Liebsten	HL		†
-----	Es liebt sich so lieblich im Lenze	LH	D-GS	†
-----	Juchhe!			†
-----	Klage	LH	FS-FS	†
-----	Liebe kam aus fernen Landen	HL	C-E	†
-----	Meine Liebe ist gruen	MLH	ES-A	†
-----	O liebliche Wangen	MLH	E-G	†
-----	Sind es Schmerzen	HL	BF-F	†
-----	Vergebliches Staendchen	LHM	E-FS	†
Hassler	Gagliarda			SIM
Haydn	Matrosenlied			
Jensen	Am Ufer des Flusses des Manzanares	H	D-FS	GSC
-----	Margreta	M	F-F	PET
-----	Murmuring zephyr	LH	E-AF	GSC
Korngold	Das Staendchen	M		SC
Loewe	Des Glockenthuermers Tochterlein	H	CS-A	SC
Mendelssohn	An die Entfernte	M	F-F	
-----	Jagdlied	HL	BF-EF	†
-----	Neue Liebe	H	CS-A	†
-----	O Jugend	H	E-A	†

Mozart	Alles fuehlt der Liebe Freuden (Die Zauberfloete)			†
-----	An Chloe	LH	EF-AF	
Schubert	Das Fischermaedchen	L	A-EF	†
-----	Der Wachtelschlag	H	DS-FS	PET
-----	Die Forelle	MLH	EF-GF	†
-----	Die Post	HML	BF-EF	†
-----	Erstarrung	HL	D-F	†
-----	Fischerweise	L	C-D	†
-----	Fruehlingssehnsucht	HL	B-E	†
-----	Heidenroeslein			
-----	Rastlose Liebe	M	B-F	†
-----	Ueber Wildemann			PET
-----	Wohin!	HL	B-E	†
Schulze	Staendchen			SIM
Schumann	Auftraege	HL	C-E	†
-----	Geisternaehe			
-----	Wanderlied	HL	A-E	†
-----	Widmung	HL	BF-F	†
Strauss, J.	Tales from the Vienna forest	H	EF-C	GSC
Strauss, R.	Heimliche Aufforderung	HL	B-E	†
-----	Kling			†
Trunk	Tanzlied			
Wolf	Ach, im Maien	HL	C-E	†
-----	Auf dem gruenen Balkon	HL		†
-----	Ein Staendchen euch zu bringen	HL		†
-----	Er ist's	H	D-G	†
-----	Fussreise	HL	D-E	†
-----	Lied vom Winde			†
-----	Nimmersatte Liebe	LH	CF-AF	†
-----	Zum neuen Jahr			PET

Italian Songs and Arias Employing Spirited Singing

Lyric Tenor

Bononcini	L'esperto nocchiero (Astarte)	HL	B-E	†
Carissimi	Filli, non t'amo più	HL	B-D	†
-----	Vittoria, mio core	HLM	B-E	†
Cavalli	Donzelle fuggite	HL	C-EF	†
Cimarosa	Brillar mi sento il core (Il Matrimonio Segreto)			RIC
D'Astorga	Vo' cercando in queste valli	H	D-G	STB

Donaudy	Ah mai non cessate			RIC
-----	Spirate pur, spirate			RIC
Durante	Danza, danza fanciulla gentile	HM	BF-F	†
Gaffi	Luci vezzose	HL	D-E	DIT
Giordano	Mia madre, la mia vecchia madre (Fedora)			BRO
Handel	Sei, mia gioja (Partenope)			CFI
Legrenzi	Che fiero costume	HML	C-D	†
Leoncavallo	Harlequin's serenade (I Pagliacci)	H	E-A	CFI
-----	Mattinata	MLH	C-AF	†
Mozart	Per pietà non ricercate			BOO
Paradies	M'ha preso alla sua ragna	M	EF-F	GSC
Porpora	Non più fra sassi			PET
Puccini	Tra voi belle (Manon Lescaut)			RIC
Respighi	Invito alla danza			BON
Rontani	Or ch'io non segno più	HL	CS-E	DIT
Scarlatti, A.	All' acquisto di gloria (Tigrane)	H	C-G	GSC
-----	Chi vuole innamorarsi	HL	D-EF	DIT
-----	Già il sole dal Gange	LH	EF-F	GSC
Scarlatti, D.	Qual farfalletta			
Tosti	The last song	HL		RIC
Verdi	Di tu se fedele (Un Ballo in Maschera)			RIC
-----	Giorno di pianto (I Vespri Siciliani)			RIC
-----	La donna è mobile (Rigoletto)	LMH	FS-AS	†
-----	Questa o quella (Rigoletto)	H	EF-AF	†

Miscellaneous Songs Employing Spirited Singing

Lyric Tenor

Dvořák	I will sing new songs of gladness	HL		†
Falla	El paño moruno	HL		AMP
-----	Seguidilla murciana	HL		AMP
Gretchaninoff	The skylark			DIT
Grieg	With a water lily			†
Mussorgsky	Hopak	HM	CS-FS	GSC
Rachmaninoff	Floods of spring	HL		DIT

Songs and Arias Employing Staccato

Lyric Tenor

Bemberg	Il neige	H	FS-G	GRU
Dupont	Chanson des noisettes			HEU
Fourdrain	Carnaval	M	C-F	RIC
Handel	Would you gain the tender creature (Acis and Galatea)			†
Hue	L'âne blanc	H	EF-G	HEU
Mozart	Das Veilchen	LMH	F-G	†
Scarlatti, A.	Rugiadose odorose (Il Pirro e Demetrio)	HL	D-E	DIT
Schubert	Der Juengling an der Quelle	LH	E-A	†
Sibella	La Girometta	HML	D-E	GSC

American and British Songs of Popular Appeal

Lyric Tenor

Arden and Wille	Roses in your hair	ML	C-EF	ROW
Balfe	Killarney	H	D-E	GSC
Bassett	Take joy home	LH	EF-BF	GSC
Beach	Ah, love but a day			ASC
Bergen	La marquita			
Bond	Just a wearyin' for you			BOS
-----	Still unexprest	HL	C-C	BOS
Bone and Fenton	Captain Kidd	MH	B-G	CFI
Brahe	Bless this house	HML	A-EF	BOO
Brodsky	Be my love			MLR
Brown	Your song from paradise	LMH	D-G	BOO
Burleigh	Jean	HML		PRE
Cadman	From the land of the sky-blue water			WHI
-----	The builder	HML	B-D	FLA
Campbell-Tipton	A spirit flower	LHM	B-G	GSC
Chanler	I rise when you enter	M	CS-G	GSC
Charles	The house on a hill	LH	D-G	GSC
-----	When I have sung my songs	HM	BF-EF	GSC
Clarke	Shy one	HL	BF-G	BOH
Clay	I'll sing thee songs of Araby	MH	EF-AF	†

566

Coates	Bird songs at eventide	LM		CHA
-----	I heard you singing	LMH	D-AF	CHA
-----	Rise up and reach the stars			CHA
-----	Sea rapture	MH	E-G	CHA
Cowen	Border ballad	LM	D-E	BOO
Crouch	Kathleen Mavourneen	HL	A-E	CFI
Curran	Life	HM	BF-F	GSC
Del Riego	O dry those tears	LMH	E-GS	CHA
De Rose	I heard a forest praying	MH	EF-GF	CHA
D'Hardelot	Because	MH	E-G	CHA
Diack	Sing a song of sixpence			
Dix	The trumpeter	HML	A-C	BOH
Dobson	Dry be that tear	H	EF-BF	GSC
Donaldson	Romance			
Dunn	The bitterness of love			JFI
Eden	What's in the air today	M	D-F	ELK
Edwards	By the bend of the river	HML	C-E	GSC
-----	Into the night	HML	C-DF	GSC
Enders	Russian picnic	HM	C-G	GSC
Forsyth	The bell man			DIT
Foster	Jeanie with the light brown hair	LH	D-G	CFI
-----	My journey's end	HLM	DF-G	GSC
Fox	The hills of home	HML	BF-DF	CFI
Friml	L'amour, toujours l'amour			HAR
Geehl	For you alone			SHU
Glover	Rose of Tralee			
Harmati	Bluebird of happiness			HAR
Head	When I think upon the maidens	LM	D-G	BOO
Henschel	Morning-hymn	MH	DS-GS	†
Herbert	La espanola			
Ireland	Sea fever	HLM	D-F	AUG
La Forge	Song of the open	MH	EF-AF	DIT
-----	To a messenger	HLM	CF-G	GSC
Lehmann	Ah, moon of my delight			BOS
Leoni	Tally-ho!	LH	E-F	GSC
Levitzki	Ah, thou beloved one	H	EF-AF	GSC
-----	Do you remember?	HML	BF-EF	GSC
Lohr	The little Irish girl	HLM	C-E	CHA
MacGimsey	To my mother	HML	C-C	CFI
Mac Murraugh	Macushla			BOO
Malotte	Blow me eyes	MH	C-G	GSC
-----	For my mother	HLM	BF-EF	GSC
Manz-Zucca	I love life	LM	F-F	PRE
-----	The big brown bear	HML	C-F	GSC
Manning	In the Luxembourg gardens	HML	BF-D	GSC

567

(Manning)	Shoes	M	EF-F	GSC
Margetson	Tommy, lad	HML	A-D	BOH
Marshall	I hear you calling me	LMH	G-A	BOO
McGill	Duna	HML	BF-D	BOO
Molloy	The Kerry Dance	LH	C-G	GSC
Moya	The song of songs	LM	D-F	CHA
Murray	She shall have music	M	A-G	CHA
Nevin	Little boy blue			BOS
-----	Mighty lak' a rose			JCH
Olcott	Mother Machree	LMH	F-A	WIT
Posford	The world is mine tonight			FOX
Rasbach	Trees	LMH	CS-GS	GSC
Rickett	Diaphenia	M	C-F	GSC
Roeckel	The green isle of Erin			
Rogers	At parting	LH	CS-FS	GSC
-----	The star	LH	C-AF	GSC
Ronald	Down in the forest	HML	C-D	ENO
-----	Drift down, drift down			BOO
-----	Prelude	HML	B-D	ENO
Rose	Our waltz			CNN
Russell	Fulfillment	LH	EF-GF	BOS
-----	Where the river Shannon flows	HML	C-D	WIT
Sacco	Brother Will, Brother John	M	C-F	GSC
Sanderson	Friend o' mine	HHM		BOO
-----	Shipmates of mine	LL	G-D	BOO
-----	Susan is her name	LM	D-E	BOH
-----	Until	LMH	E-A	BOO
Scott	Think on me	HML	D-EF	GAL
Silesu	A little love, a little kiss	LMH		CHA
Skiles	You will know my love			CFI
Speaks	In May time	HL	D-E	JCH
-----	Morning	HML	BF-D	GSC
-----	Sylvia	HML	AF-DF	GSC
Spross	Let all my life be music			JCH
Strelezki	Dreams	LMH	B-A	GSC
Sullivan	The lost chord	HL	C-F	GSC
Taylor	A song for lovers	MH	D-F	JFI
Torrence	Smilin Kitty O'Day	ML	CS-D	BOO
Tours	Mother o' mine	HML	C-D	CHA
Tyson	Noon and night	LH	F-AF	GSC
Warren	Fulfilment	H	D-BF	GAL
-----	If you have forgotten	LH	GF-GF	GSC
Weaver	Dream dawn			GAL
Westendorf	I'll take you home again Kathleen			EAS
Wilson	My lovely Celia	HL	B-E	BOO
Wolf	Iris	LMH	F-BF	FLA

Wolfe	Short'nin' bread	LHM	D-D	FLA
-----	Sugar-plum	L	CS-E	GSC
-----	Who's gonna mourn for me	LMH	D-A	ROB
Wood	A brown bird singing	HLM	FS-G	CHA
-----	Do you know my garden	MH	EF-G	CHA
-----	I look into your garden	LMH	F-AF	CHA
-----	Roses of Picardy	HML		CHA
Woodford-Finden	Kashmiri song			BOO

(See also Humorous Songs, Negro Spirituals,
Folk Songs, Operetta Songs and Opera Arias.)

Miscellaneous Songs of
Popular Appeal

Lyric Tenor

Alvarez	La partida	HL	DS-E	GSC
Bach-Gounod	Ave Maria			†
Behrend	Bonjour ma belle	LMH	E-FS	DIT
Benatsky	Ich muss wieder einmal in Grinzing sein			AMP
Bixio	Torno, picina			
Bizet	Agnus Dei	HLM	C-AF	†
-----	Chanson d'avril	H	BF-G	†
Braga	Angel's serenade	LH	D-G	†
Buzzi-Peccia	Lolita			RIC
-----	Povero pulcinella	H	E-A	GSC
Cardillo	Core'ngrato			RIC
Cavalli	Donzelle fuggite	HL	C-EF	†
Cottrau	Addio a Napoli	M	C-F	GSC
-----	Santa Lucia			
Crescenzo	Rondine al nido	HM	DS-FS	CAR
De Curtis	Non ti scordar di me			
-----	Senza nisciuno			
-----	Torna al Surriento	HM	D-F	CFI
De Koven	Recessional			
Denza	Funiculi, funicula			†
-----	Occhi turchini	LMH		RIC
D'Esposito	Anima e core			
Dicapua	Maria, mari			
-----	O sole mio			BOS
Donaudy	O del mio amato ben	M	EF-F	RIC
Dvořák	Songs my mother taught me	HM	E-E	†
Falvo	Dicitencello vuje			
Franz	Dedication	HML	BF-C	†

569

Freire	Ay, ay, ay	LH		RIC
Gastaldon	Musica proibita	MH	E-A	GSC
Gounod	Au printemps	LMH	DF-A	GSC
-----	Sérénade	LMH	D-A	GSC
Grieg	A dream			†
-----	I love thee	HML	E-F	†
Kreuder	Immer und ewig			
Lara	Granada			SOU
Lecuona	Siboney			FEI
Lehar	Ma rose blanche			
-----	Only my song			CHA
Leoncavallo	Mattinata	MLH	C-AF	†
Leroux	Le nil	LH	E-A	†
Massenet	Elégie	LM	C-GF	GSC
-----	Ouvre tes yeux bleus	MH	C-G	†
Mattei	Non é ver	HML		DIT
Mendelssohn	On wings of song			†
Merikanto	A fairy story by the fire	HML		JFI
Nutile	Mamma mia che vo' sape?			
Rabey	Tes yeux	H	EF-G	DUR
Rachmaninoff	To the children	MH	F-G	DIT
Rimsky- Korsakov	The nightingale and the rose	H	FS-FS	DIT
Rossini	La danza	MH	E-A	†
Rubinstein	Since first I met thee	H	D-G	DIT
Sadero	Amuri, Amuri	M		CHE
Schubert	An die Musik	HL	A-DS	†
-----	Ave Maria	LMH	F-F	†
-----	Hark! hark! the lark	LMH	F-G	†
-----	Staendchen			
Schumann	Widmung	HL	BF-F	†
Sibella	La Girometta	HML	D-E	GSC
Sieczynski	Vienna, city of my dreams			HAR
Sjoeberg	Visions	MH	F-AF	GAL
Stolz	Du solsst der Kaiser meiner Seele sein			DRE
-----	Im Prater blueh'n die Baeume			
Strauss, J.	Blue Danube waltz			GSC
-----	Tales from the Vienna forest	H	EF-C	GSC
-----	Wein, Weib und Gesang			
-----	Wiener Blut			
Tchaikovsky	None but the lonely heart	HLM	C-F	DIT
Tosti	À vucchella	LH	F-G	RIC
-----	Ideale			GSC
-----	L'alba separa dalla luce l'ombra			HEU
-----	Marechiare	M	D-FS	GSC

(Tosti)	The last song	HL		RIC
Weill	Da draussen in der Wachau			
Yradier	La paloma	HL	BF-EF	GSC

(See also Humorous Songs, Negro Spirituals,
Folk Songs, Operetta Songs and Opera Arias.)

Arias From British Operas

Lyric Tenor

Arne, T.	Preach not me your musty rules (Comus)	HML		ROW
Balfe	Then you'll remember me (The Bohemian Girl)	M	E-F	†
Handel	Massimo's air (Ezio)			
-----	Say to Irene (Atalanta)	H	D-AF	CFI
-----	Silent worship (Tolomeo)	LM	D-E	CUR
Purcell	Fairest isle (King Arthur)			NOV
-----	Hark! the echoing air (The Fairy Queen)			BAF
-----	I attempt from love's sickness to fly (The Indian Queen)	MH	CS-E	†
-----	Music for a while (Oedipus)	LH		SC
-----	Sweeter than roses (Pausanias)			SC
Stanford	Tell me ye flowerates (Veiled Pilgrim)			

Arias From French Operas

Lyric Tenor

Berlioz	Inutiles regrets (Les Troyens à Carthage)	MH	E-C	CHO
-----	Merci, doux crepuscule (La Damnation de Faust)			NOV
-----	Nature immense (La Damnation de Faust)			NOV
Bizet	De mon amie fleur endormie (Les Pêcheurs des Perles)			CHO
-----	Flower song (Carmen)	H	E-BF	†
-----	Je crois entendre encore (Les Pêcheurs des Perles)	H	D-A	GSC

Delibes	Fantaisie aux divins mensonges Lakmé			BRO
Gluck	Bannis la crainte (Alceste)			†
-----	S'il était vrai (Iphigénie en Aulide)			†
-----	Unis dès la plus tendre enfance (Iphigénie en Aulide)			NOV
Godard	Cachés dans cet asile (Jocelyn) Violin or cello	MH	DF-F	GSC
Gounod	Ah! lève-toi, soleil! (Roméo et Juliette)	H	F-BF	†
-----	Prête-moi ton aide (La Reine de Saba)	H		JCH
-----	Salut! demeure chaste et pure (Faust)	H	EF-C	†
Halévy	Dieu que ma voix tremblante (La Juive)			
-----	O Dieu, Dieu de nos pères (La Juive)			
-----	Rachel, quand du' Seigneur (La Juive)	H	EF-BF	CFI
Lalo	Aubade (Le Roi d'Ys)			†
Lully	Air de Sangaride (Atys)	M		ROU
-----	Air du grand prêtre (Persée)	M	E-E	ROU
-----	Bois épais (Amadis)	ML	C-EF	†
-----	Plus j'observe ces lieux (Armide)			LEM
Massenet	Ah! fuyez, douce image (Manon)	H	F-BF	GSC
-----	J'aurais sur ma poitrine (Werther)			HEU
-----	Je ne sais si je veille (Werther)			HEU
-----	Le rêve de des Grieux (Manon)	H	E-A	†
-----	O souverain! ô juge! ô père! (Le Cid)			HEU
-----	Pourquoi me reveiller (Werther)	H	FS-AS	HEU
Mehul	A peine sortir (Joseph)			
-----	Versez tous vos chagrins (Stratonice)			LEM
Messager	La maison grise (Fortuno)			CHO
Meyerbeer	O paradis (L'Africaine)	H	F-BF	†
Rameau	A l'amour rendez les armes (Hippolyte et Aricie)			CHO
-----	Dans ces doux asiles (Castor et Pollux)			LEM

(Rameau)	Tristes apprêts (Castor et Pollux)			CHE
Reyer	Esprits gardiens (Sigurd)			HEU
Rousseau	Je vais revoir ma charmante maîtresse (Le Devin du Village)			CHE
Thomas	Adieu! Mignon (Mignon)	H	F-A	HEU
-----	Elle ne croyait pas (Mignon)	H	G-A	†

Arias From German Operas

Lyric Tenor

Lortzing	Vater, Mutter, Schwestern, H Brueder (Undine)		SC
Mozart	Alles fuehlt der Liebe Freuden (Die Zauberfloete)		†
-----	Constanze, dich wieder zu sehen (Abduction from Seraglio)		
-----	Dies Bildnis ist bezaubernd schoen (Die Zauberfloete)		†
-----	Hier soll ich dich denn sehen (Abduction from Seraglio)		†
-----	Im Mohrenland (Abduction from Seraglio)		†
-----	O wie aengstlich, o wie feurig (Abduction from Seraglio)		†
-----	Wie stark ist nicht dein Zauberton (Die Zauberfloete)		†
Strauss	Arie des Saengers (Der Rosenkavalier)		BOO
Wagner	Atmest du nicht mit mir die suessen Duefte (Lohengrin)		GSC
-----	In fernem Land (Lohengrin) H	E-A	†
-----	Mein Lieber Schwan (Lohengrin)		†
Weber	Jetzt ist wohl ihr Fenster offen (Der Freischuetz)		GSC

Arias From Italian Operas

Lyric Tenor

Bellini	A te o cara amor talora (I Puritani)			RIC
-----	Meco all'altar di venere	H	D-C	RIC
	(Norma)			

(Bellini)	Vieni fra queste braccia (I Puritani)			RIC
Boito	Dai campi, dai prati (Mefistofele)			RIC
-----	Giunto, sul passo estremo (Epilogue) (Mefistofele)			RIC
Cilea	E la solita storia (Lamento di Federico) (L'Arlesiana)			
-----	La dolcissima effigie (Adriana Lecouvreur)	H		AMP
-----	L'Anima ho stanca (Adriana Lecouvreur)	H		AMP
Donizetti	Com'è gentil (Don Pasquale)			RIC
-----	Quanto è bella (L'Elisir d'Amore)			BRO
-----	Sogno soave e casto (Don Pasquale)			BRO
-----	Spirto gentil (La Favorita)	H	G-C	†
-----	Tombe degl' avi miei (Lucia di Lammermoor)	H	F-BF	BRO
-----	Una furtiva lagrima (L'Elisir d'Amore)	H	F-AF	†
-----	Una vergine, un angiol (La Favorita)	H	E-C	BRO
Flotow	M'apparì (Martha)	HLM	EF-AF	†
Giordano	Amor ti vieta (Fedora)	H		AMP
-----	Come un bel di (Andrea Chenier)	H	E-BF	AMP
---.-	Mia madre, la mia vecchia madre (Fedora)			BRO
-----	Un di all'azzurro spazio (Andrea Chenier)	H	F-BF	SON
-----	Vedi, io piango (Fedora)			SON
Leoncavallo	Harlequin's serenade (I Pagliacci)	H	E-A	CFI
-----	Testa adorata (La Boheme)			SON
-----	Vesti la giubba (I Pagliacci)	H	D-A	†
Mascagni	Addio alla madre (Cavalleria Rusticana)			GSC
-----	Apri la tua finestra (Iris)			RIC
-----	Ed anche Beppe amo (L'Amico Fritz)			JCH
-----	O amore, o bella luce (L'Amico Fritz)			GSC
-----	Siciliana (O Lola) (Cavalleria Rusticana)	H	AF-AF	†

Monteverdi	Ahi, troppo è duro (Il Balletto delle Ingrate)	HL	C-EF	DIT
-----	Lasciatemi morire (Arianna)	ML	D-D	†
Mozart	Dalla sua pace (Don Giovanni)	H	D-G	†
-----	Il mio tesoro (Don Giovanni)	H	D-A	GSC
-----	Un aura amorosa (Così Fan Tutte)			†
Pietri	Io conosco un giardino (Maristella)			
Ponchielli	Cielo e mar (La Gioconda)	H	D-BF	†
Puccini	Ah Manon, mi tradisce (Manon Lescaut)	H	E-BF	RIC
-----	Amore o grillo (Madama Butterfly)	H	F-BF	RIC
-----	Che gelida manina (La Boheme)	H	F-C	RIC
-----	Ch'ella mi creda libero (La Fanciulla del West)			RIC
-----	Donna non vidi mai (Manon Lescaut)	H	E-BF	RIC
-----	E lucevan le stelle (Tosca)	H	FS-A	RIC
-----	Firenze è come un albero fiorito (Gianni Schicchi)			RIC
-----	Guardate, pazzo son, guardate (Manon Lescaut)			RIC
-----	Nessun dorma (Turandot)			RIC
-----	Non piangere, Liù (Turandot)			RIC
-----	Or son sei mesi (La Fanciulla del West)			RIC
-----	Recondita armonia (Tosca)	H	E-BF	RIC
-----	Torna ai felici dì (Le Villi)			RIC
-----	Tra voi belle (Manon Lescaut)			RIC
Rossini	Ecco ridente in cielo (Il Barbiere di Siviglia)	H	FS-B	†
-----	O muto asil del pianto (La Cenerentola)			
-----	Se il mio nome (Il Barbiere di Siviglia)	H	GS-B	†
Verdi	Ah! si, ben mio coll'essere (Il trovatore)	H	F-AF	†
-----	Dal labbro il canto (Falstaff)	H	DS-AF	RIC

(Verdi)	De'miei bollenti spiriti (La Traviata)	H	F-AF	†
-----	Di tu se fedele (Un Ballo in Maschera)			RIC
-----	Giorno di pianto (I Vespri Siciliani)			RIC
-----	La donna è mobile (Rigoletto)	LMH	FS-AS	†
-----	La mia letizia infondere (I Lombardi)	H		RIC
-----	O, tu che in seno agli angeli (La Forza del Destino)	H	DF-BF	RIC
-----	Parmi veder le lagrime (Rigoletto)	H	F-AF	GSC
-----	Quando le sere al placido (Luisa Miller)			RIC
-----	Questa o quella (Rigoletto)	H	EF-AF	†
Wolf-Ferrari	Lucieta è un bel nome (I Quattro Rusteghi)			

Miscellaneous Opera Arias

Lyric Tenor

Borodin	Vladimir's cavatina (Prince Igor)			BES
Dvořák	Dimitrij's aria (Dimitrij)			
Gershwin	Where is my Bess? (Porgy and Bess)			BRO
Granados	Descubrase el pensamiento (Goyescas)			GSC
-----	The maja and the nightingale (Goyescas)	H	BS-A	GSC
Hartmann	Sverkel's romance (Liden Kirsten)			
Parker	In a garden (Fairyland)			GSC
Rachmaninoff	Romance of the young gypsy (Aleko)	H		AMP
Rimsky-Korsakov	Forest song (Sadko)			BRO
-----	Levko's song (May Night)			
-----	Lykow's aria (The Tsar's Bride)			
-----	Song of India (Sadko)	LH	D-G	GSC
Smetana	How is it possible? (The Bartered Bride)			BOO

(Smetana)	Ma-ma-mama so dear (The Bartered Bride)			BOO
Tchaikovsky	Forgive me bright celestial visions (Pique Dame)			GSC
-----	Lenski's aria (Eugene Onegin)			GSC

Arias From Oratorios and Latin Works

Lyric Tenor

Bach, J.S.	Ah, my soul (St. John Passion)			
-----	Benedictus (Mass in B Minor) Violin			†
-----	Haste ye shepherds (Christmas Oratorio)			
-----	'Tis thee I would be praising (Christmas Oratorio)			
-----	Ye foes of man (Christmas Oratorio)			
Beethoven	In my soul dread thoughts awaken (Mount of Olives)	H	E-A	†
Berlioz	Le repos de la Ste. Famille (L'Enfance du Christ)	MH		CST
Dvořák	O guide me in the way (Saint Ludmila)			NOV
Gaul	My soul is athirst for God (The Holy City)			
Handel	Ask if yon damask rose (Susanna)			†
-----	Comfort ye (The Messiah)	H	E-GS	†
-----	Evr'y valley (The Messiah)			†
-----	How vain is man . (Judas Maccabaeus)			†
-----	Jehovah (Occasional Oratorio)			
-----	Let me wander not unseen (L'Allegro)	M	D-G	†
-----	Love in her eyes sits playing (Acis and Galatea)			†
-----	Love sounds th' alarm (Acis and Galatea)			NOV
-----	O King of Kings (Esther)	H		CHE
-----	O sleep why dost thou leave me (Semele)	H	DS-GS	†
-----	Round about the fairy ring (Triumph of Time and Truth)			
-----	Sacred raptures cheer my breast (Solomon)	H	D-A	NOV

(Handel)	Sound an alarm!	H		†
	(Judas Maccabaeus)			
-----	The enemy said	H	D-A	NOV
	(Israel in Egypt)			
-----	Thou shalt dash them	H		†
	(The Messiah)			
-----	Thus when the sun	H	D-G	†
	(Samson)			
-----	Total eclipse (Samson)			†
-----	Waft her, angels	H	D-A	†
	(Jephtha)			
-----	War is naught but toil and			†
	trouble (Alexander's Feast)			
-----	What though I trace each		CS-E	†
	herb and flower (Solomon)			
-----	Wher'er you walk (Semele) HML		C-D	†
-----	Why does the God of			†
	Israel sleep (Samson)			
-----	Would you gain the tender			†
	creature (Acis and Galatea)			
-----	Ye verdant hills (Susanna)			
Haydn	In native worth (The	H	F-A	†
	Creation)			
-----	The trav'ler stands	H	E-A	†
	perplexed (The Seasons)			
Honegger	In the Lord I put my faith			
	(King David)			
Mendelssohn	Be thou faithful unto death MH		D-G	†
	(Saint Paul)			
-----	He counteth all your sorrows H		D-G	†
	(Hymn of Praise)			
-----	If with all your hearts	MH	F-AF	†
	(Elijah)			
-----	Then shall the righteous	H	EF-AF	†
	shine forth (Elijah)			
-----	The sorrows of death			†
	(Hymn of Praise)			
Parker	Golden Jerusalem			NOV
	(Hora Novissima)			
Rossini	Cujus animam	M	EF-DF	DIT
	(Stabat Mater)			
Saint-Saëns	Domine ego credidi			GSC
	(Christmas Oratorio)			
Verdi	Ingemisco (The Requiem)			GSC

Lyric Tenor

Bach, J.S.	Ach, ziehe die Seele (Cantata 96) Flute			
-----	Dein Blut, so meine Schuld durchstreicht (Cantata 78) Flute			BRO
-----	Die Liebe zieht mit sanften Schritten (Cantata 36) Oboe d'amore			
-----	Erbarme dich (Cantata 55) Flute			
-----	Ergiesse dich reichlich, du goettliche Quelle (Cantata 5) Viola			
-----	Erschuettre dich nur nicht (Cantata 99) Flute or violin			
-----	Es duenket mich, ich seh Dich kommen (Cantata 175) Cello			
-----	Geliebter Jesu (Cantata 16) English horn or viola			
-----	Gott ist mein Freund (Cantata 139) Violin			
-----	Handle nicht nach deinen Rechten (Cantata 101) Violin			
-----	Ich traue seiner Gnaden (Cantata 97) Violin			PET
-----	Ich will an den Himmel denken (Cantata 166) Oboe			
-----	Ja, tausendmal (Cantata 43) Violin			NOV
-----	Man halte nur ein wenig stille (Cantata 93)			NOV
-----	Mich kann kein Zweifel stoeren (Cantata 108) Violin			
-----	Nimm mich Dir zu eigen hin (Cantata 65)			NOV
-----	O Seelen Paradies (Cantata 172) Violin or viola			AUG
-----	Only be still (Cantata 93) 2 Violins, viola and cello			NOV
-----	Pan is master (Phoebus and Pan)			NOV
-----	Seht! was die Liebe tut (Cantata 85) Violin			
-----	Sheep may safely graze (Cantata 208) 2 Flutes and continuo	LM	EF-GF	GAL

(Bach, J.S.)	Tausendfaches Unglueck schrecken (Cantata 143) Violin			
, -----	Wir waren schon zu tief gesunken (Cantata 9) Violin			RIC
-----	Wo wird in diesem Jammertale (Cantata 114) Flute			
-----	Woferne du den edlen Frieden (Cantata 41) Cello			RIC
Debussy	Air d'Azaël (L'Enfant Prodigue)	H	C-A	GSC
Handel	Have mercy, Lord (Te Deum)	HM		†
Medtner	Serenade for voice and orchestra			
Mendelssohn	O come let us worship 95 Psalm			
Rameau	Air gai (L'Impatience)			DUR
-----	Quand le silence (Air Tendre) (Diane et Acteon)			
Scarlatti, D.	Tuo mi chiami (Tinto a Note di Sangue)			OXF

Operetta, Musical Comedy or Show Songs

Lyric Tenor

Berlin	A pretty girl is like a melody (Ziegfeld Follies 1919)			BER
Brodsky	I'll never love you (The Toast of New Orleans)			ROB
Caryll	Goodbye girls, I'm through (Chin Chin)			CHA
Coslow	Sing you sinners (Honey)			FAM
Coward	If you could only come with me (Bitter Sweet)			HAR
De Koven	Oh promise me (Robin Hood)	HML	C-D	†
Forrest-Grieg	Strange music (Song of Norway)			CHA
Friml	Donkey serenade (The Firefly)			WIT
-----	Giannina mia (The Firefly)			GSC
-----	Give me one hour (The White Eagle)			MRT
-----	Love me tonight (The Vagabond King)			FAM
-----	Only a rose (The Vagabond King)			GSC

580

(Friml)	Rose Marie (Rose Marie) M		EF–G	HAR
-----	The bubble (High Jinks)			GSC
Henderson	The thrill is gone (Scandals of 1931)			CRF
Herbert	Ah! sweet mystery of life LMH (Naughty Marietta)		A–A	WIT
-----	Eileen Alanna Asthore (Eileen)			WIT
-----	Gypsy love song LHM (The Fortune Teller)		C–E	WIT
-----	I'm falling in love with someone (Naughty Marietta)			WIT
-----	Isle of our dreams (The Red Mill)			WIT
-----	Life and love (The Velvet Lady)			WIT
-----	Love is like a cigarette (The Rose of Algeria)			WIT
-----	Moonbeams (The Red Mill)			WIT
-----	Neapolitan love song (Princess Pat)			WIT
-----	Personality (The Only Girl)			WIT
-----	Pretty as a picture (Sweethearts)			GSC
-----	Star of love (The Madcap Duchess)			GSC
-----	The rose of Algeria (The Rose of Algeria)			WIT
-----	The springtime of life (The Debutante)			GSC
-----	The time and the place and the girl (Mlle. Modiste)			WIT
-----	Thine alone (Eileen)			WIT
-----	When shall I again see Ireland (Eileen)			WIT
-----	When you're away (The Only Girl)			WIT
-----	Ze English language (Mlle. Modiste)			WIT
Herold	Ce soir, j'arrive donc (Le Pré aux Clercs)			BRA
Kalman	Gruess' mir mein Wien (Graefin Mariza)			BRO
-----	Komm, Zigany (Graefin Mariza)			BRO
-----	Love's own sweet song (Sari)			MAR
-----	Play gipsies, dance gipsies (Graefin Mariza)			HAR
-----	Zwei Maerchenaugen (Zirkusprinzessen)			
Kern	Make believe (Show Boat) M		CS–FS	HAR

(Kern)	Smoke gets in your eyes (Roberta)			HAR
-----	The night was made for love (The Cat and the Fiddle)	M	C-F	HAR
-----	The song is you (Music in the Air)	M	C-F	HAR
-----	The way you look tonight (Swing Time)			CHA
-----	They didn't believe me (Girl from Utah)			HAR
-----	Why do I love you (Show Boat)	M	C-F	HAR
-----	You're devastating (Roberta)			HAR
Korngold	Du bist mein Traum (Das Lied der Liebe)			SC
Kreisler	Stars in my eyes (The King Steps Out)			CHA
Kunnecke	Ich bin nur ein armer Wandergeselle (Der Vetter aus Dingsda)			
Lehar	Du bist meine Sonne (Giuditta)			CHA
-----	Fear nothing (Paganini)			SCH
-----	Freunde, das Leben ist lebenswert (Giuditta)			GLO
-----	Gern hab' ich die Frau'n gekuesst (Paganini)			GLO
-----	Girls, girls (The Merry Widow)			BRO
-----	Hab' ein blaues Himmelbett (Frasquita)			
-----	I love you so (The Merry Widow)			CHA
-----	Ich bin ein Zigeunerkind (Gypsy Love)			BRO
-----	Immer nur laecheln (The Land of Smiles)			GLO
-----	Lied und Czardas (Gypsy Love)			BRO
-----	Lippen Schweigen (The Merry Widow)	LMH	D-A	CHA
-----	Love is like a breeze in May (Paganini)			SAL
-----	Maxim's (The Merry Widow)			CHA
-----	O Maedchen, mein Maedchen (Friederike)			GLO
-----	Polenlied (The Blue Mazurka)			GLO
-----	Sah ein Knab ein Roeslein steh'n (Friederike)			SAL
-----	Schoenste der Frauen (Giuditta)			CHA

(Lehar)	Sieh dort den kleinen pavillon (The Merry Widow)			GLO
-----	So wie um den Sonnenball (Giuditta)			GLO
-----	Volgalied (Zarewitsch)			GLO
-----	Von Apfelblueten einen Kranz (The Land of Smiles)			GLO
-----	Was ich laengst ertraeumte (Goettergatte)			GLO
-----	Yours is my heart alone (The Land of Smiles)			HAR
-----	Zorika, Zorika (Gypsy Love)			BRO
Milloecker	Dunkelrote Rosen bring' ich (Mme. Dubarry)			CHA
-----	Glueckswalzer (Gasparone)			
-----	If I am dreaming (Mme. Dubarry)			CHA
-----	O wenn ich doch der Raeuber waer' (Gasparone)			
Porter	Begin the Beguine	L	BF-F	HAR
	(Jubilee)			
-----	Easy to love (Born to Dance)			CHA
-----	I love you (Mexican Hayride)			CHA
-----	In the still of the night (Rosalie)			CHA
-----	I've got you under my skin (Born to Dance)			CHA
-----	Night and day	M	BF-EF	HAR
	(Gay Divorcee)			
-----	Rosalie (Rosalie)			CHA
-----	Use your imagination (Out of This World)			CHA
-----	Were thine that special face (Kiss Me Kate)			CHA
-----	What is this thing called love (Wake Up and Dream)			HAR
-----	Why shouldn't I? (Jubilee)			HAR
Rodgers	Falling in love with love (The Boys from Syracuse)			WIL
-----	If I loved you (Carousel)			WIL
-----	It's a grand night for singing (State Fair)			CHA
-----	June is bustin' out all over (Carousel)			WIL
-----	My romance (Jumbo)			CHA
-----	Soliloquy (Carousel)			CHA
-----	That's for me (State Fair)			CHA

583

(Rodgers)	This nearly was mine (South Pacific)			WIL
-----	Who are you (The Boys from Syracuse)			CHA
-----	With a song in my heart (Spring is Here)			HAR
-----	Younger than springtime (South Pacific)			WIL
Romberg	One alone (The Desert Song)			HAR
-----	Serenade (The Student Prince)			HAR
-----	Softly as in a morning sunrise (New Moon)			BRO
-----	The Riff song (The Desert Song)	L	D-G	HAR
-----	When I grow too old to dream (The Night is Young)	HLM	C-G	ROB
-----	Who are we to say? (Girl of the Golden West)	M		FEI
-----	You will remember Vienna (Viennese Nights)			HAR
Schwartz	I love Louisa (The Band Wagon)			HAR
-----	You and the night and the music (Revenge with Music)			HAR
Spoliensky	Tell me tonight (Tell Me Tonight)			HAR
Straus	Da draussen im duftenden Garden (A Waltz Dream)			BRO
Strauss, J.	Adieu, mein kleiner Gardeoffizier (White Horse Inn)			
-----	Als flotter Geist, doch frueh verwaist (The Gypsy Baron)			CRZ
-----	Du Maerchenstadt im Donautal (Spitzentuch der Koenigin)			
-----	Komm in die Gondel (Eine Nacht in Venedig)	H		
-----	Open road, open sky (The gypsy Baron)			GSC
-----	Sei mir gegruesst, du holdes Venetia (Eine Nacht in Vendig)			
-----	Southern roses (Spitzentuch der Koenigin)			
-----	Sweetheart waltz (The Gypsy Baron)			CRZ
-----	Treu sein, das liegt mir nicht (Eine Nacht in Vendig)			
Styne	I'll walk alone (Follow the Boys)			MAY
Sullivan	A wand'ring minstrel I (The Mikado)			

(Sullivan)	Take a pair of sparkling eyes (The Gondoliers)			GSC
Suppe	Hab' ich nur deine Liebe (Boccaccio)			
Tierney	Rio Rita (Rio Rita)	M	C-F	FEI
Youmans	Great Day (Great Day)	M	EF-F	MLR
-----	More than you know (Great Day)	M	D-EF	MLR
-----	Through the years (Through the Years)	HML	A-F	MLR
-----	Without a song (Great Day)	HLM	BF-F	MLR
Zeller	Sei nicht boes! (Der Obersteiger)			

Song Cycles (Or Groups of Songs)

Lyric Tenor

Beethoven	An die ferne Geliebte	HL	C-E	†
-----	Irish songs Piano, violin and cello			
-----	Scotch songs Piano, violin and cello			
Bergsma	Six songs	H	E-BF	CFI
Berlioz	Les nuits d'été			AUG
Bliss	Lovelocks			GOT
Brahms	Romanzen aus Magelone			†
Breville	Prières d'enfant	M	D-F	ROU
Britten	Serenade Horn and string orchestra	H		BOO
-----	Seven sonnets of Michelangelo	H		BOH
-----	The holy sonnets of John Donne	H		BOO
Caplet	Les prières			DUR
Chanler	Epitaphs			ARR
Cornelius	Six Christmas songs	HL		BOS
Debussy	Ariettes oubliées	HL		†
-----	Fêtes galantes	LH	CS-A	†
-----	Proses lyriques	HL		JOB
Fauré	La bonne chanson	HL		INT
-----	Les mélodies de Venise			HAM
-----	Poème d'un jour			HAM
Finzi	A young man's exhortation (10 songs)			OXF
Hahn	Songs in gray	M		BOS
Manning	Sketches of Paris	HL	C-E	GSC
Milhaud	Les soirées de Pétrograde			DUR

585

Osma	Cantares de mi tierra	H	D-G	BOS
Rasi	Three madrigals for solo voice			
Ravel	Chansons Madécasses Flute, cello and piano			DUR
-----	Don Quichotte à Dulcinée	HM	A-F	DUR
Schubert	Die schoene Muellerin	HL		†
-----	Die Winterreise			†
Schumann	Dichterliebe			†
-----	Liederkreis			
Slonimsky	Gravestones at Hancock, New Hampshire	H	D-G	AXE
Smetana	First songs			

Vaughan
  Williams
	On Wenlock edge
	  String quartet and piano
				BOO

Watts	Vignettes of Italy			DIT

Solo Cantatas

Lyric Tenor

Bach, J.S.	Ich armer Mensch (Cantata 55)	DIT

-----	Meine Seele ruehmt und preist
	  (Cantata 189) Flute, oboe and
	  violin	

Handel	Look down, harmonious Saint Harpsichord and orchestra	

(See Solo Cantatas of Pergolesi, Handel and
Scarlatti, Kirchenkantaten of Buxtehude and
Symphoniae Sacrae of Schuetz.)

Concert Arias

Lyric Tenor

Mozart	Ah, più tremar non voglio			
-----	Clarice cora mia sposa			
-----	Con ossequio, con rispetto			
-----	Misero! o sogno	H	EF-AF	BOO
-----	Muesst ich, auch durch tausend Drachen			
-----	Per pieta, non ricercate			BOO
-----	Se al labbro mio non credi			
-----	Si mostra la sorte			
-----	Tali e cotanti sono			

Va, dal furor portata

Christmas Songs

Lyric Tenor

Adam	O Holy Night			
Attey	Sweet was the song			BOO
Bach, J.S.	Haste ye shepherds (Christmas Oratorio)			
Bax	A Christmas carol	H	DF-A	CHE
Benjamin	Before dawn			CUR
Berlioz	Le repos de la Ste. Famille (L'Enfance du Christ)	MH		CST
Black	In the sky a wondrous star	H	DF-AF	GRA
Bornschein	Babe of Bethlehem	H	EF-G	CFI
Busser	La salutation angélique	HM		DUR
Chaminade	Christmas carol of the birds	MH	D-A	GSC
Cottone	Ninna, nanna	H	FS-A	MCR
De Koven	The white Christ	L	C-D	GSC
Dickinson	The shepherds' story	H		GRA
Dunhill	To the Queen of Heaven	M	C-G	GSC
Elmore and Reed	Come all ye who weary	L	C-C	JFI
Fauré	Noël	LH	EF-AF	GSC
Franck	L'ange et l'enfant			HAM
Harker	A child is born in Bethlehem	LH	D-G	GSC
Head	Small Christmas tree	H	F-AF	BOO
-----	The little road to Bethlehem	MH	EF-AF	BOO
-----	The robin's carol	H	C-AF	BOH
-----	The three mummers			BOO
Jewell	The vision of the shepherds	HL	A-D	ASC
Kaull	Unto you is born a Savior	MH	D-AF	BOS
Lynn	The magic night of Christmas	M	D-D	DIT
Martin	The Holy Child	HML	G-G	ENO
Mc Kinney	The Holy Mother sings	MH	AF-AF	JFI
Neidlinger	The birthday of a king	LMH	C-F	GSC
-----	The manger cradle	L	EF-F	GSC
Niles	See Jesus the Savior			GSC
Reimann	Joseph tender, Joseph mine	M	F-F	GRA

Saint-Saëns	Domine ego credidi (Christmas Oratorio)			GSC
Schubert	They sang that night in Bethlehem	LMH	EF-EF	GSC
Strauss	Die heiligen drei Koenige	H	C-G	
Thorp	Come, Mary, take courage	M	DS-FS	GAL
Warlock	The first mercy	M	F-F	BOO
West	It came upon a midnight	MM	E-FS	SUM
Wolf	Schlafendes Jesuskind	HL	AS-F	

Easter Songs

Lyric Tenor

Bantock	Easter hymn	M	FS-F	CHE
Chaffin	Easter message	MH	D-G	FLA
Curran	Crucifixion			
Dennee	Easter song	HM	B-F	ASC
Gore	O sing unto the Lord a new song	H		JFI
Granier	Hosanna	HH	F-BF	DIT
Guion	At the cry of the first bird	H	D-G	GSC
Hageman	Christ went up into the hills	LH	EF-AF	CFI
Huhn	Christ is risen	HM	C-E	ASC
Lekberg	A ballad of trees and the Master	H	E-A	GAL
Mac Gimsey	I was there when they crucified my Lord	HL		CFI
Parker	Golden Jerusalem (Hora Novissima)			NOV
Rachmaninoff	Christ is risen	LM	D-F	GAL
Schubert	Ave Maria	LMH	F-F	†
Scott	Angels roll the rock away	MH	E-G	HUN
-----	The first Easter morn	LH	F-G	GSC
Stainer	My hope is in the everlasting (The Daughter of Jairus)			
Tchaikovsky	A legend	M	D-E	GSC
Wolf	Herr, was traegt der Boden	HL	B-DS	†
Yon	Christ Triumphant	MH	E-A	JFI
-----	O faithful Cross	HM	C-EF	JFI
-----	Our Paschal Joy	LH	AF-AF	JFI

Patriotic Songs

Lyric Tenor

Alberti	A nation's prayer	H		ELV
Cadman	Glory	H	EF-G	GAL
De Koven	Recessional			
Dix	The trumpeter	HML	A-C	BOH
Dungan	Eternal life	HL		PRE
Foster, F.	The Americans come	MH	F-BF	JFI
Hower	To the unknown soldier	H	D-G	GSC
Lester	Greater love hath no man	LH	B-E	CFI
O'Hara	There is no death	LMH	EF-AF	CHA
Steffe	Battle hymn of the Republic			

Sacred Songs

Lyric Tenor

Allitsen	The Lord is my light	LMH	D-AF	BOO
Bach, C.P.E.	The last judgement			
Bach, J.S.	Draw near to me	HML		GSC
-----	God, my shepherd, walks beside me	H		GRA
-----	Sheep may safely graze (Cantata 208) 2 Flutes and continuo	LM	EF-GF	GAL
Beethoven	The worship of God in nature			
Bizet	O Lord be merciful	HL		GSC
Bone and Fenton	Thy word is a lamp	LH	C-F	ROW
Brown	The twenty-third Psalm	LH		GRA
-----	What are these which are arrayed	HLM	C-F	ASC
Browning	For I am persuaded	LM	DF-G	CFI
-----	The beatitudes	HM	C-F	CFI
Buck	Fear not ye, O Israel	HLM		GSC
Campbell-Tipton	I will give thanks unto the Lord	LMH	DF-AF	GSC
Chadwick	A ballad of trees and the Master	HML	A-F	DIT
Charles	Incline Thine ear	HL	BF-D	GSC
-----	Love is of God	H	D-G	GSC
Clokey	God is in everything	LH	D-G	JFI
Creston	Psalm 23	MH	F-AF	GSC

Davis	Let not your heart be troubled	HML		WOO
-----	Trust in the Lord	MH	CS-G	GAL
Dungan	Eternal life	HL		PRE
Dvořák	God is my shepherd			AMP
-----	Hear my prayer, O Lord			AMP
-----	Turn Thee to me			AMP
Edmunds	Praise we the Lord	HL	D-D	ROW
Gore	O sing unto the Lord a new song	H		JFI
Gounod	O Divine Redeemer	LMH	C-G	GSC
-----	The King of love my Shepherd is	H	E-G	HHE
Guion	Prayer	HL		GSC
Hageman	Christ went up into the hills	LH	EF-AF	CFI
Hamblen	Trust in Him	LH	D-G	GSC
Handel	Have mercy, Lord (Te Deum)	HM		†
-----	Thanks be to Thee	M	CS-E	†
Harker	How beautiful upon the mountains	MLH	EF-G	GSC
Henschel	Morning-hymn	MH	DS-GS	†
Homer	The everlasting mercy	M	AF-F	GSC
Knapp	Open the gates of the temple	HML	A-D	PON
Kountz	Lord bless the coming year			
Liddle	How lovely are Thy dwellings	HML		BOS
MacDermid	In my Father's house are many mansions	HML		FRS
-----	Ninety first Psalm	HLM		FRS
Malotte	The beatitudes	LH	E-G	GSC
-----	The Lord's prayer			
-----	The twenty-third Psalm	HLM	C-F	GSC
Mendelssohn	Be thou faithful unto death (Saint Paul)	MH	D-G	†
-----	He counteth all your sorrows (Hymn of Praise)	H	D-G	†
-----	If with all your hearts (Elijah)	MH	F-AF	†
-----	O come let us worship 95 Psalm			
-----	Then shall the righteous shine forth (Elijah)	H	EF-AF	†
-----	The sorrows of death (Hymn of Praise)			†
Saint-Saëns	Thou, O Lord, art my protector	MH	C-A	GSC

Sanderson	Green pastures	HL	BF-EF	BOO
Scott	Come ye blessed	LMH	EF-AF	GSC
Speaks	The Lord is my light	HML		GSC
-----	Thou wilt keep him in perfect peace	HML		GSC
Stainer	My hope is in the everlasting (The Daughter of Jairus)			
Stevenson	I sought the Lord	HL	D-F	DIT
Stickles	Saith the Lord	LH	D-F	CHA
Thiman	My Master hath a garden	HL		NOV
-----	Thou wilt keep him in perfect peace	H	D-G	GRA
Thompson	My Master hath a garden	M		ECS
Van de Water	The Penitent	HM		DIT
-----	The publican	HL	C-E	DIT
Weaver	Assurance	H	EF-G	GAL
-----	Praise the Lord, His glories show	H	E-G	GAL
Widor	O Lord most Holy			
Wolf	Prayer (Gebet)			
Yon	Christ triumphant	MH	E-A	JFI

Wedding Songs

Lyric Tenor

Barnby	O perfect love	M	C-G	DIT
Beethoven	Ich liebe dich	HL	BF-DF	†
Bond	I love you truly			BOS
Clough- Leighter	Possession	MH	DF-AF	GSC
De Koven	Oh promise me (Robin Hood)	HML	C-D	†
Dello Joio	How do I love thee?	H	D-G	CFI
D'Hardelot	Because	MH	E-G	CHA
Diggle	A wedding prayer	HM	EF-F	GSC
Franck	O Lord most Holy	LM	A-FS	BOS
Geehl	For you alone			SHU
Grieg	I love thee	HML	E-F	†
Lippe	How do I love you?			BOS
Marx	Hat dich die Liebe beruehrt	MH	EF-BF	AMP
Rosa	Wedding song	F	DF-GF	GSC
Rowley	Here at thine altar, Lord			NOV
Schubert	Du bist die Ruh	LMH	EF-AF	†
-----	Ungeduld	HML		†
Schumann	Widmung	HL	BF-F	†
Sowerby	O perfect love	MH	EF-AF	GRA

591

Strauss	Seitdem dein Aug' in meines Schaute			SC
Willan	O perfect love	HM	E-FS	GRA
Youmans	Through the years (Through the Years)	HML	A-F	MLR

Songs and Arias With Added Accompanying Instrument

Lyric Tenor

Bach, J.S.	Ach, ziehe die Seele (Cantata 96) Flute	
-----	Dein Blut, so meine Schuld durchstreicht (Cantata 78) Flute	BRO
-----	Die Liebe zieht mit sanften Schritten (Cantata 36) Oboe d'amore	
-----	Erbarme dich (Cantata 55) Flute	RIC
-----	Ergiesse dich reichlich, du goettliche Quelle (Cantata 5) Viola	
-----	Erschuettre dich nur nicht (Cantata 99) Flute or violin	
-----	Es duenket mich, ich seh dich kommen (Cantata 175) Cello	
-----	Geliebter Jesu (Cantata 16) English horn or viola	
-----	Gott ist mein Freund (Cantata 139) Violin	
-----	Handle nicht nach deinen Rechten (Cantata 101) Violin	
-----	Ich will an den Himmel denken (Cantata 166) Oboe	
-----	Ja, tausendmal (Cantata 43) Violin	NOV
-----	Mich kann kein Zweifel stoeren (Cantata 108) Violin	
-----	O Seelen Paradies (Cantata 172) Violin or viola	AUG
-----	Seht! was die Liebe thut! (Cantata 85) Violin or viola	RIC
-----	Tausendfaches Unglueck schrecken (Cantata 143) Violin	

(Bach, J.S.)	Wir waren schon zu tief gesunken (Cantata 9) Violin			RIC
-----	Wo wird in diesem Jammertale (Cantata 114) Flute			
-----	Woferne du den edlen Frieden (Cantata 41) Cello			RIC
Beethoven	Irish songs Piano, violin and cello			
-----	Scotch songs Piano, violin and cello			
Braga	Angel's serenade Violin	LH	D-G	†
Britten	Serenade Horn and string orchestra	H		BOO
Campra	Air de Musette Flute, cello and harps			
Chausson	Le colibri Violin or cello	M	F-GF	BOS
Godard	Cachés dans cet asile (Jocelyn) Violin or cello	MH	DF-F	GSC
Handel	Look down, look down, harmonious Saint Harpsichord and orchestra			
Kramer	Pleading String quartet	LH	D-GF	JFI
Leroux	Le nil Cello or violin	LH	E-A	†
Rabey	Tes yeux Violin and piano	H	EF-G	DUR
Ravel	Chansons madécasses Flute, cello and piano			DUR
Vaughan Williams	On Wenlock edge String quartet and piano			BOO
Villa-Lobos	Suite Voice and violin			AMP

American Recital Songs

Dramatic Tenor

Bacon	Is there such a thing as day?	M	DS-FS	AMP
Barber	I hear an army	LH	D-AF	GSC
-----	Rain has fallen	HM	D-E	GSC
-----	Sure on this shining night	MH	D-G	GSC
-----	The daisies	M	C-F	GSC
-----	With rue my heart is laden	HL	CS-D	GSC
Beach	Ah, love but a day			ASC
-----	The year's at the spring	MH	AF-AF	ASC

593

Bone and Fenton	Captain Kidd	MH	B–G	CFI
-----	Green fields	MH	E–A	PRE
Bowles	Heavenly grass	ML	B–E	GSC
Braine	Dawn awakes	HML	A–D	ASC
Branscombe	At the postern gate	MH	DF–AF	ASC
Britain	Stillness			
Burnham	Sing me a song of a lad that is gone	HL		GSC
Campbell– Tipton	A spirit flower	LHM	B–G	GSC
-----	After sunset	HM	DS–A	GSC
-----	Rhapsodie	LMH	DF–A	GSC
-----	The crying of water	LH	FS–GS	GSC
Carpenter	Don't ceare	M	C–D	GSC
-----	If	M	D–E	GSC
-----	Light, my light	M	C–G	GSC
-----	On the day when death will knock at thy door	M	C–F	GSC
-----	The pools of peace	M	D–F	GSC
Carter	Dust of snow	M	D–E	AMP
Castelnuovo– Tedesco	O mistress mine			CHE
Chadwick	Allah	LH	CS–GS	ASC
Chanler	I rise when you enter	M	CS–G	GSC
Charles	And so, goodbye	LH	EF–AF	GSC
-----	Clouds	HML	C–EF	GSC
-----	My lady walks in loveliness	HM	C–EF	GSC
-----	When I have sung my songs	HM	BF–EF	GSC
Clough– Leighter	Who knows?	M		GSC
Crist	Knock on the door	H	EF–AF	GSC
-----	White hours like snow	HL	CS–BF	CFI
-----	You will not come again	HML	BF–CS	CFI
Davis	Nancy Hanks	H	D–G	GAL
Deis	Come down to Kew			
Diamond	David weeps for Absolom	M	D–A	MUP
Dobson	Cargoes	ML	C–EF	GSC
Duke	I've dreamed of sunsets	M	C–G	GSC
Edmunds	Billy boy	ML	BF–EF	ROW
-----	Fare you well	MH	F–AF	ROW
Elwell	In the mountains	M	DF–F	BMI
Engel	A sprig of rosemary	M	EF–F	GSC
Foote	I'm wearing awa'	HL		ASC
Giannini	Far above the purple hills	LH	CS–A	RIC
-----	Heart cry	H		RIC
-----	If I had known	H		RIC

(Giannini)	Tell me, o blue, blue sky	H		RIC
Golde	Who knows?	HM	BF-F	GSC
Griffes	An old song resung	LM	EF-F	GSC
-----	By a lonely forest pathway	HML	A-EF	GSC
-----	Elves	H	F-AF	GSC
-----	Symphony in yellow	M	D-GF	GSC
-----	The lament of Ian the proud	MH	DS-AS	GSC
-----	The rose of the night	H	CS-A	GSC
-----	Waikiki	H	DS-GS	GSC
Guion	Wild geese	M	D-F	CFI
Hadley	My shadow			ASC
-----	The time of parting	HLM	E-G	CFI
Hageman	At the well	LH	EF-AF	GSC
-----	Do not go, my love	HL	B-EF	GSC
-----	Miranda	HL		GAL
-----	Music I heard with you	MH	E-A	GAL
-----	Voices			
Hindemith	The whistling thief	M	E-F	AMP
Homer	Dearest	LMH	EF-AF	GSC
Hopkinson	My days have been so wondrous free	LH	EF-G	†
-----	My generous heart disdains			
Horsman	In the yellow dusk	MH	FS-A	GSC
-----	The bird of the wilderness	LMH	DF-BF	GSC
Kernochan	We two together	H	EF-AF	GAL
Klemm	London rain			
Kramer	For a dream's sake	HL		JFI
-----	I have seen dawn	M	DS-F	GSC
-----	Pleading	LH	D-GF	JFI
-----	The last hour	HML		JCH
La Forge	Grieve not, beloved	H	FS-G	RIC
-----	Hills	HL		RIC
Lang	Irish love song	HML	A-E	ASC
Levitzki	Ah, thou beloved one	H	EF-AF	GSC
-----	Do you remember?	HML	BF-EF	GSC
Lockwood	O, lady, let the sad tears fall	M		MER
Loeffler	To Helen	M	DF-F	GSC
MacDowell	The sea	HL	D-D	BRH
Mc Arthur	Night	H	F-AF	GSC
Mc Donald	Daybreak	H		ELV
Moore	Adam was my grandfather			GAL
Nordoff	Music I heard with you	H	DS-FS	AMP
-----	Tell me, Thyrsis	H	E-G	AMP
-----	There shall be more joy	M	CS-FS	AMP

Rogers	The last song	MLH	E-AF	GSC
-----	Time for making songs	HM	CS-F	DIT
-----	Wind song	LM	C-G	GSC
Rorem	The lordly Hudson	M	DF-G	MER
Rummel	Ecstasy	LMH	GF-AF	GSC
Sacco	Brother Will, brother John	M	C-F	GSC
-----	Spanish Johnny	HL	BF-F	GSC
Strickland	Here in the high hills	H	DF-G	GSC
Tyson	Sea moods	LH	E-AF	GSC
Warner	Hurdy gurdy	M	D-F	CFI
Warren	We two	LH	E-A	GSC
-----	White horses of the sea	LH	F-G	GSC
Watts	Blue are her eyes	H	FS-FS	DIT
Weaver	A book of verses	H	D-AF	GAL

British Recital Songs

Dramatic Tenor

Aiken	Sigh no more	HML		STB
Anon	False Phillis			
Arne, T.	Blow, blow thou winter wind	M	C-F	†
-----	Peggy			GSC
Bantock	A dream of spring	H	E-G	CHE
-----	A feast of lanterns	HM	D-F	GAL
-----	Silent strings	MH	F-G	BOO
Bartlet	What thing is love			BOO
Bax	Rann of exile	H	D-G	CHE
-----	The enchanted fiddle			
-----	The white peace			CHE
Benjamin	Calm sea and mist			CUR
-----	Hedgerow			CUR
-----	The piper			BOO
-----	The wasp			CUR
Berners	Dialogue between Tom Filuter and his man	M	D-F	CHE
-----	Theodore or the pirate king			CHE
Besley	Listening	H	E-AF	CUR
Bliss	Three jolly gentlemen	H		†
Bridge	All things that we clasp	HL		BOS
-----	Come to me in my dreams	HL	C-EF	BOH
-----	E'en as a lovely flower	HM	FS-E	BOH
-----	Love went a-riding	HL		BOS
-----	O that it were so	LMH	D-G	CHA
-----	So perverse			BOS
Butterworth	Loveliest of trees			AUG

596

(Butterworth)	When I was one and twenty			AUG
Campion	Follow thy fair sun			STB
-----	There is a garden in her face			DIT
Clarke	Shy one	HL	BF-G	BOH
Coleridge-Taylor	Life and death	HML		ASC
-----	Onaway! Awake beloved	MH	FS-BF	†
-----	She rested by the broken brook	HL		DIT
Delius	Indian love song	H		†
-----	Love's philosophy			†
-----	To the queen of my heart			†
Dowland	Come again! sweet love	M	D-E	STB
-----	Come away			BOO
-----	I saw my lady weep	M	E-E	STB
-----	Say love, if ever thou didst find			STB
-----	Shall I sue?			STB
Dunhill	The cloths of heaven	LM	EF-G	STB
Eden	What's in the air today?	M	D-F	ELK
Elgar	And King Olaf heard the cry	H	EF-BF	NOV
Ford	Now I see thy looks were feigned			BOO
-----	Since first I saw your face			DIT
Forsyth	The bell man			DIT
German	Charming Chloe	HML		NOV
-----	My song is of the sturdy north	ML		CHA
Gibbs	Five eyes	HL	D-D	BOS
Green	My lips shall speak the praise	M	E-F	OXF
Gurney	Hawk and buckle			OXF
-----	Under the greenwood tree			ROG
Head	Sea gipsy	LM	E-GS	BOO
-----	The ships of Arcady	ML	BF-EF	BOH
-----	When I think upon the maidens	LM	D-G	BOO
Hely-Hutchinson	Old mother Hubbard	HL	B-E	CFI
Henschel	Morning-hymn	MH	DS-GS	†
Holbrooke	Come not when I am dead			ENO
Holst	Journey's end			AUG
-----	The heart worships	ML	BF-D	STB
Hook	Bright Phoebus	M	EF-F	GSC
Ireland	Great things			AUG
-----	Hope the hornblower			BOO
-----	The heart's desire			ROG

597

Jones	What if I speede?			BOO
Leveridge	When dull care			BOO
Moeran	Bright cap			OXF
Morley	It was a lover and his lass	HM		DIT
Munro	My lovely Celia			BIR
Parry	To Althea	M		NOV
Purcell, E.	Passing by	HM	D-D	DIT
Purcell, H.	Had I but love			DUN
-----	If music be the food of love	M	D-G	BOO
-----	I'll sail upon the dog star	HL	A-E	†
Quilter	Blow, blow thou winter wind	HL	C-E	BOO
-----	Love's philosophy	LMH	D-A	BOO
-----	Now sleeps the crimson petal	LMH	EF-GF	BOO
Rosseter	When Laura smiles	LM	D-E	STB
Scott	The unforeseen	HML		GAL
-----	Time of day			ELK
Stanford	The fairy lough	ML	A-EF	BOO
Thomson	The knight of Bethlehem	LM		NOV
Vaughan Williams	Orpheus with his lute			PRO
-----	Silent noon			GSC
-----	The roadside fire	HML	BF-EF	BOO
-----	The vagabond	ML	A-E	BOO
Warlock	Sleep			OXF

French Recital Songs

Dramatic Tenor

Berlioz	L'absence	H	CS-FS	GSC
Bruneau	L'heureux vagabond	LH	EF-G	GSC
Caplet	Le forêt			DUR
Charpentier	Les chevaux de bois	H	E-A	HEU
Chausson	Chanson d'amour			
-----	La caravane	MH	CS-A	HAM
-----	Le colibri	M	F-GF	BOS
-----	Le temps des lilas	MH	D-GS	†
Dalayrac	Hélas! C'est près de vous			
Debussy	Beau soir	LH	C-FS	†
-----	C'est l'extase	LH	CS-A	†
-----	Chevaux de bois	H	C-G	†
-----	Colloque sentimental			DUR
-----	De fleurs	H	C-AF	†
-----	La mer est plus belle	HL		†

(Debussy)	Le faune			DUR
-----	Mandoline	HM	BF-F	†
-----	Nuits d'etoiles	LH	E-A	MAR
-----	Spleen			
Delibes	Bonjours, Suzon	LM	C-F	GSC
Duparc	Chanson triste	MH	FS-AF	†
-----	La vague et la cloche			ROU
-----	La vie antérieure	HL		†
-----	Lamento	ML	EF-EF	BOS
-----	Le manoir de Rosamunde	HL	B-F	BOS
-----	Phidylé	MH	EF-AF	BOS
-----	Testament	HL		INT
Fauré	Après un rêve	HM	C-F	†
-----	Au cimetière	LH	D-F	†
-----	Automne	MH	D-FS	GSC
-----	Clair de lune	MH	C-G	†
-----	Fleur jetée	HM	BF-FS	†
-----	L'hiver a cessé	HL		INT
-----	Madrigal	MH	F-F	HAM
-----	Mandoline	HL	F-E	†
-----	Prison	LH		†
-----	Rencontre	H	EF-AF	†
-----	Toujours	LH	F-AF	†
Février	L'intruse	M	B-DF	HEU
Fourdrain	Carnaval	M	C-F	RIC
-----	Chanson norvégienne	H	E-G	RIC
-----	Promenade au mule			
Franck	La procession	LH	E-GS	†
-----	Le mariage des roses	M	E-FS	BOS
-----	S'il est un charmant gazon			
Gounod	Medjé (Chanson arabe)	MH	G-G	BOO
-----	Vénise	HL		INT
Hahn	D'une prison	L	BF-EF	HEU
-----	L'heure exquise	M	DF-F	†
-----	Offrande	M	D-D	GSC
-----	Paysage	MH	EF-G	HEU
Hue	J'ai pleuré en rêve	HL	D-E	BOS
-----	Sonnez les matines	H	FS-G	HEU
Indy	Lied maritime	LH	B-G	†
-----	Mirage			HAM
Koechlin	Le thé	HM	C-E	BOS
Lalo	Marine	LH	DS-FS	
Lenormand	Quelle souffrance	HM	AF-F	HAM
Liszt	Oh! quand je dors	H	E-A	†
Martini	Plaisir d'amour	M	BF-EF	GSC
Massenet	Nuit d'Espagne			
Milhaud	Chant de Forgeron	M	C-FS	SC
Paladilhe	Lamento provinçal	M	CS-FS	HOM
-----	Les trois prières			

(Paladilhe)	Psyché	HM	BF–F	GSC
Pessard	Requiem du coeur			LED
Poldowski	Colombine	H	D–GF	CHE
-----	Dansons la gigue	M	EF–G	MAR
-----	L'heure exquise	LMH	DF–AF	CHE
Poulenc	Air vif	H	C–AF	ROU
-----	Bleuet	H	FS–GF	DUR
-----	La belle jeunesse	L	D–F	HEU
Ravel	Chanson à boire			DUR
-----	Kaddisch	H	C–G	DUR
Rhené-Baton	Il pleut des pétales de fleurs	M	CS–E	DUR
Rosenthal	Le marabout			ESC
Roussel	Jazz dans la nuit	H	C–A	DUR
-----	Le bachelier de Salamanque			DUR
-----	Le jardin mouillé	M	C–FS	ROU
Saint-Saëns	Guitares et mandolines			DUR
-----	Tristesse			
Satie	Le chapelier			ROU
Severac	Chanson pour le petit cheval			ROU
-----	Les hiboux			ROU

German Recital Songs

Dramatic Tenor

Bach, C.P.E.	Passionslied			SIM
Bach, J.S.	Bist du bei mir	HML	A–EF	†
Beethoven	Adelaide	HML	BF–E	†
-----	Andenken			†
-----	Delizia	M	C–F	GSC
-----	Der Wachtelschlag			†
-----	Die Ehre Gottes	HL	AF–EF	†
-----	Ich liebe dich	HL	BF–DF	†
-----	Mailied			RIC
-----	Neue Liebe, neues Leben			†
-----	Wonne der Wehmut			†
Brahms	Ach, wende diesen Blick			†
-----	Am Sonntag Morgen	L	CS–FS	†
-----	Auf dem Kirchhofe	HL	BF–EF	†
-----	Bei dir sind meine Gedanken	MH	E–FS	†
-----	Botschaft	HL	D–F	†
-----	Der Schmied	HL	EF–EF	†
-----	Der Tod, das ist die kuehle Nacht	L	AF–F	†
-----	Der Ueberlaeufer			†
-----	Die Mainacht	HL	BF–FF	†

(Brahms)	Feldeinsamkeit	HL	C-EF	†
-----	Geheimnis			†
-----	Heimkehr			†
-----	In Waldeseinsamkeit	H	ES-G	†
-----	Juchhe!			RIC
-----	Lerchengesang	LH	FS-GS	†
-----	Liebe kam aus fernan Landen	HL	C-E	†
-----	Meine Liebe ist gruen	MLH	ES-A	†
-----	Minnelied	MHL	C-EF	†
-----	Nachtigall	MHL	BF-FS	†
-----	Nicht mehr zu dir zu gehen			†
-----	O kuehler Wald	MH	A-F	†
-----	O liebliche Wangen	MLH	E-G	†
-----	O wuesst' ich doch den Weg zurueck	H	E-FS	†
-----	Schoen war, das ich dir weihte			†
-----	Sehnsucht	H	EF-AF	†
-----	Sind es Schmerzen	HL	BF-F	†
-----	Sonntag	H	D-G	†
-----	So willst du des Armen	HL	C-E	†
-----	Staendchen	HL	BF-E	†
-----	Tambourliedchen			†
-----	Vergebliches Staendchen	LMH		†
-----	Von ewiger Liebe	LMH	B-AF	†
-----	Wenn ich mit Menschen			†
-----	Wie bist du meine Koenigin	HL	C-E	†
-----	Wie froh und frisch	HL	B-E	†
-----	Wie Melodien zieht es	HL	A-E	†
-----	Willst du, dass ich geh'?	L	C-G	†
-----	Wir wandelten	LH	EF-GF	GSC
Brull	Sechse, sieben oder acht			
Cornelius	Komm, wir wandeln	H	FS-GS	SC
Franck, J.W.	Auf, auf, zu Gottes Lob			SIM
Handel	Dank sei Dir, Herr	M	CS-E	†
Haydn	Liebes Maedchen, hoer' mir zu			HSC
-----	She never told her love	HL	B-D	DIT
-----	The sailor's song			
Hildach	Der Lenz			HSC
Jensen	Margreta	M	F-F	PET
-----	Murmuring zephyr	LH	E-AF	GSC
Korngold	Nachtwanderer	M	CS-F	AMP
Liszt	Die drei Zigeuner	LM	B-G	GSC
-----	Du bist wie eine Blume	H	E-G	†
-----	Es muss ein Wunderbares sein	M	C-EF	DUR

(Liszt)	O lieb' so lang du lieben kannst	HML	B-F	†
Loehnor	O Ewigkeit			SIM
Loewe	Tom der Reimer			HSC
Mahler	Des Antonius von Padua Fischpredigt	HL	GF-F	†
-----	Ich atmet' einen linden Duft	HL		INT
-----	Ich ging mit Lust	HL		INT
-----	Revelge	H	D-A	UNI
Marx	Hat dich die Liebe beruehrt	MH	EF-BF	AMP
-----	Nocturne	H	EF-AF	AMP
-----	Selige Nacht	M	DF-GF	AMP
Mendelssohn	Gruss	M	DS-FS	†
-----	Jagdlied	HL	BF-EF	†
-----	Nachtlied			
-----	Neue Liebe	H	CS-A	†
-----	Venetianisches Gondellied	LM	E-FS	AUG
Reger	Des Kindes Gebet	H	F-G	BOT
-----	Friede	H	EF-G	UNI
Schoeck	Reiselied			
-----	Wanderlied der Prager Studenten			
Schoenberg	Erhebung			GSC
Schubert	Abschied	HL	BF-F	†
-----	Am Feierabend	HL	BF-F	†
-----	Am Meer	HML	B-D	†
-----	Am See			PET
-----	An den Mond	HL	F-GF	†
-----	An die Entfernte			PET
-----	An Silvia			†
-----	Auf dem Flusse	HL	F-E	†
-----	Auf dem Wasser zu singen	MH	EF-GF	†
-----	Aufenthalt	HLM	A-F	GSC
-----	Ave Maria	LMH	F-F	†
-----	Das Fischermaedchen	L	A-EF	†
-----	Das Wandern	HLM	E-E	†
-----	Das Wirtshaus	HL	C-D	†
-----	Dem Unendlichen	L	A-GF	†
-----	Der Atlas	HL	BF-F	†
-----	Der Doppelgaenger	HL	G-D	†
-----	Der Erlokoenig	HML	A-E	†
-----	Der Juengling an der Quelle	LH	E-A	†
-----	Der Leiermann	ML	C-D	†
-----	Der Lindenbaum	HL	A-D	†
-----	Der Musensohn	LH	FS-G	†
-----	Der Neugierige	HL	CS-EF	†

(Schubert)	Der Schiffer	LH	BF-A	†
-----	Der stuermische Morgen	HL		
-----	Der Wanderer an den Mond	LM	D-F	PET
-----	Der Wegweiser	L	D-EF	†
-----	Der zuernende Barde			PET
-----	Die Allmacht	HML	G-E	†
-----	Die boese Farbe	HL	CS-F	†
-----	Die Forelle	MLH	EF-GF	†
-----	Die Liebe hat gelogen	LM	G-F	†
-----	Die Nebensonnen	HL	F-D	†
-----	Die Post	HML	BF-EF	†
-----	Die Wetterfahne			
-----	Du bist die Ruh	LMH	EF-AF	†
-----	Du liebst mich nicht	LH	E-FS	†
-----	Erstarrung	HL	D-F	†
-----	Fragment aus dem Aeschylus			PET
-----	Fruehlingstraum	HL	C-D	†
-----	Gebet waehrend der Schlacht	M	CS-E	†
-----	Geheimes	HL	BF-EF	†
-----	Gruppe aus dem Tartarus	L	CS-EF	†
-----	Ihr Bild	HL	C-C	†
-----	Ihr Grab			PET
-----	Im Abendrot	HL	C-D	†
-----	In der Ferne	HL		†
-----	Irrlicht			
-----	Lachen und Weinen	HL	C-EF	†
-----	Liebesbotschaft	H	E-G	†
-----	Litanei	HLM	C-EF	†
-----	Mein!	HL		†
-----	Memnon	LM	AF-F	PET
-----	Nacht und Traeume	HL	C-DF	†
-----	Prometheus	HL		†
-----	Rast			
-----	Rastlose Liebe	M	B-F	†
-----	Schaefers Klagelied	HL	BF-D	†
-----	Staendchen	MH	B-E	†
-----	Ungeduld	HML		GSC
-----	Wer nie sein Brot	HL	C-EF	†
-----	Wohin?	HL	B-E	†
Schumann	Aus den Hebraeischen Gesaengen			
-----	Der Nussbaum	LMH	D-FS	†
-----	Die beiden Grenadiere			
-----	Die Lotusblume	HLM	BF-F	†
-----	Du bist wie eine Blume	HM	F-EF	†
-----	Er ist's	HL	BF-EF	†

(Schumann)	Fruehlingsfahrt	HL	B-E	†
-----	Ich grolle nicht	HL	BF-D	†
-----	Ich hab' im Traum geweinet	HL	B-D	†
-----	Ihre Stimme	LH		†
-----	Im Rhein, im heiligen Strome	HM	D-F	
-----	Lieb' Liebchen	HL	B-E	†
-----	Mein schoener Stern			
-----	Melancholie			
-----	Mondnacht	M	E-FS	†
-----	Provenzalisches Lied	LH		†
-----	Romanze	HL	C-E	†
-----	Schoene Wiege meiner Leiden	HL	C-EF	†
-----	Talismane			
-----	Waldesgespraech	HL	A-FS	†
-----	Wanderlied	HL	A-E	†
-----	Widmung	HL	BF-F	†
Sommer	Ganz leise			
Strauss	Allerseelen	HL	AS-E	†
-----	Befreit			HSC
-----	Breit ueber mein Haupt	LH	GF-AF	HSC
-----	Caecilie	MH	E-B	†
-----	Die Nacht	HL		†
-----	Freundliche Vision	HL	C-F	†
-----	Fuer fuenfzehn Pfennige			†
-----	Heimliche Aufforderung	HL	B-E	†
-----	Ich liebe dich			†
-----	Ich trage meine Minne	M		†
-----	Kling			†
-----	Madrigal	LH	EF-GF	
-----	Mit deinen blauen Augen	LH	C-GS	†
-----	Morgen	HML	E-F	†
-----	Nichts	LH	E-A	†
-----	Ruhe meine Seele			†
-----	Traum durch die Daemmerung	HML	BF-EF	†
-----	Wozu noch Maedchen	H	FS-A	
-----	Zueignung	HL	CS-FS	†
Trunk	In meiner Heimat			
Weingartner	Liebesfeier			
Wolf	Alle gingen, Herz, zu Ruh	HL	C-EF	†
-----	An die Geliebte			†
-----	Dank des Paria			PET
-----	Das Koehlerweib ist trunken			PET
-----	Denk' es, o Seele	LH	EF-F	†
-----	Der Feuerreiter			†
-----	Der Freund	HM	BF-E	PET

(Wolf)	Der Musikant	HL	CS-D	†
-----	Der Rattenfaenger	HL		†
-----	Der Soldat, 1	LH	E-FS	†
-----	Der Soldat, 2	H	EF-AF	PET
-----	Der Tambour	HL		†
-----	Er ist's	H	D-G	†
-----	Fussreise	HL	D-E	†
-----	Gebet	HL		†
-----	Gesang Weylas	HL	DF-F	†
-----	Gesellenlied			
-----	Heb' auf dein blondes Haupt	HL	G-DF	†
-----	Im Fruehling	HL	BF-F	†
-----	Jaegerlied			PET
-----	Lebe wohl	HL	BF-F	†
-----	Morgenstimmung	LH	C-GS	†
-----	Neue Liebe	LH	D-AF	†
-----	Nun wandre, Maria	HL	EF-D	†
-----	Seemanns Abschiedslied	H	C-A	†
-----	Storchenbotschaft			†
-----	Trunken muessen wir alle sein	M	ES-FS	†
-----	Ueber Nacht	LH	D-G	†
-----	Und willst du deinen Liebsten sterben	HL		†
-----	Verborgenheit	HL	B-E	†
-----	Verschwiegene Liebe	LH	DF-FS	†
-----	Wenn du zu den Blumen gehst	HL	B-EF	†
-----	Zur ruh', zur ruh'	HL	A-GF	†
Wolff	Alle Dinge haben Sprache	M	BF-GF	†
-----	Schoen strech ich aus in Bette			

Italian Recital Songs

Dramatic Tenor

Bassani	Dormi, bella, dormi tu	L	EF-F	GSC
Bimboni	Sospiri miei	M	EF-EF	GAL
Bononcini	Deh, più a me non v'ascondete	LH	EF-F	†
Caccini	Amarilli, mia bella	ML	C-D	†
Caldara	Alma del core			GSC
-----	Come raggio di sol	HL	D-F	†
-----	Sebben crudele	HML	E-DS	†
-----	Selve amiche, ombrose piante	HM	E-E	†
Carissimi	Filli, non t'amo più	HL	B-D	†

(Carissimi)	Vittoria, mio core	HLM	B-E	†
Casella	Amante sono vaghiccia di voi			RIC
Castelnuovo-Tedesco	La ermita de San Simon			
-----	L'Infinito			
Cavalli	Donzelle fuggite	HL	C-EF	†
Cesti	Intorno all'idol mio (Orontea)	MH	D-F	†
-----	Tu mancavi a tormentarmi	H	D-G	GSC
Cimara	Stornellata marinara	HM		RIC
De Luca	Non posso disperar	HL	C-E	GSC
Donaudy	Ah mai non cessate			RIC
-----	Freschi luoghi			RIC
-----	Quando ti rivedrò			RIC
-----	Spirate pur, spirate			RIC
-----	Vaghissima sembianza	H	˙E-A	RIC
Durante	Danza, danza fanciulla gentile	HM	BF-F	†
-----	Vergin, tutta amor	LM	C-EF	†
Falconieri	Non più d'amore	HL	C-D	DIT
-----	Nudo arciero	HL	AF-AF	DIT
-----	O bellissimi capelli	HL	B-D	†
Fasolo	Cangia, cangia tue voglie	H	C-G	GSC
Frescobaldi	Se l'aura spira	HL	C-EF	DIT
Gaffi	Luci vezzose	HL	D-E	DIT
Gagliano	Dormi amore	HL	CS-E	DIT
Gasparini	Caro laccio, dolce nodo	M	EF-EF	GSC
Giordani	Caro mio ben	HML	B-D	†
Handel	Ombra mai fu (Serse)	HM	BF-EF	†
-----	Semplicetto a donna credi Alcina)			DIT
Haydn	Pensi a me			
Jommelli	Chi vuol comprar la bella	H	B-G	GSC
Legrenzi	Che fiero costume	HML	C-D	†
Lonati	Tu paristi idolo amato			PET
Lotti	Pur dicesti, o bocca bella	LMH	E-FS	GSC
Malipiero	Inno a Maria Nostra Donna	H		CHE
Marcello	Il mio bel foco	LMH	C-G	GSC
Paradies	M'ha preso alla sua ragna	M	EF-F	GSC
Pergolesi	Nina	HL	CS-D	DIT
Peri	Invocazione di Orfeo (Euridice)	HL	E-CS	DIT
Pizzetti	Il clefta prigione			FRL
-----	San Basilio			
Respighi	Abbandono			BON
-----	Bella porta di rubini			RIC

606

(Respighi)	In alto mare			BON
-----	Invito alla danza			BON
-----	Mattinata			BON
-----	Nebbie			†
Rontani	Or ch'io non segno più	HL	CS-E	DIT
Rosa	Selve, voi che le speranze	MH	D-G	DIT
-----	Star vicino	HL	D-E	†
Rossini	La danza	MH	E-A	†
Scarlatti, A.	Chi vuole innamorarsi	HL	D-EF	DIT
-----	Già il sole dal Gange	LH	EF-F	GSC
-----	La fortuna			BOS
-----	Sento nel core	M	E-F	†
Secchi	Love me or not			BOO
-----	Lungi dal caro bene	HL	A-FS	DIT
Stradella	Ragion sempre addita	H	E-G	†
-----	Se nel ben			CFI
Torelli	Tu lo sai	HL	BF-F	†
Tosti	Addio	MH		RIC
-----	Mattinata			RIC
-----	The last song	HL		RIC
Traetta	Ombra cara, amorosa	HL	B-F	†
Wolf-				
Ferrari	Rispetto			HSC

Russian Recital Songs

Dramatic Tenor

Arensky	Autumn	H	CS-FS	GSC
Balakirev	The pine tree			DIT
Borodin	A dissonance	MH	E-F	†
-----	The sea	MH	DS-GS	DIT
Cui	The statue at Czarskoe-Selo	HM	DF-EF	†
Dargomijshky	O thou rose maiden	H	E-G	DIT
Gliere	Ah, twine no blossoms	HM	CS-F	DIT
Gretchaninoff	Hushed the song of the nightingale	MH	E-G	DIT
-----	Over the steppe	LM	C-G	GSC
-----	The skylark			DIT
-----	Wounded birch	HL	B-EF	†
Malashkin	O could I but express in song	LH		CHE
Mednikoff	The hills of Gruzia	H	DS-A	LAC
Mussorgsky	Death and the peasant			GSC
-----	Death the commander			
-----	Night			GSC
-----	On the Dnieper			GSC

(Mussorgsky)	The goat	HL	C-E	CFI
-----	The seminarian			GSC
Rachmaninoff	Floods of spring	HL		DIT
-----	God took away from me			GSC
-----	In the silence of night	LH	D-A	GSC
----*-	O thou billowy harvest field	HL	CS-E	GSC
-----	The island	LH	DF-F	†
-----	The songs of Grusia	H	E-A	GSC
Rubinstein	Der Asra	HM	B-F	GSC
-----	Die Thraene	M	C-G	GSC
Tchaikovsky	Farewell			DIT
-----	Regret			NOV
-----	Why	HL		†

Scandinavian Recital Songs

Dramatic Tenor

Alfven	Skogen sover			LUN
Grieg	A dream			†
-----	A swan			†
-----	By the brook			GSC
-----	Den Aergjerrige			
-----	En fuglevise			
-----	Eros	LM	C-F	†
-----	Greeting			PET
-----	I love thee	HML	E-F	†
-----	Pa skogstien	H	E-G	HAN
-----	Solnedgang			
-----	Thanks for thy counsel			DIT
-----	The first meeting			PET
-----	To Norway	M	E-F	DIT
-----	Vandring i skoven	M	D-FS	HAN
-----	With a water-lily	HM	CS-EF	†
Hartmann	Flyv fugl, flyv			
Heise	Dengang jeg var kun saa			
-----	Liden Karen			
-----	Skovensomhed			
Horneman	Kongernes Konge			HAN
Lange-Mueller	Kornmodsglandsen			
-----	Serenad			
-----	Skind ud du klare solskin			DIT
Melartin	Morgonsång			
Nordquist	Til havs			
Rung	Hvor Nilen vande Aegypterens jord			
Sibelius	Black roses	M	A-ES	AMP

608

(Sibelius)	The tryst	M		AMP
Sjoeberg	Visions	MH	F-AF	GAL
Sjoegren	Jeg ser for mit øje			
-----	Og jeg vil drage			
-----	The Seraglio's garden	HL		GSC
Soedermann	Kung Heimer och Aslog			
Stenhammer	Ballad			

Spanish Recital Songs

Dramatic Tenor

Alvarez	A granada	M	D-FS	GSC
-----	La partida	HL	DS-E	GSC
Lara	Granada			SOU
Nin	El vito			ESC

Miscellaneous Recital Songs

Dramatic Tenor

Bach-Gounod	Ave Maria			
Bizet	Agnus Dei	HLM	C-AF	
Cherubini	Ave Maria	H	E-A	GSC
Dvořák	Clouds and darkness			
-----	God is my shepherd			AMP
-----	Hear my prayer, O Lord			AMP
-----	I will sing new songs of gladness	HL		
-----	Lord, Thou art my refuge and shield			AMP
-----	Songs my mother taught me	HM	E-E	
-----	Turn Thee to me			AMP
Franck	Panis angelicus	LM		

British Songs and Arias
For Opening Recitals

Dramatic Tenor

Anon	Have you seen but a white lily grow?			GSC
Dowland	I saw my lady weep	M	E-E	STB
Green	My lips shall speak the praise	M	E-F	OXF

609

Handel	Have mercy, Lord (Te Deum)	HM		
-----	O sleep why dost thou leave me	H		†
-----	Silent worship	LM		CUR
-----	Wher'er you walk (Semele)	HML	C-D	
Purcell	An ode to Cynthia walking on Richmond Hill			
-----	If music be the food of love	M	D-G	BOO
-----	Music for a while (Oedipus)	LH		SC
-----	There's not a swain on the plain	M	B-G	BAF

German Songs For Opening Recitals

Dramatic Tenor

Bach, J.S.	Bist du bei mir	HML	A-EF	†
Beethoven	Adelaide	HML	BF-E	†
-----	Andenken			†
-----	Ich liebe dich	HL	BF-DF	†
Brahms	Nachtigall	MHL	BF-FS	†
Handel	Dank sei Dir, Herr	M	CS-E	†
Haydn	She never told her love	HL	B-D	DIT
Schubert	Das Wandern	HLM	E-E	†
-----	Liebesbotschaft	H	E-G	†
Wolf	Ueber Nacht	LH	D-G	†

Italian Songs and Arias For Opening Recitals

Dramatic Tenor

Bononcini	Deh, più a me non v'ascondete	LH	EF-F	†
Caccini	Amarilli, mia bella	ML	C-D	†
Caldara	Sebben crudele	HML	E-DS	†
Carissimi	Vittoria, mio core	HLM	B-E	†
Cavalli	Donzelle fuggite	HL	C-EF	†
Cesti	Tu mancavi a tormentarmi	H	D-G	GSC
Cimara	Stornellata marinara	HM		RIC
Donaudy	Quando ti rivedrò			RIC
Durante	Vergin, tutta amor	LM	C-EF	†
Falconieri	O bellissimi capelli	HL	B-D	†
Handel	Ombra mai fu (Serse)	HM	BF-EF	†

610

Jommelli	Chi vuol comprar la bella	H	B-G	GSC
Lotti	Pur dicesti, o bocca bella	LMH	E-FS	GSC
Marcello	Il mio bel foco	LMH	C-G	†
Peri	Invocazione di Orfeo (Euridice)	HL	E-CS	DIT
Rosa	Star vicino	HL	D-E	†
Scarlatti, A.	Già il sole dal Gange	LH	EF-F	GSC
-----	Sento nel core	M	E-F	†
Stradella	Se nel ben			CFI
Traetta	Ombra cara, amorosa	HL	B-F	†

American Songs For Closing Recitals

Dramatic Tenor

Barber	I hear an army	LH	D-AF	GSC
-----	Sure on this shining night	MH	D-G	GSC
Branscombe	At the postern gate	MH	DF-AF	ASC
Carpenter	Light, my light	M	C-G	GSC
Chanler	I rise when you enter	M	CS-G	GSC
Charles	And so, goodbye	LH	EF-AF	GSC
-----	When I have sung my songs	HM	BF-EF	GSC
Crist	Knock on the door	H	EF-AF	GSC
Curran	Life	HM	BF-F	GSC
Enders	Russian picnic	HM	C-G	GSC
Foster	My journey's end	HLM	DF-G	GSC
Golde	Who knows	HM	BF-F	GSC
Hageman	At the well	LH	EF-AF	GSC
-----	Miranda	HL		GAL
-----	Voices			
Horsman	The bird of the wilderness	LMH	DF-BF	GSC
Kernochan	We two together	H	EF-AF	GAL
La Forge	Hills	HL		RIC
-----	Song of the open	MH	EF-AF	DIT
Levitzki	Ah, thou beloved one	H	EF-AF	GSC
Malotte	Blow me eyes	MH	C-G	GSC
Mc Arthur	Night	H	F-AF	GSC
Mc Donald	Daybreak	H		ELV
Nordoff	Tell me, Thyrsis	H	E-G	AMP
Rogers	The last song	MLH	E-AF	GSC
-----	Time for making songs	HM	CS-F	DIT
Rummel	Ecstasy	LMH	GF-AF	GSC
Russell	The way to the town	H	F-AF	GAL

611

Speaks	Morning	HML	BF-D	GSC
Tyson	Sea moods	LH	E-AF	GSC
Warren	Fulfilment	H	D-BF	GAL
-----	We two	LH	E-A	GSC
-----	White horses of the sea	LH	F-G	GSC

(See also Negro Spirituals and Folk Songs.)

Miscellaneous Songs For Closing Recitals

Dramatic Tenor

Besley	Listening	H	E-AF	CUR
Bliss	Three jolly gentlemen	H		†
Brahms	Juchhe!			†
-----	Meine Liebe ist gruen	MLH	ES-A	†
-----	Wie froh und Frisch	HL	B-E	†
-----	Willst du, dass ich geh'?	L	C-G	†
Bridge	Love went a-riding	HL		BOS
Britten	Oliver Cromwell			BOH
Cimara	Canto di primavera		D-G	FRL
Cowen	Border ballad	LM	D-E	BOO
Debussy	Chevaux de bois	H	C-G	†
Delius	Love's philosophy			†
Durante	Danza, danza fanciulla gentile	HM	BF-F	†
Eden	What's in the air today?	M	D-F	ELK
German	My song is of the sturdy north	ML		CHA
Grieg	By the brook			GSC
-----	En Fuglevise			
Head	When I think upon the maidens	LM	D-G	BOO
Hely-Hutchinson	Old mother Hubbard	HL	B-E	CFI
Henschel	Morning-hymn	MH	DS-GS	†
Hughes	The leprehaun			
Ireland	Great things			AUG
Nin	El vito			ESC
Nordquist	Til havs			
Poulenc	Air vif	H	C-AF	ROU
Quilter	Blow, blow thou winter wind	HL	C-E	BOO
-----	Love's philosophy	LMH	D-A	BOO
Rachmaninoff	Floods of spring	HL		DIT
Schoenberg	Erhebung			GSC
Schubert	Die Forelle	MLH	EF-GF	†

612

Schumann	Er ist's	HL	BF-EF	†
Sibelius	The tryst	M		AMP
Strauss	Ich liebe dich			†
Vaughan Williams	The roadside fire	HML	BF-EF	BOO
Warlock	Yarmouth Fair	HL	B-E	CFI
Wolf	Er ist's	H	D-G	†
-----	Gesellenlied			
-----	Morgenstimmung	LH	C-GS	†

Atmospheric Songs

Dramatic Tenor

Bantock	A dream of spring	H	E-G	CHE
Barber	Rain has fallen	HM	D-E	GSC
Bax	The white peace			CHE
Benjamin	Calm sea and mist			CUR
Bone and Fenton	Green fields	MH	E-A	PRE
Bridge	E'en as a lovely flower	HM	FS-E	BOH
Brogi	Venitian vision	M	D-F	RIC
Burleigh	Sometimes I feel like a motherless child	HML		RIC
Carpenter	The pools of peace	M	D-F	GSC
Carter	Dust of snow	M	D-E	AMP
Charles	Clouds	HML	C-EF	GSC
-----	My lady walks in loveliness	HM	C-EF	GSC
-----	When I have sung my songs	HM	BF-EF	GSC
Cui	The statue at Czarskoe-Selo	HM	DF-EF	†
Curran	Nocturne	HML	B-DS	GSC
Davis	Nancy Hanks	H	D-G	GAL
Debussy	C'est l'extase	LH	CS-A	†
-----	Nuits d'etoiles	LH	E-A	MAR
Del Riego	O dry those tears	LMH	E-GS	CHA
Dunhill	The cloths of Heaven	LM	EF-G	STB
Eakin	What of that midnight long ago	M	D-F	GAL
Elmore and Reed	Come all ye who weary	L	C-C	JFI
Forsyth	The bell man			DIT
Grieg	På skogstien	H	E-G	HAN
Griffes	Symphony in yellow	M	D-GF	GSC
Guion	At the cry of the first bird	H	D-G	GSC

613

Hahn	L'heure exquise	M	DF-F	†
-----	Paysage	MH	EF-G	HEU
Harty	My lagan love	ML	BF-EF	BOO
Haydn	She never told her love	HL	B-D	DIT
Holst	The heart worships	ML	BF-D	STB
Hughes	A Ballynure ballad	L	BF-D	BOH
Kramer	Pleading	LH	D-GF	JFI
-----	The last hour	HML		JCH
Mac Gimsey	Sweet little Jesus boy	ML	D-D	CFI
Mahler	Ich ging mit Lust	HL		INT
McArthur	Night	H	F-AF	GSC
Niles	I wonder as I wander	HL	BF-D	GSC
-----	Jesus, Jesus rest your head	HL	A-D	GSC
-----	The gambler's lament	HL	B-E	GSC
Nordoff	Music I heard with you	H	DS-FS	AMP
Paladilhe	Psyché	HM	BF-F	GSC
Quilter	Now sleeps the crimson petal	LMH	EF-GF	BOO
Robinson	Water boy	M	B-E	BOS
Roussel	Le jardin Mouillé	M	C-FS	ROU
Schubert	Nacht und Traeume	HL	C-DF	CFI
Schumann	Der Nussbaum	LMH	D-FS	†
-----	Ich hab' im Traum geweinet	HL	B-D	†
Stanford	The fairy lough	ML	A-EF	BOO
Strauss	Die Nacht	HL		†
-----	Traum durch die Daemmerung	HML	BF-EF	†
Vaughan Williams	Silent noon			GSC
Warlock	The first mercy	M	F-F	BOO
Watts	Blue are her eyes	H	FS-FS	DIT
Wolf	Verborgenheit	HL	B-E	†

American Dramatic Songs

Dramatic Tenor

Barber	I hear an army	LH	D-AF	GSC
Beach	Ah, love but a day			ASC
-----	The year's at the spring	MH	AF-AF	ASC
Campbell-Tipton	A spirit flower	LHM	B-G	GSC
-----	The crying of water	LH	FS-GS	GSC
Carpenter	Light, my light	M	C-G	GSC
-----	On the day when death will knock at thy door	M	C-F	GSC

614

Crist	You will not come again	HML	BF-CS	CFI
Curran	Life	HM	BF-F	GSC
Diamond	David weeps for Absolom	M	D-A	MUP
Enders	Russian picnic	HM	C-G	GSC
Foster	My journey's end	HLM	DF-G	GSC
Geehl	For you alone			SHU
Giannini	Far above the purple hills	LH	CS-A	RIC
Griffes	An old song resung	LM	EF-F	GSC
-----	The lament of Ian the proud	MH	DS-AS	GSC
-----	The rose of the night	H	CS-A	GSC
-----	Waikiki	H	DS-GS	GSC
Guion	Wild geese	M	D-F	CFI
Hageman	Do not go, my love	HL	B-EF	GSC
-----	Music I heard with you	MH	E-A	GAL
Horsman	The bird of the wilderness	LMH	DF-BF	GSC
Kernochan	We two together	H	EF-AF	GAL
La Forge	Grieve not, beloved	H	FS-G	RIC
-----	Song of the open	MH	EF-AF	DIT
Loeffler	To Helen	M	DF-F	GSC
Mac Dowell	The sea	HL	D-D	BRH
Mana-Zucca	I love life	LM	F-F	PRE
Moore	Adam was my grandfather			GAL
Nordoff	Tell me, Thyrsis	H	E-G	AMP
Rogers	The last song	MLH	E-AF	GSC
-----	Time for making songs	HM	CS-F	DIT
Speaks	Morning	HML	BF-D	GSC
Strickland	Here in the high hills	H	DF-G	GSC
Tyson	Sea moods	LH	E-AF	GSC
Warren	Fulfilment	H	D-BF	GAL
-----	We two	LH	E-A	GSC
-----	White horses of the sea	LH	F-G	GSC

British Dramatic Songs and Arias

Dramatic Tenor

Arne, T.	Preach not me your musty rules (Comus)	HML		ROW
Bax	Rann of exile	H	D-G	CHE
Besley	Listening	H	E-AF	CUR
Bridge	O that it were so	LMH	D-G	CHA
Coleridge-Taylor	Life and death	HML		ASC
Cowen	Border ballad	LM	D-E	BOO
Delius	Indian love song	H		†
-----	To the queen of my heart			†
Del Riego	Homing	HML	BF-E	CHA

615

Dix	The trumpeter	HML	A-C	BOH
German	My song is of the sturdy north	ML		CHA
Handel	Sound an alarm! (Judas Maccabaeus)	H		†
-----	Total eclipse (Samson)			†
Head	Sea gipsy	LM	E-GS	BOO
Henschel	Morning-hymn	MH	DS-GS	†
Holbrooke	Come not when I am dead			ENO
Ireland	Great things			AUG
-----	Hope the hornblower			BOO
Leveridge	When dull care			BOO
Purcell	I'll sail upon the dog star	HL	A-E	†
Quilter	Blow, blow thou winter wind	HL	C-E	BOO
Ronald	Prelude	HML	B-D	ENO
Sanderson	Shipmates of mine	LL	G-D	BOO
Vaughan Williams	The vagabond	ML	A-E	BOO

French Dramatic Songs and Arias

Dramatic Tenor

Bizet	Flower song (Carmen)	H	E-BF	†
Caplet	Le forêt			DUR
Chausson	La caravane	MH	CS-A	HAM
Debussy	Chevaux de bois	H	C-G	†
-----	Colloque sentimental			DUR
-----	De fleurs	H	C-AF	†
Duparc	La vague et la cloche			ROU
-----	La vie antérieure	HL		†
-----	Le manoir de Rosamunde	HL	B-F	BOS
-----	Phidylé	MH	EF-AF	BOS
-----	Testament	HL		INT
Fauré	Automne	MH	D-FS	GSC
-----	Jetée	HM	BF-FS	†
-----	L'hiver a cessé	HL		INT
-----	Prison	LH		†
-----	Toujours	LH	F-AF	†
Février	L'intruse	M	B-DF	HEU
Fourdrain	Chanson norvégienne	H	E-G	RIC
Gounod	Ah! lève-toi, Soleil! (Roméo et Juliette)	H	F-BF	†
Grétry	Si l'univers entier m'oublie (Richard Coeur-De-Lion)			LEM
Hahn	D'une prison	L	BF-EF	HEU
-----	Offrande	M	D-D	†

Hue	J'ai pleuré en rêve	HL	D-E	BOS
Indy	Lied maritime	LH	B-G	ROU
-----	Mirage			HAM
Lalo	Marine	LH	DS-FS	
Lenormand	Quelle souffrance	HM	AF-F	HAM
Paladilhe	Lamento provinçal	M	CS-FS	HOM
Pessard	Requiem du coeur			LED
Poldowski	Dansons la gigue	M	EF-G	MAR
-----	L'heure exquise	LMH	DF-AF	CHE
Rhené-Baton	Il pleut des pétales de fleurs	M	CS-E	DUR
Severac	Chanson pour le petit cheval			ROU

German Dramatic Songs and Arias

Dramatic Tenor

Beethoven	In des Lebens Fruehlingstagen (Fidelio)			†
Brahms	Ach, wende diesen Blick			†
-----	Am Sonntag Morgen	L	CS-FS	†
-----	Nicht mehr zu dir zu gehen			†
-----	Von ewiger Liebe	LMH	B-AF	†
Liszt	Die drei Zigeuner	LM	B-G	GSC
Mahler	Um Mitternacht	HL		INT
Marx	Hat dich die Liebe beruehrt	MH	EF-BF	AMP
-----	Selige Nacht	M	DF-GF	AMP
Schoenberg	Erhebung			GSC
Schubert	Am Feierabend	HL	BF-F	†
-----	Am Meer	HML	B-D	†
-----	Auf dem Flusse	HL	F-E	†
-----	Aufenthalt	HLM	A-F	†
-----	Dem Unendlichen	L	A-GF	†
-----	Der Atlas	HL	BF-F	†
-----	Der Doppelgaenger	HL	G-D	†
-----	Der Erlkoenig	HML	A-E	†
-----	Der Lindenbaum	HL	A-D	†
-----	Der Schiffer	LH	BF-A	†
-----	Die Allmacht	HML	G-E	†
-----	Die Liebe hat gelogen	LM	G-F	†
-----	Du liebst mich nicht	LH	E-FS	†
-----	Erstarrung	HL	D-F	GSC
-----	Fragment aus dem Aeschylus			PET
-----	Fruehlingstraum	HL	C-D	†
-----	Gebet waehrend der Schlacht	M	CS-E	†

(Schubert)	Gruppe aus dem Tartarus	L	CS-EF	†
-----	In der Ferne	HL		†
-----	Prometheus	HL		†
-----	Schaefers Klagelied	HL	BF-D	†
Schumann	Fruehlingsfahrt	HL	B-E	†
-----	Ich grolle nicht	HL	BF-D	†
-----	Schoene Wiege meiner Leiden	HL	C-EF	†
-----	Talismane			
-----	Waldesgespraech	HL	A-FS	†
Strauss	Caecilie	MH	E-B	†
-----	Kling			†
-----	Madrigal	LH	EF-GF	
-----	Ruhe meine Seele			†
-----	Zueignung	HL	CS-FS	†
Wagner	Allmaecht' ger Vater (Rienzi)			PET
-----	Am stillen Herd (Die Meistersinger)	H	D-A	GSC
-----	Dir Toene Lob! (Tannhaeuser)			GSC
-----	Ein Schwert verhiess mir der Vater (Die Walkuere)			GSC
-----	Fanget an (Die Meistersinger)	H	F-A	PET
-----	Mein lieber Schwan (Lohengrin)			GSC
-----	Nothung! nothung! neidliches Schwert (Siegfried)			GSC
-----	Willst jenes Tags du nicht (Der Fliegende Hollaender)			GSC
-----	Winterstuerme wichen dem Wonnemond (Die Walkuere)	H	C-G	†
Wolf	Alle gingen, Herz, zu Ruh	HL	C-EF	†
-----	Das Koehlerweib ist trunken			PET
-----	Denk' es, o Seele	LH	EF-F	†
-----	Der Feuerreiter			†
-----	Der Freund	HM	BF-E	PET
-----	Der Rattenfaenger	HL		†
-----	Lebe wohl	HL	BF-F	†
-----	Seemanns Abschiedslied	H	C-A	†
-----	Ueber Nacht	LH	D-G	†
-----	Zur Ruh', zur Ruh'	HL	A-GF	†

Italian Dramatic Songs and Arias

Dramatic Tenor

Bellini	Meco all' altar di venere (Norma)	H	D-C	RIC
Boito	Giunto sul passo estremo (Epilogue) (Mefistofele)			RIC
Casella	Amante sono vaghiccia di voi			RIC
Cimara	Canto di primavera		D-G	FRL
Durante	Vergin, tutta amor	LM	C-EF	†
Giordano	Come un bel di (Andrea Chenier)	H	E-BF	AMP
-----	Un di all'azzurro spazio (Andrea Chenier)	H	F-BF	SON
Leoncavallo	Vesti la giubba (I Pagliacci)	H	D-A	†
Ponchielli	Cielo e mar (La Gioconda)	H	D-BF	†
Respighi	In alto mare			BON
-----	Nebbie			†
Traetta	Ombra cara, amorosa	HL	B-F	†
Verdi	Celeste Aida (Aida)	LM	D-BF	†
-----	Di quella pira (Il Trovatore)	H	G-C	†
-----	Giorno di pianto (I Vespri Siciliani)			RIC
-----	O tu che in seno agli angeli (La Forza del Destino)	H	DF-BF	RIC

Miscellaneous Dramatic Songs

Dramatic Tenor

Alvarez	La partida	HL	DS-E	GSC
Borodin	A dissonance	MH	E-F	†
Dvořák	Hear my prayer, O Lord			AMP
Gliere	Ah, twine no blossoms	HM	CS-F	DIT
Gretchaninoff	Over the steppe	LM	C-G	GSC
-----	The skylark			DIT
-----	Wounded birch	HL	B-EF	†
Grieg	A dream			†
-----	A swan			†
-----	Den Aergjerrige			
-----	Eros	LM	C-F	†
Malashkin	O could I but express in song	LH		CHE
Mussorgsky	On the Dnieper			GSC
Rachmaninoff	Christ is risen	LM	D-F	GAL

(Rachmaninoff)	Floods of spring	HL		DIT
-----	God took away from me			GSC
-----	O thou billowy harvest field	HL	CS-E	GSC
-----	To the children	MH	F-G	DIT
Sibelius	Black roses	M	A-ES	AMP
-----	The tryst	M		AMP
Tchaikovsky	None but the lonely heart	HLM	C-F	DIT
-----	Why	HL		GSC

Humorous Songs

Dramatic Tenor

Arden and Wille	Cockles and mussels	HM	E-E	ROW
Berners	Dialogue between Tom Filuter and his man	M	D-F	CHE
-----	Theodore or the pirate king			CHE
Bliss	Three jolly gentlemen	H		†
Bone and Fenton	Captain Kidd	MH	B-G	CFI
Brahms	Vergebliches Staendchen	LHM	E-FS	†
Bridge	So perverse			BOS
Britten	Oliver Cromwell			BOH
Brockway	The swapping song			GSC
Carpenter	Don't ceare	M	C-D	GSC
-----	If	M	D-E	GSC
Castelnuovo- Tedesco	La ermita de San Simon			
Chanler	I rise when you enter	M	CS-G	GSC
Clarke	Shy one	HL	BF-G	BOH
Delibes	Bonjours, Suzon	LM	C-F	GSC
Enders	Russian picnic	HM	C-G	GSC
Gibbs	Five eyes	HL	D-D	BOS
Hadley	My shadow			ASC
Head	When I think upon the maidens	LM	D-G	BOO
Hely- Hutchinson	Old mother Hubbard	HL	B-E	CFI
Hindemith	The whistling thief	M	E-F	AMP
Hughes	A Ballynure ballad	L	BF-D	BOH
-----	Kitty, my love, will you marry me?	M	C-F	BOH
-----	The stuttering lovers	MH	E-FS	CHA
Liddle	The garden where the praties grow	LMH	E-FS	STB

620

Mahler	Des Antonius von Padua Fischpredigt	HL	GF-F	†
Malotte	Blow me eyes	MH	C-G	GSC
Moore	Adam was my grandfather			GAL
Mussorgsky	The seminarian			GSC
Niles	The gambler's lament	HL	B-E	GSC
Nordoff	There shall be more joy	M	CS-FS	AMP
Poulenc	La belle jeunesse	L	D-F	HEU
Powell	The deaf woman's courtship	M		JFI
Rontani	Or ch'io non segno più	HL	CS-E	DIT
Rosenthal	Le marabout			ESC
Sacco	Brother Will, brother John	M	C-F	GSC
Satie	Le chapelier			ROU
Scarlatti, A.	Chi vuole innamorarsi	HL	D-EF	DIT
Smetana	Ma-ma-mama so dear (The Bartered Bride)			BOO
Stanford	The little admiral	L	C-G	STB
Strauss	Fuer fuenfzehn Pfennige			†
Torrence	Smilin' Kitty O'Day	ML	CS-D	BOO
Wolf	Der Musikant	HL	CS-D	INT
-----	Der Soldat 1	LH	E-FS	†
-----	Der Tambour	HL		
-----	Storchenbotschaft			†

American Folk Songs (Arr.)

Dramatic Tenor

Bacon	Careless love			
Brockway	Frog went-a-courting			GRA
-----	Sourwood mountain			GRA
-----	The swapping song			GSC
Davis	He's gone away	M	C-E	GAL
Guion	All day on the prarie	M	EF-F	GSC
Hughes	Birds' courting song			GSC
Niles	Black is the color of my true love's hair			
-----	Down in the valley			GSC
-----	I wonder as I wander	HL	BF-D	GSC
-----	Jesus, Jesus rest your head	HL	A-D	GSC
-----	The gambler's lament	HL	B-E	GSC
-----	The rovin' gambler	HL	BF-EF	GSC
Powell	The deaf woman's courtship	M		JFI
-----	The rich old woman	M		JFI

621

Robinson	Water boy	M	B-E	BOS
Russell	The way to the town	H	F-AF	GAL
Siegmeister	He's gone away			
-----	Poor way faring stranger			

British Folk Songs (Arr.)

Dramatic Tenor

Arden and Wille	Cockles and mussels	HM	E-E	ROW
Britten	Oliver Cromwell			BOH
Broadwood	Some rival has stolen my true love	LM	D-E	BOO
Gatty	Bendemeer's stream	LMH		BOO
Harty	My lagan love	ML	BF-EF	BOO
-----	The game played in Erin-Go-Bragh			CFI
Hatton	The minstrel boy			BOO
Hopekirk	Annie Laurie			DIT
-----	Flow gently, sweet Afton			DIT
-----	Loch Lomond			DIT
-----	Ye banks and braes	LM	D-C	DIT
Hughes	A Ballynure ballad	L	BF-D	BOH
-----	Down by the Sally gardens			BOO
-----	Kitty, my love, will you marry me?	M	C-F	BOH
-----	The leprehaun			
-----	The stuttering lovers	MH	E-FS	CHA
Kennedy-Fraser	An Eriskay love lilt			BOO
-----	Land of heart's desire			BOO
-----	The bens of Jura			BOO
Liddle	The garden where the praties grow	LMH	E-FS	STB
Page	The foggy dew			DIT
-----	The harp that once through Tara's halls			DIT
-----	The meeting of the waters			DIT
Peel	In summertime on Bredon	ML	BF-EF	CHA
Taylor	May day carol			JFI
Vaughan Williams	Robin Hood and the pedlar	M	D-E	OXF
-----	Rolling in the dew			OXF
Warlock	Yarmouth Fair	HL	B-E	CFI

622

Miscellaneous Folk Songs (Arr.)

Dramatic Tenor

Brahms	Erlaube mir fein's Maedchen			†
-----	Mein Maedel hat einen Rosenmund	M	F-F	†
Dvořák	Gypsy songs	LH	D-A	AMP
Falla	Jota			
-----	Seguidilla murciana	HL		AMP
Tiersot	L'amours de moi	M	EF-F	HEU
Weckerlin	Aminte	M	C-D	†
-----	Chantons les amours de Jean	H	D-G	GSC
-----	Jeune fillette	M	G-E	GSC
-----	Trop aimable Sylvia	M	D-E	GSC

Negro Spirituals

Dramatic Tenor

Boatner	Oh, what a beautiful city!	HL	D-E	GSC
-----	On mah journey	LH	EF-EF	RIC
-----	Trampin', tryin' to make Heaven my home	L	D-F	ELK
Burleigh	Balm in Gilead	HL		RIC
-----	De gospel train	HL		RIC
-----	Deep river	HML		RIC
-----	Go down, Moses	HL		RIC
-----	Hard trials	M		RIC
-----	Joshua fit de battle ob Jericho	LH	DS-E	RIC
-----	Sometimes I feel like a motherless child	HML		RIC
-----	Swing low, sweet chariot	HL		RIC
-----	Were you there?	HML		RIC
Dett	Sit down servant			GSC
Johnson	City called Heaven			ROB
-----	Dere's no hidin' place down dere			
-----	Hold on			ROB
-----	Honor, honor	HM	C-E	CFI
-----	John Henry			CFI
-----	Witness	HM	D-F	CFI
Kerby-Forrest	He's got the whole world in his hands	M	G-E	MLS
Mac Gimsey	Shadrack	HM	C-EF	CFI

623

| (Mac Gimsey) | Sweet little Jesus boy | ML | D-D | CFI |
| Price | My soul's been anchored in the Lord | | | GAM |

Songs and Arias Employing Agility

Dramatic Tenor

Aiken	Sigh no more	HML		STB
Alvarez	La partida	HL	DS-E	GSC
Arne, T.	Blow, blow thou winter wind	M	C-F	†
-----	Preach not me your musty rules (Comus)	HML		ROW
Beethoven	Mailied			RIC
Besley	Listening	H	E-AF	CUR
Bliss	Three jolly gentlemen	H		†
Bononcini	Deh più a me non v'ascondete	LH	EF-F	†
Brahms	Botschaft	HL	D-F	†
-----	O liebliche Wangen	MLH	E-G	†
Caldara	Alma del core			GSC
-----	Selve amiche, ombrose piante	HM	E-E	†
Carissimi	Filli, non t'amo più	HL	B-D	†
-----	Vittoria mio core	HLM	B-E	†
Castelnuovo-Tedesço	La ermita de San Simon			
Cesti	Tu mancavi a tormentarmi	H	D-G	GSC
Chausson	Le colibri	M	F-GF	BOS
Cherubini	Ave Maria	H	E-A	GSC
Cimara	Canto di primavera		D-G	FRL
Delibes	Bonjours, Suzon	LM	C-F	GSC
Donaudy	Ah mai non cessate			RIC
-----	Freschi luoghi			RIC
-----	Spirate pur, spirate			RIC
Durante	Danza, danza fanciulla gentile	HM	BF-F	†
Fasolo	Cangia, cangia tue voglie	H	C-G	GSC
Fauré	Mandoline	HL	F-E	†
German	Charming Chloe	HML		NOV
Green	My lips shall speak the praise	M	E-F	OXF
Grétry	Si l'univers entier m'oublie (Richard Coeur-De-Lion)			LEM
Hageman	Miranda	HL		GAL
Handel	Sound an alarm! (Judas Maccabaeus)	H		†

624

(Handel)	Thou shalt dash them (The Messiah)	H		†
-----	Wher'er you walk (Semele)	HML	C-D	†
Hely-Hutchinson	Old mother Hubbard	HL	B-E	CFI
Hook	Bright Phoebus	M	EF-F	GSC
Jommelli	Chi vuol comprar la bella	H	B-G	GSC
Lotti	Pur dicesti, O bocca bella	LMH	E-FS	GSC
Mahler	Des Antonius von Padua Fischpredigt	HL	GF-F	†
Moeran	Bright cap			OXF
Morley	It was a lover and his lass	HM		DIT
Nordoff	There shall be more joy	M	CS-FS	AMP
Pizzetti	San Basilio			
Poulenc	Air vif	H	C-AF	ROU
Purcell	I attempt from love's sickness to fly (The Indian Queen)	MH	CS-E	†
-----	If music be the food of love	M	D-G	BOO
-----	I'll sail upon the dog star	HL	A-E	†
-----	Music for a while (Oedipus)	LH		SC
Quilter	Love's philosophy	LMH	D-A	BOO
Ravel	Chanson à boire			DUR
-----	Kaddisch	H	C-G	DUR
Rossini	La danza	MH	E-A	†
Saint-Saëns	Guitares et mandolines			DUR
Scarlatti, A.	Già il sole dal Gange	LH	EF-F	GSC
-----	La fortuna			BOS
Schubert	Am See			PET
-----	Auf dem Wasser zu singen	MH	EF-GF	†
-----	Das Wandern	HLM	E-E	†
-----	Die Wetterfahne			
-----	Irrlicht			
-----	Liebesbotschaft	H	E-G	†
-----	Litanei	HLM	C-EF	†
-----	Mein!	HL		†
-----	Rast			
-----	Ungeduld	HML		†
Schumann	Mondnacht	M	E-FS	†
-----	Waldesgespraech	HL	A-FS	†
Scott	Time of day			ELK
Stradella	Ragion sempre addita	H	E-G	†
Strauss	Fuer fuenfzehn Pfennige			†
Weber	Unter bluehenden Mandelbaeumen (Euryanthe)			PET
-----	Von Jugend auf in dem Kampfgefild (Oberon)			GSC

American Songs Employing
Crescendo and Diminuendo

Dramatic Tenor

Bacon	Is there such a thing as day?	M	DS-FS	AMP
Barber	Rain has fallen	HM	D-E	GSC
-----	The daisies	M	C-F	GSC
Beach	Ah, love but a day			ASC
Campbell- Tipton	A spirit flower	LHM	B-G	GSC
-----	The crying of water	LH	FS-GS	GSC
Carpenter	The pools of peace	M	D-F	GSC
Charles	Clouds	HML	C-EF	GSC
Clough- Leighter	Who knows?	M		GSC
Elwell	In the mountains	M	DF-F	BMI
Hopkinson	My days have been so wondrous free	LH	EF-G	†
La Forge	Hills	HL		RIC
Loeffler	To Helen	M	DF-F	GSC
Niles	I wonder as I wander	HL	BF-D	GSC
-----	Jesus, Jesus rest your head	HL	A-D	GSC
Rogers	At parting	LH	CS-FS	GSC

British Songs Employing
Crescendo and Diminuendo

Dramatic Tenor

Arne, T.	Peggy			GSC
Bantock	A dream of spring	H	E-G	CHE
Benjamin	Calm sea and mist			CUR
-----	The wasp			CUR
Bridge	E'en as a lovely flower	HM	FS-E	BOH
Clarke	Shy one	HL	BF-G	BOH
Delius	Indian love song	H		†
Gurney	Under the greenwood tree			ROG
Head	The ships of Arcady	ML	BF-EF	BOH
Purcell	I attempt from love's sickness to fly (The Indian Queen)	MH	CS-E	†
Quilter	Now sleeps the crimson petal	LMH	EF-GF	BOO

French Songs Employing
Crescendo and Diminuendo

Dramatic Tenor

Bizet	Apres l'hiver			†
Debussy	C'est l'extase	LH	CS-A	†
-----	Green	H	C-AF	†
Duparc	Chanson triste	MH	FS-AF	†
-----	Phidylé	MH	EF-AF	BOS
Fauré	Adieu	MH	F-F	†
-----	Clair de lune	MH	C-G	†
-----	Les roses d'Ispahan			
Gounod	Medjé (Chanson arabe)	MH	G-G	BOO
Koechlin	L'hiver			†
Martini	Plaisir d'amour	M	BF-EF	GSC
Paladilhe	Psyché	HM	BF-F	GSC

German Songs Employing
Crescendo and Diminuendo

Dramatic Tenor

Beethoven	Andenken			†
Brahms	Geheimnis			†
-----	Sonntag	H	D-G	†
-----	Wie Melodien zieht es	HL	A-E	†
Haydn	Liebes Maedchen, hoer' mir zu			HSC
Mahler	Ich atmet' einen linden Duft	HL		INT
Mendelssohn	Venetianisches Gondellied	LM	E-FS	AUG
Reger	Des Kindes Gebet	H	F-G	BOT
Schubert	Abschied	HL	BF-F	†
-----	Am See			PET
-----	An den Mond	HL	F-GF	†
-----	Auf dem Wasser zu singen	MH	EF-GF	†
-----	Der Musensohn	LH	FS-G	†
-----	Der Wanderer an den Mond	LM	D-F	PET
-----	Fruehlingstraum	HL	C-D	†
-----	Geheimes	HL	BF-EF	†
-----	Lachen und Weinen	HL	C-EF	†
-----	Liebesbotschaft	H	E-G	†
-----	Nacht und Traeume	HL	C-DF	†
Schumann	Der Nussbaum	LMH	D-FS	†
-----	Provenzalisches Lied	LH		†
-----	Romanze	HL	C-E	†

Strauss	Die Nacht	HL		†
Wolf	Nun wandre, Maria	HL	EF-D	DIT
-----	Und willst du deinen Liebsten sterben	HL		†
-----	Verschwiegene Liebe	LH	DF-FS	†
-----	Wenn du zu den Blumen gehst	HL	B-EF	†

Italian Songs and Arias Employing
Crescendo and Diminuendo

Dramatic Tenor

Caldara	Alma del core			GSC
-----	Sebben crudele	HML	E-DS	†
-----	Selve amiche, ombrose piante	HM	E-E	†
Cesti	Intorno all'idol mio (Orontea)	MH	D-F	†
De Luca	Non posso disperar	HL	C-E	GSC
Donaudy	Freschi luoghi			RIC
Falconieri	O bellissimi capelli	HL	B-D	†
Fasolo	Cangia, cangia tue voglie	H	C-G	GSC
Frescobaldi	Se l'aura spira	HL	C-EF	DIT
Handel	Ombra mai fu (Serse)	HM	BF-EF	†
Monteverdi	Lasciatemi morire (Arianna)	ML	D-D	†
Respighi	Bella porta di rubini			RIC
-----	Mattinata			BON
Rosa	Selve, voi che le speranze	MH	D-G	DIT
Scarlatti, A.	La fortuna			BOS
-----	Sento nel core	M	E-F	†
Secchi	Love me or not			BOO

Miscellaneous Songs Employing
Crescendo and Diminuendo

Dramatic Tenor

Grieg	En fuglevise			
-----	In the boat			†
-----	It was a lovely summer evening			†
-----	Nu er aftenen lys og lang			HAN
-----	Spring tide			DIT
-----	With a water lily	HM	CS-EF	
Mussorgsky	The banks of the Don			GSC
Rachmaninoff	The lilacs	LH	E-G	†

(Rachmaninoff) The island | | LH | DF-F | †

American Songs Employing
Piano Singing

Dramatic Tenor

Barber	Rain has fallen	HM	D-E	GSC
-----	With rue my heart is laden	HL	CS-D	GSC
Burleigh	Jean	HML		PRE
Campbell-Tipton	A spirit flower	LHM	B-G	GSC
-----	The crying of water	LH	FS-GS	GSC
Carpenter	The pools of peace	M	D-F	GSC
Charles	Clouds	HML	C-EF	GSC
-----	My lady walks in loveliness	HM	C-EF	GSC
-----	When I have sung my songs	HM	BF-EF	GSC
Clough-Leighter	Who knows?	M		GSC
Crist	White hours like snow	HL	CS-BF	CFI
Davis	Nancy Hanks	H	D-G	GAL
Elwell	In the mountains	M	DF-F	BMI
Engel	A sprig of rosemary	M	EF-F	GSC
Giannini	Tell me, o blue, blue sky	H		RIC
Griffes	Symphony in yellow	M	D-GF	GSC
Hageman	Do not go, my love	HL	B-EF	GSC
Kramer	Pleading	LH	D-GF	JFI
Mac Dowell	The sea	HL	D-D	BRH
Mac Gimsey	Sweet little Jesus boy	ML	D-D	CFI
Niles	I wonder as I wander	HL	BF-D	GSC
-----	Jesus, Jesus rest your head	HL	A-D	GSC
Nordoff	Music I heard with you	H	DS-FS	AMP
Watts	Blue are her eyes	H	FS-FS	DIT

British Songs Employing
Piano Singing

Dramatic Tenor

Arden and Wille	Cockles and mussels	HM	E-E	ROW
Benjamin	Calm sea and mist			CUR

Bridge	E'en as a lovely flower	HM	FS-E	BOH
Clarke	Shy one	HL	BF-G	BOH
Coleridge-Taylor	Onaway! Awake beloved	MH	FS-BF	†
-----	She rested by the broken brook	HL		DIT
Del Riego	O dry those tears	LMH	E-GS	CHA
Dunhill	The cloths of Heaven	LM	EF-G	STB
Forsyth	The bell man			DIT
Harty	My lagan love	ML	BF-EF	BOO
Heady	The ships of Arcady	ML	BF-EF	BOH
Quilter	Now sleeps the crimson petal	LMH	EF-GF	BOO
Vaughan Williams	Orpheus with his lute			PRO
-----	Silent noon			GSC

French Songs Employing
Piano Singing

Dramatic Tenor

Debussy	Nuits d'etoiles	LH	E-A	MAR
Fauré	Après un rêve	HM	C-F	†
-----	Clair de lune	MH	C-G	†
Février	L'intruse	M	B-DF	HEU
Franck	Le mariage des roses	M	E-FS	BOS
Hahn	D'une prison	L	BF-EF	HEU
-----	L'heure exquise	M	DF-F	†
-----	Offrande	M	D-D	†
-----	Paysage	MH	EF-G	HEU
Liszt	Oh! quand je dors	H	E-A	†
Lully	Bois épais (Amadis)	ML	C-EF	†
Paladilhe	Psyché	HM	BF-F	GSC
Poldowski	L'heure exquise	LMH	DF-AF	CHE
Rabey	Tes yeux	H	EF-G	DUR
Roussel	Le jardin mouillé	M	C-FS	ROU
Weckerlin	Aminte	M	C-D	†
-----	Trop aimable Sylvia	M	D-E	GSC

German Songs Employing
Piano Singing

Dramatic Tenor

Beethoven	Ich liebe dich	HL	BF-DF	†
Brahms	Geheimnis			†

(Brahms)	In Waldeseinsamkeit	H	ES-G	†
-----	Lerchengesang	LH	FS-GS	†
-----	Staendchen	HL	BF-E	†
Haydn	Liebes Maedchen, hoer' mir zu			HSC
Mahler	Ich atmet' einen Linden Duft	HL		INT
-----	Ich ging mit Lust	HL		INT
Marx	Selige Nacht	M	DF-GF	AMP
Mendelssohn	Gruss	M	DS-FS	†
Reger	Des Kindes Gebet	H	F-G	BOT
Schubert	Abschied	HL	BF-F	†
-----	Auf dem Wasser zu singen	MH	EF-GF	†
-----	Ave Maria	LMH	F-F	†
-----	Der Wanderer an den Mond	LM	D-F	PET
-----	Du bist die Ruh	LMH	EF-AF	†
-----	Fruehlingstraum	HL	C-D	†
-----	Geheimes	HL	BF-EF	†
-----	Im Abendrot	HL	C-D	†
-----	Lachen und Weinen	HL	C-EF	†
-----	Liebesbotschaft	H	E-G	†
-----	Nacht und Traeume	HL	C-DF	†
Schumann	Der Nussbaum	LMH	D-FS	†
-----	Mondnacht	M	E-FS	†
Strauss	Allerseelen	HL	AS-E	DIT
-----	Die Nacht	HL		†
-----	Freundliche Vision	HL	C-F	†
-----	Ich trage meine Minne	M		†
-----	Traum durch die Daemmerung	HML	BF-EF	†
Trunk	In meiner Heimat			
Wolf	An die Geliebte			†
-----	Jaegerlied			PET
-----	Verborgenheit	HL	B-E	†
-----	Verschwiegene Liebe	LH	DF-FS	†

Italian Songs and Arias Employing Piano Singing

Dramatic Tenor

Bassani	Posate dormite (La Serenata)	H		GSC
Bononcini	Deh, più a me non v'ascondete	LH	EF-F	†
Brogi	Venitian vision	M	D-F	RIC

631

Castelnuovo-Tedesco	L'Infinito			
Cimara	Fiocca la neve	H	G-G	GSC
Frescobaldi	Se laura spira	HL	C-EF	DIT
Gagliano	Dormi, amore (La Flora)	HL	CS-E	DIT
Gluck	O del mio dolce ardor			†
Jommelli	Chi vuol comprar la bella	H	B-G	GSC
Monteverdi	Lasciatemi morire (Arianna)	ML	D-D	†
Secchi	Lungi dal caro bene	HL	A-FS	DIT
Tosti	Ideale			GSC

Miscellaneous Songs Employing Piano Singing

Dramatic Tenor

Cui	The statue at Czarskoe-Selo	HM	DF-EF	†
Dvořák	God is my shepherd			AMP
-----	Songs my mother taught me	HM	E-E	†
Gretchaninoff	Hushed the song of the nightingale	MH	E-G	DIT
Grieg	A dream			†
-----	A swan			†
Mednikoff	The hills of Gruzia	H	DS-A	LAC
Rachmaninoff	In the silence of night	LH	D-A	GSC
Sibelius	The tryst	M		AMP

American Songs Employing Rapid Enunciation

Dramatic Tenor

Boatner	Oh, what a beautiful city!	HL	D-E	GSC
Brockway	The swapping song			GSC
Burleigh	Joshua fit de battle ob Jericho	LH	DS-E	RIC
Carpenter	Don't ceare	M	C-D	GSC
Deis	Come down to Kew			
Griffes	Elves	H	F-AF	GSC
Hadley	My shadow			ASC
Hageman	At the well	LH	EF-AF	GSC
-----	Miranda	HL		GAL
Kountz	The sleigh	HL	D-FS	GSC

632

Rodgers	The surrey with the fringe on the top (Oklahoma)			WIL
Sacco	Brother Will, brother John	M	C-F	GSC
Warner	Hurdy gurdy	M	D-F	CFI

British Songs Employing Rapid Enunciation

Dramatic Tenor

Bantock	A feast of lanterns	HM	D-F	GAL
Bax	The enchanted fiddle			
Berners	Dialogue between Tom Filuter and his man	M	D-F	CHE
Britten	Oliver Cromwell			BOH
Cowen	Border ballad	LM	D-E	BOO
Dowland	Shall I sue?			STB
German	Charming Chloe	HML		NOV
Gibbs	Five eyes	HL	D-D	BOS
Head	When I think upon the maidens	LM	D-G	BOO
Hughes	Kitty, my love, will you marry me?	M	C-F	BOH
-----	The stuttering lovers	MH	E-FS	CHA
Liddle	The garden where the praties grow	LMH	E-FS	STB
Molloy	The Kerry Dance	LH	C-G	GSC
Morley	It was a lover and his lass	HM		DIT
Scott	Time of day			ELK

French Songs Employing Rapid Enunciation

Dramatic Tenor

Debussy	Chevaux de bois	H	C-G	†
-----	Mandoline	HM	BF-F	†
Delibes	Bonjours, Suzon	LM	C-F	GSC
Fauré	Mandoline	HL	F-E	†
-----	Toujours	LH	F-AF	†
Fourdrain	Carnaval	M	C-F	RIC
Poldowski	Dansons la gigue	M	EF-G	MAR
Poulenc	La belle jeunesse	L	D-F	HEU
Roussel	Le bachelier de Salamanque			DUR
Severac	Chanson pour le petit cheval			ROU

Weckerlin	Aminte	M	C-D	†
-----	Trop aimable Sylvia	M	D-E	GSC

German Songs Employing
Rapid Enunciation

Dramatic Tenor

Beethoven	Mailied			RIC
-----	Neue Liebe, neues Leben			†
Brahms	Juchhe!			†
-----	Meine Liebe ist gruen	MLH	ES-A	†
-----	O liebliche Wangen	MLH	E-G	†
-----	Staendchen	HL	BF-E	†
-----	Tambourliedchen			†
-----	Vergebliches Staendchen	LHM	E-FS	†
Jensen	Margreta	M	F-F	PET
Mendelssohn	Neue Liebe	H	CS-A	†
Schubert	Abschied	HL	BF-F	†
-----	Am Feierabend	HL	BF-F	†
-----	Das Wandern	HLM	E-E	†
-----	Der Musensohn	LH	FS-G	†
-----	Der Schiffer	LH	BF-A	†
-----	Der zuernende Barde			PET
-----	Die Forelle	MLH	EF-GF	†
-----	Die Post	HML	BF-EF	†
-----	Erstarrung	HL	D-F	†
-----	Mein!	HL		†
-----	Ungeduld	HML		†
-----	Wohin?	HL	B-E	†
Strauss	Fuer fuenfzehn Pfennige			†
-----	Wozu noch, Maedchen	H	FS-A	
Wolf	Der Feuerreiter			†
-----	Jaegerlied			PET

Italian Songs Employing
Rapid Enunciation

Dramatic Tenor

Buzzi-Peccia	Povero pulcinella	H	E-A	GSC
Carissimi	Vittoria, mio core	HLM	B-E	†
Cavalli	Donzelle fuggite	HL	C-EF	†
De Luca	Non posso disperar	HL	C-E	GSC
Donaudy	Ah mai non cessate			RIC
Durante	Danza, danza fanciulla gentile	HM	BF-F	†

Falconieri	Non più d'amore	HL	C-D	DIT
-----	Nudo arciero	HL	AF-AF	DIT
Legrenzi	Che fiero costume	HML	C-D	†
Paradies	M'ha preso alla sua ragna	M	EF-F	GSC
Rontani	Or ch'io non segno più	HL	CS-E	DIT
Rossini	La danza	MH	E-A	†
Scarlatti, A.	Chi vuole innamorarsi	HL	D-EF	DIT
Stradella	Ragion sempre addita	H	E-G	†

Miscellaneous Songs Employing Rapid Enunciation

Dramatic Tenor

Falla	Seguidilla murciana	HL		AMP
Grieg	In the boat			†
-----	The way of the world			†
-----	With a water lily	HM	CS-EF	†
Mussorgsky	The evening hymn			
-----	The magpie and the gypsy dancer			GSC
-----	The seminarian			GSC
Smetana	Ma-ma-mama so dear (The Bartered Bride)			BOO

American Songs Employing Sustained Singing

Dramatic Tenor

Barber	Sure on this shining night	MH	D-G	GSC
Burleigh	Deep river	HML		RIC
-----	Sometimes I feel like a motherless child	HML		RIC
-----	Were you there?	HML		RIC
Chadwick	Allah	LH	CS-GS	ASC
Charles	And so, goodbye	LH	EF-AF	GSC
Curran	Nocturne	HML	B-DS	GSC
Dunn	The bitterness of love			JFI
Edwards	By the bend of the river	HML	C-E	GSC
-----	Into the night	HML	C-DF	GSC
Foote	I'm wearing awa'	HL		ASC
Giannini	Far above the purple hills	LH	CS-A	RIC
Griffes	By a lonely forest pathway	HML	A-EF	GSC
-----	The lament of Ian the proud	MH	DS-AS	GSC
-----	The rose of the night	H	CS-A	GSC

635

Hageman	Music I heard with you	MH	E-A	GAL
Horsman	In the yellow dusk	MH	FS-A	GSC
-----	The bird of the wilderness	LMH	DF-BF	GSC
Kernochan	We two together	H	EF-AF	GAL
Kramer	For a dream's sake	HL		JFI
Levitzki	Do you remember?	HML	BF-EF	GSC
Mc Donald	Daybreak	H		ELV
Rasbach	Trees	LMH	CS-GS	GSC
Robinson	Water boy	M	B-E	BOS
Rogers	Wind song	LM	C-G	GSC
Scott	Think on me	HML	D-EF	GAL
Skiles	You will know my love			CFI
Speaks	Sylvia	HML	AF-DF	GSC

British Songs and Arias Employing Sustained Singing

Dramatic Tenor

Arne, T.	Blow, blow thou winter wind	M	C-F	†
Bantock	Silent strings	MH	F-G	BOO
Bax	The white peace			CHE
Bridge	All things that we clasp	HL		BOS
-----	O that it were so	LMH	D-G	CHA
Butterworth	Loveliest of trees			AUG
Campion	Follow thy fair sun			STB
-----	There is a garden in her face			DIT
Clarke	The blind ploughman	HML	C-D	CHA
Coleridge-Taylor	Life and death	HML		ASC
Del Riego	Homing	HML	BF-E	CHA
Dowland	I saw my lady weep	M	E-E	STB
Dunhill	To the Queen of Heaven	M	C-G	GSC
Ford	Now I see thy looks were feigned			BOO
-----	Since first I saw your face			DIT
Handel	Total eclipse (Samson)			†
-----	Wher'er you walk (Semele)	HML	C-D	†
Henschel	Morning-hymn	MH	DS-GS	†
Holbrooke	Come not when I am dead			ENO
Holst	The heart worships	ML	BF-D	STB
Purcell	Had I but love			DUN
-----	If music be the food of love	M	D-G	BOO
-----	Music for a while (Oedipus)	LH		SC

Ronald	Prelude	HML	B-D	ENO
Scott	The unforeseen	HML		GAL
Thomson	The knight of Bethlehem	LM		NOV
Warlock	Sleep			OXF

French Songs and Arias Employing Sustained Singing

Dramatic Tenor

Bizet	Flower song (Carmen)	H	E-BF	†
Caplet	Le forêt			DUR
Chausson	Le colibri Violin or cello	M	F-GF	BOS
-----	Le temps des lilas	MH	D-GS	†
Dalayrac	Hélas! c'est près de vous			
Debussy	Beau soir	LH	C-FS	†
-----	Colloque sentimental			DUR
-----	De fleurs	H	C-AF	†
Duparc	La vie antérieure	HL		†
-----	Lamento	ML	EF-EF	†
Fauré	Au cimetière	LH	D-F	†
-----	Automne	MH	D-FS	GSC
-----	Prison	LH		†
-----	Rencontre	H	EF-AF	†
Gluck	Unis dès la plus tendre enfance (Iphigénie en Aulide)			NOV
Gounod	Ah! leve-toi, Soleil! (Roméo et Juliette)	H	F-BF	†
Hue	J'ai pleuré en rêve	HL	D-E	BOS
Indy	Lied maritime	LH	B-G	†
Lalo	Marine	LH	DS-FS	
Lenormand	Quelle souffrance	HM	AF-F	HAM
Massenet	Elégie	LM	C-GF	GSC
Messager	La maison grise (Fortuno)			CHO
Paladilhe	Lamento provincal	M	CS-FS	HOM
Poulenc	Bleuet	H	FS-GF	DUR
Ravel	Kaddisch	H	C-G	DUR
Rhené-Baton	Il pleut des pétales de fleurs	M	CS-E	DUR
Severac	Les hiboux			ROU

German Songs and Arias Employing Sustained Singing

Dramatic Tenor

Bach, C.P.E.	Passionslied			SIM
Bach, J.S.	Bist due bei mir	HML	A-EF	†
Beethoven	Adelaide	HML	BF-E	†
-----	An die ferne Geliebte	HL	C-E	†
-----	Delizia	M	C-F	GSC
-----	Die Ehre Gottes	HL	AF-EF	†
-----	Wonne der Wehmut			†
Bohm	Calm as the night	HML	A-EF	†
Brahms	Auf dem Kirchhofe	HL	BF-EF	†
-----	Der Tod, das ist die kuehle Nacht	L	AF-F	†
-----	Der Ueberlaeufer			†
-----	Die Mainacht	HL	BF-FF	†
-----	Feldeinsamkeit	HL	C-EF	†
-----	Minnelied	MHL	C-EF	†
-----	Nachtigall	MHL	BF-FS	†
-----	O kuehler Wald	MH	A-F	†
-----	O wuesst' ich doch den Weg zurueck	H	E-FS	†
-----	Schoen war, das ich dir weihte			†
-----	Wie bist due meine Koenigin	HL	C-E	†
-----	Wir wandelten	LH	EF-GF	†
Cornelius	Komm, wir wandeln	H	FS-GS	SC
Haydn	She never told her love	HL	B-D	DIT
Liszt	Du bist wie eine Blume	H	E-G	GSC
-----	Es muss ein Wunderbares sein	M	C-EF	DUR
Mahler	Um Mitternacht	HL		INT
Marx	Hat dich die Liebe beruehrt	MH	EF-BF	AMP
-----	Nocturne	H	EF-AF	AMP
Mendelssohn	He counteth all your sorrows (Hymn of Praise)	H	D-G	†
-----	If with all your hearts (Elijah)	MH	F-AF	†
-----	Nachtlied			
Reger	Friede	H	EF-G	UNI
Schoenberg	Erhebung			GSC
Schubert	Am Meer	HML	B-D	†
-----	An die Musik	HL	A-DS	†
-----	Auf dem Flusse	HL	F-E	†
-----	Das Wirtshaus	HL	C-D	†

638

(Schubert)	Der Doppelgaenger	HL	G-D	†
-----	Der Leiermann	ML	C-D	†
-----	Der Lindenbaum	HL	A-D	†
-----	Der Neugierige	HL	CS-EF	†
-----	Der Wegweiser	L	D-EF	†
-----	Die Allmacht	HML	G-E	†
-----	Die Liebe hat gelogen	LM	G-F	†
-----	Die Nebensonnen	HL	F-D	†
-----	Du liebst mich nicht	LH	E-FS	†
-----	Ihr Bild	HL	C-C	†
-----	In der Ferne	HL		GSC
-----	Litanei	HLM	C-EF	†
-----	Memnon	LM	AF-F	PET
-----	Schaefers Klagelied	HL	BF-D	†
-----	Staendchen	MH	B-E	†
-----	Wer nie sein Brot	HL	C-EF	†
Schumann	Aus den Hebraeischen Gesaengen			
-----	Die Lotusblume	HLM	BF-F	†
-----	Due bist wie eine Blume	HM	F-EF	†
-----	Ich grolle nicht	HL	BF-D	†
-----	Ich hab' im Traum geweinet	HL	B-D	†
-----	Ihre Stimme	LH		†
-----	Im Rhein, im heiligen Strome	HM	D-F	
-----	Mein schoener Stern			
Strauss	Befreit			HSC
-----	Breit ueber mein Haupt	LH	GF-AF	HSC
-----	Madrigal	LH	EF-GF	
-----	Mit deinen blauen Augen	LH	C-GS	†
-----	Morgen	HML	E-F	†
-----	Ruhe meine Seele			†
Wagner	Allmaecht'ger Vater (Rienzi)			PET
-----	Am stillen Herd (Die Meistersinger)	H	D-A	GSC
-----	Atmest du nicht mit mir die suessen Duefte (Lohengrin)			GSC
-----	In fernem Land (Lohengrin)	H	E-A	GSC
-----	Mein lieber Schwan (Lohengrin)			†
-----	Willst jenes Tags du nicht (Der Fliegende Hollaender)			GSC
-----	Winterstuerme wichen dem Wonnemond (Die Walkuere)	H	C-G	†
Weber	Unter bluehenden Mandelbaeumen (Euryanthe)			PET

639

Wolf	Alle gingen, Herz zu Ruh	HL	C-EF	†
-----	Denk' es, o Seele	LH	EF-F	†
-----	Gebet	HL		†
-----	Gesang Weylas	HL	DF-F	†
-----	Heb' auf deine blondes Haupt	HL	G-DF	†
-----	Herr, was traegt der Boden	HL	B-DS	†
-----	Im Fruehling	HL	BF-F	†
-----	Lebe wohl	HL	BF-F	†
-----	Morgenstimmung	LH	C-GS	†
-----	Neue Liebe	LH	D-AF	†
-----	Zur Ruh', zur Ruh'	HL	A-GF	†
Wolff	Alle Dinge haben Sprache	M	BF-GF	†

Italian Songs and Arias Employing
Sustained Singing

Dramatic Tenor

Bellini	Meco all'altar di venere (Norma)	H	D-C	RIC
Bimboni	Sospiri miei	M	EF-EF	GAL
Boito	Giunto, sul passo estremo (Epilogue) (Mefistofele)			RIC
Braga	Angel's serenade Violin	LH	D-G	†
Caccini	Amarilli, mia bella	ML	C-D	†
Caldara	Come raggio di sol	HL	D-F	†
Cesti	Tu mancavi a tormentarmi	H	D-G	GSC
Cimara	Stornellata marinara	HM		RIC
Donaudy	Quando ti rivedrò			RIC
-----	Vaghissima sembianza	H	E-A	RIC
Durante	Vergin, tutta amor	LM	C-EF	†
Giordano	Come un bel di (Andrea Chenier)	H	E-BF	AMP
-----	Un di all'azzurro spazio (Andrea Chenier)	H	F-BF	SON
Haydn	Pensi a me			
Leoncavallo	Vesti la giubba (I Pagliacci)	H	D-A	†
Lonati	Tu paristi idolo amato			PET
Mattei	Non è ver	HML		DIT
Pergolesi	Nina	HL	CS-D	DIT
Peri	Invocazione di Orfeo (Euridice)	HL	E-CS	DIT
Ponchielli	Cielo e mar (La Gioconda)	H	D-BF	†
Respighi	Abbandono			BON

(Respighi)	Nebbie			†
Rosa	Star vicino	HL	D-E	†
Stradella	Se nel ben			CFI
Torelli	Tu lo sai	HL	BF-F	†
Verdi	Deserto sulla terra (Il Trovatore)			GSC
-----	O, tu che in seno agli angeli (La Forza del Destino)	H	DF-BF	RIC

Miscellaneous Songs Employing Sustained Singing

Dramatic Tenor

Arensky	Autumn	H	CS-FS	GSC
Borodin	A dissonance	MH	E-F	†
Cherubini	Ave Maria	H	E-A	GSC
Dvořák	Hear my prayer, O Lord			AMP
-----	Lord, Thou art my refuge and shield			AMP
-----	Turn Thee to me			AMP
Gliere	Ah, twine no blossoms	HM	CS-F	DIT
Gretchaninoff	Over the steppe	LM	C-G	GSC
-----	Wounded birch	HL	B-EF	†
Grieg	I love thee	HML	E-F	†
-----	To Norway	M	E-F	DIT
Malashkin	O could I but express in song	LH		CHE
Mussorgsky	On the Dnieper			GSC
Rachmaninoff	Christ is risen	LM	D-F	GAL
-----	O thou billowy harvest field	HL	CS-E	GSC
-----	To the children	MH	F-G	DIT
Sibelius	Black roses	M	A-ES	AMP
Sjoegren	The Seraglio's garden	HL		GSC
Tchaikovsky	None but the lonely heart	HLM	C-F	DIT
-----	Why	HL		†

American Songs Employing Spirited Singing

Dramatic Tenor

Barber	I hear an army	LH	D-AF	GSC
Beach	The year's at the spring	MH	AF-AF	ASC
Boatner	Oh, what a beautiful city!	HL	D-E	GSC

641

Burleigh	Joshua fit de battle ob Jericho	LH	DS-E	RIC
Carpenter	Don't ceare	M	C-D	GSC
-----	If	M	D-E	GSC
-----	Light, my light	M	C-G	GSC
Castelnuovo-Tedesco	O mistress mine			CHE
Chanler	I rise when you enter	M	CS-G	GSC
Curran	Life	HM	BF-F	GSC
Deis	Come down to Kew			
Dobson	Cargoes	ML	C-EF	GSC
Enders	Russian picnic	HM	C-G	GSC
Griffes	An old song resung	LM	EF-F	GSC
-----	Elves	H	F-AF	GSC
Guion	All day on the prarie	M	EF-F	GSC
-----	Wild geese	M	D-F	CFI
Hadley	My shadow			ASC
Hageman	At the well	LH	EF-AF	GSC
-----	Miranda	HL		GAL
-----	Voices			
Hindemith	The whistling thief	M	E-F	AMP
Kountz	The sleigh	HL	D-FS	GSC
La Forge	Song of the open	MH	EF-AF	DIT
Levitzki	Ah, thou beloved one	H	EF-AF	GSC
Manz-Zucca	I love life	LM	F-F	PRE
Margetson	Tommy, lad	HML	A-D	BOH
Moore	Adam was my grandfather			GAL
Niles	The rovin' gambler	HL	BF-EF	GSC
Nordoff	There shall be more joy	M	CS-FS	AMP
Rogers	The last song	MLH	E-AF	GSC
Rummel	Ecstasy	LMH	GF-AF	GSC
Sacco	Brother Will, brother John	M	C-F	GSC
Speaks	Morning	HML	BF-D	GSC
Strickland	Here in the high hills	H	DF-G	GSC
Warner	Hurdy gurdy	M	D-F	CFI
Warren	White horses of the sea	LH	F-G	GSC

British Songs Employing Spirited Singing

Dramatic Tenor

Arne, T.	Preach not me your musty rules (Comus)	HML		ROW
Bantock	A feast of lanterns	HM	D-F	GAL
Bax	The enchanted fiddle			
Benjamin	Hedgerow			CUR

Besley	Listening	H	E-AF	CUR
Bliss	Three jolly gentlemen	H		†
Bridge	Love went a-riding	HL		BOS
-----	So perverse			BOS
Butterworth	When I was one and twenty			AUG
Cowen	Border ballad	LM	D-E	BOO
Delius	To the Queen of my heart			†
Dowland	Come again! sweet love	M	D-E	STB
-----	Say love, if ever thou didst find			STB
-----	Shall I sue?			STB
Eden	What's in the air today?	M	D-F	ELK
German	Charming Chloe	HML		NOV
-----	My song is of the sturdy north	ML		CHA
Gibbs	Five eyes	HL	D-D	BOS
Head	Sea gipsy	LM	E-GS	BOO
-----	When I think upon the maidens	LM	D-G	BOO
Hook	Bright Phoebus	M	EF-F	GSC
Hopekirk	Ye banks and braes	LM	D-C	DIT
Hughes	The stuttering lovers	MH	E-FS	CHA
Ireland	Great things			AUG
-----	Hope the hornblower			BOO
Jones	What if I speede?			BOO
Leveridge	When dull care			BOO
Liddle	The garden where the praties grow	LMH	E-FS	STB
Martin	Come to the fair	HML	D-D	BOO
Moeran	Bright cap			OXF
Molloy	The Kerry Dance	LH	C-G	GSC
Morley	It was a lover and his lass	HM		DIT
Purcell	I'll sail upon the dog star	HL	A-E	†
Quilter	Blow, blow thou winter wind	HL	C-E	BOO
-----	Love's philosophy	LMH	D-A	BOO
Scott	Time of day			ELK
Vaughan Williams	The roadside fire	HML	BF-EF	BOO
-----	The vagabond	ML	A-E	BOO

French Songs and Arias Employing
Spirited Singing

Dramatic Tenor

Bruneau	L'heureux vagabond	LH	EF-G	GSC
Charpentier	Les chevaux de bois	H	E-A	HEU
Chausson	La caravane	MH	CS-A	HAM
Debussy	Chevaux de bois	H	C-G	†
-----	La mer est plus belle	HL		†
-----	Le faune			DUR
-----	Mandoline	HM	BF-F	†
Delibes	Bonjours, Suzon	LM	C-F	GSC
Duparc	Le manoir de Rosamunde	HL	B-F	BOS
-----	Testament	HL		INT
Fauré	Fleur jetée	HM	BF-FS	†
-----	L'hiver a cessé	HL		INT
-----	Mandoline	HL	F-E	†
-----	Toujours	LH	F-AF	†
Fourdrain	Chanson norvégienne	H	E-G	RIC
Gluck	Bannis la crainte (Alceste)			†
Gounod	Vénise	HL		INT
Grétry	Si l'univers entier m'oublie			LEM
	(Richard Coeur-De-Lion)			
Koechlin	Le thé	HM	C-E	BOS
Poldowski	Colombine	H	D-GF	CHE
-----	Dansons la gigue	M	EF-G	MAR
Poulenc	Air vif	H	C-AF	ROU
-----	La belle jeunesse	L	D-F	HEU
Ravel	Chanson à boire			DUR
Roussel	Le bachelier de Salamanque			DUR
Saint-Saëns	Guitares et mandolines			DUR
Severac	Chanson pour le petit cheval			ROU

German Songs and Arias Employing
Spirited Singing

Dramatic Tenor

Beethoven	Mailied			RIC
-----	Neue Liebe, neues Leben			†
Brahms	Bei dir sind meine	MH	E-FS	†
	Gedanken			
-----	Botschaft	HL	D-F	†
-----	Der Gang zur Liebsten	HL		†
-----	Der Schmied	HL	EF-EF	†
-----	Heimkehr			†
-----	Juchhe!			†

(Brahms)	Liebe kam aus fernen Landen	HL	C-E	†
-----	Meine Liebe ist gruen	MLH	ES-A	†
-----	O liebliche Wangen	MLH	E-G	†
-----	Sehnsucht	H	EF-AF	†
-----	Sind es Schmerzen	HL	BF-F	†
-----	Tambourliedchen			†
-----	Vergebliches Staendchen	LHM	E-FS	†
-----	Wie froh und frisch	HL	B-E	†
Jensen	Margreta	M	F-F	PET
-----	Murmuring zephyr	LH	E-AF	GSC
Mendelssohn	Jagdlied	HL	BF-EF	†
-----	Neue Liebe	H	CS-A	†
Schubert	Am Feierabend	HL	BF-F	†
-----	Aufenthalt	HLM	A-F	†
-----	Das Fischermaedchen	L	A-EF	†
-----	Der Schiffer	LH	BF-A	DIT
-----	Der zuernende Barde			PET
-----	Die Forelle	MLH	EF-GF	†
-----	Die Post	HML	BF-EF	†
-----	Erstarrung	HL	D-F	†
-----	Mein!	HL		†
-----	Rastlose Liebe	M	B-F	†
-----	Wohin?	HL	B-E	†
Schumann	Er ist's	HL	BF-EF	†
-----	Schoene Wiege meiner Leiden	HL	C-EF	†
-----	Waldesgespraech	HL	A-FS	†
-----	Wanderlied	HL	A-E	†
-----	Widmung	HL	BF-F	†
Strauss	Caecilie	MH	E-B	†
-----	Fuer fuenfzehn Pfennige			†
-----	Heimliche Aufforderung	HL	B-E	†
-----	Kling			†
-----	Zueignung	HL	CS-FS	†
Wagner	Dir Toene Lob! (Tannhaeuser)			GSC
-----	Fanget an (Die Meistersinger)	H	F-A	PET
Weber	Von Jugend auf in dem Kampfgefild (Oberon)			GSC
Wolf	Das Koehlerweib ist trunken			PET
-----	Der Feuerreiter			†
-----	Der Rattenfaenger	HL		†
-----	Der Soldat, 1	LH	E-FS	PET
-----	Er ist's	H	D-G	†
-----	Fussreise	HL	D-E	†
-----	Seemanns Abschiedslied	H	C-A	†
-----	Trunken muessen wir alle sein	M	ES-FS	†

Italian Songs Employing
Spirited Singing

Dramatic Tenor

Carissimi	Filli, non t'amo più	HL	B–D	†
-----	Vittoria, mio core!	HLM	B–E	†
Casella	Amante sono vaghiccia di voi			RIC
Cavalli	Donzelle fuggite	HL	C–EF	†
Cimara	Canto di primavera		D–G	FRL
Donaudy	Ah mai non cessate			RIC
-----	Spirate pur, spirate			RIC
Durante	Danza, danza fanciulla gentile	HM	BF–F	†
Falconieri	Non più d'amore	HL	C–D	DIT
-----	Nudo arciero	HL	AF–AF	DIT
Gaffi	Luci vezzose	HL	D–E	DIT
Legrenzi	Che fiero costume	HML	C–D	†
Marcello	Il mio bel foco	LMH	C–G	†
Parādies	M'ha preso alla sua ragna	M	EF–F	GSC
Respighi	In alto mare			BON
-----	Invito alla danza			BON
Rontani	Or ch'io non segno più	HL	CS–E	DIT
Scarlatti, A.	Chi vuole innamorarsi	HL	D–EF	DIT
-----	Già il sole dal Gange	LH	EF–F	GSC
Tosti	The last song	HL		RIC

Miscellaneous Songs Employing
Spirited Singing

Dramatic Tenor

Dvořák	I will sing new songs of gladness	HL		†
-----	Sing ye a joyful song			AMP
-----	Tune thy fiddle gypsy			SIM
Gretchaninoff	The skylark			DIT
Grieg	With a water lily			†
Mussorgsky	Hopak	HM		GSC
Rachmaninoff	Floods of spring	HL		DIT
-----	God took away from me			GSC
-----	Oh, no, I pray do not depart			DIT
-----	Sorrow in spring			
Sandoval	Sin tu amor	H	E–G	GSC
Tchaikovsky	At the ball	MH		GSC

Dramatic Tenor

Arden and Wille	Roses in your hair	ML	C-EF	ROW
Beach	Ah, love but a day			ASC
Bond	Still unexprest	HL	C-C	BOS
Bone and Fenton	Captain Kidd	MH	B-G	CFI
Burleigh	Jean	HML		PRE
Campbell-Tipton	A spirit flower	LHM	B-G	GSC
Chanler	I rise when you enter	M	CS-G	GSC
Charles	And so, goodbye	LH	EF-AF	GSC
-----	When I have sung my songs	HM	BF-EF	GSC
Clarke	Shy one	HL	BF-G	BOH
-----	The blind ploughman	HML	C-D	CHA
Cowen	Border ballad	LM	D-E	BOO
Curran	Life	HM	BF-F	GSC
Del Riego	Homing	HML	BF-E	CHA
-----	O dry those tears	LMH	E-GS	CHA
D'Hardelot	Because	MH	E-G	CHA
Dix	The trumpeter	HML	A-C	BOH
Dobson	Cargoes	ML	C-EF	GSC
Dunn	The bitterness of love			JFI
Eden	What's in the air today?	M	D-F	ELK
Edwards	By the bend of the river	HML	C-E	GSC
-----	Into the night	HML	C-DF	GSC
Elgar	Land of hope and glory			BOO
Enders	Russian picnic	HM	C-G	GSC
Forsyth	The bell man			DIT
Foster	My journey's end	HLM	DF-G	GSC
Fox	The hills of home	HML	BF-DF	CFI
Friml	L'amour, toujours, l'amour			HAR
Geehl	For your alone			SHU
Head	When I think upon the maidens	LM	D-G	BOO
Hely-Hutchinson	Old mother Hubbard	HL	B-E	CFI
Henschel	Morning-hymn	MH	DS-GS	†
Ireland	Sea fever	HLM	D-F	AUG
La Forge	Song of the open	MH	EF-AF	DIT
Levitzki	Ah, thou beloved one	H	EF-AF	GSC
-----	Do you remember?	HML	BF-EF	GSC
Malotte	Blow me eyes	MH	C-G	GSC
-----	For my mother	HLM	BF-EF	GSC

Mana-Zucca	I love life	LM	F-F	PRE
Margetson	Tommy, lad	HML	A-D	BOH
Martin	Come to the fair	HML	D-D	BOO
O' Hara	The song is the thing			CHA
Rasbach	Trees	LMH	CS-GS	GSC
Rogers	At parting	LH	CS-FS	GSC
Ronald	Prelude	HML	B-D	ENO
Sacco	Brother Will, brother John	M	C-F	GSC
Sanderson	Shipmates of mine	LL	G-D	BOO
-----	Until	LMH	E-A	BOO
Scott	Think on me	HML	D-EF	GAL
Skiles	You will know my love			CFI
Speaks	Morning	HML	BF-D	GSC
-----	Sylvia	HML	AF-DF	GSC
Stanford	The little admiral	L	C-G	STB
Strelezki	Dreams	LMH	B-A	GSC
Torrence	Smilin' Kitty O'Day	ML	CS-D	BOO
Tours	Mother o' mine	HML	C-D	CHA
Warren	Fulfilment	H	D-BF	GAL

(See also Humorous Songs, Negro Spirituals,
Folk Songs, Operetta Songs and Opera Arias.)

Miscellaneous Songs of Popular Appeal

Dramatic Tenor

Alvarez	La partida	HL	DS-E	GSC
Bixio	Torno, picina			
Bizet	Agnus Dei	HLM	C-AF	†
Bohm	Calm as the night	HML	A-EF	†
Braga	Angel's serenade Violin	LH	D-G	†
Brogi	Venitian vision	M	D-F	RIC
Buzzi-Peccia	Povero pulcinella	H	E-A	GSC
Cavalli	Donzelle fuggite	HL	C-EF	†
Cimara	Canto di primavera		D-G	FRL
De Curtis	Torna al Surriento	HM	D-F	CFI
Dvořák	Songs my mother taught me	HM	E-E	†
Grieg	A dream			†
-----	I love thee	HML	E-F	†
Lara	Granada			SOU
Massenet	Elégie	LM	C-GF	GSC
Mattei	Non è ver	HML		DIT
Rabey	Tes yeux	H	EF-G	DUR
Rachmaninoff	To the children	MH	F-G	DIT

Rossini	La danza	MH	E-A	†
Schubert	An die Musik	HL	A-DS	DIT
-----	Ave Maria	LMH	F-F	†
-----	Staendchen			
Schumann	Widmung	HL	BF-F	†
Sjoeberg	Visions	MH	F-AF	GAL
Strauss, J.	Wein, Weib, und Gesang			
Strauss, R.	Zueignung	HL	CS-FS	†
Tchaikovsky	None but the lonely heart	HLM	C-F	DIT
Tosti	The last song	HL		RIC
Yradier	La paloma	HL	BF-EF	GSC

(See also Humorous Songs, Negro Spirituals,
Folk Songs, Operetta Songs and Opera Arias.)

Arias From French Operas

Dramatic Tenor

Bizet	Flower song (Carmen)	H	E-BF	†
Gluck	Bannis la crainte (Alceste)			†
-----	Unis dès la plus tendre enfance (Iphigénie en Aulide)			NOV
Gounod	Ah! lève-toi, soleil! (Roméo et Juliette)	H	F-BF	†
Grétry	Si l'univers entier m'oublie (Richard Coeur-De-Lion)			LEM
Lully	Bois épais (Amadis)	ML	C-EF	†
Mehul	Versez tous vos chagrins (Stratonice)			LEM
Messager	La maison grise (Fortuno)			CHO
Meyerbeer	Plus blanche que la blanche hermine (Les Huguenots)			BRO
Reyer	Esprits gardiens (Sigurd)			HEU

Arias From German Operas

Dramatic Tenor

Beethoven	In des Lebens Fruehlingstagen (Fidelio)			†
Lortzing	Vater, Mutter, Schwestern, Brueder (Undine)	H		SC
Wagner	Allmaecht'ger Vater (Rienzi)			PET
-----	Am stillen Herd (Die Meistersinger)	H	D-A	GSC

(Wagner)	Atmest du nicht mit mir die suessen Duefte (Lohengrin)			GSC
-----	Dir Toene Lob! (Tannhaeuser)			GSC
-----	Ein Schwert verhiess mir der Vater (Die Walkuere)			GSC
-----	Fanget an (Die Meistersinger)	H	F-A	PET
-----	Ihr nicht beim Feste (Rienzi)	H		†
-----	Inbrunst im Herzen (Tannhaeuser)	H	DS-A	GSC
-----	In fernem Land (Lohengrin)	H	E-A	†
-----	Morgentlich leuchtend (Preislied) (Die Meistersinger)			
-----	Mein lieber Schwan (Lohengrin)			†
-----	Nothung! Nothung! Neidliches Schwert (Siegfried)			GSC
-----	Nur eine Waffe taugt (Parsifal)			GSC
-----	Schmiede mein Hammer ein hartes Schwert (Siegfried)			GSC
-----	Was ruht dort schlummernd (Siegfried)			GSC
-----	Wie sie selig hehr und milde wandelt (Tristan und Isolde)			†
-----	Willst jenes Tags du nicht (Der Fliegende Hollaender)			GSC
-----	Winterstuerme wichen dem Wonnemond (Die Walkuere)	H	C-G	†
Weber	Unter bluehenden Mandelbaeumen (Euryanthe)			PET
-----	Von Jugend auf in dem Kampfgefild (Oberon)			GSC

Arias From Italian Operas

Dramatic Tenor

Bellini	Meco all'altar di venere (Norma)	H	D-C	RIC
Boito	Giunto sul passo estremo (Epilogue) (Mefistofele)			RIC
Giordano	Come un bel di (Andrea Chenier)	H	E-BF	AMP
-----	Un di all'azzurro spazio (Andrea Chenier)	H	F-BF	SON

Leoncavallo	Vesti la giubba (I Pagliacci)	H	D-A	†
Monteverdi	Lasciatemi morire (Arianna)	ML	D-D	†
Ponchielli	Cielo e mar (La Gioconda)	H	D-BF	†
Puccini	Recondita armonia (Tosca)	H	E-BF	RIC
Rossini	O muto asil del pianto (La Cenerentola)			
Verdi	Ah! si, ben mio coll' essere (Il Trovatore)	H	F-AF	†
-----	Celeste Aida (Aida)	LM	D-BF	†
-----	Deserto sulla terra (Il Trovatore)			GSC
-----	Di quella pira (Il Trovatore)	H	G-C	†
-----	Giorno di pianto (I Vespri Siciliani)			RIC
-----	Mort d'Otello (Otello)			RIC
-----	O tu che in seno agli angeli (La Forza del Destino)	H	DF-BF	RIC

Miscellaneous Opera Arias

Dramatic Tenor

Arne, T.	Preach not me your musty rules (Comus)	HML		ROW
Britten	Peter's dreams (Peter Grimes)			BOH
Purcell	I attempt from love's sickness to fly (The Indian Queen)	MH	CS-E	
-----	Music for a while (Oediups)	LH		SC
Smetana	Ma-ma-mama so dear (The Bartered Bride)			BOO

Arias From Oratorios and Latin Works

Dramatic Tenor

| Beethoven | In my soul dread thoughts awaken (Mount of Olives) | H | E-A | † |
| Gaul | My soul is athirst for God (The Holy City) | | | |

651

Handel	Sound an alarm!	H		†
	(Judas Maccabaeus)			
-----	Thou shalt dash them	H		†
	(The Messiah)			
-----	Total eclipse (Samson)			†
-----	Wher'er you walk	HML	C-D	†
	(Semele)			
Honegger	In the Lord I put my faith			ECS
	(King David)			
Mendelssohn	He counteth all your sorrows	H	D-G	†
	(Hymn of Praise)			
-----	If with all your hearts	MH	F-AF	†
	(Elijah)			

Operetta, Musical Comedy
or Show Songs

Dramatic Tenor

Benatsky	Drei Musketiere			
	(Drei Musketiere)			
-----	Muetterlein, bleib immer bei mir			
	(Drei Musketiere)			
-----	Zuschau'n kann ich nicht			
	(Das Weisse Roessl)			
Coward	I'll see you again	M	C-F	HAR
	(Bitter Sweet)			
De Koven	Oh promise me	HML	C-D	†
	(Robin Hood)			
Friml	Rose Marie	M	EF-G	HAR
	(Rose Marie)			
Herbert	Ah! sweet mystery of life	LMH	A-A	WIT
	(Naughty Marietta)			
-----	❋ Gypsy love song	LHM	C-E	WIT
	(The Fortune Teller)			
-----	I'm falling in love with someone			WIT
	(Naughty Marietta)			
-----	I want what I want when			WIT
	I want it (Mlle. Modiste)			
-----	Neapolitan love song			WIT
	(Princess Pat)			
-----	Tramp, tramp, tramp			WIT
	(Naughty Marietta)			
Kern	The song is you	M	C-F	HAR
	(Music in the Air)			
Lehar	Du bist meine Sonne			CHA
	(Giuditta)			
-----	Fear nothing (Paganini)			SCH

(Lehar)	Freunde, das Leben ist lebenswert (Giuditta)			GLO
-----	Hab' ein blaues Himmelbett (Frasquita)			
-----	Immer nur laecheln (The Land of Smiles)			GLO
-----	Liebste, glaub' an mich (Schoen ist die Welt)			OCT
-----	Polenlied (The Blue Mazurka)			GLO
-----	Sah ein Knab' ein Roeslein steh'n (Friederike)			SAL
-----	Sieh dort den kleinen Pavillon (The Merry Widow)			GLO
-----	Volgalied (Zarewitsch)			GLO
-----	Von Apfelblueten einen Kranz (The Land of Smiles)			GLO
-----	Yours is my heart alone (The Land of Smiles)			HAR
Rodgers	The surrey with the fringe on the top (Oklahoma)			WIL
-----	Younger than springtime (South Pacific)			WIL
Romberg	The Riff Song (The Desert Song)	L	D-G	HAR
Youmans	Through the years (Through The Years)	HML	A-F	MLR
-----	Without a song (Great Day)	HLM	BF-F	MLR
Zeller	Lass dir Zeit (Der Kellermeister)			

Song Cycles (Or Groups of Songs)

Dramatic Tenor

Beethoven	An die ferne Geliebte	HL	C-E	†
-----	Sechs Geistliche Lieder			
Brahms	Romanzen aus Magelone			†
-----	Zigeunerlieder			
Cornelius	Six Christmas songs	HL		BOS
Dvořák	Biblical songs	HL		AMP
Mussorgsky	Songs and dances of death			INT
Ravel	Don Quichotte à Dulcinée	HM	A-F	DUR
-----	Histoires naturelles			DUR
Schubert	Die schoene Muellerin	HL		†
-----	Die Winterreise			†

653

(Schubert)	Gesaenge des Harfners, 1, 2 and 3			PET
Schumann	Dichterliebe			†
Smetana	Evening songs			
Vaughan Williams	On Wenlock edge String quartet and piano			BOO

Concert Arias

Dramatic Tenor

| Mozart | Per pietà, non ricercate | | | BOO |

Christmas Songs

Dramatic Tenor

Adam	O Holy Night	LMH	EF-G	†
Benjamin	Before dawn			CUR
De Koven	The white Christ	L	C-D	GSC
Dunhill	To the Queen of Heaven	M	C-G	GSC
Eakin	What of that midnight long ago	M	D-F	GAL
Elmore and Reed	Come all ye who weary	L	C-C	JFI
Fischer	Calm on the listening ear of night	MH	EF-AF	DIT
Grieg	Christmas song			AUG
Harker	A child is born in Bethlehem	LH	D-G	GSC
Head	The little road to Bethlehem	MH	EF-AF	BOO
-----	The three mummers			BOO
Kountz	The sleigh	HL	D-FS	GSC
Martin	The Holy Child	HML	G-G	ENO
Mc Kinney	The Holy Mother sings	MH	AF-AF	JFI
Neidlinger	The birthday of a king	LMH	C-F	GSC
Niles	Our Lovely Lady singing	M	EF-F	GSC
Schubert	Ave Maria	LMH	F-F	†
Strauss	Die Heiligen Drei Koenige	H	C-G	
Warlock	The first mercy	M	F-F	BOO

Easter Songs

Dramatic Tenor

Bach, J.S.	Jesus from the grave is risen	M	F-EF	CFI
Bantock	Easter hymn	M	FS-F	CHE
Curran	Crucifixion			
Granier	Hosanna	HH	F-BF	DIT
Guion	At the cry of the first bird	H	D-G	GSC
Hageman	Christ went up into the hills	LH	EF-AF	CFI
Huhn	Christ is risen	HM	C-E	ASC
La Forge	Before the Crucifix	HML	BF-EF	GSC
Lekberg	A ballad of trees and the Master	H	E-A	GAL
Mac Farlane	On wings of living light	MH	D-G	GSC
Mac Gimsey	I was there when they crucified my Lord	HL		CFI
Mahler	Um Mitternacht	HL		INT
O'Hara	There is no death	LMH	EF-AF	CHA
Parker	Golden Jerusalem (Hora Novissima)			NOV
Rachmaninoff	Christ is risen	LM	D-F	GAL
Schubert	Ave Maria	LMH	F-F	†
Scott	Angels roll the rock away	MH	E-G	HUN
-----	The first Easter morn	LH	F-G	GSC
Wolf	Herr, was traegt der Boden	HL	B-DS	†
Yon	Christ triumphant	MH	E-A	JFI
-----	O faithful Cross	HM	C-EF	JFI
-----	Our Paschal Joy	LH	AF-AF	JFI

Patriotic Songs

Dramatic Tenor

De Koven	Recessional			
Dix	The trumpeter	HML	A-C	BOH
Dungan	Eternal life	HL		PRE
Elgar	Land of hope and glory			BOO
Howe	To the unknown soldier	H	D-G	GSC
Lester	Greater love hath no man	LH	B-E	CFI
O'Hara	There is no death	LMH	EF-AF	CHA
Steffe	Battle hymn of the Republic			

Sacred Songs

Dramatic Tenor

Allitsen	The Lord is my light	LMH	D-AF	BOO
Bach, J.S.	Draw near to me	HML		GSC
Beethoven	The worship of God in nature			
Bizet	O Lord be merciful	HL		GSC
Bone and Fenton	Thy word is a lamp	LH	C-F	ROW
Brown	What are these which are arrayed	HLM	C-F	ASC
Buck	Fear not ye, O Israel	HLM		GSC
Campbell-Tipton	I will give thanks unto the Lord	LMH	DF-AF	GSC
Chadwick	A ballad of trees and the Master	HML	A-F	DIT
Charles	Love is of God	H	D-G	GSC
Creston	Psalm 23	MH	F-AF	GSC
Davis	Let not your heart be troubled	HML		WOO
-----	Trust in the Lord	MH	CS-G	GAL
Dungan	Eternal life	HL		PRE
Dvořák	God is my Shepherd			AMP
-----	Hear my prayer, O Lord			AMP
-----	Turn Thee to me			AMP
Edmunds	Praise we the Lord	HL	D-D	ROW
Fauré, J.	The palms	HM	C-EF	DIT
Goodhall	The mountain	M	D-E	GAL
Guion	Prayer	HL		GSC
Handel	Thanks be to Thee	M	CS-E	
Henschel	Morning-hymn	MH	DS-GS	†
Holst	The heart worships	ML	BF-D	STB
Liddle	How lovely are Thy dwellings	HML		BOS
Mac Dermid	In my Father's house are many mansions	HML		FRS
-----	Ninety-first Psalm	HLM		FRS
Malotte	The Lord's prayer			
-----	The twenty-third Psalm	HLM	C-F	GSC
Mendelssohn	He counteth all your sorrows (Hymn of Praise)	H	D-G	†
-----	If with all your hearts (Elijah)	MH	F-AF	†
Sanderson	Green pastures	HL	BF-EF	BOO
Schubert	The Omnipotent			
Scott	Come ye blessed	LMH	EF-AF	GSC
-----	Ride on, ride on	HML		FLA

Speaks	Thou wilt keep him in perfect peace	HML		GSC
Stevenson	I sought the Lord	HL	D-F	DIT
-----	Praise	M	F-F	CFI
Stickles	Saith the Lord	LH	D-F	CHA
Tchaikovsky	Lord, Almighty God (Moscow Cantata)	M		GRA
Thiman	Thou wilt keep him in perfect peace	H	D-G	GRA
Van de Water	The penitent	HM		DIT
-----	The publican	HL	C-E	DIT
Ware	The greatest of these	LH	EF-AF	BOS
Weaver	Assurance	H	EF-G	GAL
-----	Praise the Lord, His glories show	H	E-G	GAL
Wolf	Gebet	HL		†
-----	Morning prayer (Morgenstimme)			

Wedding Songs

Dramatic Tenor

Beethoven	Ich liebe dich	HL	BF-DF	†
De Koven	Oh promise me (Robin Hood)	HML	C-D	†
Dello Joio	How do I love thee?	H	D-G	CFI
D'Hardelot	Because	MH	E-G	CHA
Franck	O Lord most Holy	LM	A-FS	BOS
Geehl	For you alone			SHU
Grieg	I love thee	HML	E-F	†
Lippe	How do I love you?			BOS
Marx	Hat dich die Liebe beruehrt	MH	EF-BF	AMP
Schubert	Du bist die Ruh	LMH	EF-AF	†
-----	Ungeduld	HML		†
Schumann	Widmung	HL	BF-F	†
Sowerby	O perfect love	MH	EF-AF	GRA
Strauss	Ich liebe dich			†
Thiman	The God of love my Shepherd is	ML	A-D	NOV
Willan	O perfect love	HM	E-FS	GRA
Youmans	Through the years (Through the Years)	HML	A-F	MLR

Songs With Added Accompanying Instrument

Dramatic Tenor

Braga	Angel's serenade	LH	D-G	†
	Violin			
Chausson	Le colibri	M	F-GF	BOS
	Violin or cello			
Curran	Nocturne Violin	HML	B-DS	GSC
Kramer	Pleading String quartet	LH	D-GF	JFI
Rabey	Tes yeux	H	EF-G	DUR
	Violin and piano			
Vaughan Williams	On Wenlock edge			BOO
	String quartet and piano			

American Recital Songs

Baritone

Bacon	Brady			BOO
-----	Casey Jones			
Barber	Bessie Bobtail	M	C-F	GSC
-----	Dover Beach	M	BF-F	GSC
	String quartet			
-----	Here in this spot with you			
-----	I hear an army	LH	D-AF	GSC
-----	I ride the great black horses			
-----	Rain has fallen	HM	D-E	GSC
-----	Sure on this shining night	MH	D-G	GSC
-----	The daisies	M	C-F	GSC
-----	The Queen's face on the	L	C-E	GSC
	summery coin			
-----	With rue my heart is	HL	CS-D	GSC
	laden			
Barnett	Music, when soft voices	M	C-E	GSC
	die			
Bartholomew	When we are parted	M	CS-E	GAL
Beach	Ah, love but a day			ASC
-----	The year's at the spring	MH	AF-AF	ASC
Bloch	Psalm 22	M	B-F	GSC
Bone and Fenton	Captain Kidd	MH	B-G	CFI
-----	Everything that I can spy	M	E-GF	CFI
-----	Green fields	MH	E-A	PRE
-----	Tryst	MH	FS-G	CFI
Bowles	Cabin	ML	CS-CS	GSC
-----	David	M	E-D	AMP

(Bowles)	Heavenly grass	ML	B-E	GSC
-----	I went to see my love			
-----	Lonesome man	M	DF-EF	GSC
-----	Once a lady was here	ML	C-EF	GSC
Boyd	Cape Horn gospel	L	BF-D	GAL
Braine	Dawn awakes	HML	A-D	ASC
Branscombe	At the postern gate	MH	DF-AF	ASC
-----	By St. Lawrence waters	HL		ASC
Burnham	Sing me a song of a lad that is gone	HL		GSC
Buzzi-Peccia	London bridge	ML	BF-DF	CFI
Cadman	Service	HML	BF-D	FLA
Campbell-Tipton	If I were king	HML	C-EF	GSC
-----	The crying of water	LH	FS-GS	GSC
Carpenter	Berceuse de guerre	M	C-G	GSC
-----	Don't ceare	M	C-D	GSC
-----	Go, lovely rose	M	DF-EF	GSC
-----	Looking glass river	M	B-D	GSC
-----	May the maiden			DIT
-----	On the day when death will knock at thy door	M	C-F	GSC
-----	Serenade	LH	CS-A	GSC
-----	Slumber song	ML	BF-F	GSC
-----	The cock shall crow	M	B-E	GSC
-----	The green river	M	B-E	GSC
-----	Young man chieftan	L	B-E	GSC
Carter	Dust of snow	M	D-E	AMP
Castelnuovo-Tedesco	Apemantus grace			CHE
-----	O mistress mine			CHE
-----	Springtime	M		CHE
-----	The horn			CHE
Chadwick	Allah	LH	CS-GS	ASC
-----	Drake's drum			
-----	O let night speak of me	HM	C-F	ASC
-----	The admirals			
-----	The danza	HM		ASC
Chanler	I rise when you enter	M	CS-G	GSC
Charles	Clouds	HML	C-EF	GSC
-----	My lady walks in loveliness	HM	C-EF	GSC
-----	Song of exaltation	M		GSC
-----	Sweet song of long ago	HML	A-D	GSC
-----	When I have sung my songs	HM	BF-EF	GSC
Clifton	If music be the food of love, play on			
Coombs	Her rose	ML	D-C	GSC

659

Copland	Long time ago			
Cowell	The donkey	M	D-F	MER
Crist	Into a ship dreaming	LMH	EF-GS	CFI
Davis	The jolly fat friar			
Dello Joio	Mill doors	M	D-E	CFI
-----	The assassination			CFI
-----	There is a lady sweet and kind	M	C-F	CFI
Diamond	David weeps for Absolom	M	D-A	MUP
Dobson	Cargoes	ML	C-EF	GSC
Dougherty	Blow ye winds	L	C-D	GSC
-----	Declaration of independence	L	C-C	GSC
-----	Hush'd be the camps today	M	BF-G	GSC
-----	Loveliest of trees	HM	C-E	BOH
-----	The bird and the beast			
Duke	Capri			
-----	Central Park at dusk	M		BOO
-----	Here in this spot with you	M	B-F	GSC
-----	I ride the great black horses	M	C-G	GSC
-----	Loveliest of trees	L	C-D	GSC
-----	Luke Havergal	M	BF-F	CFI
-----	Miniver Cheevy	L	G-F	CFI
-----	On a March day	M	B-GF	BOH
-----	Reveille			
-----	Richard Cory	L	A-EF	CFI
-----	White in the moon the long road lies	M		VLP
Edmunds	Billy boy	ML	BF-EF	ROW
-----	Fare you well	MH	F-AF	ROW
Elwell	Music I heard	M		AMP
-----	The road not taken	M	B-FS	GSC
Engel	Sea shell	M	EF-EF	GSC
Foote	I'm wearing awa'	HL		ASC
-----	Tranquillity	HL	BF-E	ASC
Foster, S.C.	Ah, may the red rose live always			GSC
-----	De Glendy Burke			GSC
-----	Ellen Bayne			DIT
-----	Gentle Annie			
Galloway	Alone upon the housetops			
Ganz	A memory	HM	B-D	GSC
Gilbert	Pirate song	L	C-EF	GRA
Golde	O beauty, passing beauty	MH	CS-GS	GSC
-----	Who knows	HM	BF-F	GSC
Griffes	An old song resung	LM	EF-F	GSC
-----	By a lonely forest pathway	HML	A-EF	GSC
-----	Phantoms	M	BF-F	GSC

(Griffes)	Sorrow of Mydath	M		GSC
-----	Symphony in yellow	M	D-GF	GSC
Guion	Black oxen			
Hadley	My shadow			ASC
Hageman	Don Juan Gomez	M		GAL
-----	Miranda	HL		GAL
-----	Music I heard with you	MH	E-A	GAL
-----	The donkey			BOO
-----	The rich man	M		GAL
Hammond	The pipes of Gordon's men	HL	D-F	GSC
Harris	Agatha Morley	M	C-D	CFI
Helm	She is not fair			
Hindemith	The whistling thief	M	E-F	AMP
Homer	Sing me a song of a lad that is gone	HL	C-EF	GSC
Hopkinson	Come fair Rosina			
-----	My days have been so wondrous free	LH	EF-G	†
-----	My generous heart disdains			
-----	O'er the hills	LH	C-G	†
Horsman	In the yellow dusk	MH	FS-A	GSC
-----	The bird of the wilderness	LMH	DF-BF	GSC
Howard	Love in thy youth			
Howe	When I died in Berners Street	H	C-G	GSC
Huhn	Courage	HML	BF-EF	GSC
Ives	Charlie Rutlage	M		ARR
-----	General William Booth enters into Heaven			
-----	The greatest man	M		ARR
-----	The white gulls			
James	The victory riders			
Kagen	Never more will the wind			
-----	Upstream	H	CS-F	WTR
Kernochan	Out of the rolling ocean			
-----	Smuggler's song			GAL
-----	We two together	H	EF-AF	GAL
Kingsford	Courage	M	C-F	GSC
Kleinsinger	The courtship of old Joe Clark			
Klemm	Animal man			CFI
Kramer	For a dream's sake	HL		JFI
-----	Minnelied	M	C-E	JFI
-----	Pleading	LH	D-GF	JFI
-----	Swans	HL		RIC
Kubik	I bought a bright sword			
-----	Shoe song			
La Forge	Hills	HL		RIC

(La Forge)	To a messenger	HLM	CF-G	GSC
-----	Voodoo spirits			CFI
Lang	Irish love song	HML	A-E	ASC
Levitzki	Do you remember?	HML	BF-EF	GSC
Loeffler	To Helen	M	DF-F	GSC
Mac Dowell	The sea	HL	D-D	BRH
-----	Thy beaming eyes	ML	BF-EF	ASC
Mac Gimsey	O Lord you made a Moses	M		CFI
-----	Thunderin' wonderin'	L	C-D	CFI
Malotte	One, two, three	M	C-F	GSC
-----	Upstream	M	C-F	GSC
Mana Zucca	I shall know			CNG
-----	Rachem	HML		CHA
-----	Thy will be done			CNG
Manning	In the Luxembourg gardens	HML	BF-D	GSC
Mason	A prophet	M	BF-GF	GSC
-----	A sea dirge			WIT
Mc Feeters	Exultation	HL	C-E	GSC
Metcalf	At nightfall	HML	C-DF	ASC
Miller	Boats of mine	HML	BF-EF	FLA
Mitchell	I must go down to the sea	M	BF-F	GAH
Moore	Adam was my grandfather			GAL
Naginski	Night song at Amalfi	M	D-EF	GSC
-----	Richard Cory	ML	A-E	GSC
Nordoff	Tell me, Thyrsis	H	E-G	AMP
Olmstead	The ladies of St. James's	L	BF-EF	GSC
-----	Thy sweet singing	HL	BF-EF	GSC
Paxson	Dusk at sea	HL	A-EF	GSC
-----	Laughing song	M	C-F	CFI
Porter, Q.	Music, when soft voices die	HM	D-C	MUP
-----	The desolate city			
Protheroe	The pilot			
Robertson	The Jolly Roger	HML	C-D	GSC
Rogers	War			DIT
-----	The last song	MLH	E-AF	GSC
-----	Time for making songs	HM	CS-F	DIT
-----	Wind song	LM	C-G	GSC
Rorem	From an unknown past			
Rose	Roadways			GAM
Russell	Fulfillment	LH	EF-GF	BOS
Sacco	Brother Will, brother John	M	C-F	GSC
-----	Drum of peace	M	D-F	CFI
-----	Johnny the one	HL	BF-D	GSC
-----	Mexican serenade	HL	D-EF	BOS

662

(Sacco)	Revelation	HL	DF-EF	BOS
-----	Spanish Johnny	HL	BF-F	GSC
-----	The ragpicker	MH	C-AF	GSC
Sachs	Grandma			FLA
-----	The three riders	M	C-F	GSC
Schindler	From a city window			
Schuman	Holiday song	M	C-F	GSC
Scott	Cherry ripe	L	B-E	ELK
Singer	This want of you	L	E-FS	BOH
Speaks	Shepherd, see thy horse's foaming mane			FLA
Spencer	For whom the bell tolls	MH	F-AF	BOS
Swanson	Joy	M	BF-EF	LEE
-----	The negro speaks of rivers	M		LEE
-----	The valley	L	BF-DF	LEE
Taylor	A song for lovers	MH	D-F	JFI
-----	Captain Stratton's fancy	L	CS-F	JFI
Thompson	Velvet shoes	M	C-E	ECS
Tureman	A winter sunset	L	BF-E	GSC
Tyson	Noon and night	LH	F-AF	GSC
-----	One little cloud	HL	BF-D	GSC
-----	Sea moods	LH	E-AF	GSC
Warner	Hurdy gurdy	M	D-F	CFI
Warren	By a fireside	HL	C-EF	GSC
-----	My parting gift			DIT
-----	Through my open window	HL	C-E	GSC
-----	We two	LH	E-A	GSC
-----	White horses of the sea	LH	F-G	GSC
Watts	Blue are her eyes	H	FS-FS	DIT
-----	Falmouth Town	M	B-FS	GSC
-----	Joy	HL	D-F	GSC
-----	Like music on the waters	H		GSC
-----	The poet sings	MH	EF-AF	DIT
Weaver	A book of verses	H	D-AF	GAL
-----	The Abbot of Derry	HL	B-EF	GSC
Wolfe	The hand-organ man	M	B-FS	GSC
Worth	The evening is hushed			

British Recital Songs

Baritone

Aiken	Sigh no more	HML		STB
Anon	False Phillis			
-----	Have you seen but a white lily grow?	H	E-F	GSC
Arne, T.	By the gaily circling glass	L		DIT

663

(Arne, T.)	Now Phoebus sinketh in the west			GSC
-----	Why so pale and wan?			GSC
Bainton	Ring out, wild bells	M	C-EF	OXF
Bantock	A feast of lanterns	HM	D-F	GAL
-----	Lament of Isis	L		AMP
-----	Silent strings	MH	F-G	BOO
-----	The celestial weaver			
-----	The golden nenuphar	HM	B-E	ELK
Bartlet	What thing is love			BOO
-----	Whither runneth my sweetheart			BOO
Bax	The enchanted fiddle			
Benjamin	Hedgerow			CUR
-----	The wasp			CUR
Berners	Dialogue between Tom Filuter and his man	M	D-F	CHE
-----	Theodore or the pirate king			CHE
Blow	The self banished	L	C-F	NOV
Boughton	Immanence	M	B-E	CUR
Bridge	All things that we clasp	HL		BOS
-----	Come to me in my dreams	HL	C-EF	BOH
-----	E'en as a lovely flower	HM	FS-E	BOH
-----	Isobel	HML		CHA
-----	Love went a-riding	HL		BOS
-----	O that it were so	LMH	D-G	CHA
Britten	The birds	M		BOO
Bury	There is a lady	HM	CS-E	CFI
Butterworth	Loveliest of trees			AUG
-----	When I was one and twenty			AUG
Campion	Follow thy fair sun			STB
-----	There is a garden in her face			DIT
-----	When to her lute Corinna sings			STB
Clarke	Shy one	HL	BF-G	BOH
Coleridge-Taylor	Eleanore	HML		NOV
-----	She rested by the broken brook	HL		DIT
Delius	Love's philosophy			†
-----	Twilight fancies	M	D-FS	CFI
Dowland	Awake, sweet love	M	E-F	STB
-----	Come again! sweet love	M	D-E	STB
-----	Come away			BOO
-----	Deare, if you change			BOO
-----	Fine knacks for ladies	M	E-F	STB
-----	Flow, my tears	M	D-E	STB
-----	I saw my lady weep	M	E-E	STB
-----	Say love, if ever thou didst find			STB

664

(Dowland)	Shall I sue?			STB
-----	Sorrow, sorrow stay	M	D-D	BOS
-----	The lowest trees have tops			STB
-----	What if I never speede?	M	D-D	BOS
-----	White as lilies was her face			STB
Dunhill	The cloths of heaven	LM	EF-G	STB
Elgar	My old tunes	M	D-EF	ELK
-----	To the children	M	C-E	ELK
Fisher	At Tankerton Inn	LM	B-G	BOO
-----	Spanish gold			BOO
Ford	Now I see thy look were feigned			BOO
-----	Since first I saw your face			DIT
-----	There is a lady sweet and kind	M	D-E	STB
Forsyth	The bell man			DIT
German	Charming Chloe	HML		NOV
-----	My song is of the sturdy north	ML		CHA
-----	Rolling down to Rio	ML	G-D	NOV
Gibbs	Five eyes	HL	D-D	BOS
-----	The market			CUR
Green	My lips shall speak the praise	M	E-F	OXF
Gurney	An epitaph			OXF
Hammond	Ballad of the bony fiddler			
Handel	On love's wings			
Harty	Homeward	L	C-E	NOV
Head	A vagabond song			BOO
-----	Money, O!			BOO
-----	Sweet chance that led my steps abroad	LM	C-F	BOH
-----	The ships of Arcady	ML	BF-EF	BOH
-----	When I think upon the maidens	LM	D-G	BOO
-----	Why have you stolen my delight?	LH		BOH
Hely-Hutchinson	Old mother Hubbard	HL	B-E	CFI
Henschel	The angels dear	M		PRE
Holst	Creation			GSC
-----	The heart worships	ML	BF-D	STB
-----	The Sergeant's song			ASH
-----	Weep ye no more	M		STB
Hook	Bright Phoebus	M	EF-F	GSC
Howells	Old skinflint	M	D-F	CUR
Hughes	Old mother Hubbard			CRA
Humphrey	I pass all my hours			DIT
Ireland	Great things			AUG
-----	I was not sorrowful	ML		BOO

(Ireland)	The soldier	HLM		BOO
-----	When lights go rolling round the sky			
Johnson	As I walked forth one summer day			DIT
Jones	Love is a bable			STB
-----	What if I speede?			BOO
Lawes	I am confirmed			BOO
Leveridge	The beggar's song	L	G-D	BOO
-----	The maiden's resolution			GSC
-----	When dull care			BOO
Longsteffe	When the Sergeant Major's on parade			CHA
Milford	So sweet love seemed	HL	D-D	GRA
Molloy	Punchinello	L	A-D	GSC
Morgan	Clorinda	HM	C-EF	ENO
Morley	It was a lover and his lass	HM		DIT
-----	Sweet nymph, come to thy lover	M	D-B	BOS
Munro	My lovely Celia			BIR
Novello	A page's road song			ENO
Parry	To Althea	M		NOV
-----	To Lucasta			
Peterkin	A curse on a closed gate (Voice and viola)	M	D-E	OXF
Pilkington	Rest, sweet nymphs			STB
Purcell, E.	Passing by	HM	D-D	DIT
Purcell, H.	Ah, how pleasant 'tis to love			AUG
-----	Cease, o my sad soul			POT
-----	Evening hymn	M	C-F	OXF
-----	Hark! how all things with one sound rejoice			NOV
-----	If music be the food of love	M	D-G	BOO
-----	I'll sail upon the dog star	HL	A-E	†
-----	Man is for woman made			
-----	Not all my torments			NOV
-----	Since from my dear			
-----	Sylvia, now your scorn give over			FSY
Quilter	Blow, blow thou winter wind	HL	C-E	BOO
-----	Drink to me only	LMH	GF-GF	BOH
-----	Go, lovely rose	LHM	F-GF	CHA
-----	Hey, ho the wind and the rain			BOO
-----	It was a lover and his lass	HL	CS-E	BOO

(Quilter)	I will go with my father a-plowing	MH	D-G	ELK
-----	Now sleeps the crimson petal	LMH	EF-GF	BOO
Rosseter	What then is love but mourning			STB
-----	When Laura smiles	LM	D-E	STB
Rowley	Cherry song			
-----	In Twinkledown valley			
-----	On Newlyn Hill			BOH
-----	The toll gate house			ROG
Russell	Poor man's garden	HML	A-D	BOO
Sanderson	Drumadune			BOH
-----	Quiet	ML	AF-EF	BOH
-----	The company Sergeant major			BOH
Shaw	Song of the Palanquin bearers	LH	E-F	CUR
Somervell	A kingdom by the sea	ML	DF-F	BOO
Stanford	Drake's drum			BOO
-----	The bold unbiddable child	ML	B-DF	STB
-----	The fairy lough	ML	A-EF	BOO
-----	The pilbroch			
Stephenson	Love is a sickness	HML	C-D	BOO
-----	Ships that pass in the night	HML	DF-DF	BOO
Taylor	The wind mill	M		OXF
Toye	The inn	L	C-E	CUR
Treharne	The fly			
Vaughan Williams	Boy Jonny	LH		BOH
-----	Bright is the ring of words	L		BOH
-----	Joy shipmate, joy			OXF
-----	Let beauty awake			
-----	Linden Lea	HML	C-D	BOS
-----	Orpheus with his lute			PRO
-----	See the chariot at hand			
-----	Silent noon			GSC
-----	The infinite shining heavens			BOH
-----	The roadside fire	HML	BF-EF	BOO
-----	The vagabond	ML	A-E	BOO
-----	The water mill	L	C-D	OXF
Walton	Sunset			
Warlock	As ever I saw	MH	DF-GF	ROG
-----	Captain Stratton's fancy			AUG
-----	Fair and true	M	EF-EF	CFI
-----	Good ale			AUG
-----	Jillian of Berry			OXF
-----	Milkmaids			
-----	My own country	M	C-E	CFI
-----	One more river	L	C-F	ROG
-----	Passing by	M	D-G	CFI
-----	Piggesnie	ML	B-E	AUG

667

(Warlock)	Pretty ring time	H	D-G	CFI
-----	Robin good-fellow			
-----	Sigh no more	M	EF-F	CFI
-----	Sleep			OXF
-----	The droll lover			
-----	The sweet o' the year			ELK
White	So we'll go no more a-roving			CHA
Wilson	Phillis has such charming graces	ML	CS-EF	BOO
-----	The sailor's life	M		BOO
-----	The pretty creature	L		BOO

French Recital Songs

Baritone

Aubert	La lettre			DUR
Auric	Le gloxinia			AMP
Benati	Air crois en mon coeur fidèle			ROU
Berton	Hymne d'amour	HM	B-DS	LRO
Beydts	Dans les ombres de mon âme			
Boieldieu	C'est la Princesse de Navane			DIT
Busser	Notre père qui êtes aux cieux			
Caplet	La ronde	M		DUR
-----	Le forêt			DUR
-----	Viens, une flûte invisible			DUR
Chabrier	Ballade des gros dindons	HL		†
-----	L'Île heureuse	M	B-F	†
-----	Villanelle des petits canards	HML	B-E	†
Chaminade	Ronde d'amour			
-----	Tu me dirais	LH	BF-AF	DIT
Charpentier	La ronde des compagnons			
Chausson	Apaisement	MH	EF-G	HAM
-----	Chanson de clown	M	D-EF	ROU
-----	Le charme	HM	BF-EF	HAM
-----	Le colibri	M	F-GF	BOS
-----	Le temps des lilas	MH	D-GS	†
-----	Les papillons	M	C-F	GSC
Debussy	Ballade des femmes de Paris			DUR
-----	Beau soir	LH	C-FS	†
-----	Chevaux de bois	H	C-G	†
-----	Colloque sentimental			DUR
-----	De soir	HL		†
-----	Green	H	C-AF	†
-----	Je tremble en voyant ton visage			DUR

668

(Fauré)	Lydia	MH	G-G	†
-----	Madrigal	MH	F-F	HAM
-----	Nell	LH	FS-AF	†
-----	Nocturne	H	F-A	MAR
-----	Notre amour	H	DS-B	†
-----	Prison	LH		†
-----	Rencontre	H	EF-AF	†
-----	Soir	LH	D-GS	†
-----	Spleen	H	E-FS	MAR
-----	Toujours	LH	F-AF	†
Ferrari	Le miroir	M	E-F	GSC
Février	L'intruse	M	B-DF	HEU
Fourdrain	Alger le soir	M		RIC
-----	Carnaval	M	C-F	RIC
-----	Promenade au mule			
Franck	Le mariage des roses	M	E-FS	BOS
-----	Lied	LH	FS-FS	†
-----	Nocturne	HL		†
Gevaert	Lamentation napolitaine			
Gounod	A la brise			
-----	Adore and be still	HL		GSC
-----	Au printemps	LMH	DF-AF	GSC
-----	Au rossignol	LMH	D-G	CHO
-----	Ce que je suis sans toi			SC
-----	Dernières volontés			
-----	Envoi de fleurs	MH	G-G	SC
-----	L'absent			
-----	Le soir	M	CS-FS	GSC
-----	Medjé (Chanson arabe)	MH	G-G	BOO
-----	O ma belle rebelle			
-----	Prière			
-----	Vénise	HL		INT
Hahn	D'une prison	L	BF-EF	HEU
-----	L'enamourée			HEU
-----	L'heure exquise	M	DF-F	†
-----	L'incrédule			HEU
-----	Les cygnes			HEU
-----	Offrande	M	D-D	†
-----	Paysage	MH	EF-G	HEU
-----	Phyllis			HEU
-----	Tous deux			BOS
-----	Trois jours de vendange	M		HEU
Holmès	Au pays	HM	C-F	CFI
-----	L'oiseau bleu			HEU
-----	La belle du roi			HEU
Honegger	Automne			
-----	Chanson (Ronsard)			SEN
	Flute and string quartet			
Hue	J'ai pleuré en rêve	HL	D-E	BOS

Indy	La chevauchée du cid	M		HAM
-----	Lied maritime	LH	B-G	†
-----	Madrigal			DIT
-----	Mirage			HAM
Koechlin	Le thé	HM	C-E	BOS
Lalo	Marine	LH	DS-FS	
Leguerney	L'adieu	M	B-FS	DUR
Lemaire	Chanson à manger	M	B-E	GSC
Lenormand	Quelle souffrance	HM	AF-F	HAM
Levade	Les vieilles de chez nous			
Martini	Plaisir d'amour	M	BF-EF	GSC
Massenet	Crépuscule	M	D-E	GSC
-----	Pensée d'automne	HML	B-E	GSC
Milhaud	Chant d'amour	M	C-GF	ESC
-----	Chant de Forgeron	M	C-FS	SC
-----	La tourterelle	M	B-G	DUR
Paladilhe	Lamento provinçal	M	CS-FS	HOM
-----	Les trois prières			
-----	Psyché	HM	BF-F	GSC
Pessard	L'adieu du matin	ML	BF-D	GSC
-----	Requiem du coeur			LED
Pierné	En barque	L	D-DF	GSC
Pillois	Mon feu			SEN
Poldowski	Colombine	H	D-GF	CHE
-----	Dansons la gigue	M	EF-G	MAR
Poulenc	A sa guitare	M	D-FS	DUR
-----	Chanson à boire	L	B-E	HEU
-----	Chanson d'Orkenise			AMP
-----	Couplets bachiques	L	C-FF	HEU
-----	Dans le jardin d'Anna			SAL
-----	Fleurs	M	DF-F	ROU
-----	Hôtel			AMP
-----	Invocation aux Parques			HEU
-----	L'anguille			ROU
-----	La belle jeunesse	L	D-F	HEU
-----	La grenouillère			DEI
-----	Le bal masque			SAL
-----	Le disparu			ROU
-----	Montparnasse	H	EF-G	ESC
-----	Priez pour paix	ML		ROU
-----	Reine des mouettes	M	FF-F	SAL
-----	Sanglots			AMP
-----	Sérénade			
-----	Voyage à Paris			AMP
Rameau	Le grillon			DUR
Ravel	Chanson à boire			DUR
-----	Chanson française			
-----	Chanson romanesque			DUR
-----	D'Anne qui me jecta	HM	CS-FS	GSC

(Ravel)	Dansant l'amique			
-----	Kaddisch	H	C-G	DUR
-----	La pintade			DUR
-----	Le martin-pêcheur			DUR
-----	Le paon	M	C-F	DUR
-----	Manteau de fleurs	H		INT
-----	Nicolette	L	B-FS	ELK
-----	Ronsard à son âme	L	CS-E	DUR
-----	Sainte	M	C-G	ELV
-----	Sur l'herbe	MH	C-G	DUR
-----	Tout gai!	MH	EF-F	
-----	Trois beaux oiseaux du paradis			DUR
Rhené-Baton	Nuit d'autrefois			DUR
Riquier	Chanson religieuse (Troubador song)			
Roussel	Coeur en péril			DUR
-----	Le jardin mouillé	M	C-FS	ROU
Saint-Saëns	Aimons-nous			DUR
-----	Danse macabre	L	BF-EF	AXE
-----	La cloche	LH	DF-AF	†
-----	Le lever de la lune			DUR
-----	Les pas d'armes du Roi Jean	HML	A-F	RIC
-----	Mai	H	G-FS	DUR
-----	Tournoiement			DUR
Satie	Daphénéo			ROU
-----	La statue da bronze			ROU
-----	Le chapelier			ROU
Severac	Chanson de la nuit durable			SAL
-----	Les hiboux			ROU
Szulc	Dansons la gigue	M		ROU
Tiersot	Les filles de la rochelle	H		GRA
Weckerlin	Bergère légère	M	D-E	BOS
Widor	Je ne veux pas autre chose	HL	C-EF	HAM

German Recital Songs

Baritone

Ahle	Bruenstiges Verlangen	M	E-E	GSC
Bach, J.S.	Bist due bei mir	HML	A-EF	†
-----	Gedenke doch, mein Geist, zurueck			PET
-----	Komm suesser Tod	MH	C-G	†
-----	Mein Jesu, was fuer Seelenweh			
-----	O Jesulein suess			
Beethoven	Adelaide	HML	BF-E	†
-----	An die Geliebte	M	E-E	†

672

(Beethoven)	An die Hoffnung	H	B-A	†
-----	Andenken			†
-----	Auf dem Huegel sitz' ich spaehend			†
-----	Aus Goethes Faust			
-----	Bitten			†
-----	Busslied			†
-----	Das Geheimnis			
-----	Delizia	M	C-F	GSC
-----	Der Kuss			†
-----	Der Wachtelschlag			†
-----	Die Ehre Gottes	HL	AF-EF	†
-----	Diese Wolken in den Hoehen			†
-----	Es kehret der Maien			
-----	Faithfu' Johnie			
-----	Ich liebe dich	HL	BF-DF	†
-----	In questa tomba	ML	A-CS	†
-----	Leichte Segler in den Hoehen			
-----	Nimm sie hin denn, diese Lieder			†
-----	Vom Tode	L	A-EF	GSC
-----	Wo die Berge so blau			†
-----	Wonne der Wehmut			†
Brahms	Am Sonntag Morgen	L	CS-FS	†
-----	An den Mond	HL	CS-EF	†
-----	An die Tauben	HL	CS-E	†
-----	Auf dem Kirchhofe	HL	BF-EF	†
-----	Auf dem See	HL	D-F	†
-----	Bei dir sind meine Gedanken	MH	E-FS	†
-----	Blinde Kuh			†
-----	Botschaft	HL	D-F	†
-----	Dein blaues Auge	MH	BF-G	†
-----	Denn es gehet dem Menschen	HL		†
-----	Der Schmied	HL	EF-EF	†
-----	Der Tod, das ist die kuehle Nacht	L	AF-F	†
-----	Der Ueberlaeufer			†
-----	Die Mainacht	HL	BF-FF	†
-----	Ein Sonett			†
-----	Feldeinsamkeit	HL	C-EF	†
-----	Geheimnis			†
-----	Heimkehr			†
-----	Ich wandte mich und sahe an	HL		†
-----	In Waldeseinsamkeit	H	ES-G	†
-----	Juchhe!			RIC
-----	Kein Haus, keine Heimat	HL	D-D	†
-----	Klage	LH	FS-FS	†

(Brahms)	Lerchengesang	LH	FS-GS	†
-----	Liebe kam aus fernen Landen	HL	C-E	†
-----	Meine Lieder	HL	D-DS	†
-----	Minnelied	MHL	C-EF	†
-----	Mit vierzig Jahren	HL	FS-D	†
-----	Muss es eine Trennung geben?	LH	FS-FS	†
-----	Nachtwandler			
-----	Nicht mehr zu dir zu gehen			†
-----	O kuehler Wald	MH	A-F	†
-----	O liebliche Wangen	MLH	E-G	†
-----	O wuesst' ich doch den Weg zurueck	H	E-FS	†
-----	Regenlied	HL	CS-F	†
-----	Ruhe, Suessliebchen	HL	BS-E	†
-----	Sapphische Ode	HML		†
-----	Schwermut			†
-----	Schwesterlein			†
-----	Sehnsucht	H	EF-AF	†
-----	Sind es Schmerzen	HL	BF-F	†
-----	Sonntag	H	D-G	†
-----	So willst du des Armen	HL	C-E	†
-----	Staendchen	HL	BF-E	†
-----	Steig' auf, geliebter Schatten	HL	BF-EF	CFI
-----	Tambourliédchen			†
-----	Treue Liebe	LMH	DS-E	†
-----	Unueberwindlich			†
-----	Vergebliches Staendchen	LMH		†
-----	Verrat	HL	FS-EF	†
-----	Verzagen	MH	CS-FS	†
-----	Von ewiger Liebe	LMH	B-AF	†
-----	Von waldbekraenzter Hoehe			†
-----	Wehe, so willst du mich wieder			†
-----	Wenn du nur zuweilen laechelst			†
-----	Wenn ich mit Menschen			†
-----	Wie bist du meine Koenigin	HL	C-E	†
-----	Wie froh und frisch	HL	B-E	†
-----	Wie Melodien zieht es	HL	A-E	†
-----	Willst du, dass ich geh'?	L	C-G	†
-----	Wir wandelten	LH	EF-GF	†
Bungert	Der Sandtraeger			
-----	Ich hab' ein kleines Lied erdacht			
Franz	For music	ML	C-D	†
-----	Im Herbst	HM	A-F	†
-----	Marie	HL	D-F	†
-----	Sonnenuntergang	HL	CS-FS	†

(Franz)	Sterne mit den gold'nen Fuesschen	HL	DS-E	DIT
-----	Stille Sicherheit	M	E-F	†
Gluck	Ode an den Tod			
Handel	Dank sei Dir, Herr	M	CS-E	†
Hassler	Tanzlied			SIM
Haydn	Liebes Maedchen, hoer' mir zu			HSC
-----	She never told her love	HL	B-D	DIT
-----	The sailor's song			
-----	The spirit's song	M	B-GF	†
-----	The wanderer			
Hildach	Wo du hingehst			
Humperdinck	Am Rhein			AMP
Jensen	Margreta	M	F-F	PET
Liszt	Am Rhein			
-----	Die drei Zigeuner	LM	B-G	GSC
-----	Die Lorelei	LH	BF-BF	†
-----	Es muss ein Wunderbares sein	M	C-EF	DUR
-----	Nimm einen Strahl der Sonne			DUR
-----	Wieder moecht' ich dir begegnen			DUR
Loewe	Archibald Douglas			†
-----	Der Noeck			SC
-----	Die Uhr	HML	AF-EF	†
-----	Edward	HL	F-E	†
-----	Erkennen			SC
-----	Erlkoenig	M	G-F	†
-----	Friedericus Rex			SC
-----	Heinrich der Vogler			SC
-----	Hochzeitlied			HSC
-----	Kleiner Haushalt			HSC
-----	Odins Meeresritt			SC
-----	Prinz Eugen			SC
-----	Suesses Begraebnis			SC
-----	Tom der Reimer			HSC
Mahler	Der Tamboursgesell	HL		INT
-----	Des Antonius von Padua Fischpredigt	HL	GF-F	†
-----	Die zwei blauen Augen	M	A-G	†
-----	Ging heut Morgen uebers Feld	M	A-FS	INT
-----	Ich bin der Welt abbanden gekommen	HL		INT
-----	Ich hab' ein gluehend Messer	M	BF-GF	WEI
-----	Urlicht	L	DF-E	†

(Schubert)	Ave Maria	LMH	F-F	†
-----	Das Fischermaedchen	L	A-EF	†
-----	Das Lied im Gruen			PET
-----	Das Wandern	HLM	E-E	†
-----	Das Wirtshaus	HL	C-D	†
-----	Dass sie hier gewesen!			PET
-----	Dem Unendlichen	L	A-GF	†
-----	Der Atlas	HL	BF-F	†
-----	Der Blumenbrief	L	F-EF	†
-----	Der Doppelgaenger	HL	G-D	†
-----	Der entsuehnte Orest			PET
-----	Der Erlkoenig	HML	A-E	†
-----	Der Juengling an der Quelle	LH	E-A	†
-----	Der Juengling und der Tod	M	DF-FF	†
-----	Der Leiermann	ML	C-D	†
-----	Der Lindenbaum	HL	A-D	†
-----	Der Musensohn	LH	FS-G	†
-----	Der Neugierige	HL	CS-EF	†
-----	Der Pilgrim	LH	D-F	†
-----	Der Schiffer	LH	BF-A	†
-----	Der stuermische Morgen	HL		
-----	Der Wanderer	HML	FS-D	†
-----	Der Wanderer an den Mond	LM	D-F	PET
-----	Der Wegweiser	L	D-EF	†
-----	Der Zwerg	M	A-GF	PET
-----	Der zuernende Barde			PET
-----	Die Allmacht	HML	G-E	†
-----	Die Forelle	MLH	EF-GF	†
-----	Die junge Nonne	LH	C-GF	†
-----	Die Kraehe	HL	A-E	†
-----	Die liebe Farbe			
-----	Die Liebe hat gelogen	LM	G-F	†
-----	Die Nebensonnen	HL	F-D	†
-----	Die Post	HML	BF-EF	†
-----	Die Stadt	HL	A-E	†
-----	Die Sterne	LH		DIT
-----	Die Taubenpost	HL	D-EF	†
-----	Du liebst mich nicht	LH	E-FS	†
-----	Erstarrung	HL	D-F	†
-----	Erster Verlust	M	C-F	†
-----	Fahrt zum Hades	HL	G-DF	PET
-----	Fischerweise	L	C-D	†
-----	Florio			PET
-----	Fragment aus dem Aeschylus			PET
-----	Freude der Kinderjahre	LH	C-G	†
-----	Fruehlingsglaube	M	EF-F	†
-----	Fruehlingssehnsucht	HL	B-E	†

677

(Schubert)	Fruehlingstraum	HL	C-D	†
-----	Ganymed	LH	EF-G	†
-----	Gebet waehrend der Schlacht	M	CS-E	†
-----	Geheimes	HL	BF-EF	†
-----	Gruppe aus dem Tartarus	L	CS-EF	†
-----	Gute Nacht	LH	C-FS	†
-----	Heideroeslein			†
-----	Ihr Bild	HL	C-C	†
-----	Ihr Grab			PET
-----	Im Abendrot	HL	C-D	†
-----	Im Fruehling	LH	D-FS	†
-----	In der Ferne	HL		†
-----	Irrlicht			
-----	Kriegers Ahnung	HL	G-EF	†
-----	Lachen und Weinen	HL	C-EF	†
-----	Liebesbotschaft	H	E-G	GSC
-----	Liebeslauschen			PET
-----	Lied eines Schiffers an die Dioskuren	HL	A-C	†
-----	Litanei	HLM	C-EF	†
-----	Lob der Thraenen	LM	F-F	†
-----	Meeresstille	HL	B-D	†
-----	Mein!	HL		†
-----	Memnon	LM	AF-F	PET
-----	Mut	HL		†
-----	Nachtgesang			PET
-----	Nachtstueck	LH	D-G	†
-----	Nacht und Traeume	HL	C-DF	†
-----	Prometheus	HL		†
-----	Schwanengesang			†
-----	Sei mir gegruesst	LH	G-G	†
-----	Seligkeit			
-----	Staendchen			
-----	Totengraebers Heimweh	HL	G-EF	†
-----	Ueber Wildemann			PET
-----	Ungeduld	HML		†
-----	Vor meiner Wiege	HL	C-E	†
-----	Wanderers Nachtlied, 1	HL		†
-----	Wanderers Nachtlied, 2	LH	F-F	†
-----	Wehmuth	HL	B-D	†
-----	Wer nie sein Brot	HL	C-EF	†
-----	Wer sich der Einsamkeit ergibt	M	C-FS	†
-----	Widerschein			PET
-----	Wohin?	HL	B-E	†
Schuetz	Aus dem 119th Psalm			
-----	Eile mich, Gott, zu erretten			BAR
Schumann, C.	Er ist gekommen			

678

Schumann, R.	Alte Laute	HL	DF-DF	†
-----	An den Sonnenschein	HL	A-D	†
-----	Auftraege	HL	C-E	†
-----	Aus den Hebraeischen Gesaengen			
-----	Dein Angesicht	HL	B-EF	†
-----	Der Hidalgo	HL	BF-F	†
-----	Der Husar, trara			
-----	Der Knabe mit dem Wunderhorn			†
-----	Der Nussbaum	LMH	D-FS	†
-----	Der Sandmann	HL	AF-DF	†
-----	Der Soldat			
-----	Die beiden Grenadiere			
-----	Die Lotusblume	HLM	BF-F	†
-----	Du bist wie eine Blume	HM	F-EF	†
-----	Er ist's	HL	BF-EF	†
-----	Fruehlingsfahrt	HL	B-E	†
-----	Ich grolle nicht	HL	BF-D	†
-----	Ich hab' im Traum geweinet	HL	B-D	†
-----	Ich wandelte unter den Baeumen	HL	A-D	†
-----	Ihre Stimme	LH		CFI
-----	Im Rhein, im heiligen Strome	HM	D-F	
-----	Im Walde	HL	A-D	†
-----	In der Fremde	HL		†
-----	Jeden Morgen			
-----	Lieb, Liebchen	HL	B-E	†
-----	Melancholie			
-----	Mit Myrthen und Rosen	HL	A-D	†
-----	Mondnacht	M	E-FS	†
-----	Provenzalisches Lied	LH		†
-----	Requiem			†
-----	Romanze	HL	C-E	†
-----	Schoene Wiege meiner Leiden	HL	C-EF	†
-----	Staendchen			
-----	Stille Traenen	HL		†
-----	Talismane			
-----	Waldesgespraech	HL	A-FS	†
-----	Wanderlied	HL	A-E	†
-----	Wenn ich in deine Augen seh'	HL	EF-FF	†
-----	Wer machte dich so krank?			
-----	Widmung	HL	BF-F	†
Strauss	Ach wehe mir unglueckhaftem Manne			
-----	Allerseelen	HL	AS-E	†

(Strauss)	Befreit			HSC
-----	Caecilie	MH	E-B	†
-----	Die Nacht	HL		DIT
-----	Du meines Herzens Kroenelein	HL	CS-E	†
-----	Freundliche Vision	HL	C-F	†
-----	Fuer fuenfzehn Pfennige			†
-----	Geduld	LH	C-G	
-----	Heimkehr	HL	B-E	†
-----	Heimliche Aufforderung	HL	B-E	†
-----	Ich trage meine Minne	M		†
-----	Liebeshymnus			†
-----	Madrigal	LH	EF-GF	
-----	Mit deinen blauen Augen	LH	C-GS	†
-----	Morgen	HML	E-F	†
-----	Nachtgang			†
-----	Ruhe meine Seele			†
-----	Schlechtes Wetter			†
-----	Traum durch die Daemmerung	HML	BF-EF	†
-----	Waldseligkeit			†
-----	Wie sollten wir geheim sie halten	LH	D-A	
-----	Winterliebe			†
-----	Winterweihe			†
Trunk	In meiner Heimat			
-----	Mir traeumte von einem Koenigskind			
-----	Schnitterlied			
Weber	Reigen			PET
Weingartner	Die Post im Walde			
-----	Hochsommer			
-----	Liebesfeier			
Wolf	Abschied			†
-----	Ach, des Knaben Augen	HL		†
-----	Ach, im Maien	HL	C-E	†
-----	Alle gingen, Herz, zu Ruh	HL	C-EF	†
-----	Alles endet, was entstehet	HL	F-C	†
-----	Anakreons Grab	HL	D-D	†
-----	An die Geliebte			†
-----	Auch kleine Dinge	HM	D-E	†
-----	Auf dem gruenen Balkon	HL		†
-----	Auf ein altes Bild	HL	E-DS	†
-----	Auf einer Wanderung	HL		†
-----	Auftrag	HL		†
-----	Bedeckt mich mit Blumen	HL	B-D	†
-----	Begegnung	M	EF-GF	PET
-----	Benedeit die sel'ge Mutter	H	D-G	PET
-----	Biterolf	HL	D-F	DIT

(Wolf)	Cophtisches Lied, 2			†
-----	Dank des Paria			PET
-----	Das Koehlerweib ist trunken			PET
-----	Das Staendchen	HL		†
-----	Dass doch gemalt all deine Reize waeren			†
-----	Denk' es, o Seele	LH	EF-F	†
-----	Der Feuerreiter			†
-----	Der Freund	HM	BF-E	PET
-----	Der Gaertner	HL		†
-----	Der Genesene an die Hoffnung	H	BF-AF	PET
-----	Der Musikant	HL	CS-D	†
-----	Der Rattenfaenger	HL		†
-----	Der Schreckenberger			†
-----	Der Soldat, 1	LH	E-FS	†
-----	Der Soldat, 2	H	EF-AF	PET
-----	Der Tambour	HL		†
-----	Ein Staendchen euch zu bringen	HL		†
-----	Epiphanias	HL	B-D	†
-----	Er ist's	H	D-G	†
-----	Fuehlt meine Seele	L	A-D	†
-----	Fussreise	HL	D-E	†
-----	Ganymed	HL	CS-D	†
-----	Gesang Weylas	HL	DF-F	†
-----	Gesegnet sei, durch den die Welt	HL		†
-----	Hatt ich irgend wohl Bedenken			PET
-----	Heb' auf dein blondes Haupt	HL	G-DF	†
-----	Heimweh (Eichendorff Lieder)	M		†
-----	Heimweh (Moerike Lieder)			†
-----	Hoch beglueckt in deiner Liebe	HL	DF-F	†
-----	Im Fruehling	HL	BF-F	†
-----	In der Fruehe	HL	C-C	†
-----	Jaegerlied			PET
-----	Lebe wohl	HL	BF-F	†
-----	Lied eines Verliebten			†
-----	Morgenstimmung	LH	C-GS	†
-----	Morgentau	HL	D-D	†
-----	Nachtzauber	HL	B-E	†
-----	Neue Liebe	LH	D-AF	†
-----	Nimmersatte Liebe	LH	CF-AF	†
-----	Nun wandre, Maria	HL	EF-D	†
-----	Prometheus			PET
-----	Seemanns Abschiedslied	H	C-A	†

(Wolf)	Selbstgestaendnis			PET
-----	Trunken muessen wir alle sein	M	ES-FS	†
-----	Ueber Nacht	LH	D-G	†
-----	Um Mitternacht	HL	G-EF	†
-----	Und willst du deinen Liebsten sterben	HL		†
-----	Verborgenheit	HL	B-E	GSC
-----	Verschwiegene Liebe	LH	DF-FS	†
-----	Wenn du zu den Blumen gehst	HL	B-EF	†
-----	Wer sich der Einsamkeit	HL	B-F	†
-----	Wer tat deinen Fuesslein weh?			
-----	Wiegenlied			
-----	Wohl denk' ich oft	M	C-EF	†
-----	Zur Ruh', zur Ruh'	HL	A-GF	†
Wolff	Alle Dinge haben Sprache	M	BF-GF	†
-----	Der Steinklopfer	M	BS-F	HMP
-----	Du bist so jung			HMP
-----	Es ist alles wie ein wunderbarer Garten			HMP
-----	Es werde Licht			†
-----	Ewig			
-----	Faeden			
-----	Knabe und Veilchen	M	D-D	HMP
-----	Landschaft			
-----	Seidenschuh' ueber Leisten von Gold			
-----	Since you're near	M	BF-GF	†
-----	Sommernacht			
-----	Tag meines Lebens			
-----	Und alles gehoeret uns			HMP

Italian Recital Songs

Baritone

Bassani	Dormi, bella, dormi tu	L	EF-F	GSC
Bimboni	Sospiri miei	M	EF-EF	GAL
Bononcini	L'esperto nocchiero (Astarte)	HL	B-E	†
-----	Per la gloria	HL	C-EF	†
-----	Suol dar la vita all'or			CFI
Brogi	Un ricordo			
Caccini	Amarilli, mia bella	ML	C-D	†
Caldara	Alma del core			GSC
-----	Come raggio di sol	HL	D-F	†
-----	Mirti, faggi			PET

(Caldara)	Sebben crudele	HML	E-DS	†
-----	Selve amiche, ombrose piante	HM	E-E	†
Carissimi	A morire!	ML	C-D	
-----	Filli, non t'amo più	HL	B-D	†
-----	Vittoria, mio core!	HLM	B-E	†
Castelnuovo-Tedesco	La barba bianca			
Cavalli	Beato chi può (Serse)			HEU
-----	Donzelle fuggite	HL	C-EF	†
-----	Troppo soavi i gusti	HM	E-E	DIT
Cesti	Ah, quanto è vero (Il Pomo d'Oro)	HL	F-F	DIT
-----	Che angoscia, che affanno (Il Pomo d'Oro)	HL	C-DF	DIT
-----	E dove t'aggiri (Il Pomo d'Oro)	HM	D-EF	DIT
-----	Intorno all'idol mio (Orontea)	MH	D-F	†
Cimara	Fiocca la neve	H	G-G	GSC
-----	Stornellata marinara	HM		RIC
De Leva	Canta il mare			
Del Leuto	Dimmi, amor	M	C-F	GSC
De Luca	Non posso disperar	HL	C-E	GSC
Denza	Gallop my steed			GSC
Donaudy	O del mio amato ben	M	EF-F	RIC
-----	Quando ti rivedrò			RIC
-----	Spirate pur, spirate			RIC
-----	Vaghissima sembianza	H	E-A	RIC
Durante	Danza, danza fanciulla gentile	HM	BF-F	†
-----	Vergin, tutta amor	LM	C-EF	†
Falconieri	Bella fanciulla			
-----	Non più d'amore	HL	C-D	DIT
-----	Nudo arciero	HL	AF-AF	DIT
-----	O bellissimi capelli	HL	B-D	†
Fatuo	Mattinata	M		RIC
Frescobaldi	Se l'aura spira	HL	C-EF	DIT
Gaffi	Luci vezzose	HL	D-E	DIT
Gagliano	Dormi, amore	HL	CS-E	DIT
-----	Valli profonde (Il Dannato)			HEU
Gasparini	Caro laccio, dolce nodo	M	EF-EF	GSC
Giordani	Caro mio ben	HML	B-D	†
Gluck	Spiagge amate (Paride ed Elena)			†
Handel	Affani del pensier (Ottone)			†
-----	Alma mia (Floridante)	HM	CS-E	†
-----	Col raggio placido (Agrippina)			

(Handel)	Dammi pace (Tamerlano)			
-----	Furibondo spira (Partenope)			KIS
-----	No soffrir non può (Berenice)			MUP
-----	Non lo dirò (Tolomeo)			
-----	O rendetemi il mio bene (Amadigi)	L	CS-EF	CFI
-----	Ombra mai fu (Serse)	HM	BF-EF	†
-----	Sento la gioja			
-----	Si, tra i ceppi (Berenice)	L	B-D	†
-----	V'adoro pupille (Julius Caesar)			BOO
-----	Volate più dei venti (Muzio Scevola)			MUP
Legrenzi	Che fiero costume	HML	C-D	GSC
Lotti	Pur dicesti, o bocca bella	LMH	E-FS	GSC
Malipiero	Ballata	H		CHE
-----	Inno a Maria, Nostra Donna	H		CHE
Marcello	Non m'è grave morir per amore	L	C-E	GSC
Monteverdi	Lettera amorosa			
-----	Maledetto sia l'aspetto			PET
Mozart	Ridente la calma			BOS
Paisiello	Lode al ciel			
-----	Nel cor più non mi sento	HL	C-EF	†
Paradies	M'ha preso alla sua ragna	M	EF-F	GSC
Pasquini	Sussurrate interno a clori			
Pergolesi	Bella mia (Il Maestro di Musica)			GSC
-----	Nina	HL	CS-D	DIT
-----	Ogni pena più spietata	L	B-E	GSC
Peri	Invocazione di Orfeo (Euridice)	HL	E-CS	DIT
-----	Nel puro ardor (Euridice)	HL	EF-C	DIT
Piccini	O nuit, dresse du mystere (Le Faux Lord)			GSC
Pizzetti	Angeleca			
-----	Oscuro è il ciel	M		RIC
Quagliati	Apra il suo verde seno	HL	E-CS	DIT
Respighi	Bella porta di rubini			RIC
-----	E se un giorno tornasse	M		RIC
-----	Nebbie			†
-----	Notte			BON
-----	Pioggia			BON
Rontani	Or ch'io non segno più	HL	CS-E	DIT
-----	Se bel rio	ML	D-C	†
Rosa	Selve, voi che le speranze	MH	D-G	DIT

(Rosa)	Star vicino	HL	D-E	†
Rossellini	La chambre vide			
-----	Le cennamelle			
Rossini	La danza	MH	E-A	†
Sadero	Amuri, Amuri	M		CHE
Santoliquido	Canzone Araba			
-----	Nel giardino			FOR
-----	Riflessi			FOR
Sarti	Lungi dal caro bene	HL	G-D	GSC
	(Armide)			
Scarlatti, A.	Chi vuole innamorarsi	HL	D-EF	DIT
-----	Già il sole dal Gange	LH	EF-F	GSC
-----	La fortuna			BOS
-----	Le violette			
-----	O cessate di piagarmi	HL	DS-E	†
-----	Rugiadose odorose	HL	D-E	DIT
	(Il Pirro e Demetrio)			
-----	Sento nel core	M	E-F	†
-----	Son tutta duolo	M	D-EF	GSC
Scarlatti, D.	Consolati e spara amante	L	BF-E	GSC
Secchi	Love me or not			BOO
-----	Lungi dal caro	HL	A-FS	DIT
Sibella	La Girometta	HML	D-E	GSC
-----	Sotto il ciel	HM	C-F	GSC
Stradella	Col mio sangue comprenderei	HL	E-F	DIT
	(Il Floridoro)			
-----	Per pietà (Il Floridoro)	HM	D-F	DIT
-----	Pietà, Signore	HM	C-F	GSC
-----	Se nel ben			CFI
Torelli	Tu lo sai	HL	BF-F	†
Toselli	Serenade			HEU
Tosti	À vucchella	LH	F-G	RIC
-----	Addio	MH		RIC
-----	Aprile	LMH		RIC
-----	La serenata	HLM	D-EF	GSC
-----	Mattinata			RIC
-----	The last song	HL		RIC
-----	Voi dormite signora			
-----	Vorrei morir	HM		RIC
Verdi	Tre romanze			RIC
Vivaldi	Piango gemo			
-----	Un certo no so che	HL	BF-EF	†
Wolf-Ferrari	Sonnets from Dante's "La Vita Nuova"			

Baritone

Arensky	Autumn	H	CS-FS	GSC
-----	Let me dream			
-----	Revery	MH	DS-FS	DIT
Blumenfeld	The starving peasant			
Cui	Hunger song	LM	E-F	DIT
-----	The statue at Czarskoe-Selo	HM	DF-EF	†
Davidenko	The blacksmith			
Gliere	Now forgotten is my lyre			
Glinka	The midnight review			
Gretchaninoff	Freedom			
-----	Hushed the song of the nightingale	MH	E-G	DIT
-----	My native land	L	C-EF	GSC
-----	Night			
-----	Over the steppe	LM	C-G	GSC
-----	Quand la hache tombe			
-----	The captive			DIT
-----	To a cup bearer			
-----	Wounded birch	HL	B-EF	†
Koeneman	The blacksmith	L		CHE
-----	When the king went forth to war	ML	A-E	CHE
Malashkin	O could I but express in song	LH		CHE
Mednikoff	The hills of Gruzia	H	DS-A	LAC
Mussorgsky	After the battle			GSC
-----	Death and the peasant			GSC
-----	Death the commander			
-----	In my attic			GSC
-----	Le chef d'armes			
-----	My little room			
-----	Night			GSC
-----	On the Dnieper			GSC
-----	Savishna			BES
-----	Serenade			BES
-----	Sphinx			BRH
-----	The banks of the Don			GSC
-----	The classic			BRH
-----	The evening prayer	M	C-E	GSC
-----	The goat	HL	C-E	CFI
-----	The grave			BRH
-----	The seminarian			GSC
-----	The song of the flea	L	AS-G	GSC
-----	Tiny star where art thou	LH	DF-F	BOS

Rachmaninoff	A dream	H		BOO
-----	Fair maiden			
-----	Floods of spring	HL		DIT
-----	God took away from me			GSC
-----	How fair this spot	MH		GSC
-----	In the silence of night	LH	D-A	GSC
-----	Morning	ML	B-DS	GSC
-----	No prophet, I			BOO
-----	Oh, no, I pray do not depart	H		DIT
-----	O thou billowy harvest field	HL	CS-E	GSC
-----	The island	LH	DF-F	†
-----	The raising of Lazarus			BRH
Rimsky-Korsakov	In silent woods			GSC
-----	On the Georgian hills	HM		GSC
-----	The prophet			
Rubinstein	Extases			
-----	When I see those little feet	MH		GSC
Tchaikovsky	At the ball	MH		GSC
-----	Don Juan's serenade	HLM	B-E	GSC
-----	Evening	HM		GSC
-----	Night	H		GSC
-----	Pilgrim's song	HLM	B-E	GSC
-----	To the forest			BOO

Scandinavian Recital Songs

Baritone

Alnaes	Sidste reis			
-----	Til en ung mann			
Grieg	A dream			†
-----	A swan			†
-----	Autumnal gale	HL	A-F	CFI
-----	By the brook			GSC
-----	Eros	LM	C-F	†
-----	Good morning			†
-----	Hunter's song	L	DS-E	GSC
-----	I love thee	HML	E-F	†
-----	In the boat	LM	D-ES	†
-----	Når jeg vil dø	L	CS-EF	HAN
-----	Nu er aftenen lys og lang	L	C-E	HAN
-----	Ragna			†
-----	Saint John's Eve	L	DF-E	CFI
-----	Serenade til Welhaven			

(Grieg)	Spillemand			
-----	Thanks for thy counsel			DIT
-----	The way of the world			DIT
-----	The wounded heart			PET
-----	Til en II	M	E-F	HAN
-----	Vaer hilset, I Damer	M	D-F	HAN
-----	Vandring i skoven	M	D-FS	HAN
-----	Ved Moders grav	M	C-F	HAN
Heise	Arnes sang			
-----	Kongesønnens romance			
Kilpinen	Sprich Geliebte, o sprich			
-----	Summer night			
Lassen, E.	Ich hatte einst ein Vaterland	HML	B-E	GSC
Melartin	O Herre			
Nielson	Den Danske sang			
-----	Havet omkring Danmark			
-----	Irmelin rose			HAN
Rangstroem	Klunkom, Welam Welamsson			
-----	Song to Karin			
-----	Vingar i natten			
Sibelius	Black roses	M	A-ES	AMP
-----	Come away death			AMP
-----	Die stille Stadt			DIT
-----	Reeds, reeds rustle			
-----	The origin of fire			
-----	Under strandens granar			
Sinding	Light	M	BF-F	GSC
-----	Sylvelin	M	E-E	GSC
Sjoeberg	Visions	MH	F-AF	GAL
-----	The Seraglio's garden	HL		GSC
Soedermann	Kung Heimer och Aslog			

Spanish Recital Songs

Baritone

Alvarez	La partida	HL	DS-E	GSC
Calleia	Granadinas			DIT
Eakin	Ay gitanos			
Ginastera	Triste			RIC
Guastavino	Campanas			
-----	Déjame estavoz			
-----	La rose y la sauce			RIC
-----	Paisaje			RIC
-----	Se equivoca			
Lara	Granada			SOU
Lecuona	Dame de tus rosas			

(Lecuona)	Por eso te quiero			MAR
Mompou	Combat del somni			
Padilla	Princesita	M		BOS
Sandoval	Madrigal	HL	A-E	GSC
-----	Sin tu amor	H	E-G	GSC
Serrano	Marinela			

Miscellaneous Recital Songs

Baritone

Bach-Gounod	Ave Maria			
Bartok	Ujdalok			
Bizet	Agnus Dei	HLM	C-AF	
Chajes	Adarim			TRA
Dvořák	Clouds and darkness			
-----	God is my shepherd			AMP
-----	I will sing new songs of gladness	HL		
-----	Lord, Thou art my refuge and shield			AMP
-----	Songs my mother taught me	HM	E-E	
-----	Turn Thee to me			AMP
Franck	Panis angelicus	LM		
Gustaldon	Musica probita			
Kodaly	Kit kene elvenni			
Kotilainen	Kun joulu on			
Monteverdi	Laudate Dominum			
Ravel	Mayerke mein suhn			RAV
Saint-Saëns	Ave Maria	HM		DIT
-----	Ave Verum			DUR
Schubert	Ave Maria			
Schuetz	Fili mi Absalom			
	4 Trombones and harpsichord			
Villa-Lobos	A Viola			
-----	Cantilena no. 3			
-----	Remeiro de San Francisco			
-----	Xango			AMP

British Songs and Arias For Opening Recitals

Baritone

| Dowland | I saw my lady weep | M | E-E | STB |
| Green | My lips shall speak the praise | M | E-F | OXF |

689

Handel	Have mercy, Lord (Te Deum)	HM		†
-----	Hear me, ye winds and and waves (Scipione)	ML	G-EF	BOO
-----	Let me wander not unseen (L'Allegro)	M	D-G	†
-----	Silent worship (Tolomeo)	LM	D-E	CUR
-----	Tears such as tender fathers shed (Deborah)	L		†
-----	Wher'er you walk (Semele)	HML	C-D	†
Purcell	Ah, how pleasant 'tis to love			AUG
-----	Evening hymn	M	C-F	OXF
-----	If music be the food of love	M	D-G	BOO
-----	Music for a while (Oedipus)	LH		SC
-----	Not all my torments			NOV

German Songs for Opening Recitals

Baritone

Bach, J.S.	Bist du bei mir	HML	A-EF	†
-----	O Jesulein suess			
Beethoven	Adelaide	HML	BF-E	†
-----	Andenken			†
-----	Ich liebe dich	HL	BF-DF	†
Brahms	Verzagen	MH	CS-FS	†
Bungert	Der Sandtraeger			
Gluck	Ode an den Tod			
Handel	Dank sei Dir, Herr	M	CS-E	†
Schubert	Das Wandern	HLM	E-E	†
-----	Ganymed	LH	EF-G	†
-----	Liebesbotschaft	H	E-G	†
Schuetz	Eile mich, Gott, zu erretten			BAR
Schumann	Mit Myrthen und Rosen	HL	A-D	†
Wolf	Ueber Nacht	LH	D-G	†

Italian Songs and Arias For Opening Recitals

Baritone

Caccini	Amarilli, mia bella	ML	C-D	†
Caldara	Sebben crudele	HML	E-DS	†
Carissimi	Vittoria, mio core	HLM	B-E	†
Cavalli	Beato chi può (Serse)			HEU
-----	Donzelle fuggite	HL	C-EF	†

Cesti	Ah, quanto è vero (Il Pomo d'Oro)	HL	F-F	DIT
-----	Che angoscia, che affanno (Il Pomo d'Oro)	HL	C-DF	DIT
-----	E dove t'aggiri (Il Pomo d'Oro)			DIT
Cimara	Stornellata marinara	HM		RIC
Donaudy	Quando ti rivedrò			RIC
Durante	Vergin, tutta amor	LM	C-EF	†
Falconieri	O bellissimi capelli	HL	B-D	†
Gluck	Spiagge amate (Paride ed Elena)			†
Handel	Affani del pensier (Ottone)			†
-----	Furibondo spira (Partenope)			KIS
-----	Lascia ch'io pianga (Rinaldo)	HM	EF-F	†
-----	O rendetemi il mio bene (Amadigi)	L	CS-EF	CFI
-----	Sei mia gioia (Pathenope)	HL	C-F	CFI
-----	Si, tra i ceppi (Berenice)	L	B-D	GSC
-----	V'adoro pupille (Julius Caesar)			BOO
Lotti	Pur dicesti, o bocca bella	LMH	E-FS	GSC
Monteverdi	Ahi, troppo è duro (Il Balletto delle Ingrate)	HL	C-EF	DIT
Mozart	Ridente la calma			BOS
Paisiello	Nel cor più non mi sento	HL	C-EF	†
Pergolesi	Salve Regina			
Peri	Invocazione di Orfeo (Euridice)	HL	E-CS	DIT
Piccini	O nuit, dresse du mystere (Le Faux Lord)			GSC
Rosa	Star vicino	HL	D-E	†
Sarti	Lungi dal caro bene (Armide)	HL	G-D	GSC
Scarlatti, A.	Già il sole dal Gange	LH	EF-F	GSC
-----	Sento nel core	M	E-F	†
Stradella	Per pietà (Il Floridoro)	HM	D-F	DIT
-----	Pietà, Signore	HM	C-F	GSC
-----	Se nel ben			CFI
Vivaldi	Piango gemo			
-----	Un certo no so che	HL	BF-EF	†

Baritone

Bacon	Casey Jones			
Barber	Bessie Bobtail	M	C-F	GSC
-----	I hear an army	LH	D-AF	GSC
-----	Sure on this shining night	MH	D-G	GSC
Branscombe	At the postern gate	MH	DF-AF	ASC
Carpenter	Serenade	LH	CS-A	GSC
Castelnuovo-Tedesco	Springtime	M		CHE
Chanler	I rise when you enter	M	CS-G	GSC
Charles	When I have sung my songs	HM	BF-EF	GSC
Copland	Old American songs			
Curran	Life	HM	BF-F	GSC
Dougherty	Everyone sang			
Duke	I ride the great black horses	M	C-G	GSC
-----	On a March day	M	B-GF	BOH
Foster	My journey's end	HLM	DF-G	GSC
Golde	Who knows	HM	BF-F	GSC
Hageman	Don Juan Gomez	M		GAL
-----	Miranda	HL		GAL
Horsman	The bird of the wilderness	LMH	DF-BF	GSC
Kernochan	We two together	H	EF-AF	GAL
Kingsford	Courage	M	C-F	GSC
Kleinsinger	The courtship of old Joe Clark			
La Forge	Hills	HL		RIC
-----	Song of the open	MH	EF-AF	DIT
-----	To a messenger	HLM	CF-G	GSC
Mac Gimsey	Jeri Jericho	M	C-G	CFI
-----	Land uv degradashun	M	BF-F	CFI
-----	O Lord you made a Moses	M		CFI
-----	Thunderin' wonderin'	L	C-D	CFI
Malotte	Blow me eyes	MH	C-G	GSC
-----	Mister Jim	M	D-F	GSC
-----	Song of the open road			ABC
-----	Upstream	M	C-F	GSC
Mana Zucca	Rachem	HML		CHA
Nordoff	Tell me, Thyrsis	H	E-G	AMP
Paxson	Laughing song	M	C-F	CFI
Rogers	The last song	MLH	E-AF	GSC
-----	Time for making songs	HM	CS-F	DIT
Sacco	Drum of peace	M	D-F	CFI
-----	Johnny the one	HL	BF-D	GSC

Sachs	The three riders	M	C-F	GSC
Schindler	From a city window			
Schuman	Holiday song	M	C-F	GSC
Singer	This want of you	L	E-FS	BOH
Swanson	Joy	M	BF-EF	LEE
Taylor	Captain Stratton's fancy	L	CS-F	JFI
Tyson	Sea moods	LH	E-AF	GSC
Warren	My parting gift			DIT
-----	We two	LH	E-A	GSC
-----	White horses of the sea	LH	F-G	GSC
Watts	Joy	HL	D-F	GSC
Weaver	The Abbot of Derry	HL	B-EF	GSC
Wolfe	Bone come a-knittin'			FLA
-----	Who's gonna mourn for me	LMH	D-A	ROB

(See also Negro Spirituals and Folk Songs.)

Miscellaneous Songs For
Closing Recitals

Baritone

Brahms	Juchhe!			†
-----	Wenn du nur zuweilen laechelst			†
-----	Wie froh und frisch	HL	B-E	†
-----	Willst du, dass ich geh'?	L	C-G	†
Bridge	Love went a-riding	HL		BOS
Britten	Oliver Cromwell			BOH
Cimara	Canto di primavera		D-G	FRL
Cowen	Border ballad	LM	D-E	BOO
Debussy	Chevaux de bois	H	C-G	†
De Lamarter	Break, new born year			WIT
Delius	Love's philosophy			†
Durante	Danza, danza fanciulla gentile	HM	BF-F	†
Eakin	Ay gitanos			
Falla	Jota	LH		AMP
-----	Polo	HL		AMP
German	My song is of the sturdy north	ML		CHA
Gretchaninoff	My native land	L	C-EF	GSC
Grieg	By the brook			GSC
-----	Good morning			†
-----	Hunter's song	L	DS-E	GSC
-----	Vaer hilset, I Damer	M	D-F	HAN
Head	A vagabond song			BOO

(Head)	When I think upon the maidens	LM	D-G	BOO
Hely- Hutchinson	Old mother Hubbard	HL	B-E	CFI
Hughes	Old mother Hubbard			CRA
Ireland	Great things			AUG
-----	When lights go rolling round the sky			
Keel	Trade winds	HL	BF-EF	BOH
Marx	Der Ton	M	C-F	AMP
Quilter	Blow, blow thou winter wind	HL	C-E	BOO
-----	Over the mountains			BOS
Rachmaninoff	Floods of spring	HL		DIT
-----	Oh, no, I pray do not depart	H		DIT
Rangstroem	Song to Karin			
Respighi	Pioggia			BON
Schubert	Die Forelle	MLH	EF-GF	†
-----	Ueber Wildemann			PET
Schumann	Er ist's	HL	BF-EF	†
Sinding	Light	M	BF-F	GSC
Strauss	Ich liebe dich			†
Vaughan Williams	The roadside fire	HML	BF-EF	BOO
Warlock	Yarmouth Fair	HL	B-E	CFI
Wolf	Er ist's	H	D-G	
-----	Morgenstimmung	LH	C-GS	†

American Atmospheric Songs

Baritone

Barber	Rain has fallen	HM	D-E	GSC
Bone and Fenton	Green fields	MH	E-A	PRE
-----	Tryst	MH	FS-G	CFI
Burleigh	Sometimes I feel like a motherless child	HML		RIC
Carpenter	Go, lovely rose	M	DF-EF	GSC
-----	Looking glass river	M	B-D	GSC
-----	Slumber song	ML	BF-F	GSC
-----	The green river	M	B-E	GSC
Carter	Dust of snow	M	D-E	AMP
Charles	Clouds	HML	C-EF	GSC
-----	My lady walks in loveliness	HM	C-EF	GSC

(Charles)	When I have sung my songs	HM	BF-EF	GSC
Crist	Into a ship dreaming	LMH	EF-GS	CFI
Curran	Nocturne Violin	HML	B-DS	GSC
Dougherty	Loveliest of trees	HM	C-E	BOH
Duke	Central Park at dusk	M		BOO
-----	Loveliest of trees	L	C-D	GSC
Ganz	A memory	HM	B-D	GSC
Griffes	Symphony in yellow	M	D-GF	GSC
Kramer	Minnelied	M	C-E	JFI
-----	Pleading	LH	D-GF	JFI
-----	Swans	HL		RIC
Loeffler	To Helen	M	DF-F	GSC
Mac Dowell	The sea	HL	D-D	BRH
Mac Gimsey	Sweet little Jesus boy	ML	D-D	CFI
Naginski	Night song at Amalfi	M	D-EF	GSC
Niles	I wonder as I wander	HL	BF-D	GSC
-----	Jesus, Jesus rest your head	HL	A-D	GSC
-----	The gambler's lament	HL	B-E	GSC
Robinson	Water boy	M	B-E	BOS
Sacco	The ragpicker	MH	C-AF	GSC
Tureman	A winter sunset	L	BF-E	GSC
Tyson	Noon and night	LH	F-AF	GSC
Watts	Blue are her eyes	H	FS-FS	DIT

British Atmospheric Songs

Baritone

Anon	Have you seen but a white lily grow?	H	E-F	GSC
Bridge	E'en as a lovely flower	HM	FS-E	BOH
Del Riego	O dry those tears	LMH	E-GS	CHA
Dunhill	The cloths of heaven	LM	EF-G	STB
Forsyth	The bell man			DIT
Handel	O sleep why dost thou leave me (Semele)	H	DS-GS	†
Harty	My lagan love	ML	BF-EF	BOO
Holst	The heart worships	ML	BF-D	STB
Hughes	A Ballynure ballad	L	BF-D	BOH
Quilter	Now sleeps the crimson petal	LMH	EF-GF	BOO
Sanderson	Quiet	ML	AF-EF	BOH
Somervell	A kingdom by the sea	ML	DF-F	BOO
Stanford	The fairy lough	ML	A-EF	BOO

695

Vaughan Williams			
Williams	Bright is the ring of words L		BOH
-----	Silent noon		GSC
-----	The infinite shining heavens		BOH
Warlock	Sleep		OXF

French Atmospheric Songs and Arias

Baritone

Chausson	Apaisement	MH	EF-G	HAM
-----	Les papillons	M	C-F	GSC
Debussy	Nuits d'etoiles	LH	E-A	MAR
Delibes	Lakmé, ton doux regards (Lakmé)			HEU
Duparc	La vie antérieure	HL		†
Fauré	En sourdine	HL	C-EF	†
Ferrari	Le miroir	M	E-F	GSC
Février	L'ihtruse	M	B-DF	HEU
Gluck	Un ruisselet bien clair (La Rencontre Imprévue)			LEM
Gounod	Sérénade	LMH	D-A	GSC
Hahn	D'une prison	L	BF-EF	HEU
-----	L'heure exquise	M	DF-F	†
-----	Paysage	MH	EF-G	HEU
Holmès	Au pays	HM	C-F	CFI
Leguerney	L'adieu	M	B-FS	DUR
Massenet	Chanson de la Touraine (Panurge)	M	EF-EF	HEU
Paladilhe	Psyché	HM	BF-F	GSC
Poulenc	Fleurs	M	DF-F	ROU
Ravel	Sainte	M	C-G	ELV
-----	Sur l'herbe	MH	C-G	DUR
Roussel	Le jardin mouillé	M	C-FS	ROU

German Atmospheric Songs and Arias

Baritone

Brahms	Nachtwandler			
-----	Steig' auf, geliebter Schatten	HL	BF-EF	†
Franz	Sterne mit den gold'nen Fuesschen	HL	DS-E	†
Haydn	She never told her love	HL	B-D	DIT
Schubert	Gute Nacht	LH	C-FS	†
-----	Nacht und Traeume	HL	C-DF	†

Schumann	Dein Angesicht	HL	B-EF	†
-----	Der Nussbaum	LMH	D-FS	†
-----	Ich hab' im Traum geweinet	HL	B-D	†
-----	Im Walde	HL	A-D	†
Strauss	Die Nacht	HL		†
-----	Traum durch die Daemmerung	HML	BF-EF	†
Wolf	Verborgenheit	HL	B-E	†

Miscellaneous Atmospheric Songs

Baritone

Cui	The statue at Czarskoe-Selo	HM	DF-EF	†
Grieg	A dream			†
-----	A swan			†
-----	In the boat	LM	D-ES	†
-----	Når jeg vil dø	L	CS-EF	HAN
-----	Ragna			†
-----	Til En II	M	E-F	HAN
Mussorgsky	My little room			
-----	Tiny star where art thou	LH	DF-F	BOS
Rachmaninoff	Morning	ML	B-DS	GSC
Sibelius	Reeds, reeds rustle			
Sinding	Sylvelin	M	E-E	GSC

American Dramatic Songs

Baritone

Barber	Bessie Bobtail	M	C-F	GSC
-----	I hear an army	LH	D-AF	GSC
Beach	Ah, love but a day			ASC
-----	The year's at the spring	MH	AF-AF	ASC
Bloch	Psalm 22	M	B-F	GSC
Campbell-Tipton	The crying of water	LH	FS-GS	GSC
Carpenter	Berceuse de guerre	M	C-G	GSC
-----	On the day when death will knock at thy door	M	C-F	GSC
-----	Slumber song	ML	BF-F	GSC
-----	The green river	M	B-E	GSC
Chadwick	O let night speak of me	HM	C-F	ASC
Curran	Life	HM	BF-F	GSC
Damrosch	Danny Deever	L	A-F	PRE
Diamond	David weeps for Absolom	M	D-A	MUP

697

Duke	Capri			
-----	Here in this spot with you	M	B-F	GSC
-----	I ride the great black horses	M	C-G	GSC
-----	On a March day	M	B-GF	BOH
Foster	My journey's end	HLM	DF-G	GSC
Geehl	For you alone			SHU
Gilbert	Pirate song	L	C-EF	GRA
Griffes	An old song resung	LM	EF-F	GSC
-----	Phantoms	M	BF-F	GSC
-----	Sorrow of Mydath	M		GSC
Hageman	Don Juan Gomez	M		GAL
-----	Music I heard with you	MH	E-A	GAL
Horsman	The bird of the wilderness	LMH	DF-BF	GSC
Huhn	Invictus	ML	BF-DF	ASC
Ives	Charlie Rutlage	M		ARR
Johnson	Roll, Jerd'n roll	M	EF-F	GSC
Kernochan	We two together	H	EF-AF	GAL
La Forge	Song of the open	MH	EF-AF	DIT
Loeffler	To Helen	M	DF-F	GSC
Mac Dowell	The sea	HL	D-D	BRH
Mac Gimsey	Land uv degradashun	M	BF-F	CFI
Malotte	Song of the open road			ABC
Manz-Zucca	I love life	LM	F-F	PRE
Moore	Adam was my grandfather			GAL
Nordoff	Tell me, Thyrsis	H	E-G	AMP
Rogers	The last song	MLH	E-AF	GSC
-----	Time for making songs	HM	CS-F	DIT
Singer	This want of you	L	E-FS	BOH
Speaks	Morning	HML	BF-D	GSC
-----	Shepherd, see thy horse's foaming mane			FLA
Taylor	Captain Stratton's fancy	L	CS-F	JFI
Tyson	Sea moods	LH	E-AF	GSC
Warren	We two	LH	E-A	GSC
-----	White horses of the sea	LH	F-G	GSC
Wolfe	De glory road	L	A-F	GSC
-----	Gwine to Hebb'n	LM	B-E	GSC
-----	Who's gonna mourn for me	LMH	D-A	ROB

British Dramatic Songs and Arias

Baritone

Arne, T.	Preach not me your musty rules (Comus)	HML		ROW

698

Bainton	Ring out, wild bells	M	C-EF	OXF
Bridge	O that it were so	LMH	D-G	CHA
Cowen	Border ballad	LM	D-E	BOO
Delius	Twilight fancies	M	D-FS	CFI
Del Riego	Homing	HML	BF-E	CHA
Dix	The trumpeter	HML	A-C	BOH
Dowland	Fine knacks for ladies	M	E-F	STB
German	My song is of the sturdy north	ML		CHA
-----	Rolling down to Rio	ML	G-D	NOV
Grainger	Shallow brown	M	F-F	GSC
Handel	But who may abide (The Messiah)	L	G-E	†
-----	Why do the nations (The Messiah)	L	B-E	†
Holst	The Sergeant's song			ASH
Ireland	Great things			AUG
Leveridge	When dull care			BOO
Purcell	I'll sail upon the dog star	HL	A-E	†
Quilter	Blow, blow thou winter wind	HL	C-E	BOO
Ronald	Prelude	HML	B-D	ENO
Sanderson	Shipmates of mine	LL	G-D	BOO
Sullivan	The lost chord	HL	C-F	GSC
Templeton	Wi' a hundred pipers	L	BF-EF	GSC
Vaughan Williams	Joy, shipmate joy			OXF
-----	The vagabond	ML	A-E	BOO

French Dramatic Songs and Arias

Baritone

Bizet	Chanson du toreador (Carmen)	HL	BF-F	†
-----	L'orage s'est calmé (Les Pêcheurs des Perles)			CHO
-----	Quand la flamme de l'amour (Le Jolie Fille de Perth)			CHO
Caplet	Le forêt			DUR
Charpentier	Les pauvre gens peuvent-ils être heureux (Louise)			HEU
Debussy	Chevaux de bois	H	C-G	†
-----	Colloque sentimental			DUR
-----	Noël des enfants qui n'ont plus de maisons			DUR
Duparc	La vague et la cloche			ROU
-----	La vie antérieure	HL		†
-----	Le manoir de Rosamunde	HL	B-F	BOS

699

(Duparc)	Phidylé	MH	EF-AF	BOS
-----	Testament	HL		INT
Fauré	Automne	MH	D-FS	GSC
-----	Poème d'un jour			HAM
-----	Prison	LH		†
-----	Toujours	LH	F-AF	†
Février	L'intruse	M	B-DF	HEU
Hahn	D'une prison	L	BF-EF	HEU
-----	Offrande	M	D-D	†
Holmès	Au pays	HM	C-F	CFI
Hue	J'ai pleuré en rêve	HL	D-E	BOS
Indy	Lied maritime	LH	B-G	ROU
-----	Mirage			HAM
Lalo	Marine	LH	DS-FS	
Lenormand	Quelle souffrance	HM	AF-F	HAM
Massenet	Promesse de mon avenir (Le Roi de Lahore)	L	DF-GF	GSC
-----	Salomé, Salomé (Hérodiade)			GSC
-----	Vision fugitive (Hérodiade)	LM	C-GF	GSC
Meyerbeer	Adamastor, roi des vagues profondes (L'Africaine)	L	D-E	GSC
-----	Fille des rois (L'Africaine)			BRO
-----	Nonnes qui reposez (Robert le Diable)			GSC
Offenbach	Scintille diamant (Tales of Hoffman)	M		GSC
Paladilhe	Lamento provincal	M	CS-FS	HOM
Pessard	Requiem du coeur			LED
Poldowski	Dansons la gigue	M	EF-G	MAR
Saint-Saëns	Danse macabre	L	BF-EF	AXE
-----	Les pas d'armes du Roi Jean	HML	A-F	RIC
Thomas	Chanson bachique (O vin dissipe) (Hamlet)			GSC
-----	Comme une pâle fleur (Hamlet)			HEU

German Dramatic Songs and Arias

Baritone

Beethoven	In questa tomba	ML	A-CS	†
Brahms	Am Sonntag Morgen	L	CS-FS	†
-----	Nicht mehr zu dir zu gehen			†
-----	Treue Liebe	LMH	DS-E	†
-----	Verrat	HL	FS-EF	†
-----	Von ewiger Liebe	LMH	B-AF	†
Franz	Im Herbst	HM	A-F	†
Liszt	Die drei Zigeuner	LM	B-G	GSC

(Liszt)	Die Lorelei	LH	BF-BF	†
Loewe	Archibald Douglas			†
-----	Edward	HL	F-E	†
-----	Erkennen			SC
-----	Odins Meeresritt			SC
Mahler	Der Tamboursgesell	HL		INT
-----	Ich hab' ein gluehend Messer	M	BF-GF	WEI
-----	Lieder eines fahrenden Gesellen	M		INT
Marx	An einen Herbstwald	M	CS-FS	UNI
-----	Hat dich die Liebe beruehrt	MH	EF-BF	AMP
Mendelssohn	Is not His word like a fire (Elijah)	M	B-F	†
-----	It is enough (Elijah)	L	A-E	†
-----	Schilflied	M	F-FS	
Schubert	Am Feierabend	HL	BF-F	GSC
-----	Am Meer	HML	B-D	†
-----	An Schwager Kronos	HL	G-E	†
-----	Auf dem Flusse	HL	F-E	†
-----	Aufenthalt	HLM	A-F	†
-----	Dem Unendlichen	L	A-GF	†
-----	Der Atlas	HL	BF-F	†
-----	Der Doppelgaenger	HL	G-D	†
-----	Der Erlkoenig	HML	A-E	†
-----	Der Lindenbaum	HL	A-D	†
-----	Der Schiffer	LH	BF-A	†
-----	Die Allmacht	HML	G-E	†
-----	Die junge Nonne	LH	C-GF	†
-----	Die Kraehe	HL	A-E	†
-----	Die Liebe hat gelogen	LM	G-F	†
-----	Die Stadt	HL	A-E	†
-----	Du liebst mich nicht	LH	E-FS	†
-----	Erstarrung	HL	D-F	†
-----	Fahrt zum Hades	HL	G-DF	PET
-----	Fragment aus dem Aeschylus			PET
-----	Fruehlingstraum	HL	C-D	†
-----	Ganymed	LH	EF-G	†
-----	Gebet waehrend der Schlacht	M	CS-E	†
-----	Gruppe aus dem Tartarus	L	CS-EF	†
-----	In der Ferne	HL		†
-----	Kriegers Ahnung	HL	G-EF	†
-----	Mut	HL		GSC
-----	Prometheus	HL		†
-----	Totengraebers Heimweh	HL	G-EF	†
Schumann	Der arme Peter	HL	B-G	†

(Schumann)	Der Husar, Trara!			
-----	Der Soldat			
-----	Fruehlingsfahrt	HL	B-E	†
-----	Ich grolle nicht	HL	BF-D	†
-----	Mit Myrthen und Rosen	HL	A-D	†
-----	Schoene Wiege meiner Leiden	HL	C-EF	†
-----	Talismane			
-----	Waldesgespraech	HL	A-FS	†
Strauss	Caecilie	MH	E-B	†
-----	Madrigal	LH	EF-GF	
-----	Ruhe meine Seele			†
Wagner	Die Frist ist um (Der Fliegende Hollaender)			†
-----	Leb' wohl, du kuehnes, herrliches Kind (Die Walkuere)	L	B-E	†
Weber	Wo berg' ich mich (Euryanthe)			†
Wolf	Alle gingen, Herz, zu Ruh	HL	C-EF	†
-----	Das Koehlerweib ist trunken			PET
-----	Denk' es, o Seele	LH	EF-F	†
-----	Der Feuerreiter			†
-----	Der Freund	HM	BF-E	PET
-----	Der Rattenfaenger	HL		INT
-----	Epiphanias	HL	B-D	†
-----	Lebe wohl	HL	BF-F	†
-----	Nachtzauber	HL	B-E	†
-----	Prometheus			PET
-----	Seemanns Abschiedslied	H	C-A	†
-----	Ueber Nacht	LH	D-G	†
-----	Zur Ruh', zur Ruh'	HL	A-GF	†

Italian Dramatic Songs and Arias

Baritone

Cimara	Canto di primavera		D-G	FRL
Donizetti	Vien, Leonora a piedi tuoi (La Favorita)			BRO
Durante	Vergin, tutta amor	LM	C-EF	†
Giordano	Nemico della patria (Andrea Chenier)	L	B-FS	SON
Leoncavallo	Zaza, piccola zingara (Zaza)			SON
Mascagni	Il cavallo scalpita (Cavalleria Rusticana)			GSC
Piccini	O nuit, dresse du mystere (Le Faux Lord)			GSC
Ponchielli	O monumento (La Gioconda)			RIC

702

Puccini	Se la giurata fede (Tosca)	M	DF-F	RIC
Respighi	Nebbie			†
Verdi	Cortigiani, vil razza (Rigoletto)			GSC
-----	Credo (Otello)	M	AS-FS	JCH
-----	Eri tu (Un Ballo in Maschera)	M	A-G	†
-----	Ford's monologue (E sogno) (Falstaff)			RIC
-----	Il mio sangue (Luisa Miller)			RIC
-----	In braccio alle dovizie (I Vespri Siciliani)			RIC
-----	O de' verd'anni miei (Ernani)			RIC
-----	O vecchio cor, che batti (I Due Foscari)			RIC
-----	Per me giunto (Don Carlos)			RIC
-----	Urna fatale (La Forza del Destino)			RIC

Miscellaneous Dramatic Songs

Baritone

Alvarez	La partida	HL	DS-E	GSC
Cui	Hunger song	LM	E-F	DIT
Dvořák	Hear my prayer, O Lord			AMP
Gliere	Now forgotten is my lyre			
Gretchaninoff	Over the steppe	LM	C-G	GSC
-----	The captive			DIT
-----	Wounded birch	HL	B-EF	†
Grieg	A dream			†
-----	A swan			†
-----	Autumnal gale	HL	A-F	CFI
-----	Eros	LM	C-F	†
-----	In the boat	LM	D-ES	†
-----	Vaer hilset, I Damer	M	D-F	HAN
Koeneman	When the king went forth to war	ML	A-E	CHE
Korbay	Had a horse, a finer no one ever saw			SC
Malashkin	O could I but express in song	LH		CHE
Mussorgsky	After the battle			GSC
-----	On the Dnieper			GSC
-----	Siege of Kazan (Boris Godunoff)	L	F-E	GSC

(Mussorgsky)	The song of the flea	L	AS-G	GSC
Rachmaninoff	Christ is risen	LM	D-F	GAL
-----	Floods of spring	HL		DIT
-----	God took away from me			GSC
-----	Oh, no, I pray, do not depart	H		DIT
-----	O thou billowy harvest field	HL	CS-E	GSC
-----	To the children	MH	F-G	DIT
Rimsky-Korsakov	On the Georgian hills	HM		GSC
Sibelius	Black roses	M	A-ES	AMP
Sinding	Light	M	BF-F	GSC
Tchaikovsky	None but the lonely heart	HLM	C-F	DIT
-----	Pilgrim's song	HLM	B-E	GSC

American Humorous Songs

Baritone

Bone and Fenton	Captain Kidd	MH	B-G	CFI
Brockway	The swapping song			GSC
Carpenter	Don't ceare	M	C-D	GSC
Chanler	I rise when you enter	M	CS-G	GSC
Dougherty	Declaration of independence	L	C-C	GSC
Guion	What shall we do with a drunken sailor	HML	C-D	GSC
Hadley	My shadow			ASC
Hindemith	The whistling thief	M	E-F	AMP
Mac Gimsey	Egg-a-bread			MCG
-----	Jonah and the whale	M	BF-EF	CFI
Malotte	Blow me eyes	MH	C-G	GSC
-----	Mister Jim	M	D-F	GSC
Mana-Zucca	The big brown bear	HML	C-F	GSC
Mason	A grain of salt	L	A-D	GSC
-----	I ain't afeared of the Admiral	L	A-E	GSC
-----	Nautical lays of a landsman	L	A-E	GSC
-----	The constant cannibal maiden	L	C-FS	GSC
Moore	Adam was my grandfather			GAL
Niles	The gambler's lament	HL	B-E	GSC
Paxson	Laughing song	M	C-F	CFI
Powell	The deaf woman's courtship	M		JFI
Rodgers	Soliloquy (Carousel)			CHA

704

Romberg	The fireman's bride (Up in Central Park)	M	D-EF	WIL
Sacco	Brother Will, brother John	M	C-F	GSC
-----	Mexican serenade	HL	D-EF	BOS
Schuman	Holiday song	M	C-F	GSC
Scott	The drunken sailor			
Taylor	Captain Stratton's fancy	L	CS-F	JFI
Weaver	The Abbot of Derry	HL	B-EF	GSC
Wolfe	Sailormen	HM	D-FS	GSC
-----	Short'nin' bread	LHM	D-D	FLA

British Humorous Songs

Baritone

Arden and Wille	Cockles and mussels	HM	E-E	ROW
Arne, T.	Why so pale and wan?			GSC
Berners	Dialogue between Tom Filuter and his man	M	D-F	CHE
-----	Theodore or the pirate king			CHE
Britten	Oliver Cromwell			BOH
Charles, W.	The green eyed dragon	M	BF-E	BOH
Clarke	Shy one	HL	BF-G	BOH
Coates	Stone cracker John	L		BOO
Gibbs	Five eyes	HL	D-D	BOS
-----	The market			CUR
Head	When I think upon the maidens	LM	D-G	BOO
Hely- Hutchinson	Old mother Hubbard	HL	B-E	CFI
Hughes	A Ballynure ballad	L	BF-D	BOH
-----	Kitty, my love, will you marry me?	M	C-F	BOH
-----	Old mother Hubbard			CRA
-----	The stuttering lovers	MH	E-FS	CHA
Johnston	Because I were shy	L	B-E	CRA
Jones	Love is a bable			STB
Lawes	I am confirmed			BOO
Leveridge	The maiden's resolution			GSC
Liddle	The garden where the praties grow	LMH	E-FS	STB
Lohr	The little Irish girl	HLM	C-E	CHA
Old English	Young Richard			PRE
Sanderson	Captain Mac	ML	G-E	BOO
-----	Laughing cavalier	LM	BF-F	BOO
Stanford	The little admiral	L	C-G	STB

Sullivan	The Lord Chancellor's insomnia (Iolanthe)			
Torrence	Smilin' Kitty O'Day	ML	CS-D	BOO
Warlock	The droll lover			

French Humorous Songs and Arias

Baritone

Bizet	Quand la flamme de l'amour (Le Jolie Fille de Perth)			CHO
Chabrier	Ballade des gros dindons	HL		†
-----	Villanelle des petits canards	HML	B-E	†
Debussy	Ballade des femmes de Paris			DUR
Grétry	Nièces, neuveux (Les Deux Avares)			JOB
Lemaire	Chanson à manger	M	B-E	GSC
Messager	Long ago in Alcala	M		CHA
Poulenc	Chanson à boire	L	B-E	HEU
-----	La belle jeunesse	L	D-F	HEU
-----	Le bestiaire String quartet, flute, clarinet and bassoon	M		AMP
Ravel	Sur l'herbe	MH	C-G	DUR
Satie	La statue de bronze			ROU
-----	Le chapelier			ROU

German Humorous Songs and Arias

Baritone

Beethoven	Aus Goethes Faust			
-----	Der Kuss			†
Brahms	Vergebliches Staendchen	LHM	E-FS	†
Mahler	Des Antonius von Padua Fischpredigt	HL	GF-F	†
Mendelssohn	Ich bin ein vielgerister Mann (Heimkehr aus der Fremde)	ML		DIT
Mozart	Der Vogelfaenger bin ich ja (Die Zauberfloete)	L	D-E	†
-----	Warnung	HM	C-D	
Reichardt	Rhapsodie			MOS
Schubert	Heidenroeslein			
Strauss, J.	Open road, open sky (The Gypsy Baron)			GSC
Strauss, R.	Fuer fuenfzehn Pfennige			†

Wolf	Abschied			†
-----	Der Musikant	HL	CS-D	†
-----	Der Soldat, 1	LH	E-FS	†
-----	Der Tambour	HL		†
-----	Epiphanias	HL	B-D	†
-----	Nimmersatte Liebe	LH	CF-AF	†

Italian Humorous Songs and Arias

Baritone

Mozart	Ho capito, Signor (Don Giovanni)			
-----	Aprite un po' quegli occhi (Le Nozze di Figaro)			
-----	Der Vogelfaenger bin ich ja (Zauberfloete)			†
-----	Madamina! Il catalogo e questo (Don Giovanni)			†
-----	Non più andrai (Le Nozze di Figaro)	L	C-E	†
Pergolesi	Son imbrogliato io gia (La Serva Padrona)	L		RIC
Rontani	Or ch'io non segno più	HL	CS-E	DIT
Rossini	Largo al factotum (Il Barbieri di Siviglia)			†
Scarlatti, A.	Chi vuole innamorarsi	HL	D-EF	DIT
Wolf-Ferrari	Aprila, o bella (Jewels of the Madonna)	HL	D-FS	GSC

Miscellaneous Humorous Songs

Baritone

Grieg	The way of the world			DIT
Mussorgsky	Song of the parrot (Boris Godunoff)			DIT
-----	The evening prayer	M	C-E	GSC
-----	The seminarian			GSC
-----	The song of the flea	L	AS-G	GSC

American Folk Songs (Arr.)

Baritone

Bacon	Adam and Eve	M	B-D	CFI
-----	The Erie canal	L	D-C	CFI
Bartholomew	Pretty Saro	M	D-D	GSC
-----	Little Mawhee			GSC
Brockway	Barbara Allen			GRA
-----	Frog went-a-courting			GRA
-----	Sourwood mountain			GRA
-----	The barnyard song			GRA
-----	The swapping song			GSC
Burleigh	The dove and the lily	HL		RIC
Copland	I bought me a cat			
-----	Old American songs			
Davis	He's gone away	M	C-E	GAL
Dougherty	Across the western ocean	M	D-D	GSC
-----	Five sea chanties	L	A-EF	GSC
-----	Mobile bay	M	BF-EF	GSC
-----	Rio Grande	M	EF-EF	GSC
-----	Shenandoah	L	A-D	GSC
Guion	All day on the prarie	M	EF-F	GSC
-----	Home on the range	HLM	C-F	GSC
-----	What shall we do with a drunken sailor	HML	C-D	GSC
Hughes	The warranty deed			GSC
Niles	Black is the color of my true love's hair			
-----	Down in the valley			GSC
-----	Gambler, don't lose your place	HM	C-F	GSC
-----	Gambler's song of the Big Sandy River	HM	CS-FS	GSC
-----	I wonder as I wander	HL	BF-D	GSC
-----	Jesus, Jesus rest your head	HL	A-D	GSC
-----	The black oak tree			CFI
-----	The gambler's lament	HL	B-E	GSC
-----	The rovin' gambler	HL	BF-EF	GSC
Paxson	Bid your love			
-----	Blow ye winds			
-----	Sally Brown			
-----	Shenandoah			
Powell	At the foot of Yonders mountain	M		JFI
-----	Five Virginian folk songs			JFI
-----	The deaf woman's courtship	M		JFI

(Powell)	The rich old woman	M		JFI
Robinson	Water boy	M	B-E	BOS
Scott	Blow the man down			
-----	The drunken sailor			
-----	Wailie, wailie	M	D-E	JCH
Shaw	Black is the color of my true love's hair	M	C-F	DIT
Siegmeister	Bury me not on the lone prairie			
-----	Poor way faring stranger			
Wellesley	Sing me a chanty	HLM	B-E	FOX

British Folk Songs (Arr.)

Baritone

Arden and Wille	Cockles and mussels	HM	E-E	ROW
Britten	Oliver Cromwell			BOH
-----	The ash grove			BOH
Broadwood	Some rival has stolen my true love	LM	D-E	BOO
Clayton	O men from the fields	M	C-F	BOS
Corder	The Bailiff's daughter of Islington			JWM
Gatty	Bendemeer's stream	LMH		BOO
Grainger	Shallow Brown	M	F-F	GSC
Harty	My lagan love	ML	BF-EF	BOO
-----	The game played in Erin-Go-Bragh			CFI
Hatton	The minstrel boy			BOO
Hopekirk	Annie Laurie			DIT
-----	Loch Lomond			DIT
-----	Ye banks and braes	LM	D-C	DIT
Hughes	A Ballynure ballad	L	BF-D	BOH
-----	Down by the Sally gardens			BOO
-----	Has sorrow thy young days shaded			BOO
-----	Kitty, my love, will you marry me?	M	C-F	BOH
-----	Oft in the stilly night			
-----	The lark in clear air	ML	BF-D	BOO
-----	The stuttering lovers	MH	E-FS	CHA
Johnston	Because I were shy	L	B-E	CRA
Kennedy-Fraser	An Eriskay love lilt			BOO
-----	The bens of Jura			BOO
-----	The farmer's pride			CHA

709

(Kennedy-Fraser)	The road to the isles			BOO
Lawson	Turn ye to me	M	B-E	GSC
Liddle	The garden where the praties grow	LMH	E-FS	STB
Mc Gill	Lord Randall			BOO
Moss	The floral dance	HML	A-D	CHA
Old English	Young Richard			PRE
Page	The foggy dew			DIT
-----	The harp that once through Tara's halls			DIT
Peel	In summertime on Bredon	ML	BF-EF	CHA
-----	The bonnie Earl o' Moray			
Peterkin	I wish and I wish	M	B-E	OXF
Quilter	Over the mountains			BOS
Reid	Turn ye to me			BOO
Scott	Lord Randal	L	E-F	GAL
Shaw	The land of heart's desire	M	C-E	CUR
Somervell	David of the white rock			
Stanford	Trottin' to the fair	M		BOO
Tarrnsch	Early one morning			
Taylor	May day carol			JFI
Templeton	Wi' a hundred pipers	L	BF-EF	GSC
Vaughan Williams	And all in the morning	L	D-E	GAL
-----	Rolling in the dew			OXF
Warlock	Yarmouth Fair	HL	B-E	CFI
Welsh	All through the night			
Wilson	Come let's be merry			BOO
-----	Mary of Allendale	HML	BF-EF	BOO

Miscellaneous Folk Songs (Arr.)

Baritone

Brahms	In stiller Nacht			†
-----	Mein Maedel hat einen Rosenmund	M	F-F	†
Falla	Asturiana	HL		AMP
-----	El paño moruno	HL		AMP
-----	Jota	LH		AMP
-----	Nana	HL		AMP
-----	Polo	HL		AMP
-----	Seguidilla murciana	HL		AMP
-----	Siete canciones	HL		AMP
Ferrari	Valparaiso			
Korbay	Had a horse, a finer no one ever saw			SC

710

Milhaud	Two bretonne folk songs			ESC
Obradors	Con amores a mi madre			RIC
Ravel	Chanson espagnole	LH	D-BF	DUR
-----	Chanson italienne			DUR
-----	Là-bas, vers l'église	MH	GS-E	DUR
-----	Quel galant!	M	D-F	DUR
Serradell	La golondrina	H	C-A	GSC
Tiersot	J'ai vu la beauté ma mie			
-----	L'amours de moi	M	EF-F	HEU
Weckerlin	Aminte	M	C-D	†
-----	Chantons les amours de Jean	H	D-G	GSC
-----	Lison dormait	M	D-D	CFI
-----	Menuet d'Exaudet	H	D-G	GSC
-----	O ma tendre musette	LM	A-E	GSC
-----	Trop aimable Sylvia	M	D-E	GSC
-----	Venez, agréable printemps	M	C-F	

Negro Spirituals

Baritone

Boatner	Oh, what a beautiful city!	HL	D-E	GSC
-----	On mah journey	LH	EF-EF	RIC
-----	Trampin' (Tryin' to make heaven my home)	L	D-F	ELK
Brown	Dere's no hidin' place down dere			CFI
-----	Every time I feel de spirit			AMP
-----	Sometimes I feel like a motherless child	L		AMP
Burleigh	Balm in Gilead	HL		RIC
-----	De gospel train	HL		RIC
-----	Deep river	HML		RIC
-----	Go down, Moses	HL		RIC
-----	Hard trials	M		RIC
-----	He's just de same today	HL		RIC
-----	I stood on de ribber ob Jerdon	HL		RIC
-----	Joshua fit de battle ob Jericho	LH	DS-E	RIC
-----	My Lord, what a mornin'			RIC
-----	Nobody knows de trouble I've seen	HL		RIC
-----	Oh, didn't it rain	LH		RIC
-----	Oh, Peter, go ring-a-dem bells			RIC

(Burleigh)	Sometimes I feel like a motherless child	HML		RIC
-----	Were you there?	HML		RIC
Dett	Sit down servant			GSC
Johnson	At the feet of Jesus	L		
-----	City called Heaven			ROB
-----	Dere's no hidin' place down dere			
-----	Fix me, Jesus	L	BF-DF	GSC
-----	Hold on			ROB
-----	Honor, honor	HM	C-E	CFI
-----	John Henry			CFI
-----	Oh, glory			
-----	Ride on, King Jesus			CFI
-----	Roll Jerd'n roll	M	EF-F	GSC
-----	Take my mother home	M	BF-EF	CFI
-----	Witness	HM	D-F	CFI
Kerby-Forrest	He's got the whole world in His hands	M	G-E	MLS
Lawrence	Let us break bread together	HML	BF-EF	MCR
Mac Gimsey	Daniel in the lion's den	M		CFI
-----	Land uv degradashun	M	BF-F	CFI
-----	Shadrack	HM	C-EF	CFI
-----	Sweet little Jesus boy	ML	D-D	CFI
Payne	Crucifixion	L	C-C	GSC
Price	My soul's been anchored in the Lord			GAM
Ryder	Let us break bread together	LH	D-G	JFI
Saunders	The Lord's prayer	L	BF-C	BOH
Singer	Go down Moses	M	E-E	CFI

American Songs Employing Agility

Baritone

Barber	I hear an army	LH	D-AF	GSC
Diack	Little Jack Horner			CFI
Dichmont	Ma little banjo	ML	E-CS	GSC
Hageman	Miranda	HL		GAL
Hopkinson	O'er the hills	LH	C-G	†
Manning	Shoes	M	EF-F	GSC
Nordoff	There shall be more joy	M		AMP
Schuman	Holiday song	M	C-F	GSC
Speaks	In May time	HL	D-E	JCH

Baritone

Aiken	Sigh no more	HML		STB
Arne, T.	Now Phoebus sinketh in the west			GSC
-----	Preach not me your musty rules (Comus)	HML		ROW
German	Charming Chloe	HML		NOV
-----	Rolling down to Rio	ML	G-D	NOV
Green	My lips shall speak the praise	M	E-F	OXF
Handel	Arm, arm ye brave (Judas Maccabaeus)	L	B-E	†
-----	O ruddier than the cherry (Acis and Galatea)	L	G-F	DIT
-----	O sleep why dost thou leave me (Semele)	H	DS-GS	†
-----	Revenge, Timotheus cries (Alexander's Feast)	L	G-D	†
-----	See the raging flames arise (Joshua)			†
-----	The trumpet shall sound (The Messiah) Trumpet	L		†
-----	Thy glorious deeds (Samson)	M	C-F	†
-----	Why do the nations? (The Messiah)	L	B-E	†
Hely-Hutchinson	Old mother Hubbard	HL	B-E	CFI
Hook	Bright Phoebus	M	EF-F	GSC
Hughes	Old mother Hubbard			CRA
Morgan	Clorinda	HM	C-EF	ENO
Morley	It was a lover and his lass	HM		DIT
-----	Sweet nymph, come to thy lover	M	D-B	BOS
Purcell	Hark! how all things with one sound rejoice			NOV
-----	I attempt from love's sickness to fly (The Indian Queen)	MH	CS-E	†
-----	I'll sail upon the dog star	HL	A-E	†
Wilson	Come let's be merry			BOO
-----	Phillis has such charming graces	ML	CS-EF	BOO

713

French Songs and Arias Employing Agility

Baritone

Berlioz	Sérénade de Mephisto (La Damnation de Faust)			DIT
Chausson	Le colibri	M		BOS
-----	Les papillons	M	C-F	GSC
Gounod	Au rossignol	LMH	D-G	CHO
-----	Sérénade	LMH	D-A	GSC
Grétry	O Richard, O mon roi (Richard Coeur-De-Lion)			
Lemaire	Chanson a manger	M	B-E	GSC
Meyerbeer	Adamastor, roi des vagues profondes (L'Africaine)	L	D-E	GSC
Ravel	Chanson à boire			DUR
-----	Kaddisch	H	C-G	DUR
Spontini	Dans le sein d'un Ami (La Vestale)			

German Songs and Arias Employing Agility

Baritone

Bach, J.S.	Doch weichet, ihr tollen vergeblichen (Cantata 8) Flute			NOV
-----	Wie will ich lustig lachen (Cantata 205)			OXF
Brahms	Botschaft	HL	D-F	†
-----	O liebliche Wangen	MLH	E-G	†
Haydn	Rolling in foaming billows (The Creation)	L	C-F	†
-----	With joy th' impatient husbandman (The Seasons)	L	B-E	†
Mahler	Des Antonius von Padua Fischpredigt	HL	GF-F	†
-----	Ich bin der Welt abbanden gekommen	HL		INT
Mendelssohn	Is not His word like a fire (Elijah)	M	B-F	†
Mozart	Der Vogelfaenger bin ich ja (Die Zauberfloete)	L	D-E	†
Schubert	Am See			PET
-----	Auf dem Wasser zu singen	MH	EF-GF	†
-----	Das Wandern	HLM	E-E	†
-----	Irrlicht			
-----	Liebesbotschaft	H	E-G	†

714

(Schubert)	Mein!	HL		†
-----	Ungeduld	HML		†
Schumann	Auftraege	HL	C-E	†
-----	Mondnacht	M	E-FS	GSC
-----	Waldesgespraech	HL	A-FS	†
Strauss	Fuer fuenfzehn Pfennige			†

Italian Songs and Arias Employing Agility

Baritone

Bononcini	L'esperto nocchiero (Astarte)	HL	B-E	†
-----	Per la gloria	HL	C-EF	†
Caldara	Alma del core			GSC
-----	Selve amiche, ombrose piante	HM	E-E	†
Carissimi	Filli, non t'amo più	HL	B-D	†
-----	Vittoria, mio core	HLM	B-E	†
Cimara	Canto di primavera		D-G	FRL
Donaudy	Spirate pur, spirate			RIC
Donizetti	Cruda funesta smania (Lucia di Lammermoor)			BRO
Durante	Danza, danza fanciulla gentile	HM	BF-F	†
Handel	Affani del pensier (Ottone)			†
-----	Furibondo spira (Partenope)			KIS
-----	Sei mia gioia (Parthenope)	HL	C-F	CFI
-----	Si, tra i ceppi (Berenice)	L	B-D	†
-----	Volate più dei venti (Muzio Scevola)			MUP
Lotti	Pur dicesti, o bocca bella	LMH	E-FS	GSC
Mozart	Aprite un po quegl' occhi (Le Nozze di Figaro)			†
-----	Mentre ti lascio	L		BOO
Pergolesi	Ogni pena più spietata	L	B-E	GSC
Rossini	La danza	MH	E-A	†
-----	Largo al factotum (Il Barbiere di Siviglia)	L	D-G	†
Scarlatti, A.	Già il sole dal Gange	LH	EF-F	GSC
-----	La fortuna			BOS
-----	Rugiadose odorose (Il Pirro e Demetrio)	HL	D-E	DIT
Scarlatti, D.	Consolati e spara amante	L	BF-E	GSC
Verdi	Il mio sangue (Luisa Miller)			RIC

715

Vivaldi	Un certo no so che	HL	BF-EF	†

**Miscellaneous Songs
Employing Agility**

Baritone

Alvarez	La partida	HL	DS-E	GSC
Falla	Nana murciana	HL		AMP
-----	Polo	HL		AMP
-----	Seguidilla	HL		AMP
Grieg	Good morning			†
Mussorgsky	Oriental chant (Josua Navine Cantata)	ML	BF-E	GSC
-----	Tiny star, where art thou	LH	DF-F	BOS

**American Songs Employing
Crescendo and Diminuendo**

Baritone

Barber	Rain has fallen	HM	D-E	GSC
--ʌ---	The daisies	M	C-F	GSC
Beach	Ah, love but a day			ASC
Campbell-Tipton	The crying of water	LH	FS-GS	GSC
Carpenter	Go, lovely rose	M	DF-EF	GSC
-----	Looking glass river	M	B-D	GSC
Charles	Clouds	HML	C-EF	GSC
Duke	Loveliest of trees	L	C-D	GSC
Engel	Sea shell	M	EF-EF	GSC
Hopkinson	My days have been so wondrous free	LH	EF-G	†
La Forge	Hills	HL		RIC
Loeffler	To Helen	M	DF-F	GSC
Niles	I wonder as I wander	HL	BF-D	GSC
-----	Jesus, Jesus rest your head	HL	A-D	GSC
Rogers	At parting	LH	CS-FS	GSC
Thompson	Velvet shoes	M	C-E	ECS

Baritone

Benjamin	The wasp			CUR
Bridge	E'en as a lovely flower	HM	FS-E	BOH
Clarke	Shy one	HL	BF-G	BOH
Handel	Let me wander not unseen (L'Allegro)	M	D-G	†
-----	O sleep why dost thou leave me (Semele)	H	DS-GS	†
Head	The ships of Arcady	ML	BF-EF	BOH
Leveridge	The maiden's resolution			GSC
Morley	Sweet nymph, come to thy lover	M	D-B	BOS
Purcell	I attempt from love's sickness to fly (The Indian Queen)	MH	CS-E	†
-----	Sylvia, now your scorn give over			FSY
Quilter	Now sleeps the crimson petal	LMH	EF-GF	BOO
Shaw	Song of the Palanquin bearers	LH	E-F	CUR
Vaughan Williams	The infinite shining heavens			BOH

French Songs and Arias Employing
Crescendo and Diminuendo

Baritone

Berlioz	Le repos de la Ste. Famille (L'Enfance du Christ)	MH		CST
Debussy	Green	H	C-AF	†
-----	Les ingénus			DUR
Duparc	Chanson triste	MH	FS-AF	†
-----	L'invitation au voyage	HM	E-F	†
-----	Phidylé	MH	EF-AF	BOS
-----	Sérénade	HL		INT
Fauré	Adieu	MH	F-F	†
-----	Arpège	MH	E-FS	HAM
-----	Clair de lune	MH	C-G	†
-----	En prière	H	F-F	†
-----	Green	HL	CS-GF	†
-----	Le secret	LH	F-G	†
-----	Les roses d'Ispahan	HM	D-FS	†

(Fauré)	Lydia	MH	G-G	†
-----	Nell	LH	FS-AF	†
-----	Spleen	H	E-FS	MAR
Gounod	Envoi de fleurs	MH	G-G	SC
-----	Medjé (Chanson arabe)	MH	G-G	BOO
Martini	Plaisir d'amour	M	BF-EF	GSC
Mehul	Femme sensible (Ariodant)			
Paladilhe	Psyché	HM	BF-F	GSC
Rameau	A l'amour rendez les armes (Hippolyte et Aricie)			CHO
-----	Dans ces doux asiles (Castor et Pollux)			LEM
-----	Le grillon			DUR
Satie	Daphénéo			ROU

German Songs Employing
Crescendo and Diminuendo

Baritone

Beethoven	Andenken			†
Brahms	Auf dem See	HL	D-F	†
-----	Geheimnis			†
-----	Sonntag	H	D-G	†
-----	Wie Melodien zieht es	HL	A-E	†
Franz	Sterne mit den gold'nen Fuesschen	HL	DS-E	†
-----	Stille Sicherheit	M	E-F	†
Haydn	Liebes Maedchen, hoer' mir zu			HSC
Mendelssohn	Venetianisches Gondellied	LM	E-FS	AUG
Schubert	Abschied	HL	BF-F	†
-----	Am See			PET
-----	An den Mond	HL	F-GF	†
-----	Auf dem Wasser zu singen	MH	EF-GF	†
-----	Das Lied im Gruenen			PET
-----	Der Musensohn	LH	FS-G	†
-----	Der Wanderer	HML	FS-D	†
-----	Der Wanderer an den Mond	LM	D-F	PET
-----	Die Taubenpost	HL	D-EF	†
-----	Fruehlingstraum	HL	C-D	†
-----	Geheimes	HL	BF-EF	†
-----	Hark! hark! the lark	LMH	F-G	†
-----	Im Fruehling	LH	D-FS	GSC
-----	Lachen und Weinen	HL	C-EF	†
-----	Liebesbotschaft	H	E-G	†
-----	Nacht und Traeume	HL	C-DF	†

718

Schumann	Der Nussbaum	LMH	D-FS	†
-----	Der Sandmann	HL	AF-DF	†
-----	Provenzalisches Lied	LH		†
-----	Romanze	HL	C-E	†
-----	Staendchen			
Strauss	Die Nacht	HL		†
Wolf	Auch kleine Dinge	HM	D-E	†
-----	Der Gaertner	HL		†
-----	Morgentau	HL	D-D	†
-----	Nun wandre, Maria	HL	EF-D	†
-----	Und willst du deinen Liebsten sterben	HL		†
-----	Verschwiegene Liebe	LH	DF-FS	†
-----	Wenn du zu den Blumen gehst	HL	B-EF	†
Wolff	Faeden			
-----	Knabe und Veilchen	M	D-D	HMP

Italian Songs and Arias Employing Crescendo and Diminuendo

Baritone

Bononcini	Per la gloria	HL	C-EF	†
Caldara	Alma del core			GSC
-----	Sebben crudele	HML	E-DS	†
-----	Selve amiche, ombrose piante	HM	E-E	†
Cesti	Intorno all'idol mio (Orontea)	MH	D-F	†
De Luca	Non posso disperar	HL	C-E	GSC
Falconieri	O bellissimi capelli	HL	B-D	†
Frescobaldi	Se l'aura spira	HL	C-EF	DIT
Handel	Affani del pensier (Ottone)			†
-----	Ombra mai fu (Serse)	HM	BF-EF	†
Marcello	Non m'é grave morir per amore	L	C-E	GSC
Monteverdi	Lasciatemi morire (Arianna)	ML	D-D	†
Respighi	Bella porta di rubini			RIC
Rontani	Se bel rio	ML	D-C	†
Rosa	Selve, voi che le speranze	MH	D-G	DIT
Scarlatti, A.	La fortuna			BOS
-----	Sento nel core	M	E-F	†
Secchi	Love me or not			BOO

Miscellaneous Songs Employing
Crescendo and Diminuendo

Baritone

Gretchaninoff	My native land	L	C-EF	GSC
Grieg	En fuglevise			
-----	In the boat	LM	D-ES	†
-----	Nu er aftenen lys og lang	L	C-E	HAN
-----	Springtide			
Mussorgsky	Oriental chant (Josua Navine Cantata)	ML	BF-E	GSC
-----	The banks of the Don			GSC
-----	The evening prayer	M	C-E	GSC
Rachmaninoff	The island	LH	DF-F	†

American Songs Employing
Piano Singing

Baritone

Barber	With rue my heart is laden	HL	CS-D	GSC
Burleigh	Jean	HML		PRE
Carpenter	May the maiden			DIT
-----	The green river	M	B-E	GSC
Charles	My lady walks in loveliness	HM	C-EF	GSC
-----	When I have sung my songs	HM	BF-EF	GSC
De Rose	I heard a forest praying	MH	EF-GF	CHA
Foote	Tranquillity	HL	BF-E	ASC
Ganz	A memory	HM	B-D	GSC
Griffes	Symphony in yellow	M	D-GF	GSC
Guion	Mam'selle Marie	M	D-E	GSC
Kramer	Minnelied	M	C-E	JFI
-----	Pleading	LH	D-GF	JFI
-----	Swans	HL		RIC
Mac Dowell	The sea	HL	D-D	BRH
Mac Gimsey	Sweet little Jesus boy	ML	D-D	CFI
Manning	In the Luxembourg gardens	HML	BF-D	GSC
-----	Shoes	M	EF-F	GSC
Naginski	Night song at Amalfi	M	D-EF	GSC
Taylor	A song for lovers	MH	D-F	JFI
Watts	Blue are her eyes	H	FS-FS	DIT

British Songs Employing
Piano Singing

Baritone

Anon	Have you seen but a white lily grow?	H	E-F	GSC
Arden and Wille	Cockles and mussels	HM	E-E	ROW
Coleridge-Taylor	She rested by the broken brook	HL		DIT
Delius	So white, so soft, is she	LH	B-FS	BOH
-----	Twilight fancies	M	D-FS	CFI
Del Riego	O dry those tears	LMH	E-GS	CHA
Dunhill	The cloths of heaven	LM	EF-G	STB
Forsyth	The bell man			DIT
Gurney	An epitaph			OXF
Handel	Silent worship (Tolomeo)	LM	D-E	CUR
Harty	My lagan love	ML	BF-EF	BOO
Ireland	I was not sorrowful	ML		BOO
Pilkington	Rest, sweet nymphs			STB
Sanderson	Quiet	ML	AF-EF	BOH
Shaw	The land of heart's desire	M	C-E	CUR
Vaughan Williams	Orpheus with his lute			PRO
-----	Silent noon			GSC

French Songs and Arias Employing
Piano Singing

Baritone

Aubert	La lettre			DUR
Berlioz	Voici des roses (La Damnation de Faust)			CST
Debussy	La grotte			DUR
-----	Nuits d'etoiles	LH	E-A	MAR
Delibes	Lakmé, ton doux regards (Lakmé)			HEU
Dukas	Sonnet			DUR
Duparc	Extase	LMH	FS-A	†
Fauré	Après un rêve	HM	C-F	†
-----	C'est l'extase	HL	C-FF	GSC
-----	Dans les ruines d'une abbaye	M	E-FS	†
-----	En sourdine	HL	C-EF	†
Ferrari	Le miroir	M	E-F	GSC

721

Février	L'intruse	M	B-DF	HEU
Franck	Le mariage des roses	M	E-FS	BOS
Gounod	Au rossignol	LMH	D-G	CHO
-----	Sérénade	LMH	D-A	GSC
Hahn	D'une prison	L	BF-EF	HEU
-----	L'heure exquise	M	DF-F	†
-----	Offrande	M	D-D	†
-----	Paysage	MH	EF-G	HEU
Lully	Bois épais (Amadis)	ML	C-EF	†
Massenet	Crépuscule	M	D-E	GSC
-----	Légende de la sauge (Jongleur de Notre-Dame)	M	CS-F	HEU
Pessard	L'adieu du matin	ML	BF-D	GSC
Poulenc	Invocation aux Parques			HEU
-----	Montparnasse	H	EF-G	ESC
Ravel	D'Anne qui me jecta	HM	CS-FS	GSC
-----	Sainte	M	C-G	ELV
-----	Sur l'herbe	MH	C-G	DUR
-----	Trois beaux oiseaux du paradis			DUR
Roussel	Le jardin mouillé	M	C-FS	ROU
Saint-Saëns	Mai	H	G-FS	DUR
Weckerlin	Aminte	M	C-D	†
-----	Bergère légère	M	D-E	BOS
-----	Menuet d'Exaudet	H	D-G	GSC
-----	O ma tendre musette	LM	A-E	GSC
-----	Trop aimable Sylvia	M	D-E	GSC
Widor	Je ne veux pas autre chose	HL	C-EF	HAM

German Songs and Arias Employing
Piano Singing

Baritone

Beethoven	Ich liebe dich	HL	BF-DF	†
Brahms	In Waldeseinsamkeit	H	ES-G	†
-----	Lerchengesang	LH	FS-GS	†
-----	Nachtwandler			
-----	Sapphische Ode	HML		†
-----	Staendchen	HL	BF-E	†
-----	Steig' auf, geliebter Schatten	HL	BF-EF	†
Franz	Marie	HL	D-F	†
Hassler	Tanzlied			SIM
Mahler	Die zwei blauen Augen	M	A-G	†
-----	Ich bin der Welt abbanden gekommen	HL		INT

Marx	Der Rauch			UNI
Mendelssohn	It is enough (Elijah)	L	A-E	†
-----	Lord God of Abraham (Elijah)	L	B-E	†
Schubert	Ave Maria	LMH	F-F	†
-----	Du bist die Ruh	LMH	EF-AF	†
-----	Im Abendrot	HL	C-D	†
-----	Lob der Thraenen	LM	F-F	†
-----	Totengraebers Heimweh	HL	G-EF	†
Schumann	Mondnacht	M	E-FS	†
-----	Requiem			†
Strauss	Allerseelen	HL	AS-E	†
-----	Freundliche Vision	HL	C-F	BOO
-----	Heimkehr	HL	B-E	†
-----	Ich trage meine Minne	M		†
-----	Nachtgang			†
-----	Traum durch die Daemmerung	HML	BF-EF	†
Trunk	In meiner Heimat			
Wagner	O du, mein holder Abendstern (Tannhaeuser)	L	BF-E	†
Wolf	Ach, des Knaben Augen	HL		†
-----	An die Geliebte			†
-----	Auf ein altes Bild	HL	E-DS	†
-----	Jaegerlied			PET
-----	Nachtzauber	HL	B-E	†
-----	Schlafendes Jesuskind	HL	AS-F	†
-----	Verborgenheit	HL	B-E	†

Italian Songs and Arias Employing Piano Singing

Baritone

Bononcini	Deh, più a me non v'ascondete	LH		†
Brogi	Venitian vision	M	D-F	RIC
Cimara	Fiocca la neve	H	G-G	GSC
Durante	Vergin tutto amor			†
Gagliano	Dormi, amore (La Flora)	HL	CS-E	DIT
Gluck	O del mio dolce ardor (Paride ed Elena)			GSC
Mozart	Deh vieni alla finestra (Don Giovanni)	L	D-E	†
Respighi	Notte			BON
Scarlatti, A.	Già mai			
Secchi	Lungi dal caro bene	HL	A-FS	DIT

723

Miscellaneous Songs Employing
Piano Singing

Baritone

Arensky	Revery	MH	DS-FS	DIT
Cui	The statue at Czarskoe-Selo	HM	DF-EF	†
Dvořák	God is my shepherd			AMP
-----	Goin' home			DIT
-----	Songs my mother taught me	HM	E-E	†
Gretchaninoff	Hushed the song of the nightingale	MH	E-G	DIT
Grieg	A dream			†
-----	A swan			†
-----	Ragna			†
-----	Til En II	M	E-F	HAN
Mednikoff	The hills of Gruzia	H	DS-A	LAC
Mussorgsky	My little room			
Rachmaninoff	In the silence of night	LH	D-A	GSC
Rimsky-Korsakov	In silent woods			GSC
Sibelius	Die stille Stadt			DIT
Sinding	Sylvelin	M	E-E	GSC
Tchaikovsky	Evening	HM		GSC

American Songs Employing
Rapid Enunciation

Baritone

Boatner	Oh, what a beautiful city!	HL	D-E	GSC
Brockway	The swapping song			GSC
Burleigh	Joshua fit de battle ob Jericho	LH	DS-E	RIC
Carpenter	Don't ceare	M	C-D	GSC
-----	The cock shall crow	M	B-E	GSC
Guion	What shall we do with a drunken sailor	HML	C-D	GSC
Hadley	My shadow			ASC
Hageman	Don Juan Gomez	M		GAL
Kernochan	Smuggler's song			GAL
Kountz	The sleigh	HL	D-FS	GSC
Leoni	Tally-ho!			GSC
Mac Gimsey	Egg-a-bread			MCG
Mana-Zucca	The big brown bear	HML	C-F	GSC
Naginski	Richard Cory	ML	A-E	GSC

724

Sacco	Brother Will, brother John	M	C-F	GSC
-----	Mexican serenade	HL	D-EF	BOS
Speaks	Shepherd see thy horse's foaming mane			FLA
Warner	Hurdy gurdy	M	D-F	CFI
Weaver	The Abbot of Derry	HL	B-EF	GSC
Wolfe	De glory road	L	A-F	GSC
-----	Short'nin' bread	LHM	D-D	FLA

British Songs Employing Rapid Enunciation

Baritone

Bantock	A feast of lanterns	HM	D-F	GAL
Bartlet	Whither runneth my sweetheart			BOO
Bax	The enchanted fiddle			
Berners	Dialogue between Tom Filuter and his man	M	D-F	CHE
Britten	Oliver Cromwell			BOH
Charles	The green eyed dragon	M	BF-E	BOH
Cowen	Border ballad	LM	D-E	BOO
Dowland	Shall I sue?			STB
Fisher	At Tankerton Inn	LM	B-G	BOO
Gibbs	Five eyes	HL	D-D	BOS
Head	When I think upon the maidens	LM	D-G	BOO
Hughes	Kitty, my love, will you marry me?	M	C-F	BOH
-----	The stuttering lovers	MH	E-FS	CHA
Lehmann	Myself when young	LL	A-E	GSC
Leveridge	The beggar's song	L	G-D	BOO
Liddle	The garden where the praties grow	LMH	E-FS	STB
Molloy	The Kerry dance	LH	C-G	GSC
Moss	The floral dance	HML	A-D	CHA
Old English	Young Richard			PRE
Sanderson	Susan is her name	LM	D-E	BOH
Shaw	Song of the Palanquin bearers	LH	E-F	CUR
Sullivan	Ho, Jolly Jenkin (Ivanhoe)	LM	C-F	CHA
Templeton	Wi' a hundred pipers	L	BF-EF	GSC
Vaughan Williams	The water mill	L	C-D	OXF
Warlock	Good ale			AUG

French Songs Employing
Rapid Enunciation

Baritone

Caplet	La ronde	M		DUR
Chabrier	Villanelle des petits canards	HML	B-E	†
Debussy	Ballade des femmes de Paris			DUR
-----	Chevaux de bois	H	C-G	†
-----	Green	H	C-AF	†
-----	Le temps a laissié son manteau			DUR
-----	Mandoline	HM	BF-F	†
Fauré	Dans les ruines d'une abbaye	M	E-FS	†
-----	Notre amour	H	DS-B	†
-----	Poème d'un jour			HAM
-----	Toujours	LH	F-AF	†
Fourdrain	Carnaval	M	C-F	RIC
Gounod	Ballade de la reine Mab (Roméo et Juliette)			JCH
Milhaud	La tourterelle	M	B-G	DUR
Pessard	L'adieu du matin	ML	BF-D	GSC
Poldowski	Dansons la gigue	M	EF-G	MAR
Poulenc	Couplets bachiques	L	C-FF	HEU
-----	La belle jeunesse	L	D-F	HEU
Ravel	Manteau de fleurs	H		INT
-----	Nicolette	L	B-FS	ELK
Saint-Saëns	Danse macabre	L	BF-EF	AXE
-----	Mai	H	G-FS	DUR
-----	Tournoiement			DUR
Weckerlin	Aminte	M	C-D	†
-----	Chantons les amours de Jean	H	D-G	GSC
-----	Trop aimable Sylvia	M	D-E	GSC

German Songs Employing
Rapid Enunciation

Baritone

Brahms	Blinde Kuh			†
-----	Juchhe!			†
-----	Staendchen	HL	BF-E	†
-----	Tambourliedchen			†
-----	Vergebliches Staendchen	LHM	E-FS	†

Jensen	Margreta	M	F-F	PET
Mendelssohn	An die Entfernte	M	F-F	
Mozart	Warnung	HM	C-D	
Schubert	Abschied	HL	BF-F	†
-----	Am Feierabend	HL	BF-F	†
-----	Das Lied im Gruenen			PET
-----	Der Musensohn	LH	FS-G	†
-----	Der Schiffer	LH	BF-A	†
-----	Der zuernende Barde			PET
-----	Die Forelle	MLH	EF-GF	†
-----	Die Post	HML	BF-EF	†
-----	Erstarrung	HL	D-F	†
-----	Fischerweise	L	C-D	†
-----	Fruehlingssehnsucht	HL	B-E	†
-----	Ueber Wildemann			PET
-----	Wohin?	HL	B-E	†
Wolf	Der Feuerreiter			†
-----	Ein Staendchen euch zu bringen	HL		†
-----	Jaegerlied			PET

Italian Songs and Arias Employing Rapid Enunciation

Baritone

Cavalli	Donzelle fuggite	HL	C-EF	†
De Luca	Non posso disperar	HL	C-E	GSC
Falconieri	Non più d'amore	HL	C-D	DIT
-----	Nudo arciero	HL	AF-AF	DIT
Legrenzi	Che fiero costume	HML	C-D	†
Malipiero	Ballata	H		CHE
Mascagni	Il cavallo scalpita (Cavalleria Rusticana)			GSC
Mozart	Finch' han dal vino (Don Giovanni)	L	D-EF	†
-----	Ho capito, Signor (Con Giovanni)			
-----	Non più andrai (Le Nozze di Figaro)	L	C-E	†
-----	Se vuol ballare (Le Nozze di Figaro)	L		†
Paradies	M'ha preso alla sua ragna	M	EF-F	GSC
Pergolesi	Son imbrogliato io già (La Serva Padrona)	L		RIC
Rontani	Or ch'io non segno più	HL	CS-E	DIT
Scarlatti, A.	Chi vuole innamorarsi	HL	D-EF	DIT
Tosti	À vucchella	LH	F-G	RIC

Miscellaneous Songs Employing
Rapid Enunciation

Baritone

Falla	Seguidilla murciana	HL		AMP
Grieg	In the boat	LM	D-ES	†
-----	Nu er aftenen lys og lang	L	C-E	HAN
-----	The way of the world			DIT
-----	With a water lily	HM	CS-EF	†
Mussorgsky	The evening prayer	M	C-E	GSC
-----	Siege of Kazan (Boris Godunoff)			GSC
-----	The seminarian			GSC

American Songs Employing
Sustained Singing

Baritone

Andrews	Sea fever	L	A-D	GSC
Barber	Sure on this shining night	MH	D-G	GSC
Burleigh	Deep river	HML		RIC
-----	Sometimes I feel like a motherless child	HML		RIC
-----	Were you there?	HML		RIC
Carpenter	Slumber song	ML	BF-F	GSC
Chadwick	Allah	LH	CS-GS	ASC
-----	O let night speak of me	HM	C-F	ASC
Coombs	Her rose	ML	D-C	GSC
Curran	Nocturne	HML	B-DS	GSC
Edwards	By the bend of the river	HML	C-E	GSC
-----	Into the night	HML	C-DF	GSC
Foote	I'm wearing awa'	HL		ASC
Foster, S.C.	Ah, may the red rose live always			GSC
-----	Gentle Annie			BOS
Golde	O beauty, passing beauty	MH	CS-GS	GSC
Griffes	By a lonely forest pathway	HML	A-EF	GSC
Guion	Home on the range	HLM	C-F	GSC
Hageman	Music I heard with you	MH	E-A	GAL
Horsman	In the yellow dusk	MH	FS-A	GSC
-----	The bird of the wilderness	LMH	DF-BF	GSC
Kernochan	We two together	H	EF-AF	GAL
Kramer	For a dream's sake	HL		JFI
Lang	Irish love song	HML	A-E	ASC
Levitzki	Do you remember?	HML	BF-EF	GSC
Mac Dowell	Thy beaming eyes	ML	BF-EF	ASC

728

Mana-Zucca	Nichavo	HLM	F-G	JCH
Metcalf	At nightfall	HML	C-DF	ASC
Nevin	The Rosary	HML	C-D	BOS
Porter, Q.	Music, when soft voices die	HM	D-C	MUP
Rasbach	Trees	LMH	CS-GS	GSC
Robinson	Water boy	M	B-E	BOS
Rogers	Wind song	LM	C-G	GSC
Scott	Think on me	HML	D-EF	GAL
Speaks	Sylvia	HML	AF-DF	GSC
Tyson	Noon and night	LH	F-AF	GSC
Watts	The poet sings	MH	EF-AF	DIT

British Songs and Arias Employing Sustained Singing

Baritone

Balfe	The heart bowed down (The Bohemian Girl)			†
Bantock	Silent strings	MH	F-G	BOO
Blow	The self banished	L	C-F	NOV
Bridge	All things that we clasp	HL		BOS
-----	Isobel	HML		CHA
-----	O that it were so	LMH	D-G	CHA
Bury	There is a lady	HM	CS-E	CFI
Butterworth	Loveliest of trees			AUG
Campion	Follow thy fair sun			STB
-----	There is a garden in her face			DIT
-----	When to her lute Corinna sings			STB
Clarke	The blind ploughman	HML	C-D	CHA
Del Riego	Homing	HML	BF-E	CHA
Dowland	Flow, my tears	M	D-E	STB
-----	I saw my lady weep	M	E-E	STB
-----	Sorrow, sorrow stay	M	D-D	BOS
Dunhill	To the Queen of Heaven	M	C-G	GSC
Elgar	I am the good shepherd (Light of Life)			NOV
Ford	Now I see thy looks were feigned			BOO
-----	Since first I saw your face			DIT
-----	There is a lady sweet and kind	M	D-E	STB
Glover	Rose of Tralee	LMH	E-G	MOV
Handel	But who may abide (The Messiah)	L	G-E	†
-----	Defend her! Heaven (Theodora)			STB
-----	Hear me, ye winds and waves (Scipione)	ML	G-EF	BOO

729

(Handel)	Loathsome urns disclose your treasure (Triumph of Time and Truth)			DIT
-----	Shall I in Mamre's fertile plain (Joshua)	L	G-EF	DIT
-----	Tears such as tender fathers shed (Deborah)	L		†
-----	The people that walked in darkness (The Messiah)			†
-----	Wher'er you walk (Semele)	HML	C-D	†
Holst	The heart worships	ML	BF-D	STB
Humphrey	I pass all my hours			DIT
Johnson	As I walked forth one summer day			DIT
Mc Gill	Duna	HML	BF-D	BOO
Milford	So sweet love seemed	HL	D-D	GRA
Purcell	Cease, o my sad soul			POT
-----	If music be the food of love	M	D-G	BOO
-----	Music for a while (Oedipus)	LH		SC
-----	Since from my dear			
Quilter	Drink to me only	LMH	GF-GF	BOH
-----	Go, lovely rose	LHM	F-GF	CHA
Ronald	Prelude	HML	B-D	ENO
Sanderson	Drumadune			BOH
Scott	Lord Randal	L	E-F	GAL
Stephenson	Love is a sickness	HML	C-D	BOO
Sullivan	The lost chord	HL	C-F	GSC
Vaughan Williams	Bright is the ring of words	L		BOH
-----	Linden Lea	HML	C-D	BOS
Warlock	Passing by	M	D-G	CFI
-----	Sleep			OXF
Welsh	All through the night			
Wood	I look into your garden	LMH	F-AF	CHA

French Songs and Arias Employing Sustained Singing

Baritone

Bizet	L'orage s'est calmé (Les Pecheurs des Perles)			CHO
Caplet	Le forêt			DUR
Chausson	Apaisement	MH	EF-G	HAM
-----	Chanson de clown	M	D-EF	ROU
-----	Le charme	HM	BF-EF	HAM

730

(Chausson)	Le colibri	M	F-GF	BOS
-----	Le temps des lilas	MH	D-GS	†
Debussy	Beau soir	LH	C-FS	†
-----	Colloque sentimental			DUR
-----	Faites silence! écoutez tous! (L'Enfant Prodigue)			DUR
-----	Je tremble en voyant ton visage			DUR
-----	Le son du cor	HL		†
-----	Romance	HM	C-E	†
Duparc	Elégie	HM		ROU
-----	La vie antérieure	HL		†
-----	Lamento	ML	EF-EF	†
Fauré	Au cimetière	LH	D-F	†
-----	Aurore	H	D-G	†
-----	Automne	MH	D-FS	GSC
-----	Le parfum impérissable	LH	GF-GF	
-----	Les berceaux	LMH	BF-G	†
-----	Nocturne	H	F-A	MAR
-----	Prison	LH		†
-----	Rencontre	H	EF-AF	MAR
-----	Soir	LH	D-GS	†
Franck	Nocturne	HL		†
Gounod	Avant de quitter ces lieux (Faust)	HM	DF-F	†
Grétry	O Richard, ô mon Roi (Richard Coeur-De-Lion)	L	BF-G	LEM
-----	Songe enchanteur (Anacréon)			LEM
Honegger	Chanson (Ronsard)			SEN
Hue	J'ai pleuré en rêve	HL	D-E	BOS
Indy	Lied maritime	LH	B-G	†
-----	Madrigal			DIT
Lalo	Marine	LH	DS-FS	
Leguerney	L'adieu	M	B-FS	DUR
Lenormand	Quelle souffrançe	HM	AF-F	HAM
Massenet	Elégie	LM	C-GF	GSC
-----	Promesse de mon avenir (Le Roi de Lahore)	L	DF-GF	GSC
-----	Salomé, Salomé (Hérodiade)			GSC
-----	Vision fugitive (Hérodiade)	LM	C-GF	GSC
Messager	La maison grise (Fortuno)			CHO
Monsigny	Adieu, chère Louise (Le déserteur)			JOB
Offenbach	Scintille diamant (Tales of Hoffman)	M		GSC
Paladilhe	Lamento provinçal	M	CS-FS	HOM
Poulenc	A sa guitare	M	D-FS	DUR
-----	Chanson à boire	L	B-E	HEU
-----	Fleurs	M	DF-F	ROU

731

Ravel	Chanson italienne			DUR
-----	Kaddisch	H	C-G	DUR
-----	Là-bas vers l'église	MH	GS-E	DUR
-----	Le martin-pêcheur			DUR
-----	Le paon	M	C-F	DUR
-----	Ronsard à son âme	L	CS-E	DUR
Saint-Saëns	Aimons-nous			DUR
-----	La cloche	LH	DF-AF	†
-----	Le lever de la lune			DUR
Severac	Les hiboux			ROU
Spontini	Dans le sein d'un ami (La Vestale)			PET
Thomas	Comme une pâle fleur (Hamlet)			HEU
Tiersot	L'amours de moi	M	EF-F	HEU
Weckerlin	Venez, agréable printemps	M	C-F	

German Songs and Arias Employing Sustained Singing

Baritone

Ahle	Bruenstiges Verlangen	M	E-E	GSC
Bach, J.S.	Bist du bei mir	HML	A-EF	†
-----	Consider, O my soul (St. John Passion)			†
-----	Hier in meines Vaters Staette (Cantata 32) Violin			AUG
Beethoven	Adelaide	HML	BF-E	†
-----	An die ferne Geliebte	HL	C-E	†
-----	Das Geheimnis			
-----	Delizia	M	C-F	GSC
-----	Die Ehre Gottes	HL	AF-EF	†
-----	Faithfu' Johnie			
-----	In questa tomba	ML	A-CS	†
-----	Vom Tode	L	A-EF	GSC
-----	Wonne der Wehmut			†
Brahms	An den Mond	HL	CS-EF	†
-----	Auf dem Kirchhofe	HL	BF-EF	†
-----	Dein blaues Auge	MH	BF-G	†
-----	Der Tod, das ist die kuehle Nacht	L	AF-F	†
-----	Der Ueberlaeufer			†
-----	Die Mainacht	HL	BF-FF	†
-----	Feldeinsamkeit	HL	C-EF	†
-----	Minnelied	MHL	C-EF	†
-----	Mit vierzig Jahren	HL	FS-D	†

732

(Brahms)	Muss es eine Trennung geben?	LH	FS-FS	CFI
-----	O kuehler Wald	MH	A-F	†
-----	O wuesst' ich doch den Weg zurueck	H	E-FS	†
-----	Ruhe, Suessliebchen	HL	BS-E	†
-----	Schwermut			†
-----	Treue Liebe	LMH	DS-E	†
-----	Verzagen	MH	CS-FS	†
-----	Wenn du nur zuweilen laechelst			†
-----	Wie bist du meine Koenigin	HL	C-E	†
-----	Wir wandelten	LH	EF-GF	†
Franz	Dedication	HML	BF-C	†
-----	For music	ML	C-D	†
-----	Im Herbst	HM	A-F	†
Haydn	Now heav'n in fullest glory shone (The Creation)	L		†
-----	She never told her love	HL	B-D	DIT
Humperdinck	Am Rhein			AMP
Liszt	Es muss ein Wunderbares sein		C-EF	DUR
Loewe	Suesses Begraebnis			SC
Mahler	Wenn mein Schatz Hochzeit			WEI
Marx	Der Ton	M	C-F	AMP
-----	Hat dich die Liebe beruehrt	MH	EF-BF	AMP
Mendelssohn	O God, have mercy (Saint Paul)	L	B-D	GSC
-----	On wings of song			†
Mozart	Abendempfindung	M	E-F	
-----	Verdankt sei es dem Glanz			DIT
Schubert	Am Bach im Fruehling			PET
-----	Am Flusse			PET
-----	Am Meer	HML	B-D	†
-----	An die Leier	LM	BF-F	†
-----	An die Musik	HL	A-DS	†
-----	An die Tueren	HL		†
-----	Auf dem Flusse	HL	F-E	†
-----	Das Wirtshaus	HL	C-D	†
-----	Der Doppelgaenger	HL	G-D	†
-----	Der Leiermann	ML	C-D	†
-----	Der Lindenbaum	HL	A-D	†
-----	Der Neugierige	HL	CS-EF	†
-----	Der Wegweiser	L	D-EF	†
-----	Die Allmacht	HML	G-E	†
-----	Die Kraehe	HL	A-E	†
-----	Die Liebe hat gelogen	LM	G-F	†
-----	Die Nebensonnen	HL	F-D	†

(Schubert)	Die Stadt	HL	A-E	†
-----	Du liebst mich nicht	LH	E-FS	†
-----	Erster Verlust	M	C-F	†
-----	Fruehlingsglaube	M	EF-F	†
-----	Ganymed	LH	EF-G	†
-----	Gute Nacht	LH	C-FS	
-----	Ihr Bild	HL	C-C	†
-----	In der Ferne	HL		†
-----	Lied eines Schiffers an die Dioskuren	HL	A-C	†
-----	Litanei	HLM	C-EF	†
-----	Memnon	LM	AF-F	PET
-----	Nachtgesang			PET
-----	Sei mir gegruesst	LH	G-G	†
-----	Wanderers Nachtlied, 1	HL		†
-----	Wanderers Nachtlied, 2	LH	F-F	†
-----	Wehmuth	HL	B-D	†
-----	Wer nie sein Brot	HL	C-EF	†
-----	Wer sich der Einsamkeit ergibt	M	C-FS	†
Schuetz	Aus dem 119th Psalm			
Schumann	An den Sonnenschein	HL	A-D	†
-----	Aus den Hebraeischen Gesaengen			
-----	Dein Angesicht	HL	B-EF	†
-----	Die Lotusblume	HLM	BF-F	†
-----	Du bist wie eine Blume	HM	F-EF	†
-----	Ich grolle nicht	HL	BF-D	†
-----	Ich hab' im Traum geweinet	HL	B-D	†
-----	Ich wandelte unter den Baeumen	HL	A-D	†
-----	Ihre Stimme	LH		†
-----	Im Rhein, im heiligen Strome	HM	D-F	
-----	In der Fremde	HL		DIT
-----	Mit Myrthen und Rosen	HL	A-D	†
-----	Stille Traenen	HL		†
-----	Wenn ich in deine Augen seh'	HL	EF-FF	†
-----	Wer machte dich so krank?			
Strauss	Befreit			HSC
-----	Liebeshymnus			†
-----	Madrigal	LH	EF-GF	
-----	Mit deinen blauen Augen	LH	C-GS	†
-----	Morgen	HML	E-F	†
-----	Ruhe meine Seele			†
Wolf	Alle gingen, Herz, zu Ruh	HL	C-EF	†
-----	Alles endet, was entstehet	HL	F-C	†

(Wolf)	Anakreons Grab	HL	D-D	†
-----	Bedeckt mich mit Blumen	HL	B-D	†
-----	Biterolf	HL	D-F	†
-----	Das Staendchen	HL		†
-----	Denk' es, o Seele	LH	EF-F	INT
-----	Der Genesene an die Hoffnung	H	BF-AF	PET
-----	Fuehlt meine Seele	L	A-D	†
-----	Gebet	HL		†
-----	Gesang Weylas	HL	DF-F	†
-----	Gesegnet sei, durch den die Welt	HL		†
-----	Heb' auf dein blondes Haupt	HL	G-DF	†
-----	Heimweh (Eichendorff Lieder)	M		†
-----	Herr, was traegt der Boden	HL	B-DS	†
-----	Im Fruehling	HL	BF-F	†
-----	In der Fruehe	HL	C-C	†
-----	Lebe wohl	HL	BF-F	†
-----	Morgenstimmung	LH	C-GS	†
-----	Neue Liebe	LH	D-AF	†
-----	Um Mitternacht	HL	G-EF	†
-----	Wohl denk' ich oft	M	C-EF	†
-----	Zur Ruh', zur Ruh'	HL	A-GF	†
Wolff	Alle Dinge haben Sprache	M	BF-GF	†
-----	Du bist so jung			HMP
-----	Ewig			

Italian Songs and Arias Employing Sustained Singing

Baritone

Bimboni	Sospiri miei	M	EF-EF	GAL
Caccini	Amarilli, mia bella	ML	C-D	†
Caldara	Come raggio di sol	HL	D-F	†
Cavalli	Beato chi può (Serse)			HEU
-----	Troppo soavi i gusti	HM	E-E	DIT
Cesti	Che angoscia, che affanno (Il Pomo d'Oro)	HL	C-DF	DIT
-----	E dove t'aggiri (Il Pomo d'Oro)			DIT
Cimara	Stornellata marinara	HM		RIC
Del Leuto	Dimmi, amor	M	C-F	GSC
Diaz	O splendore infinito (Benvenuto)	L	A-F	GRU

735

Donaudy	O del mio amato ben	M	EF-F	RIC
-----	Quando ti rivedrò			RIC
-----	Vaghissima sembianza	H	E-A	RIC
Donizetti	Ambo nati in questa valle (Linda di Chamounix)			RIC
-----	Bella siccome un angelo (Don Pasquale)			BRO
Durante	Vergin, tutta amor	LM	C-EF	†
Giordano	Nemico della patria (Andrea Chenier)	L	B-FS	SON
Gluck	Spiagge amate (Paride ed Elena)			CFI
Handel	Lascia ch'io pianga (Rinaldo)	HM	EF-F	†
-----	No soffrir non può (Berenice)			MUP
-----	O rendetemi il mio bene (Amadigi)	L	CS-EF	CFI
-----	V'adoro pupille (Julius Caesar)			BOO
Leoncavallo	Prologue (I Pagliacci)	M	BF-A	CFI
-----	Zaza, piccola zingara (Zaza)			SON
Mattei	Non è ver	HML		DIT
Monteverdi	Ahi, troppo è duro (Il Balletto delle Ingrate)	HL	C-EF	DIT
Mozart	Ridente la calma			BOS
Paisiello	Nel cor più non mi sento	HL	C-EF	†
Pergolesi	Bella mia (Il Maestro di Musica)			GSC
-----	Nina	HL	CS-D	DIT
Peri	Invocazione di Orfeo (Euridice)	HL	E-CS	DIT
Piccini	O nuit, dresse du mystere (Le Faux Lord)			GSC
Puccini	Se la giurata fede (Tosca)	M	DF-F	RIC
Respighi	Nebbie			†
Rosa	Star vicino	HL	D-E	†
Santoliquido	Nel giardino			FOR
Scarlatti, A.	O cessate di piagarmi	HL	DS-E	GSC
-----	Son tutta duolo	M	D-EF	GSC
Stradella	Col mio sangue comprenderei (Il Floridoro)	HL	E-F	DIT
-----	Per pietà (Il Floridoro)	HM	D-F	DIT
-----	Pietà, Signore	HM	C-F	GSC
-----	Se nel ben			CFI
Torelli	Tu lo sai	HL	BF-F	†
Tosti	Aprile	LMH		RIC

Baritone

Arensky	Autumn	H	CS-FS	GSC
Dvořák	Hear my prayer, O Lord			AMP
-----	Lord, thou art my refuge and shield			AMP
-----	Turn Thee to me			AMP
Gretchaninoff	Over the steppe	LM	C-G	GSC
-----	The captive			DIT
-----	Wounded birch	HL	B-EF	†
Grieg	I love thee	HML	E-F	†
Malashkin	O could I but express in song	LH		CHE
Mussorgsky	In my attic			GSC
-----	On the Dnieper			GSC
-----	Sphinx			BRH
-----	The grave			BRH
Rachmaninoff	Christ is risen	LM	D-F	GAL
-----	O thou billowy harvest field	HL	CS-E	GSC
-----	To the children	MH	F-G	DIT
Rimsky-Korsakov	On the Georgian hills	HM		GSC
Sibelius	Black roses	M	A-ES	AMP
Sjoegren	The Seraglio's garden	HL		GSC
Tchaikovsky	A legend	M	D-E	GSC
-----	None but the lonely heart	HLM	C-F	DIT
-----	Pilgrim's song	HLM	B-E	GSC

American Songs Employing
Spirited Singing

Baritone

Barber	I hear an army	LH	D-AF	GSC
Beach	The year's at the spring	MH	AF-AF	ASC
Boatner	Oh, what a beautiful city!	HL	D-E	GSC
Boyd	Cape Horn gospel	L	BF-D	GAL
Burleigh	Joshua fit de battle ob Jericho	LH	DS-E	RIC
Carpenter	Don't ceare	M	C-D	GSC
-----	Serenade	LH	CS-A	GSC
-----	The cock shall crow	M	B-E	GSC
Castelnuovo-Tedesco	O mistress mine			CHE

Chadwick	Drake's drum			
-----	The admirals			
Chanler	I rise when you enter	M	CS-G	GSC
Curran	Life	HM	BF-F	GSC
Damrosch	Danny Deever	L	A-F	PRE
Dobson	Cargoes	ML	C-EF	GSC
Duke	On a March day	M	B-GF	BOH
Elwell	The road not taken	M	B-FS	GSC
Griffes	An old song resung	LM	EF-F	GSC
Guion	All day on the prarie	M	EF-F	GSC
-----	What shall we do with a drunken sailor	HML	C-D	GSC
Hadley	My shadow			ASC
Hageman	Don Juan Gomez	M		GAL
-----	Miranda	HL		GAL
Hindemith	The whistling thief	M	E-F	AMP
Hopkinson	O'er the hills	LH	C-G	†
Johnson	Roll Jerd'n roll	M	EF-F	GSC
Kountz	The sleigh	HL	D-FS	GSC
La Forge	Song of the open	MH	EF-AF	DIT
Malotte	Mister Jim	M	D-F	GSC
Mana-Zucca	I love life	LM	F-F	PRE
Margetson	Tommy, lad	HML	A-D	BOH
Mason	A sea dirge			WIT
Moore	Adam was my grandfather			GAL
Niles	The rovin' gambler	HL	BF-EF	GSC
Rogers	The last song	MLH	E-AF	GSC
Sacco	Brother Will, brother John	M	C-F	GSC
-----	Mexican serenade	HL	D-EF	BOS
Schuman	Holiday song	M	C-F	GSC
Speaks	Morning	HML	BF-D	GSC
-----	On the road to Mandalay	HL	BF-F	PRE
-----	Shepherd, see thy horse's foaming mane			FLA
Taylor	Captain Stratton's fancy	L	CS-F	JFI
Warner	Hurdy gurdy	M	D-F	CFI
Warren	White horses of the sea	LH	F-G	GSC
Weaver	The Abbot of Derry	HL	B-EF	GSC
Wolfe	Short'nin' bread	LHM	D-D	FLA

British Songs and Arias Employing
Spirited Singing

Baritone

| Arne, T. | By the gaily circling glass | L | | DIT |

738

(Arne, T.)	Now Phoebus sinketh in the west			GSC
-----	Preach not me your musty rules (Comus)	HML		ROW
-----	Why so pale and wan			GSC
Bantock	A feast of lanterns	HM	D-F	GAL
Bartlet	Whither runneth my sweetheart			BOO
Bax	The enchanted fiddle			
Benjamin	Hedgerow			CUR
Bridge	Love went a-riding	HL		BOS
Butterworth	When I was one and twenty			AUG
Charles, W.	The green eyed dragon	M	BF-E	BOH
Cowen	Border ballad	LM	D-E	BOO
Dowland	Awake, sweet love	M	E-F	STB
-----	Come again! sweet love	M	D-E	STB
-----	Say love, if ever thou didst find			STB
-----	Shall I sue?			STB
-----	What if I never speede?	M	D-D	BOS
German	Charming Chloe	HML		NOV
-----	My song is of the sturdy north	ML		CHA
-----	Rolling down to Rio	ML	G-D	NOV
Gibbs	Five eyes	HL	D-D	BOS
Handel	Arm, arm, ye brave (Judas Maccabaeus)	L	B-E	†
-----	O ruddier than the cherry (Acis and Galatea)	L	G-F	DIT
-----	Revenge, Timotheus cries (Alexander's Feast)	L	G-D	†
-----	See the raging flames arise (Joshua)			†
-----	Thy glorious deeds (Samson)	M	C-F	†
Head	Money, o!			BOO
-----	When I think upon the maidens	LM	D-G	BOO
Holst	The Sergeant's song			ASH
Hook	Bright Phoebus	M	EF-F	GSC
Hopekirk	Ye banks and braes	LM	D-C	DIT
Hughes	The stuttering lovers	MH	E-FS	CHA
Ireland	Great things			AUG
Johnston	Because I were shy	L	B-E	CRA
Jones	Love is a bable			STB
-----	What if I speede			BOO
Keel	Trade winds	HL	BF-EF	BOH
Lawes	I am confirmed			BOO
Leveridge	The beggar's song	L	G-D	BOO

(Leveridge)	When dull care			BOO
Liddle	The garden where the praties grow	LMH	E-FS	STB
Martin	Come to the fair	HML	D-D	BOO
Molloy	The Kerry Dance	LH	C-G	GSC
Morgan	Clorinda	HM	C-EF	ENO
Morley	It was a lover and his lass	HM		DIT
Moss	The floral dance	HML	A-D	CHA
Purcell	Hark! how all things with one sound rejoice			NOV
-----	I'll sail upon the dog star	HL	A-E	†
Quilter	Blow, blow thou winter wind	HL	C-E	BOO
-----	It was a lover and his lass	HL	CS-E	BOO
-----	I will go with my father a-plowing	MH	D-G	ELK
Rowley	The toll gate house			ROG
Sanderson	Captain Mac	ML	G-E	BOO
-----	Laughing cavalier	LM	BF-F	BOO
Sullivan	Ho, Jolly Jenkin (Ivanhoe)	LM	C-F	CHA
Toye	The inn	L	C-E	CUR
Vaughan Williams	Joy shipmate, joy			OXF
-----	The roadside fire	HML	BF-EF	BOO
-----	The vagabond	ML	A-E	BOO
Warlock	As ever I saw	MH	DF-GF	ROG
-----	Captain Stratton's fancy			AUG
-----	Good ale			AUG
-----	Pretty ring time	H	D-G	CFI

French Songs and Arias Employing Spirited Singing

Baritone

Berlioz	Chanson de la puce (La Damnation de Faust)			CST
-----	Sérénade de Mephisto (La Damnation de Faust)			DIT
Bizet	Chanson du toreador (Carmen)	HL	BF-F	†
-----	Quand la flamme de l'amour (Le Jolie Fille de Perth)			CHO
Caplet	La ronde	M		DUR
Chabrier	L'ile heureuse	M	B-F	†
-----	Villanelle des petits canards	HML	B-E	†
Chausson	Les papillons	M	C-F	GSC

740

Composer	Title	Voice	Range	Pub
Debussy	Ballade des femmes de Paris			DUR
-----	Chevaux de bois	H	C-G	†
-----	De soir	HL		†
-----	Le faune			DUR
-----	Le temps a laissié son manteau			DUR
-----	Mandoline	HM	BF-F	†
-----	Noël des enfants qui n'ont plus de maisons			DUR
Duparc	Le manoir de Rosamunde	HL	B-F	BOS
-----	Testament	HL		INT
Fauré	Noël	LH	EF-AF	GSC
-----	Notre amour	H	DS-B	†
-----	Poème d'un jour			HAM
-----	Toujours	LH	F-AF	MAR
Gluck	C'est en vain que l'enfer compte (Alceste)			†
-----	Un ruisselet bien clair (La Rencontre Imprévue)			LEM
Gounod	Au printemps	LMH	DF-AF	GSC
-----	Ballade de la reine Mab (Roméo et Juliette)			JCH
-----	Vénise	HL		INT
Grétry	Nièces neuveux (Les Deux Avares)			JOB
Koechlin	Le thé	HM	C-E	BOS
Lully	Il faut passer (Alceste)			LEM
Massenet	Chanson de la Touraine (Panurge)	M	EF-EF	HEU
Meyerbeer	Adamastor, roi des vagues profondes (L'Africaine)	L	D-E	GSC
-----	Fille des rois (L'Africaine)			BRO
Milhaud	Chant d'amour	M	C-GF	ESC
-----	La tourterelle	M	B-G	DUR
Poldowski	Colombine	H	D-GF	CHE
-----	Dansons la gigue	M	EF-G	MAR
Poulenc	La belle jeunesse	L	D-F	HEU
Ravel	Chanson à boire			DUR
-----	Chanson espagnole	LH	D-BF	DUR
-----	Manteau de fleurs	H		INT
-----	Nicolette	L	B-FS	ELK
-----	Quel galant!	M	D-F	DUR
Saint-Saëns	Danse macabre	L	BF-EF	AXE
-----	Les pas d'armes du roi Jean	HML	A-F	RIC
-----	Qui donc commande (Henry VIII)			GSC
-----	Tournoiement			DUR
Weckerlin	Chantons les amours de Jean	H	D-G	GSC

German Songs and Arias Employing
Spirited Singing

Baritone

Beethoven	An die Geliebte	M	E-E	†
-----	Aus Goethes Faust			
-----	Busslied			†
-----	Der Kuss			†
Brahms	Bei dir sind meine Gedanken	MH	E-FS	†
-----	Blinde Kuh			†
-----	Botschaft	HL	D-F	†
-----	Der Gang zur Liebsten	HL		†
-----	Der Schmied	HL	EF-EF	†
-----	Heimkehr			†
-----	Juchhe!			†
-----	Klage	LH	FS-FS	†
-----	Liebe kam aus fernen Landen	HL	C-E	†
-----	Meine Lieder	HL	D-DS	†
-----	O liebliche Wangen	MLH	E-G	†
-----	Sehnsucht	H	EF-AF	†
-----	Sind es Schmerzen	HL	BF-F	†
-----	Tambourliedchen			†
-----	Vergebliches Staendchen	LHM	E-FS	†
-----	Wie froh und frisch	HL	B-E	†
Franz	Sonnenuntergang	HL	CS-FS	DIT
Haydn	Rolling in foaming billows (The Creation)	L	C-F	†
-----	With joy th' impatient husbandman (The Seasons)	L	B-E	†
Jensen	Margreta	M	F-F	PET
Mahler	Ging heut Morgen uebers Feld	M	A-FS	INT
-----	Ich hab' ein gluehend Messer	M	BF-GF	WEI
-----	Lieder eines fahrenden Gesellen	M		INT
Mendelssohn	An die Entfernte	M	F-F	
-----	Ich bin ein vielgereister Mann (Heimkehr aus der Fremde)	ML		DIT
-----	Is not His word like a fire? (Elijah)	M	B-F	†
-----	Jagdlied	HL	BF-EF	†
Mozart	Der Vogelfaenger bin ich ja (Die Zauberfloete)	L	D-E	†
Schubert	Am Feierabend	HL	BF-F	†
-----	Aufenthalt	HLM	A-F	†

(Schubert)	Das Fischermaedchen	L	A-EF	†
-----	Der Schiffer	LH	BF-A	†
-----	Der zuernende Barde			PET
-----	Die Forelle	MLH	EF-GF	†
-----	Die Post	HML	BF-EF	†
-----	Erstarrung	HL	D-F	†
-----	Fischerweise	L	C-D	†
-----	Fruehlingssehnsucht	HL	B-E	
-----	Heidenroeslein			
-----	Mein!	HL		†
-----	Mut	HL		†
-----	Ueber Wildemann			PET
-----	Wohin?	HL	B-E	†
Schumann	Auftraege	HL	C-E	†
-----	Der Husar, trara!			
-----	Er ist's	HL	BF-EF	†
-----	Im Walde	HL	A-D	†
-----	Schoene Wiege meiner Leiden	HL	C-EF	†
-----	Waldesgespraech	HL	A-FS	†
-----	Wanderlied	HL	A-E	†
-----	Widmung	HL	BF-F	†
Strauss	Caecilie	MH	E-B	†
-----	Fuer fuenfzehn Pfennige			†
-----	Heimliche Aufforderung	HL	B-E	†
-----	Schlechtes Wetter			†
Weber	Reigen			PET
Wolf	Ach, im Maien	HL	C-E	†
-----	Auf dem gruenen Balkon	HL		†
-----	Auf einer Wanderung	HL		†
-----	Begegnung	M	EF-GF	PET
-----	Das Koehlerweib ist trunken			PET
-----	Der Feuerreiter			†
-----	Der Rattenfaenger	HL		†
-----	Der Soldat 1	LH	E-FS	†
-----	Ein Staendchen euch zu bringen	HL		†
-----	Er ist's	H	D-G	†
-----	Fussreise	HL	D-E	†
-----	Nimmersatte Liebe	LH	CF-AF	†
-----	Seemanns Abschiedslied	H	C-A	†
-----	Trunken muessen wir alle sein	M	ES-FS	†

Italian Songs and Arias Employing
Spirited Singing

Baritone

Bononcini	L'esperto nocchiero (Astarte)	HL	B-E	†
Carissimi	Filli, non t'amo più	HL	B-D	†
-----	Vittoria, mio core	HLM	B-E	†
Cavalli	Donzelle fuggite	HL	C-EF	†
Cimara	Canto di primavera		D-G	FRL
Donaudy	Spirate, pur spirate			RIC
Durante	Danza, danza fanciulla gentile	HM	BF-F	†
Falconieri	Non più d'amore	HL	C-D	DIT
-----	Nudo arciero	HL	AF-AF	DIT
Gaffi	Luci vezzose	HL	D-E	DIT
Handel	Furibondo spira (Partenope)			KIS
-----	Si, tra i ceppi (Berenice)	L	B-D	†
-----	Volate più dei venti (Muzio Scevola)			MUP
Legrenzi	Che fiero costume	HML	C-D	†
Leoncavallo	Mattinata	MLH	C-AF	†
Mascagni	Il cavallo scalpita (Cavalleria Rusticana)			GSC
Mozart	Aprite un po quegl' occhi (Le Nozze di Figaro)			RIC
-----	Finch' han dal vino (Don Giovanni)	L	D-EF	†
-----	Non più andrai (Le Nozze di Figaro)	L	C-E	†
Paradies	M' ha preso alla sua ragna	M	EF-F	GSC
Pergolesi	Son imbrogliato io già (La Serva Padrona)	L		RIC
Respighi	Pioggia			BON
Rontani	Or ch'io non segno più	HL	CS-E	DIT
Scarlatti, A.	Chi vuole innamorarsi	HL	D-EF	DIT
-----	Già il sole dal Gange	LH	EF-F	GSC
Scarlatti, D.	Consolati e spara amante	L	BF-E	GSC
Tosti	The last song	HL		RIC
Verdi	Cortigiani, vil razza (Rigoletto)			GSC
Wolf-Ferrari	Aprila, o bella (Jewels of the Madonna)	HL	D-FS	GSC

Miscellaneous Songs Employing
Spirited Singing

Baritone

Dvořák	I will sing new songs of gladness	HL		†
Falla	El paño moruno	HL		AMP
-----	Seguidilla murciana	HL		AMP
-----	Siete canciones	HL		AMP
Grieg	Good morning			†
-----	Hunter's song	L	DS-E	GSC
-----	Vaer hilset, I Damer	M	D-F	HAN
Koeneman	When the King went forth to war	ML	A-E	CHE
Mussorgsky	Siege of Kazan (Boris Godunoff)	L	F-E	GSC
Rachmaninoff	Floods of spring	HL		DIT
-----	God took away from me			GSC
-----	Oh, no, I pray, do not depart	H		DIT
Sandoval	Sin tu amor	H	E-G	GSC
Tchaikovsky	At the ball	MH		GSC
-----	Don Juan's serenade	HLM	B-E	GSC

Songs and Arias Employing Staccato

Baritone

Beethoven	Bitten			†
Fourdrain	Carnaval	M	C-F	RIC
Mozart	Se vuol ballare (Le Nozze di Figaro)	L		†
Mussorgsky	The song of the flea	L	AS-G	GSC
Paxson	Laughing song	M	C-F	CFI
Scarlatti, A.	Rugiadose odorose (Il Pirro e Demetrio)	HL	D-E	DIT
Schubert	Der Juengling an der Quelle	LH	E-A	†
Sibella	La Girometta	HML	D-E	GSC

Baritone

Andrews	Sea fever	L	A-D	GSC
Arden and Wille	Roses in your hair	ML	C-EF	ROW
Beach	Ah, love but a day			ASC
Bond	Still unexprest	HL	C-C	BOS
Bone and Fenton	Captain Kidd	MH	B-G	CFI
Brahe	Bless this house	HML	A-EF	BOO
Brown	Your song from paradise	LMH	D-G	BOO
Burleigh	Jean	HML		PRE
Cadman	The builder	HML	B-D	FLA
Chanler	I rise when you enter	M	CS-G	GSC
Charles	The house on a hill	LH	D-G	GSC
-----	When I have sung my songs	HM	BF-EF	GSC
-----	The green eyed dragon	M	BF-E	BOH
Clarke	Shy one	HL	BF-G	BOH
-----	The blind ploughman	HML	C-D	CHA
Coates	Sea rapture	MH	E-G	CHA
-----	Stone cracker John	L		BOO
Cowen	Border ballad	LM	D-E	BOO
Crouch	Kathleen Mavourneen	HL	A-E	CFI
Curran	Life	HM	BF-F	GSC
Damrosch	Danny Deever	L	A-F	PRE
Del Riego	Homing	HML	BF-E	CHA
-----	O dry those tears	LMH	E-GS	CHA
-----	Shadow march			CHA
De Rose	I heard a forest praying	MH	EF-GF	CHA
-----	Wagon wheels			SHA
D' Hardelot	I know a lovely garden			CHA
Dichmont	Ma little banjo	ML	E-CS	GSC
Dobson	Cargoes	ML	C-EF	GSC
Donaldson	My buddy			REM
Dougherty	Everyone sang			
Edwards	By the bend of the river	HML	C-E	GSC
-----	Can this be summer			
-----	Into the night	HML	C-DF	GSC
Enders	Hangman, hangman	M	C-E	GSC
Fenner	Night song	L	BF-EF	FEN
Fisher	At Tankerton Inn	LM	B-G	BOO
-----	Tavern song			BOO
Forsyth	The bell man			DIT
Foster	My journey's end	HLM	DF-G	GSC
Foster, S.C.	Gentle Annie			BOS

Fox	The hills of home	HML	BF-DF	CFI
German	Rolling down to Rio	ML	G-D	NOV
Glover	Rose of Tralee	LMH	E-G	MOV
Guion	Mam'selle Marie	M	D-E	GSC
-----	When the work's all done this fall	L	B-D	CFI
Hageman	Don Juan Gomez	M		GAL
Harmati	Bluebird of happiness			HAR
Head	When I think upon the maidens	LM	D-G	BOO
Hely- Hutchinson	Old mother Hubbard	HL	B-E	CFI
Hughes	Old mother Hubbard			CRA
Huhn	Invictus	ML	BF-DF	ASC
Kern	The last time I saw Paris			CHA
Kountz	Prayer of the Norwegian child	ML	C-C	GSC
La Forge	Song of the open	MH	EF-AF	DIT
-----	To a messenger	HLM	CF-G	GSC
Leoni	Tally-ho!			GSC
Lehmann	Myself when young	LL	A-E	GSC
Levitzki	Do you remember?	HML	BF-EF	GSC
Lohr	The little Irish girl	HLM	C-E	CHA
Mac Gimsey	Down to de river	M	B-G	CFI
-----	Egg-a-bread			MCG
-----	Jeri Jericho	M	C-G	CFI
-----	Jonah and the whale	M	BF-EF	CFI
-----	Thunderin' wonderin'	L	C-D	CFI
-----	To my mother	HML	C-C	CFI
Malotte	Blow me eyes	MH	C-G	GSC
-----	For my mother	HLM	BF-EF	GSC
-----	Mister Jim	M	D-F	GSC
-----	Sing a song of sixpence	M	C-F	GSC
-----	Song of the open road			ABC
Mana-Zucca	I love life	LM	F-F	PRE
-----	Nichavo	HLM	F-G	JCH
-----	The big brown bear	HML	C-F	GSC
Manning	In the Luxembourg gardens	HML	BF-D	GSC
-----	Shoes	M	EF-F	GSC
Margetson	Tommy, lad	HML	A-D	BOH
Marshall	I hear you calling me	LMH	G-A	BOO
Martin	Come to the fair	HML	D-D	BOO
Mason	A grain of salt	L	A-D	GSC
-----	I ain't afeared o' the Admiral	L	A-E	GSC
-----	The constant cannibal maiden	L	C-FS	GSC
McGill	Duna	HML	BF-D	BOO
Molloy	The Kerry Dance	LH	C-G	GSC

Moya	The song of songs	LM	D-F	CHA
Murray	She shall have music	M	A-G	CHA
Nevin	The Rosary	HML	C-D	BOS
Oberbrunner	Giuseppe, da barber	HML	E-E	GSC
Olcott	Mother Machree	LMH	F-A	WIT
Paxson	Laughing song	M	C-F	CFI
Posford	At the Balalaika	L	BF-EF	FEI
Quilter	Drink to me only	LMH	GF-GF	BOH
Rasbach	Overtones	HL	B-D	GSC
-----	Trees	LMH	CS-GS	GSC
Rogers	At parting	LH	CS-FS	GSC
Ronald	Prelude	HML	B-D	ENO
Russell	Children of men	HL	EF-F	FLA
-----	Fulfillment	LH	EF-GF	BOS
-----	Where the river Shannon flows	HML	C-D	WIT
Sacco	Brother Will, brother John	M	C-F	GSC
Sachs	Grandma			FLA
Sanderson	Captain Mac	ML	G-E	BOO
-----	Friend o' mine	HHM		BOO
-----	Laughing cavalier	LM	BF-F	BOO
-----	Shipmates of mine	LL	G-D	BOO
-----	Susan is her name	LM	D-E	BOH
-----	The company Sergeant Major			BOH
-----	Until	LMH	E-A	BOO
Schuman	Holiday song	M	C-F	GSC
Scott	Think on me	HML	D-EF	GAL
Somervell	A kingdom by the sea	ML	DF-F	BOO
Speaks	In May time	HL	D-E	JCH
-----	Morning	HML	BF-D	GSC
-----	On the road to Mandalay	HL	BF-F	PRE
-----	Sylvia	HML	AF-DF	GSC
Stanford	The bold unbiddable child	ML	B-DF	STB
-----	The little admiral	L	C-G	STB
Stickles	The open road			DIT
Stothart	Cuban love song	L	BF-G	ROB
-----	Ride cossack ride			FEI
-----	Rogue song			ROB
-----	The song of the shirt	L	A-E	ROB
-----	When I'm looking at you	F	C-F	ROB
Strelezki	Dreams	LMH	B-A	GSC
Suesse	Another mile			WOR
-----	The night is young and you're so beautiful	M	B-E	WOR
Sullivan	The lost chord	HL	C-F	GSC
Taylor	A song for lovers	MH	D-F	JFI
Torrence	Smilin' Kitty O'Day	ML	CS-D	BOO
Tours	Mother o' mine	HML	C-D	CHA

Tyson	Noon and night	LH	F-AF	GSC
Weaver	The Abbot of Derry	HL	B-EF	GSC
Wolfe	Betsy's boy	HL	A-E	GSC
-----	Bone come-a-knittin'			FLA
-----	De glory road	L	A-F	GSC
-----	Gwine to Hebb'n	LM	B-E	GSC
-----	Sailormen	HM	D-FS	GSC
-----	Short'nin' bread	LHM	D-D	FLA
-----	Spring plowing	LHM	CS-FS	GSC
-----	Who's gonna mourn for me	LMH	D-A	ROB
Wood	Do you know my garden	MH	EF-G	CHA
-----	I look into your garden	LMH	F-AF	CHA
Woodford-Finden	Kashmiri song			BOO
-----	Will the sun never set?			

(See also Humorous Songs, Negro Spirituals,
Folk Songs, Operetta Songs and Opera Arias.)

Miscellaneous Songs of Popular Appeal

Baritone

Alvarez	La partida	HL	DS-E	GSC
Bach-Gounod	Ave Maria			†
Berger	They all dance the samba	M	A-FS	GSC
Billi	E canta il grillo	HM		RIC
Bizet	Agnus Dei	HLM	C-AF	†
Brogi	Venitian vision	M	D-F	RIC
Buzzi-Peccia	Lolita			RIC
Cardillo	Core'ngrato			RIC
Cimara	Canto di primavera		D-G	FRL
De Curtis	Tu, ca nun chaigne			
Denza	Occhi de fata	HML		RIC
-----	Se	H	E-AF	GSC
Donaudy	O del mio amato ben	M	EF-F	RIC
Dvořák	Goin' home			DIT
-----	Songs my mother taught me	HM	E-E	†
Franz	Dedication	HML	BF-C	†
Freire	Ay, ay, ay	LH		RIC
Gounod	Au printemps	LMH	DF-AF	GSC
-----	Sérénade	LMH	D-A	GSC
Grieg	A dream			†
-----	I love thee	HML	E-F	†
Hubay	Hejre kati			BRE
Lara	Granada			SOU
Leoncavallo	Mattinata	MLH	C-AF	GSC

Massenet	Elégie	LM	C-GF	GSC
Mattei	Non è ver	HML		DIT
Mendelssohn	On wings of song			†
Messager	Long ago in Alcala	M		CHA
Mussorgsky	The evening prayer	M	C-E	GSC
Rachmaninoff	To the children	MH	F-G	DIT
Ravel	Dansant l'amique			
Rossini	La danza	MH	E-A	†
Sadero	Amuri, Amuri	M		CHE
Saint-Saëns	Danse macabre	L	BF-EF	AXE
Schubert	An die Musik	HL	A-DS	†
-----	Ave Maria	LMH	F-F	†
-----	Hark! hark! the lark	LMH	F-G	†
-----	Staendchen			
Schumann	Widmung	HL	BF-F	†
Sibella	La Girometta	HML	D-E	GSC
Sjoeberg	Visions	MH	F-AF	GAL
Straus	Song in my heart	M	C-G	GSC
Tchaikovsky	None but the lonely heart	HLM	C-F	DIT
-----	Pilgrim's song	HLM	B-E	GSC
Tosti	À vucchella	LH	F-G	RIC
-----	Marechiare	M	D-FS	GSC
-----	The last song	HL		RIC
Veláquez	Bésame mucho	M	CS-D	SOU
Yradier	La paloma	HL	BF-EF	GSC

(See also Humorous Songs, Negro Spirituals,
Folk Songs, Operetta Songs and Opera Arias.)

Arias From American Operas

Baritone

Dello Joio	The creed of Pierre Cochon (The Triumph of Joan)			
Gershwin	A woman is a sometime thing (Porgy and Bess)			GER
-----	I got plenty o' nuttin' (Porgy and Bess)	L	B-D	CHA
-----	It ain't necessarily so (Porgy and Bess)			CHA
Gruenberg	Standin' in de need of prayer (Emperor Jones)			CSC
Hanson	Oh, 'tis an earth defiled (Merry Mount)			HAR
Taylor	Nay, Maccus, lay him down (The King's Henchman)			JFI

| (Taylor) | The Colnel's air (Peter Ibbetson) | | | JFI |
| Thomson | Saint Ignatius' vision (Four Saints in Three Acts) | | | BRO |

Arias from British Operas

Baritone

Arne, T.	Preach not me your musty rules (Comus)	HML		ROW
Balfe	The heart bowed down (The Bohemian Girl)			†
Gay	If the heart of a man (The Beggar's Opera)			BOO
-----	In the days of my youth (The Beggar's Opera)			BOO
German	The English rose (Merrie England)			
Handel	Hear me, ye winds and waves (Scipione)	ML	G-EF	BOO
-----	Silent worship (Tolomeo)	LM	D-E	CUR
Purcell	I attempt from love's sickness to fly (The Indian Queen)	MH	CS-E	†
-----	Music for a while (Oedipus)	LH		SC
Sullivan	Ho, Jolly Jenkin (Ivanhoe)	LM	C-F	CHA

Arias From French Operas

Baritone

Berlioz	Chanson de la puce (La Damnation de Faust)			CST
-----	Inutiles regrets (Les Troyens à Carthage)	MH	E-C	CHO
-----	Sérénade de Mephisto (La Damnation de Faust)			DIT
-----	Voici des roses (La Damnation de Faust)			CST
Bizet	Chanson du Toreador (Carmen)	HL	BF-F	†
-----	L'orage s'est calmé (Les Pêcheurs des Perles)			CHO
-----	Quand la flamme de l'amour (Le Jolie Fille de Perth)			CHO

Charpentier	Les pauvre gens peuvent- ils être heureux? (Louise)			HEU
Debussy	Faites silence! Ecoutez tous! (L'Enfant Prodigue)			
Delibes	Lakmé, ton doux regards (Lakmé)			HEU
Gluck	Air d'Agamemnon (Iphigenie en Aulide)			LEM
-----	C'est en vain que l'enfer compte (Alceste)			†
-----	Un ruisselet bien clair (La Rencontre Imprévue)			LEM
Gounod	Avant de quitter ces lieux (Faust)	HM	DF-F	†
-----	Ballade de la reine Mab (Roméo et Juliette)			JCH
Grétry	Nièces, neuveux (Les Deux Avares)			JOB
-----	O Richard, ô mon Roi (Richard Coeur-De-Lion)	L	BF-G	LEM
-----	Songe enchanteur (Anacréon)			LEM
Lully	Air de Cadmus (Cadmus et Hermione)			ROU
-----	Air de Mecure (Persée)			
-----	Air des Songes (Persée)			
-----	Bois épais (Amadis)	ML	C-EF	†
-----	Il faut passer (Alceste)			LEM
Massenet	Chanson de la Touraine (Panurge)	M	EF-EF	HEU
-----	Dors ô cité perverse (Hérodiade)			
-----	Promesse de mon avenir (Le Roi de Lahore)	L	DF-GF	GSC
-----	Salomé, Salomé (Hérodiade)			GSC
-----	Vision fugitive (Hérodiade)	LM	C-GF	GSC
-----	Voila donc la terrible cité (Thaïs)			
Mehul	Femme sensible (Ariodant)			
Messager	La maison grise (Fortuno)			CHO
Meyerbeer	Adamastor, roi des vagues profondes (L'Africaine)	L	D-E	GSC
-----	Fille des rois (L'Africaine)			BRO
-----	Nonnes qui reposez (Robert le Diable)			GSC
-----	Se vendicata assai (Dinorah)	M	DF-GF	BRO
Offenbach	J'ai des yeux (Tales of Hoffman)			GSC
-----	Scintille diamant (Tales of Hoffman)	M		GSC

Rameau	A l'amour rendez les armes (Hippolyte et Aricie)	CHO
-----	Air of Theseus (Hippolyte et Aricie)	CHE
-----	Dans ces doux asiles (Castor et Pollux)	LEM
-----	Invocation et hymne au soleil (Les Indes Galantes)	LEM
Reyer	Et toi Fréia (Sigurd)	HEU
Saint-Saëns	Qui donc commande (Henry VIII)	GSC
Spontini	Dans le sein d'un ami (La Vestale)	PET
Thomas	Chanson bachique (O vin dissipe) (Hamlet)	GSC
-----	Comme une pâle fleur (Hamlet)	HEU

Arias From German Operas

Baritone

Humperdinck	Peter's song (Haensel und Gretel)			SC
-----	Spielmann's air (Die Koenigskinder)			
Korngold	Pierrot's dance song (The Dead City)			AMP
Lortzing	Es wohnt am Seegestade (Undine)			
Mendelssohn	Ich bin ein vielgereister Mann ML (Heimkehr aus der Fremde)			DIT
Mozart	Air d'Alazim (Zaïde)			INT
-----	Der Vogelfaenger bin ich ja L (Die Zauberfloete)		D-E	†
-----	Ein Maedchen oder Weibchen wuenscht (Die Zauberfloete)			†
-----	Invocation to the sun (King Thamos in Egypt)			
Wagner	Als du in kuehnem Sange (Tannhaeuser)			†
-----	Blick' ich umher (Tannhaeuser)	M	B-EF	†
-----	Darf ich die Antwort sagen (Tristan und Isolde)			
-----	Die Frist ist um (Der Fliegende Hollaender)			†
-----	Durch dich musst' ich verlieren (Lohengrin)	H	B-F	GSC

(Wagner)	Koenig's Gebet (Lohengrin) M		F-EF	GSC
-----	Leb' wohl, du kuehnes, L		B-E	†
	herrliches Kind (Die Walkuere)			
-----	O du, mein holder L		BF-E	†
	Abendstern (Tannhaeuser)			
-----	O Himmel, lass dich jetzt			GSC
	erflehen (Tannhaeuser)			
-----	Wahn! Wahn! ueberall L		A-E	†
	Wahn! (Die Meistersinger)			
-----	Was duftet doch der Flieder			
	(Die Meistersinger)			
-----	Wohl wusst' ich hier sie im			GSC
	Gebet zu finden (Tannhaeuser)			
Weber	Wo berg' ich mich (Euryanthe)			†

Arias From Italian Operas

Baritone

Bellini	Ah! per sempre (I Puritani)			RIC
Cilea	Come due tizzi accesi			SON
	(L'Arlesiana)			
-----	Ecco il monologo			SON
	(Adriana Lecouvreur)			
Diaz	O splendore infinito L		A-F	GRU
	(Benvenuto)			
Donizetti	A tanto amor (La Favorita)			BRO
-----	Ambo nati in questa valle			RIC
	(Linda di Chamounix)			
-----	Bella siccome un angelo			BRO
	(Don Pasquale)			
-----	Cruda funesta smania			BRO
	(Lucia di Lammermoor)			
-----	Vien, Leonora a piedi tuoi			BRO
	(La Favorita)			
Franchetti	Ferito prigionier (Germania)			RIC
Giordano	Nemico della patria L		B-FS	SON
	(Andrea Chenier)			
Leoncavallo	Prologue (I Pagliacci) M		BF-A	CFI
-----	Zaza, piccola zingara (Zaza)			SON
Mascagni	Il cavallo scalpita			GSC
	(Cavalleria Rusticana)			
Montemezzi	Suonata è l'ora			RIC
	(L'Amore dei Tre Re)			
Monteverdi	Ahi, troppo è duro HL		C-EF	DIT
	(Il Balletto delle Ingrate)			
-----	Lasciatemi morire ML		D-D	†
	(Arianna)			

(Monteverdi)	Qual honor (Orfeo)			BRO
Mozart	Aprite un po quegl' occhi			†
	(Le Nozze di Figaro)			
-----	Deh vieni alla finestra	L	D-E	†
	(Don Giovanni)			
-----	Finch' han dal vino	L	D-EF	†
	(Don Giovanni)			
-----	Ho capito, Signor (Don Giovanni)			
-----	Non più andrai	L	C-E	†
	(Le Nozze di Figaro)			
-----	Se vuol ballare	L		†
	(Le Nozze di Figaro)			
Pergolesi	Son imbrogliato io già	L		RIC
	(La Serva Padrona)			
Ponchielli	O monumento (La Gioconda)			RIC
-----	Pescator, affonda l'esca			RIC
	(La Gioconda)			
Puccini	Minnie, dalla mia casa son			RIC
	partito (La Fanciulla del West)			
-----	Se la giurata fede	M	DF-F	RIC
	(Tosca)			
-----	Scorri fiume eterno (Il Tabarro)			RIC
Rossini	Largo al factotum	L	D-G	†
	(Il Barbiere di Siviglia)			
Verdi	Alla vita che t'arride			RIC
	(Un Ballo in Maschera)			
-----	Cortigiani, vil razza			GSC
	(Rigoletto)			
-----	Credo (Otello)	M	AS-FS	JCH
-----	Di provenza il mar	M	DF-GF	GSC
	(La Traviata)			
-----	Egli è salvo!			RIC
	(La Forza del Destino)			
-----	Era la notte (Otello)			GSC
-----	Eri tu	M	A-G	
	(Un Ballo in Maschera)			
-----	Ford's monologue (E sogno)			RIC
	(Falstaff)			
-----	Il balen del suo sorriso	M	A-G	†
	(Il Trovatore)			
-----	Il mio sangue (Luisa Miller)			RIC
-----	In braccio alle dovizie			RIC
	(I Vespri Siciliani)			
-----	L'onore! ladri! (Falstaff)			RIC
-----	Le menaccie fieri accenti			RIC
	(La Forza del Destino)			
-----	O de' verd' anni miei			RIC
	(Ernani)			

(Verdi)	O vecchio cor, che batti (I Due Foscari)			RIC
-----	Pari siamo (Rigoletto)			GSC
-----	Per me giunto (Don Carlos)			RIC
-----	Quand' ero paggio (Falstaff)	MH	DS-AF	RIC
-----	Urna fatale (La Forza del Destino)			RIC
Wolf-Ferrari	Aprila, o bella (Jewels of the Madonna)	HL	D-FS	GSC

Miscellaneous Opera Arias

Baritone

Borodin	No sleep, no rest (Prince Igor)			BOO
Kodaly	I am going to plow the Emperor's courtyard (Hary Janos)			
-----	Red apple (Hary Janos)			
Mussorgsky	Monologue and Hallucination Scene (Boris Godunoff)			BES
-----	Shaklovitov's aria (Khovantchina)			
-----	Siege of Kazan (Boris Godunoff)	L	F-E	GSC
-----	Song of the parrot (Boris Godunoff)			DIT
Rimsky-Korsakov	Song of the Venetian guest (Sadko)			BRO
Rubinstein	The demon's song (The Demon)			
Tchaikovsky	Onegin's aria (Eugene Onegin)			GSC
-----	Prince Yeletsky's aria (Pique Dame)			GSC
-----	Who can compare? (Iolanthe)			

Arias From Oratorios and Latin Works

Baritone

Bach, J.S.	Consider, O my soul (St. John Passion)	†
-----	Mighty Lord (Christmas Oratorio)	

(Bach, J.S.)	My darkened heart (Christmas Oratorio)			
Berlioz	Le repos de la Ste. Famille (L'Enfance du Christ)	MH		CST
Dubois	God, my father (Seven Last Words)			GSC
Dvořák	Give ear, ye people (St. Ludmilla)			
-----	I was not deceived (St. Ludmilla)			
Elgar	I am the good shepherd (Light of Life)			NOV
Handel	But who may abide (The Messiah)	L	G-E	†
-----	Chi sprezzando il somo bene (La Passione)			
-----	Defend her! Heaven (Theodora) Edited and set for strings			STB
-----	Let me wander not unseen (L'Allegro)	M	D-G	†
-----	Loathsome urns disclose your treasure (Triumph of Time and Truth)			DIT
-----	More sweet is that name (Semele)			
-----	O ruddier than the cherry (Acis and Galatea)	L	G-F	DIT
-----	O sleep why dost thou leave me (Semele)	H	DS-GS	†
-----	Revenge, Timotheus cries (Alexander's Feast)	L	G-D	†
-----	See, the conqu'ring hero comes (Judas Maccabaeus)			†
-----	See the raging flames arise (Joshua)			†
-----	Shall I in Mamre's fertile plain (Joshua)	L	G-EF	DIT
-----	Tears such as tender fathers shed (Deborah)	L		†
-----	The people that walked in darkness (The Messiah)			†
-----	The trumpet shall sound (The Messiah) Trumpet	L		†
-----	Thy glorious deeds (Samson)	M	C-F	†
-----	Wher'er you walk (Semele)	HML	C-D	†
-----	Why do the nations (The Messiah)	L	B-E	†
Haydn	Now heav'n in fullest glory shone (The Creation)	L		†
-----	Rolling in foaming billows (The Creation)	L	C-F	†

(Haydn)	With joy th' impatient husbandman (The Seasons)	L	B-E	GSC
Mendelssohn	But the mountains shall depart (Elijah)			
-----	For know ye not (Saint Paul)			
-----	Is not His word like a fire (Elijah)	M	B-F	†
-----	It is enough (Elijah)	L	A-E	†
-----	Lord God of Abraham (Elijah)	L	B-E	†
-----	O God, have mercy (Saint Paul)	L	B-D	†
Sullivan	Honor the Lord with they substance (The Prodigal Son)			

Cantata Arias

Baritone

Bach, J.S.	Doch weichet, ihr tollen vergeblichen (Cantata 8) Flute			NOV
-----	Gleich wie die wilden Meereswellen (Cantata 178) Violin			
-----	Good fellows be merry (The Peasant Cantata)			†
-----	Hier in meines Vaters staette (Cantata 32) Violin			
-----	Sheep may safely graze (Cantata 208) 2 Flutes and continuo	LM	EF-GF	GAL
-----	So oft ich meine Tabakspfeife (The Coffee Cantata)			BRH
-----	Wie will ich lustig lachen (Cantata 205)			OXF
Handel	Have mercy, Lord (Te Deum)	HM		†
Mussorgsky	Oriental chant (Josua Navine Cantata)	ML	BF-E	GSC
Pasquini	Air in Riva del Giordano (Erminia)			
Tchaikovsky	Prayer (Moscow Cantata)	M	A-GF	GAL

Baritone

Arlen	My shining hour			MOR
	(The Sky's the Limit)			
Berlin	The girl that I marry			BER
	(Annie Get Your Gun)			
-----	White Christmas			BER
	(Holiday Inn)			
Brown	Singing in the rain			ROB
	(Hollywood Review)			
-----	You are my lucky star			ROB
	(Broadway Melody of 1936)			
Coward	Dear little cafe			HAR
	(Bitter Sweet)			
-----	I'll see you again	M	C-F	HAR
	(Bitter Sweet)			
-----	Imagine the Duchess's feelings			CHA
	(Conversation Piece)			
-----	Tokay (Bitter Sweet)			HAR
Forrest-Grieg	Strange music			CHA
	(Song of Norway)			
Friml	Donkey Serenade			WIT
	(The Firefly)			
-----	Gather the rose			MLS
	(The White Eagle)			
-----	Give me one hour			MRT
	(The White Eagle)			
-----	Ma belle			HAR
	(The Three Musketeers)			
-----	March of the musketeers			HAR
	(The Three Musketeers)			
-----	Only a rose			GSC
	(The Vagabond King)			
-----	Rose Marie (Rose Marie)	M	EF-G	HAR
-----	Song of the vagabond	M	C-F	FAM
	(The Vagabond King)			
-----	The mounties (Rose Marie)			HAR
Gershwin	Love walked in			CHA
	(Goldwyn Follies 1938)			
-----	Song of the Flame			CHA
	(Song of the Flame)			
-----	Soon (Strike Up the Band)			BRO
-----	Swanee (Sinbad)			CHA
Henderson	The thrill is gone			CRF
	(Scandals of 1931)			

Herbert	Absinthe frappe			WIT
	(It Happened in Nordland)			
-----	Ah! sweet mystery of	LMH	A-A	WIT
	life (Naughty Marietta)			
-----	Every day is ladies' day with me			WIT
	(The Red Mill)			
-----	Free trade and a misty moon			WIT
	(Eileen)			
-----	Good-a-bye, John			WIT
	(The Red Mill)			
-----	Gypsy love song	LHM	C-E	WIT
	(The Fortune Teller)			
-----	I'm falling in love with someone			WIT
	(Naughty Marietta)			
-----	I want what I want when I			WIT
	want it (Mlle. Modiste)			
-----	I wish I was an island in an			WIT
	ocean of girls (Princess Pat)			
-----	Neapolitan love song			WIT
	(Princess Pat)			
-----	'Neath the southern moon			
	(Naughty Marietta)			
-----	The love of the Lorelei			GSC
	(The Debutante)			
-----	Thine alone (Eileen)			WIT
-----	Tramp, tramp, tramp			WIT
	(Naughty Marietta)			
Hirsch	Learn to smile			VIC
	(The O'Brien Girl)			
Howard	I wonder who's kissing her			BMI
	now (The Prince of Tonight)			
Kalman	Play gipsies, dance gipsies			HAR
	(Graefin Mariza)			
Kern	Any moment now			HAR
	(Can't Help Singing)			
-----	Look for the silver lining			CHA
	(Sally)			
-----	Lovely to look at (Roberta)			CHA
-----	More and more			CHA
	(Can't Help Singing)			
-----	Ol' man river (Show Boat)	LM	BF-G	HAR
-----	The song is you	M	C-F	HAR
	(Music in the Air)			
-----	They didn't believe me			HAR
	(Girl From Utah)			
-----	Try to forget			HAR
	(The Cat and the Fiddle)			
Kreisler	You are free (Apple Blossoms)			HAR
Kirsch	The love nest (Mary)			HAR

Lehar	Yours is my heart alone (The Land of Smiles)			HAR
Loewe	I talk to the trees (Paint Your Wagon)			
-----	There but for you go I (Brigadoon)			FOX
Luders	Fall in (The Prince of Pilsen)			WIT
-----	Message of the violet (The Prince of Pilsen)			WIT
Monsigny	Adieu, chère Louise (Le Déserteur)			JOB
Porter	All thru the night (Anything Goes)			BRO
-----	Begin the Beguine (Jubilee)	L	BF-F	HAR
-----	Blow, Gabriel, blow (Anything Goes)			BRO
-----	I get a kick out of you (Anything Goes)			BRO
-----	Night and Day (Gay Divorcee)	M	BF-EF	HAR
-----	So in love (Kiss Me Kate)			CHA
Rodgers	Getting to know you (The King and I)			BRO
-----	Hello young lovers (The King and I)			BRO
-----	If I love you (Carousel)			WIL
-----	June is bustin' out all over (Carousel)			WIL
-----	Kansas City (Oklahoma)			WIL
-----	Mountain greenery (The Garrick Gaities)			HAR
-----	Oh, what a beautiful morning (Oklahoma)			WIL
-----	Soliloquy (Carousel)			CHA
-----	Some enchanted evening (South Pacific)	M	C-E	CHA
-----	The surrey with the fringe on the top (Oklahoma)			WIL
-----	Where or when? (Babes in Arms)			CHA
-----	You are never away (Allegro)			BRO
-----	You'll never walk alone (Carousel)			WIL
-----	Younger than springtime (South Pacific)			WIL

Romberg	Auf Wiedersehen (The Blue Paradise)	HL		GSC
-----	Lover come back to me (New Moon)	H	D-G	HAR
-----	Once to every heart (Blossom Time)			FEI
-----	One alone (The Desert Song)			HAR
-----	Senorita (Girl of the Golden West)	M		FEI
-----	Soldiers of fortune (Girl of the Golden West)	M		FEI
-----	Stouthearted men (New Moon)	L	C-F	HAR
-----	Sun up to sundown (Girl of the Golden West)			FEI
-----	The desert song (The Desert Song)			HAR
-----	The fireman's bride (Up in Central Park)	M	D-EF	WIL
-----	The Riff song (The Desert Song)	L	D-G	HAR
-----	Wanting you (New Moon)			BRO
-----	When I grow too old to dream (The Night is Young)	HLM	C-G	ROB
-----	Who are we to say? (Girl of the Golden West)	M		FEI
-----	Zing, zing, zoom, zoom (Up in Central Park)			ROB
Schwartz	I'll never leave you (Prince Charming)			HAR
Sloane	What's the matter with the moon? (The Mocking Bird)			MAR
Spoliensky	Tell me tonight (Tell Me Tonight)			HAR
Straus	Life is a dream (The Prodigal)			ROB
-----	My hero (The Chocolate Soldier)	H	D-G	WIT
Strauss, J.	Ach wie so herrlich (Eine Nacht in Venedig)			
-----	Als flotter Geist, doch frueh verwaist (The Gypsy Baron)			CRZ
-----	Ja, das Schreiben und das Lesen (The Gypsy Baron)			CRZ
-----	Love can be dreamed (The Gypsy Baron)			GSC
-----	Mine alone (The Gypsy Baron)			CRZ

(Strauss, J.)	Open road, open sky			GSC
	(The Gypsy Baron)			
Sullivan	The Lord Chancellor's insomnia			
	(Iolanthe)			
-----	Tit willow (The Mikado)			GSC
-----	When I was a lad			GSC
	(H.M.S. Pinafore)			
Tierney	Ranger's song (Rio Rita)			FEI
-----	Rio Rita (Rio Rita)	M	C-F	FEI
Weill	Soliloquy			BRO
	(Lost in the Stars)			
Youmans	Drums in my heart			HAR
	(Through the Years)			
-----	Great day (Great Day)	M	EF-F	MLR
-----	Hallelujah!	L	BF-F	HAR
	(Hit the Deck)			
-----	Tea for two (No, no, Nanette)			HAR
-----	Without a song	HLM	BF-F	MLR
	(Great Day)			
Zeller	Lass dir zeit			
	(Der Kellermeister)			
-----	Sei nicht boes!			
	(Der Obersteiger)			

Song Cycles (Or Groups of Songs)

Baritone

Babin	Beloved stranger	L		AUG
Barber	Three songs for voice and			GSC
	piano, Op. 10			
Beethoven	An die ferne Geliebte	HL	C-E	†
-----	Sechs geistliche Lieder			
Berger	Four sonnets	M	A-G	GSC
	Piano or string quartet			
Bloch	Poèmes d'automne	M	B-G	GSC
Brahms	Romanzen auz Magelone			†
-----	Vier ernste Gesaenge			†
-----	Zigeunerlieder			
Copland	Old American songs			
Cornelius	Six Christmas songs	HL		BOS
Debussy	Le promenoir des deux			DUR
	amants			
-----	Trois ballades de Francois			DUR
	Villon			
-----	Trois chansons de France			DUR
Dougherty	Five sea chanties	L	A-EF	GSC
Dvořák	Biblical songs	HL		AMP

763

Falla	Siete canciones	HL		AMP
Fauré	L'horizon chimérique	M		DUR
-----	La bonne chanson	HL		INT
-----	Poème d'un jour			HAM
Finzi	Earth and air and rain (10 songs)			OXF
Griffes	Five poems of ancient China and Japan	M	AS-EF	GSC
Honegger	Trois chansons String quartet and flute			SEN
Kilpinen	Lieder um den Tod	M		AMP
-----	Spielmannslieder			
Mahler	Kindertotenlieder	L	G-GF	INT
-----	Lieder eines fahrenden Gesellen	M		INT
Mason	Nautical lays of a landsman	L	A-E	GSC
-----	Russians (Song cycle)			
Milhaud	Quatre chants hébraïques			
Mussorgsky	Songs and dances of death			INT
-----	Sunless			CHE
-----	The nursery	M	C-G	INT
Niles	Five gambling songs	M		GSC
Poulenc	Banalités			AMP
-----	Chansons Gaillardes	L		HEU
-----	Chansons villageoises	M	C-G	ESC
-----	Le bestiaire String quartet, flute, clarinet and bassoon	M		AMP
-----	Métamorphoses			SAL
-----	Tel jour, telle nuit	M	B-A	DUR
-----	12 Poems of Guillaume Appollinaire			ESC
Powell	Five Virginian folk songs			JFI
Ravel	Chansons madécasses Flute, cello and piano			DUR
-----	Don Quichotte à Dulcinée	HM	A-F	DUR
-----	Histoires naturelles			DUR
-----	Quatre chants populaires	M		DUR
Schubert	Die schoene Muellerin	HL		†
-----	Die Winterreise			†
-----	Gesaenge des Harfners, 1, 2 and 3			PET
Schumann	Der arme Peter	HL	B-G	†
-----	Dichterliebe			†
-----	Liederkreis			
-----	Vier Husarenlieder	L	D-EF	BRH
Somervell	Maud			BOH
Stravinsky	Trois histoires pour enfants			CHE

Vaughan		
Williams	Songs of travel	BOH
-----	The house of life	ASH
Wolf	Harfenspieler Lieder (1, 2 and 3)	
-----	Michelangelo Lieder	†
Woodford-		
Finden	Indian love lyrics	BOO

Solo Cantatas

Baritone

Bach, J.S.	Ich habe genug (Cantata 82)		
	Oboe, strings and continuo		
Foss	Song of anguish		
Pergolesi	Salve Regina		
Porpora	Salve Regina		
Rameau	La Musette		
Stradella	Se amor m'annoda	L	BF-F
Telemann	Kleine Kantate		
	(Von Wald und Au)		

(See Solo Cantatas of Pergolesi, Handel and
Scarlatti, Kirchenkantaten of Buxtehude and
Symphoniae Sacrae of Schuetz.)

Concert Arias

Baritone

Mozart	Io ti lascio, o cara, addio	L	BF-D	AUG
-----	Mentre ti lascio	L		BOO

Christmas Songs

Baritone

Adam	O holy night	LMH	EF-G	†
Andrews	I heard the bells on	L	A-E	GAL
	Christmas day			
Bach, J.S.	Mighty Lord (Christmas Oratorio)			
-----	My darkened heart			
	(Christmas Oratorio)			
-----	So appears Thy natal day	L		GAL
Berlin	White Christmas			BER
	(Holiday Inn)			

765

Berlioz	Le repos de la Ste. Famille (L'Enfance du Christ)	MH		CST
Branscombe	Hail ye time of holidays			
Chaminade	Christmas carol of the birds	MH	D-A	GSC
De Koven	The white Christ	L	C-D	GSC
Dickinson	Joseph, tender Joseph	M		GRA
Dunhill	To the Queen of Heaven	M	C-G	GSC
Eakin	What of that midnight long ago	M	D-F	GAL
Elmore and Reed	Come all ye who weary	L	C-C	JFI
Evans	The Virgin had a baby	L	C-EF	BOH
Fauré	Noël	LH	EF-AF	GSC
Grieg	Christmas song			AUG
Harris	The feast of Christmas	M	C-F	OXF
Head	The three mummers			BOO
Jewell	The vision of the shepherds	HL	A-D	ASC
Kountz	The sleigh	HL	D-FS	GSC
Kramer	Dark and wondrous night	HML	C-E	DIT
Lynn	Gently little Jesus	L	BF-BF	DIT
Mac Gimsey	A new Christmas morning hallelujah	M	DF-F	CFI
Martin	The Holy Child	HML	G-G	ENO
Massenet	Légende de la sauge (Jongleur de Notre-Dame)	M	CS-F	HEU
Matthews	Voices of the sky	HL	BF-D	GSC
Mc Kinney	The Holy Mother sings	MH	AF-AF	JFI
Murphy	O little town of Bethlehem	M	D-F	SUM
Neidlinger	The birthday of a King	LMH	C-F	GSC
-----	The manger cradle	L	EF-F	GSC
Niles	The cherry tree			GSC
Prokoff	Christmas cradle song	LM	D-E	CHA
Rodney	A dream of Bethlehem	MML	G-DF	ENO
Russell	Child Redeemer	HL		GAL
Schubert	Ave Maria	LMH	F-F	†
-----	They sang that night in Bethlehem	LMH	EF-EF	GSC
Taylor	Christmas folk song	L	BF-EF	GRA
Thiman	In the bleak midwinter	L	A-E	NOV
Trunk	The Christ child in the manger	HM		AMP
Walsh	Christmas story			REM
West	It came upon a midnight	MM	E-FS	SUM
Wild	The Christ child	M	EF-EF	CFI
Wolf	Schlafendes Jesuskind	HL	AS-F	†

Baritone

Bach, J.S.	Jesus from the grave is risen	M	F-EF	CFI
Curran	Crucifixion			
Dennee	Easter song	HM	B-F	ASC
Dubois	God, my father (Seven Last Words)			GSC
Guion	At the cry of the first bird	H	D-G	GSC
Hageman	Christ went up into the hills	LH	EF-AF	CFI
Handel	The trumpet shall sound (The Messiah) Trumpet	L		†
Huhn	Christ is risen	HM	C-E	ASC
Kountz	Palm Sunday	HL		GAL
La Forge	Before the Crucifix	HML	BF-EF	GSC
Mac Farlane	On wings of living light	MH	D-G	GSC
Mac Gimsey	I was there when they crucified my Lord	HL		CFI
O'Hara	There is no death	LMH	EF-AF	CHA
Rachmaninoff	Christ is risen	LM	D-F	GAL
Schubert	Ave Maria	LMH	F-F	†
Scott	Angels roll the rock away	MH	E-G	HUN
Tchaikovsky	A legend	M	D-E	GSC
Turner	Hail your risen Lord	HL	C-D	GSC
Vaughan Williams	Easter			GAL
Wolf	Herr, was traegt der Boden	HL	B-DS	†
Yon	Christ triumphant	MH	E-A	JFI
-----	O faithful Cross	HM	C-EF	JFI
-----	Our Paschal joy	LH	AF-AF	JFI

Patriotic Songs

Baritone

Bone and Fenton	Prayer for a waiting world	L		CFI
Bowles	An American hero	M	E-E	AXE
Candlyn	O God of armies	L	DF-DF	GRA
Chadwick	He maketh wars to cease	ML		ASC
De Koven	Recessional			
Dix	The trumpeter	HML	A-C	BOH

Dungan	Eternal life	HL		PRE
Foster, F.	The Americans come	MH	F-BF	JFI
Handel	Arm, arm ye brave (Judas Maccabaeus)	L	B-E	†
Lester	Greater love hath no man	LH	B-E	CFI
O'Hara	Guns	M	C-F	DBH
-----	There is no death	LMH	EF-AF	CHA

Sacred Songs

Baritone

Bach, J.S.	Draw near to me	HML		GSC
Beethoven	The worship of God in nature			
Bizet	O Lord be merciful	HL		GSC
Bone and Fenton	First Psalm	LM	DF-F	CFI
-----	Thy word is a lamp	LH	C-F	ROW
Brown	The twenty-third Psalm	LH		GRA
-----	What are these which are arrayed	HLM	C-F	ASC
Browning	For I am persuaded	LM	DF-G	CFI
-----	The beatitudes	HM	C-F	CFI
Buck	Fear not ye, O Israel	HLM		GSC
Campbell-Tipton	I will give thanks unto the Lord	LMH	DF-AF	GSC
Candlyn	God that madest earth and heaven	M	C-F	GRA
Chadwick	A ballad of trees and the Master	HML	A-F	DIT
Charles	Incline Thine ear	HL	BF-D	GSC
Clokey	God is in everything	LH	D-G	JFI
Davis	Be ye kind, one to another	L		GAL
-----	Let not your heart be troubled	HML		WOO
-----	Trust in the Lord	MH	CS-G	GAL
Dvořák	God is my shepherd			AMP
-----	Hear my prayer, O Lord			AMP
-----	Turn Thee to me			AMP
Edmunds	Praise we the Lord	HL	D-D	ROW
Faure	The palms	HM	C-EF	DIT
Franck	O Lord most holy	LM	A-FS	BOS
Goodhall	The mountain	M	D-E	GSL
Green	Praised be the Lord	M	C-F	OXF
Guion	Prayer	HL		GSC
-----	The cross bearer	HM	B-DS	GSC
Handel	Thanks be to Thee	M	CS-E	†

768

Hinchliffe	Tranquillity	M	E-F	CFI
Holst	The heart worships	ML	BF-D	STB
Knapp	Open the gates of the temple	HML	A-D	PON
La Forge	They that trust in the Lord	HL	BF-EF	GAL
-----	What shall I render unto the Lord?	HL	C-D	GSC
Lederer	Psalm 104	L	A-E	CFI
Liddle	How lovely are Thy dwellings	HML		BOS
Mac Dermid	In my Fathers house are many mansions	HML		FRS
-----	Ninety first Psalm	HLM		FRS
Mac Gimsey	Think on these things	LM	BF-EF	CFI
Malotte	The beatitudes	LH	E-G	GSC
-----	The Lord's Prayer			
-----	The twenty-third Psalm	HLM	C-F	GSC
Mc Feeters	A Psalm of praise	M		CFI
Mc Gill	Thine eternal peace	HL	A-CS	GSC
Mendelssohn	But the mountains shall depart (Elijah)			
-----	For know ye not (Saint Paul)			
-----	Lord God of Abraham (Elijah)	L	B-E	†
-----	O God, have mercy (Saint Paul)	L	B-D	†
Noble	Souls of the righteous	M		GRA
O'Connor-Morris	Fill thou my life, O Lord	L	BF-EF	CFI
Rorem	Song of David	M		AMP
Sanderson	Green pastures	HL	BF-EF	BOO
Schubert	The Omnipotent			
-----	To the Infinite			
Scott	Consider the lilies	HL	C-E	GSC
-----	Ride on, ride on	HML		FLA
Speaks	The Lord is my light	HML		GSC
-----	Thou wilt keep him in perfect peace	HML		GSC
Stevenson	I sought the Lord	HL	D-F	DIT
-----	Praise	M	F-F	CFI
Stickles	Saith the Lord	LH	D-F	CHA
Sullivan	Honor the Lord with thy substance (The Prodigal Son)			
Tchaikovsky	Lord Almighty God (Moscow Cantata)	M		GRA
-----	Pilgrim's song	HLM	B-E	GSC
Thiman	My master hath a garden	HL		NOV
Thompson	My Master hath a garden	M		ECS
Van de Water	The penitent	HM		DIT

(Van de Water)	The publican	HL	C-E	DIT
Weaver	Build thee more stately mansions	M	C-E	GAL
Wolf	Morning prayer (Morgenstimme)			
-----	Prayer (Gebet)			

Wedding Songs

Baritone

Barnby	O perfect love	M	C-G	DIT
Beethoven	Ich liebe dich	HL	BF-DF	†
Bond	I love you truly			BOS
Clough-Leighter	Possession	MH	DF-AF	GSC
De Koven	Oh promise me (Robin Hood)	HML	C-D	†
Delius	So white, so soft, is she	LH	B-FS	BOH
D'Hardelot	Because	MH	E-G	CHA
Diggle	A wedding prayer	HM	EF-F	GSC
Franck	O Lord most holy	LM	A-FS	BOS
Geehl	For you alone			SHU
Grieg	I love thee	HML	E-F	†
La Forge	How much I love you	HM	DF-F	GSC
Lippe	How do I love you?			BOS
Marx	Hat dich die Liebe beruehrt	MH	EF-BF	AMP
Sacco	With this ring	M	F-F	BVC
Schubert	Du bist die Ruh	LMH	EF-AF	†
-----	Ungeduld	HML		†
Schumann	Widmung	HL	BF-F	†
Sharp	Possession	MH	D-A	DIT
Sowerby	O perfect love	MH	EF-AF	GRA
Strauss	Ich liebe dich			†
Thiman	The God of love my Shepherd is	ML	A-D	NOV
Youmans	Through the years (Through the Years)	HML	A-F	MLR

Songs and Arias With Added Accompanying Instrument

Baritone

Bach, J.S.	Gleich wie die wilden Meereswellen (Cantata 178) Violin	

(Bach, J.S.)	Hier in meines Vaters Staette (Cantata 32) Violin			AUG
Barber	Dover Beach String quartet	M	BF-F	GSC
Berger	Four sonnets Piano or string quartet	M	A-G	GSC
Chausson	Le colibri Violin or cello	M	F-GF	BOS
Curran	Nocturne Violin	HML	B-DS	GSC
Handel	Defend her! Heaven (Theodora) Edited and set for strings			STB
-----	The trumpet shall sound (The Messiah) Trumpet	L		†
Honegger	Chanson (Ronsard) Flute and string quartet			SEN
-----	Trois chansons String quartet and flute			SEN
Kramer	Pleading String quartet	LH	D-GF	JFI
Mana-Zucca	Rachem Trumpet	HML		CHA
Milford	So sweet love seemed Cello	HL	D-D	GRA
Peterkin	A curse on a closed gate Voice and viola	M	D-E	OXF
Poulenc	Le bestiaire String quartet, flute, clarinet and bassoon	M		AMP
Ravel	Chansons madécasses Flute, cello and piano			DUR

American Recital Songs

Bass

Athay	City streets	M	E-EF	CFI
Bacon	A clear midnight			NEM
-----	Brady			BOO
Barber	I hear an army	LH	D-AF	GSC
-----	Nocturne	HM	CS-FS	GSC
-----	Rain has fallen	HM	D-E	GSC
-----	With rue my heart is laden	HL	CS-D	GSC
Bauer	Songs in the night	HL	A-C	GSC
Billings	David's lamentation			BIR
Binder	Abraham Lincoln walks at midnight			
Boyd	Cape Horn gospel	L	BF-D	GAL
Braine	Dawn awakes	HML	A-D	ASC

Cadman	Service	HML	BF-D	FLA
Campbell- Tipton	The crying of water	LH	FS-GS	GSC
Carpenter	Dansons la gigue	M	B-E	GSC
-----	Don't ceare	M	C-D	GSC
-----	Go, lovely rose	M	DF-EF	GSC
-----	Looking glass river	M	B-D	GSC
-----	The cock shall crow	M	B-E	GSC
-----	The day is no more	M	GS-DS	GSC
-----	The green river	M	B-E	GSC
-----	To one unknown	M	A-DS	GSC
Chanler	The policeman in the park	L		GSC
Charles	Sweet song of long ago	HML	A-D	GSC
-----	When I have sung my songs	HM	BF-EF	GSC
Coombs	Her rose	HL	D-C	GSC
Deis	Reflection	HM	B-F	
Dougherty	Blow ye winds	L	C-D	GSC
-----	Declaration of independence	L	C-C	GSC
-----	Loveliest of trees	HM	C-E	BOH
Dreier	They call me vagabond			
Duke	Calvary	L	G-F	CFI
-----	Deep sea mood			
-----	Here in this spot with you	M	B-F	GSC
-----	Loveliest of trees	L	C-D	GSC
-----	Richard Cory	L	A-EF	CFI
Dungan	Down the wild song	HL	AF-F	CFI
Edmunds	Billy boy	ML	BF-EF	ROW
Farwell	These saw visions			GAL
Foote	I'm wearing awa'	HL		ASC
Ganz	A woman's last word	HL	BF-F	GRA
Golde	Calls	HL	BF-EF	GSC
Griffes	An old song resung	LM	EF-F	GSC
Harris	Agatha Morley	M	C-D	CFI
Haubiel	Terry, my son	M		CMP
Hawley	Ah, 'tis a dream	L	G-C	JCH
Huhn	Cato's advice	L	G-C	GSC
Ives	Charlie Rutlage	M		ARR
-----	General William Booth enters into Heaven			
Kramer	Minnelied	M	C-E	JFI
La Forge	To a messenger	HLM	CF-G	GSC
Levitzki	Do you remember?	HML	BF-EF	GSC
Mac Gimsey	Thunderin' wonderin'	L	C-D	CFI
-----	Trouble	ML	C-D	CFI
Malotte	Upstream	M	C-F	GSC
Mana-Zucca	Thy will be done			CNG
Manning	In the Luxembourg gardens	HML	BF-D	GSC
Mason	A prophet	M	BF-GF	GSC

772

(Mason)	A sea dirge			WIT
Mc Gill	O sleep	L	A-CS	GSC
Mead	The wanderer	LMH	D-A	CFI
Metcalf	At nightfall	HML	C-DF	ASC
Miller	Boats of mine	HML	BF-EF	FLA
Naginski	The ship starting	M	BF-B	GSC
Paxson	Dusk at sea	HL	A-EF	GSC
Pinsuti	Bedouin love song	HL	FS-DS	GSC
Robinson	Joe Hill			MRR
Rogers	The last song	MLH	E-AF	GSC
Sachs	The three riders	M	C-F	GSC
Schuman	Holiday song	M	C-F	GSC
Singer	This want of you	L	E-FS	BOH
Sonneck	To Helen	M	B-F	GSC
Speaks	Shepherd, see thy horse's foaming mane			FLA
Still	If you should go			LEE
Swanson	Pierrot	L	B-D	WTR
-----	The valley	L	BF-DF	LEE
Taylor	Captain Stratton's fancy	L	CS-F	JFI
Thompson	Velvet shoes	M	C-E	ECS
Thomson	Dirge	M	D-F	GSC
Tyson	Noon and night	LH	F-AF	GSC

British Recital Songs

Bass

Aiken	Sigh no more	HML		STB
Anon	False Phillis			
Arne, T.	By the gaily circling glass	L		DIT
-----	Now Phoebus sinketh in the west			GSC
-----	Why so pale and wan?			GSC
Bantock	Silent strings	MH	F-G	BOO
Berners	Dialogue between Tom Filuter and his man	M	D-F	CHE
Boyce	Rail no more ye learned asses	L	G-D	OXF
-----	The song of Momus to Mars	M	BF-EF	CFI
Campion	Follow thy fair sun			STB
-----	There is a garden in her face			DIT
Coleridge-Taylor	She rested by the broken brook	HL		DIT
Dibdin	Blow high, blow low			POT

Dowland	Shall I sue?			STB
Dunhill	The cloths of Heaven	LM	EF-G	STB
Ford	Since first I saw your face			DIT
Forsyth	The bell man			DIT
German	My song is of the sturdy north	ML		CHA
-----	Rolling down to Rio	ML	G-D	NOV
Gibbs	Five eyes	HL	D-D	BOS
-----	The ballad of Semmerwater	L	AF-EF	CUR
-----	Toll the bell			
Goossens	Melancholy	M		CHE
Handel	Droop not young lover		G-E	
-----	The birds no more shall sing			
Harrison	I hear an army			CRA
Harty	Homeward	L	C-E	NOV
Head	Sweet chance that led my steps abroad	LM	C-F	BOH
-----	The ships of Arcady	ML	BF-EF	BOH
-----	When I think upon the maidens	LM	D-G	BOO
Hely-Hutchinson	Old mother Hubbard	HL	B-E	CFI
Holst	Creation			GSC
-----	The heart worships	ML	BF-D	STB
-----	The Sergeant's song			ASH
Jones	Love is a babble			STB
Keel	Trade winds	HL	BF-EF	BOH
Lawes	I am confirmed			BOO
Leveridge	The beggar's song	L	G-D	BOO
Longsteffe	When the Sergeant Major's on parade			CHA
Milford	So sweet love seemed Cello	HL	D-D	GRA
Munro	My lovely Celia			BIR
Parry	Why so pale and wan, fond lover	L		NOV
Purcell, E.	Passing by	HM	D-D	DIT
Purcell, H.	Arise, ye subterranean winds			GSC
-----	Evening hymn	M	C-F	OXF
-----	If music be the food of love	M	D-G	BOO
-----	I'll sail upon the dog star	HL	A-E	†
Quilter	It was a lover and his lass	HL	CS-E	BOO
-----	Music and moonlight	L	C-EF	CUR
-----	Now sleeps the crimson petal	LMH	EF-GF	BOO
-----	O mistress mine	HML		BOO
-----	Take, o take those lips away			BOO
Rosseter	When Laura smiles	LM	D-E	STB

Russell	Poor man's garden	HML	A-D	BOO
Sanderson	Quiet	ML	AF-EF	BOH
Scott	Song of London	M	BF-E	ELK
Shaw	Song of the Palanquin bearers		E-F	CUR
Singer	This want of you	L	E-FS	BOH
Stanford	A soft day	ML	DF-DF	STB
-----	Faith			BOH
-----	Farewell	M	BF-E	STB
-----	She is far from the land			
-----	Windy nights			
Stephenson	Love is a sickness	HML	C-D	BOO
Taylor	The banks o' Doon	ML		JFI
-----	The wind mill	M		OXF
Toye	The inn	L	C-E	CUR
Vaughan Williams	Four nights	L	AF-EF	OXF
-----	How can the tree but wither?			OXF
-----	The roadside fire	HML	BF-EF	BOO
-----	The water mill	L	C-D	OXF
Warlock	Good ale			AUG

French Recital Songs

Bass

Bruneau	L'heureux vagabond	LH	EF-G	GSC
Chausson	Le colibri Violin or cello	M	F-GF	BOS
-----	Le temps des lilas	MH	D-GS	†
Debussy	Beau soir	LH	C-FS	†
-----	Colloque sentimental			DUR
-----	La mer est plus belle	HL		†
-----	Le faune			DUR
-----	Le temps a laissié son manteau			DUR
Duparc	Chanson triste	MH	FS-AF	†
-----	La vague et la cloche			ROU
-----	Lamento	ML	EF-EF	†
-----	Le manoir de Rosamunde	HL	B-F	BOS
-----	L'invitation au voyage	HM	E-F	†
-----	Phidylé	MH	EF-AF	BOS
Dupont	Les boeufs			SAL
Fauré	Après un rêve	HM	C-F	†
-----	Automne	MH	D-FS	GSC
-----	Dans les ruines d'une abbaye	M	E-FS	†
-----	Fleur jetée	HM	BF-FS	†
-----	Le parfum impérissable	LH	GF-GF	
-----	Les berceaux	LMH	BF-G	†

(Fauré)	Nocturne	H	F-A	MAR
-----	Prison	LH		MAR
-----	Rencontre	H	EF-AF	†
-----	Sérénade toscane	MH	G-AF	HAM
Ferrari	Le lazzarone			
-----	Le miroir	M	E-F	GSC
Fourdrain	Promenade au mule			
Garat	Dans le printemps de mes années	M		DUR
Georges	Le flibustier			
Gounod	Au printemps	LMH	DF-AF	GSC
-----	Au rossignol	LMH	D-G	CHO
-----	Que les songes heureux			GSC
Hahn	D'une prison	L	BF-EF	HEU
-----	Je me metz en vostre mercy			HEU
-----	L'heure exquise	M	DF-F	†
-----	Offrande	M	D-D	†
-----	Paysage	MH	EF-G	HEU
-----	The gay vagabond			
-----	Trois jours de vendange	M		HEU
Holmès	Au pays	HM	C-F	CFI
Honegger	Chanson (Ronsard) Flute and string quartet			SEN
-----	Psalm 34 (I will bless the Lord at all times)			SAL
-----	Psalm 130 (Mimaamaquim)			SAL
-----	Psalm 138 (I will give Thee thanks with my whole heart)			SAL
Hue	J'ai pleuré en rêve	HL	D-E	BOS
Ibert	Chanson de la mort			
Indy	Madrigal			DIT
Lenormand	Quelle souffrance	HM	AF-F	HAM
Martini	Plaisir d'amour	M	BF-EF	GSC
Milhaud	Le chant du veilleur			
Paladilhe	Les trois prières			
Pessard	L'adieu du matin	ML	BF-D	GSC
Poulenc	Chanson à boire	L	B-E	HEU
-----	Fêtes galantes			SAL
-----	Invocation aux Parques			HEU
-----	La belle jeunesse	L	D-F	HEU
-----	Madrigal			
-----	Sérénade			
Ravel	Ronsard à son âme	L	CS-E	DUR
Saint-Saëns	Danse macabre	L	BF-EF	AXE
-----	Les pas d'armes du Roi Jean	HML	A-F	RIC
Severac	Les hiboux			ROU
Widor	Je ne veux pas autre chose	HL	C-EF	HAM

Beethoven	Adelaide	HML	BF-E	†
-----	An die Geliebte	M	E-E	†
-----	Auf dem Huegel sitz' ich spaehend			†
-----	Aus Goethes Faust			
-----	Der Kuss			†
-----	Der Wachtelschlag			†
-----	Die Ehre Gottes	HL	AF-EF	†
-----	Die Liebe des Naechsten			
-----	Diese Wolken in den Hoehen			†
-----	God is my song			
-----	Ich liebe dich	HL	BF-DF	†
-----	In questa tomba	ML	A-CS	†
-----	Vom Tode	L	A-EF	GSC
-----	Wonne der Wehmut			†
Brahms	Am Sonntag Morgen	L	CS-FS	†
-----	An die Nachtigall	H	DS-G	†
-----	Auf dem Kirchhofe	HL	BF-EF	†
-----	Botschaft	HL	D-F	†
-----	Dein blaues Auge	MH	BF-G	†
-----	Denn es gehet dem Menschen	HL		†
-----	Der Ueberlaeufer			†
-----	Die Mainacht	HL	BF-FF	†
-----	Ein Sonett			†
-----	Ein Wanderer	LH	E-AF	†
-----	Erinnerung	H	E-G	†
-----	Feldeinsamkeit	HL	C-EF	GSC
-----	Ich wandte mich und sahe an	HL		†
-----	In Waldeseinsamkeit	H	ES-G	†
-----	Kein Haus, keine Heimat	HL	D-D	†
-----	Maienkaetzchen	L	D-E	†
-----	Meine Liebe ist gruen	MLH	ES-A	†
-----	Minnelied	MHL	C-EF	†
-----	Mit vierzig Jahren	HL	FS-D	†
-----	Nachtigall	MHL	BF-FS	†
-----	Nicht mehr zu dir zu gehen			†
-----	O kuehler Wald	MH	A-F	†
-----	O liebliche Wangen	MLH	E-G	†
-----	O wuesst' ich doch den Weg zurueck	H	E-FS	†
-----	Ruhe Suessliebchen	HL	BS-E	†
-----	Sandmaennchen	LH	F-G	†
-----	Sapphische Ode	HML		†

(Brahms)	Sonntag	H	D-G	†
-----	Staendchen	HL	BF-E	†
-----	Steig' auf, geliebter Schatten	HL	BF-EF	†
-----	Tambourliedchen			†
-----	Treue Liebe	LMH	DS-E	†
-----	Unbewegte laue Luft			†
-----	Unueberwindlich			†
-----	Vergebliches Staendchen	LMH		†
-----	Verrat	HL	FS-EF	GSC
-----	Von ewiger Liebe	LMH	B-AF	†
-----	Vor dem Fenster			†
-----	Wenn ich mit Menschen			†
-----	Wie bist du meine Koenigin	HL	C-E	†
-----	Wie Melodien zieht es	HL	A-E	†
-----	Wie rafft ich mich auf			†
-----	Wir wandelten	LH	EF-GF	†
Franz	Es ragt ins Meer der Runenstein	HL	G-F	†
-----	For music	ML	C-D	†
-----	Im Herbst	HM	A-F	†
-----	Mutter, o sing mich zur Ruh	HL	E-G	†
Handel	Dank sei Dir, Herr	M	CS-E	†
Haydn	The spirit's song	M	B-GF	†
-----	The wanderer			
Liszt	Die Lorelei	LH	BF-BF	†
-----	Ueber allen Gipfeln ist Ruh			DUR
Loewe	Der heilige Franziskus	L	A-E	SC
-----	Der Noeck			SC
-----	Der selt'ne Beter			SC
-----	Die Uhr	HML	AF-EF	†
-----	Edward	HL	F-E	†
-----	Friedericus Rex			SC
-----	Odins Meeresritt			SC
-----	Tom der Reimer			HSC
Mozart	An Chloe	LH	EF-AF	
-----	Die Verschweigung			
-----	Warnung	HM	C-D	
Pfitzner	Der Gaertner			
-----	Ist der Himmel im Lenz so blau			
Schubert	Am Bach im Fruehling			PET
-----	Am Meer	HML	B-D	†
-----	An die Leier	LM	BF-F	†
-----	An Schwager Kronos	HL	G-E	†
-----	An Silvia			†
-----	Aufenthalt	HLM	A-F	†
-----	Aus Heliopolis			PET

778

(Schubert)	Ave Maria	LMH	F-F	†
-----	Das Wirtshaus	HL	C-D	†
-----	Der Atlas	HL	BF-F	†
-----	Der Doppelgaenger	HL	G-D	†
-----	Der Erlkoenig	HML	A-E	†
-----	Der Goldschmiedsgesell			PET
-----	Der Juengling an der Quelle	LH	E-A	†
-----	Der Juengling auf dem Huegel	L	G-F	†
-----	Der Kampf			PET
-----	Der Leiermann	ML	C-D	†
-----	Der Lindenbaum	HL	A-D	†
-----	Der Schiffer	LH	BF-A	†
-----	Der stuermische Morgen	HL		
-----	Der Wanderer	HML	FS-D	†
-----	Der Wegweiser	L	D-EF	†
-----	Der Zwerg	M	A-GF	PET
-----	Der zuernende Barde			PET
-----	Die Allmacht	HML	G-E	†
-----	Die Forelle	MLH	EF-GF	†
-----	Die Kraehe	HL	A-E	†
-----	Die Post	HML	BF-EF	†
-----	Die Stadt	HL	A-E	†
-----	Fahrt zum Hades	HL	G-DF	PET
-----	Fischerweise	L	C-D	†
-----	Fruehlingsglaube	M	EF-F	†
-----	Gebet waehrend der Schlacht	M	CS-E	†
-----	Gruppe aus dem Tartarus	L	CS-EF	†
-----	Gute Nacht	LH	C-FS	†
-----	Heidenroeslein			
-----	Ihr Grab			PET
-----	Il modo di prender moglie			
-----	Il traditor deluso			
-----	Im Abendrot	HL	C-D	†
-----	Kriegers Ahnung	HL	G-EF	†
-----	L'incanto degli occhi			
-----	Lachen und Weinen	HL	C-EF	†
-----	Mein!	HL		†
-----	Mut	HL		†
-----	Rastlose Liebe	M	B-F	†
-----	Sei mir gegruesst	LH	G-G	†
-----	Seligkeit			
-----	Staendchen	MH	B-E	†
-----	Tischlied			PET
-----	Totengraebers Heimweh	HL	G-EF	†
-----	Ungeduld	HML		†
-----	Wohin?	HL	B-E	†

Schuetz	Aus dem 119th Psalm			
-----	Herr, nun laessest Du Deinen Diener			BAR
Schumann	An den Sonnenschein	HL	A-D	†
-----	Der Soldat			
-----	Die beiden Grenadiere			
-----	Die Lotusblume	HLM	BF-F	†
-----	Du bist wie eine Blume	HM	F-EF	†
-----	Fruehlingsfahrt	HL	B-E	†
-----	Ich grolle nicht	HL	BF-D	†
-----	Im Rhein, im heiligen Strome	HM	D-F	
-----	Im Walde	HL	A-D	†
-----	Lieb' Liebchen	HL	B-E	†
-----	Romanze	HL	C-E	GSC
-----	Wanderlied	HL	A-E	†
-----	Wenn ich in deine Augen seh'	HL	EF-FF	†
-----	Wer nie sein Brot			†
-----	Widmung	HL	BF-F	†
Strauss	Breit ueber mein Haupt	LH	GF-AF	HSC
-----	Caecilie	MH	E-B	†
-----	Der Einsame			†
-----	Die Nacht	HL		†
-----	Freundliche Vision	HL	C-F	†
-----	Heimliche Aufforderung	HL	B-E	†
-----	Im Spaetboot			
-----	Madrigal	LH	EF-GF	
-----	Mit deinen blauen Augen	LH	C-GS	†
-----	Morgen	HML	E-F	†
-----	Nachtgang			†
-----	Ruhe meine Seele			†
-----	Staendchen	HM	A-FS	†
-----	Traum durch die Daemmerung	HML	BF-EF	†
-----	Wie sollten wir geheim sie halten	LH	D-A	
-----	Zueignung	HL	CS-FS	†
Wolf	Abschied			†
-----	Alles endet, was entstehet	HL	F-C	†
-----	Anakreons Grab	HL	D-D	†
-----	An die Geliebte			†
-----	Auf einer Wanderung	HL		†
-----	Biterolf	HL	D-F	†
-----	Cophtisches Lied, 1			†
-----	Der Freund	HM	BF-E	PET
-----	Der Gaertner	HL		†
-----	Der Musikant	HL	CS-D	†
-----	Der Rattenfaenger	HL		†

(Wolf)	Der Schreckenberger			†
-----	Der Soldat, 1	LH	E–FS	†
-----	Der Tambour	HL		†
-----	Er ist's	H	D–G	†
-----	Fuehlt meine Seele	L	A–D	†
-----	Fussreise	HL	D–E	†
-----	Gesang Weylas	HL	DF–F	†
-----	Gesegnet sei das Gruen	HL		†
-----	Gesegnet sei, durch den die Welt	HL		†
-----	Heb' auf dein blondes Haupt	HL	G–DF	†
-----	In der Fruehe	HL	C–C	†
-----	Nun lass uns Frieden schliessen	HL		†
-----	Nun wandre, Maria	HL	EF–D	†
-----	Prometheus			PET
-----	Seemanns Abschiedslied	H	C–A	†
-----	Trunken muessen wir alle sein	M	ES–FS	†
-----	Ueber Nacht	LH	D–G	†
-----	Um Mitternacht	HL	G–EF	†
-----	Und steht ihr frueh am Morgen auf			†
-----	Verborgenheit	HL	B–E	†
-----	Wenn du zu den Blumen gehst	HL	B–EF	†
-----	Wohl denk' ich oft	M	C–EF	†
Wolff	Ewig			
-----	Sommernacht			

Italian Recital Songs

Bass

Bassani	Dormi, bella, dormi tu	L	EF–F	GSC
Bononcini	L'esperto nocchiero (Astarte)	HL	B–E	†
-----	Pupille nere			
Caccini	Amarilli, mia bella	ML	C–D	†
Caldara	Alma del core			GSC
-----	Come raggio di sol	HL	D–F	†
-----	Mirti, faggi			PET
-----	Sebben crudele	HML	E–DS	†
-----	Selve amiche, ombrose piante	HM	E–E	†
Carissimi	A morire!	ML	C–D	
-----	Filli, non t'amo più	HL	B–D	†
-----	No, no, non si speri!	HL	C–EF	†

(Carissimi)	Vittoria, mio core!	HLM	B-E	†
Castelnuovo-Tedesco	Ninna Nanna			
Cavalli	Beato chi può (Serse)			HEU
-----	Donzelle fuggite	HL	C-EF	†
Cesti	Che angoscia, che affanno (Il Pomo d'Oro)	HL	C-DF	DIT
-----	E dove t'aggiri (Il Pomo d'Oro)	HM	D-EF	DIT
-----	Intorno all'idol mio (Orontea)	MH	D-F	†
Cimara	Fiocca la neve	H	G-G	GSC
Coscia	Dormi, dormi			
Durante	Danza, danza fanciulla gentile	HM	BF-F	†
-----	Vergin, tutta amor	LM	C-EF	†
Falconieri	O bellissimi capelli	HL	B-D	†
-----	Vezzosette e care	M	CS-E	GSC
Frescobaldi	Se l'aura spira	HL	C-EF	DIT
Gagliano	Dormi, amore	HL	CS-E	DIT
Gasparini	Caro laccio, dolce nodo	M	EF-EF	GSC
Giordani	Caro mio ben	HML	B-D	†
Handel	Alma mia (Floridante)	HM	CS-E	†
---†---	Cara sposa (Radamisto)	M	CS-D	†
-----	Col raggio placido (Agrippina)			
-----	Del minnacciar del vento (Ottone)	L		†
-----	Ombra mai fu (Serse)	HM	BF-EF	†
-----	Si, tra i ceppi (Berenice)	L	B-D	†
Legrenzi	Che fiero costume	HML	C-D	†
Lotti	Pur dicesti, o bocca bella	LMH	E-FS	GSC
Marcello	Non m'è grave morir per amore	L	C-E	GSC
-----	Perchè mai non m'uccise il dolore			
Monteverdi	Addio di Seneca			
Paisiello	Nel cor più non mi sento	HL	C-EF	†
Pergolesi	Bella mia (Il Maestro di Musica)			GSC
-----	Nina	HL	CS-D	DIT
Peri	Invocazione di Orfeo (Euridice)	HL	E-CS	DIT
Pizzetti	L'annuncie			
Provenzale	La stellidaura vendicata (A. of Armidoro)			
Respighi	Nebbie			†
Rontani	Se bel rio	ML	D-C	†
Rosa	Star vicino	HL	D-E	†
Sadero	L'amor xe una pietanza	M		CHE

782

Sarti	Lungi dal caro bene (Armide)	HL	G-D	GSC
Scarlatti, A.	Chi vuole innamorarsi	HL	D-EF	DIT
-----	Già il sole dal Gange	LH	EF-F	GSC
----	La fortuna			BOS
-----	Rugiadose odorose (Il Pirro e Demetrio)	HL	D-E	DIT
Scarlatti, D.	Consolati e spara amante	L	BF-E	GSC
Sibella	La Girometta	HML	D-E	GSC
-----	Non ho parole	HL	C-F	GSC
Stradella	Per pietà (Il Floridoro)	HM	D-F	DIT
-----	Pietà, Signore	HM	C-F	
Torelli	Tu lo sai	HL	BF-F	†
Tosti	La serenata	HLM	D-EF	GSC
-----	Sogno			RIC
-----	The last song	HL		RIC
Zandonai	I due tarli	M		RIC

Russian Recital Songs

Bass

Borodin	Love			
Cui	Hunger song	LM	E-F	DIT
Dargomijshky	The old corporal			
Glazounoff	Song of Bacchus			
Gretchaninoff	Death			AMP
-----	My native land	L	C-EF	GSC
-----	Over the steppe	LM	C-G	GSC
-----	Voices of night			
-----	Wounded birch	HL	B-EF	†
Koeneman	When the King went forth to war	ML	A-E	CHE
Malashkin	O could I but express in song	LH		CHE
Mednikoff	The hills of Gruzia	H	DS-A	LAC
Mussorgsky	After the battle			GSC
-----	Death and the peasant			GSC
-----	Death the commander			
-----	Serenade			BES
-----	Song of the old man			
-----	Sphinx			BRH
-----	The banks of the Don			GSC
-----	The classic			BRH
-----	The grave			BRH
-----	The seminarian			GSC
-----	Trepak			BES
-----	Within four walls			CHE

Rachmaninoff	All things depart			BOO
-----	Floods of spring	HL		DIT
-----	How fair this spot	MH		GSC
-----	Oh, never sing to me again	H		BOO
-----	O thou billowy harvest field	HL	CS-E	GSC
-----	Spring waters	M	D-GS	CHE
-----	When yesterday we met			BOH
Revutzki	My beloved			
-----	The merry fiddler			
Rimsky- Korsakov	The prophet			
Rubinstein	Ballad			
-----	Do not weep my child			
-----	Gold rolls here below me			
-----	The prisoner			
Shostakovich	In the fields			
Tchaikovsky	At the ball	MH		GSC
-----	Be it a bright day			
-----	Don Juan's serenade	HLM	B-E	GSC
-----	Moment of fear			
-----	Pilgrim's song	HLM	B-E	GSC

Scandinavian Recital Songs

Bass

Grieg	A swan			†
-----	Autumnal gale	HL	A-F	CFI
-----	I love thee	HML	E-F	†
-----	Jeg lever et liv i laengsel	L	BF-E	HAN
-----	The old mother	ML	D-D	DIT
-----	The tryst			DIT
-----	Two brown eyes	LM	EF-F	GSC
Kilpinen	Elegia satakielle			
Palmgren	Var ar vägens mål?			HAN
Sibelius	Black roses	M	A-ES	AMP

Spanish Recital Songs

Bass

De Cola	Sarie Marías			
Nin	El canto de los pájaros			ESC
-----	Granadina			AMP
-----	Minué cantado			ESC
Obradors	El vito			

784

Miscellaneous Recital Songs

Bass

Bizet	Agnus Dei	HLM	C-AF	
Chopin	The little ring	HL		GSC
Dvořák	Clouds and darkness			
-----	God is my shepherd			AMP
-----	I will sing new songs of gladness	HL		†
-----	Lord, Thou art my refuge and shield			AMP
-----	Songs my mother taugh me	HM	E-E	†
-----	Turn Thee to me			AMP
Franck	Panis angelicus	LM		
Haydn	O Jesus, Deus Pacis			
Sinadinos	The Eagle			

British Songs and Arias
For Opening Recitals

Bass

Blow	Music's the cordial of a troubled breast (Begin the Song)	L	D-E	PET
Boyce	The song of Momus to Mars	M	BF-EF	CFI
Handel	Hear me, ye winds and waves (Scipione)	ML	G-EF	BOO
-----	Silent worship (Tolomeo)	LM	D-E	CUR
-----	Wher'er you walk (Semele)	HML	C-D	†
Purcell	Arise, ye subterranean winds			GSC
-----	Evening hymn	M	C-F	OXF
-----	If music be the food of love	M	D-G	BOO
-----	Music for a while (Oedipus)	LH		SC
Wilson	When dull care			BOO

German Songs For Opening Recitals

Bass

Beethoven	Adelaide	HML	BF-E	†
-----	God is my song			
-----	Ich liebe dich	HL	BF-DF	†
Brahms	Ein Wanderer	LH	E-AF	†
-----	Nachtigall	MHL	BF-FS	†
Handel	Dank sei Dir, Herr	M	CS-E	†
Haydn	She never told her love	HL		DIT
Mozart	An Chloe	LH	EF-AF	
Schubert	Das Wandern	HLM	E-E	†
Wolf	Ueber Nacht	LH	D-G	†

Italian Songs and Arias
For Opening Recitals

Bass

Caccini	Amarilli, mia bella	ML	C-D	†
Caldara	Sebben crudele	HML	E-DS	†
Carissimi	Vittoria, mio core	HLM	B-E	†
Cavalli	Beato chi può (Serse)			HEU
-----	Donzelle fuggite	HL	C-EF	†
Cesti	Che angoscia, che affanno	HL	C-DF	DIT
	(Il Pomo d'Oro)			
Durante	Vergin, tutta amor	LM	C-EF	†
Falconieri	O bellissimi capelli	HL	B-D	†
Handel	Cara sposa (Radamisto)	M	CS-D	†
-----	Confusa si miri	L	B-D	CFI
	(Rodelinda)			
-----	Ombra mai fu (Serse)	HM	BF-EF	†
-----	Si, tra i ceppi (Berenice)	L	B-D	†
Lotti	Pur dicesti, o bocca bella	LMH	E-FS	GSC
Monteverdi	Ahi, troppo è duro	HL	C-EF	DIT
	(Il Balletto delle Ingrate)			
Mozart	Mentre ti lascio	L		BOO
Paisiello	Nel cor più non mi sento	HL	C-EF	†
Peri	Invocazione di Orfeo	HL	E-CS	DIT
	(Euridice)			
Rosa	Star vicino	HL	D-E	RIC
Sarti	Lungi dal caro bene	HL	G-D	GSC
	(Armide)			
Scarlatti, A.	Già il sole dal Gange	LH	EF-F	GSC
Stradella	Per pietà (Il Floridoro)			
-----	Pietà, Signore	HM	C-F	GSC

Bass

Barber	I hear an army	LH	D-AF	GSC
Charles	When I have sung my songs	HM	BF-EF	GSC
Copland	I bought me a cat			
-----	Old American songs			
Diack	Little Jack Horner			CFI
Dougherty	Everyone sang			
Foster	My journey's end	HLM	DF-G	GSC
La Forge	To a messenger	HLM	CF-G	GSC
Mac Gimsey	Jwri Jericho	M	C-G	CFI
-----	Land uv degradashun	M	BF-F	CFI
-----	Thunderin' wonderin'	L	C-D	CFI
Malotte	Blow me eyes	MH	C-G	GSC
-----	Song of the open road			ABC
-----	Upstream	M	C-F	GSC
Niles	The rovin' gambler	HL	BF-EF	GSC
Rogers	The last song	MLH	E-AF	GSC
Sachs	The three riders	M	C-F	GSC
Singer	This want of you	L	E-FS	BOH
Swanson	Pierrot	L	B-D	WTR
Taylor	Captain Stratton's fancy	L	CS-F	JFI
Wolfe	Who's gonna mourn for me?	LMH	D-A	ROB

(See also Negro Spirituals and Folk Songs.)

Miscellaneous Songs For Closing Recitals

Bass

Brahms	Feinsliebchen, du sollst nicht barfuss geh'n			†
-----	Meine liebe ist Gruen	MLH	ES-A	†
Cowen	Border ballad	LM	D-E	BOO
Durante	Danza, danza fanciulla gentile	HM	BF-F	†
German	My song is of the sturdy north	ML		CHA
Gretchaninoff	My native land	L	C-EF	GSC
Grieg	Jeg lever et liv i laengsel	L	BF-E	HAN
Head	When I think upon the maidens	LM	D-G	BOO

Hely-Hutchinson	Old Mother Hubbard	HL	B-E	CFI
Keel	Trade winds	HL	BF-EF	BOH
Lara	Granada			
Obradors	El vito			
Quilter	Over the mountains			BOS
Rachmaninoff	Floods of spring	HL		DIT
Schubert	Die Forelle	MLH	EF-GF	†
Sinadinos	The eagle			
Strauss	Staendchen	HM	A-FS	†
Vaughan Williams	The roadside fire	HML	BF-EF	BOO
Warlock	Yarmouth Fair	HL	B-E	CFI
Wilson	When dull care			BOO
Wolf	Er ist's	H	D-G	†

Atmospheric Songs and Arias

Bass

Barber	Rain has fallen	HM	D-E	GSC
Brahms	Steig' auf, geliebter Schatten	HL	BF-EF	†
Burleigh	Sometimes I feel like a motherless child	HML		RIC
Carpenter	Go, lovely rose	M	DF-EF	GSC
-----	Looking glass river	M	B-D	GSC
-----	The day is no more	M	GS-DS	GSC
-----	The green river	M	B-E	GSC
Charles	When I have sung my songs	HM	BF-EF	GSC
Cimara	Fiocca la neve	H	G-G	GSC
Delibes	Lakmé ton doux regards (Lakmé)			HEU
Dougherty	Loveliest of trees	HM	C-E	BOH
Duke	Loveliest of trees	L	C-D	GSC
Dunhill	The cloths of Heaven	LM	EF-G	STB
Elmore and Reed	Come all ye who weary	L	C-C	JFI
Ferrari	Le miroir	M	E-F	GSC
Forsyth	The bell man			DIT
Grieg	A swan			†
Hahn	D'une prison	L	BF-EF	HEU
-----	L'heure exquise	M	DF-F	†
-----	Paysage	MH	EF-G	HEU
Holmès	Au pays	HM	C-F	CFI
Holst	The heart worships	ML	BF-D	STB
Hughes	A Ballynure ballad	L	BF-D	BOH

Kramer	Minnelied	M	C-E	JFI
Lynn	Gently little Jesus	L	BF-BF	DIT
-----	The magic night of Christmas	M	D-D	DIT
Massenet	Chanson de la Touraine (Panurge)	M	EF-EF	HEU
Niles	I wonder as I wander	HL	BF-D	GSC
-----	Jesus, Jesus rest your head	HL	A-D	GSC
Quilter	Now sleeps the crimson petal	LMH	EF-GF	BOO
Robinson	Water boy	M	B-E	BOS
Sanderson	Quiet	ML	AF-EF	BOH
Schubert	Gute Nacht	LH	C-FS	†
Schumann	Im Walde	HL	A-D	†
Strauss	Die Nacht	HL		†
-----	Traum durch die Daemmerung	HML	BF-EF	†
Tyson	Noon and night	LH	F-AF	GSC
Vaughan Williams	Four nights	L	AF-EF	OXF
Wolf	Verborgenheit	HL	B-E	†

American Dramatic Songs

Bass

Barber	I hear an army	LH	D-AF	GSC
Campbell-Tipton	The crying of water	LH	FS-GS	GSC
Carpenter	The green river	M	B-E	GSC
-----	To one unknown	M	A-DS	GSC
Damrosch	Danny Deever	L	A-F	PRE
Duke	Calvary	L	G-F	CFI
-----	Here in this spot with you	M	B-F	GSC
Foster	My journey's end	HLM	DF-G	GSC
Griffes	An old song resung	LM	EF-F	GSC
Huhn	Cato's advice	L	G-C	GSC
-----	Invictus	ML	BF-DF	ASC
Ives	Charlie Rutlage	M		ARR
Mac Gimsey	Land uv degradashun	M	BF-F	CFI
Malotte	Song of the open road			ABC
Mana-Zucca	I love life	LM	F-F	PRE
Rogers	The last song	MLH	E-AF	GSC
Romberg	Stouthearted men (New Moon)	L	C-F	HAR
Schuman	Holiday song	M	C-F	GSC
Singer	This want of you	L	E-FS	BOH

Speaks	Shepherd, see thy horse's foaming mane			FLA
Taylor	Captain Stratton's fancy	L	CS-F	JFI
Wolfe	Who's gonna mourn for me	LMH	D-A	ROB

British Dramatic Songs and Arias

Bass

Arne, T.	Preach not me your musty rules (Comus)	HML		ROW
Cowen	Border ballad	LM	D-E	BOO
Del Riego	Homing	HML	BF-E	CHA
Dix	The trumpeter	HML	A-C	BOH
German	My song is of the sturdy north	ML		CHA
-----	Rolling down to Rio	ML	G-D	NOV
Grainger	Shallow brown	M	F-F	GSC
Handel	But who may abide (The Messiah)	L	G-E	†
-----	Why do the nations (The Messiah)	L	B-E	†
Harrison	I hear an army			CRA
Holst	The Sergeant's song			ASH
Purcell	Arise, ye subterranean winds			GSC
-----	I'll sail upon the dog star	HL	A-E	†
Sanderson	Shipmates of mine	LL	G-D	BOO
Sullivan	The lost chord	HL	C-F	GSC
Templeton	Wi' a hundred pipers	L	BF-EF	GSC

French Dramatic Songs and Arias

Bass

Berlioz	O misère des rois (L'Enfance du Christ)			CST
Bizet	Quand la flamme de l'amour (Le Jolie Fille de Perth)			CHO
Debussy	Colloque sentimental			DUR
Duparc	La vague et la cloche			ROU
-----	Le manoir de Rosamunde	HL	B-F	BOS
-----	Phidylé	MH	EF-AF	BOS
Fauré	Automne	MH	D-FS	GSC
-----	Fleur jetée	HM	BF-FS	†
-----	Prison	LH		†

790

Gounod	Au bruit des lourds marteaux (Philémon et Baucis)	L	AF-EF	†
Hahn	D'une prison	L	BF-EF	HEU
-----	Offrande	M	D-D	†
Holmès	Au pays	HM	C-F	CFI
Hue	J'ai pleuré en rêve	HL	D-E	BOS
Lenormand	Quelle souffrance	HM	AF-F	HAM
Massenet	Les grands mots (Manon)			GSC
Meyerbeer	Nonnes qui reposez (Robert le Diable)			GSC
Saint-Saëns	Danse macabre	L	BF-EF	AXE
-----	Les pas d'armes du Roi Jean	HML	A-F	RIC
Thomas	Le tambour major (Le Caid)			HEU

German Dramatic Songs and Arias

Bass

Beethoven	Ha! welch ein Augenblick (Fidelio)			†
-----	In questa tomba	ML	A-CS	†
Brahms	Am Sonntag Morgen	L	CS-FS	†
-----	Nicht mehr zu dir zu gehen			†
-----	Treue Liebe	LMH	DS-E	†
-----	Verrat	HL	FS-EF	†
-----	Von ewiger Liebe	LMH	B-AF	†
Franz	Im Herbst	HM	A-F	†
Liszt	Die Lorelei	LH	BF-BF	†
Loewe	Der selt'ne Beter			SC
-----	Edward	HL	F-E	†
-----	Odins Meeresritt			SC
Mendelssohn	Is not His word like a fire? (Elijah)	M	B-F	†
-----	It is enough (Elijah)	L	A-E	
Schubert	Am Meer	HML	B-D	†
-----	An Schwager Kronos	HL	G-E	†
-----	Aufenthalt	HLM	A-F	†
-----	Der Atlas	HL	BF-F	†
-----	Der Doppelgaenger	HL	G-D	†
-----	Der Erlkoenig	HML	A-E	†
-----	Der Lindenbaum	HL	A-D	†
-----	Der Schiffer	LH	BF-A	†
-----	Der Zwerg	M	A-GF	PET
-----	Die Allmacht	HML	G-E	GSC
-----	Die Kraehe	HL	A-E	†
-----	Die Stadt	HL	A-E	†

791

(Schubert)	Fahrt zum Hades	HL	G-DF	PET
-----	Gebet waehrend der Schlacht	M	CS-E	†
-----	Gruppe aus dem Tartarus	L	CS-EF	†
-----	Kriegers Ahnung	HL	G-EF	†
-----	Mut	HL		†
-----	Totengraebers Heimweh	HL	G-EF	†
Schumann	Der Soldat			
-----	Fruehlingsfahrt	HL	B-E	†
-----	Ich grolle nicht	HL	BF-D	†
-----	Wer nie sein Brot			†
Strauss	Caecilie	MH	E-B	†
-----	Madrigal	LH	EF-GF	
-----	Ruhe meine Seele			†
-----	Zueignung	HL	CS-FS	†
Wagner	Jerum! jerum! (Die Meistersinger)			†
-----	Leb' wohl, du kuehnes herrliches Kind (Die Walkuere)	L	B-E	†
-----	Pogners Anrede (Die Meistersinger)	L	A-F	†
Wolf	Der Freund	HM	BF-E	PET
-----	Der Rattenfaenger	HL		†
-----	Prometheus			PET
-----	Seemanns Abschiedslied	H	C-A	†
-----	Ueber Nacht	LH	D-G	INT

Italian Dramatic Songs and Arias

Bass

Boito	Son lo spirito (Mefistofele)	L	G-E	RIC
Donizetti	Vieni la mia vendetta (Lucrezia Borgia)			BRO
Durante	Vergin, tutta amor	LM	C-EF	†
Ponchielli	Si, morir ella de' (La Gioconda)			RIC
Respighi	Nebbie			†
Verdi	Ella giammai m'amò (Don Carlos)	L	A-E	RIC
-----	Infelice è tu credevi (Ernani)	L	GF-EF	GSC
-----	O tu Palermo (I Vespri Siciliani)			RIC

Miscellaneous Dramatic Songs

Bass

Cui	Hunger song	LM	E-F	DIT
Gretchaninoff	Over the steppe	LM	C-G	GSC
-----	Wounded birch	HL	B-EF	†
Grieg	A swan			†
-----	Autumnal gale	HL	A-F	CFI
-----	Jeg lever et liv i laengsel	L	BF-E	HAN
Koeneman	When the King went forth to war	ML	A-E	CHE
Korbay	Shepherd, see thy horse's foaming mane	L	B-DS	SC
Malashkin	O could I but express in song	LH		CHE
Mussorgsky	After the battle			GSC
-----	Siege of Kazan (Boris Godunoff)	L	F-E	GSC
-----	The song of the flea	L	AS-G	GSC
Rachmaninoff	Christ is risen	LM	D-F	GAL
-----	Floods of spring	HL		DIT
-----	O thou billowy harvest field	HL	CS-E	GSC
Sibelius	Black roses	M	A-ES	AMP
Tchaikovsky	Pilgrim's song	HLM	B-E	GSC

American Humorous Songs

Bass

Carpenter	Don't ceare	M	C-D	GSC
Diack	Little Jack Horner			CFI
Dougherty	Declaration of independence	L	C-C	GSC
Guion	What shall we do with a drunken sailor	HML	C-D	GSC
Malotte	Blow me eyes	MH	C-G	GSC
Mana-Zucca	The big brown bear	HML	C-F	GSC
Mason	A grain of salt	L	A-D	GSC
-----	I ain't afeared o' the Admiral	L	A-E	GSC
-----	Nautical lays of a landsman	L	A-E	GSC
Romberg	The fireman's bride (Up in Central Park)	M	D-EF	WIL
Schuman	Holiday song	M	C-F	GSC
Taylor	Captain Stratton's fancy	L	CS-F	JFI

British Humorous Songs

Bass

Arne, T.	Why so pale and wan?			GSC
Berners	Dialogue between Tom Filuter and his man	M	D-F	CHE
Boyce	The song of Momus to Mars	M	BF-EF	CFI
Charles, W.	The green eyed dragon	M	BF-E	BOH
Gibbs	Five eyes	HL	D-D	BOS
Head	When I think upon the maidens	LM	D-G	BOO
Hely-Hutchinson	Old mother Hubbard	HL	B-E	CFI
Hughes	A Ballynure ballad	L	BF-D	BOH
Johnston	Because I were shy	L	B-E	CRA
Jones	Love is a babble			STB
Lawes	I am confirmed			BOO
Liddle	The garden where the praties grow	LMH	E-FS	STB
Lohr	The little Irish girl	HLM	C-E	CHA
Sanderson	Captain Mac	ML	G-E	BOO
Torrence	Smilin' Kitty O'Day	ML	CS-D	BOO

German Humorous Songs

Bass

Beethoven	Aus Goethes Faust			
-----	Der Kuss			†
Brahms	Vergebliches Staendchen	LHM	E-FS	†
Mendelssohn	Ich bin ein vielgereister Mann (Heimkehr aus der Fremde)	ML		DIT
Mozart	Solche hergelaufne Laffen (Abduction from Seraglio)			†
-----	Warnung	HM	C-D	
Schubert	Heidenroeslein			
Wolf	Abschied			†
-----	Der Musikant	HL	CS-D	†
-----	Der Soldat 1	LH	E-FS	†
-----	Der Tambour	HL		†

Italian Humorous Songs

Bass

Mozart	La vendetta (Le Nozze di Figaro)			†
-----	Madamina (Don Giovanni)	L	A-E	†
-----	Non più andrai (Le Nozze di Figaro)	L	C-E	†
Pergolesi	Son imbrogliato io già (La Serva Padrona)	L		RIC
Rossini	La calunnia (Il Barbiere di Siviglia)			†
Scarlatti, A.	Chi vuole innamorarsi	HL	D-EF	DIT

Miscellaneous Humorous Songs

Bass

Bizet	Quand la flamme de l'amour (Le Jolie Fille de Perth)			CHO
Gounod	Sérénade de Mephistopheles (Faust)	L	G-G	CHO
Mussorgsky	The seminarian			GSC
-----	The song of the flea	L	AS-G	GSC
Poulenc	Chanson à boire	L	B-E	HEU
-----	La belle jeunesse	L	D-F	HEU

American Folk Songs (Arr.)

Bass

Bacon	Adam and Eve	M	B-D	CFI
-----	The Erie Canal	L	D-C	CFI
Brockway	Barbara Allen			GRA
-----	Sourwood mountain			GRA
Copland	I bought me a cat			
-----	Old American songs			
Davis	He's gone away	M	C-E	GAL
Dougherty	Across the western ocean	M	D-D	GSC
-----	Five sea chanties	L	A-EF	GSC
-----	Mobile bay	M	BF-EF	GSC
-----	Rio Grande	M	EF-EF	GSC
-----	Shenandoah	L	A-D	GSC
Guion	Home on the range	HLM	C-F	GSC

(Guion)	What shall we do with a drunken sailor	HML	C-D	GSC
Niles	Black is the color of my true love's hair			
-----	Down in the valley			GSC
-----	I wonder as I wander	HL	BF-D	GSC
-----	Jesus, Jesus rest your head	HL	A-D	GSC
-----	Oh who's goin' to shoe your pretty little foot			GSC
-----	The rovin' gambler	HL	BF-EF	GSC
Robinson	Water boy	M	B-E	BOS
Siegmeister	Bury me not on the lone prairie			
Wellesley	Sing me a chanty	HLM	B-E	FOX

British Folk Songs (Arr.)

Bass

Bantock	There was a jolly miller			
Britten	The ash grove			BOH
Broadwood	Some rival has stolen my true love	LM	D-E	BOO
Grainger	Shallow Brown	M	F-F	GSC
Harty	The game played in Erin-Go-Bragh			CFI
Hatton	The minstrel boy			BOO
Hopekirk	Annie Laurie			DIT
-----	Loch Lomond			DIT
-----	Ye banks and braes	LM	D-C	DIT
Hughes	A Ballynure ballad	L	BF-D	BOH
-----	Down by the Sally gardens			BOO
-----	The lark in clear air	ML	BF-D	BOO
Johnston	Because I were shy	L	B-E	CRA
Kennedy-Fraser	An Eriskay love lilt			BOO
Lawson	Turn ye to me	M	B-E	GSC
Liddle	The garden where the praties grow	LMH	E-FS	STB
Moss	The floral dance	HML	A-D	CHA
Page	The harp that once through Tara's halls			DIT
Quilter	Over the mountains			BOS
-----	Three poor mariners			BOO
Reid	Turn ye to me			BOO
Taylor	May day carol			JFI
Templeton	Wi' a hundred pipers	L	BF-EF	GSC

Vaughan				
Williams	King William	L	D-D	OXF
-----	Lullaby of the Madonna	L	BF-D	GRA
-----	Rollin in the dew			OXF
Warlock	Yarmouth Fair	HL	B-E	CFI
Welsh	All through the night			
Wilson	Come let's be merry			BOO
-----	When dull care			BOO

Miscellaneous Folk Songs (Arr.)

Bass

Brahms	Da unten in Thale			†
-----	Erlaube mir, fein's Maedchen			†
-----	Feinsliebchen, du sollst nicht barfuss geh'n			†
-----	In stiller Nacht			†
-----	Mein Maedel hat einen Rosenmund	M	F-F	†
Koeneman	The song of the Volga boatmen	L		CHE
Korbay	Marishka, Marishka			SC
-----	Shepherd, see thy horse's foaming mane		B-DS	SC
Liddle	An old French carol	LM	F-F	BOO
Obradors	Con amores a mi madre			RIC
Sinigaglia	Il cacciatore del bosco			
-----	Il maritino			
-----	Novara la bella			
Tiersot	L'amours de moi	M	EF-F	HEU
Weckerlin	Aminte	M	C-D	†
-----	Chanson normande			
-----	L'etoile du matin			
-----	O ma tendre musette	LM	A-E	GSC
-----	Pêche des moules			
-----	Trop aimable Sylvia	M	D-E	GSC

Negro Spirituals

Bass

Boatner	On mah journey	LH	EF-EF	RIC
-----	Trampin' (Tryin' to make Heaven my home)	L	D-F	ELK
Brown	Every time I feel de spirit	L		AMP
-----	Hammer song	L	A-C	AMP

Burleigh	Balm in Gilead	HL		RIC
-----	By and by	HL		RIC
-----	De gospel train	HL		RIC
-----	Deep river	HML		RIC
-----	Go down, Moses	HL		RIC
-----	Hard trials	M		RIC
-----	I stood on de ribber ob Jerdon	HL		RIC
-----	Nobody knows de trouble I've seen	HL		RIC
-----	Oh, Peter, go ring-a-dem bells			RIC
-----	Scandalize my name	M		RIC
-----	Weepin' Mary	HL		RIC
-----	Were you there?	HML		RIC
Collins	Safe by de Lawd			
Dett	Sit down servant			GSC
Johnson	At the feet of Jesus	L		
-----	City called Heaven			ROB
-----	Dere's no hidin' place down dere			
-----	Fix me Jesus	L	BF-DF	GSC
-----	Hold on			ROB
-----	John Henry			CFI
-----	Take my mother home	M	BF-EF	CFI
Kerby-Forrest	He's got the whole world in His hands	M	G-E	MLS
Mac Gimsey	Land uv degradashun	M	BF-F	CFI
Payne	Crucifixion	L	C-C	GSC
Ryder	Let us break bread together	LH	D-G	JFI
Saunders	The Lord's prayer	L	BF-C	BOH
Singer	Go down Moses	M	E-E	CFI

British Songs and Arias Employing Agility

Bass

Aiken	Sigh no more	HML		STB
Arne, T.	Now Phoebus sinketh in the west			GSC
-----	Preach not me your musty rules (Comus)	HML		ROW
German	Rolling down to Rio	ML	G-D	NOV
Handel	Arm, arm ye brave (Judas Maccabaeus)	L	B-E	†
-----	But who may abide (The Messiah)	L	G-E	†

(Handel)	His scepter is the rod of righteousness (Occasional Oratorio)	L	G-E	GSC
-----	Honour and arms (Samson)	L	G-EF	†
-----	How willing my paternal love (Samson)	L	B-E	DIT
-----	O ruddier than the cherry (Acis and Galatea)	L	G-F	DIT
-----	Revenge, Timotheus cries (Alexander's Feast)	L	G-D	†
-----	The trumpet shall sound (The Messiah)	L		†
-----	Thy glorious deeds (Samson)	M	C-F	†
-----	Wher'er you walk (Semele)	HML	C-D	†
-----	Why do the nations (The Messiah)	L	B-E	†
Hely-Hutchinson	Old mother Hubbard	HL	B-E	CFI
Purcell	Arise, ye subterranean winds			GSC
-----	If music be the food of love	M	D-G	BOO
-----	I'll sail upon the dog star	HL	A-E	†
-----	Music for a while (Oedipus)	LH		SC
Wilson	Come let's be merry			BOO

French Songs and Arias Employing Agility

Bass

Berlioz	Sérénade de Mephisto (La Damnation de Faust)			DIT
Chausson	Le colibri	M	F-GF	BOS
Gounod	Au bruit des lourds marteaux (Philémon et Baucis)	L	AF-EF	†
-----	Au rossignol	LMH	D-G	CHO
-----	Sous les pieds d'une femme (La Reine de Saba)			GSC
Meyerbeer	Piff, paff! (Les Huguenots)			BRH
Thomas	Le tambour major (Le Caid)			HEU

German Songs and Arias
Employing Agility

Bass

Bach, J.S.	Aechzen und erbaermlich L Weinen (Cantata 13) Violin or flute		G-EF	PET
-----	Come blessed cross (St. Matthew Passion) Cello			†
-----	Doch weichet, ihr tollen vergeblichen (Cantata 8) Flute			NOV
-----	Endlich, endlich wird mein Joch (Cantata 56) Oboe			RIC
-----	Give, O give me back my Lord (St. Matthew Passion)			†
-----	Gladly will I all resigning (St. Matthew Passion)			†
-----	Gute Nacht, du Weltgetuemmel (Cantata 27) 2 Violins, viola and continuo			
-----	Hier in meines Vaters Staette (Cantata 32) Violin			AUG
-----	Make thee clean my heart from sin (St. Matthew Passion)			†
Brahms	Botschaft	HL	D-F	†
-----	O liebliche Wangen	MLH	E-G	GSC
Handel	Zweier Augen Majestaet (Almira)			MUP
Haydn	Now Heav'n in fullest L glory shone (The Creation)			†
-----	Rolling in foaming billows L (The Creation)		Ċ-F	†
-----	With joy th' impatient L husbandman (The Seasons)		B-E	†
Mendelssohn	Is not His word like a fire M (Elijah)		B-F	†
Mozart	Solche hergelaufne Laffen (Abduction from Seraglio)			†
Schubert	Fruehlingsglaube	M	EF-F	†
-----	Mein!	HL		†
-----	Ungeduld	HML		†
Strauss	Staendchen	HM	A-FS	†
Weber	Hier im Ird'schen Jammertal (Der Freischuetz)			†

Italian Songs and Arias
Employing Agility

Bass

Bellini	Vi ravviso, o luoghi ameni (La Sonnambula)			DIT
Bononcini	L'esperto nocchiero (Astarte)	HL	B-E	†
Caldara	Alma del core			GSC
-----	Selve amiche, ombrose piante	HM	E-E	†
Carissimi	Filli, non t'amo più	HL	B-D	†
-----	Vittoria, mio core	HLM	B-E	†
Cavalli	Beato chi può (Serse)			HEU
Donizetti	Vieni la mia vendetta (Lucrezia Borgia)			BRO
Durante	Danza, danza fanciulla gentile	HM	BF-F	†
Handel	Confusa si miri (Rodelinda)	L	B-D	CFI
-----	Del minnacciar del vento (Ottone)	L		†
-----	Si, tra i ceppi (Berenice)	L	B-D	†
-----	Sei mia gioia (Parthenope)	HL	C-F	CFI
Mozart	Aprite un po quegl' occhi (Le Nozze di Figaro)			†
Pergolesi	Bella mia (Il Maestro di Musica)			GSC
Rossini	A un dottore (Il Barbiere di Siviglia)			GSC
Scarlatti, A.	Già il sole dal Gange	LH	EF-F	GSC
-----	La fortuna			BOS
-----	Rugiadose odorose (Il Pirro e Demetrio)	HL	D-E	DIT
Scarlatti, D.	Consolati e spara amante	L	BF-E	GSC
Verdi	Infelice è tu credevi (Ernani)	L	GF-EF	GSC
-----	O tu Palermo (I Vespri Siciliani)			RIC

American Songs Employing
Crescendo and Diminuendo

Bass

Bacon	A clear midnight			NEM
Barber	Rain has fallen	HM	D-E	GSC

Campbell-Tipton	The crying of water	LH	FS-GS	GSC
Carpenter	Go, lovely rose	M	DF-EF	GSC
-----	Looking glass river	M	B-D	GSC
-----	The day is no more	M	GS-DS	GSC
Duke	Loveliest of trees	L	C-D	GSC
Niles	I wonder as I wander	HL	BF-D	GSC
-----	Jesus, Jesus rest your head	HL	A-D	GSC
Rogers	At parting	LH	CS-FS	GSC
Thompson	Velvet shoes	M	C-E	ECS

German Songs Employing Crescendo and Diminuendo

Bass

Brahms	Maienkaetzchen	L	D-E	†
-----	Sandmaennchen	LH	F-G	†
-----	Sonntag	H	D-G	†
-----	Wie Melodien zieht es	HL	A-E	†
Schubert	Der Juengling an der Quelle	LH	E-A	†
-----	Der Juengling auf dem Huegel	L	G-F	†
-----	Der Wanderer	HML	FS-D	†
-----	Lachen und Weinen	HL	C-EF	†
Schumann	Romanze	HL	C-E	†
Strauss	Die Nacht	HL		†
Wolf	Der Gaertner	HL		†
-----	Nun lass uns Frieden schliessen	HL		†
-----	Nun wandre, Maria	HL	EF-D	†
-----	Wenn du zu den Blumen gehst	HL	B-EF	†

Italian Songs Employing Crescendo and Diminuendo

Bass

Caldara	Alma del core			GSC
-----	Sebben crudele	HML	E-DS	†
-----	Selve amiche, ombrose piante	HM	E-E	†
Carissimi	No, no, non si speri	HL	C-EF	†

Cesti	Intorno all' idol mio (Orontea)	MH	D-F	†
Falconieri	O bellissimi capelli	HL	B-D	†
-----	Vezzosette e care	M	CS-E	GSC
Frescobaldi	Se l'aura spira	HL	C-EF	DIT
Handel	Ombra mai fu (Serse)	HM	BF-EF	†
Marcello	Non m'è grave morir per amore	L	C-E	GSC
Monteverdi	Lasciatemi morire (Arianna)	ML	D-D	†
Mozart	Se vuol ballare (Le Nozze di Figaro)	L		†
Rontani	Se bel rio	ML	D-C	†
Scarlatti, A.	La fortuna			BOS

Miscellaneous Songs Employing
Crescendo and Diminuendo

Bass

Duparc	Chanson triste	MH	FS-AF	†
-----	L'invitation au voyage	HM	E-F	†
-----	Phidylé	MH	EF-AF	BOS
Goosens	Melancholy	M		CHE
Gretchaninoff	My native land	L	C-EF	GSC
Head	The ships of Arcady	ML	BF-EF	BOH
Martini	Plaisir d'amour	M	BF-EF	GSC
Mussorgsky	The banks of the Don			GSC
Nin	Minué cantado			ESC
Quilter	Now sleeps the crimson petal	LMH	EF-GF	BOO
Shaw	Song of the Palanquin bearers	LH	E-F	CUR

American Songs Employing
Piano Singing

Bass

Bacon	A clear midnight			NEM
Barber	Rain has fallen	HM	D-E	GSC
-----	With rue my heart is laden	HL	CS-D	GSC
Burleigh	Jean	HML		PRE
Campbell-Tipton	The crying of water	LH	FS-GS	GSC
Carpenter	Go, lovely rose	M	DF-EF	GSC

(Carpenter)	Looking glass river	M	B-D	GSC
-----	The cock shall crow	M	B-E	GSC
-----	The day is no more	M	GS-DS	GSC
-----	The green river	M	B-E	GSC
Charles	When I have sung my songs	HM	BF-EF	GSC
Farwell	These saw visions			GAL
Kramer	Minnelied	M	C-E	JFI
Manning	In the Luxembourg gardens	HML	BF-D	GSC
Niles	I wonder as I wander	HL	BF-D	GSC
-----	Jesus, Jesus rest your head	HL	A-D	GSC
Thompson	Velvet shoes	M	C-E	ECS

British Songs Employing
Piano Singing

Bass

Coleridge-Taylor	She rested by the broken brook	HL		DIT
Dunhill	The cloths of Heaven	LM	EF-G	STB
Forsyth	The bell man			DIT
Handel	Silent worship (Tolomeo)	LM	D-E	CUR
Head	The ships of Arcady	ML	BF-EF	BOH
Liddle	The garden where the praties grow	LMH	E-FS	STB
Quilter	Now sleeps the crimson petal	LMH	EF-GF	BOO
-----	O mistress mine	HML		BOO
Sanderson	Quiet	ML	AF-EF	BOH

French Songs and Arias Employing
Piano Singing

Bass

Debussy	La mer est plus belle	HL		†
Delibes	Lakmé ton doux regards (Lakmé)			HEU
Fauré	Après un rêve	HM	C-F	†
-----	Dans les ruines d'une abbaye	M	E-FS	†
Ferrari	Le miroir	M	E-F	GSC
Gounod	Au rossignol	LMH	D-G	CHO
Hahn	D'une prison	L	BF-EF	HEU
-----	L'heure exquise	M	DF-F	†

(Hahn)	Offrande	M	D–D	†
-----	Paysage	MH	EF–G	HEU
Lully	Bois épais (Amadis)	ML	C–EF	
Pessard	L'adieu du matin	ML	BF–D	GSC
Poulenc	Invocation aux Parques			HEU
Ravel	Don Quichotte à Dulcinée	HM	A–F	DUR
Thomas	De son coeur j'ai calmé la fièvre (Mignon)	L	A–D	HEU
Weckerlin	Aminte	M	C–D	†
-----	O ma tendre musette	LM	A–E	GSC
-----	Trop aimable Sylvia	M	D–E	GSC
Widor	Je ne veux pas autre chose	HL	C–EF	HAM

German Songs and Arias Employing
Piano Singing

Bass

Beethoven	Ich liebe dich	HL	BF–DF	†
Brahms	Botschaft	HL	D–F	†
-----	Der Gang zur Liebsten	HL		†
-----	In Waldeseinsamkeit	H	ES–G	†
-----	Sandmaennchen	LH	F–G	†
-----	Sapphische Ode	HML		†
-----	Staendchen	HL	BF–E	†
-----	Steig' auf, geliebter Schatten	HL	BF–EF	†
-----	Vergebliches Staendchen	LHM	E–FS	†
Mendelssohn	It is enough (Elijah)	L	A–E	†
-----	Lord God of Abraham (Elijah)	L	B–E	†
Mozart	An Chloe	LH	EF–AF	
Schubert	Ave Maria	LMH	F–F	†
-----	Du bist die Ruh	LMH	EF–AF	†
-----	Im Abendrot	HL	C–D	†
-----	Lachen und Weinen	HL	C–EF	†
-----	Totengraebers Heimweh	HL	G–EF	†
-----	Wohin?	HL	B–E	†
Schumann	Im Walde	HL	A–D	†
Strauss	Die Nacht	HL		†
-----	Freundliche Vision	HL	C–F	BOO
-----	Nachtgang			†
-----	Traum durch die Daemmerung	HML	BF–EF	†
Wolf	An die Geliebte			†
-----	Der Gaertner	HL		†
-----	Verborgenheit	HL	B–E	†

Italian Songs and Arias Employing
Piano Singing

Bass

Bononcini	Deh, più a me non v'ascondete	LH	EF-F	†
Castelnuovo-Tedesco	Ninna Nanna			
Cimara	Fiocca la neve	H	G-G	GSC
Durante	Vergin, tutta amor			
Frescobaldi	Se l'aura spira	HL	C-EF	DIT
Gagliano	Dormi, amore (La Flora)	HL	CS-E	DIT
Monteverdi	Lasciatemi morire (Arianna)	ML	D-D	†
Mozart	Deh vieni alla finestra (Don Giovanni)	L	D-E	†
Rontani	Se bel rio	ML	D-C	†
Secchi	Lungi dal caro bene	HL		DIT

Miscellaneous Songs Employing
Piano Singing

Bass

Cui	Dusk fallen	LH	E-GS	DIT
-----	The statue at Czarskoe-Selo	HM		†
Dvořák	God is my shepherd			AMP
-----	Goin' home			DIT
-----	I will life mine eyes			AMP
-----	Songs my mother taught me	HM	E-E	†
Grieg	A swan			†
-----	In the boat	LM	D-ES	†
-----	Snegl, Snegl	M	B-F	HAN
Mednikoff	The hills of Gruzia	H	DS-A	LAC

American Songs Employing
Rapid Enunciation

Bass

Boatner	Oh! what a beautiful city!	HL	D-E	GSC
Carpenter	Don't ceare	M	C-D	GSC
-----	The cock shall crow	M	B-E	GSC
Dichmont	Ma little banjo	ML	E-CS	GSC

British Songs Employing
Rapid Enunciation

Bass

Berners	Dialogue between Tom Filuter and his man	M	D-F	CHE
Charles, W.	The green eyed dragon	M	BF-E	BOH
Cowen	Border ballad	LM	D-E	BOO
Dowland	Shall I sue?			STB
Fisher	At Tankerton Inn	LM	B-G	BOO
German	Rolling down to Rio	ML	G-D	NOV
Gibbs	Five eyes	HL	D-D	BOS
Head	When I think upon the maidens	LM	D-G	BOO
Lehmann	Myself when young	LL	A-E	GSC
Leveridge	The beggar's song	L	G-D	BOO
Liddle	The garden where the praties grow	LMH	E-FS	STB
Moss	The floral dance	HML	A-D	CHA
Shaw	Song of the Palanquin bearers	LH	E-F	CUR
Sullivan	Ho, Jolly Jenkin (Ivanhoe)	LM	C-F	CHA
Templeton	Wi' a hundred pipers	L	BF-EF	GSC
Vaughan Williams	The water mill	L	C-D	OXF
Warlock	Good ale			AUG

French Songs and Arias Employing
Rapid Enunciation

Bass

Chausson	Le colibri Violin or cello	M	F-GF	BOS
Debussy	Le temps a laissié son manteau			DUR
Fauré	Dans les ruines d'une abbaye	M	E-FS	†
Meyerbeer	Piff, paff. (Les Huguenots)			BRH
Pessard	L'adieu du matin	ML	BF-D	GSC
Poulenc	La belle jeunesse	L	D-F	HEU
Saint-Saëns	Danse macabre	L	BF-EF	AXE
Thomas	Le tambour major (Le Caid)			HEU
Weckerlin	Aminte	M	C-D	†
-----	Trop aimable Sylvia	M	D-E	GSC

807

German Songs and Arias Employing
Rapid Enunciation

Bass

Beethoven	Hat man nicht auch Gold beineben (Fidelio)			†
Brahms	Meine liebe ist Gruen	MLH	ES-A	†
-----	O liebliche Wangen	MLH	E-G	†
-----	Staendchen	HL	BF-E	†
-----	Tambourliedchen			†
-----	Vergebliches Staendchen	LHM	E-FS	†
Mendelssohn	Ich bin ein vielgereister Mann (Heimkehr aus der Fremde)	ML		DIT
-----	O God, have mercy (Saint Paul)	L	B-D	†
Mozart	Solche hergelaufne Laffen (Abduction from Seraglio)			†
-----	Warnung	HM	C-D	
Schubert	Der Schiffer	LH	BF-A	†
-----	Der zuernende Barde			PET
-----	Die Forelle	MLH	EF-GF	†
-----	Die Post	HML	BF-EF	†
-----	Fischerweise	L	C-D	†
-----	Mein!	HL		†
-----	Ungeduld	HML		†
-----	Wohin?	HL	B-E	†
Strauss	Staendchen	HM	A-FS	†

Italian Songs and Arias Employing
Rapid Enunciation

Bass

Boito	Son lo spirito (Mefistofele)	L	G-E	RIC
Carissimi	Vittoria, mio core	HLM	B-E	†
Cavalli	Donzelle fuggite	HL	C-EF	†
Donizetti	Ah, un foco insolito (Don Pasquale)			RIC
-----	Udite, udite o rustici (L'Elisir d'Amore)			BRO
Durante	Danza, danza fanciulla gentile	HM	BF-F	†
Legrenzi	Che fiero costume	HML	C-D	†
Mozart	Aprite un po quegl' occhi (Le Nozze di Figaro)			†

(Mozart)	Finch' han dal vino (Don Giovanni)	L	D-EF	†
-----	Ho capito, Signor (Don Giovanni)			
-----	La vendetta (Le Nozze di Figaro)			†
-----	Madamina (Don Giovanni)	L	A-E	†
-----	Non più andrai (Le Nozze di Figaro)	L	C-E	†
-----	Se vuol ballare (Le Nozze di Figaro)	L		†
Pergolesi	Son imbrogliato io già (La Serva Padrona)	L		RIC
Rossini	A un dottore (Il Barbiere di Siviglia)			GSC
-----	La calunnia (Il Barbiere di Siviglia)			†
Scarlatti, A.	Chi vuole innamorarsi	HL	D-EF	DIT

Miscellaneous Songs Employing
Rapid Enunciation

Bass

Grieg	In the boat	LM	D-ES	†
-----	Nu er aftenen lys og lang	L	C-E	HAN
-----	The way of the world			DIT
Korbay	Shepherd see thy horse's foaming mane			
Mussorgsky	The siege of Kazan (Boris Godunor)			
-----	The seminarian			GSC

American Songs Employing
Sustained Singing

Bass

Andrews	Sea fever	L	A-D	GSC
Bacon	A clear midnight			NEM
Barber	Rain has fallen	HM	D-E	GSC
-----	With rue my heart is laden	HL	CS-D	GSC
Burleigh	Deep river	HML		RIC
-----	Jean	HML		PRE
-----	Sometimes I feel like a motherless child	HML		RIC

(Burleigh)	Were you there?	HML		RIC
Campbell-Tipton	The crying of water	LH	FS-GS	GSC
Carpenter	Go, lovely rose	M	DF-EF	GSC
-----	Looking glass river	M	B-D	GSC
-----	The day is no more	M	GS-DS	GSC
-----	The green river	M	B-E	GSC
-----	To one unknown	M	A-DS	GSC
Charles	When I have sung my songs	HM	BF-EF	GSC
Coombs	Her rose	ML	D-C	GSC
Edwards	By the bend of the river	HML	C-E	GSC
-----	Into the night	HML	C-DF	GSC
Farwell	These saw visions			GAL
Foote	I'm wearing awa'	HL		ASC
Guion	Home on the range	HLM	C-F	GSC
Hawley	Ah, 'tis a dream	L	G-C	JCH
Kramer	Minnelied	M	C-E	JFI
Levitzki	Do you remember?	HML	BF-EF	GSC
Manning	In the Luxembourg gardens	HML	BF-D	GSC
Metcalf	At nightfall	HML	C-DF	ASC
Naginski	The ship starting	M	BF-B	GSC
Robinson	Water boy	M	B-E	BOS
Rogers	At parting	LH	CS-FS	GSC
Skiles	You will know my love			CFI
Speaks	Sylvia	HML	AF-DF	GSC
Tyson	Noon and night	LH	F-AF	GSC

British Songs and Arias Employing Sustained Singing

Bass

Bantock	Silent strings	MH	F-G	BOO
Campion	Follow thy fair			STB
-----	There is a garden in her face			DIT
Clarke	The blind ploughman	HML	C-D	CHA
Coleridge-Taylor	She rested by the broken brook	HL		DIT
Del Riego	Homing	HML	BF-E	CHA
Dunhill	The cloths of Heaven	LM	EF-G	STB
Ford	Since first I saw your face			DIT
Forsyth	The bell man			DIT
Goossens	Melancholy	M		CHE
Handel	But who may abide (The Messiah)	L	G-E	†

(Handel)	Hear me, ye winds and waves (Scipione)	ML	G-EF	BOO
-----	How willing my paternal love (Samson)	L	B-E	DIT
-----	Leave me, loathsome light (Semele)	L		DIT
-----	Shall I in Mamre's fertile plain (Joshua)	L	G-EF	DIT
-----	Silent worship (Tolomeo)	LM	D-E	CUR
-----	Thy glorious deeds (Samson)	M	C-F	NOV
-----	Vouchsafe, O Lord (Dettingen Te Deum)	HM		ELV
-----	Wher'er you walk (Semele)	HML	C-D	†
Head	The ships of Arcady	ML	BF-EF	BOH
Holst	The heart worships	ML	BF-D	STB
Keel	Trade winds	HL	BF-EF	BOH
Mc Gill	Duna	HML	BF-D	BOO
Milford	So sweet love seemed Cello	HL	D-D	GRA
Purcell	If music be the food of love	M	D-G	BOO
-----	Music for a while (Oedipus)	LH		SC
-----	Next winter comes slowly (The Faery Queen)			GSC
Quilter	Now sleeps the crimson petal	LMH	EF-GF	BOO
Sanderson	Quiet	ML	AF-EF	BOH
Stephenson	Love is a sickness	HML	C-D	BOO
Sullivan	The lost chord	HL	C-F	GSC
Vaughan Williams	Four nights	L	AF-EF	OXF
-----	The roadside fire	HML	BF-EF	BOO
Wood	I look into your garden	LMH	F-AF	CHA

French Songs and Arias Employing Sustained Singing

Bass

Berlioz	O misère des rois (L'Enfance du Christ)			CST
Chausson	Le colibri Violin or cello	M	F-GF	BOS
-----	Le temps des lilas	MH	D-GS	†
Debussy	Beau soir	LH	C-FS	†
-----	Colloque sentimental			DUR

811

Delibes	Lakmé ton doux regards (Lakmé)			HEU
Duparc	Chanson triste	MH	FS-AF	†
-----	Lamento	ML	EF-EF	†
-----	L'invitation au voyage	HM	E-F	†
-----	Phidylé	MH	EF-AF	BOS
Fauré	Après un rêve	HM	C-F	†
-----	Automne	MH	D-FS	GSC
-----	Le parfum impérissable	LH	GF-GF	
-----	Les berceaux	LMH	BF-G	†
-----	Nocturne	H	F-A	MAR
-----	Prison	LH		†
-----	Rencontre	H	EF-AF	†
Ferrari	Le miroir	M	E-F	GSC
Gounod	Au rossignol	LMH	D-G	CHO
-----	Que les songes heureux			GSC
-----	Sous les pieds d'une femme (La Reine de Saba)			GSC
Hahn	D'une prison	L	BF-EF	HEU
-----	L'heure exquise	M	DF-F	†
-----	Paysage	MH	EF-G	HEU
Halévy	Si la rigeur (La Juive)			†
-----	Vous qui du Dieu vivant (La Juive)			
Honegger	Chanson (Ronsard) Flute and string quartet			SEN
Hue	J'ai pleuré en rêve	HL	D-E	BOS
Indy	Madrigal			DIT
Lenormand	Quelle souffrance	HM	AF-F	HAM
Lully	Bois épais (Amadis)	ML	C-EF	†
Martini	Plaisir d'amour	M	BF-EF	GSC
Massenet	Elégie	LM	C-GF	GSC
-----	Les grands mots (Manon)			GSC
Poulenc	Chanson à boire	L	B-E	HEU
Ravel	Ronsard à son âme	L	CS-E	DUR
Severac	Les hiboux			ROU
Thomas	De son coeur j'ai calmé la fièvre (Mignon)	L	A-D	HEU
Tiersot	L'amours de moi	M	EF-F	HEU
Weckerlin	O ma tendre musette	LM	A-E	GSC
Widor	Je ne veux pas autre chose	HL	C-EF	HAM

Bass

Bach, J.S.	Aechzen und erbaermlich Weinen (Cantata 13) Violin or flute	L	G-EF	PET
-----	Consider, O my soul (St. John Passion)			†
-----	Come blessed cross (St. Matthew Passion) Cello			†
-----	Gute Nacht, du Weltgetuemmel (Cantata 27) 2 Violins, viola and continuo			
-----	Hier in meines Vaters Staette (Cantata 32) Violin			AUG
-----	Ich will den Kreuzstab (Cantata 56)			BRO
-----	Make thee clear my heart from sin (St. Matthew Passion)			†
Beethoven	Adelaide	HML	BF-E	†
-----	An die ferne Geliebte	HL	C-E	†
-----	Die Ehre Gottes	HL	AF-EF	†
-----	Ich liebe dich	HL	BF-DF	†
-----	In questa tomba	ML	A-CS	†
-----	Vom Tode	L	A-EF	GSC
-----	Wonne der Wehmut			†
Brahms	An die Nachtigall	H	DS-G	†
-----	Auf dem Kirchhofe	HL	BF-EF	CFI
-----	Dein blaues Auge	MH	BF-G	†
-----	Der Ueberlaeufer			†
-----	Die Mainacht	HL	BF-FF	†
-----	Erinnerung	H	E-G	†
-----	Feldeinsamkeit	HL	C-EF	†
-----	In Waldeseinsamkeit	H	ES-G	†
-----	Minnelied	MHL	C-EF	†
-----	Mit vierzig Jahren	HL	FS-D	†
-----	Nachtigall	MHL	BF-FS	†
-----	O kuehler Wald	MH	A-F	†
-----	O wuesst' ich doch den Weg zurueck	H	E-FS	†
-----	Ruhe, Suessliebchen	HL	BS-E	†
-----	Sapphische Ode	HML		†
-----	Steig' auf, geliebter Schatten	HL	BF-EF	†
-----	Treue Liebe	LMH	DS-E	†
-----	Wie bist du meine Koenigin	HL	C-E	†

(Brahms)	Wie Melodien zieht es	HL	A-E	†
-----	Wir wandelten	LH	EF-GF	†
Franz	Dedication	HML	BF-C	†
-----	Es ragt ins Meer der Runenstein	HL	G-F	†
-----	For music	ML	C-D	†
-----	Im Herbst	HM	A-F	†
-----	Mutter, o sing mich zur Ruh	HL	E-G	GSC
Haydn	Now Heav'n in fullest glory shone (The Creation)	L		†
Loewe	Der heilige Franziskus	L	A-E	SC
Mendelssohn	It is enough (Elijah)	L	A-E	†
-----	Lord God of Abraham (Elijah)	L	B-E	†
-----	O God, have mercy (Saint Paul)	L	B-D	†
Mozart	In diesen heiligen Hallen (Die Zauberfloete)	L	FS-C	†
-----	O Isis und Osiris (Die Zauberfloete)			†
-----	Wer ein Liebchen hat gefunden (Abduction from Seraglio)			†
Schubert	Am Bach im Fruehling			PET
-----	Am Meer	HML	B-D	†
-----	An die Leier	LM	BF-F	†
-----	Ave Maria	LMH	F-F	†
-----	Das Wirtshaus	HL	C-D	†
-----	Der Doppelgaenger	HL	G-D	†
-----	Der Juengling an der Quelle	LH	E-A	†
-----	Der Juengling auf dem Huegel	L	G-F	†
-----	Der Leiermann	ML	C-D	†
-----	Der Lindenbaum	HL	A-D	†
-----	Der Wanderer	HML	FS-D	†
-----	Der Wegweiser	L	D-EF	†
-----	Die Allmacht	HML	G-E	GSC
-----	Die Kraehe	HL	A-E	†
-----	Die Stadt	HL	A-E	†
-----	Du bist die Ruh	LMH	EF-AF	†
-----	Fruehlingsglaube	M	EF-F	†
-----	Gute Nacht	LH	C-FS	†
-----	Im Abendrot	HL	C-D	†
-----	Sei mir gegruesst	LH	G-G	†
-----	Staendchen	MH	B-E	†
Schuetz	Aus dem 119th Psalm			
Schumann	An den Sonnenschein	HL	A-D	†
-----	Die Lotusblume	HLM	BF-F	†

814

(Schumann)	Du bist wie eine Blume	HM	F-EF	†
-----	Ich grolle nich	HL	BF-D	†
-----	Im Rhein, im heiligen Strome	HM	D-F	
-----	Romanze	HL	C-E	†
-----	Wenn ich in deine Augen seh'	HL	EF-FF	†
-----	Wer nie sein Brot			†
Strauss	Breit ueber mein Haupt	LH	GF-AF	HSC
-----	Der Einsame			†
-----	Die Nacht	HL		†
-----	Freundliche Vision	HL	C-F	†
-----	Heimliche Aufforderung	HL	B-E	†
-----	Im Spaetboot			
-----	Madrigal	LH	EF-GF	
-----	Mit deinen blauen Augen	LH	C-GS	DIT
-----	Morgen	HML	E-F	†
-----	Nachtgang			†
-----	Ruhe meine Seele			†
-----	Traum durch die Daemmerung	HML	BF-EF	†
Wagner	Auf wolkigen Hoeh'n (Siegfried)			†
-----	Gebet des Amfortas (Parsifal)			GSC
-----	Koenigs Gebet (Lohengrin)	M	F-EF	GSC
-----	Leb' wohl du kuehnes, herrliches Kind (Die Walkuere)	L	B-E	†
-----	Moegst du, mein Kind (Der Fliegende Hollaender)			†
-----	Pogners Anrede (Die Meistersinger)	L	A-F	†
Wolf	Alles endet, was entstehet	HL	F-C	†
-----	Anakreons Grab	HL	D-D	†
-----	An die Geliebte			†
-----	Biterolf	HL	D-F	†
-----	Fuehlt meine Seele	L	A-D	†
-----	Gebet	HL		†
-----	Gesang Weylas	HL	DF-F	†
-----	Gesegnet sei, durch den die Welt	HL		†
-----	Heb' auf dein blondes Haupt	HL	G-DF	†
-----	Herr, was traegt der Boden	HL	B-DS	INT
-----	In der Fruehe	HL	C-C	†
-----	Michelangelo Lieder			†
-----	Nun lass uns Frieden schliessen	HL		†

(Wolf)	Nun wandre, Maria	HL	EF-D	†
-----	Um Mitternacht	HL	G-EF	†
-----	Verborgenheit	HL	B-E	†
-----	Wenn du zu den Blumen gehst	HL	B-EF	†
-----	Wohl denk' ich oft	M	C-EF	†
Wolff	Ewig			

Italian Songs and Arias Employing Sustained Singing

Bass

Bellini	Vi ravviso, o luoghi ameni (La Sonnambula)			DIT
Caccini	Amarilli, mia bella	ML	C-D	†
Caldara	Alma del core			GSC
-----	Come raggio di sol	HL	D-F	†
Carissimi	No, no, non si speri!	HL	C-EF	†
Castelnuovo-Tedesco	Ninna Nanna			
Cavalli	Beato chi può (Serse)			HEU
Cesti	Che angoscia, che affanno (Il Pomo d'Oro)	HL	C-DF	DIT
-----	Intorno all'idol mio (Orontea)	MH	D-F	†
Cimara	Fiocca la neve	H	G-G	GSC
Diaz	O splendore infinito (Benvenuto)	L	A-F	GRU
Donizetti	Udite, udite o rustici (L'Elisir d'Amore)			BRO
-----	Vieni la mia vendetta (Lucrezia Borgia)			BRO
Durante	Vergin, tutta amor	LM	C-EF	†
Gagliano	Dormi, amore (La Flora)	HL	CS-E	DIT
Handel	Ombra mai fu (Serse)	HM	BF-EF	†
Mattei	Non è ver	HML		DIT
Monteverdi	Ahi, troppo è duro (Il Balletto delle Ingrate)	HL	C-EF	DIT
-----	Lasciatemi morire (Arianna)	ML	D-D	†
Mozart	Deh vieni alla finestra (Don Giovanni)	L	D-E	†
Paisiello	Nel cor più non mi sento	HL	C-EF	†
Pergolesi	Bella mia (Il Maestro di Musica)			GSC
-----	Nina	HL	CS-D	DIT
Peri	Invocazione di Orfeo (Euridice)	HL	E-CS	DIT

Ponchielli	Si, morir ella de' (La Gioconda)			RIC
Respighi	Nebbie			†
Rosa	Star vicino	HL	D-E	†
Stradella	Per pietà (Il Floridoro)	HM	D-F	DIT
-----	Pietà, Signore	HM	C-F	GSC
Torelli	Tu lo sai	HL	BF-F	†
Tosti	The last song	HL		RIC
Verdi	Ella giammai m'amò (Don Carlos)	L	A-E	RIC
-----	Il lacerato spirito (Simon Boccanegra)	L	FS-D	GSC
-----	Infelice è tu credevi (Ernani)	L	GF-EF	GSC
-----	O tu Palermo (I Vespri Siciliani)			RIC
-----	Tu sul labbro de' veggenti (Nabucco)			RIC

Miscellaneous Songs Employing Sustained Singing

Bass

Dvořák	God is my shepherd			AMP
-----	Hear my prayer, O Lord			AMP
-----	I will life mine eyes			AMP
-----	Lord thou art my refuge and shield			AMP
-----	Songs my mother taught me	HM	E-E	†
-----	Turn Thee to me			AMP
Gretchaninoff	Over the steppe	LM	C-G	GSC
-----	Wounded birch	HL	B-EF	†
Grieg	A swan			†
-----	I love thee	HML	E-F	†
-----	The old mother	ML	D-D	DIT
-----	Two brown eyes	LM	EF-F	GSC
Malashkin	O could I but express in song	LH		CHE
Mussorgsky	Sphinx			BRH
-----	The grave			BRH
Rachmaninoff	Christ is risen	LM	D-F	GAL
-----	O thou billowy harvest field	HL	CS-E	GSC
Sibelius	Black roses	M	A-ES	AMP
Tchaikovsky	Don Juan's serenade	HLM	B-E	GSC
-----	Pilgrim's song	HLM	B-E	GSC

American Songs Employing
Spirited Singing

Bass

Bacon	The Erie canal	L	D-C	CFI
Barber	I hear an army	LH	D-AF	GSC
Boyd	Cape Horn gospel	L	BF-D	GAL
Carpenter	Dansons la gigue	M	B-E	GSC
-----	Don't ceare	M	C-D	GSC
-----	The cock shall crow	M	B-E	GSC
Damrosch	Danny Deever	L	A-F	PRE
Griffes	An old song resung	LM	EF-F	GSC
Guion	What shall we do with a drunken sailor	HML	C-D	GSC
Huhn	Cato's advice	L	G-C	GSC
Kountz	The sleigh	HL	D-FS	GSC
Mana-Zucca	I love life	LM	F-F	PRE
Margetson	Tommy, lad	HML	A-D	BOH
Mason	A sea dirge			WIT
Niles	The rovin' gambler	HL	BF-EF	GSC
Rogers	The last song	MLH	E-AF	GSC
Schuman	Holiday song	M	C-F	GSC
Speaks	On the road to Mandalay	HL	BF-F	PRE
-----	Shepherd, see thy horse's foaming mane			FLA
Taylor	Captain Stratton's fancy	L	CS-F	JFI
Wolfe	Short'nin' bread	LHM	D-D	FLA

British Songs and Arias Employing
Spirited Singing

Bass

Arne, T.	By the gaily circling glass	L		DIT
-----	Now Phoebus sinketh in the west			GSC
-----	Preach not me your musty rules (Comus)	HML		ROW
-----	Why so pale and wan?			GSC
Charles, W.	The green eyed dragon	M	BF-E	BOH
Cowen	Border ballad	LM	D-E	BOO
Dowland	Shall I sue			STB
German	My song is of the sturdy north	ML		CHA
-----	Rolling down to Rio	ML	G-D	NOV
Gibbs	Five eyes	HL	D-D	BOS

818

Handel	Arm, arm ye brave (Judas Maccabaeus)	L	B-E	†
-----	His scepter is the rod of righteousness (Occasional Oratorio)	L	G-E	GSC
-----	Honour and arms (Samson)	L	G-EF	†
-----	O ruddier than the cherry (Acis and Galatea)	L	G-F	DIT
-----	Revenge, Timotheus (Alexander's Feast)	L	G-D	†
-----	Thy glorious deeds (Samson)	M	C-F	†
Harrison	I hear an army			CRA
Head	When I think upon the maidens	LM	D-G	BOO
Holst	The sergeant's song			ASH
Hopekirk	Ye banks and braes	LM	D-C	DIT
Johnston	Because I were shy	L	B-E	CRA
Jones	Love is a babble			STB
Keel	Trade winds	HL	BF-EF	BOH
Lawes	I am confirmed			BOO
Leveridge	The beggar's song	L	G-D	BOO
Liddle	The garden where the praties grow	LMH	E-FS	STB
Martin	Come to the fair	HML	D-D	BOO
Moss	The floral dance	HML	A-D	CHA
Purcell	Arise, ye subterranean winds			GSC
-----	I'll sail upon the dog star	HL	A-E	†
Quilter	It was a lover and his lass	HL	CS-E	BOO
-----	O mistress mine	HML		BOO
Sanderson	Captain Mac	ML	G-E	BOO
Shaw	Song of the Palanquin bearers	LH	E-F	CUR
Sullivan	Ho, Jolly Jenkin (Ivanhoe)	LM	C-F	CHA
Toye	The inn	L	C-E	CUR
Vaughan Williams	The roadside fire	HML	BF-EF	BOO
Warlock	Good ale			AUG

French Songs and Arias Employing
Spirited Singing

Bass

Berlioz	Chanson de la puce (La Damnation de Faust)			CST
-----	Sérénade de Mephisto (La Damnation de Faust)			DIT

Bruneau	L'heureux vagabond	LH	EF–G	GSC
Debussy	La mer est plus belle	HL		†
-----	Le faune			DUR
-----	Le temps a laissié son manteau			DUR
Duparc	Le manoir de Rosamunde	HL	B–F	BOS
Fauré	Fleur jetée	HM	BF–FS	†
Gluck	C'est en vain que l'enfer compte (Alceste)			†
Gounod	Au bruit des lourds marteaux (Philémon et Baucis)	L	AF–EF	†
-----	Au printemps	LMH	DF–AF	GSC
-----	Le veau d'or (Faust)	L	C–EF	†
Hahn	The gay vagabond			
Lully	Il faut passer (Alceste)			LEM
Massenet	Chanson de la Touraine (Panurge)	M	EF–EF	HEU
Meyerbeer	Piff, paff! (Les Huguenots)			BRH
Poulenc	La belle jeunesse	L	D–F	HEU
Saint-Saëns	Danse macabre	L	BF–EF	AXE
-----	Les pas d'armes du roi Jean	HML	A–F	RIC
Thomas	Le tambour major (Le Caid)			HEU

German Songs and Arias Employing Spirited Singing

Bass

Bach, J.S.	Doch weichet, ihr tollen vergeblichen (Cantata 8) Flute			NOV
-----	Endlich, endlich wird mein Joch (Cantata 56) Oboe			RIC
Beethoven	An die Geliebte	M	E–E	†
-----	Aus Goethes Faust			
-----	Der Kuss			†
-----	Ha! welch ein Augenblick (Fidelio)			†
-----	Hat man nicht auch Gold beineben (Fidelio)			†
Brahms	Botschaft	HL	D–F	†
-----	Der Gang zur Liebsten	HL		†
-----	Meine Liebe ist gruen	MLH	ES–A	†
-----	O liebliche Wangen	MLH	E–G	†
-----	Tambourliedchen			†
-----	Vergebliches Staendchen	LHM	E–FS	†
Haydn	Rolling in foaming billows (The Creation)	L	C–F	†

(Haydn)	With joy th' impatient husbandman (The Seasons)	L	B-E	†
Mendelssohn	Ich bin ein vielgereister Mann (Heimkehr aus der Fremde)	ML		DIT
-----	Is not His word like a fire? (Elijah)	M	B-F	GSC
Mozart	An Chloe	LH	EF-AF	
-----	Solche hergelaufne Laffen (Abduction from Seraglio)			†
Nicolai	Als Bueblein klein (Die Lustigen Weiber)			GSC
Schubert	Aufenthalt	HLM	A-F	†
-----	Der Schiffer	LH	BF-A	†
-----	Der zuernende Barde			PET
-----	Die Forelle	MLH	EF-GF	†
-----	Die Post	HML	BF-EF	†
-----	Fischerweise	L	C-D	†
-----	Heidenroeslein			
-----	Lachen und Weinen	HL	C-EF	†
-----	Mein!	HL		†
-----	Mut	HL		†
-----	Rastlose Liebe	M	B-F	†
-----	Wohin?	HL	B-E	†
Schumann	Im Walde	HL	A-D	†
-----	Wanderlied	HL	A-E	†
-----	Widmung	HL	BF-F	†
Strauss	Caecilie	MH	E-B	†
-----	Heimliche Aufforderung	HL	B-E	†
-----	Staendchen	HM	A-FS	†
-----	Wie sollten wir geheim sie halten	LH	D-A	
-----	Zueignung	HL	CS-FS	†
Wagner	Jerum! jerum! (Die Meistersinger)			GSC
-----	Moegst du, mein Kind (Der Fliegende Hollaender)			†
Weber	Hier im Ird' shen Jammertal (Der Freischuetz)			†
Wolf	Auf einer Wanderung	HL		†
-----	Der Rattenfaenger	HL		†
-----	Der Soldat 1	LH	E-FS	†
-----	Er ist's	H	D-G	†
-----	Fussreise	HL	D-E	†
-----	Seemanns Abschiedslied	H	C-A	†
-----	Trunken muessen wir alle sein	M	ES-FS	†

Italian Songs and Arias Employing
Spirited Singing

Bass

Bononcini	L'esperto nocchiero (Astarte)	HL	B-E	†
Caldara	Sebben crudele	HML	E-DS	†
Carissimi	Filli, non t'amo più	HL	B-D	†
-----	Vittoria, mio core!	HLM	B-E	†
Cavalli	Donzelle fuggite	HL	C-EF	†
Donizetti	Ah, un foco insolito (Don Pasquale)			RIC
-----	Udite, udite o rustici (L'Elisir d'Amore)			BRO
-----	Vieni la mia vendetta (Lucrezia Borgia)			BRO
Durante	Danza, danza fanciulla gentile	HM	BF-F	†
Falconieri	Vezzosette e care	M	CS-E	GSC
Handel	Confusa si miri (Rodelinda)	L	B-D	CFI
-----	Del minnacciar del vento (Ottone)	L		†
-----	Si, tra i ceppi (Berenice)	L	B-D	†
Legrenzi	Che fiero costume	HML	C-D	†
Mozart	Aprite un po quegl' occhi (Le Nozze di Figaro)			†
-----	Finch' han dal vino (Don Giovanni)	L	D-EF	†
-----	La Vendetta (Le Nozze di Figaro)			†
-----	Madamina (Don Giovanni)	L	A-E	GSC
-----	Non più andrai (Le Nozze di Figaro)	L	C-E	†
-----	Se vuol ballare (Le Nozze di Figaro)	L		†
Pergolesi	Son imbrogliato io già (La Serva Padrona)	L		RIC
Ponchielli	Si, morir ella de' (La Gioconda)			RIC
Rossini	A un dottore (Il Barbiere di Siviglia)			GSC
Scarlatti, A.	Chi vuole innamorarsi	HL	D-EF	DIT
-----	Già il sole dal Gange	LH	EF-F	GSC
Scarlatti, D.	Consolati e spara amante	L	BF-E	GSC
Tosti	The last song	HL		RIC

822

Miscellaneous Songs Employing
Spirited Singing

Bass

Alnaes	Nu brister i all de klofter	L	A-F	HAN
Dvořák	I will sing new songs of gladness	HL		†
-----	Sing ye a joyful song			AMP
Grieg	Hunter's song	L	DS-E	GSC
-----	Jeg lever et liv i laengsel	L	BF-E	HAN
Koeneman	When the King went forth to war	ML	A-E	CHE
Mussorgsky	Siege of Kazan (Boris Godunoff)	L	F-E	GSC
Rachmaninoff	Floods of spring	HL		DIT
Tchaikovsky	At the ball	MH		GSC
-----	Don Juan's serenade	HLM	B-E	GSC

American and British Songs
of Popular Appeal

Bass

Andrews	Sea fever	L	A-D	GSC
Arden and Wille	Roses in your hair	ML	C-EF	ROW
Brown	Your song from paradise	LMH	D-G	BOO
Burleigh	Jean	HML		PRE
Cadman	The builder	HML	B-D	FLA
Charles, E.	When I have sung my songs	HM	BF-EF	GSC
Charles, W.	The green eyed dragon	M	BF-E	BOH
Clarke	The blind ploughman	HML	C-D	CHA
Cowen	Border ballad	LM	D-E	BOO
Damrosch	Danny Deever	L	A-F	PRE
Del Riego	Homing	HML	BF-E	CHA
D'Hardelot	Because	MH	E-G	CHA
Diack	Little Jack Horner			CFI
Dichmont	Ma little banjo	ML	E-CS	GSC
Dix	The trumpeter	HML	A-C	BOH
Dougherty	Everyone sang			
Edwards	By the bend of the river	HML	C-E	GSC
-----	Into the night	HML	C-DF	GSC
Elvey	Great and fair is she			
Fisher	At Tankerton Inn	LM	B-G	BOO

823

(Fisher)	Tavern song			BOO
Forsyth	The bell man			DIT
Foster	My journey's end	HLM	DF-G	GSC
Fox	The hills of home	HML	BF-DF	CFI
German	Rolling down to Rio	ML	G-D	NOV
Guion	Home on the range	HLM	C-F	GSC
-----	What shall we do with a drunken sailor	HML	C-D	GSC
Head	When I think upon the maidens	LM	D-G	BOO
Hely-Hutchinson	Old mother Hubbard	HL	B-E	CFI
Huhn	Invictus	ML	BF-DF	ASC
Ireland	Sea fever	HLM	D-F	AUG
Johnston	Because I were shy	L	B-E	CRA
Kountz	Prayer of the Norwegian child	ML	C-C	GSC
-----	The sleigh	HL	D-FS	GSC
La Forge	To a messenger	HLM	CF-G	GSC
Lehmann	Myself when young	LL	A-E	GSC
Levitzki	Do you remember?	HML	BF-EF	GSC
Lohr	The little Irish girl	HLM	C-E	CHA
Mac Gimsey	Down to de river	M	B-G	CFI
-----	Jeri Jericho	M	C-G	CFI
-----	Land uv degradashun	M	BF-F	CFI
-----	Thunderin' wonderin'	L	C-D	CFI
-----	To my mother	HML	C-C	CFI
-----	Trouble	ML	C-D	CFI
-----	Twilight meditation			MCG
Malotte	Blow me eyes	MH	C-G	GSC
-----	For my mother	HLM	BF-EF	GSC
-----	Song of the open road			ABC
Mana-Zucca	I love life	LM	F-F	PRE
-----	The big brown bear	HML	C-F	GSC
Manning	In the Luxembourg gardens	HML	BF-D	GSC
Margetson	Tommy, lad	HML	A-D	BOH
Martin	Come to the fair	HML	D-D	BOO
Mason	A grain of salt	L	A-D	GSC
-----	I ain't a'feared o' the Admiral	L	A-E	GSC
Mc Gill	Duna	HML	BF-D	BOO
Rogers	At parting	LH	CS-FS	GSC
Sanderson	Captain Mac	ML	G-E	BOO
-----	Shipmates of mine	LL	G-D	BOO
-----	Until	LMH	E-A	BOO
Schuman	Holiday song	M	C-F	GSC
Shields	The friar of orders gray			
Skiles	You will know my love			CFI

Speaks	Fuzzy wuzzy			JCH
-----	On the road to Mandalay	HL	BF-F	PRE
-----	Sylvia	HML	AF-DF	GSC
Spross	Gunga Din			JCH
Squire	Three for Jack			CHA
Stickles	The open road			DIT
Stothart	The song of the shirt	L	A-E	ROB
Strelezki	Dreams	LMH	B-A	GSC
Sullivan	The lost chord	HL	C-F	GSC
Tours	Mother o' mine	HML	C-D	CHA
Tyson	Moon and night	LH	F-AF	GSC
Wellesley	Sing me a chanty	HLM	B-E	FOX
Wolfe	Who's gonna mourn for me	LMH	D-A	ROB
Wood	I look into your garden	LMH	F-AF	CHA

(See also Humorous Songs, Negro Spirituals,
Folk Songs, Operetta Songs and Opera Arias.)

Miscellaneous Songs of
Popular Appeal

Bass

Cavalli	Donzelle, fuggite	HL	C-EF	†
D' Esposito	Anima e core			
Dvořák	Songs my mother taught me	HM	E-E	†
Flégier	Le cor	ML	D-D	GSC
Franz	Dedication	HML	BF-C	†
Gounod	Au printemps	LMH	DF-AF	GSC
Grieg	I love thee	HML	E-F	†
Lara	Granada			
Massenet	Elégie	LM	C-GF	GSC
Mattei	Non è ver	HML		DIT
Saint-Saëns	Danse macabre	L	BF-EF	AXE
Schubert	Ave Maria	LMH	F-F	†
-----	Staendchen			
Schumann	Widmung	HL	BF-F	†
Sibella	La Girometta	HML	D-E	GSC
Strauss	Staendchen	HM	A-FS	†
-----	Zueignung	HL	CS-FS	†
Tagliaferri	Nun me sceta			
Tchaikovsky	Pilgrim's song	HLM	B-E	GSC
Tosti	The last song	HL		RIC

Arias From British Operas

Bass

Arne, T.	Preach not me your musty rules (Comus)	HML		ROW
Handel	Hear me, ye winds and waves (Scipione)	ML	G-EF	BOO
-----	Leave me, loathsome light (Semele)	L		DIT
-----	Silent worship (Tolomeo)	LM	D-E	CUR
Purcell	Music for a while (Oedipus)	LH		SC
-----	Next winter comes slowly (The Faery Queen)			GSC
-----	Ye twice hundred deities			
Sullivan	Ho, Jolly Jenkin (Ivanhoe)	LM	C-F	CHA

Arias From French Operas

Bass

Berlioz	Chanson de la puce (La Damnation de Faust)			CST
-----	Sérénade de Mephisto (La Damnation de Faust)			DIT
Debussy	Récit d'Arkel (Pelléas et Melisande)			DUR
Delibes	Lakmé, ton doux regards (Lakmé)			HEU
Gluck	C'est en vain que l'enfer compte (Alceste)			†
Gounod	Au bruit des lourds marteaux (Philémon et Baucis)	L	AF-EF	†
-----	Le veau d'or (Faust)	L	C-EF	†
-----	Que l'hymne nuptial (Roméo et Juliette)			CHO
-----	Sérénade de Mephistopheles (Faust)	L	G-G	CHO
-----	Sous les pieds d'une femme (La Reine de Saba)			GSC
Halévy	Si la rigueur (La Juive)			†
-----	Vous qui du Dieu vivant (La Juive)			
Lully	Bois épais (Amadis)	ML	C-EF	†
-----	Il faut passer (Alceste)			LEM
Massenet	Chanson de la Touraine (Panurge)	M	EF-EF	HEU
-----	Les grands mots (Manon)			GSC

Meyerbeer	Nonnes qui reposez (Robert le Diable)			GSC
-----	O jours heureux (L'Etoile du Nord)			BRO
-----	Piff! paff! (Les Huguenots)			BRH
Offenbach	J'ai des yeux (Tales of Hoffman)			GSC
Paladilhe	Pauvre martyr obscur (Patrie)			
Rameau	Invocation et hymne au soleil (Les Indes Galantes)			LEM
Thomas	De son coeur j'ai calmé la fièvre (Mignon)	L	A-D	HEU
-----	Fugitif et tremblant (Mignon)			HEU
-----	Le tambour major (Le Caid)			HEU

Arias From German Operas

Bass

Beethoven	Ha! welch ein Augenblick (Fidelio)			†
-----	Hat man nicht auch Gold beineben (Fidelio)			†
Handel	Zweier Augen Majestaet (Almira)			MUP
Lortzing	Auch ich war ein Juengling (Der Waffenschmied)	L	A-D	CFI
Mendelssohn	Ich bin ein vielgereister Mann (Heimkehr aus der Fremde)	ML		DIT
Mozart	In diesen heiligen Hallen (Die Zauberfloete)	L	FS-C	†
-----	O Isis und Osiris (Die Zauberfloete)			†
-----	Solche hergelaufne Laffen (Abduction from Seraglio)			†
-----	Wer ein Liebchen hat gefunden (Abduction from Seraglio)			†
Nicolai	Als Bueblein klein (Die lustigen Weiber)			GSC
Strauss	Waltz scene (Der Rosenkavalier)			BOO
Wagner	Auf wolkigen Hoeh'n (Siegfried)			†
-----	Gebet des Amfortas (Parsifal)			GSC
-----	Jerum! Jerum! (Die Meistersinger)			†
-----	Koenigs Gebet (Lohengrin)	M	F-EF	GSC

(Wagner)	Leb' wohl, du kuehnes herrliches Kind (Die Walkuere)	L	B-E	†
-----	Moegst du, mein Kind (Der Fliegende Hollaender)			†
-----	Pogners Anrede (Die Meistersinger)	L	A-F	†
-----	Wahn! wahn! ueberall wahn! (Die Meistersinger)	L	A-E	†
-----	Was duftet doch der Flieder (Die Meistersinger)			
Weber	Hier im Ird'schen Jammertal (Der Freischuetz)			†

Arias From Italian Operas

Bass

Bellini	Tu non sai (La Sonnambula)			RIC
-----	Vi ravviso, o luoghi ameni (La Sonnambula)			DIT
Boito	Prologue (Ave Signor) (Mefistofele)			RIC
-----	Son lo spirito (Mefistofele)	L	G-E	RIC
Diaz	O splendore infinito (Benvenuto)	L	A-F	GRU
Donizetti	Ah, un foco insolito (Don Pasquale)			RIC
-----	Udite, udite o rustici (L'Elisir d'Amore)			BRO
-----	Vieni la mia vendetta (Lucrezia Borgia)			BRO
Monteverdi	Ahi, troppo è duro (Il Balletto delle Ingrate)	HL	C-EF	DIT
-----	Lasciatemi morire (Arianna)	ML	D-D	†
-----	Oblivian soave (L'Incoronazione di Poppea)			HEU
Mozart	Aprite un po quegl' occhi (Le Nozze di Figaro)			†
-----	Deh vieni alla finestra (Don Giovanni)	L	D-E	†
-----	Finch' han dal vino (Don Giovanni)	L	D-EF	†
-----	Ho capito, Signor (Don Giovanni)			
-----	La vendetta (Le Nozze di Figaro)			†
-----	Madamina (Don Giovanni)	L	A-E	†

(Mozart)	Non più andrai (Le Nozze di Figaro)	L	C-E	†
-----	Se vuol ballare (Le Nozze di Figaro)	L		†
Pergolesi	Son imbrogliato io già (La Serva Padrona)	L		RIC
Ponchielli	Si, morir ella de' (La Gioconda)			RIC
Porrino	Io per l'antico diritto (Gli Orazi)			
Puccini	Colline's song (La Boheme)			RIC
Rossini	A un dottore (Il Barbiere di Siviglia)			GSC
-----	Eterno! immenso! (Mose in Egitto)			
-----	La calunnia (Il Barbiere di Siviglia)			†
Verdi	Ella giammai m'amò (Don Carlos)	L	A-E	RIC
-----	Il lacerato spirito (Simon Boccanegra)	L	FS-D	GSC
-----	Infelice è tu credevi (Ernani)	L	GF-EF	GSC
-----	O tu Palermo (I Vespri Siciliani)			RIC
-----	Tu sul labbro de' veggenti (Nabucco)			RIC

Miscellaneous Opera Arias

Bass

Borodin	I hate a dreary life (Prince Igor)			BOO
-----	Konchak's aria (Prince Igor)			
Dvořák	Alas, alas (Air of the water fay) (Rusalka)			
-----	Burgrave's aria (The Jacobin)			
Gershwin	I got plenty o' nuttin' (Porgy and Bess)	L	B-D	CHA
-----	It ain't necessarily so (Porgy and Bess)			CHA
Glinka	Prayer of Susanin (A Life for the Czar)			
Mussorgsky	Clock scene (Ah give me air, this suffocates my soul) (Boris Godunoff)			BES
-----	Death scene (Boris Godunoff)			BES

(Mussorgsky)	Monologue and hallucination scene (Boris Godunoff)			BES
-----	Pimen's monologue (Boris Godunoff)			BES
-----	Siege of Kazan (Boris Godunoff)	L	F-E	GSC
Rachmaninoff	Aleko's aria (Aleko)			
Rimsky-Korsakov	Song of the Viking guest (Sadko)		A-EF	BRO
Rubinstein	The demon's song (The Demon)			
Smetana	Everything is ready (The Bartered Bride)			BOO
Tchaikovsky	Prince Gremin's aria (Eugene Onegin)			GSC

Arias From Oratorios and Latin Works

Bass

Bach, J.S.	At evening hour of calm and peace (St. Matthew Passion)			†
-----	Consider o, my soul (St. John Passion)			†
-----	Come blessed cross (St. Matthew Passion) Cello			†
-----	Give, o give me back my Lord (St. Matthew Passion)			†
-----	Gladly will I all resigning (St. Matthew Passion)			†
-----	Make Thee clean my heart from sin (St. Matthew Passion)			
-----	Mighty Lord (Christmas Oratorio)			
-----	My darkened heart (Christmas Oratorio)			
Berlioz	O misère des rois (L'Enfance du Christ)			CST
Dvořák	Give ear, ye people (St. Ludmilla)			
-----	I was not deceived (St. Ludmilla)			
Handel	Arm, arm ye brave (Judas Maccabaeus)	L	B-E	• †
-----	But who may abide (The Messiah)	L	G-E	†
-----	His scepter is the rod of righteousness (Occasional Oratorio)	L	G-E	GSC

830

(Handel)	Honour and arms (Samson)	L	G-EF	†
-----	How willing my paternal love (Samson)	L	B-E	DIT
-----	O ruddier than the cherry (Acis and Galatea)	L	G-F	DIT
-----	Revenge, Timotheus cries (Alexander's Feast)	L	G-D	†
-----	Shall I in Mamre's fertile plain (Joshua)	L	G-EF	DIT
-----	The Lord worketh wonders (Judas Maccabeus)			
-----	The people that walked in darkness (The Messiah)			†
-----	The trumpet shall sound (The Messiah) Trumpet	L		†
-----	Thy glorious deeds (Samson)	M	C-F	†
-----	Turn not, O Queen, thy face away (Esther)			DIT
-----	What though I trace each herb and flower (Solomon)		CS-E	†
-----	Wher'er you walk (Semele)	HML	C-D	†
-----	Why do the nations (The Messiah)	L	B-E	†
-----	With pious hearts (Judas Maccabaeus)	L	G-E	†
Haydn	Behold along the dewy grass (The Seasons)			
-----	Now heav'n in fullest glory shone (The Creation)	L		†
-----	Rolling in foaming billows (The Creation)	L	C-F	†
-----	With joy th' impatient husbandman (The Seasons)	L	B-E	GSC
Mendelssohn	But the mountains shall depart (Elijah)			
-----	Consume them all (Saint Paul)			
-----	For know ye not (Saint Paul)			
-----	Is not His word like a fire (Elijah)	M	B-F	†
-----	It is enough (Elijah)	L	A-E	†
-----	Lord God of Abraham (Elijah)	L	B-E	†
-----	O God, have mercy (Saint Paul)	L	B-D	†
Rossini	Pro peccatis (Stabat Mater)			DIT

831

Sullivan	Honor the Lord with thy substance (Prodigal Son)			
Verdi	Confutatis maledictis (The Requiem)			GSC

Cantata Arias

Bass

Bach, J.S.	Aechzen und erbaermlich Weinen (Cantata 13) Violin or flute	L	G-EF	PET
-----	Die Welt mit allen Koenigreichen (Cantata 59) Violin	A-D		
-----	Doch weichet, ihr tollen vergeblichen (Cantata 8) Flute			NOV
-----	Endlich, endlich wird mein Joch (Cantata 56) Oboe			
-----	Es ist vollbracht (Cantata 159) Oboe			AUG
-----	Gleich wie die Wilden Meereswellen (Cantata 178) Violin			
-----	Greifet zu, fasst das Heil (Cantata 174) Violin or viola			
-----	Gute Nacht, du weltgetuemmel (Cantata 27) 2 Violins, viola and continuo			
-----	Herr, nun laessest du 'deinen Diener (Cantata 83) Violin or viola			
-----	Lass, o Welt, mich aus Verachtung (Cantata 123) Flute			PET
-----	Wenn Trost und Huelf' (Cantata 117) Violin			
Blow	Music's the cordial of a troubled breast (Begin the Song)	L	D-E	PET
Buck	The virgin's lullaby (The Coming of the King)	HL	B-CS	GSC
Elgar	Oh, my warriors (Caractacus)			NOV
Handel	Vouchsafe, O Lord (Dettingen Te Deum)	HM		ELV
Righini	Al nome tuo temuto (La Selva Incantata)			CFI

Berlin	A pretty girl is like a melody (Ziegfeld Follies 1919)			BER
-----	The girl that I marry (Annie Get Your Gun)			BER
-----	White Christmas (Holiday Inn)			BER
De Koven	Armorer's song (Robin Hood)	L		GSC
-----	Brown October ale (Robin Hood)	L	E-E	GSC
Herbert	Every day is ladies' day with me (The Red Mill)			WIT
-----	Gypsy love song (The Fortune Teller)	LHM	C-E	WIT
-----	Thine alone (Eileen)			WIT
Kern	Ah still suits me (Show Boat)			BRO
-----	Ol' man river (Show Boat)	LM	BF-G	HAR
-----	The song is you (Music in the Air)	M	C-F	HAR
-----	The way you look tonight (Swing Time)			CHA
-----	Yesterdays (Roberta)			CHA
Loewe	I still love Elisa (Paint Your Wagon)			
-----	I talk to the trees (Paint Your Wagon)			
Milloecker	Dunkelrote Rosen bring'ich (Mme. Dubarry)			CHA
Porter	So in love (Kiss Me Kate)			CHA
Rodgers	If I loved you (Carousel)			WIL
-----	Oh, what a beautiful morning (Oklahoma)			WIL
-----	Some enchanted evening (South Pacific)	M	C-E	CHA
-----	This nearly was mine (South Pacific)			WIL
Romberg	Stouthearted men (New Moon)	L	C-F	HAR
-----	The fireman's bride (Up in Central Park)	M	D-EF	WIL
Strauss, J.	Ja, mein idealer Lebenszweck (The Gypsy Baron)			CRZ
Weill	September song (Knickerbocker Holiday)			CHA

Song Cycles (Or Groups of Songs)

Bass

Babin	Beloved stranger	L		AUG
Beethoven	An die ferne Geliebte	HL	C-E	†
Brahms	Vier ernste Gesaenge			†
Copland	Old American songs			
Cornelius	Six Christmas songs	HL		BOS
Dougherty	Five sea chanties	L	A-EF	GSC
Dvořák	Biblical songs	HL		AMP
Mahler	Kindertotenlieder	L	G-GF	INT
Mason	Nautical lays of a landsman	L	A-E	GSC
Poulenc	Chansons gaillardes	L		HEU
Ravel	Don Quichotte à Dulcinée	HM	A-F	DUR
Schubert	Die Winterreise			†
-----	Gesaenge des Harfners, 1, 2 and 3			PET
-----	Three Italian songs			
Schumann	Dichterliebe			†
-----	Vier Husarenlieder	L	D-EF	BRH
Wolf	Harfenspieler Lieder (1, 2 and 3 Goethe)			
-----	Michelangelo Lieder			

Solo Cantatas

Bass

Bach, J.S.	Ich habe genug (Cantata 82) Oboe, strings and continuo			RIC
-----	Ich will den Kreuzstab (Cantata 56)			BRO

(See Solo Cantatas of Pergolesi, Handel and
Scarlatti, Kirchenkantaten of Buxtehude and
Symphoniae Sacrae of Schuetz.)

Concert Arias

Bass

Mozart	Alcandro, lo confesso			INT
-----	Così dunque tradisci			INT
-----	Io ti lascio, o cara addio			
-----	Mentre ti lascio	L		BOO

(Mozart)	Per questa bella mano			INT
-----	Rivolgete a lui lo sguardo			INT
-----	Un bacio di mano			INT

Christmas Songs

Bass

Andrews	I heard the bells on Christmas day	L	A-E	GAL
Bach, J.S.	Mighty Lord (Christmas Oratorio)			
-----	My darkened heart (Christmas Oratorio)			
-----	So appears thy natal day	L		GAL
Berlin	White Christmas (Holiday Inn)			BER
Berlioz	O misère des rois (L'Enfance du Christ)			CST
Branscombe	Hail ye time of holidays			
Buck	The Virgin's lullaby (The Coming of the King)	HL	B-CS	GSC
Coerne	A rhyme for Christmas-tide	L	CS-CS	DIT
Coombs	Bethlehem	HM	D-F	GSC
De Koven	The white Christ	L	C-D	GSC
Elmore and Reed	Come all ye who weary	L	C-C	JFI
Evans	The Virgin had a baby	L	C-EF	BOH
Harker	A Child is born in Bethlehem	LH	D-G	GSC
-----	There's a song in the air	HL	BF-D	GSC
Jewell	The vision of the shepherds	HL	A-D	ASC
Liddle	An old French carol	LM	F-F	BOO
Lynn	Gently little Jesus	L	BF-BF	DIT
-----	The magic night of Christmas	M	D-D	DIT
Neidlinger	The manger cradle	L	EF-F	GSC
Niles	The cherry tree			GSC
Prokoff	Christmas cradle song	LM	D-E	CHA
Rodney	A dream of Bethlehem	MML	G-DF	ENO
Taylor	Christmas folk song	L	BF-EF	GRA
Thiman	In the bleak midwinter	L	A-E	NOV

Easter Songs

Bass

Cadman	Hail joyous morn	HL	BF-DF	WIL
Duke	Calvary	L	G-F	CFI
Granier	Hosanna	HH	F-BF	DIT
Handel	The trumpet shall sound (The Messiah) Trumpet	L		†
Harker	As it began to dawn	ML	G-DF	GSC
La Forge	Before the crucifix	HML	BF-EF	GSC
Mac Farlane	On wings of living light	MH	D-G	GSC
O' Hara	There is no death	LMH	EF-AF	CHA
Parker	Come see the place	HL		GSC
Rachmaninoff	Christ is risen	LM	D-F	GAL
Turner	Hail your risen Lord	HL	C-D	GSC
Wolf	Herr, was traegt der Boden	HL	B-DS	†

Patriotic Songs

Bass

Bone and Fenton	Prayer for a waiting world	L		CFI
Candlyn	O God of armies	L	DF-DF	GRA
Chadwick	He maketh wars to cease	ML		ASC
De Koven	Recessional			
Dix	The trumpeter	HML	A-C	BOH
Dungan	Eternal life	HL		PRE
Handel	Arm, arm ye brave (Judas Maccabaeus)	L	B-E	†
Lester	Greater love hath no man	LH	B-E	CFI
O' Hara	Guns	M	C-F	DBH
-----	There is no death	LMH	EF-AF	CHA
Steffe	Battle hymn of the Republic			

Sacred Songs

Bass

Beethoven	The worship of God in nature			
Bone and Fenton	First Psalm	LM	DF-F	CFI
-----	Thy word is a lamp	LH	C-F	ROW
Brown	The twenty-third Psalm	LH	E-G	GRA

(Brown)	What are these which are arrayed	HLM	C-F	ASC
Buck	Blessed are they which love Thee	L	BF-D	GSC
-----	Fear not ye, O Israel	HLM		GSC
-----	Judge me, O God	L	GS-D	GSC
-----	O ye that hear and understand	L	A-D	GSC
Campbell-Tipton	I will give thanks unto the Lord	LMH	DF-AF	GSC
Candlyn	O God of armies	L	DF-DF	GRA
Chadwick	A ballad of trees and the Master	HML	A-F	DIT
-----	He maketh wars to cease	ML		ASC
Charles	Incline Thine ear	HL	BF-D	GSC
Clokey	God is in everything	LH	D-G	JFI
Davis	Be ye kind, one to another	L		GAL
Dungan	Eternal life	HL		PRE
Dvořák	God is my shepherd			AMP
-----	Hear my prayer, O Lord			AMP
-----	I will lift mine eyes			AMP
-----	Turn Thee to me			AMP
Edmunds	Praise we the Lord	HL	D-D	ROW
Eville	Psalm 130 (Out of the Deep)	HML		BOO
Faure, J.	The palms	HM	C-EF	DIT
Franck	O Lord most Holy	LM	A-FS	BOS
Godard	Lead kindly light			
Guion	The cross bearer	HM	B-DS	GSC
Handel	Thanks be to Thee	M	CS-E	†
Holst	The heart worships	ML	BF-D	STB
Kountz	What shall I ask	L		GAL
La Forge	They that trust in the Lord	HL	BF-EF	GAL
-----	What shall I render unto the Lord	HL	C-D	GSC
Lederer	Psalm 104	L	A-E	CFI
Liddle	How lovely are Thy dwellings?	HML		BOS
Mac Dermid	In my Fathers house are many mansions	HML		FRS
Mac Dermid	Ninety-first Psalm	HLM		FRS
Mac Gimsey	Think on these things	LM	BF-EF	CFI
Malotte	The Lord's Prayer			
-----	The twenty-third Psalm	HLM	C-F	GSC
Mc Gill	Thine eternal peace	HL	A-CS	GSC
Mendelssohn	But the mountains shall depart (Elijah)			

(Mendelssohn)	For know ye not (Saint Paul)			
-----	Lord God of Abraham (Elijah)	L	B-E	†
-----	O God, have mercy (Saint Paul)	L	B-D	†
Milligan	Hear my cry	HM	C-EF	GSC
O'Connor-Morris	Fill Thou my life, O Lord	L	BF-EF	CFI
O'Hara	Art Thou the Christ	HML	A-D	GSC
-----	Let God rule the world			
Rogers	Great peace have they which love Thy law	HML	B-CS	GSC
Sanderson	Green pastures	HL	BF-EF	BOO
Schubert	The Omnipotent			
-----	To the Infinite			
Scott	Repent ye	HML	A-D	GSC
Sowerby	The Lord is my shepherd			GRA
Speaks	Thou wilt keep him in perfect peace	HML		GSC
Stickles	Saith the Lord	LH	D-F	CHA
Sullivan	Honor the Lord with thy substance (The Prodigal Son)			
Tchaikovsky	Pilgrim's song	HLM	B-E	GSC
Van de Water	The publican	HL	C-E	DIT
Weaver	Build thee more stately mansions	M	C-E	GAL
Wolf	Give praise to Him through whom the world arose			
-----	Prayer (Gebet)			

Wedding Songs

Bass

Beethoven	Ich liebe dich	HL	BF-DF	†
De Koven	Oh promise me (Robin Hood)	HML	C-D	†
D'Hardelot	Because	MH	E-G	CHA
Grieg	I love thee	HML	E-F	†
Lippe	How do I love you?			BOS
Schubert	Du bist die Ruh	LMH	EF-AF	†
-----	Ungeduld	HML		†
Schumann	Widmung	HL	BF-F	†
Sharp	Possession	MH	D-A	DIT
Thiman	The God of love my Shepherd is	ML	A-D	NOV
Youmans	Through the years (Through the Years)	HML	A-F	MLR

Songs and Arias With Added
Accompanying Instrument

Bass

Bach, J.S.	Aechzen und erbaermlich L G-EF			PET
	Weinen (Cantata 13)			
	Violin or flute			
-----	Come blessed cross			†
	(St. Matthew Passion)			
	Cello			
-----	Die Welt mit allen Koenigreichen A-D			
	(Cantata 59) Violin			
-----	Endlich, endlich wird mein Joch			RIC
	(Cantata 56) Oboe			
-----	Es ist vollbracht (Cantata 159)			AUG
	Oboe			
-----	Gleich wie die wilden Meereswellen			
	(Cantata 178) Violin			
-----	Greifet zu, fasst das Heil			
	(Cantata 174) Violin or viola			
-----	Herr, nun laessest du deinen Diener			
	(Cantata 83) Violin or viola			
-----	Hier in meines Vaters Staette			AUG
	(Cantata 32) Violin			
-----	Ich habe genug (Cantata 82)			RIC
	Oboe, strings and continuo			
-----	Lass, o Welt, mich aus Verachtung			PET
	(Cantata 123) Flute			
-----	Wenn Trost und Huelf'			
	(Cantata 117) Violin			
Buxtehude	Mache dich, mein Herz, bereit			
	Trumpet and strings			
Chausson	Le colibri	M	F-GF	BOS
	Violin or cello			
Handel	The trumpet shall sound	L		†
	(The Messiah) Trumpet			
Honegger	Chanson (Ronsard)			SEN
	Flute and string quartet			
Milford	So sweet love seemed	HL	D-D	GRA
	Cello			
Mozart	Per questa bella mano			INT
	Cello			